W9-BPL-174

POPES

EVERY QUESTION ANSWERED

R F
S P

POPES

EVERY QUESTION ANSWERED

RUPERT MATTHEWS

METRO BOOKS
New York

METRO BOOKS
New York

An Imprint of Sterling Publishing
387 Park Avenue South
New York, NY 10016

METRO BOOKS and the distinctive Metro Books logo are trademarks of Sterling Publishing Co., Inc.

This 2013 edition published by Metro Books by arrangement with Moseley Road Inc.

Moseley Road Inc, www.moseleyroad.com
Publisher: Sean Moore
General Manager: Karen Prince
Editorial Director: Damien Moore
Art Director: Tina Vaughan
Production Director: Adam Moore

Design Philippa Baile and Duncan Youel, www.oiloften.co.uk

ISBN 978-1-4351-4571-9

For information about custom editions, special sales, and premium and corporate purchases, please contact Sterling Special Sales at 800-805-5489 or specialsales@sterlingpublishing.com.

Manufactured in China

2 4 6 8 10 9 7 5 3 1

www.sterlingpublishing.com

CONTENTS

CHAPTER 1

The Late Roman Empire 1st to 4th Centuries

CHAPTER 2

The Dark Ages 5th to 9th Centuries

CHAPTER 3

The Middle Ages
10th to 13th Centuries

CHAPTER 4

The Early Modern Period
14th to 16th Centuries

CHAPTER 5

The Modern Period 17th to 21st Centuries

CHAPTER 6

Papal Bulls and Teachings

INTRODUCTION

The papacy is one of the oldest and most enduring institutions in the world. It has lasted for almost two millennia, seeing off duchies, kingdoms, and empires that sought to eclipse it and bring the popes to heel. As a religious office that has exercised temporal rule, the papacy is unique in European history. Although its fortunes have fluctuated and its holders have been a varied group of humans, the papacy has never deviated from its appointed task to lead Christianity and follow in the sacred footsteps of its founder St. Peter.

Jesus Christ lived and performed His ministry in the Middle East. He was born in Bethlehem, preached around Galilee and Judea, before being crucified in Jerusalem. His Resurrection and the events that followed were the defining moments of Christianity, confirming His status as the Son of God and firing His disciples with the zeal to go out and spread the faith that became known as Christianity.

The leading figure among those disciples was St. Peter, formerly known as Simon, on whom Jesus had promised to build His Church. The biblical book Acts of the Apostles shows Peter as playing a leading role in Christianity after Christ ascended into Heaven. It was Peter who organized the election of Matthias to replace Judas Iscariot as a disciple, and it was Peter who ruled on a variety of issues. He left Jerusalem to preach the faith in Lydda, Joppa, and Caesarea. Two letters by Peter are included in the New Testament.

Peter later traveled to Rome and became the leader of the nascent Christian community in that great city. At the time, Rome was the largest city on Earth with a population of over a million. It was also the capital of the mighty Roman Empire, a melting pot of faiths and peoples as well as a hotbed of political intrigue and military power. Quite what Peter's role as leader of the Christians in Rome was is not entirely clear. Later writers referred to him as bishop of Rome, but the term "bishop" was then poorly defined. He most certainly had a leading role but, just as certainly, that role was not as rigidly defined as the term bishop of Rome would imply.

According to Church tradition, St. Peter taught with St. Paul in Rome where both men met their deaths in about the year 67, during the reign of the emperor Nero and because of their faith. Traditionally, Peter was executed in the Circus of Nero on the Vatican Hill and his body buried nearby. The site of his burial was later chosen as the site for a grand Basilica of St. Peter. The current basilica of that name is a sixteenth-century replacement. Both the site of the execution and the burial are now regular pilgrimage spots in the city of Rome.

Before he was taken away for execution, Peter appointed a man named Linus to take over his role as leader of the Christians in Rome. Although neither the nature of Peter's role nor the terms that he handed over to Linus have been preserved, the move was the key moment in the foundation of the papacy. In many ways, it was the moment the papacy was born.

Jesus Christ had handed to Peter authority over his flock, and now Peter was handing that authority to Linus. Thus was set in train the Apostolic Succession, the unbroken line of authority passed from person to person down the centuries that links the current pope directly to the ministry of Christ.

The functions that the current pope performs—those of preaching, governing, and ordaining—were the same as the Apostles had performed in the years

The imposing statue of St. Paul outside St. Peter's Basilica in Rome, Italy. A key founder of Church Law alongside St. Peter, St. Paul is depicted with his traditional attributes: the scrolls of scriptures and the sword of his martyrdom.

A portrait of St. Linus, Peter's successor as bishop of Rome, from an icon in the Basilica of St. Paul Outside the Walls in Rome, Italy.

immediately after Christ ascended into Heaven. And each bishop of Rome was ordained into office by bishops who had themselves been ordained by the previous pope. Thus there was an unbroken line of men who had been put into office by their predecessors by the laying on of hands right back to Christ.

Because the bishopric of Rome had been founded by St. Peter himself, the bishops of Rome maintained that they had a special leading role over other bishops. This claim was not always accepted—the patriarchs of Antioch stated that Peter

THE POPE

The title of "Pope" was in origin more of a nickname than a formal title. It derives from the Greek world for "father" and, by about the year 200, was being applied to any bishop who showed particular pastoral care for his flock. By around 470, the bishops of Rome were being given the title whether or not they were of a particularly pastoral nature. It was not until the reign of Pope Gregory VII that an edict was issued that formalized both the use of the title for the bishop of Rome and banned its use by other bishops.

The majestic interior of St. Peter's Basilica in Rome, Italy. The four pillars of St. Peter's baldachin, built by Bernini, rise above the tomb of St. Peter that was once marked by a simple rock.

The Crucifixion of St. Peter by Michelangelo Merisi da Caravaggio was painted for the Cerasi Chapel of Santa Maria del Popolo in Rome, Italy. In a final act of humility, St. Peter asked that he be crucified upside-down so as not to imitate the death of Jesus Christ.

had been bishop of Antioch before going to Rome and thus claimed precedence, while the patriarchs of Constantinople regarded themselves as equals to the bishop of Rome.

The question of precedence by the bishops of Rome was to be a constant feature of the early centuries of the papacy. The niceties of the disputes kept theologians and lawyers busy for years but, gradually, the primacy of the bishop of Rome became accepted. If nothing else, the increasing prestige of the bishop of Rome attracted to Rome the finest thinkers and administrators, so that the

THE VATICAN

The papacy is today centered on the Vatican, but it was not always so. Before 311, the bishops of Rome lived and officiated at a wide variety of locations in the city—sometimes on the run from pagan persecutors. In 311, Emperor Constantine gave Pope St. Miltiades the Lateran Palace to serve as a home and office for himself and his staff. The Lateran Basilica was built on adjacent land and became the Cathedral of Rome, a status it retains. The Vatican Hill was surrounded by stout defensive walls and by the sixteenth century had become the citadel of Rome. When the Kingdom of Italy annexed the Papal States in 1870, Pope Pius IX retreated into the Vatican fortress and vowed never to emerge. In 1929, a treaty between Italy and the papacy recognized the Vatican as an independent city state within Rome, and the popes have resided there ever since.

A fresco depicting *The Baptism of Constantine*, painted by Gianfrancesco Penni in the early sixteenth century. The event was a key turning point in the history of Christianity when it became the dominant religion of the Roman Empire.

institution came to have a near monopoly on talent, culminating in the wonders of the Renaissance.

The bishops of Rome were called upon to adjudicate in disputes across Christendom. Whether the point at issue was a theological definition or the more concrete question of which of two rivals should be appointed to a position, it was the bishop of Rome who, by the fifth century, was looked upon as being the person with the authority to make a final decision.

Not that all the men who held the position of bishop of Rome in these early years were quite up to the job—one absconded with the money collected for good works, while a second hired a gang of gladiators to slaughter his opponents—but slowly the institution came to have a prestige and power that attracted to Rome the finest brains and most elevated souls. When the Western Roman Empire fell in the later fifth century, it was the Church that survived, providing a continuity and an anchor for the citizens of the defunct Empire now forced to live under the secular rule of barbarians, many of whom where not Christians. The Church copied the old administrative system of the Empire with bishops and archbishops taking the place of provincial governors, all looking to Rome for guidance, instruction, and preferment.

In the very earliest days, the Christians of Rome had met in a field near the city to elect a new bishop. Apparently, the election was held by show of hands or acclamation. But as the number of Christians increased and the importance of the papacy grew, such a procedure would no longer suffice. From the seventh century onward, there were increasingly bitter disputes over how a new pope should be elected and who should be entitled to a vote. The people, clergy, and nobles all claimed to have a right to take part in elections, often trying to marginalize the influence of other groups.

For a while it was the nobles of the Papal States who controlled the elections of a new pope. Popes were elected for the benefit of local families and, predictably, not all popes proved to be honest or even pious. Eventually, however, it was the clergy who won the struggle for dominance at election time. By the mid-eleventh century it was established that the clergy of the parishes

The stunning mosaic in the apse of St. Paul Outside the Walls in Rome, Italy. The enthroned Christ appears with St. Peter and St. Andrew to His left and St. Paul and St. Luke to His right. In the foreground is the Gothic baldachin by Arnolfo di Cambio.

within Rome should be the sole electors. These cardinals, as they were known, at first suffered bullying and bribery, but over the decades the modern system of a secret election within a closed conclave developed. Thereafter, the influence of the secular world on the choice of a new pope declined to almost nothing.

At first, the cardinals were simply the parish priests and deacons of the parish churches in Rome. However, popes soon began to appoint as cardinals men of talent and skills from elsewhere. A local priest was hired to do the actual work of the parish, while the cardinal concentrated on serving the papacy in a higher capacity. Thus the electorate gradually lost its exclusively Roman nature, acquiring first an Italian then European profile and, finally, a more global nature.

It is that global nature of the papacy that dominates today. With the coming of Pope Francis to the Vatican the old European monopoly has been smashed. The Catholic Church has adherents across the World. Europe is no longer the center of balance for the Church as there are far more Catholics outside Europe than within it.

Nor are the old rituals and ceremonials entirely in keeping with the modern face of the Church. Many date back to the days when the pope was the secular ruler of a large swathe of central Italy and claimed respect and obedience from counts and kings. The Church no longer has such secular power but has instead gained a new mantle of spiritual and moral authority. As the papacy moves into the twenty-first century, it is right that a new pope from the New World should arise to introduce new ways of doing business and new methods of expression. The papacy has changed before to reflect the changing world. It would appear to be doing so again.

SCS VITALIS

The Late Roman Empire
1st to 4th Centuries

CHAPTER ONE

The very earliest popes were leaders of the small Christian community in pagan Rome. The nature and form of the office they held is unclear, but by the year 300 the bishop of Rome had emerged as a powerful, spiritual force within Christianity and the Roman Empire. What had begun as a religion of foreigners, the impoverished, and slaves—that met with mistrust and, at times, terrible persecution—had become the mainstream faith of Rome. Wealth and lands flowed in to the hands of the Church so the bishop of Rome took on the roles of caring for the poor, building churches, and managing finances. But, just as the papacy was finding its feet, disaster struck with the Fall of Rome.

ST. PETER ✠ The 1st Pope c.33–c.64

Born Bethsaida, Palestine; c.1
Parents Father, Jonah; Mother, unknown
Died Rome, Italy; probably October 13, 64

St. Peter was both a personal disciple of Jesus Christ and the first person to organize a community of Christians in Rome. Together with the unique mission entrusted to him by Jesus, these facts mean that Peter is today recognized as having been the first pope. This was not always the case—the early Christians in Rome reserved the title of "pope" for St. Peter's successors.

Ruins of the fishing village of Bethsaida on the northern shores of the Sea of Galilee in modern-day Israel.

Peter was born as Simon in Bethsaida on the shores of the Sea of Galilee. Together with his brother Andrew, he became a fisherman and moved to Capernaum where he married a local girl. Peter spent some time with John the Baptist but, when Jesus began His ministry, he became one of the very first disciples to give up his home to follow Christ. From the start, Peter was recognized as a leader among the disciples and seems to have been present with Jesus at every important event in His life. Peter was there to hear most of Jesus's sermons and parables and witnessed the raising of Jairus's daughter, the Transfiguration, the Last Supper, and the Agony in the Garden.

UPON THIS ROCK I WILL BUILD MY CHURCH AND THE GATES OF HELL WILL NOT PREVAIL AGAINST IT

MATTHEW 16

LEADER OF THE DISCIPLES

The particular favor with which Jesus viewed Peter is illustrated several times in the New Testament. When Jesus asked the disciples who they thought He was, it was Peter who stated that they took Him to be the Messiah, the Son of the living God. Jesus then told Peter that he was blessed because of his insight and gave him the name or title of Cephas, the Aramaic word for "rock." This name was later rendered into Greek as "Peter," the name by which the fisherman born as Simon is today best known.

Of crucial importance to the papacy, Jesus then went on to tell the disciples that "upon this rock (i.e., Peter) I will build my church and the gates of hell will not prevail against it." Jesus continued, speaking directly to Peter, "I will give you the keys of the kingdom of heaven, and whatever you bind on earth shall be bound in heaven, and whatever you loose on earth shall be loosed in heaven."

These passages, found in the Gospel of Matthew, are taken to mean that Jesus entrusted the care of His followers to St. Peter, a duty that Peter then passed on to his successors. It was largely on this basis that later popes established their claim to supremacy over other bishops. Exactly what Jesus intended in this incident has been disputed, particularly by Protestant theologians, but there can be no doubt at all that He intended Peter to have a special role of some kind.

Throughout the Gospels, Peter comes across as being generous and warm hearted but somewhat hot-tempered. This latter trait was shown most clearly when Jesus was arrested in the Garden of Gethsemane. Jesus had gone to the garden to pray, taking with Him three disciples of which Peter was one. Just as Jesus finished praying another disciple, Judas, arrived at the head of a group of men, some of whom were armed. Judas kissed Jesus, a pre-arranged signal to the servants of the high priest who Judas had brought with him. Those men surged forward to seize Jesus and Peter leapt to His defense. In the struggle that ensued, Peter cut

c.33

Jesus Christ is crucified along with two thieves at "the Place of the Skull." He is charged with claiming to be "King of the Jews."

37

Following the death of Rome's Emperor Tiberius, aged 78, his nephew Gaius Caesar, known as Caligula, takes charge of the Empire. His brief reign is notorious for its cruel excesses.

Opposite This statue of St. Peter stands in front of St. Peter's Basilica in the Vatican. He is holding the key to the kingdom of heaven and a scroll containing the names of those fit to enter.

When the disciples gathered in Jerusalem for what turned out to be the Last Supper, Jesus began washing the feet of His followers—a traditional act of hospitality at the time. Peter objected to Jesus washing his feet, but Jesus insisted and turned the incident into a lesson for his disciples: "If I then, your Lord and Teacher, have washed your feet, you also ought to wash one another's feet. For I have given you an example, that you should do as I have done to you." Peter then replied, "Lord, not my feet only, but also my hands and my head."

off the ear of Malchus, the high priest's servant. Jesus rebuked Peter, miraculously healed Malchus, and allowed Himself to be arrested.

That night, Jesus was put on trial. As Christ predicted, Peter was asked three times if he was a follower of Jesus, and each time Peter denied that this was the case. Peter was no doubt justifiably frightened of being arrested himself, or of being set upon by a mob.

Peter is absent from the Crucifixion, when only Christ's mother Mary, Mary Magdalene, and St. John seem to have been present, but he reappears as a witness to the Resurrection. He was the first of the disciples to see the risen Christ and remained a key player during the 40 days that Christ stayed on Earth.

Thereafter, the sources for Peter's later life become less extensive. The Acts of the Apostles shows that Peter played a very important leadership role in the early Christian community in Jerusalem. He preached a major sermon on Pentecost and insisted on a new disciple being selected as a replacement for Judas. Peter is recorded as having been arrested and put on trial in front of the Sanhedrin where, although he openly defied the judges, he was set free. He was later imprisoned by King Herod but escaped—set free by an angel. Peter then traveled to Lydda, Joppa, and Caesarea to speak to followers of Jesus and keep their faith alive. It was about this time that Peter began preaching the message of Christ to non-Jews and it seems to have been Peter who first set out rules for allowing Gentiles to enter the Christian community.

THE SECOND EPISTLE

Unlike the First Epistle, the Second is quite vague in its intention. It also has a number of features that seem to refer to events that took place after the year 80, by which time Peter had been martyred. Some scholars believe that while the First Epistle was written—or at least dictated—by Peter, the Second Epistle was not.

LETTERS OF ST. PETER

Two letters thought to have been written by Peter are included in the New Testament. The First Epistle of St. Peter is addressed to people living in Roman provinces in Asia Minor; it speaks of Jesus and urges the recipients to be steadfast in their faith during apparently difficult times.

The Second Epistle is addressed to churches generally and has a less specific message than the First. In this letter, Peter urges his readers to lead lives of good Christian virtue. He then condemns "false teachers" who were already twisting the true Christian message for their own purposes. The letter then explains why Christ had not returned in the Second Coming as soon as many had expected.

41

Emperor Caligula is murdered by a tribune of the guard. Caligula is succeeded by Emperor Claudius, who leads an expedition to conquer Britain in 43.

44

The Apostle James becomes the first Christian martyr, executed by order of the Judean king Herod Agrippa. Agrippa dies, aged 54, and Judea returns to being a procuratorial province of Rome.

54

Emperor Claudius is poisoned in a plot led by his wife, the empress Agrippina, who seeks to rule Rome through her 16-year-old son Nero.

Peter attacks Malchus to protect Jesus. Jesus then ordered Peter to sheathe his sword, and laid hands on Malchus to heal his wound. He then rebuked Peter saying "those who live by the sword shall die by the sword."

There has been considerable debate as to whether the two letters were, in fact, written by Peter. They were originally written in Greek, and both contain fine rhetorical flourishes. Peter, however, was an illiterate fisherman whose first language was Aramaic. It is therefore unlikely that he could have written these letters with his own hand. However, Peter is known to have had a secretary called Silvanus who may well have helped with the composition of the letters.

Where Peter was when he wrote the Epistles is likewise much debated. The First Epistle states that the writer was in Babylon. This cannot have been literally true, and is likely a coded reference to the fact that he was living in the capital of a great empire, i.e., Rome.

BISHOP OF ROME

As an Apostle with a direct personal link to Christ, Peter would have enjoyed enormous respect among the Christian community in Rome. He would also have been in a position to lay down the law and rebuke those who broke the teachings of Christ. He may have been referred to as the *presbyter* or *episkopoi* of the community. The two words seem to have been used interchangeably in early Christian times and mean "overseer" or "organizer." Our modern word "bishop" is derived from *episkopoi*, so it is likely that during his lifetime Peter was regarded as bishop of Rome. Given the small number of Christians living in Rome and the very different conditions of the time, however, a bishop at this date would have been a very different type of official to modern bishops.

A few years after Peter arrived in Rome, there was a devastating fire. Many people suspected that the fire had been caused by arson and Emperor Nero quickly blamed the Christians, ordering that they should be executed in "degrading" ways. Some were thrown to wild dogs, some were burned, and still more were crucified. It would seem that most of the Christians executed were killed during festivals marking the tenth anniversary of Nero assuming power, October 13, 64, which is recognized as the date of Peter's martyrdom.

Condemned to crucifixion, as Peter was being led to the cross he declared that he was unfit to die in the same manner as Jesus and so asked the soldiers to nail him upside down.

His body was later taken down and carried over the river to the Vatican Hill for burial. At the time, this was open country—a suitable place for the burial of a criminal. The surviving Christians marked the spot with a large red stone, symbolizing the "rock" of Peter's name. A few decades later, the rock was replaced by a proper shrine and, later still, the Basilica.

THE BASILICA

In 318, Emperor Constantine ordered that a vast basilica should be built over the tomb of St. Peter. This was demolished in the early sixteenth century and a new basilica was completed on the site by 1626 with the old altar remaining in place. In the 1950s, an excavation under the altar found an ancient tomb containing the bones of a man aged in his sixties that dated back to the mid-first century. These were declared to be the remains of St. Peter.

58

The Apostle Paul arrives at Jerusalem but is arrested and held for trial before the procurator of Judea. He is released in 62.

61

Emperor Nero executes his mother at the urging of his councilor Lucius Annaeus Seneca.

64

In July, almost two thirds of Rome is destroyed by fire. Persecution of Christians begins at Rome.

ST. LINUS ✠ The 2nd Pope c.64–c.76

Born Volterra, Italy; date unknown

Parents Father, Herculanus; Mother, Claudia

Papacy c.64–c.76

Died Rome, Italy; September 23, c.76

Not much is known for certain about Pope Linus—a reflection of the lack of written records relating to the early Church rather than of his importance. As the first bishop of Rome after St. Peter, Linus was instrumental in establishing the succession of office that stretches from today right back to Jesus.

Perhaps the earliest mention of Linus comes in the biblical book 2 Timothy. This book is a letter written by St. Paul to his friend and supporter Timothy. Almost certainly, the letter was written from Rome when Paul was expecting his martyrdom and so dates to about the year 65. In the closing section Paul writes, "Eubulus greets you, and so do Pudens, Linus, Claudia, and all the brothers and sisters." It is often held that this Linus is the same man recorded by later historians as Pope Linus, and that Claudia was his mother.

Linus's time as bishop of Rome was relatively peaceful for the Christian community. The persecution of Christians by the emperor Nero, in which St. Peter had been martyred, lasted only a few months. The Christians seem to have thereafter been more or less ignored by Roman officialdom—for a while at least.

Ruins of the old city of Volterra, Italy—the birthplace of St. Linus.

There are only two recorded actions of Linus as pope. The first was to issue an edict enforcing a rule laid down by St. Paul in his First Epistle to the Corinthians stating that women had to cover their heads in church. The second was the appointment of 15 men, none of whose names are recorded, as "bishops." The duties, rights, and status of bishops at this date are not certain. They certainly had no diocese to preside over, nor were they priests in the modern sense of the word. These bishops seem to have been those men who had learned enough about the teachings of Jesus Christ to be in a position to instruct others and to have the authority to rebuke those who misbehaved. There are indications that the bishops met in council, with Linus as a sort of chairman or convenor. It seems that men holding the office of deacon looked after the more practical side of organizing the community.

The dates of Linus's time as pope are rather obscure. He is usually said to have taken over on the death of St. Peter, though he may have assumed his duties when Peter was arrested. That would put his assumption of office in the year 64. However, the early writer Jerome dates it to 67, which might indicate a gap of three years or might mean the date of death for Peter was in 67. Linus held office until his death, which is variously given as taking place in the year 76, 78, or 80, though the sources do agree that he died on September 23. He was buried on Vatican Hill, close to the grave of St. Peter.

64

After 84 years under construction, Jerusalem's Third Temple is completed.

65

The Gospel according to St. Mark is transcribed.

67

St. Paul is executed on the *Via Ostia*, three miles outside Rome.

68

Emperor Nero commits suicide after being sentenced to death by the Roman Senate. He is succeeded by Galba, who is murdered just six months later.

69

Emperor Otho commits suicide following defeat in the Battle of Bedriacum. His successor, the emperor Vitellius, is later killed in a street battle and Emperor Vespasian ascends to power.

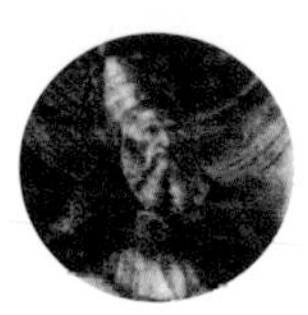

ST. ANACLETUS ✠ The 3rd Pope c.76–c.92

Born Rome, Italy; date unknown

Parents Father, Emilianus; Mother, unknown

Papacy c.79–c.92

Died Rome, Italy; c.92

Ruins of the old city of Rome—birthplace of St. Anacletus.

The confusion that surrounds the early papacy, due to a lack of reliable records, is exemplified by Anacletus. His name is given in different sources as Anacletus, Anencletus, and Cletus; and for many years it was thought that Cletus had been a different person to Anacletus.

This original confusion led to scholarly disputes over both the order in which Cletus and Anacletus had held office and their respective dates. However, it is now officially held that the three names actually refer to a single person, a saint whose day is celebrated on April 26.

The name Anacletus is Greek, but this pope is recorded as having been born in Rome. It is assumed that his parents were Greeks resident in Rome and some have suggested that they were slaves. The name Anacletus seems to have been most common among educated slaves and to have meant "blameless." One of the accusations thrown at the early Church by its pagan opponents was that it was a religion of slaves and the poor, so the origins of Anacletus may have been of the lowest social order.

That Anacletus took over from Linus is certain, but his dates are not. Some sources say he held the papacy from 76, others give the year 77, 79, or 80. Likewise, his death is recorded as having taken place in 88 or 92. It is generally agreed that this pope is the same man as the Cletus who was made a bishop by St. Peter.

His only recorded act is that one December he ordained 25 priests to minister to the Christian community of Rome. Even that fact is disputed however. It is recorded in the *Liber Pontificalis*, which was drawn up about the year 250. By that date, Rome was divided into 25 parishes and some historians think that the compilers of the book, knowing nothing for certain about Anacletus, decided to record that he had created this division of the city to give him credit for something.

The *Liber Pontificalis* also claims that "he was crowned with martyrdom." There is no evidence that this is true and, so far as we know, the emperor Domitian, who ruled Rome at this date, had nothing against the Christians. Again, the tradition may have arisen to give Anacletus some posthumous honor. However, Domitian is known to have insisted at times on being addressed as "Dominus and Deus" (Lord and God). No Christian would have agreed to that, so there is an outside chance that Anacletus may have fallen foul of the emperor for this reason.

Anacletus was traditionally buried on April 26, on the Vatican Hill, close to the red rock erected over the grave of St. Peter.

EARLY SOURCES

No contemporary written records of the earliest popes survive. Our knowledge of papal history before about 200 comes from a variety of later sources, which may or may not be reliable. From about 200 onward there are references in letters and other documents to the then pope, but for the earlier popes historians rely on a mix of documents. Potentially, the most useful of these is the *Liber Pontificalis*, a book that lists all popes, giving their dates and any noteworthy actions. The book was compiled in about 250 from earlier records, now lost, and oral traditions. For the earliest popes, the recorded details are scanty and often contradictory.

70
The Siege of Jerusalem ends with Rome victorious and the Third Temple is destroyed just six years after its completion.

79
Emperor Vespasian is succeeded by his son Titus. Mount Vesuvius erupts and the cities of Heraculaneum and Pompei are buried in lava and ash.

80
Three months of celebration mark the opening of the Colosseum in Rome. Hundreds of gladiators die in games to amuse the populace.

81
The Roman emperor Titus dies, aged 40, and is succeeded by his brother, the emperor Domitian

84
The Gospels according to St. John and St. Matthew are transcribed.

ST. CLEMENT I ✠ The 4th Pope c.92–c.100

Born Rome, Italy; date unknown

Parents Father, Faustinus; Mother, unknown

Papacy c.92–c.100

Died Rome, Italy; possibly November 24, c.100

That Clement was widely respected during his lifetime is almost certain because by the year 92 he was one of the few men still alive who had been an adult old enough to meet with St. Peter and St. Paul.

Around the year 60, St. Paul wrote a letter to the Christians in Philippi referring to a respected worker for Christ named Clement. This was the same Clement who St. Peter appointed to be a deacon in Rome. That this was the man who 30 years later became pope is almost certain.

Clement is known to have written a number of books and letters. Of these, the only one known to have survived intact is the letter he wrote to the Christians of Corinth in about 96 and known today as The First Epistle of Clement.

The letter is important for a number of reasons. First, references to the letters of St. Paul prove these were already available in both Rome and Corinth at this early date. It also demonstrates that the bishop of Rome was being asked to resolve a dispute within another Christian community. Whether this was because the bishop of Rome was recognized as superior to the bishop of Corinth or because Clement had a personal authority is not clear. It did, however, set a precedent for later bishops of Rome.

ST. EVARISTUS  The 5th Pope c.100–c.109

Born Antioch, now Antakya, Turkey; date unknown

Parents Father, Judah; Mother, unknown

Papacy c.100–c.109

Died Rome, Italy; possibly October 27, c.109

Evaristus was the first pope who had known neither Jesus nor any of the Apostles. This was a difficult time for early Christianity as the first generation of adherents died out.

When Evaristus was bishop of Rome there was a growing tendency among Christians to debate the teachings of Jesus Christ and the exact nature of His person—was he human, divine, or both? As the people who had known Jesus either directly or at second hand died, the Christians turned increasingly to the written records of Christ. It was now that the Gospels acquired the importance they would retain to the present day.

The structure of the Church was likewise in flux. Gradually, the bishops would come to wield considerable power over priests and the faithful, but that process had barely started. Nor was the primacy of the bishop of Rome accepted as yet. The bishops of Jerusalem, Antioch, Alexandria, and Constantinople also claimed their offices went back to the Apostles.

Given this ferment of ideas and events, it is a shame that Evaristus is such a shadowy figure. The only facts really known about him are that his father was born in Bethlehem and that he was buried on the Vatican Hill.

96

The Roman emperor Domitian is murdered in a plot led by his wife Domitia. He is succeeded by Emperor Nerva.

98

Emperor Nerva dies, aged 63, and is succeeded by his adopted son who reigns for nearly two decades as Emperor Trajan. Trajan will lead many successful campaigns to expand the Empire.

105

Paper is invented by the Chinese eunuch Ts'ai Lun.

117

Emperor Trajan dies and is succeeded by Emperor Hadrian.

ST. ALEXANDER I ✠ The 6th Pope c.109–c.116

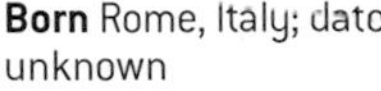

Born Rome, Italy; date unknown

Parents Father, Alexander; Mother, unknown

Papacy c.109–c.116

Died Rome, Itlay; possibly May 3, c.116

Later tradition has it that reading a narration of the Last Supper as part of the Eucharist was an idea of Alexander's. Whether this was true or not is unknown, but it may reflect genuine changes to the Eucharist.

We know from other sources that the ritual of the Eucharist was at about this time emerging from the earlier Agape, or communal feast, open only to Christians. The two eventually separated, with the eucharist being held as a disparate event—usually on a Sunday.

Similarly, Alexander has been credited with originating the practice of blessing water mixed with salt for the purpose of sprinkling in Christian homes to drive out evil influences, but there is no concrete evidence for this.

A Christian named Alexander was martyred by being beheaded beside the seventh milestone from Rome on the *Via Nomentana* in the second century. His tomb stood beside the road near the site of his execution. For many years it was believed that this Alexander was identical to Pope Alexander I, but there is no documentary link. In 1960, Pope John XXIII officially broke the link between the martyr Alexander and the pope Alexander, recognizing them to have probably been two different men.

ST. SIXTUS I ✠ The 7th Pope c.116–c.125

Born Rome, Italy; date unknown

Parents Father, Pastor; Mother, unknown

Papacy c.116–c.125

Died Rome, Italy; possibly April 3, c.125

Although his name is conventionally given as "Sixtus," this pope's real name was probably "Xystus" as this is the more correct Greek form of the name current at this date.

Of all the early popes, Sixtus I is one of the most poorly known. Although the later sources give his dates with apparent authority, they do not agree with each other. It is generally agreed, however, that he held office for ten years during the reign of the emperor Hadrian.

The most important act attributed to St. Sixtus by later historians is that it was he who introduced to the Mass the Sanctus—a short hymn that in translation runs: "Holy, Holy, Holy, Lord God of hosts. Heaven and earth are full of your glory. Hosanna in the highest. Blessed is he who comes in the name of the Lord. Hosanna in the highest."

The Sanctus is based in part on a verse from Isaiah in the Old Testament. That verse is recited during some Jewish rituals, and some believe that the Sanctus is therefore derived from Judaic practice, which would make it an ancient part of Christian ritual. However, whether St. Sixtus truly introduced it or not is not known for certain.

122

Hadrian's Wall is constructed in Britain following the arrival of Emperor Hadrian to the Roman province. The wall is designed to provide a protective barrier against the Picts.

123

Emperor Hadrian averts a war with the Parthians by meeting in person with the king of Parthia.

125

Plague sweeps across North Africa killing as many as 500,000 in Numidia before moving to Italy where it claims so many lives that entire towns are abandoned.

ST. TELESPHORUS ✠ The 8th Pope c.125–c.136

Born Terranova da Sibari, Italy; date unknown
Parents Unknown
Papacy c.125–c.136
Died Rome, Italy; possibly January 2, c.136

As with most early popes, firm information about Telesphorus is hard to come by. However, most early sources agree that he held office for 11 years and was born in southern Italy of Greek parentage.

A key source for knowledge of early Christian thinking is Irenaeus, a Greek who died in about 202. His writings include several references to the bishops of Rome. The actual dates of Telesphorus's pontificate are disputed however, nor is anyone certain what powers or obligations he held as bishop of Rome. The one fact that the early historians agree on is that Telesphorus was martyred by order of the Roman emperor, though whether that was Hadrian or Antoninus Pius is uncertain. At this time, the growing number of Christians were incurring the wrath of the Roman government. The key problem was that Christians refused to accept that other gods existed and would not pour libations on the altars of the state gods. Some years earlier, Emperor Trajan had decided that Christians should be punished only if they openly flaunted their contempt of the official gods. It seems that Telesphorus must have done just this for he was executed and his body was buried on the Vatican Hill near to that of St. Peter.

ST. HYGINUS  The 9th Pope c.138–c.142

Born Athens, Greece; date unknown
Parents Unknown
Papacy c.138–c.142
Died Rome, Italy; date unknown

The *Liber Pontificalis* says that Hyginus was an Athenian philosopher who traveled to Rome. The length of his time in office is unclear, with some sources giving four years, others as much as ten.

Although details of Hyginus's time as pope are almost entirely lacking, sources from elsewhere show that the office of bishop was changing at this time. As the numbers of Christians grew it was no longer possible for a single leader to minister to them all. Other presbyters emerged to minister to groups of the faithful, although the bishop of a city remained the most respected Christian there. We know that in Antioch, for example, the bishop was asserting a real authority over the presbyters, as opposed to the vague moral authority he had possessed before. In Antioch, nobody could act as a presbyter without the bishop's consent. In this way they sought to weed out those men insufficiently knowledgeable in Christ's teachings.

A later account credits Hyginus with similar actions in Rome and, since the ordering of ranks of clergy and decisions about who was fit to serve and who wasn't were occupying bishops elsewhere, this may be have been true. Hyginus is likewise credited with moving Easter Day from the day of the Jewish Passover to the nearest Sunday.

130

The Temple of Zeus, which was begun in 530 BC, is completed at Athens by the Roman emperor Hadrian. It is the largest temple in Greece.

135

Roman legionnaires sack Jerusalem following the Jewish War of Freedom that began in 132. The leader of the Jewish rebellion, Simon Bar Kokhba, is killed.

138

Roman emperor Hadrian dies, aged 62. He is succeeded by Emperor Antoninus Pius.

Born Aquileia, Italy; date unknown

Parents Father, Rufinus; Mother, unknown

Papacy c.142–c.155

Died Rome, Italy; date unknown

Aquileia was one of the largest and wealthiest cities of the early Roman Empire. It was destroyed by Attila the Hun in the mid-fifth century.

ST. PIUS I ✦ The 10th Pope c.142–c.155

It is during the papacy of St. Pius I that the bishopric of Rome begins to emerge into certain history. Even so, the length of his time in office is not certain, with dates varying from 140 to 146 being given for the start of his papacy.

Several early writers state that Pius was the brother of Hermas, who wrote a famous book called *The Shepherd*, which likened the established Church to a shepherd and Christian people to its flock. We know Hermas was born a slave, so many have speculated that Pius was likewise of servile origin.

Pius is often credited with being the first bishop of Rome in the modern sense of the words. The evidence for this is slim but persuasive. We know that another prominent Christian left Rome in a huff at this time, having failed to become bishop of Rome, so there must have been such a position for him to hope to gain. We also know that within a couple of decades of Pius's time writers were talking about the powers of the bishop of Rome as having been of long standing and predating Anicetus, who followed Pius. Other clues point to it having been Pius who managed to secure the authority of the bishop of Rome over all the Christian communities in and near the city. For example, Pius decreed that Easter should be celebrated on Sunday—illustrating that he was in a position to issue a decree with the expectation that it would be obeyed, at least in and around Rome.

Pius played a leading role in a bitter dispute within early Christianity. Marcion, a wealthy shipowner from Sinope, began preaching an idiosyncratic version of Christianity that became popular throughout Asia Minor. In 144, he came to Rome and proclaimed that only some Christian writings were true, denouncing others. Concerned by the validity and popularity of Marcion's views, Pius summoned a council of learned Christians to question him and, in July 144, Marcion was excommunicated, becoming perhaps the first person to suffer this fate for his views—earlier excommunications had been on the grounds of sin, especially fornication or worshiping pagan gods. His teachings were later condemned as heretical—another first.

A rather more welcome visitor to Rome at this time was St. Justin, who stayed in the city several times between 140 and 165, when he was martyred. Justin wrote many important theological works, on subjects such as the Resurrection and the Logos.

Later writers claim that Pius was himself martyred, something taken as fact from the ninth century onward. However, the research that followed the decision of the Second Vatican Council that "accounts of martyrdom are to accord with the facts of history" failed to find any real evidence that Pius had suffered anything other than a natural death.

MARCIONISM

Marcion taught that the God proclaimed by Jesus was a separate deity to that of the Old Testament, effectively cutting Christ off from his Jewish heritage. He also proclaimed the teachings of St. Paul showed that the God of Christ was a perfect spiritual entity, while the God of the Old Testament was a malicious, material creature.

139

Rome's Castel Sant'Angelo is completed as a mausoleum for the late Emperor Hadrian and his successors.

140

Emperor Antonius Pius builds a wall in Britain stretching for 37 miles from the Firth of Forth to the Firth of Clyde, extending Roman territories in the province.

144

Marcion of Sinope forms his own church in Rome.

ST. ANICETUS ✠ The 11th Pope c.155–c.166

Born Homs, Syria; date unknown

Parents Father, John; Mother, unknown

Papacy c.155–c.166

Died Rome, Italy; possibly April 20, c.166

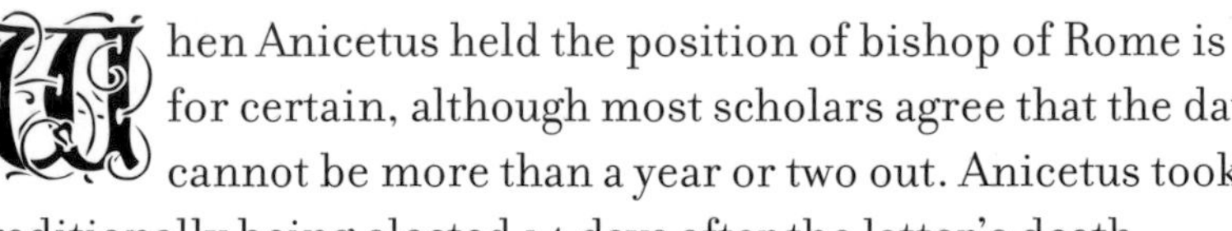

When Anicetus held the position of bishop of Rome is not known for certain, although most scholars agree that the dates 155 to 166 cannot be more than a year or two out. Anicetus took over from Pius, traditionally being elected 14 days after the latter's death.

While the method by which he was chosen is unknown, Anicetus certainly inherited wide-ranging powers and authority similar to those enjoyed by later bishops. However, the limits of the power that the bishop of Rome could exercise at this date are shown by the fact that Cerdo the Gnostic openly preached in Rome his message that there were two equal, but opposed deities—God and Satan—and that Satan created and ruled the world, while God held sway over the spiritual realm. The Gnostic sect was extremely active at the time and gained numerous adherents. Anicetus and others considered the teachings to be heretical.

St. Polycarp miraculously extinguishes the fire prepared for his execution.

The chief event of Anicetus's time as bishop came when Polycarp, bishop of Smyrna, visited Rome. Polycarp was well into his eighties at this date and, as a young man, had met and listened to John the Apostle who had known Christ. He was, as a result, highly respected.

The purpose of the visit was to allow the two leaders of Christianity to resolve various doctrinal issues, such as agreeing the date on which the Resurrection of Christ should be celebrated. Polycarp and most Christians in the East celebrated the date on the Jewish Passover, regardless of on which day of the week it fell. Most in the West preferred to celebrate it on the nearest Sunday, since it was held to be the Lord's Day. After much debate neither managed to convince the other, so they agreed to accept that each should do as they thought fit. They parted as friends, having agreed on many other matters, which is more than can be said for many of their successors as leaders of Eastern and Western Christianity. Polycarp was martyred in Smyrna soon after he left Rome. According to tradition, he was sentenced to be burned at the stake but when the flames miraculously went out, he was beheaded. Later tradition has it that Anicetus himself was martyred on April 20, perhaps alongside Justin the Martyr, but there is no conclusive evidence to support this claim.

GNOSTICISM

The basis of Gnosticism was the claim that its adherents had access to a hidden knowledge—*gnosis*—that was additional and superior to the accepted Gospels and letters of the Apostles. This knowledge was often in the form of gospels or letters that, the Gnostics claimed, St. Paul had hidden as being too sublime or powerful to be circulated to ordinary people. Other forms of hidden knowledge came in the shape of special interpretations of accepted apostolic writings. Many Gnostics passed on verbal secrets to each other, holding these to be so sacred that they should not be written down.

161

Roman emperor Antonius Pius dies of fever, aged 75, and is succeeded by his adopted son Emperor Marcus Aurelius.

165

A plague that may have been smallpox, spread by Roman legions returning from the East, drastically depopulates the Empire.

167

The first full-scale barbarian assault on Rome is repelled by Emperor Marcus Aurelius.

174

Emperor Marcus Aurelius defeats the Quadi in a victory that will be commemorated by a great column in Rome.

ST. SOTER ✠ The 12th Pope c.166–c.174

Born Fondi, Italy; date unknown
Parents Unknown
Papacy c.166–c.174
Died Rome, Italy; date unknown

It was Soter who began a process by which the ability to undertake sacred tasks was increasingly reserved only to clergy properly appointed by a bishop.

Soter issued a decree that a marriage would be considered valid only if it had been properly solemnized by a priest. Previously, Christians had followed pagan practice in seeing marriage as being primarily a civil matter.

At some point, Soter wrote a strongly worded letter to Bishop Eusebius of Corinth. The letter has not survived, but it seems to have criticized Eusebius for a lax attitude toward sinners and the conditions under which they should be readmitted to the Christian community. The reply from Corinth was apologetic and promised to put things right, but rather pointedly did not accept that the bishop of Rome had any right to dictate to the bishop of Corinth. The exchange is seen as an early attempt by the bishop of Rome to exercise the type of authority over other bishops that later popes would take for granted.

Later tradition has it that Soter spoke out against the teachings of Montanus (*see* p.28). Later accounts of the martyrdom of Soter are now considered to be apocryphal.

ST. ELEUTERUS ✠ The 13th Pope c.174–189

Born Nicopolis, Greece; date unknown
Parents Father, Habundius; Mother, unknown
Papacy c.174–189
Died Rome, Italy; 189

The first firm date in the history of the papacy is the death of Eleuterus in 189. Apart from that, however, little is known about this elusive pope. His later fame rests largely on a passage in the *Liber Pontificalis*.

The passage reads as follows: "He (Eleuterus) received a letter from Lucius, king of Britain, asking him to appoint a way by which Lucius might become a Christian." Eleuterus has therefore been credited with beginning the conversion to Christianity of the British Isles. However, at this date there were no kings in Britain, then the Roman province of Britannia, firmly under the control of Rome. Later generations sought to explain the statement by saying that the word "king" should be taken to mean "nobleman," or that the king in question was a king of an area outside Roman control.

Eleuterus was the first bishop of Rome to be faced by what would become the Montanist heresy (*see* p.28). The Christians of Lyon, led by Irenaeus who was later to gain fame as a theologian, asked Eleuterus for the opinion of the Church of Rome on the new movement within Christianity. No firm record of Eleuterus's response has survived, but he is thought to have sent at least one letter to Montanus.

177
A systematic persecution of Christians begins in Rome—the Christians are seen as a threat to the established order because of their opposition to emperor-worship.

180
Roman emperor Marcus Aurelius dies, aged 58, and is succeeded by his son, the emperor Commodus, famed for his tyrannical rule.

183
Emperor Commodus survives an assassination plot led by his sister Lucilla and a group of Roman senators. Commodus executes many distinguished Romans who he perceives to be enemies.

ST. VICTOR I ✠ The 14th Pope 189–198

Born Africa; date unknown
Parents Father, Felix; Mother, unknown
Papacy 189–198
Died Rome, Italy; 198

The first pope to have Mass celebrated in Latin instead of Greek, Victor was a formidable character who ruthlessly tackled the Gnostic writer and priest Florinus, excommunicating him from the Church.

Next to feel his wrath was Theodotus of Byzantium who had suggested that Jesus had been a normal human until the Holy Spirit descended on Him during His baptism. Theodotus, too, was excommunicated. Victor also definitively declared Montanism to be a heresy. This New Prophecy movement adhered to mainstream Christian theology in almost every respect. The hostility of the Church seems to have been driven by the claim by the self-proclaimed prophets who founded the movement to have the ability to forgive sins, something the Church reserved to ordained priests. The Montanists also held that women could become priests and bishops, again in defiance of the established Church.

Victor is the first bishop of Rome known to have had any dealings with the imperial government. A Christian servant named Marcia became the mistress of Emperor Commodus. She asked Victor for a list of fellow Christians held in slavery or prison for their faith and managed to secure their release.

ST. ZEPHYRINUS ✠ The 15th Pope 198–217

Born Rome, Italy; date unknown
Parents Father, Habundius; Mother, unknown
Papacy 198–217
Died Rome, Italy; perhaps August 26, 217

Zephyrinus was a controversial character. According to some he was a disgrace to his position as bishop of Rome; to others he was a brave man heroically defending the Faith in difficult circumstances.

Zephyrinus held office in trying times. Marcionism, Montanism, and Gnosticism were all strong and growing heresies. Moreover, a rich banker named Theodotus tried to set up a rival bishop of Rome who would espouse the heresy that Christ had been a mere man until his baptism. This plot was uncovered when the would-be rival bishop threw himself at the feet of a startled Zephyrinus and begged forgiveness.

In about 197, the emperor Septimius Severus announced a policy of religious syncretism, whereby the followers of different gods would be encouraged to identify their local deity with its Roman equivalent. Neither the Christians nor the Jews had a Roman equivalent for their God, and persecutions began. In 202, large numbers of Christians were executed in North Africa. In 211, another wave of martyrdoms followed in western North Africa and Gaul.

What action, if any, Zephyrinus took to counter this persecution is unknown. Later accounts claim that he, too, fell victim to the persecutions and was martyred on August 26, 217. He was buried on the Appian Way.

192	193	197	200
The Roman emperor Commodus is murdered on December 31 following a plot led by his Christian mistress Marcia.	On March 28, the Roman emperor Pertinax is murdered by members of the Praetorian Guard who invade the imperial palace. Septimius Severus marches into the capital with his army on June 1 and takes control of the Empire.	Byzantium is sacked by the emperor Septimius Severus.	Afghanistan is invaded by the Huns.

ST. CALLIXTUS I ✠ The 16th Pope 217–222

Born Rome, Italy; date unknown

Parents Father, Domitius; Mother, unknown

Papacy 217–222

Died Rome, Italy; perhaps August 14, 222

One of the most controversial popes, Callixtus is notorious for splitting the Church of Rome, inadvertently creating the first schism and the first antipope. Born into slavery, as a youth he worked for Carpophorus who was responsible for handling money as an investor .

As a young man Callixtus, or Callistus, worked for a Christian named Carpophorus who was responsible for handling money invested for charitable purposes by local Christians. Carpophorus put Callixtus in charge of managing the substantial funds. When the money (and Callixtus) went missing, Callixtus was arrested and put to work on a treadmill. Upon his release, he tried to extract some of the money from a Jew to whom he claimed to have lent the money. The Jew denied it and a fight broke out. Callixtus was again arrested and sentenced to slavery in mines in Sardinia.

Callixtus was freed, some years later, thanks to the mistress of Emperor Commodus (*see* p.28). When Pope Victor died, Callixtus entered the household of the new pope, Zephyrinus. By about 210, Zephyrinus had handed over to Callixtus the effective running of the Church.

When Zephyrinus died, there was a bitter dispute over who should succeed him. The majority of those entitled to vote went for Callixtus, while a vocal minority chose a priest named Hippolytus. Both men announced that they were now bishop of Rome and inevitable confusion ensued.

Callixtus took over from his predecessor in attempting to deal with doctrinal disputes, including Modalism: the idea that the Holy Trinity represents three modes of a single deity rather than three persons in one. Callixtus condemned the idea but not those who espoused it, incurring the ire of those who wanted the Modalists excommunicated.

Callixtus's death was as dramatic as his life. In August 222, rioting broke out in Rome following the murder of the emperor Elagabalus by the Praetorian Guard. Callixtus was somehow caught up in the riot, and the next day his body was found stuffed down a well.

ANTIPOPE HIPPOLYTUS

Rich, cultured, educated, and freeborn, Hippolytus was everything that Callixtus was not. When Callixtus was elected bishop of Rome, Hippolytus condemned both the election and the man and led a sizeable faction of Roman Christians into schism. Hippolytus was the author of a number of important theological and liturgical works, including the *Apostolic Tradition* and the *Refutation of All Heresies*. Traditionally, he was martyred by being dragged behind a chariot.

211	217	218	222
Rome's Septimius Severus dies in Britain and is succeeded by his eldest son Augustus, who rules as Emperor Caracalla.	Emperor Caracalla is murdered by a group of his officers and succeeded briefly by Emperor Macrinus	Emperor Macrinus is slain near Antioch on June 8 and is succeeded by a grandnephew of Septimius Severus, the 14-year-old Emperor Elagabalus who proceeds to drain the treasury of Rome with his spectacular excesses.	Emperor Elagabalus is murdered by the Praetorian Guard on March 11 and is succeeded by his 14-year-old cousin Emperor Severus Alexander.

ST. URBAN I ✢ The 17th Pope 222–230

Born Rome, Italy; date unknown
Parents Father, Pontianus; Mother, unknown
Papacy 222–230
Died Rome, Italy; 230

There are many colorful legends about Urban but little certain knowledge. This was a quiet time for Christianity with no recorded persecutions or martyrdoms.

Against this background of stable obscurity, later generations credited Urban with being the first bishop of Rome to use a silver goblet and platter for Mass, and to provide similar silver utensils to every church in Rome. For a religion that was at first largely the preserve of the impoverished, this was a remarkable step.

Also ascribed to Urban by later generations was a decree concerning the use of money given during Mass: "The gifts of the faithful that are offered to the Lord can only be used for ecclesiastical purposes, for the common good of the Christian community, and for the poor; for they are the consecrated gifts of the faithful, the atonement offering of sinners, and the patrimony of the needy." Rather more fanciful are the legends that Urban toppled a pagan idol by the power of prayer alone and that he had a tiara made for himself.

Later generations believed that he was martyred by being beheaded with a sword, and he is often shown in art with this attribute.

ST. PONTIAN  The 18th Pope 230–235

Born Rome, Italy; date unknown
Parents Father, Calpurnius; Mother, unknown
Papacy 230–235
Died Sardinia, Italy; 237

The papacy of Pontian began as quietly as that of his predecessor. In about 231, however, he was involved in a dispute in Egypt over the status of the formidably intelligent scholar and theologian Origen.

In 230, Origen spent some months in Caesarea Maritima in Palestine, where he was ordained by the local bishop. On his return to his native Alexandria, however, he found that the bishop there, Demetrius, refused to accept him as a priest. When Pontian was asked for his opinion on the matter, he judged that as Origen was from Alexandria he was wrong to have accepted elevation to the priesthood from any bishop other than the bishop of Alexandria. This incident is taken as clear evidence that Christians were starting to look to the bishop of Rome for judgement.

In March 235, Emperor Maximinus Thrax came to power and turned on the Christians. Pontian was one of the first to be arrested and sentenced to perpetual slavery in Sardinia. Just before leaving Rome, on September 28, 235, he stood down as bishop to allow someone else to take over. At the same time he was reconciled to the antipope Hippolytus (*see* p.29). Both men died in Sardinia a couple of years later.

235
Emperor Severus Alexander is killed on March 18 by his troops on the Rhine. Maximinus Thrax succeeds him and rules for just three years.

238
Roman subjects revolt in Africa, Emperor Gordian III takes control of the Roman Empire.

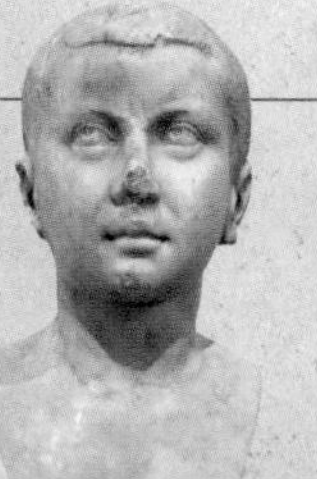

244
Emperor Gordian III drives the Persian army back across the Euphrates, but he is murdered by mutinous soldiers led by the next emperor Philippus.

ST. ANTERUS ✠ The 19th Pope 235–236

Born Petilia Policastro, Italy; date unknown
Parents Father, Romulus; Mother, unknown
Papacy 235–236
Died Rome, Italy; January 3, 236

Anterus took over as bishop of Rome at a time when Emperor Maximinus Thrax had instituted the first official, empire-wide persecution of Christians. Anterus died less than two months after taking office.

Religion in the Roman Empire was complex, with a large variety of gods and goddesses vying for attention. What all these deities had in common was that their adherents practiced their rites in public and recognized that the other gods were, in fact, gods. Governors and emperors believed that the well-being of the Empire rested on the favor of the state gods: Jupiter, Juno, and Minerva. Everyone in the Empire was expected to attend the public festivals in honor of these gods and to pour libations onto their altars. Christians pointedly refused to do so, making them obvious scapegoats when a disaster befell the Empire. Most persecutions followed either a disaster, such as famine or invasion, or were sparked by local civil unrest. Either way, the Christians were easy targets to blame and to strike.

Anterus was buried in the Catacomb of Callixtus, where his tomb was unearthed in 1854. No documented evidence exists for the later legend that he was martyred.

ST. FABIAN ✠ The 20th Pope 236–250

Born unknown, probably Italy; date unknown
Parents Father, Fabius; Mother, unknown
Papacy 236–250
Died Rome, Italy; January 20, 250

Fabian is referred to in several contemporary documents, where he is always treated with respect. He clearly made a deep impact on his fellow Christians, and it is a shame that we know little about him.

With the new persecution ordered by Emperor Maximinus Thrax, the Christians met secretly to choose a new leader. There were several distinguished candidates but legend has it that a dove settled on the head of Fabian, an otherwise unnoticed member of the crowd. Taking this as a sign from God, the Christians appointed Fabian.

Meanwhile, the persecutions of Maximinus came to an end when civil war broke out and a new emperor, Gordian III, left the Christians in peace. Fabian continued building the burial Catacomb of St. Callixtus and other cemeteries, undertook a reformation of the structure of clergy in Rome, and had the bodies of Pontian and Hippolytus returned from Sardinia.

In January 250, the next emperor, Decius, announced that everyone had to honor the state gods. Fabian was among the first to refuse and the first to be arrested. A few days later he died in prison, presumably murdered by the guards. He was buried in the Catacombs of Callixtus, where his tomb was found in 1854.

248
Emperor Philippus II holds elaborate games to celebrate the 1,000th anniversary of the founding of Rome.

249
Troops proclaim Roman commander Gaius Decius as emperor and Decius defeats and kills Emperor Philippus in battle.

250
Emperor Decius institutes the wholesale persecution of Christians.

ST. CORNELIUS ✝ The 21st Pope 251–253

Born unknown, probably Italy; date unknown

Parents Father, Castinus; Mother, unknown

Papacy March 251–June 253

Died Civitavecchia, Italy; June 253

Having ordered the death of Fabian (*see* p.31), the emperor Decius was not about to tolerate a new bishop of Rome. His men patrolled with such efficiency that it was impossible for Christians to organize a new election. It was over a year before Cornelius was finally elected in March 251.

It was arranged that any decisions that needed taking would be made by whichever priests could meet in safety. Novatian, a respected theologian, became spokesman for the priests of Rome. In February 251, Decius marched out of Rome to fight the Goths (and be killed by them), easing the pressure on the Christians.

The surprise election of a fairly junior priest as bishop of Rome seems to have been prompted by a number of factors. Cornelius was a genial character from a well-connected family who favored taking a lenient line with the thousands of lapsed Christians who had buckled under the persecution and attended pagan rites. Novatian wanted to impose harsh penalties.

Novatian promptly announced the election of Cornelius had been fraudulent and summoned his supporters to elect him bishop of Rome. There were thus two bishops of Rome, both of whom appealed to Christians elsewhere to support them. The highly regarded Bishop Cyprian of Carthage and Bishop Dionysius of Alexandria sent envoys to Rome to find out what had happened, and both declared that the election of Cornelius was valid.

Cornelius wrote several letters, mostly about the dispute of the treatment of lapsed Christians. In one of these he gives some useful figures about the Christian community in Rome. He says that the Roman Church consisted of 46 priests, 7 deacons, 7 sub-deacons, 42 acolytes, 52 ostiarii, over 1,500 widows and persons in distress, and about 50,000 followers. The population of Rome at the time was around 800,000, making the Christians a sizeable minority.

When Decius died his place was taken by Trebonianus Gallus, who had barely arrived in Rome when a plague broke out. Gallus chose the Christians as scapegoats and restarted their persecution although with less vigor than Decius. Cornelius was arrested and sent to live in a small house in the port of Centumcellae (now Civitavecchia). For almost a year, Cornelius ran the Church of Rome from exile using messengers to carry out his wishes. He died in June 253, apparently of the plague.

The busy port of Civitavecchia on the Tyrrhenian Sea, west of Rome, to which Cornelius was exiled and where he died in June 253.

ANTIPOPE NOVATIAN, 251–258

Novatian first gained fame as the author of a groundbreaking theological work on the Trinity. During the persecution by the emperor Decius he showed considerable courage in organizing the Church in Rome. Though he failed to find support from other bishops, he did initiate splits in Christian communities between those who favored rehabilitation of lapsed Christians and those who supported his hard-line stance. These factions split off to form rival communities with their own bishops. In the Eastern provinces of the empire these Novatian factions survived for over a century. Novatian himself died in 258, apparently martyred.

251

The Roman emperor Decius and his son are killed in battle against the Goths. General Gaius Vibius Trebonianus Gallus, commander of the legions on the Danube, makes peace with the Goths and marches on Rome. He rules as Emperor Gallus.

253

Campaigning soldiers rebel against Emperor Gallus and elect a new emperor Aemilianus. Although Aemilianus defeats Gallus in battle he, himself, dies soon afterward. Emperor Valerian begins a seven-year reign.

ST. LUCIUS I ✠ The 22nd Pope 253–254

Born Rome, Italy; date unknown

Parents Father, Purphirius; Mother, unknown

Papacy June 253–March 254

Died Rome, Italy; March 4, 254

Almost everything we know about Lucius comes from two letters written to him by Bishop Cyprian of Carthage. His first act was to declare the rival "bishop of Rome" (*see* p.32) to be banished.

His second act was to go into exile himself on the orders of the emperor Gallus. In October 253, however, Lucius received news that Gallus was dead. He returned to Rome to find that the persecution had been lifted. Lucius then received his first letter from Cyprian, written before news of Valerian's religious policy had reached North Africa. The letter congratulated Lucius on his decision to return to Rome and expressed the hope that he would be able to achieve the distinction of being martyred.

Lucius did die shortly afterward and was buried in the Catacomb of Callixtus. His bones were later moved to the Church of Santa Cecilia. In 1100, however, word came from Denmark that a group of demons would not leave Roskilde until they had been banished by a pope in person. Not wanting to go himself, Pope Paschal II (*see* p.146) sent the skull of Lucius encased in a small reliquary. With the demons gone, the skull was moved to Copenhagen Cathedral. It is now in the National Museum of Denmark.

ST. STEPHEN I  The 23rd Pope 254–257

Born Rome, Italy; date unknown

Parents Father, Iobius; Mother, unknown

Papacy May 12, 254–August 2, 257

Died Rome, Italy; August 2, 257

Stephen's short time as bishop of Rome was dominated by the dispute over how to treat those Christians who had lapsed during the reign of Emperor Decius. Generally, he adopted a lenient attitude.

The first decision Stephen had to take was in 254 when two Spanish bishops, expelled by their flocks for having lapsed, appealed to him. Stephen ordered that they should be reinstated, while Bishop Cyprian of Carthage decided they should be expelled. That matter was still unresolved when the bishops of Gaul wrote to Stephen asking him to expel from office Bishop Marcian of Arles who took an extreme view of lapsed Christians, refusing to reinstate them even on their deathbeds. A third dispute overshadowed all others. At this date there were a number of heretical branches of Christianity that baptized pagans into the faith. When these converts wanted to join a regular church the question arose as to whether they had to be rebaptized. Stephen and most Christians in Italy, Spain, and Greece thought they did not; Cyprian and most Christians in Africa disagreed. Stephen declared firmly that as bishop of Rome his decision was final. A serious split seemed inevitable by the time of Stephen's death.

254

Plague grips the Roman Empire and, lasting more than a decade, decimates the population. The pandemic encourages thousands to embrace Christianity.

255

Bishop Cyprian of Carthage writes *De Mortalitate*, in which he describes a pandemic that will spread from Ethiopia in Africa, through Egypt, extending through Europe as far as the British Isles.

ST. SIXTUS II ✝ The 24th Pope 257–258

Born probably Italy; date unknown

Parents Father, Iobius; Mother, unknown

Papacy August 30, 257–August 6, 258

Died Rome, Italy; August 6, 258

Sixtus was a gentle man chosen in the hope that he could solve the disputes that marred the reign of his predecessor. In the event, his rule was brief and he was dramatically martyred.

A few weeks after Sixtus took office, Emperor Valerian won a great victory against the Persians and commanded that everyone in the Empire pay due tribute to the state triad of gods. Realizing that the Christians would oppose him, Valerian ordered the immediate arrest of all bishops and priests, with bishops being earmarked for execution and priests for slavery. Fines were to be levied on anyone else who refused to obey.

On August 6, 258, Sixtus was conducting a service in the chapel in the private cemetery of Praetextatus, well outside the city of Rome. Without warning, a group of soldiers burst in to arrest the Christians. Sixtus stood up and urged the soldiers to let the congregation go and arrest only him. A ferocious blow from a sword sliced off his head, causing his body to slump back into his chair. Six deacons were killed on the spot and a seventh, Lawrence, arrested and killed three days later. The congregation fled, but Sixtus's body was later recovered and buried in the Catacomb of St. Callixtus.

ST. DIONYSIUS ✝ The 25th Pope 260–268

Born unknown, perhaps southern Italy; date unknown

Parents Father, unknown; Mother, unknown

Papacy July 22, 260–December 26, 268

Died Rome, Italy; probably December 26, 268

The bloody persecution of Christians that led to the death of Sixtus was pursued by Emperor Valerian so harshly that it proved impossible to elect a successor until a new emperor came to power in 260.

In 260, Valerian was captured by the Persians, and his son Gallienus issued the Edict of Toleration in 260. The edict removed neither the popular distrust of Christians among pagans nor the legal basis for the earlier persecutions; it merely confirmed that the state would not prosecute Christians for their beliefs. It also allowed the Roman Christians to elect a new bishop, their choice falling on the presbyter Dionysius who had earlier advised Sixtus II on healing a breach with the African bishops.

As bishop of Rome, Dionysius presided over the restoration to the Church and to individual Christians of property confiscated by Valerian, and funds were sent to the Eastern provinces to pay the ransoms of Christians captured in the recent wars. He also reorganized the Church in Rome and, while the details are not certain, he seems to have allocated cemeteries, chapels, and property to particular priests, thus establishing the system of parishes that persists to this day. He died peacefully in Rome.

258

"Valerian's Massacre": the Roman emperor issues an edict ordering the immediate execution of all Christian bishops, presbyters, and deacons, including Sixtus II, Novatian, and Cyprian of Carthage.

260

Rome's Emperor Valerian is defeated by Persia's Shapur I at Edessa and is taken prisoner treacherously at a parley.

269

A Gothic invasion of the Balkans is repelled by Emperor Claudius II.

ST. FELIX I ✠ The 26th Pope 269–274

Born Rome, Italy; date unknown

Parents Father, Constantius; Mother, unknown

Papacy January 3, 269–December 30, 274

Died Rome, Italy; December 30, 274

Virtually nothing remains of contemporary documents relating to Felix. The only innovation ascribed to him (probably anachronistically) was that he ordered that masses be said over the graves of the martyrs.

The only knowledge we have of Felix's activities comes second-hand from Antioch, then the second largest city in the Roman Empire. Bishop Paul of Samosata had preached that Jesus was "adopted" as the Son of God only at the time of His baptism. This was deemed heretical and, late in 268, Paul was deposed by a local synod. Bishop Maximus of Alexandria wrote to Dionysius asking him to confirm the ousting of Paul, but Dionysius died and it was Felix who replied. The letter has been lost, but Felix clearly found against Paul for he was soon writing to Paul's replacement—Domnus. Paul, however, refused to leave his church and house in Antioch. Felix, or a close associate, referred the matter to the emperor Aurelian who had Paul forcibly evicted. Given that it was barely a decade since Pope Sixtus had been butchered by order of an emperor, it is quite astonishing to find the Church asking an emperor to intervene to sort out its problems. On his death in 274, Felix was buried in the Catacomb of St. Callixtus.

ST. EUTYCHIAN ✠ The 27th Pope 275–283

Born Luna, near Florence, Italy; date unknown

Parents Father, Marinus; Mother, unknown

Papacy January 4, 275–December 7, 283

Died Probably in Rome, Italy; December 7, 283

All records from the time of Eutychian were destroyed during the Great Persecution that followed soon after Eutychian's death. It is assumed he enjoyed a relatively peaceful and uncontroversial papacy.

Eutychian is known to have been born in the port-city of Luna, which lay north of Rome on the coast of the Gulf of La Spezia. This made him an Etruscan by birth and, although such distinctions were becoming lost by the third century, he would perhaps have been considered a foreigner by native Romans. We know that at this date the Christian cemeteries near Rome were expanded, indicating either that there were more Christians or that they had more money to buy land for such purposes. In 275, Emperor Aurelian was murdered, and political turmoil ensued with no less than six emperors ruling over the next decade. Diocletian eventually declared himself emperor in 284. He completely reformed the Empire's military and civilian bureaucracies, standardized the tax system, and established a sound financial basis to the economy. However, he was also utterly ruthless, frequently cruel, and responsible for the bloodiest persecution of Christians ever seen.

272

Three Christians are beheaded on the road to the Temple of Mercury on top of a hill that will be named *Mont Martre* (Mountain of Martyrs) in Lucretia, later to be called Paris.

275

Rome's legions retreat from Transylvania and the Black Forest and fall back to the Rhine and the Danube. Emperor Aurelian pushes construction of fortifications for Rome begun four years earlier as the threat of invasion increases. The murder of Emperor Aurelian heralds a decade of murderous political mayhem.

ST. CAIUS ✠ The 28th Pope 283–296

Born perhaps Dalmatia; date unknown

Parents Father, Caius; Mother, unknown

Papacy December 17, 283–April 22, 296

Died probably near Rome, Italy; April 22, 296

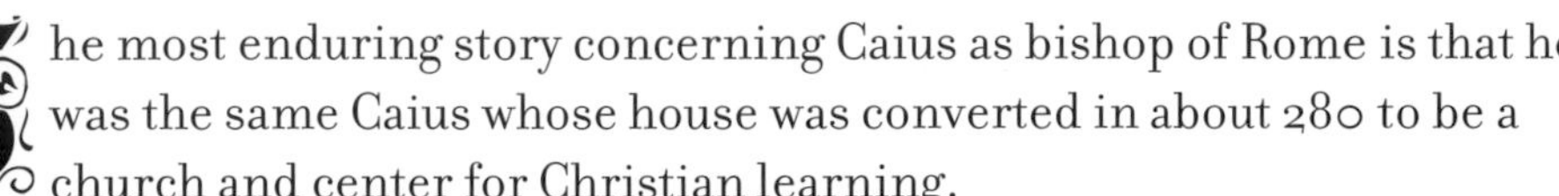

The most enduring story concerning Caius as bishop of Rome is that he was the same Caius whose house was converted in about 280 to be a church and center for Christian learning.

During the Great Persecution (*see* below), a young Christian named Susanna was martyred at Caius's house. The property had belonged to her father Gabinus and her uncle Caius, and it remained in Christian hands until about 795 when it was demolished and the site used for a basilica dedicated to St. Susanna. Recent excavations have found the original house of 280, which—assuming it belonged to Caius the pope and not to another man called Caius—provides a remarkable link to an early pope.

Caius is said to have been a friend of St. Sebastian, the soldier who fell foul of an early edict by the emperor Diocletian that banned Christians from serving in the army. According to legend, Sebastian was used for target practice by a group of archers. He miraculously survived the ordeal, only to be martyred a few years later. Legend has it that Caius himself died while in hiding in the Catacombs of St. Callixtus. Certainly he was buried there—his tomb was discovered in the nineteenth century.

ST. MARCELLINUS ✠ The 29th Pope 296–304

Born Rome, Italy; date unknown

Parents Father, Projectus; Mother, unknown

Papacy June 30, 296–perhaps April 304

Died probably Rome, Italy; perhaps October 25, 304

When Marcellinus assumed office, Christianity was a rapidly growing, but still minority, religion within the Empire and had begun to attract wealthier adherents who donated valuable property to the Church.

Some time in early 303, Emperor Diocletian sought the advice of the oracle of Apollo at Didyma. The oracle replied: "The impious on Earth hinder the ability of the god Apollo to offer his wisdom." Taking the "impious" to mean the Christians, Diocletian embarked on the Great Persecution. All Church property was to be confiscated, no Christians were to assemble for worship, and all sacred books had to be handed over. When a fire broke out in the imperial palace, Diocletian blamed Christian agents and ordered that all Christians had to make sacrifice to the pagan gods or be executed.

How Marcellinus responded has been disputed ever since. Some allege that he stood up to the government and was imprisoned, then beheaded. Others say that Marcellinus handed over the books of the diocese of Rome and performed a sacrifice to the pagan gods. Whatever the truth, he does seem to have ceased being bishop of Rome some months before his death in October 304.

284

The Roman emperor Numerian is assassinated and succeeded by Emperor Diocletian. He will later appoint Maximian Augustus as co-emperor, and Galerius and Constantius as Caesars, ruling the Empire as a tetrarchy.

303

The Great Persecution of Christians by order of Diocletian. Christians are massacred and scriptures burned.

305

Emperor Diocletian abdicates and Galerius assumes the title Augustus, ruling alongside Constantius.

ST. MARCELLUS I ✠ The 30th Pope 306–309

Born Rome, Italy; Date: unknown

Parents Father, Benedictus; Mother, unknown

Papacy perhaps December 306–309

Died place unknown; probably late 309

There was a gap of at least two years before Marcellus was elected to office. A relaxation of the persecution did not come until Emperor Maxentius took over and reduced the anti-Christian activity.

The first task facing Marcellus was to reorganize the Christian community after the upheavals of the Persecution. The second was to decide how to treat the many thousands who sacrificed to the pagan gods rather than suffer martyrdom. It was Marcellus who divided the city of Rome up into a number of districts, traditionally 25, and put over each a presbyter responsible for baptisms, burials, and penances. He also acquired a large, new burial ground for Christians on the Via Salaria.

Marcellus had been one of those who had remained true to his faith during the Great Persecution and he had little tolerance for those who had been less steadfast. There were far more Christians that had lapsed than had stayed true, and survived, and the dispute between the two groups led to violence. Ironically, Emperor Maxentius stepped in and ordered Marcellus to be more conciliatory. When the Pope refused, Maxentius banished him, probably in January 309. Marcellus died a few months later.

ST. EUSEBIUS  The 31st Pope 310

Born unknown; Date: unknown

Parents Unknown

Papacy April 18, 310–perhaps August 17, 310

Died Sicily; October 21, 310

Eusebius was elected because he was known to favor more tolerance toward the "lapsis" who had sacrificed to pagan gods rather than face persecution, but he proved to be just as intransigent as his predecessor.

Whereas Marcellus had wanted the lapsis treated extremely harshly, Eusebius wanted them readmitted to the Church after the lightest of penalties. This led to bitter disputes with those Christians who had remained faithful through the Great Persecution and resented such leniency. Led by a presbyter named Heraclius, those favoring harsh penalties rioted against Eusebius, and again Christian-on-Christian violence wracked the streets of Rome. Once again, the emperor Maxentius stepped in to enforce order on his Christian subjects. This time he exiled to Sicily both Eusebius and Heraclius. There Eusebius died very soon after, making two successive bishops of Rome who had died just months after being exiled by Emperor Maxentius—clearly getting on the wrong side of Maxentius was not a healthy option for a bishop of Rome. The body of Eusebius, but apparently not that of Heraclius, was brought back to Rome and buried in the Catacomb of St. Callixtus.

306

Constantius dies during a campaign against the Picts in Britain. Severus is elevated to role of co-emperor.

307

Co-emperor Severus dies and is succeeded by Emperor Licinius (right).

309

Anthrax or a similar plague begins to spread across the Roman Empire, sharply reducing the population over the next five years.

ST. MILTIADES ✠ The 32nd Pope 311–314

Born probably North Africa; date unknown
Parents Unknown
Papacy July 2, 311–January 10, 314
Died Rome, Italy; January 10, 314

The Basilica of San Giovanni is situated next to the Lateran Palace, which is now a museum dedicated to the history of the Papal States.

It is not known how long the bishopric of Rome lay vacant after the death of Eusebius as there is some dispute over when he ceased to be bishop. Eventually, on July 2, 311, a presbyter named Miltiades (or Melchiades), who had originally come from North Africa, was elected bishop of Rome.

Miltiades took over at a propitious time for the Christian Church in Rome. The Great Persecution of Diocletian had ended and Christianity was about to enjoy a massive growth in wealth, numbers, and respectability. The first sign of this came just a few weeks after Miltiades took office. The emperor Galerius in the Eastern provinces lifted the persecution that had continued there, his only condition being that the Christians had to include prayers for the safety of the emperor and Empire whenever they held a service. Of more direct importance to Miltiades was the order of Galarius's successor, Maxentius, that all property confiscated from the Christians during the persecutions should be restored. Miltiades sent his deacons, each armed with a written imperial order, to take back the houses, cemeteries, shrines, and other places that had formerly belonged to the Church.

In October 312, a battle was fought just outside Rome beside the Milvian Bridge. Maxentius was defeated and killed by his rival in a civil war, the emperor Constantine I, later called "the Great." The new emperor of the West was far more sympathetic to Christianity than any of his predecessors and would later convert to the new faith. As he entered Rome after his victory, Constantine met with Miltiades. The main result of that meeting was that Constantine gave to the bishop of Rome the Lateran Palace to serve as the main residence and administrative center for Christians in the city. The palace remained the official residence of the pope for centuries. It is now a museum, though not much remains of the original fourth-century building.

The disputes that had dogged his predecessors then returned to haunt Miltiades. Early in 313, a new bishop of Carthage had been appointed in the form of Caecilian. However, one of the clergy officiating at the ceremony had been Bishop Felix of Aptunga, a man accused of having handed over sacred books to state officials during the recent persecutions. This made him a traitor and, in the eyes of some Christians, ineligible to perform rites. Those who opposed Felix appointed a rival bishop of Carthage named Donatus. Both sides appealed to Constantine, who referred the matter to Miltiades. Miltiades summoned a synod of Italian bishops to decide the matter, thus turning an imperial commission into a Church hearing and ensuring that internal Church business did not become a matter for the state government. The synod ruled in favor of Caecilian on October 3, 313.

DONATISM

After the synod summoned by Miltiades ruled against him, Donatus refused to recognize Caecilian and returned to Carthage. Declaring that the Christian Church should be composed of saints, not of sinners, Donatus established a rival Church that spread rapidly across North Africa. It was not until 409 that Donatism was denounced as a heresy and some persecution of Donatists followed. The sect survived, however, and was still active as late as the 590s.

311	312	313	314
The Roman emperor Galerius dies in May after he is driven out by Maxentius. Constantine begins to march on Rome.	Constantine kills Maxentius at the Battle of Milvian Bridge and takes control of the Western Roman Empire.	Constantine and his co-emperor Licinius accept Chritianity. They return property confiscated from Christians under terms of the Edict of Milan.	The Battle of Cibalae in which Constantine defeats his co-emperor Licinius and captures the Balkans.

ST. SYLVESTER I ✦ The 33rd Pope 314–335

Born Rome, Italy; date unknown

Parents Father, Rufinus; Mother, unknown

Papacy 31 January, 314–31 December, 335

Died Rome, Italy; 31 December, 335

Holding office as bishop of Rome for 21 years, 11 months, and 1 day, Sylvester was the longest-reigning pope at the time he died. He was also highly respected and considered to be a man of wisdom. It is a shame, therefore, that we possess little certain knowledge about his papacy.

Legend has it that the emperor Constantine had long suffered from leprosy when he finally decided to convert from the pagan cult of the Invincible Sun to Christianity. It was Sylvester who baptized Constantine and, as the sacred water flowed over the emperor's skin, it miraculously washed away the disease. After the ceremony, Sylvester mounted his horse to ride back to the Lateran Palace. Instead of likewise mounting, the emperor held the pope's bridle and walked back as if he were a humble groom.

Rather more certain is the fact that Sylvester used the wealth and property given to the Church by Constantine to construct, repair, or embellish a wide array of Christian buildings. In 318, he began to build perhaps the most famous church in the world: St. Peter's Basilica on the Vatican Hill. The high altar was placed over the site of a tomb that was believed to be that of St. Peter himself, and the rest of the immense church built around it. The building was designed as a typical Roman basilica, or meeting hall, with a central nave and four side aisles. It was so large it could hold 4,000 people and was completed with much ornamentation. It was demolished in the sixteenth century to make way for the new basilica that still stands today.

Also built while Sylvester was bishop of Rome was the Basilica of Santa Croce in Gerusalemme. This church was built to celebrate the finding of the wooden cross on which Jesus had been crucified. Helena, mother of Constantine, traveled to the Holy Land in 324 to build a church over the tomb of Christ, and while there found the hiding place of the True Cross. That cross was taken to Constantinople, but soil from its hiding place was brought to Rome to underlay the floor of Santa Croce. The Archbasilica of St. John Lateran—the Cathedral of Rome—and several other churches were also built or begun by Sylvester.

During Sylvester's reign, the First Council of Nicaea was held, but he was too ill to attend. Sylvester died in Rome, in 335, and he was buried in the cemetery of St. Priscilla.

Interior of St. Peter's Basilica in Rome. Construction of the original basilica began in 310, during the papacy of St. Sylvester.

THE DONATION OF CONSTANTINE

The Donation of Constantine is a document that was supposedly given to Pope Sylvester by the emperor Constantine stating that, in gratitude for his miraculous cure, the emperor makes the bishop of Rome supreme over all other churches throughout the entire world. Until about the mid-fifteenth century, it was considered genuine and was used by the papacy to underpin its claims to vast political power. In 1457, Bishop Pecock, of Chichester, England, denounced it as a fake. It was not until around 1600 that the Church accepted that it was a forgery produced in about 770.

315	324	325	330
The Arch of Constantine constructed to commemorate the emperor's victory at the Battle of Milvian Bridge.	Constantine has his co-emperor Licinius executed and reunites the Empire under his rule.	The Council of Nicaea summoned by the Roman emperor Constantine is the first ecumenical council of the Church.	Constantinople is dedicated on May 11 and becomes the new capital of the Roman Empire. The emperor has spent four years building the new city on the site of ancient Byzantium.

ST. MARK ✠ The 34th Pope 336

Born Rome, Italy; date unknown

Parents Father, Priscus; Mother, unknown

Papacy January 18, 336–October 7, 336

Died Rome, Italy; October 7, 336

Not a huge amount is known about Mark. He was a native Roman and was probably the same Mark mentioned as a senior member of the city's clergy in a letter written by the emperor Constantine in the year 313.

When Mark became bishop of Rome he donated his house to the Church and either converted it to be a church or had a church built adjacent to it. This simple little complex grew steadily over the centuries and by about the year 1000 had become a church dedicated to St. Mark the Evangelist and a residence for visiting cardinals. In 1469, it was massively rebuilt to be a palace for the use of the pope, then handed over to the Venetian Republic to be that state's embassy in Rome. On the unification of Italy in the nineteenth century, it became state property and Mussolini's offices. Today, it is a museum.

Mark gave permission for the bishop of Ostia also to wear a pallium and it later became customary for a pope to give a pallium to favored bishops. During the Middle Ages, some popes charged a hefty fee to bishops being given the pallium, which thus acquired a rather unsavory reputation linked to corruption.

Mark died of natural causes and his bones now lie in St. Mark's Basilica.

ST. JULIUS I ✠ The 35th Pope 337–352

Born Rome, Italy; date unknown

Parents Father, Rusticus; Mother, unknown

Papacy February 6, 337–April 12, 352

Died Rome, Italy; April 12, 352

Julius became bishop of Rome just three months before Emperor Constantine the Great died. He found himself needing to deal with a complex political situation and doctrinal disputes within the Church.

At this time, the Church and Empire were similarly divided between East and West. In the West, Julius led those who accepted the decisions of the First Council of Nicaea against those, mostly in the East, who did not. Bishop Athanasius of Alexandria and Bishop Marcellus of Ancyra supported the Nicaean position, and were expelled by their diocesan priests. In 340, Julius held a synod in Rome to debate the issue, but the Easterners instead held their own Council of Antioch. Predictably, the Roman meeting found in favor of the ousted bishops, while the Antioch meeting found against them.

Julius turned to the joint emperors, Constans I and Constantius II, who summoned all their bishops to a meeting in Sofia in 342. That meeting decided that a bishop could be deposed by his diocese, but that he had the right of appeal to the pope. Later, Julius seems to have concentrated on internal Roman issues, reforming the papal administrative offices to match those of the imperial government.

337	350	354	359
Constantine dies leaving three sons and two nephews. The nephews are quickly disposed of by the sons, who then divide the Empire between themselves. Rome falls to Constantine II, who in 340 is killed by his brother Constans I. The Empire is thus divided between Constans in the West and his brother Constantius II in the East.	*Codex Sinaiticus*, the earliest Christian bible, is transcribed.	Birth of St. Augustine in Thagaste (modern Algeria), North Africa.	Council of Rimini; Pope Liberius rejects the Arian creed of council.

LIBERIUS ✠ The 36th Pope 352–366

Born Rome, Italy; date unknown

Parents Father, Augustus; Mother, unknown

Papacy May 17, 352–September 24, 366

Died Rome, Italy; September 24, 366

Liberius assumed office as war raged over Italy with Emperor Constantius II battling the pretender Magnentius. The war was also waged in the theological field for the Westerner Magnentius supported the Nicaean orthodoxy, while Constantius favored the Arian heresy.

By 353, Constantius had disposed of Magnentius and reunited the entire Empire under his own rule. Liberius took the opportunity to send messengers to the emperor at Arles suggesting that a great council of all the Eastern and Western bishops be held at the fortress-city of Aquileia. Instead, Constantius held a synod at Arles that simply confirmed the deposition of Bishop Athanasius of Alexandria (*see* p.40) but ignored the underlying theological issues.

That did not satisfy Liberius who demanded that a general council of the Church be held. This took place in Milan in October 355. Again Constantius did not allow theological discussions but only debate on the narrow issue of whether Athanasius had been properly ousted. Using bribery, threats, and intimidation, Constantius got his way. Liberius was then ordered to attend and, when he refused to accept the verdict of the council, was exiled to Thrace.

Bartolomé Murillo painting shows the wealthy patrician John revealing his dream to Pope Liberius.

In Rome, Constantius arranged the election of a more pliable bishop of Rome, Felix II. That prompted riots and demonstrations that continued, off and on, for months. By 358, both Constantius and Liberius were desperate for a solution. The emperor wanted order restored in his capital city; the bishop wanted to return to Rome. The two met at Sirmium (now Mitrovica) and Liberius signed a document that fudged the theological position.

Back in Rome, Liberius had to accept Felix as joint bishop and kept his head down. After Constantius died, Liberius began a policy of reconciliation with the Eastern bishops. He recognized those bishops who, while not being entirely orthodox in their teachings, were willing to recognize the supremacy of Rome and to accept the reinstatement of Athanasius.

It was in Liberius's time that the great Basilica of Santa Maria Maggiore became a church. The details are overlain by legend, but a rich Roman patrician named John and his wife donated their vast fortune to the Church for the service of St. Mary, mother of Christ, who appeared to John in a dream. Liberius chose the summit of the Esquiline Hill, taking land then owned by the Sicinini family that, according to the legend, was indicated by a miraculous fall of snow in mid-summer. Liberius ordered the construction of a church on the spot, possibly converting buildings already there. The current basilica was constructed in the 430s.

360
The Huns invade Europe. Picts and Scots cross Hadrian's Wall and attack Roman forces in Britain.

361
Emperor Constantius dies. Constantinople acknowledges his cousin Julian as sole ruler of the Empire. Emperor Julian begins an 18-month reign as the last non-Christian Roman emperor.

363
Emperor Julian is mortally wounded in battle with the Persians. He is succeeded by Emperor Jovian.

364
Emperor Jovian signs a humiliating treaty with the Persian king Shapur II, yielding most Roman holdings in Persia. He is found dead on the journey back to Constantinople.

ST. DAMASUS ✢ The 37th Pope 366–384

Born Egitânia (now Idanha), Portugal; c.305

Parents Father, Antonius; Mother, Laurentia

Papacy October 1, 366–December 11, 384

Died Rome, Italy; December 11, 384

Damasus is one of the most controversial of early popes. He did much to establish the shape of the papacy and of Christianity as they emerged in early medieval times and sought to rigidly (and sometimes ruthlessly) enforce the superiority of the bishop of Rome over other bishops.

Damasus served as a deacon under Liberius, but then served the antipope Felix II before returning to work for Liberius around the year 360. When Liberius died in 366, the Roman clergy were split between those who had remained loyal to Liberius in exile and those who had found accommodation with Felix. The former met in the Julian Basilica and elected a deacon named Ursinus to be bishop of Rome. Damasus, as leader of the other faction, hired a group of gladiators who stormed the Julian Basilica, massacring those within. Damasus was installed as bishop of Rome and persuaded the city prefect to expel Ursinus and his followers. Several hundred people had died in the disturbances and although other bishops accepted Damasus as bishop of Rome his standing was badly damaged.

Damasus himself moved easily through the higher levels of Roman society, probably as he came from a patrician family himself. Christianity had earlier had a reputation for being a religion of slaves and plebeians, but Damasus adopted the clothes, manners, and lifestyle of Roman nobility and made them an integral part of the papacy. He was an insider in the circles of power in Rome, in a way earlier popes had not been.

In his efforts to enforce the superiority of the bishop of Rome over other bishops, Damasus did not base his claims on synod decisions, which could be changed, but on the unique mission given by Christ to St. Peter. He persuaded the Roman government to recognize the authority of the bishop of Rome over all Christians and to exempt him from taxes.

Damasus was just as indefatigable in opposing heresy. He cracked down on teachings not to his liking in the West, but attempts to do the same in the East served to antagonize many in those provinces who were seeking compromise with the Arians.

Damasus's cultured tastes led him to compose poetry in praise of the martyrs and he encouraged many arts in service of Christianity. He was almost 80 years old when he died. His remains lie in the Church of San Lorenzo in Rome.

ARIANISM

The Arian Heresy began as a questioning by the Egyptian priest Arius of the precise nature of the relationship between God the Father and God the Son. Arius noted that, in the Bible, Jesus says both that "The Father is greater than I" and "The Lord created me." Arius concluded that this meant that God the Father had always existed, while God the Son was created later and was subservient to the Father. In 321, Arius was condemned as a heretic by a synod in Egypt, but his views spread rapidly and soon were supported by the majority of Christians in the Eastern provinces of the Roman Empire.

The Church of San Lorenzo, Rome—burial site of the controversial pope Damasus.

371	375	376	380	382
The neo-Persian Empire reaches the height of its power under Shapur II as Romans and Persians renew their wars.	The Roman emperor Valentinian I dies. Emperor Gratian assumes power.	The Battle of Adrianople ends in disaster for the Romans who are routed by mounted Visigoths. The victory presages a revolution in the art of war, with the advent of cavalry.	Emperor Theodosius I issues the Edict of Thessalonica declaring Nicene Christianity as the state church of the Roman Empire.	The Council of Rome under Pope Damasus sets the Biblical Canon, listing the inspired books of the Old Testament and the New Testament.

ST. SIRICIUS ✠ The 38th Pope 384–399

Born Rome, Italy; date unknown
Parents Father, Tiburtius; Mother, unknown
Papacy December 384–November 26, 399
Died Rome, Italy; November 26, 399

A deacon under both Liberius and Damasus, Siricius was unanimously elected by the clergy and confirmed by the emperor in February 385—imperial confirmation would soon be regarded as essential.

Siricius introduced a number of innovations that built on the work of Damasus to integrate the Christian Church into Roman high society and structures of government. He introduced the "decretal"—a letter that delivers a decision that is binding on the person to whom it is addressed. The first decretal, the *Directa Decretal*, was written to Bishop Himerius of Tarragona in answer to a letter asking a series of questions. In it Siricius stipulated that priests had to be celibate.

Siricius was the first bishop of Rome to use the title Pontifex Maximus. This ancient title means "Chief Priest" and had originated around 500 BC when it referred to the most senior of the pagan priests in Rome. After 36 BC the title was held by the emperors, with Gratian being the last to use it around 376. Siricius adopted the vacant title, using it in a Christian context to make the point that he was the most senior priest in the Empire. Later sources claimed Siricius was also the first bishop of Rome to use the title of "pope."

ST. ANASTASIUS I ✠ The 39th Pope 399–401

Born Rome, Italy; date unknown
Parents Father, Maximus; Mother, unknown
Papacy November 27, 399–December 19, 401
Died Rome, Italy; December 19, 401

Anastasius was a supporter of the ascetic movement before his elevation as bishop of Rome but any hopes the ascetics had of his support were dashed by the eruption of the Origen dispute.

Early in 400, Anastasius received a letter from Bishop Theophilus of Alexandria alerting him to the views of the theologian Origen and the way they were permeating Christian communities in the East. In particular, Theophilus was opposed to the concept of *Apokatastasis*, which held that all beings would be ultimately reconciled to God and denied the existence of Hell. Once Anastasius had understood the teachings of Origen he convened a synod at which they were declared anathema.

Anastasius would prove equally forthright in confronting other disputes. The bishops of North Africa were seeking a compromise with the still flourishing Donatists (*see* p.38), but Anastasius slapped them down with firm instructions to continue to fight against the separatist sect. He also issued instructions on ritual, establishing that priests and bishops had to stand with bowed heads when the Gospels were read in church. Anastasius's death may have been sudden. He was buried in the Pontian Cemetery.

386	395	399	401
Augustine converts to Christianity.	The Roman Empire splits into Eastern and Western empires following the death at Milan of Emperor Theodosius, aged 49. The split is considered temporary but will prove to be permanent.	*Confessions* by St. Augustine, in which he writes, "How small are grains of sand! Yet if enough are placed in a ship they sink it."	Visigoths penetrate the northern defenses of Italy and begin to ravage the countryside.

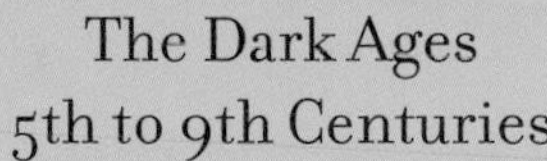

The Dark Ages
5th to 9th Centuries

CHAPTER TWO

As the government structures of Rome collapsed, the Church stepped in to provide secular as well as moral and religious leadership to the former Empire. The Papacy went from strength to strength, but was wracked by disputes over essential, though often detailed, matters of theology and philosophy. As scholars attempted to define the nature of Christ, a host of heresies sprang up to cause disruption to the Church and an agony of soul searching among the faithful. Meanwhile, the establishment of secular rule by the pope over much of Italy led the Italian nobles to taken an interest in the papacy, with potentially disastrous results.

ST. INNOCENT I ✣ The 40th Pope 401–417

Born Rome, Italy; date unknown

Parents Father, Anastasius I; Mother, unknown

Papacy December 21, 401–March 12, 417

Died Rome, Italy; March 12, 417

The shift in status of the bishop of Rome from being the leader of a small and despised religious sect to being at the heart of the governing elite was in many ways completed under Innocent I. It is ironic that this elevation of status came just as the Roman Empire was crumbling.

While the economic and political situation declined, the Christian Church struggled both to keep the Christian faith alive and to remain united and strong. Innocent was to play a key role in this effort. He was assiduous in asserting both the primacy of the bishop of Rome and adherence to the orthodox faith, which he increasingly defined as being whatever the bishop of Rome said it was. In 416, for instance, a council of African bishops condemned the teachings of the monk Pelagius as being unorthodox and then asked Innocent to add his condemnation. Innocent replied thanking the African bishops for submitting the matter to him for decision (which was not what they had done) and then confirming their view.

The Sack of Rome by the Barbarians in 410 by French artist Joseph-Noël Sylvestre.

Innocent's main dispute came over Bishop John Chrysostom of Constantinople. John was an outspoken critic of opulence, corruption, and paganism. His tactlessness led to the Eastern emperor banishing him from his diocese. Innocent waded in to the dispute, taking the side of John against the emperor and getting involved with the Eastern bishops. John died in 407 before the matter was resolved.

Politically, the great event of Innocent's pontificate was the fall of Rome to the Goths. Just before the siege began, in the autumn of 408, Innocent had left the city to lead a delegation to the Western emperor Honorius to beg for help. No help came and Rome fell (*see below*). When Innocent returned two years later he found a city that had been partly burned, widely looted, and which had lost perhaps a third of its population.

THE SACK OF ROME

King Alaric of the Goths marched on Rome in 408 but found the walls impenetrable. Alaric withdrew and opened negotiations with Emperor Honorius, which dragged on until 410 when a new Roman army from the East arrived, giving Honorius the courage to insult Alaric. Alaric returned to Rome. Goth slaves inside the city opened the Salarian Gate at dawn on August 24 and the Goths poured in to loot, rape, and pillage. It was the first time the city had been captured in 800 years. The news sent shock waves across the Empire and beyond.

404

Last gladiator fight takes place in Rome.

410

The Sack of Rome by Alaric the Goth.

411

The Alans establish their rule in the Roman province of Lusitania (Portugal).

413

St. Augustine of Hippo starts work on his key book *City of God*.

ST. ZOSIMUS ✠ The 41st Pope 417–418

Born perhaps Greece; date unknown

Parents Father, Abraham; Mother, unknown

Papacy March 18, 417–December 26, 418

Died Rome, Italy; December 26, 418

Zosimus came to Rome sometime before 406, bringing with him a letter of recommendation from John Chrysostom of Constantinople. He proved to be a great scholar and talented administrator.

Zosimus ran into trouble when he met Caelestius, a pupil of Pelagius who had been condemned as a heretic by Innocent I. Deciding that the two men had reformed, Zosimus wrote a letter to the African bishops ordering them to lift their declaration of heresy. The Africans pointed out that neither Pelagius nor Caelestius had actually renounced their heretical views and appealed to Emperor Honorius who ordered Zosimus to reissue the finding of heresy. Zosimus reluctantly backed down, but he was determined to reassert papal authority. In 418, the Carthaginian presbyter Apiarius arrived in Rome to complain that he had been unjustly excommunicated and deprived of his office by Bishop Urbanus of Sicca. Zosimus at once declared in favor of Apiarius and sent messages to the African bishops ordering them to reinstate the renegade and to stop appealing to the emperor on ecclesiastical matters. The dispute looked set to escalate when Zosimus died. He was buried in the Church of San Lorenzo, Rome.

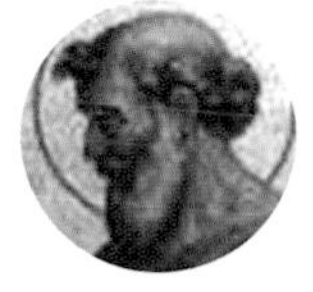

ST. BONIFACE I ✠ The 42nd Pope 418–422

Born Rome, Italy; date unknown

Parents Father, Locundus; Mother, unknown

Papacy December, 28 418–September 4, 422

Died Rome, Italy; September 4, 422

When Zosimus died, the deacons elected Archdeacon Eulalius to be bishop of Rome, while the presbyters elected the presbyter Boniface. Emperor Honorius referred the matter to a council of bishops.

Honorius ordered both candidates to stay away from Rome until June 419 when the council was scheduled to take place, but Eulalius promptly rushed to Rome to celebrate Easter in the Lateran Basilica hoping this would ensure his victory. In fact, it merely prompted the furious Honorius to confirm Boniface as bishop.

As bishop of Rome, Boniface restored peace to the Gallic Christians by repealing the act by Zosimus that had given authority over the province to the bishop of Arles; and he mollified the African bishops by agreeing a compromise in the dispute over the defrocked priest Apiarius (*see* above). Having restored peace in the West, he got into a dispute with the East. The churches of the Balkans traditionally looked to the bishop of Rome, but the area had been transferred from the Western to the Eastern Empire and it was unclear if the ecclesiastical authority should transfer as well. Boniface was adamant it should not. He died in 422 and was buried in a chapel dedicated to St. Felicity, which he had built himself.

415
King Wallia of the Goths agrees a peace treaty with Emperor Honorius.

417
King Wallia of the Goths is granted rule over Aquitaine by Emperor Honorius in return for military help against the Vandals.

420
Emperor Wu establishes the Liu Song Dynasty in China.

421
What will become Venice is founded when the church of San Giacomo is dedicated on the marshy Rialto Island.

422
An earthquake damages large parts of Rome, cracking the walls of the Colosseum from top to bottom.

ST. CELESTINE I ✠ The 43rd Pope 422–432

Born southern Italy; date unknown

Parents Father, Priscus; Mother, unknown

Papacy September 10, 422–July 27, 432

Died Rome, Italy; July 27, 432

As a young man Celestine had worked in Milan under the famous St. Ambrose, but he had moved to Rome by 416 when he is recorded as being a deacon. He was clearly popular among the Roman clergy for he was elected unopposed to be bishop of Rome.

Celestine was deeply interested in the unity of the Christian Church and spent much of his pontificate trying to make it a reality. His first move was in Rome itself, where several communities of Novatianist Christians (*see* p.32) were still in place. Celestine declared that the churches and other property used by the Novatianists were really the property of the bishop of Rome and, with the support of the prefect of Rome, seized it all. Thereafter, the Novatianist sect rapidly faded away. He also took action against the teachings of Pelagius, which had reached Britain. Celestine sent Germanus, the bishop of Auxerre, on an extended mission to Britain to explain why Pelagius was a heretic and to summon the British Church back to obedience to Rome.

A depiction of St. Germanus, the bishop of Auxerre, with his bishop's crook and mitre, from a stained-glass window in Truro Cathedral, Cornwall, England.

Celestine was less successful in his dealings with the African bishops. The controversial priest Apiarius (*see* p.46) was again expelled from his church and again appealed to Rome. In 426, Celestine found in favor of Apiarius and ordered the Africans to reinstate him. The papal position was undermined when Apiarius confessed to all the charges against him.

In 428, the newly appointed Archbishop Nestorius of Constantinople expressed his belief that Christ could not have been wholly divine and wholly human at the same time. Celestine ordered him to recant this heresy or be excommunicated. A council of bishops held at Antioch in 431 failed to reach a decision on Nestorius or his teachings. The Eastern emperor Theodosius II then stepped in to force Nestorius and 17 of his supporters to be removed as bishops and live as simple monks. Celestine continued to claim his right to decide on ecclesiastical matters in the Eastern provinces but, in practice, he was reduced to effectively agreeing with what the emperor had done. Celestine died before the Nestorian controversy was fully resolved. He was buried in the Cemetery of St. Priscilla, but his tomb was later moved to the Basilica of St. Praxedes, where it remains.

NESTORIANISM

When Nestorius was condemned by the Eastern Roman Emperor, the Christians further east refused to accept the ruling and split from the Christian Church inside the Roman Empire. That Church of the East continued to believe in the Nestorian doctrine of Christ having two natures in one body and enjoyed much success. However, in the 14th century, it was nearly destroyed by the Muslim leader Tamerlane. Today, it survives as the Assyrian Church with about half a million adherents in Iraq and neighboring areas.

423	425	426	427	429
Western Emperor Honorius dies to be replaced by usurper John.	After a civil war, John is killed and replaced as Western emperor by Valentinian III, nephew of Honorius.	The stadium and temples of Olympia are demolished to stop the pagan Olympic Games being revived.	The founding of Copan by Kinich Yax Kukmo marks the accepted start of the Mayan civilization in Central America.	The Parthenon in Athens is sacked by Christians, who then turn it into a church.

ST. SIXTUS III ✣ The 44th Pope 432–440

Born Rome, Italy; date unknown

Parents Father, Sixtus; Mother, unknown

Papacy July 31, 432–August 19, 440

Died Rome, Italy; August 19, 440

Sixtus was a key insider within the growing bureaucracy that surrounded Pope Celestine. When he became pope, Sixtus broadly continued the policies of his predecessor. However, Sixtus is best remembered for the massive contribution he made to the buildings of Rome

Sixtus's first acts were to work with the Eastern Roman emperor Theodosius II to heal the scars left by the Nestorian dispute. A compromise was reached whereby those bishops and clergy who had supported Nestorius and been expelled from office as a result could return to their positions. All they had to do was formally repudiate Nestorius. Given that by this date the Christian Church had become a wealthy institution enjoying impressive tax exemptions, expulsion from office was a serious blow that former Nestorians were keen to avoid. By the summer of 433, the affair was over.

Sixtus continued Celestine's moves to ensure Roman authority over churches in the Balkans. In 434, he wrote to the clergy of the area instructing them to ignore any messages from the patriarch of Constantinople.

When Sixtus became bishop of Rome the city had not recovered from the sacking by the Goths in 410. Large areas of the city lay in ruins, the population was in decline, and the drains and roads were falling apart. Sixtus persuaded both the Eastern emperor Valentinian III and Theodosius to donate vast sums of money to rebuild Rome. In part, the effort proved to be successful as ruins were cleared and infrastructure restored but, ultimately, it failed because the economic underpinnings of the city had gone and a long decline was inevitable. Among the building projects that Sixtus began were the construction of the Basilica of Santa Maria Maggiore, which still stands largely intact. He also built the Basilica of Santa Sabina, recently restored to its original form. Of perhaps more lasting importance, he built the first monastery in Rome, that of San Sebastiano, of which nothing now remains.

MONASTICISM

None of the accepted Scriptures make any provision for monks. This style of religious life arose first in Syria during the late-second century. Some Christians felt the need to abandon secular life and live in remote places to devote themselves to theological study and prayer. St. Antony the Great was one such, but his reputation for learning was such that dozens of followers had come to live with him by the 290s. Antony instituted strict rules based on manual labor and prayer and his community became the model for later groups. Soon, monasteries were being established in or near towns. The Monastery of San Sebastiano built by Sixtus marks the emergence of monasticism in the West.

Pope Sixtus began construction on the Basilica of Santa Maria Maggiore, replacing the original Liberian Basilica.

434

Attila becomes ruler of the Huns.

435

King Genseric of the Vandals secures his rule over much of North Africa.

439

Greek replaces Latin as the official language of the Eastern Roman Empire.

440

The Buddhist school at Nalandar is founded on the banks of the Ganges in India.

ST. LEO I ✠ The 45th Pope 440–461

Born Tuscany, Italy; Date: c.400

Parents Father, Quintianus; Mother, unknown

Papacy August 440–November 10, 461

Died Rome, Italy; November 10, 461

Born into an aristocratic family of wealth, pedigree, and influence, Leo was undoubtedly the most important of the 5th-century popes and fully deserves the epithet of "the Great" that later generations bestowed upon him. He stamped his authority on the Church and on its doctrine with firmness and consistency, while avoiding the tactlessness of some of his predecessors.

Leo served as a deacon under Celestine I and was a key adviser to Sixtus III, being credited with ensuring the latter's firm opposition to Pelagianism (*see* p.56). That Leo moved easily in the highest secular—as well as ecclesiastical—circles is shown by the fact that he was absent in Gaul on a diplomatic mission on behalf of Emperor Valentinian III when Sixtus III died. Despite being several weeks' journey away at the time, Leo was promptly elected to be bishop of Rome. He hurried back to the city, dating his assumption of office to September 29, the day he reached Rome.

This etching shows Pope Leo I before a humbled Atilla. Legend has it that a vision of St. Peter appeared warning the Hun ruler that he would die if he attacked Rome.

Coming from a family and social background fully accustomed to exercising power and well versed in the constitutional underpinnings of Roman law, Leo had no trouble either exercising the powers of the bishop of Rome over other bishops or justifying it to his full satisfaction. Leo declared that Christ had bestowed supreme and universal authority over all Christians to St. Peter and that on his martyrdom St. Peter had passed that authority on to the bishops of Rome, with the authority continuing down through the line of bishops to himself and his successors. The bishop of Rome was to other bishops what Peter had been to the other Apostles.

Every year on September 29, Leo preached a special anniversary sermon, which was afterward circulated as a letter. Those that have survived show him to have been stern against heresy but willing to guide and instruct gently those in error or who were uncertain of the true path. He insisted that the usual practice of the clergy as it had developed in Rome was the correct guide to ritual and liturgy and insisted that it was followed everywhere.

In 447, he received from Spain an appeal for help from Catholic bishops who were getting into trouble with the new Vandal rulers, who were followers of the Arian heresy. Leo replied with detailed advice and guidance that was, presumably, helpful since there seem to have been no further problems. North Africa had traditionally been keen to assert its rights in

442

Eogan mac Niall is baptized by St. Patrick and becomes the first Christian to be high king of Ireland.

449

Rebellion of Germanic mercenaries led by brothers Hengest and Horsa against their Romano-British employers, traditionally seen as the start of the conversion of Roman Britain to pagan England.

450

Traditional date of the discovery of Hawaii by Polynesian settlers led by Hawaii Loa.

451

The Battle of Chalons ends in defeat for the Huns at the hands of a Roman force under Flavius Aetius with help from the Visigoths. The Council of Chalcedon declares Jesus to be both human and divine in one.

MONOPHYSITISM AND MONOTHELITISM

In contrast to the orthodox position that Christ had been human and divine, Monophysitism saw Jesus as being identical to God the Son and having only one nature—divine. It was particularly popular in Egypt and neighboring provinces of the Eastern Roman Empire. After Monophysitism was condemned at Chalcedon it continued to have adherents in Egypt and spread to Ethiopia, Sudan, Syria, and adjacent areas. Monothelitism was a development of the Monophysite position. It stated that Jesus Christ had two natures but only one will. The position enjoyed considerable popularity and led to centuries of confusion and disputes but was denounced as heretical in 681.

Coin depicting Honoria, sister of the emperor Valentinian III. Attila the Hun requested her hand in marriage—along with half the Roman Empire as her dowry.

the face of papal authority, but with Leo things were different. While still emphasizing their distinctive position, the African bishops eagerly sought Leo's opinion and, without demur, followed his advice. In the early 440s, Bishop Hilary of Arles began trying to exercise an authority over other bishops in Gaul—authority that he did not possess but which the bishops of Arles had long sought. Leo slapped him down in no uncertain terms, confining him to his diocese. Leo even obtained an imperial rescript—a document with the force of law—stating that the bishop of Rome had authority over all the Western Roman Empire. The effectiveness of this ruling was hampered by the fact that, although Valentinian III had in theory retained authority over the entire Western Empire, large areas of it were in fact ruled by barbarian kings.

In 448, Leo received an appeal from a monk named Eutychus who had been expelled by Patriarch Flavian of Constantinople, for preaching the teachings of Monophysitism. Leo replied supporting Flavian in a letter that has become famous as the "Tome of Leo." The Eastern emperor Theodosius II called a meeting of bishops at Ephesus, which ignored the Tome, ignored Flavian, and reinstated Eutychus. Leo and Flavian were furious and responded by summoning what became the Fourth General Council of the Church, at Chalcedon in 451. There the Tome was read out and the doctrine established that Christ had been "perfect in godhead and perfect in manhood... to be acknowledged in two natures, inconfusedly, unchangeably, indivisibly, inseparably."

The Council went on to issue a number of canon laws forbidding a priest from serving in the army, a bishop from engaging in business, and a monk from getting married. More controversially, it announced that the bishop of Constantinople was on an equal footing to the bishop of Rome since both were imperial capital cities. Leo accepted all the Council's findings except this last one, advancing a series of reasons why it was illegal.

In 452, Attila the Hun invaded Italy, bringing with him all the horrors and bloodshed that a campaign by the Huns usually brought in its wake. City after city fell to the Huns amid unprecedented scenes of slaughter and brutality. Attila declared he wanted to marry Honoria, sister of Emperor Valentinian III, and expected half the Empire as her dowry. Valentinian was powerless to intervene, his meager armies being busy elsewhere. Leo took it upon himself to ride unarmed to the camp of the Huns and beg Attila for mercy. According to later legend, St. Peter himself appeared in a vision to Attila vowing instant death to him if he attacked Rome. Be that as it may, Attila retreated north back over the Alps and never again threatened Rome.

Leo was buried in the porch of St. Peter's Basilica, the first bishop of Rome to be buried in that church (although some of the very first popes had been interred on the site before the church was built). His remains were later moved inside and are now interred beneath a special altar dedicated to his memory.

453

Death of Attila the Hun. His followers are driven out of Italy by Roman troops with barbarian reinforcements.

455

Rome is sacked by the Vandals. The devastation is such that the name "vandal" becomes a generic term for a wanton destroyer.

458

Death of Merovich, founder of the Merovingian Dynasty of the Franks.

460

A famine that will last for several years begins in the neo-Persian Empire.

ST. HILARIUS ✣ The 46th Pope 461–468

Born Sardinia, Italy; date unknown

Parents Father, Crispinus; Mother, unknown

Papacy November 19, 461–Feburary 29, 468

Died Rome, Italy; Feburary 29, 468

At the Council of Ephesus in 449 it was Hilarius who was entrusted by Leo to read out the famous Tome message. During his own papacy he was keen to counter the Monophysitism that Leo had opposed.

When Hilarius read out Leo's Tome, he provoked a riot. He fled and hid in the tomb of St. John the Evangelist, just outside the city. His first act as pope was to build a chapel to St. John in thanks for saving his life. He wrote again to the Eastern bishops repeating Leo's Tome and praising the Council of Chalcedon and its decisions, while emphasizing the primacy of the bishop of Rome.

Hilarius's papacy was beset by problems in Spain and in Gaul. As travel became difficult with barbarian rulers taking power, Hilarius sought increasingly to act through deputies. In Gaul, he chose the bishopric of Arles to act as a staging post for papal instructions. However, the other Gallic bishops were unwilling to accept the superiority of Arles and the Germanic rulers each wanted to have their own bishop on an equal footing with the others. Spain had the added the problem that its new rulers were of the Arian heresy, but at least the bishops there were more amenable to Roman superiority and generally did as Hilarius instructed.

ST. SIMPLICIUS ✣ The 47th Pope 468–483

Born Tivoli, Italy; date unknown

Parents Father, Castinus; Mother, unknown

Papacy March 3, 468–March 10, 483

Died Rome, Italy; March 10, 483

The early life of Simplicius is unknown. As pope, he proved to be energetic. He built the unusual Church of Santo Stefano on the site of an abandoned temple to the god Mithras, where it still stands today.

Simplicius also acquired a large hall on the Esquiline Hill that he made into the Church of San Andrea—the first time an old civilian building had been converted in this way.

In September 476, the Western emperor Romulus Augustulus abdicated at the command of one of the Germanic warlords. The Roman Senate sent the imperial regalia to the Eastern Emperor Zeno, telling him that he was now also the Emperor of the West. In reality, however, imperial power in the West was dead. Acacius, Bishop of Constantinople, immediately declared that ecclesiastical authority should also move and claimed that his see was now superior to that of Rome. To gain support for the change, Acacius approached the numerous followers of Monophysitism with a compromise definition of Christ's status. This "Henoticon" outraged Simplicius who denounced it as heresy. The dispute was rapidly escalating when Simplicius died. He was buried in the porch of St. Peter's Basilica, close to Leo the Great.

466

The Huns attack Constantinople but are unable to breach the city walls.

476

Romulus Augustulus, the last emperor of Rome, abdicates.

477

The Buddhist Shaolin Temple is founded on the slopes of Mount Song, one of the four sacred mountains of China.

484

Peroz, ruler of the Persian Empire, is killed by the Huns at the Battle of Herat.

ST. FELIX III ✠ The 48th Pope 483–492

Born Rome, Italy; date unknown

Parents Father, Felix of Fasciola; Mother, unknown

Papacy March 13, 483–March 1, 492

Died Rome, Italy; March 1, 492

Felix came to office as Bishop Acacius of Constantinople was seeking to supplant the pope as head of Christianity. The conflict led to a schism between East and West that lasted for over three decades.

Felix wrote a long letter to Acacius and another to the emperor Zeno insisting that the pope in Rome was superior and chastising them for seeking a compromise with the heretic Monophysitists. Felix's messengers delivered the note but, in fact, agreed to support Acacius. The furious Felix reacted by excommunicating his own ambassadors and Acacius and deposing a number of Eastern bishops. The messenger sent to announce the move to Acacius did so while he was celebrating mass at the altar of his own cathedral. As a result, the Christian churches of the Eastern Empire repudiated Roman authority and cut off all communication.

In the 480s, King Genseric of the Vandals, eased the Arian persecution of Catholics and thousands of former Catholics flocked back to their faith. Felix viewed them as weaklings who should have suffered martyrdom and imposed such harsh penances on the returnees that many died before they could be completed, while others gave up and stayed as Arians.

ST. GELASIUS I ✠ The 49th Pope 492–496

Born Rome, Italy; date unknown

Parents Father, Valerius; Mother, unknown

Papacy March 1, 492–November 21, 496

Died Rome, Italy; November 21, 496

Although unpopular among the people of Rome, Gelasius was highly regarded by the clergy. In contemporary writings his personal virtues were praised more highly than any other pope of the time.

After the death of Acacia, the East had dropped its demand for the patriarch of Constantinople to supplant the pope as leader of Christians and sought reconciliation. Gelasius replied that no communication was possible until the Eastern bishops accepted the excommunication of Acacia. Bishop Euphemius of Constantinople refused, so the schism continued. Gelasius had meanwhile propounded a new doctrine that was to have a lasting impact throughout Christendom. In this *Duo Sunt* Gelasius claimed that the pope and the emperor each had a unique and separate mission from God: the pope was to look after the Church and spiritual matters, while the emperor was to look after the material well-being of the people.

In Rome, Gelasius got involved in a long dispute with the citizens by preaching against the three days of revelry during the popular pagan festival of Lupercalia, which he condemned as sacrilegious. When preaching failed, he banned the festivities.

491
Death of Zeno, Eastern Roman emperor. He is succeeded by Anastasius I.

492
King Theodoric the Great invades Italy and begins his long career of conquest.

494
A powerful earthquake devastates Syria and neighboring areas.

494
Emperor Xiao Wen Di makes Chinese the official state language of China, replacing a number of earlier languages and dialects.

496
King Clovis of the Franks abandons Arianism and is baptized as a Catholic Christian.

ANASTASIUS II ✠ The 50th Pope 496–498

Born Rome, Italy; date unknown

Parents Father, Peter; Mother, unknown

Papacy November 24, 496–November 16, 498

Died Rome, Italy; November 16, 498

he first action of Pope Anastasius II was to send a formal letter to the emperor Anastasius I in Constantinople announcing his election and expressing his desire to reunite Christianity.

The letter was controversial because it did not insist that the Eastern bishops had to accept the excommunication of Acacius, nor that clergy appointed by Acacius had to be reconsecrated, nor that the controversial Henoticon (*see* p.52) had to be denounced as heresy. Alongside the messenger from the pope traveled ambassadors from Theodoric, the Gothic king of Italy, who wanted imperial sanction for agreements he had made with neighboring rulers and formal recognition that he would rule Italy for life.

The negotiations might have been over quickly, but the emperor Anastasius asked Theodoric to persuade Pope Anastasius to accept the Henoticon. The pope remained firm, but when he welcomed to Rome the deacon Photinus, who was a known supporter of the Henoticon, rumors spread that he was about to give in. Several Roman priests and Western bishops stopped communicating with Anastasius and seemed on the point of refusing to acknowledge him as pope when Anastasius died.

ST. SYMMACHUS ✠ The 51st Pope 498–514

Born Sardinia, Italy; date unknown

Parents Father, Fortunatus; Mother, unknown

Papacy November 22, 498–July 19, 514

Died Rome, Italy; July 19, 514

n the final days of Anastasius's papacy there had been widespread plotting. The anti-Anastasius faction elected Symmachus, while the pro-Anastasius faction elected the archpriest Lawrence.

The city then collapsed into rioting as the factions attacked each other. King Theodoric stepped in to settle the dispute, ruling that Symmachus was pope as he had been elected first.

Symmachus's election was so violent and shambolic that one of his first actions was to lay down rules about future elections. He then turned his attention to the schism with Constantinople, rejecting all the compromises agreed by his predecessor and refusing to budge for the rest of his pontificate. In 500, however, Symmachus was accused of performing incorrect rituals, misusing church property, and having an affair. Instead of agreeing to appear in front of a synod of bishops, Symmachus barricaded himself inside St. Peter's, which was seen by Theodoric as an admission of guilt. After several years, Theodoric accepted the delayed judgement of the synod that only God can judge a pope and Symmachus settled down to a quiet decade of administration and the enlargement of the papal quarters at St. Peter's.

497

Indian mathematician Arybhata calculates the correct value of pi to four decimal places.

498

Kavadh wins the civil war in the Persian Empire with the help of Hun mercenaries.

500

Battle of Dijon at which the Franks crush the Burgundians, later recognized as the founding event of the Frankish empire.

501

Akhal Mo Naab becomes ruler of the Mayan city of Palenque in Central America.

ST. HORMISDAS ✠ The 52nd Pope 514–523

Born Frosinone, Italy; date unknown

Parents Father, Justus; Mother, unknown

Papacy July 20, 514–August 6, 523

Died probably Rome, Italy; August 6, 523

Hormisdas had been a close associate of Symmachus for some time and seems to have been put forward for the papal throne by the pope on his deathbed. Hormisdas was a keen supporter of the hardline views of Symmachus and anticipated clashes with the emperor in Constantinople.

Hormisdas was no fool, and he carefully prepared the ground for his stand against the emperor. He first made conciliatory moves to the supporters of Lawrence (*see* p.54) restoring them to their positions and toning down the rhetoric against the antipope, who had died in 508. He then turned to King Theodoric of Italy who, although an Arian Christian, took a great interest in the views of his Catholic subjects. Hormisdas made certain that the political master of Italy was on his side before turning his attention to the East.

Anagni Cathedral, in the province of Frosinone where Pope Hormisdas was born.

Hormisdas refused an invitation from the emperor to preside over a council of bishops in Heraclia, Thrace, to thrash out the various divisive issues. He insisted that the Council of Chalcedon had ruled definitively against Monophysitism, that the Tome of Leo clearly set out the theological position, that Acacia of Constantinople had been properly excommunicated, and that any clergy consecrated by Acacia had to be reconsecrated by Roman clergy. Anastasius felt he had no choice but to reject the pope's statement.

In July 518, however, Anastasius died and was replaced as emperor by the general Justin, a firm opponent of Monophysitism. Justin sent a message to Hormisdas inviting him to send a delegation to Constantinople to end the schism. Hormisdas did just that, including in the delegation the deacon Dioscorus—a gifted orator who spoke fluent Greek. The mission appeared to be a total triumph for Rome. The Eastern Church accepted the Chalcedonian position entirely, repudiated Monophysitism, and recognized Rome as the apostolic see.

An illustration showing the persecution of heretics during the reign of the Byzantine emperor Justin I (r.518–527).

In 520, Hormisdas was asked to decide if the writings of the Gallic theologian Faustus of Riez should be banned. During his lifetime, Faustus had been a bishop and was highly regarded both for his great learning and for his saintly lifestyle. More recently, however, his ideas that a human had a part to play in the saving of his or her own soul and that this redemption was not the work of God only had begun to be questioned. Aware that Faustus was still popular, Hormisdas compromised. He said that the books should not be banned, but that people reading them must take care not to be led astray by any false information they contained.

512

Earliest known writing in the Arabic script is completed at Zabad, Syria.

517

Emperor Wu Di converts to Buddhism and introduces the religion to central China.

520

King Theodoric the Great of Italy orders the construction of his architecturally important tomb at Ravenna.

521

The philosopher Boethius introduces the Greek style of music notation to Western Europe.

ST. JOHN I ✠ The 53rd Pope 523–526

Born Tuscany, Italy; date unknown

Parents Father, Constantius; Mother, unknown

Papacy August 13, 523–May 18, 526

Died Ravenna, Italy; May 18, 526

John had been a key supporter of the antipope Lawrence (*see* p.54) but had been reconciled to Pope Symmachus by 506 and, under Hormisdas, had risen to be the senior deacon of Rome. He was destined to suffer one of the most humiliating pontificates of all time.

John was on good terms with King Theodoric of Italy, the Emperor Justin of Constantinople, all the bishops, and most secular rulers. He was also a friend and frequent correspondent of the philosopher Boethius who, like him, had been born into Roman aristocracy. It was a friendship that he would come to regret.

In 524, Emperor Justin I of Constantinople decided that his support for the Chalcedonian interpretation of Christianity was not enough. The Arian Christians in his empire were, he decided, heretics who had to be stamped out. Arian churches and church property were confiscated, Arians were expelled from employment by the state, and a range of persecution measures taken that forced many Arians to choose between penury and conversion to orthodox Christianity. The vast majority of Arians in the empire were Goths or related tribes living in northern parts of the empire. This worried Theodoric—who was himself both Goth and Arian—whose lands bordered the northern regions of the Empire where the persecution was at its strongest.

Theodoric summoned John to Ravenna and ordered him to lead an embassy to Constantinople to persuade Justin to call off the persecution. Worried what Theodoric might do to orthodox Christians if he refused, John agreed. When he arrived in Constantinople John was welcomed with great splendor and ceremony, even being allowed to celebrate Easter in Constantinople according to Roman rituals. Justin agreed to stop the persecution, but said that those who had converted from Arianism would not be allowed to return to their old faith.

Thinking he had done all required of him, John returned to Ravenna to find Theodoric apoplectic with fury. Theodoric had just executed Boethius for treasonous correspondence with Justin and viewed John's reception in Constantinople as a sign that he, too, was involved in secret plots with the emperor. John was thrown into prison where he died. His body was taken back to Rome and buried in the nave of St. Peter's on May 27.

PELAGIANISM

The heresy of Pelagianism was named for the British monk Pelagius, even though he neither held nor espoused many of its key tenets. It was his writings that set off the train of thought that was to lead to the full-blown heresy. Working in Rome from about 380, Pelagius was a highly regarded theologian whose personal life was held up by contemporaries as being a fine example for other Christians to follow. Pelagius came to believe that humans were not condemned by the sins of Adam, but merely that Adam had set a bad example. Humans, he thought, had the free will to choose to be sinful or not and that God's grace helped them in their good works.

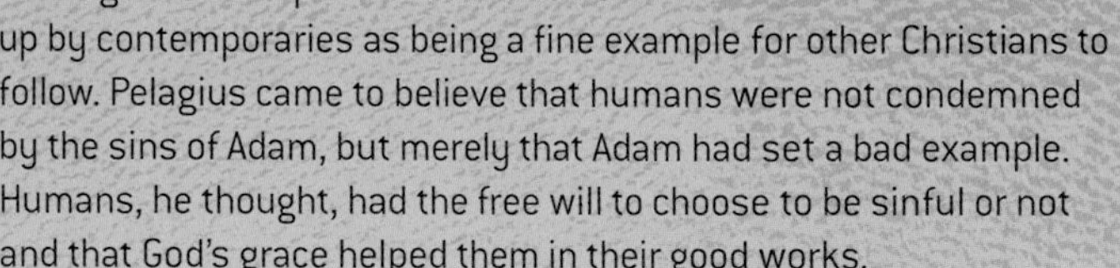

532 Hilderic becomes King of the Vandals in North Africa, favoring the Catholic branch of Christianity.

524 Clodoald, heir to the Frankish throne, retires to a monastery to escape assassination, finding later fame as St. Cloud of France.

525 A shroud, said to be that in which Christ was buried, is found in Edessa during building works after a great flood.

526 Theodoric the Great dies, aged 72. He is succeeded as king of the Ostrogoths by his son Athalaric.

527 Constantinople's Emperor Justin dies aged 77. His son Justinian begins a 38-year reign.

FELIX IV ✠ The 54th Pope 526–530

Born Samnium, Italy; date unknown

Parents Father, Castorius; Mother, unknown

Papacy July 12, 526–September 22, 530

Died Rome, Italy; September 22, 530

In 526, the clergy of Rome was split between those wanting to appease Theodoric and those favoring closer ties to Constantinople. After 58 days Theodoric stepped in and told the clergy to elect Felix.

Theodoric died just a few weeks later, leaving his crown to his grandson Athalaric with Queen Amalasuntha as regent. Felix got on well with both and managed to extract some valuable concessions to the Church. As well as getting a good deal of money from the king, Felix obtained a number of public buildings in the Forum as Church property and converted them to be churches. In one, Saints Cosma and Damiano, he installed a mosaic portrait of himself. He also secured an agreement that any priest accused of a crime would be tried by the pope, not by the king's judges—counted among the greatest privileges of the Church.

Pelagianism (*see* p.56) had meanwhile become popular in France. Felix wrote to Bishop Caesarius of Arles in 529 with a list of 25 Propositions explaining why the heresy was wrong. He then fell ill and, feeling death coming upon him, summoned the Roman clergy and announced that he wanted his successor to be the archdeacon Boniface.

BONIFACE II ✠ The 55th Pope 530–532

Born Rome, Italy; date unknown

Parents Father, Sigibuld; Mother, unknown

Papacy September 22, 530–October 17, 532

Died Rome, Italy; October 17, 532

As Felix IV lay dying he bequeathed the papacy to Archdeacon Boniface, but the senate insisted on a proper election. When the clergy gathered at the Lateran Basilica they elected the Greek deacon Dioscorus.

Immediately following the election, a smaller number of clergy hurried to a nearby hall and elected Boniface. Schism seemed imminent but, three weeks later, Dioscorus died. The triumphant Boniface summoned a meeting of Roman clergy where he produced a document condemning Dioscorus and affirming that Felix's wishes should have been upheld. Thus he forced those who had backed Dioscorus to sign in conditions of abject humiliation.

Having established himself firmly in power, Boniface pushed his luck by insisting that all the Roman clergy swear that they would choose the deacon Vigilius as his successor. The Senate objected and strongly worded messages came from Queen Amalasuntha. It was Boniface's turn to be humiliated, and he was forced to absolve the clergy from their oath. As pope, his only decision of real importance was to confirm the 25 Propositions against Pelagianism issued by his predecessor Felix, making them the definitive Catholic position on God's grace. Boniface seems to have died suddenly and was buried in St. Peter's.

528

Traditional date for Buddhism reaching what is now Korea.

529

The Benedictine order of monks is founded at Monte Cassino by Benedict of Nursia who formulates strict rules for monasticism in his *Regula Monachorum*.

530

King Hilderic of the Vandals famously responds to a message from Byzantine Emperor Justinian, saying "nothing is more befitting a monarch than that he minds his own business."

531

Khosrau I becomes ruler of the Persian Empire and agrees a peace treaty with the Byzantine Empire.

532

The Nike Riots take place in Constantinople costing the lives of 30,000 people and destroying large areas of the city.

JOHN II ✠ The 56th Pope 533–535

Born Rome, Italy; date unknown

Parents Father, Projectus; Mother, unknown

Papacy January 2, 533–May 8, 535

Died Rome, Italy; May 8, 535

The elderly deacon Mercurius came to power largely because nobody objected to him strongly and many hoped he would soon die anyway. As his name honored a pagan god, he changed it to John.

The election that followed the death of Boniface II was a scandal that horrified the Christian world; the rival candidates openly touted for votes and paid bribes to secure them—raiding funds intended to help the poor and selling off Church treasures. After two months, the senate stepped in to force a vote that put John II into office. King Athalaric of Italy was so incensed that he had a large marble slab erected in the porch of St. Peter's on which were engraved rules for the conduct of future elections.

John received a letter and lavish gifts from the new Emperor Justinian I in Constantinople who was keen to find a formula of words to describe Christ that, although orthodox, could be accepted by moderate Monophysitists. The phrase he proposed, that Christ was "one of the Trinity suffered in the flesh," had been rejected by Hormisdas. John, to the delight of the emperor, chose to accept it. John then fulfilled the expectations of those who had elected him by dying and clearing the way for a new election.

ST. AGAPETUS I ✠ The 57th Pope 535–536

Born Rome, Italy; date unknown

Parents Father, Gordianus; Mother, unknown

Papacy May 13, 535–April 22, 536

Died Constantinople; April 22, 536

Only five days after the death of John II, Agapetus was elected in his place. Agapetus came from one of the richest families in Rome and was highly educated in both Christianity and pagan philosophy.

One of Agapetus's first moves was to found a library in Rome containing Latin translations of Greek writers. He also ceremonially burned the document condemning Dioscorus that had been forced on the clergy by Boniface II (*see* p.57).

The main crisis of Agapetus's reign began when Queen Amalasuntha, Gothic ruler of Italy, was murdered by her cousin Theodahad. The Byzantine emperor Justinian announced that he had been asked for help by Amalasuntha and would now punish the usurper Theodahad.

Theodahad summoned Pope Agapetus and begged him to go to Constantinople to persuade Justinian to call off the coming war. Agapetus arrived in the imperial capital in February 536, persuaded Justinian to oust from office the patriarch Anthimus, then promptly died of exhaustion. Rome was thrown into turmoil. The Byzantine general Belisarius was marching north from Sicily to conquer Italy, King Theodahad was marching south to fight him, and the city was caught in the middle.

533

Citing a revolt by orthodox Christians against the Arian Vandals as an excuse, Emperor Justinian of Constantinople invades North Africa.

534

Byzantine general Belisarius completes the conquest of North Africa for Justinian.

535

Massive eruption of the volcano Krakatoa in Indonesia spews so much ash into the upper atmosphere that the world's climate is cooled for the next three years.

535

Chinese author Jia Sixia writes a treatise on agriculture that influences Chinese landholding and cultivation for centuries.

ST. SILVERIUS ✠ The 58th Pope 536–537

Born Frosinone, Italy, date unknown

Parents Father, Pope Hormisdas; Mother unknown

Papacy June 8, 536–November 11, 537

Died Palmaria, Italy; November 11, 537

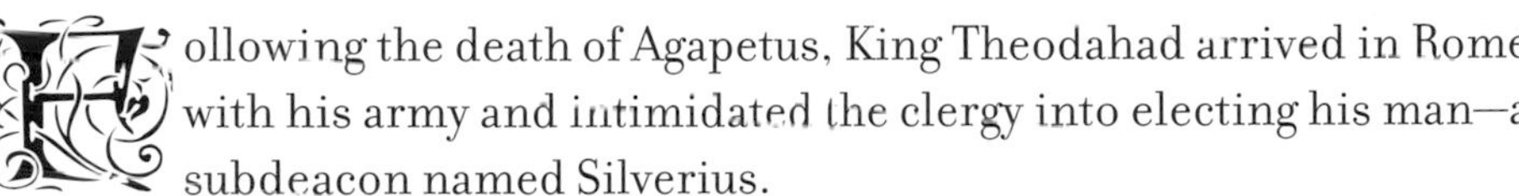

Following the death of Agapetus, King Theodahad arrived in Rome with his army and intimidated the clergy into electing his man—a subdeacon named Silverius.

Early in December 536, Belisarius and his army arrived outside the gates of Rome. Silverius met the senate and together they decided to open the gates to Belisarius to avoid bloodshed. A few weeks later the deacon Vigilius, who had been with Agapetus in Constantinople, arrived back in Rome. He brought secret messages from the Empress Theodora to Belisarius who plotted to make Vigilius pope and reinstate Anthimus as patriarch of Constantinople. Belisarius wasted little time in arresting Silverius and forcing him to become a monk. Silverius was then sent off to Patara in the heart of the Byzantine Empire. From there he managed to get a message to the emperor Justinian who instructed that Silverius be sent back to Rome for an open trial. However, his return to Rome was intercepted by troops of Belisarius who took him to the island of Palmaria, where he was handed over to two henchmen of Vigilius. On November 11, 537, Silverius abdicated. Four weeks later he was dead, no doubt murdered by the servants of Vigilius.

VIGILIUS ✠ The 59th Pope 537–555

Born Rome, Italy; date unknown

Parents Father, John; Mother, unknown

Papacy March 29, 537–June 7, 555

Died Syracus, Sicily; June 7, 555

Rich, noble, and learned, Vigilius had been chosen by Pope Boniface II to be his successor but the Roman clergy chose first John II then Agapetus I and then Silverius instead. Vigilius was not easily thwarted.

Vigilius was in Constantinople when Agapetus died, and he won the support of Empress Theodora by promising to reinstate Patriarch Anthimus (*see* p.58). Arriving in Rome, Vigilius arranged the murder of Pope Silverius and took over the papal throne. He conspicuously failed to reinstate Anthimus. Late in 543, Justinian condemned a group of 5th-century writings known as the Three Chapters, which categorically denounced Monophysitism as supporting the Nestorian heresy. Most Eastern bishops agreed under protest, but the Western bishops and Vigilius did not. On 22 November, 545, Justinian's soldiers marched into St. Peter's and arrested Vigilius while he was conducting Mass. The pope was taken to Constantinople and thrown into prison. Justinian summoned the Council of Constantinople of 553, which condemned the Three Chapters and deposed numerous Western bishops. In 554, Vigilius agreed to all the emperor's demands. He was released but died in Sicily en route to Rome.

536	537	540	544	547	552
Traditional date of the death of Emperor Ankan of Japan.	Traditional date of the Battle of Camlann, at which the British king Arthur was killed.	Antioch falls to the Persians, who loot the city before retiring to Persia.	Persia is defeated by the Byzantines at Dara and Edessa.	King Ida seizes Bamburgh to establish the first English kingdom in northern Britain.	Traditional date on which Buddhism reaches Japan.

PELAGIUS I ✠ The 60th Pope 556–561

Born Rome, Italy; c.490
Parents Father, John; Mother, unknown
Papacy April 16, 556–March 3, 561
Died Rome, Italy; March 3, 561

Born into a noble Roman family, Pelagius was wealthy, talented, highly educated, and rose steadily through the ranks of the Church. He would, however, prove to be one of the most controversial popes in history.

Pelagius had traveled to Constantinople with Agapetus and was a firm supporter of Vigilius. So much so that when the pope was absent from Rome it was Pelagius who was appointed papal representative. As such, it was Pelagius who endured the Gothic siege of Rome in 546 and who negotiated a surrender with King Totila.

In 556, Emperor Justinian declared that he wanted Pelagius to be pope and with imperial troops swarming over the city the clergy agreed without a formal election. Nevertheless, large sections of the Church refused to accept him as pope and he was shunned by Roman society. Gaul and northern Italy split from Rome completely, refusing to have anything to do with the new pope. Although much of his work as pope was wasted because his instructions were often ignored, Pelagius reorganized the way the papal estates were administered, reformed the papal finances to root out corruption, and made strenuous efforts to raise the quality of monastic institutions. He was buried in St. Peter's.

JOHN III ✠ The 61st Pope 561–574

Born Rome, Italy; date unknown
Parents Father, Anastasius; Mother, unknown
Papacy July 17, 561–July 13, 574
Died Rome, Italy; July 13, 574

John was chosen by the Roman clergy who, with imperial troops in the city, were unlikely to elect someone hostile to Constantinople. His father was a senior member of the senate of Rome.

The early years of John's reign were quiet as he worked to reestablish Roman authority over those areas that had refused to accept Pope Pelagius. He may also have sponsored the growth of the library and completed the Church of St. Philip and St. James (now the Church of the Twelve Holy Apostles), begun by his predecessor in thanks for the Byzantine victories over the Goths.

In 565, the Emperor Justinian died and was succeeded by his nephew Justin II. The new emperor withdrew troops from Italy and North Africa, which opened the way for the Lombards to invade. By 570, the Germanic tribe had captured the entire Po Valley and were moving south. John hurried to Naples where the Byzantine army was camped. The army marched to Rome, and General Narses was installed in the old imperial Palace. The move halted the Lombards, but friction between the Romans and the Byzantines flared up and John was forced out of the city to the Church of St. Tiburtius. There he died, and was buried in St. Peter's.

557
The Avars arrive in Europe and send an embassy to Constantinople.

558
Fleeing the Avars, the Lombards move southwest toward Italy.

559
First manned flight occurs when condemned prisoner Yuan Huangtou is forced to fly in a giant kite at Ye, China.

562
War between the major Maya states of Tikal and Caracol ends in victory for Caracol.

568
A Lombard kingdom that will rule northern and central Italy is founded by the Lombard ruler Alboin.

BENEDICT I ✠ The 62nd Pope 575–579

Born Rome, Italy; date unknown

Parents Father, Boniface; Mother, unknown

Papacy June 2, 575–July 30, 579

Died Rome, Italy; July 30, 579

Benedict seems to have been elected very soon after the death of John III but, because imperial approval was required, he had to wait 11 months while messengers tried to get past the invading Lombards.

From the fortress city of Ravenna, the imperial governors did their best—with limited resources—to maintain some sort of order in Italy. From Rome, Benedict tried to liaise with the governors, though their interests did not always coincide. The invading Lombards were actually refugees fleeing the barbaric Avars who had surged out of Asia some years earlier. They were divided up into a number of different tribes, each led by a nobleman, which could unite on occasion but were just as often divided.

In 578, the Lombards finally reached Rome and laid siege to the city. They did not have the weapons needed to break the walls, but instead relied on starvation to subdue the Romans. Emperor Justin II sent a fleet of grain ships from Constantinople that managed to get through to the city but, by the summer of 579, famine struck. Benedict died as the famine worsened, apparently of a minor disease exacerbated by malnutrition. He was buried in St. Peter's as was becoming normal for a pope.

PELAGIUS II ✠ The 63rd Pope 579–590

Born Rome, Italy; date unknown

Parents Father, Unigild; Mother, unknown

Papacy November 26, 579–February 7, 590

Died Rome, Italy; February 7, 590

Benedict I died when Rome was besieged by the Lombards. Feeling an urgent need for a new pope, the Romans elected Pelagius within hours but had to wait until November for imperial confirmation.

As well as asking for his confirmation from Constantinople, Pelagius asked for military help against the invading Lombards. Emperor Tiberius II replied that he was too busy fighting the Persians but advised the pope to bribe the Lombards and to appeal to the king of the Franks for men. Lacking funds for bribes, Pelagius wrote to Bishop Aunarius of Auxerre asking him to persuade the Frankish king Chilperic to intervene. Chilperic turned out, like Tiberius, to be busy with his own wars.

Relief finally came from Ravenna when the imperial governor secured peace with the Lombards in 585. It was in 589 that the conversion of the Visigoths in Spain from Arian to Catholic Christianity was declared complete. Pelagius was also responsible for reconstruction work in St. Peter's Basilica that moved the high altar to stand over the tomb of St. Peter. In the winter of 589 the Tiber flooded Rome, causing raw sewage to run down the streets. An epidemic broke out and claimed Pelagius.

574

Having lost the fortress of Dara to the Persians, Emperor Justin II abdicates leaving the throne to the successful general Tiberius II.

576

The Visigoths firmly establish their capital at Toledo from where they will cement their rule over Spain.

583

Earthquake and fire destroy large areas of Constantinople.

585

The Visigothic king Leovigild finishes the Visigothic conquest of the Spanish Peninsula.

ST. GREGORY I ✠ The 64th Pope 590–604

Born Rome, Italy; c.540
Parents Father, Gordianus; Mother, unknown
Papacy September 3, 590–March 12, 604
Died Rome, Italy; March 12, 604

Gregory the Great was born into a wealthy, noble family of central Italy and was related to both Felix III and Agapetus I. He was thus assured of an easy entry into a good career. His father chose the imperial civil service for young Gregory, and it was probably family influence that got him the job of prefect of Rome in 572. Gregory, however, favored the Church.

When his father died in 574, Gregory turned the family mansion on the Caelian Hill into a monastery and became a monk. He devoted himself to prayer and theological study, famously making himself ill with an ascetic denial of food and wine.

In 578, Benedict I made him a deacon and gave him a series of tasks to perform—a pattern followed by later popes. Pelagius II sent him as ambassador to Constantinople with the task of getting military aid against the Lombards. He stayed in the imperial capital for almost three years, building up a network of contacts in the imperial civil service and in the Eastern church. He returned to Rome in 586 and went back to his monastic house, though he was summoned almost daily to give advice, write letters, and assist with papal administration.

When Pelagius died, Gregory believed he would be released from papal service and began preparing to move to an estate outside Rome where he had set up another monastery. He attended the meeting of clergy to elect a successor and was horrified when he heard his own name put forward as a candidate. He tried to protest but was shouted down by clerics who thought he was merely being modest, and he was swiftly elected pope. His first action was to write to Emperor Maurice asking him to refuse to ratify the election. Maurice instead confirmed Gregory in office.

Although there was still an imperial prefect in Rome, his influence was waning rapidly. Gregory stepped in to use his formidable talents as an administrator to organize the civil government of Rome and the surrounding area. He also enforced a strict regime of managing the estates belonging to the pope, whether they were near Rome, in Sicily, Spain, or France. All of this put the papacy on a secure financial footing from which it never again slipped. Nor was Gregory above military service. When the Lombard King Agilulf besieged Rome in 593, it was Gregory who organized the defence, and then negotiated a deal that saw the Lombards retreat in return for a cash payment. Although he readily accepted the legality of the imperial sovereignty over Rome and Italy, Gregory did not let this interfere with his practical work of ruling the city himself.

Bronze coin depicting Emperor Maurice in consular uniform.

THE CHANGING FORTUNES OF ROME

The great flood of 589 marked a turning point in the fortunes of the city of Rome. During early imperial times over a million people lived in the city. That number was down to perhaps 800,000 by the time the city fell to the Goths in 410, but had plunged to about 80,000 by 589. There was no longer an economic case for Rome to be a big city. The imperial largesse that had so long maintained the city had moved east to Constantinople. By 590, there was simply not enough money to repair the damage to the drains and roads, so they went unrepaired. By 620, the population had sunk to 40,000.

590
Traditional date of the death of Urien Rheged, Christian ruler of northern Britain who enjoyed many successes against the pagan English.

592
Civil war in the Persian Empire ends with the triumph of Khosrau II at the Battle of Blarathon.

595
Theudebert II becomes king of the Austrasian Franks.

595
Construction of the Zhaozhou Bridge in Zhao, China. It is the world's oldest open-spandrel, stone-arch bridge and the first known arch of less than half a semicircle.

Rome fared well under the rule of Gregory I: aqueducts were repaired, courts were reformed, and people were fed with doles of grain as they were under the old imperial rule.

In ecclesiastical matters, Gregory was just as hardworking. Learning that most of Britain had in the previous century turned pagan, as it was overrun by the English, Gregory sent St. Augustine to convert the country back to Christianity. He even cracked a joke. Seeing some English children being sold as slaves in Rome he said they were not "Angli" (English) but "Angeli" (angels). As a monk himself, the first to become pope, he tirelessly promoted the foundation and expansion of monasteries by granting them important financial privileges. Gregory introduced a number of liturgical and musical changes, though it is thought that many later ascribed to him were later inventions.

A gilded bronze forehead plate of a lamellar helmet depicting the coronation of Lombard King Agilulf who besieged Rome in 593.

His only real failure came in his relations with the patriarch of Constantinople. Like Pelagius before him, Gregory objected to the patriarch calling himself an "ecumenical patriarch," with its implications of authority beyond his diocese. The Eastern patriarch did not give in, and was supported by the emperor. Perhaps as a riposte, Gregory adopted the modest title "servant of the servants of God" for the pope.

The last known act of the senate of Rome came during Gregory's pontificate, thus bringing to an end an institution that had lasted over a thousand years. The senate had its origins somewhere before 700 BC as the council of village elders when Rome was a collection of wooden huts. During the time of the emperors, the senate gradually lost its political power though not its social standing. By 400, the senate had the power to run the city of Rome itself and conduct treason trials, but little else. After the last Western emperor abdicated in 476, the senate began to reassume its former importance. Theoretical power lay with the emperor in Constantinople, but he was too far away to exercise day-to-day decision-making, so the senate stepped in to fill the void. However, the long wars against the Goths cost the lives of many senators. By the mid-6th century, ambitious noblemen were increasingly seeking a career in the papal curia, which was largely running Rome by this date, and in the Church itself. Gregory himself was representative of this shift. In 603, toward the end of Gregory's papacy, the senate approved the erection of a statue of the emperor Phocas. After that there is no further record of it ever meeting again.

On the announcement of his death, the people of Rome at once acclaimed Gregory a saint. He has been recognized as a saint ever since. He was buried in St. Peter's, as tradition by this date decreed.

597

St. Augustine founds the King's School in Canterbury, now the oldest school in Britain.

603

Battle of Degasaston sees the defeat of Picts and Scots, handing control of what is now northern England to the English.

604

Prince Shotoku of Japan publishes the Seventeen Articles by which he will judge the behavior and worth of civil servants. It has never been repealed and remains in force.

SABINIAN ✠ The 65th Pope 604–606

Born Volterra, Italy; date unknown

Parents Unknown

Papacy September 13, 604–February 22, 606

Died Near Rome, Italy; February 22, 606

Sabinian's promotion through Church ranks has been characterized as slow, though it must have been fairly steady for it is as a deacon of some years standing that he first enters the written record in 593.

In 593, Sabinian was sent as Gregory's ambassador to the imperial court in Constantinople. He was elected within days of the death of Gregory but had to wait several months before the emperor in Constantinople, Phocas, approved the election. Once in power, he reversed Gregory's policy of using primarily monks for Church business, preferring to promote and employ lay clergy. When war again broke out with the Lombards, the enemy cut off the grain supplies to the city. In similar circumstances, Gregory had thrown open the doors of the huge state granaries to allow the people to help themselves. Sabinian kept the grain under lock and key, carefully rationing it and selling it instead of giving it away. He was immediately accused of profiteering and his popularity plummeted. He died in the midst of peace negotiations with the Lombards. His funeral procession had to go around Rome to reach St. Peter's to avoid a demonstration against his rationing system.

BONIFACE III ✠ The 66th Pope 607

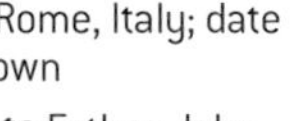

Born Rome, Italy; date unknown

Parents Father, John Cataadiocce; Mother, unknown

Papacy February 19, 607–November 12, 607

Died Rome, Italy; November 12, 607

Boniface II is renowned for persuading the emperor to issue a formal declaration that "the See of Blessed Peter the Apostle should be the head of all the Churches."

The emperor also agreed that the patriarch of Constantinople could know longer use the title "ecumenical patriarch," which had overtones of universal authority that challenged the power of Rome. Despite this success, Boniface's election seems to have been another at which the behavior of the clergy was improper. Emperor Phocas delayed confirming the election for almost a year, which indicates that an investigation was taking place. Boniface held a synod in Rome for the sole purpose of setting down election rules. The synod banned discussion of a likely successor to the papacy until three days after the pope's death to allow the funeral to be conducted with some sense of decorum. The penalty imposed for breaking the ban was immediate excommunication. Those wishing to take a positive view of Boniface suggest that he was disgusted by the election and wished to avoid a repetition, but it may be that he was himself guilty of misconduct and the synod was the price demanded by Phocas.

605

Emperor Yang Guang orders the construction of the Grand Canal linking Beijing to Hangzhou, a distance of 1,100 miles.

607

Construction of the Horyu-ji Buddhist temple and monastery complex in Nara, Japan.

609

Death of Zuhayr, Arab poet.

610

The Byzantine emperor Phocas is overthrown by his African governor Heraclius and is lynched by the mob at Constantinople.

610

According to Islamic belief, Muhammed has his first vision of the Archangel Gabriel who begins the revelation of the Koran.

ST. BONIFACE IV ✠ The 67th Pope 608–615

Born Valeria, Italy; date unknown

Parents Father, John; Mother, unknown

Papacy September 15, 608–May 8, 615

Died Rome, Italy; May 8, 615

Boniface was a deacon who served as a senior treasurer to Gregory I. Like Gregory, he was a firm supporter of monks, as opposed to lay clergy, although he may not have been a monk himself.

On election to the papacy, Boniface converted his own extensive house into a monastery and used the resources of the papacy to encourage monasticism throughout Western Christendom. He was on good terms with Emperor Phocas who, in 609, allowed him to convert the Roman Pantheon into a church. Boniface went to work with a will, ripping out every sign of the pagan gods to which the temple had been dedicated. He then brought 28 cartloads of sacred bones, probably those of Christian martyrs, from the catacombs and buried them under the floor. The newly decorated church was dedicated to St. Mary and the Martyrs, as it still is.

In 610, Boniface held a synod in Rome aimed at regulating and improving the discipline and learning in monasteries. In early 615, he received a strongly worded letter from the Irish monk St. Columban, condemning the Three Chapters (*see* p.59) and asking the pope to take action. Boniface died before he could reply, and he was buried in St. Peter's.

ST. ADEODATUS I ✠ The 68th Pope 615–618

Born Rome, Italy; date unknown

Parents Father, Stephen; Mother, unknown

Papacy October 19, 615–November 8, 618

Died Rome, Italy; November 8, 618

Adeodatus was the first pope known to use a bulla, or lead seal, to authenticate a formal document. For some centuries after, a bulla was used on all sorts of documents to emphasize their importance.

The name Adeodatus is sometimes given as Deusdedit or Deodatus, all of which mean "God has given." He came from a family of Church officials—his father had been a subdeacon—and he was firmly opposed to the monastic party of Gregory and Boniface IV. He ordained 14 new priests, the first in more than a decade, and assiduously promoted men who were not monks. At this distance in time it is difficult to understand the issues at stake, and it may have been simply a matter of personal ambition that divided the monastic and non-monastic factions in Rome.

In 61 6, the Byzantine troops in Italy mutinied and slaughtered any imperial official they could lay hands on. Adeodatus remained loyal to the emperor, closing the gates of Rome against the rebels. In 618, an earthquake hit Rome, causing widespread damage. This was followed by a disease, characterized by scabs. Adeodatus fell victim and, in his will, left every priest in Rome the equivalent of a year's pay.

613
Chlothar II murders his aunt, nephew, cousin, and other family members to reunite the kingdom of the Franks under his own rule.

615
Jerusalem is sacked by the Persians, who take the "True Cross" as part of the booty.

616
Traditional date for the founding of a Christian chapel to St. Peter on Thorn Island in the Thames River, now Westminster Abbey.

616
Khosrau II of Persia invades the Byzantine Empire, looting Alexandria in Egypt before returning to Persia.

618
The Tang Dynasty takes control of China. The dynasty lasted to 907 and is recognized as a golden age for Chinese culture.

BONIFACE V ✠ The 69th Pope 619–625

Born Naples, Italy; date unknown

Parents Father, John; Mother, unknown

Papacy December 23, 619–October 25, 625

Died Rome, Italy; October 25, 625

Like Adeodatus before him, Boniface V favored priests over monks and enacted several regulations to protect their position within the Church. For instance, he ruled that only priests could perform baptisms.

Boniface also altered Church law to bring it into line with imperial law on matters of bequests and confirmed that churches could offer asylum to fugitives in some circumstances. He is known to have been a keen letter writer. Among his correspondents was Mellitus, archbishop of Canterbury, and Justus, bishop of Rochester. He also wrote to Ethelburga, a Christian princess of Kent who had married the pagan King Edwin of Northumbria urging her to convert her husband to Christianity. She succeeded in 627, but five years later Edwin was killed in battle and his kingdom reverted to paganism.

It was during the papacy of Boniface V, in June 622, that an event occurred that would have a massive impact on Christianity. The prophet Muhammed, leader of the fledgling Islamic religion, heard of a plot to murder him in his home town of Mecca and fled to Yathrib (now Medina). Muslims date their calendar from Muhammed's flight from Mecca, an event known as the Hijra.

HONORIUS I ✠ The 70th Pope 625–638

Born Near Naples, Italy; date unknown

Parents Father, Petronius; Mother, unknown

Papacy October 27, 625–October 12, 638

Died Rome, Italy; October 12, 638

During his lifetime, the papacy of Honorius was considered stable and unspectacular. With hindsight, however, it has become one of the most controversial in papal history.

The key moment came in 634 when Honorius received a letter from Sergius I, patriarch of Constantinople. The Eastern Church had for a long time been struggling with the heresy of Monophysitism (*see* p.50). The vast majority of popes had taken a strong line on the heresy and opposed any compromise. Now Sergius suggested that Christ should be described as having "two distinct natures but one operation." Sergius explained why he thought this form of words was consistent with orthodox teaching yet allowed moderate Monophysitists to accept it. Honorius agreed, approved the wording, and welcomed converts from the heresy. Fifty years later, the Third Council of Constantinople declared the wording to be the heresy of "Monothelitism" and repudiated it, anathematizing those who supported it. In the 14th century, when the doctrine of papal infallibility was being developed, the actions of Honorius in supporting a heresy caused a great deal of difficulty, as they have ever since.

623

Frankish merchant Samo is elected king of the Slavs in what is now the Czech Republic, going on to throw off Avar overlordship.

624

Battle of Badr. Muhammed leads his Muslims to victory over the Quraysh tribe of Mecca.

627

Battle of Nineveh. Byzantine emperor Heraclius crushes the Persians, finally ending the long wars between the two empires.

SEVERINUS ✣ The 71st Pope 640

Born Rome, Italy; date unknown

Parents Father, Avienus; Mother, unknown

Papacy May 28, 640–August 2, 640

Died Rome, Italy; August 2, 640

Elected soon after the death of Honorius, Severinus was forced to wait for imperial confirmation because he refused to accept the description of Christ as having "two distinct natures but one operation" (*see* p.66).

Severinus believed the new description of Christ was too close to the Monophysitist heresy (*see* p.50) and sent an embassy to meet with Emperor Heraclius to sort the issue out. Meanwhile, the imperial troops in Italy were in serious arrears with their pay. In an effort to appease them, the imperial paymaster Maurice told them that the money was in the papal treasury in Rome and that he would get it as soon as he could. The army promptly marched on Rome, stormed into the city, and forced Severinus and his monks to barricade themselves into the Lateran. The exarch Isaac of Ravenna arrived and ordered both the troops and the pope out of the city. He then plundered the papal vaults himself—though he was careful to sent some of the gold to his emperor. The papal embassy returned from Constantinople to declare that Heraclius had given permission for the consecration so long as Severinus promised to consider the new description of Christ. The consecration took place but Severinus died soon after.

JOHN IV ✣ The 72nd Pope 640–642

Born Ravenna, Italy; date unknown

Parents Father, Venantius; Mother, unknown

Papacy December 24, 640–October 12, 642

Died Rome, Italy; October 12; 642

John was archdeacon of Rome when elected, but his father had been the senior legal adviser to Exarch Isaac in Ravenna, so the new pope had a foot in both camps in disputes between pope and emperor.

Disputes were not long in coming because Emperor Heraclius was still keen to gain acceptance for his description of Christ (*see* p.66). Just two months after his consecration, John held a synod that condemned the Eastern formula of words as being the heresy Monothelitism. Heraclius decided to climb down and blamed the patriarch Sergius I, now safely dead, for having proposed the heresy.

John benefited from this predecessor's skill at financial organization and was able to refill the papal treasury after it had been looted under Severinus. He spent large sums of money buying freedom for Christians enslaved by the pagan Avars and Slavs. He built a chapel in the Lateran dedicated to the saints of Dalmatia, his family's original home, and brought important relics to give it added importance. He was less successful in his efforts to persuade the native British Church to accept the Roman method of calculating Easter. Despite a lively exchange of letters, the northerners stuck to their old ways.

633	638	640	641	641	642
Muslim Arab armies invade Syria and Iraq.	Jerusalem falls to Muslim Arab armies under Umar ibn al Khattab.	Emperor Heraclius sends missionaries to begin the conversion of the pagan Croats.	Alexandria falls to Muslim Arabs under Amr ibn al As.	Caesarea falls to the Muslim Arabs.	Battle of Nehavand sees Muslim Arabs under Sad ibn Abi Waqqas destroy the Persian army, opening the way for the Muslim conquest of Persia.

THEODORE I ✣ The 73rd Pope 642–649

Born Jerusalem, Byzantine Empire; date unknown
Parents Father, unknown; Mother, unknown
Papacy November 24, 642–May 14, 649
Died Place unknown; May 14, 649

The son of a bishop, it is presumed that Theodore fled his home in Jerusalem to escape the Muslims as they erupted out of Arabia to find the Byzantine and Persian empires exhausted after years of warfare.

When he arrived in Rome Theodore was already known as an opponent of the heresy Monothelitism (*see* p.51). As pope, he promptly wrote to the emperor Constans II and Patriarch Paul II asking why the Monothelitic form of words was still acceptable in the East. The situation was complicated by the fact that Paul II had been put in place after the previous patriarch, Pyrrhus, had been ousted. When Pyrrhus came to Rome denouncing Monothelitism he was welcomed by Theodore as if he were still patriarch. When Pyrrhus later recanted and approved the heresy, Theodore was so angry that he wrote out the instrument of excommunication in consecrated wine using the tomb of St. Peter as a desk. Constans was heartily sick of the whole business. He issued an edict, the *Typos*, which banned discussion of the nature of Christ entirely. When the papal ambassador tried to bring up the subject, Constans had him thrown into prison. The news of this diplomatic outrage was still en route to Rome when Theodore died.

ST. MARTIN I ✣ The 74th Pope 649–653

Born Todi, Italy; date unknown
Parents unknown
Papacy July 5, 649–June 17, 653
Died Cherso, Crimea; September 16, 655

Following his election, without waiting for imperial approval, Martin I had himself consecrated as pope. He then summoned a synod of 105 Western bishops to meet in the Lateran.

The synod condemned the Emperor Constans's *Typos* edict. Letters were then sent to Constans and the Eastern bishops demanding that they fall in line with Rome. Incensed, Constans sent the Exarch Olympius with an army to arrest the pope. Arriving in Italy, however, Olympius found the country fully supportive of Martin. Rather than arrest the pope, he supported him. He declared himself the Byzantine Emperor and raised a revolt against Constans but succumbed to disease during his invasion of Sicily. Apopleptic with rage, Constans sent a new army under Exarch Theodore Calliopas. This time Rome was captured, and Martin was arrested and deposed. He was taken to Constantinople and tried for treason. Found guilty, he was publicly flogged and exiled for life to the Crimea. The final humiliation came when he learned that the clergy of Rome had accepted his deposition and elected a successor. Despite several requests, Rome sent him no money to ease the conditions of his exile. In 655, he died of malnutrition.

643	645	649	650	651
The Muslim Arabs conquer Tripoli.	The Byzantines recapture Alexandria from the Arabs.	The Muslim Arabs conquer Cyprus.	The world's first paper money is issued in China by a private bank.	The Koran is compiled in its modern form by Caliph Uthman.

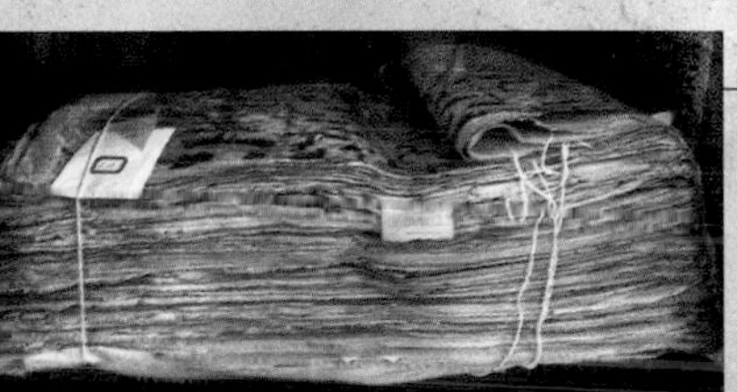

ST. EUGENE I ✣ The 75th Pope 654–657

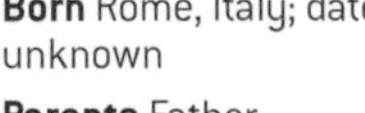

Born Rome, Italy; date unknown

Parents Father, Rufinanius; Mother, unknown

Papacy August 10, 654–June 2, 657

Died Rome, Italy; June 2, 657

When Martin I was deposed, the electors of Rome were initially inclined to support him but, as the city was under Byzantine military rule, they obeyed the emperor and elected Eugene I.

Every contemporary source emphasizes the genial nature of the new pope. He did much work for the poor and worked tirelessly for the good of others. Unfortunately, he took over the papacy in desperately difficult circumstances that proved to be beyond his powers to remedy. Eugene sent an embassy to Constantinople to try to resolve the dispute over Monothelitism (*see* p.51). The embassy was welcomed by the new patriarch Peter, who proposed a compromise stating that Christ had two natures, human and divine, each with its own will (the Roman position) but that as a person he had one single will (the Byzantine position). Eugene welcomed it but before he could confirm it there was a near riot in the Basilica of Santa Maria Maggiore when the assembled clergy heard the form of words. Eugene reluctantly sent a message to Constantinople rejecting the new compromise. Furious, Constans threatened to lead an army to Rome to bring the troublesome priests to heel. Eugene died before Constans arrived.

ST. VITALIAN ✣ The 76th Pope 657–672

Born Segni, Italy; date unknown

Parents Father, Anastasius; Mother, unknown

Papacy July 30, 657–January 27, 672

Died Rome, Italy; January 27, 672

Following his election, Vitalian wrote to Emperor Constans II and the Eastern patriarch Peter very tactfully stating the position of Rome regarding Monothelitism (*see* p.51).

Peter was so pleased that he added the pope's name to those prayed for at Mass in Constantinople—the first pope in fifty years to be so honored. Constans, too, was mollified and announced that he was now coming to Italy in peace. The visit by the emperor finally took place in July 663, but did not go quite as Vitalian hoped. Constans began by stripping many ancient Roman buildings of their metal, then he made the archbishop of Ravenna (the base of Byzantine power in Italy) independent of the pope and imposed new taxes. Finally, a decision to take up residence in Sicily proved too much for the civil service. Constans was murdered in his bath. Vitalian moved quickly to support the heir, Constantine IV, and the Monothelitist dispute was forgotten for a while.

Outside of the doctrinal dispute, Vitalian was a champion of church music. He enlarged the musical school at the Lateran and is credited, perhaps correctly, with introducing organ music to churches.

652

Sigebert II becomes king of Essex. His accession marks the resumption of the conversion of the English to Christianity after a generation of pagan resurgence.

654

Arabs invade Rhodes, melting down the famous statue, the *Colossus of Rhodes.*

656

Civil war breaks out in the Islamic empire between the supporters of Ali (Muhammed's cousin) and Aisha (Muhammed's wife).

661

Islamic Caliph Ali is murdered. Muawiyah I founds the Umayyad caliphate to rule the lands conquered by the Muslims.

673

Birth of English monk, scholar, and historian later to be known as the Venerable Bede.

ADEODATUS II ✠ The 77th Pope 672–676

Born Rome, Italy; date unknown

Parents Father, Jovinianus; Mother, unknown

Papacy April 11, 672–June 17, 676

Died Rome, Italy; June 17, 676

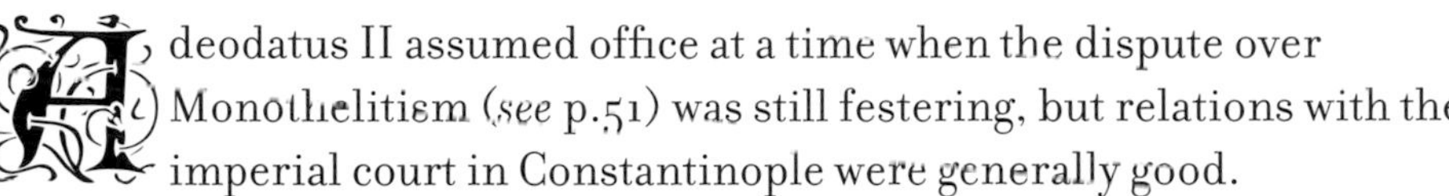

Adeodatus II assumed office at a time when the dispute over Monothelitism (*see* p.51) was still festering, but relations with the imperial court in Constantinople were generally good.

Before his election as pope, he had been a Benedictine monk in the cloister of St. Erasmus. It used to be considered that Adeodatus had granted important favors to two major monasteries. St. Peter's monastery in Canterbury, England, was granted complete freedom from supervision by the archbishops of Canterbury and was subject only to control or instruction direct from the pope, which made the monastery effectively independent. Similar privileges were granted to the monastery of St. Martin at Tours, France. However, both documents are now thought to be early medieval forgeries concocted at the monasteries concerned. Whether they encapsulated genuine grants from Adeodatus or were simply made up is unknown. In contrast, help that Adeodatus reportedly gave to pilgrims is considered genuine. Surviving records indicate that, as pope, Adeodatus was generally generous to the poor but seems not to have accomplished a great deal during his papacy.

DONUS ✠ The 78th Pope 676–678

Born Rome, Italy; date unknown

Parents Father, Maurice; Mother, unknown

Papacy November 2, 676–April 11, 678

Died Rome, Italy; April 11, 678

Donus was an elderly, respectable, and learned priest when he was elected to follow Adeodatus II. It was widely expected that his papacy would be dominated the dispute over Monothelitism (*see* p.51).

The patriarch of Constantinople, Theodore I, wrote a letter to Donus emphasizing the need to work together for the good of all Christians but skating over the issues at dispute. The reply Donus sent has not survived but was presumably just as friendly without giving ground on the theological differences. Donus also put out placatory feelers to Archbishop Reparatus of Ravenna with a view to bringing that archdiocese back under Roman authority. Then a scandal exploded at the heart of Rome. The monks of one of the best-known monasteries in Rome were revealed to be adherents of the Nestorian heresy (*see* p.48). Donus moved swiftly to deal with the crisis—forcibly expelling the monks from the monastery.

The peace moves to Constantinople had, meanwhile, borne fruit. Emperor Constantine IV wrote to Donus inviting him to send delegates to a conference where the Monothelitic dispute could be sorted out once and for all. Donus died before the letter arrived.

674
Arabs under Muawiyah I attack the city of Constantinople, but are driven off.

674
The vast Frankish realm is divided between Theuderic I and Childeric II.

675
The murder of Childeric of the Franks leads to civil war and anarchy in the Frankish kingdom.

676
Death of Chinese poet Wang Bo, famous for the work *Friendships Across the World Make Near Neighbors of Far Horizons*.

ST. AGATHO — The 79th Pope 678–681

Born Rome, Italy; date unknown

Parents Father, Emilianus; Mother, unknown

Papacy June 27, 678–January 10, 681

Died Rome, Italy; January 10, 681

Agatho's pontificate was short but momentous as it finally marked the end to the split with Constantinople over the dispute over Monothelitism (*see* p.51). One of his first problems as pope, however, was not doctrinal but financial—the papacy was almost bankrupt.

Agatho sacked the papal treasurer and took over the job himself, firstly persuading the emperor Constantine IV to forego the charge usually made for confirming a pope in office. By the time he died, Agatho had reformed practice in the papal finances and bequeathed a more solvent institution to his successors.

It was Agatho who received a letter sent to his predecessor Donus by Emperor Constantine IV proposing a meeting to sort out the issue of Monothelitism once and for all. Constantine's idea was for a panel of theologians from East and West to debate the issue and find a way forward. Before sending the delegation, Agatho took the precaution of holding a series of synods across the West to establish a joint position. As expected, the delegation was of a very high quality, including two future popes: John V and Constantine. When the delegation arrived in Constantinople the emperor had cancelled the theological debate and instead summoned what became the Sixth General Council, or Third Council of Constantinople, in November 680. The primary task was to end the division between East and West over Monothelitism, and to reach a decision on Monophysitism as well. The papal delegation read out a long letter composed by Agatho that summarized the findings of the Western synods. The Council, chaired by the emperor himself, discussed the matter for months, but finally decided that Agatho was correct in every particular. Both Monophysitism and Monothelitism were condemned and their followers anathematized—including Pope Honorius (*see* p.66). Going further, the Council confirmed that Christ had given the true faith to the Church of Rome through St. Peter and that St. Peter had been speaking through Agatho.

Agatho would have been delighted and thrilled to have the orthodox faith and papal authority confirmed in this unambiguous way. However, he died before the decisions of the Council could be brought to Rome.

Mosaic in the Basilica of Sant'Apollinare in Ravenna depicting Pope Agatho making the papal oath.

THE PAPAL OATH

It has been suggested that Agatho was the first pope to take what has become known as "The Papal Oath." The oath pledged the incoming pope to uphold canon law, adhere rigidly to orthodox teaching, and excommunicate heretics. The actual form of this oath is a matter of dispute, as is the question of for how many centuries it remained in use. It may have fallen out of use in the 12th century. Some historians doubt if there ever was a formal Papal Oath as such but suggest, instead, that each pope made such pledges as seemed relevant at the time.

677	678	680	680
Hungarian tribes fleeing the Avars complete their move into what had until then been Pannonia, but now becomes known as Hungary.	Death of Uija, ruler of the Korean state of Baekje. After his death, the state breaks up and Korea falls under Chinese and Japanese control.	Death of the Caliph Muawiyah I, who is succeeded by Yazid I as head of Islam. The Battle of Kerbela on October 10 ends the life of Husain, a descendant of the prophet Muhammed.	The Bulgars complete their conquest of what is now Bulgaria.

ST. LEO II ✠ The 80th Pope 682–683

Born Sicily, Italy; date unknown
Parents unknown
Papacy August 17, 682–July 3, 683
Died Rome, Italy; July 3, 683

Leo was elected within days of the death of Agatho and messengers were sent to Constantinople requesting the imperial approval for consecration to take place. The messengers arrived at a delicate time.

The Sixth General Council (*see* p.71) was near to agreement but had not yet produced a final statement. One sticking point was whether those who had accepted Monothelitism should be anathematized by name—as the emperor Constantine IV wanted, presumably so that blame could be shared with the West. If so, Pope Honorius would have to be named.

When Constantine had agreed to forego the tax usually charged by the emperor on an incoming pope, he had insisted in return that the emperor's personal seal was needed before a pope could be enthroned. Now he used that effective veto on Leo taking office to insist that he got his way. Honorius was anathematized as a heretic and condemned for having "by his betrayal allowed to be overthrown the immaculate faith." Humiliating as this was for the papacy, the split with the East was over and the two heresies had been definitively condemned. Leo must have felt it a price worth paying, though later generations were not so sure.

ST. BENEDICT II ✠ The 81st Pope 684–685

Born Rome, Italy; date unknown
Parents unknown
Papacy June 26, 684–May 8, 685
Died Rome, Italy; May 8, 685

Benedict was a local Roman who joined the Church as a boy, apparently as a choirboy. He had subsequently served in every order in the Church up to that of priest—the rank he held when elected.

Imperial confirmation of Benedict's papacy took nearly a year and one of Benedict's top priorities was to bring an end to this process, which was time-consuming and humiliating for the papacy. Emperor Constantine IV, having used his power to get his way with Leo II, was surprisingly willing to surrender it. In future, it was decreed, imperial confirmation could be given by the exarch in Ravenna—the confirmation would be little more than a rubber stamp. As an added token of imperial favor, Constantine sent the pope locks of the hair from his two sons: Justinian (later the emperor Justinian II) and Heraclius. In a solemn ceremony, Benedict adopted the two boys by proxy. Meanwhile, although the Sixth General Council had condemned the heresy of Monothelitism, there was still a lot of tidying up to do. Many Eastern Monothelitics had been sent to Rome for punishment, whereupon Leo sent them to various monasteries to be re-educated in orthodox theology.

682	682	683	684
A prolonged drought brings famine and mass starvation to China.	Emperor Temmu of Japan overhauls the military and court system of the country, with the latter seeing the introduction of many Chinese customs.	Death of Pacal the Great of the Maya city state of Palenque in Central America after a reign of 70 years that saw Palenque reach its height of prosperity and political power.	Marwan takes over as Umayyad Caliph, head of the Islamic state and religion, establishing his branch of the family that would remain in control to the end of the Umayyad Caliphate.

JOHN V ✠ The 82nd Pope 685–686

Born Antioch, Syria; date unknown
Parents Father, Cyriacus; Mother, unknown
Papacy July 23, 685–August 2, 686
Died Rome, Italy; August 2, 686

John marked a return to native Greek-speakers in the papacy after the local Roman Benedict II. He had been born in Antioch and probably came to Rome to escape the new Muslim rulers of the area.

Since he was able to speak Greek fluently, he performed well at the Sixth General Council, becoming perhaps the leading spokesman of the Roman delegation. At the end of the Council, he went back to Rome taking with him the formal decrees. By 685, he was archdeacon of Rome and was elected unopposed to succeed Benedict II.

No sooner was John in office than he received word that Archbishop Citonatus of Cagliari in Sardinia had consecrated a bishop without first passing the name to Rome for confirmation. This was a usurpation of power since the archbishop of Cagliari had no right to act on his own initiative. John suspended the bishop, then summoned everyone involved to Rome where a synod reaffirmed papal authority and, once the Sardinians had agreed to this, installed the disputed bishop in office.

John continued building works begun by Benedict II, with work under way in St. Peter's, the Pantheon, and at San Lorenzo in Lucina. He died after barely a year in office.

CONON ✠ The 83rd Pope 686–687

Born perhaps Sicily, Italy; date unknown
Parents Father, unknown; Mother, unknown
Papacy October 21, 686–September 21, 687
Died Rome, Italy; September 21, 687

The militia of Rome decided that since the pope now had effective command of the armed forces, they should have a say in the papal election. The elderly Conon, an ex-soldier, was chosen as pope.

Conon was the son of a successful Thracian general and, perhaps because of his family's background in imperial service, he got on well with the new emperor Justinian II. The emperor reduced taxes on the papal estates in Italy and confirmed his intention to abide by the decisions of the Sixth General Council (*see* p.71). Conon had another success when he welcomed to Rome the Irish priest St. Kilian who he sent to Franconia (now in Bavaria) where Kilian had great success converting the locals.

When the position of rector of the Sicilian estates fell vacant, Conon appointed Deacon Constantine of Syracuse on the grounds that he thought him the best man for the task of managing the extensive estates. However, the position was a highly lucrative one that usually went to one of the Roman clergy, and those clerics now felt seriously snubbed. Moreover they worried that other similarly coveted jobs might go to outsiders. Trouble was averted by Conon's death.

685
Founding of the Al-Aqsa Mosque, the third holiest in Islam, in Jerusalem by the Caliph Abd al-Malik.

685
Battle of Nechtansmere sees the Picts defeat the Northumbrians and restrict English settlement to south of the Firth of Forth.

687
The two parts of the Frankish kingdom, Neustria and Austrasia, are reunited under Theuderic III, though real power lay with the mayor of the palace Pepin.

687
Death of St. Cuthbert of Lindisfarne, later patron saint of the northern English.

ST. SERGIUS I ✠ The 84th Pope 687–701

Born Palermo, Sicily; date unknown

Parents Unknown

Papacy December 15, 687–September 9, 701

Died probably Rome, Italy; September 9, 701

When Conon died, the Roman militia rushed to the Lateran, installing their favored priest Theodore in the papal apartments. Archdeacon Paschal arrived next and took over the rest of the Lateran.

Paschal had already written to Ravenna, promising the imperial exarch a fortune if he used Byzantine troops to back his election. Meanwhile, the leading citizens of Rome met at the imperial palace and elected the priest Sergius. A crowd then carried him to the Lateran and stormed inside. Theodore gave in at once, but Paschal waited for the exarch, who arrived and confirmed Sergius in office.

Sergius devoted himself to improving sacred music, introducing the singing of the Agnus Dei, and to restoring churches that were in need of repair. He also moved the remains of Leo I to an ornate tomb in the heart of St. Peter's. His quiet work was disrupted by news that the Quinisext Council—held in Constantinople without Western bishops—had issued 102 new canon laws. Sergius flatly refused to endorse the laws. Emperor Justinian sent a small army to Rome, but the imperial soldiers in Italy sided with the pope. Relations with the emperor subsided to an angry silence, while Sergius returned to his quiet work.

JOHN VI ✠ The 85th Pope 701–705

Born probably Ephesus, Byzantine Empire; date unknown

Parents Unknown

Papacy October 30, 701–January 11, 705

Died Rome, Italy; January 11, 705

In 695, Emperor Justinian II was overthrown in a military coup that ushered in a period known as "The Twenty Year Anarchy" when the Byzantine Empire had seven emperors and numerous pretenders.

The imperial exarch Theophylact was in Rome at the time of the coup but did not have enough money to pay his troops, who promptly mutinied. John stepped in to resolve the dispute without bloodshed. While some took advantage of the confusion in Byzantine government to declare independence, John preferred to remain loyal but nevertheless exploited the situation to gather more authority to the papacy.

The limits of this papal authority, however, were clearly demonstrated by a dispute between Bishop Wilfrid of York and Archbishop Theodore in England. King Egfrith of Northumbria sided with Theodore and sent Wilfrid into exile. Although John VI decreed that Wilfrid was in the right and should be restored to his archdiocese of York, King Egfrith contemptuously refused even to read the documents from Rome. John had more success with the Lombard king Aripert II, who returned to papal ownership vast estates in the southwestern Alps, apparently without taking payment.

691	694	697	701
The Dome of the Rock is completed in Jerusalem.	King Egica of Spain accuses the Jews of aiding a Muslim invasion and sentences all Jews to slavery.	Paolo Lucio Anafesto becomes the first Doge of Venice. Apparently, he was subject to the Byzantine emperor and may have been appointed by him or elected by the citizens of Venice.	Muslim Arab forces capture Adulis, driving Christian residents inland to Ethiopia.

JOHN VII ✠ The 86th Pope 705–707

Born Rossano, Calabria; c.650

Parents Father, Plato; Mother, Blatta

Papacy March 1, 705–October 18, 707

Died Rome, Italy; October 18, 707

The son of an imperial official, John rose to be an administrator of papal estates. As pope, he set himself two tasks: to adore the Virgin Mary and to establish good relations with the notorious Lombards.

To achieve the former, John built an oratory attached to St. Peter's dedicated to Mary Theotokos—the "God-bearer." He also restored the Ancient Church of St. Mary in the Roman Forum. Finally, he commissioned a huge icon of the Blessed Virgin Mary that he installed in the Church of Our Lady in Trastevere. To achieve his more secular ambition, he sent numerous embassies and letters to the Lombard nobles, keeping in close touch with them and working hard to keep them on side.

In 706, Justinian was restored to the Byzantine throne. In a bloodbath of epic proportions, he slaughtered anyone he suspected had had a hand in his deposition. He then sent a blunt message to John telling him to agree to the canons declared at the Quinisext Council (*see* p.74). John dared not snub the emperor by refusing but dared not antagonize his own clergy by agreeing. Instead, he delayed answering while slavishly supporting the emperor in everything else. John was still delaying when he died.

SISINNIUS ✠ The 87th Pope 708

Born probably Syria; date unknown

Parents Father, John; Mother, unknown

Papacy January 15, 708–February 4, 708

Died Rome, Italy; February 4, 708

Sisinnius was probably elected within a few days of the death of John VII, but his official reign does not begin until imperial approval arrived in January 708.

At this date the papal election took place in the Lateran Basilica and all the clergy and citizens of Rome were invited to take part. Although the army had no formal role in itself, the soldiers are recorded to have made their views forcibly known at several elections. It is inconceivable that they did not take part in papal elections at this time, perhaps muscling in to the basilica as individual voters. The process of voting at this time is not recorded, but would probably have been by way of a recorded ballot.

Whatever the precise process by which he was elected, Sisinnius had to wait nearly three months before confirmation was received from the imperial exarch in Ravenna. He had meanwhile ordered the manufacture of a large quantity of lime so that the city walls of Rome could be repaired and improved. Sisinnius, who was already old at the time of his election and reportedly afflicted with chronic gout, would not live to see the work carried out for he died suddenly and was buried in St. Peter's Basilica.

704	705	706	706	707
Death of St. Adamnan of Iona, Scotland.	Arabs complete the conquest of Armenia, but fail to convert the population to Islam.	The Grand Mosque of Damascus is begun by Caliph Al-Walid I.	Death of Yuquan Shenxiu, perhaps the most influential of the Zen Buddhist thinkers during the Chinese Tang Dynasty.	The Balearic Islands are captured by the Muslim Arabs.

CONSTANTINE ✠ The 88th 708–715

Born probably Syria; date unknown

Parents Father, perhaps John; Mother, unknown

Papacy March 25, 708–April 9, 715

Died Rome, Italy; April 9, 715

The ponitifcate of Constantine I was dominated by relations with the Byzantine emperors. Constantine was a Syrian and was therefore able to speak Greek fluently and probably had contacts in the Eastern Church, which may explain his election as pope.

One of the first actions of the new pope was to consecrate Archbishop Felix of Ravenna. This Constantine did willingly enough but, in response, Felix subtly changed the usual oath of obedience and tokens of submission in such a way that they could be interpreted as reviving the independence of the archbishop of Ravenna from the jurisdiction of Rome. Constantine was still considering how best to respond when a Byzantine army stormed into Ravenna and arrested Felix on charges of plotting to overthrow Emperor Justinian II. The hapless archbishop was dragged to Constantinople where he underwent a show trial before being found guilty, blinded, and thrown into prison.

It must, therefore, have been with great trepidation that Constantine received an abrupt summons from Justinian to come to Constantinople. The object of the visit, the emperor wrote, was to reach agreement over the canons declared at the Quinisext Council (*see* p.74), which Pope Sergius I had refused to ratify and Pope John VII had so carefully avoided dealing with. Constantine was as opposed to the disputed ecclesiastical rules as had been Sergius. With the horrible fate of Felix of Ravenna vividly in mind, Constantine set out for Constantinople in October 710.

In fact, Constantine was received with all the favors usually reserved for the arrival of the emperor. The pope and his entourage were then escorted to the city of Nicomedia to meet Justinian. The emperor ostentatiously bowed to the pope before handing the negotiations over to officials and leaving to get on with the business of running the empire.

For his part, Constantine delegated talks to the deacon Gregory (later Pope Gregory II). It soon became clear that the main objectives of Justinian had been to humiliate the pope, demonstrate imperial superiority by forcing the pontiff to come to Constantinople, and to terrify everyone by a round of murders and mutilations. These objectives achieved, Justinian proved to be not especially interested in the Quinisext Canons. Once Constantine had agreed to a few of the disputed rules, and mumbled vague promises about the others, he was allowed to return to Rome.

The pope had been back in Rome only a few weeks when news arrived that Justinian had himself been murdered and replaced by the nobleman Philippikos Bardanes. This Bardanes was an adherent of the Monothelitic heresy (*see* p.50), and his first action was to demand that Constantine approve the doctrine. Constantine refused, as had so many of his predecessors, and again the imperial exarch marched on Rome. This time, however, the people of Rome rallied to the pope and a series of bloody riots followed that forced the exarch to withdraw. Meanwhile, Bardanes was in his turn ousted by an army rebellion. The new emperor, Anastasius II, at once rejected Monothelitism and sent messages of peace to Rome. Constantine was thus able to enjoy his last few months as pope in peace.

Emperor Philippikos Bardanes replaced the Byzantine emperor Justinian II. This document shows him ordering the decapitation of his enemy Tiberius.

709
King Cenred of Mercia in England abdicates and travels to Rome to become a monk.

711
Muslim Arabs invade Spain under Tariq ibn Ziyad, and within 5 years they subdue the entire Iberian Peninsula.

713
Work begins on the Leshan Buddha, China; at 233 feet tall, it will be the world's biggest stone Buddha.

716
The monastery of Iona, Scotland, celebrates Easter according to the Roman tradition ending the independence of the Celtic Church.

717
Leo the Isaurian leads a coup to become Byzantine emperor Leo III, ending the Twenty Years of Chaos and founding the Isaurian Dynasty that will last until 802.

ST. GREGORY II ✠ The 89th Pope 715–731

Born Rome, Italy; date unknown
Parents Unknown
Papacy May 19, 715–February 11, 731
Died Rome, Italy; February 11, 731

Following on from a succession of short-lived popes, Gregory II's reign of 15 years brought some much needed stability to the papacy. The ultimate papal insider, Gregory had been born in Rome and grew up in the Lateran Palace where he rose to become Librarian.

Gregory accompanied Pope Constantine to Constantinople and was largely responsible for the successful negotiations with Emperor Justinian II at that time. When Constantine died, Gregory was the obvious successor.

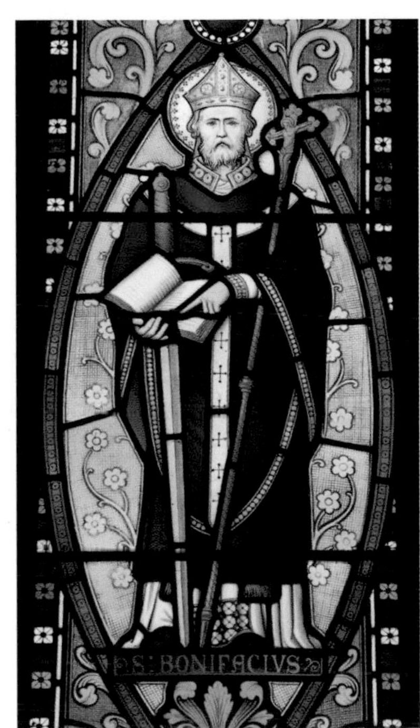

In 718, an English monk named Winfrid arrived in Rome with an ambitious plan to convert the pagans of north Germany. Gregory enthusiastically embraced Winfrid and gave him a new name—Boniface. Boniface became the patron saint of Germany.

Gregory's first act was to repair the walls of Rome against a threatened Muslim invasion from North Africa. He then persuaded King Liutprand of the Lombards to hand back to papal control the key fortresses of Cumae and Sutri, along with the surrounding lands. By 717, Gregory had secured the defenses of Rome.

Meanwhile, trouble was brewing with the new and powerful Byzantine emperor Leo III. In 722, Leo imposed new taxes on Italy, which came as the Italians were suffering from a bad harvest. Gregory led the formal protests, while the Roman mob drove the Byzantine prefect of Rome out of the city. At the time this move was not considered very important, but with hindsight it is clear that this was a key step in the process of papal secular rule over central Italy independent of the Byzantine Empire.

In 726, the dispute with Leo entered a new phase when the emperor issued an edict banning the veneration of icons and ordering the destruction of all images of the saints. This iconoclasm was popular in Constantinople but bitterly opposed in the West. The Italian provinces rose in rebellion and, in 727, Gregory summoned a synod to discuss the issue. With the synod's approval Gregory wrote a famous letter to Leo declaring "the dogmas of the Church are not a matter for the emperor, but for the bishops."

Leo responded by sending a fresh army to Italy commanded by a military hard man named Eutychius. This Eutychius formed an alliance with Liutprand, then sent men in disguise to Rome with orders to murder Gregory. The plot was discovered before any bloodshed occurred, but it did nothing to improve relations between Rome and Constantinople. In 729, Liutprand and Eutychius arrived outside the gates of Rome with their armies. Gregory crept into the Lombard camp and exploited doctrinal disputes between the Catholic Liutprand and Orthodox Eutychius to break up the alliance against him. Liutprand entered Rome on foot and symbolically laid his sword on the tomb of St. Peter before leaving for his lands in the north. Eutychius agreed a treaty with Gregory that in theory reaffirmed Byzantine sovereignty over Italy, but in practice increased the independence of the pope.

Gregory then turned to sorting out disputes over primacy and privileges among the Italian bishops but he had made little progress before his death. He was buried in St. Peter's Basilica.

718
Pelagius of Asturias wins the Battle of Covadonga to free his small state in northern Spain from Muslim rule. It is today seen as the start of the Christian *Reconquista* of the Iberian Peninsula.

720
The Moors cross the Pyrenees and capture Narbonne.

723
The world's first mechanical clock is built in China.

726
Greece revolts against Byzantine rule. A Greek fleet sets out for Constantinople with an antiemperor but is destroyed by the imperial fleet who use an incendiary weapon called Greek Fire.

731
An ecclesiastical history of England is completed by "the Venerable Bede."

ST. GREGORY III ✠ The 90th 731–741

Born probably Syria; date unknown

Parents unknown

Papacy March 18, 731–November 28, 741

Died Rome, Italy; November 28, 741

The funeral of Pope Gregory II in St. Peter's on February 11, 731, was interrupted by a sudden scuffle in the crowd. The disturbance grew louder and larger until a section of the crowd was seen to be lifting to their shoulders a Syrian-born Greek cleric, who was also named Gregory.

Cheering erupted and the crowd surged off toward the Lateran with Gregory struggling to be set free. Arriving at the Lateran, the crowd began chanting that Gregory should be the next pope and, with nobody willing to stand up to the mob, they got their way.

Gregory dutifully wrote to the Byzantine exarch to seek confirmation of his papacy. When the confirmation was received, the consecration took place on March 18. Seeking a good relationship with the East, Gregory wrote to Emperor Leo III seeking to clarify where the emperor stood on iconoclasm—the burning religious issue of the day. Leo threw the papal messenger in prison and refused to reply.

Understandably angry, Gregory called a synod, which, in November 731, issued a blunt denunciation of iconoclasm and proclaimed excommunication on anyone who indulged in the destructive practice. The messenger sent to deliver the excommunication was also put in prison, but that was not enough for Leo. He decided that the papacy needed to be taught a lesson. He confiscated all papal estates in Sicily and Calabria, then under imperial rule, and told the bishops of the Balkans that they now came under the jurisdiction of the patriarch of Constantinople. He also sent a war fleet to attack Rome, but the fleet was hit by a storm and so badly battered that it crept back home.

Despite imperial hostility, Gregory helped Exarch Eutychius against King Liutprand of the Lombards. Beaten at Ravenna, Liutprand turned on Rome. He found the city impregnable behind newly restored walls, but he captured several nearby fortresses and looted the surrounding lands. Gregory quickly concluded alliances with Liutprand's rebellious vassals Duke Trasamund of Spoleto and the Duke of Benevento. He also sent ambassadors to Charles Martel, the effective ruler of the Franks, offering to make him a consul and patrician if he came to help. However, the Franks were allies of the Lombards against the Arabs of Spain, while the two dukes proved to be treacherous. The alliance he had so carefully fostered began to fall apart, at which point Gregory himself died.

Tremissis coin from the reign of King Liutprand of the Lombards.

ICONOCLASM

The iconoclasts declared images of saints to be no better than pagan idols. Images of Christ were also held to be sacrilegious since, by depicting the outward semblance of Christ's human body, they were divorcing His human nature from His divine nature—a heresy. Those supporting the use of icons countered by pointing to uses of images in the Bible and by the apostles. Emperor Leo III took up the cause of iconoclasm and began the systematic destruction of religious art in the Byzantine Empire, a policy continued by his son Constantine V.

731	732	732	735	738	739	740
Muslim advance into central Asia halted by Turgesh forces at the Battle of the Defile.	Muslim advance into Europe halted at the Battle of Tours by a Frankish army led by Charles Martel.	Bubonic plague strikes Constantinople; it will kill up to 200,000 people over the next four years.	Death of English monk, historian, and theologian: the Venerable Bede.	Mayan city state Quirigua defeats Copan, ending Copan dominance of the Mayan cultural area.	Charles Martel drives the last Muslim forces out of France and back into Spain.	The Khazars of eastern Europe convert to Judaism.

ST. ZACHARY ✠ The 91st Pope 741–752

Born Calabria, Italy; date unknown

Parents Unknown

Papacy December 10, 741–March 22, 752

Died Rome, Italy; March 22, 752

Zachary was of Greek ancestry and his first priority on coming to power in Rome was to get on better terms with the Byzantine emperor Constantine V. He sent ambassadors to Constantinople to announce his election to the emperor and deliver formal letters to the patriarch.

Constantine gave the pope vast and lucrative estates in central Italy to make up for those lost in Sicily. Although Constantine was a keen iconoclast, whereas Zachary was a supporter of icons, they chose not to mention the subject—each having troubles closer to home.

The main problem for Zachary was the Lombards. King Liutprand was as powerful and belligerent as ever, while Duke Trasamund of Spoleto was showing no signs of helping Rome. Zachary traveled to Terni to meet with Liutprand and agreed to lend the support of the papal armed forces to help Liutprand and handed over lavish gifts. Zachary was meanwhile deeply involved with events among the Franks. In 750, an embassy came from Pepin, son of Charles Martel, asking if formal kingship should be invested in the man who held real power or the man who had inherited the title but held no power. Zachary decided in favor of the former. Pepin then promptly deposed King Childeric III, forced him to become a monk, and proclaimed himself king of the Franks.

In 749, Liutprand's son Aistulf became king of the Lombards and at once attacked Ravenna. This time Zachary could not broker peace, and soon the last Byzantine foothold in northern Italy had fallen to Aistulf. The conqueror made no secret of the fact that Rome would be next. Soon after learning this dread news, Zachary passed away. He was buried in an oratory he had constructed in St. Peter's Basilica.

The origins of the pope's unique headwear has been traced back to Zachary who is thought to have adopted the formal headgear of a Byzantine nobleman.

PAPAL TIARA

It was Pope Zachary who first took to wearing cone-shaped headgear. This resembled an upright pyramid of stiff white linen, folded into shape and with a band of decoration around the base. In the course of the 10th century, when the popes asserted their formal rule over the papal states, they added around the base a small golden crown to symbolize their temporal power. Some time in the 13th century, a second crown was added above the first, probably to symbolize the pope's spiritual power. The third tier of crown first appeared in the early 14th century and it is this triple tiara that appears on papal arms and insignia. This takes the form of a domed hat surmounted by a cross and ringed by three circlets or open crowns, one above the other. In that form it was used in every papal coronation from 1314 to 1963, after which coronations ceased to be held.

744	746	747	748	750	751
In Morocco, Muslim leader Salah ibn Tarif declares himself to be a prophet and founds a heretical branch of Islam that lasts three centuries.	A Byzantine fleet and army reconquer Cyprus from the Muslims.	Chinese emperor Xuanzong abolishes the death penalty—the first state known to have done so. It is later reintroduced.	Death of Empress Gensho of Japan—a key figure in the development of Japanese legal systems.	Approximate date of the destruction by fire of Teotihuacan, largest city in the Americas with a population of around 125,000.	Chinese and Muslim forces clash for the first time near Samarkand in the Battle of Talas—a Muslim victory.

STEPHEN II ✠ The 92nd Pope 752–757

Born Rome; date unknown

Parents Unknown

Papacy March 26, 752–April 26, 757

Died Rome, Italy; April 26, 757

A few days after the death of Pope Zachary, the clergy and people of Rome elected a presbyter named Stephen. On March 23, he moved into the Lateran but died suddenly two days later. Gathering in Santa Maria Maggiore, the clergy elected another Stephen to replace him.

Statue of King Pepin of the Franks in Würzburg, Germany.

Pope Stephen II was at once confronted with a truculent king: Aistulf of the Lombards. Backed by his army, Aistulf declared that the Duchy of Rome (the administrative unit of the Byzantine Empire that included Rome) belonged to him and began levying taxes accordingly. The Romans had just been getting used to being free of Constantinople and resented the new impositions. Stephen therefore traveled north over the Alps—the first pope to do so—to visit King Pepin of the Franks. He reminded Pepin that he owed his throne to Pope Zachary and asked for his help.

Pepin led the mighty Frankish army over the Alps into Italy and defeated Aistulf. The cowed Lombard handed over to the pope not only the sovereignty over the Duchy of Rome and disputed border fortresses, but also the lands the Lombards had so recently taken from the Byzantines. When Pepin returned home, Aistulf reneged on the deal, so Pepin returned and crushed Lombard military power, forcing Aistulf to give the pope Emilia as well as the former concessions.

At this point, an envoy from Emperor Constantine V arrived to announce that the lands being given to the pope were really the property of the Empire. Pepin retorted that he had fought Aistulf for the benefit of St. Peter, not a mortal emperor, and that he would give the lands to nobody but the heir of St. Peter. Faced by the Frankish army, the Byzantines went home. The incident proved momentous. The papacy, Italy, and all the old Western provinces of the Roman Empire were now free of Byzantine control. While rulers in Constantinople still claimed legal sovereignty over their former provinces, such claims were a dead letter with no force and were ignored in the West. The Franks were now the real power in Western Europe.

Stephen, meanwhile, set about consolidating his rule over what would soon become known as the Papal States. The lands were wealthy and dotted with rich towns that could be taxed to provide a large income for the papal treasury. Combined with papal estates in other countries, this income made the pope a wealthy prince as well as spiritual head of Western Christendom. Stephen had given his successors the financial tools they needed to exert pressure on those rulers who might prove recalcitrant about obeying papal edicts.

THE NUMBERING OF THE STEPHENS

The death of the first Stephen elected in 752 came before he had been consecrated, which at the time was considered necessary before he officially held the post of pope. However, in the 16th century it was decided that a pope should take office from the moment he is elected. By this criteria, the first Stephen of 752 was Stephen II, with his replacement becoming Stephen III. Subsequent Stephens were renumbered accordingly on official papal documents.

753	754	755	757
The wealthy central Asian city of Samarkand falls to the Muslims.	Emperor Constantine V restarts the destruction of holy images in the Byzantine Empire as he continues his father's iconoclastic policies.	The general An Lu-Shan revolts against the Tang emperors of China and captures the capital of Chang'an.	Offa becomes king of Mercia, England, and soon becomes the most powerful ruler in Britain.

ST. PAUL I ✠ The 93rd Pope 757–767

Born Rome, Italy; date unknown

Parents Unknown

Papacy May 29, 757–June 28, 767

Died Rome, Italy; June 28, 767

Stephen II's reign was considered so successful in Rome that when he died his younger brother Paul was elected in his place. As a result of his brother's work, much of Paul's reign would be taken up with duties more usually associated with a prince than a bishop.

Paul's first act was to write to Emperor Constantine V in Constantinople to announce the news of his election. Significantly, he did not ask for permission for a consecration. He wrote an almost identical letter to King Pepin of the Franks, thus emphasizing the importance to the papacy of its relationship with the Franks.

The situation in Rome was not quite as straightforward as Paul would have the two rulers believe. The archdeacon Theophylact led a sizeable faction of the clergy that opposed the new relationship with the Franks, preferring the traditional friendship with the emperors. Paul delayed his consecration until he had come to an arrangement with Theophylact. Once consecrated, Paul had to deal with King Desiderius of the Lombards who had grabbed back several towns and fortresses handed over by Aistulf to Stephen.

St. Paul's Basilica in Rome. The mural's central image depicts Christ with St. Peter at His right hand and St. Paul at his left hand.

Desiderius came to Rome to discuss the matter. He explained that he had taken the towns because Pepin had not, as promised, released some Lombard nobles being held hostage. While this was true, Desiderius was really in league with the emperor. Desiderius had promised to return Ravenna to the Empire in return for imperial recognition of his rule over Rome and Spoleto. Learning of Lombard duplicity, Paul wrote to Pepin asking for the release of the hostages, a letter he showed to Desiderius. But by the same messenger he sent a second letter urging Pepin to ignore the first letter and march into Italy to attack the Lombards. Pepin, however, was busy fighting the Muslim rulers of Spain. Pepin sent ambassadors armed with threats of Frankish invasion who persuaded Desiderius to hand back some, but not all, of his acquisitions.

Meanwhile, the emperor had been continuing his persecution of those who venerated icons, with the result that hundreds of monks and clergy had fled west. Paul had given them sanctuary and handed over to them the monastery of Saints Stefano and Silvestro. Now came news that Constantine had sent envoys to Pepin asking him to support iconoclasm, or at least to use his influence to force Paul to send the refugees home for punishment. Paul was deeply worried, but summoned a synod of northern bishops at Gentilly, which found in favor of the icons. The Byzantine envoys were sent home without any concessions from Pepin.

The news from Gentilly reached Rome in the late spring of 757. Soon afterward, a scorching heat wave hit Rome, forcing the elderly Paul to seek relief inside the cool stone walls of St. Paul's Basilica. The heat still proved too much and Paul succumbed. He was at first buried in St. Paul's but later his body was moved to St. Peter's.

757	760	762	763
Chinese general and rebel An Lu Shan is murdered by his own son, who continues the civil war against the Tang Dynasty for another six years.	The Mayan city of Dos Pilas is abandoned, marking another stage in the collapse of central American civilization.	Caliph Al Mansur moves the political capital of the Islamic world to Baghdad.	Death of Jianzhen—the highly regarded Japanese Buddhist monk.

STEPHEN III ✠ The 94th 768–772

Born Sicily, Italy; date unknown

Parents Unknown

Papacy August 7, 768–January 24, 772

Died Rome, Italy; 24 January, 772

Stephen's election was among the bloodiest in papal history. His first move as pope was to write to King Pepin of the Franks to announce his election. By the time the letter arrived Pepin was dead, but his sons Charles and Carloman quickly approved Stephen's papacy.

When Pope Paul died, an unintended consequence of the recent papal move into temporal rule became bloodily apparent. Now that the popes were secular rulers of a great swathe of central Italy, the local nobles wanted to have some say in the government. Duke Toto of Nepi, one of those newly subject to papal rule, decided that the answer was to install a pope who saw the nobles' point of view. He chose his brother Constantine and led an army into Rome to seize the Lateran. There, the bishop of Praeneste consecrated Constantine to be a subdeacon, deacon, and priest before two more bishops were found and Constantine was consecrated as pope. There had been no election, so the bulk of the Roman clergy, led by the notary Christopher and his son Sergius, opposed Constantine.

In July 768, Christopher, Sergius, and their supporters announced that rather than serve Constantine they would become monks and leave Rome. In fact, they made straight for King Desiderius of the Lombards and asked him to invade Rome to oust Constantine. The delighted Desiderius obliged and sent an army led by Sergius into Rome. Toto was killed and Constantine was thrown into prison.

At this point, the priest Waldipert, acting on the instructions of Desiderius, led a gang of soldiers and armed Romans to the monastery of St. Vito. There they grabbed the chaplain, Philip, and marched him to the Lateran where they proclaimed him pope. Hearing what was happening, Sergius led a mob to the Lateran where he packed Philip off back to his monastery and imprisoned Waldipert.

Constantine was then put on trial before the clergy of Rome. They denounced his consecration, citing the fact that he was married and had kept his wife after becoming a priest. Constantine countered with ancient writings in favor of married clergy. This so angered the clerics, all of whom were celibate, that they gouged out his eyes and threw him out of the city.

An election was then held and a Sicilian priest named Stephen was elected to be Stephen III. Stephen set about a brutal purge of Constantine's supporters. Those who were not murdered were blinded, beaten, and expelled.

King Desiderius now took advantage of the debt owed him by Stephen. He sent an agent, Paul Afiarta, to Rome to put pressure on Stephen and so acquired control of Ravenna and surrounding lands that were by now part of the Papal States. Desiderius also sought friendship with the Franks, sending his daughter Desiderata to marry King Charles, now the sole ruler of the Franks. However, Charles rejected Desiderata and instead married a 13-year-old princess from Swabia, which meant war with Lombardy. Both Charles and Desiderius called on Stephen for papal support, at which crucial moment the pope died. He was hailed a saint in his native Sicily but the sainthood, not surprisingly, has never been made official by the Church.

King Pepin's son Charles, would become the first Holy Roman emperor, known today as Charlemagne.

768
Birth of Han Yu, leading poet, essayist and philosopher of Tang China.

770
Foundation of the port of Hedeby, later to become the leading port and market of Scandinavia.

771
Deaths of King Carloman of the Franks and his illegitimate half brother Remigius leave the third brother Charles the sole ruler of the Franks.

773
Arab scholars in Baghdad establish the concept of zero in mathematics.

ADRIAN I ✠ The 95th Pope 772–795

Born Rome, Italy; traditionally 700

Parents Father, Theodore; Mother, unknown

Papacy February 1, 772–December 25, 795

Died Rome, Italy; December 25, 795

In 787, the Second Council of Nicaea took place. Adrian sent representatives and a thesis supporting icons that was applauded when it was read out. This was the last of the great Seven Ecumenical Councils that are recognized as gathering together all Christendom. It succeeded in finding a form of words about icons acceptable to both East and West.

The long pontificate of Adrian began in turbulent fashion but became one of the most settled and productive periods for Rome in the 8th or 9th centuries. Adrian was born into one of the noblest families in Rome. His parents died when he was young and he was raised by his uncle.

As pope, Adrian found himself overshadowed by the rich and powerful Paul Afiarta, who had been appointed papal chamberlain by Pope Stephen III and who was the agent of King Desiderius of the Lombards. Adrian asked Afiarta to take an important message to Desiderius and, as soon as his rival was out of the city, he proclaimed an amnesty on all those Afiarta had imprisoned. He then ordered that Afiarta was to be arrested if he returned to Rome.

Realizing this almost certainly meant war with the Lombards, Adrian sent a message to King Charles of the Franks reminding him that he was pledged to aid the papacy and begging for help against the Lombards. No reply had arrived when, in December 772, Desiderius launched a surprise attack on the Papal States. Adrian sent a stern message to the Lombard king promising to excommunicate him if he came within sight of Rome. Desiderius halted his march, but occupied his gains with every intention of keeping them.

When spring melted the Alpine snows in early 773, messengers from Charles reached Desiderius and threatened war if he did not return his conquests to papal control. The Lombard king contemptuously refused. A few weeks later, Charles marched over the Alps with a huge army, swept all before him, and besieged Desiderius in Pavia.

The siege was still dragging on when, in 774, Charles suddenly arrived in Rome to attend the Easter services in St. Peter's and hold talks with Adrian. The pope probably produced the faked document known as the *Donation of Constantine* (*see* p.39). He certainly claimed that the pope should be the ruler of all Italy south of the River Po and asked Charles to give these lands to him. Charles promised to give the papacy everything promised by his father Pepin.

In June 774, Desiderius surrendered and Charles sent him to live out the rest of his life as a monk in Corbie. Charles then gave the papacy all that had been promised, but not all that Adrian wanted. Tuscany, Spoleto, and numerous other lands were left in the hands of their Lombard dukes. The reason soon became clear. Charles had himself crowned king of the Lombards and took control of all the lands that Adrian had wanted for the papacy.

Despite this setback, Adrian was now in secure control of more territory than any pope before him. He put great efforts into ensuring a steady flow of taxes into Rome. The money was spent repairing the walls of Rome, strengthening the embankments along the Tiber to stop flooding, rebuilding four aqueducts to secure the supply of fresh water to Rome, and beautifying several churches.

778	784	786	788	789
King Charles of the Franks invades Spain to fight the Muslims. His rearguard is defeated by Basques at Roncesvalles, an incident made famous by the epic poem *The Song of Roland*.	The paddle-wheel ship powered by slaves is invented by Chinese engineer Li Gao.	Harun al Rashid becomes Caliph, ruling the Abassid Empire until 809.	King Charles of the Franks conquers Saxony.	First Viking raid on England.

ST. LEO III ✠ The 96th 795–816

Born Rome, Italy; 750
Parents Unknown
Papacy December 26, 795–June 12, 816
Died Rome, Italy; June 12, 816

Leo was born in Rome but his family came from southern Italy and he was viewed as something of an outsider. His father, moreover, had been a tradesman, not a noble. A highly controversial character, Leo was responsible for one of the most momentous acts of any pope—the hailing of King Charles of the Franks as emperor.

It was probably due to his exceptional intelligence that Leo was promoted within the papal curia and rose to be the cardinal priest of Santa Susanna. His election the day after the funeral of Adrian I was unanimous.

Leo's first act was to send the keys to the tomb of St. Peter and a sacred banner to King Charles of the Franks, today known as Charlemagne. Charles replied in terms calculated to define the relationship between himself and the papacy. He said it was his role to defend the Church and to convert the pagans to the true faith, while it was the pope's job to pray for the safety of the Frankish realm and the victories of its armies.

Paschalis and Campulus plotted the downfall of Pope Leo III.

Leo then set to work to reform the administration of the Papal States and of the huge estates owned by the papacy in other lands. He was ruthless at rooting out corruption and clamped down hard on those lining their own pockets from papal revenues. Combined with his lowly family origins, these actions roused the anger of the noble families of Rome. Over the preceding centuries, the nobles had managed to more or less monopolize the office of pope and the senior church positions for themselves. They liked neither the upstart commoner nor his stringent reforms—two relatives of Adrian, who he had raised to high office, hatched a plot against Leo.

Paschalis, chief notary, and Campulus, chief purse keeper, hired a gang of Roman cutthroats to attack Leo. The plot was launched on April 25, 799, as Leo was riding to mass. The gang overpowered Leo's guard, dragged him from his horse and wrestled him to the ground. A knife was produced with which to cut out the pope's eyes and tongue. This would have rendered him unfit for office and cleared the way for the election of a new pope more to the liking of the nobles. However, a troop of Frisian soldiers stationed in Rome by Charlemagne was nearby. They cut their way through the crowd, hacked down the assailants, and rescued Leo.

Paschalis and Campulus continued to plot against Leo. A court was hurriedly convened that convicted Leo of adultery and perjury, then declared him deposed. He was sentenced to be locked up for life in a monastery. Fearing for his life, Leo broke out of the monastery, borrowed a horse and money from friends, and fled Rome. Learning that Leo had gone, his enemies rightly guessed he was heading for Charlemagne and sent messengers to the king of the Franks. Both Leo and the messengers reached Charlemagne at Paderborn. Charlemagne sent them all back to Rome with a powerful force of soldiers

793
Vikings sack the Abbey of Lindisfarne, their first major raid on England.

793
Emir Hashim of Cordoba declared a jihad, or holy war, against the remaining Christian states of Spain.

798
King Coenwulf of Mercia conquers Kent, ending Kentish independence.

799
Death of Huai Su, leading calligrapher of Tang Dynasty China.

HOLY ROMAN EMPIRE

Exactly what Leo meant by crowning Charlemagne is not entirely clear. Some think he was reviving the Western Roman Empire, abolished in 476 (*see* p.52). Others point out that that title had not been abolished, but transferred to the emperor in Constantinople. However, Emperor Constantine VI had been overthrown in 797 and power now rested with Empress Irene whom many considered to be an illegal ruler. He may have merely intended to flatter Charlemagne with an exalted title. Whatever the motives of Leo and Charlemagne, they had founded the Holy Roman Empire—an institution that would last for a thousand years.

to keep order and a group of noblemen to investigate events and report back.

By the end of the year the Frankish nobles had concluded that Leo was almost certainly guilty of adultery and probably of perjury but could not decide if these crimes were grounds for his deposition. They sent for Charlemagne. The king was busy and did not arrive in Rome until November 800. After studying the evidence, Charlemagne announced on December 23 that Leo had to take an oath of purgation for his crimes, while those who had conspired against him were sentenced to death—a sentence that was postponed indefinitely on condition they left the Papal States and never returned.

Two days later, at Christmas Day mass, Leo produced an imperial crown, placed it on Charlemagne's head and proclaimed him emperor of the Romans. Leo then fell to his knees and did homage to Charlemagne. Contemporaries claimed the move came as a surprise to Charlemagne, but modern scholars doubt this. Surprised or not, Charlemagne did not object.

Thereafter, Leo was undisputed as pope. He was, however, generally subservient to Charlemagne and usually did as the emperor told him. He raised the bishop of Salzburg to the rank of archbishop, organized bishops in new Frankish conquests as ordered, and dated his coins according to Frankish custom. The only time he refused an order from Charlemagne came in 810 when Charlemagne wanted the words "and from the Son" added to the doctrine of the Holy Spirit coming from God the Father. He did, however, accept the theological position behind the wording. Known as the Filioque, the form of words would later be adopted by the papacy and would be instrumental in the schism between Rome and Constantinople in 1054.

Leo devoted the rest of his reign to enforcing his reforms in the curia and administrative machinery of the papacy. He assiduously promoted clergy who did not come from Rome and was ever reluctant to allow the nobility of the Papal States any formal role in government. He also restored several churches and spent a great deal of money enlarging and beautifying the Lateran Palace.

On Christmas Day, 800, Leo declared Charlemagne Holy Roman emperor.

803

Venice becomes independent of the Byzantine Empire.

810

The *Book of Kells*, an illuminated manuscript of the four gospels in Latin, is completed in Ireland.

812

Chinese Tang Dynasty issues the first paper money underwritten by a government.

814

Death of Emperor Charlemagne, also known as King Charles of the Franks.

ST. STEPHEN IV ✠ The 97th Pope 816–817

Born Rome, Italy; c.770
Parents Father, Marinus; Mother, unknown
Papacy June 22, 816–January 24, 817
Died Rome, Italy; January 24, 817

After the controversial reign of the commoner Leo III, the Roman clergy went back to a Roman nobleman in the shape of Stephen IV. He would be pope for less than a year but would achieve much.

Stephen's first act as pope was to get the people of Rome to swear allegiance to Louis the Pious, son of Charlemagne. He then asked for a personal meeting with Louis, which took place at Rheims in October. Louis welcomed Stephen with immense hospitality, even prostrating himself on the ground. There then followed an elaborate mass in which Stephen crowned Louis, using a golden circlet said to have once belonged to Constantine the Great. The ceremony was advantageous to both men. Louis gained divine sanction for his use of the title "emperor"; Stephen gained tacit admission that papal approval was needed for the anointing of a new emperor. When he returned to Rome, Stephen took with him the banished conspirators against Leo (*see* p.84), who Louis agreed could now return home. Although Stephen thus favored his aristocratic heritage, he was also popular with non-aristocratic clergy. Two months after he returned to Rome, Stephen died and was buried in St. Peter's.

ST. PASCHAL I ✠ The 98th Pope 817–824

Born Rome, Italy; date unknown
Parents Father, Bonosus; Mother, Theodora
Papacy January 24, 817–February 11, 824
Died Rome, Italy; February 11, 824

Paschal had worked nearly all his life in the papal bureaucracy and rose to be abbot of St. Stephen's Monastery. The very morning after the death of Pope Stephen IV, Paschal was proclaimed as his successor.

Paschal's first action was to send a letter to Louis announcing his election. Louis replied with the *Pactum Ludovicianum*—a document confirming the pope's possession of the Papal States and agreeing that future papal elections would be conducted without imperial interference.

In 823, Lothair, Louis's son and heir, visited Italy. Paschal crowned Lothair as co-emperor, giving him a sword to symbolize his secular power. Lothair then chose to act as arbiter in a tax dispute between the papal treasury and the Abbey of Farfa, deciding in favor of Farfa. Soon afterward, two papal officials known to be friendly with Lothair were murdered. Other murders followed and the crimes were traced to Paschal's household. Louis sent a team to investigate, whereupon Paschal took an oath of innocence. Faced by a wall of silence, the investigators returned to Louis who allowed the matter to drop. A few weeks later, however, Paschal himself was dead. He was buried in the Church of Santa Prassede, which he had built.

816

Execution of the Muslim general Harthama ibn Ayan by al Mamun, Caliph of the Abbasid Empire.

817

The Bulgarians lay siege to Constantinople, but are driven off.

820

Arab mathematician Muhammed ibn Musa al-Kwarismi lays the foundations of the branch of mathematics known as algebra.

EUGENE II ✢ The 99th Pope 824–827

Born Rome, Italy; date unknown

Parents Father, perhaps Boemund; Mother, unknown

Papacy June 824–August 27, 827

Died Rome, Italy; August 27, 827

When Paschal died, riots broke out as the nobles and clergy put forward rival candidates. Emperor Louis sent the learned monk Wala to sort things out. Wala favored the candidate of the nobles—Eugene II.

Co-emperor Lothair traveled to Rome to set the relationship between pope and emperor on a formal footing, resulting in the *Constitutio Romana*, published in November 824, stating that the Papal States were a fief of the empire. All citizens of the Papal States had to swear allegiance to the emperor, as did a new pope before his election could be considered valid. Papal elections were to involve Roman citizens, not just the clergy as had been the case in recent years, and the papal government was to be inspected by two officials—one appointed by the emperor, one by the pope. Although Eugene thus gave in to imperial demands regarding his temporal rule, on Church matters he was more intransigent. He issued new rules on the way bishops were chosen, clergy educated, and monasteries organized. He refused to compromise over iconoclasm with the Eastern church, stating that the matter was resolved at the Second Council of Nicaea. The cause of Eugene's death and place of burial are unknown.

VALENTINE ✢ The 100th Pope 827

Born Rome, Italy; date unknown

Parents Father, Leontius; Mother, unknown

Papacy mid August, 827–mid October, 827

Died Rome, Italy; perhaps October 10, 827

After the death of Eugene III, the terms of the *Constitutio Romana* concerning the papal election were adhered to. The clergy, nobility, and citizens gathered to choose a successor—Archdeacon Valentine.

Valentine was the son of a leading Roman noble named Leontius who lived on the *Via Lata*, one of the most prestigious addresses in Rome. He had entered the Church when a very young man and was ordained by Paschal I, who greatly favored Valentine. Eugene II also promoted Valentine and entrusted him with delicate tasks. His youth was much remarked upon and he may have been as young as 30 when elected pope.

The enthusiasm that marked Valentine's election was widespread. He was carried to the Lateran and placed on the papal throne immediately his election was over—the first time that any pope had been enthroned before being consecrated as bishop of Rome. The imperial official whose duty it was to report on papal government had not been in Rome when Eugene died and Valentine was elected. Valentine's first task would therefore be to write to Emperor Louis to pledge his loyalty. However, just 30 days after his election Valentine died of some unspecified cause.

823

Four year civil war in the Byzantine Empire ends with victory for Michael II.

825

Clerics are documented as teaching students at Oxford, England, an event later claimed as the founding of Oxford University.

827

The Mayan city of Copan is abandoned, marking the final phase of the collapse of urban civilization in the area.

GREGORY IV ✠ The 101st 827–844

Born Place unknown ; date unknown
Parents Unknown
Papacy October/ November 827–January 25, 844
Died Rome, Italy; January 25, 844

Gregory was from a noble family and, like many younger sons unlikely to inherit, had entered the Church both to find a career and increase the influence of his family in the government of the Papal States. He gained a reputation for learning and for being mild tempered and diplomatic.

When Valentine died, the nobility were in sudden need of a new candidate and chose Gregory—then cardinal priest of San Marco. The election that followed was carried out according to the new rules (*see* p.87) with Gregory unopposed. Gregory at once started planning his consecration, but the imperial legate stopped him, declaring that first the emperor had to be satisfied the election had been conducted fairly. The Romans objected but gave way rather than risk Frankish anger. The consecration took place on March 29, 828.

Gregory ordered the construction of a powerful fortress to guard the port of Ostia. He named it Gregoriopolis.

In 831, Gregory received a visit from the missionary Anskar, who was trying to convert the Danes and northern Germans. Gregory proclaimed him legate to Scandinavia and gave him a pallium. That same year, Gregory sent senior clerics north over the Alps to visit the bishops there and teach them Roman-style liturgy and ritual. He also declared that All Saints Day should be observed throughout Christendom and persuaded the emperor Louis the Pious to enforce this decision. Indeed, it was relations with the imperial family that were to dominate Gregory's pontificate. In 833, Emperor Louis gave his youngest son, Charles the Bald, the kingdom of Aquitaine. The other brothers—Lothair, Pepin, and Louis the German—rebelled. Lothair invited Gregory to act as mediator, so Gregory crossed the Alps.

St. Anskar, missionary to the Danes, was proclaimed legate to Scandinavia by Pope Gregory IV.

Arriving in France, Gregory found that all the local bishops had sided with Louis and resented Gregory arriving in the entourage of the rebel Lothair. Gregory retorted with a furious message declaring that, as pope, he had every right to work for the peace and unity of the Empire. He went to see Louis to negotiate a deal, but he had been duped. The sons had invited Gregory only to play for time while they bribed nobles into joining them. Louis was betrayed and flung into prison. Gregory hurriedly returned to Rome, angry and humiliated.

By 834, Emperor Louis was free and back in control. However, when he died in 840 his sons at once went to war against each other. In 843, three surviving brothers agreed the Treaty of Verdun. Charles took what is now France; Louis took most of modern Germany, plus Switzerland, Austria, and the northern Balkans; Lothair took a strip of land running from the mouth the Rhine south to the Alps and all of Italy. He also inherited the title of emperor. Gregory, himself, died soon after receiving the news from Verdun.

827

Sicily is invaded by Saracens from North Africa who begin a 50-year war of conquest.

828

The Christians in Egypt revolt against Muslim rule, but the rebellion is bloodily put down.

829

The Byzantine emperor Michael II dies and is succeeded by Theophilus, who will reign until 842.

835

The Ganlu Incident sees Chinese court officials and court eunuchs turn on each other. Thousands are killed in the riots, which end with the eunuch faction in firm control of the government. The Tang emperors are reduced to a figurehead role.

SERGIUS II ✠ The 102nd Pope 844–847

Born Rome, Italy; date unknown

Parents Unknown

Papacy January 844–January 27, 847

Died Rome, Italy; January 27, 847

The emperor Lothair (above) sent his son Louis to Rome to investigate the scandalous election of Sergius II.

Elderly and crippled with gout, Sergius nevertheless quickly became one of the most energetic builders in early papal history, restoring the great Marcian aqueduct and embellishing many churches. All this cost money, which Sergius acquired by plumbing new depths in simony.

As Gregory IV lay dying, men were plotting in quiet corners. However, for once, it was not the aristocratic families who ruled the Papal States and dominated the papacy but rather the citizens of Rome who were doing the plotting. The moment that Gregory's death was announced, they struck. A huge crowd of men poured into the streets and surged toward the Lateran Palace and Basilica. They stormed the complex, then barricaded themselves inside along with a respected deacon—and non-aristocrat—named John. They enthroned John as pope and sent a message north to the emperor Lothair announcing the election. The nobles, however, were not easily outmaneuvered. They had already agreed to meet at St. Martino to choose their favored candidate and went ahead as planned. They chose an aristocratic priest named Sergius, a close relative of Stephen IV.

The armed retainers of the nobles were summoned to Rome and rampaged through the streets, cutting down any supporters of the papal pretender. They stormed the defenses of the Lateran, slaughtered anyone who offered resistance, and captured John. Sergius spared John's life on condition he retire to a monastery and never appear in public again. That done, Sergius was consecrated immediately.

Emperor Lothair was unimpressed by the news from Rome. He sent his son Louis and Archbishop Drogo of Metz marching south with an army to investigate. The imperial troops entered Rome and imposed martial law while Louis summoned a synod of Italian bishops to investigate the election. The synod found that Sergius's election was valid, but that he should have awaited confirmation from the emperor before being consecrated. Thus vindicated, Sergius crowned Louis king of the Lombards and appointed Drogo his representative for all lands north of the Alps. The imperial army then left and Sergius could enjoy his new position.

However, in August 846, a large force of Muslim Saracens landed at the mouth of the Tiber. The garrison of Gregoriopolis (*see* p.88), which was supposed to protect Rome, simply fled. Sergius ordered the city gates shut and manned the walls. The pirates pillaged St. Peter's Basilica and St. Paul's—both outside the walls—and fled back to sea with as much as they could carry. Many Roman citizens claimed the raid was a punishment for Sergius's crimes. Sergius's health deteriorated further after the raid and he never recovered.

SIMONY

Sergius was notorious for indulging in the illegal practice of charging bishops, abbots, and other clerics a sum of money before they were confirmed in office. It was a vice that the Church had never quite been able to eradicate, and which Sergius took to new depths. Some guilty of simony go further and accept straight bribes for appointing somebody quite unsuitable to office. Favors other than clerical positions might also be put on sale, including pardons and holy relics.

837 Naples is attacked by Muslim pirates for the first time.

840 The Holy Roman Emperor Louis the Pious dies, aged 62. His 45-year-old son, Lothair, succeeds him as emperor.

844 Rhodri Mawr becomes Prince of Gwynedd, later uniting all the Welsh under his rule.

845 A force of Vikings led by Ragnar Lodbrok captures Paris and extorts a huge payment to leave peacefully.

845 A persecution of Buddhists begins in China that will result in the destruction of 4,600 monasteries and 40,000 temples.

846 Death of Harald Klak, king of Denmark.

ST. LEO IV The 103rd 847–855

Born Rome, Italy; date unknown
Parents Father, Radaold; Mother, unknown
Papacy April 10, 847–July 17, 855
Died Rome, Italy; July 17, 855

When Sergius II died nobody in Rome wanted any trouble, so Leo was elected unopposed before sunset. Leo sent the usual messages to the emperor, Lothair, but the urgency of dealing with the Saracens prompted him to be consecrated before official imperial permission arrived.

Leo began by repairing the existing city walls and, when funds arrived from Lothair, he extended the old Aurelian Walls to embrace the Vatican Hill and St. Peter's Basilica—an area that became known as the Leonine City. He also moved the population of the vulnerable coastal town of Centumcellae to a new, more easily defended site surrounded by stout walls, and so created what is now Civitavecchia (though he called it Leopolis). Knowing that strong walls would not be enough, Leo organized a league between the naval city states of Naples, Amalfi, and Gaeta. That league proved its worth in 849 at the Battle of Ostia. The combined Christian fleets intercepted a massive Saracen fleet heading for Ostia and destroyed it utterly. Rome was never again threatened by the Muslims.

Feeling Rome to be secure, Leo ordered a massive programme of rebuilding. The badly damaged Basilica of St. Peter was restored to its former grandeur—including decorating the high altar with 206 pounds of gold. The restored basilica was topped with a metal statue of a cockerel, before the crowing of which St. Peter had denied Christ three times. Other buildings were restored, including the Monastery of San Martino where Leo had begun his clerical career. San Clemente was also repaired, and Leo's portrait can still be seen in a fresco there.

Leo was not one to be shy about exercising the supreme authority of the popes. He slapped down Patriarch Ignatius of Constantinople for deposing the bishop of Syracuse without checking with Rome first, issued lengthy instructions to the English churches, and told Bishop Calcrius of Tripoli to stick rigidly to rules on penances even in the face of hostile Muslim government. He even went so far as to declare the entire Synod of Soisson of 853 null and void when he did not like its decisions. He was also a great champion of music in the rituals of the Church.

After his death, Leo's body was buried, but his bones were later transferred into a single tomb containing the remains of the first four Leos. In the 18th century, the bones of Leo the Great were taken out and given their own resting place, leaving Leo IV with the two other Leos.

KING ALFRED THE GREAT

Leo welcomed a young English prince to Rome in 853. He blessed the boy and sent him on a tour of the city, allowing him to be taught by the finest minds in Rome. The boy was the fourth son of King Ethelwulf of Wessex and was being educated for a career in the Church. However, his three elder brothers died and so the prince became king. As Alfred the Great, he defeated the pagan Vikings to save England for Christianity.

847
The city of Bari in Italy is captured by the Muslims.

847
Pope Leo IV builds the Leonine Wall to protect St. Peter's.

848
Foundation of the Chola Dynasty that would rule much of southern India to 1279.

851
Canterbury Cathedral is sacked by Danish forces who navigate the Thames estuary. The Vikings are defeated at Ockley by King Ethelwulf.

BENEDICT III ✠ The 104th Pope 855–858

Born Possibly Rome, Italy; date unknown

Parents Unknown

Papacy September 29, 855–April 17, 858

Died Rome, Italy; April 17, 858

Benedict is usually said to have been a native Roman, but all that is really known of his life before he became pope is that he was educated at the Lateran school and was ordained by Gregory IV before being made cardinal priest of St. Callisto by Leo IV.

When Leo IV died, the clergy and people of Rome quickly elected Adrian, priest of San Marco, to be pope. Adrian refused the honor, however, and Benedict was elected in his place. He could not be consecrated until the approval of Emperor Lothair arrived. A faction of aristocrats led by a man called Arsenius used the delay to conspire against Benedict. They wrote to the emperor alleging fraud in the election and declaring their support for the priest Anastasius, nephew of Arsenius. This Anastasius was staying with the co-emperor Louis II and had a great reputation for learning, but unfortunately he had been excommunicated by Leo IV after an earlier argument.

Louis sent Anastasius to Rome with an army. The imperial troops stormed the Lateran, bundled Benedict into prison, and installed Anastasius in his place. The bishops of Ostia and Albano were in Rome, but they both refused to consecrate Anastasius. Meanwhile, the people of Rome were on the streets attacking the imperial troops. After three days of bloodshed the imperial troops pulled out, taking Anastasius with them and allowing Benedict to be consecrated.

Unknown to anyone in Rome, Emperor Lothair had died on the day Benedict was consecrated and Louis II, the sponsor of Anastasius, became Holy Roman emperor. Benedict is reported to have acted as a mediator between Louis and his brothers Lothair II and Charles the Bald over the division of their inheritance, though details have not survived.

Benedict was vigorous in claiming the primacy of the pope over other bishops, but did so in a tactful way. When Patriarch Ignatius of Constantinople deposed some bishops and then sought Benedict's approval, the pope insisted that all the information be sent to him for detailed study but then endorsed the deposition anyway. This was a tactic that he would employ on many occasions during his time as pope.

POPE JOAN

One of the most persistent legends about the papacy circulating in the Middle Ages concerned the female pope Joan. Different versions of the tale give widely varying details, but most agree that she lived in the 9th century and some specify that she was elected after the death of Leo IV. According to most versions, Joan was a highly intelligent and talented young woman who resented the fact that, as a woman, she was banned from holding high office in the Church. She therefore adopted the name John and began dressing as a man. Moving from her native Mainz to Rome, she worked her way up to become a cardinal priest and, eventually, pope. However, her true sex was soon revealed and she was ousted from office—the whole affair being hushed up.

855

Holy Roman Emperor Lothair dies, aged 60, after dividing his lands between his three sons. He is succeeded as emperor by his 33-year-old son, who will reign for 20 years as Louis II.

855

Death of Ahmad ibn Hanbal, Islamic scholar, lawyer, and theologian.

856

A series of earthquakes shakes the Middle East from Corinth to Persia, killing perhaps as many as 700,000 people.

858

Massive floods strike northern China, killing an estimated 70,000 people and causing widespread damage that undermines the economy and begins the decline of the Tang Dynasty.

ST. NICHOLAS I ✠ The 105th 858–867

Born Place unknown; date unknown

Parents Unknown

Papacy April 24, 858–November 13, 867

Died Rome, Italy; November 13, 867

While he was a trusted adviser to Benedict III, Nicholas had been foremost in pushing the view that the pope was the supreme head of the Christian Church. Now that he was pope himself, Nicholas formulated a view of the position of the pope in the world that would prove to be highly influential in the Catholic Church for centuries to come.

When Benedict III died, Holy Roman Emperor Louis II was close to Rome. He hurriedly marched to Rome to stop any repeat of the debacles that had attended recent papal elections. By the time Louis arrived, he found that all of Rome and the Papal States had agreed that Adrian, cardinal priest of San Marco, should be pope. Louis agreed and all seemed set for a trouble-free succession. But (as he had done in the papal elections three years earlier) Adrian refused to be pope, so another candidate had to be found. After some bickering the choice fell on Nicholas—a man well connected through the Church and Papal States.

Emperor Michael III stood as sponsor, by proxy, for Boris I of Bulgaria at his baptism. Boris's conversion to Eastern-style Christianity was imposed by the peace settlement in 864 following the Byzantine invasion of Bulgaria.

Nicholas's first action, however, took everyone by surprise. He sent for Anastasius, the excommunicated priest who had tried to become pope in 855, and made him abbot of Santa Maria in Trastevere. Anastasius went on to become a key adviser to Nicholas, giving the pope the benefit of his deep knowledge of Church procedures and the imperial court. A dispute with Constantinople broke out almost at once. In December 858, Byzantine emperor Michael III ousted Patriarch Ignatius of Constantinople and replaced him with a layman, Photius, who was hurriedly consecrated a priest. Nicholas refused to recognize Photius and sent a team to investigate the matter. The papal envoys found that everything had been done according to Byzantine law and recommended that Nicholas recognize Photius. Instead, Nicholas summoned a synod in Rome at which he denounced and excommunicated Photius. When Michael III sent a letter of objection, Nicholas replied with a lengthy and bluntly worded missive telling Michael not to interfere in Church business and stating Rome's authority over Constantinople. In response, Photius called his own synod and excommunicated Nicholas. The dispute was still continuing at the time of Nicholas's death.

The new pope was no less confrontational with the Holy Roman emperors. The Germans had traditionally seen marriage as an agreement between the two partners. Those

859	861	862	863	865
The university of Al Karaouine is founded in Fes, North Africa. It is now the oldest continually active university in the world.	Paris, Cologne, Aix-le-Chapelle, Worms, and Toulouse are sacked by Vikings.	Rurik the Viking captures Novgorod and founds the Rurik Dynasty that would rule Russia for eight centuries.	The Battle of Lalakaon is a significant victory for the Byzantines over the Arabs that starts a period of resurgence for the Byzantine Empire.	Constantinople is attacked by Russian Norsemen.

GOD'S REPRESENTATIVE

The pope was, Nicholas firmly believed, God's representative on Earth. He therefore had absolute authority over the Church, with the various bishops, synods, and clergy being there simply to ensure that his instructions were properly carried out, quickly and efficiently. Nicholas also believed that the pope was the sole legitimate arbiter of morals and social norms. His views on the relationship between spiritual and secular rulers was clear: secular rulers had no right whatsoever to interfere in anything that the Church did, but the Church did have an absolute right to lay down the law to secular rulers on matters of morals or when secular actions affected the Church. These attitudes, and the tactless force with which Nicholas chose to express and enforce them, were not calculated to win friends. They did, however, earn him the lasting respect and gratitude of later popes and explain why he was made a saint.

civil agreements very often included conditions under which a marriage could end and what payments should be made for the support of children or for other purposes. The role of the vows before God was to ensure the terms were adhered to. The Church, however, took the view that marriage was for life and was a sacred act in the eyes of God.

In 862, Lothair II, brother to Emperor Louis II, separated from his wife Theutberga and married a woman named Waldrada instead. A synod of Frankish bishops met at Metz to deal with many issues, one of which was the approval of the new marriage as being in line with Frankish custom. The archbishops of Cologne and Trier traveled to Rome with the decisions of the synod to seek papal confirmation. They were shocked when Nicholas excommunicated them on the spot for approving bigamy. The archbishops appealed to Emperor Louis II who sent an army to Rome. Nicholas shut himself up behind the new defenses around the Vatican Hill and refused to give way. The imperial troops could not get in, so Louis capitulated. He told the archbishops to accept their sentences and instructed his brother to take back his old wife.

Patriarch Photius of Constantinople

Nicholas intervened in another imperial marriage dispute when Judith, daughter of Charles the Bald, married Count Baldwin of Flanders without her father's consent. The bishops in the realm of Charles met and excommunicated her until such time as she returned to her father's house. Nicholas investigated and found that the wedding had been conducted properly according to Church law. He declared the marriage valid and the excommunication invalid.

Nicholas also got his way over the right of the pope to intervene in the actions of bishops and archbishops within their dioceses. In 861, Archbishop Hincmar of Reims held a synod at Soissons that deposed Bishop Rothad of Soissons for having himself deposed a priest on spurious grounds. Rothad appealed to Nicholas, while Hincmar declared that the synod had the right to act without the need to seek approval from the pope. Nicholas cited as proof of his right to intervene a collection of early canon law, known as the Decretals—forgeries made in the mid-9th century. Whether or not Nicholas knew them to be forgeries is an open question.

Archbishop John of Ravenna was going about his business when he received a summons from Nicholas to travel to Rome to answer allegations that he had stripped parishes of money. Since the days when Ravenna had been the seat of the Byzantine exarch of Italy, the prelates of Ravenna enjoyed a number of privileges, including that they did not need to obey a summons from the pope in person but could conduct any necessary business through letters. This John now did but, on February 24, 861, he received a letter from Nicholas telling him that he had been deposed and excommunicated. John appealed to Emperor Louis who advised him that if he surrendered the ancient privileges of his see all would be well. In November, John formally submitted to Nicholas and was reinstated.

866

Viking Ivar the Boneless captures York and establishes a Viking kingdom in northern England.

866

The emperor Michael III consents to the assassination of his Uncle Caesar Bardas and rewards the assassin, his Armenian chamberlain Basil, by making him co-emperor.

867

Michael III is murdered by his co-emperor Basil, who founds the Macedonian dynasty that will rule the Byzantine Empire until 1054.

ADRIAN II ✠ The 106th 867–872

Born Rome, Italy; 792

Parents Father, Theodore; Mother, unknown

Papacy December 14, 867–December 14, 872

Died Rome, Italy; December 14, 872

Adrian came from one of the richest families in Rome and was related to Stephen IV and Sergius II. He had not originally been intended for a Church career and married. However, he was later separated from his wife and became a deacon and, in 842, cardinal priest of San Marco.

Holy Roman Emperor Louis II defeats the Saracens at the Muslim stronghold of Bari in 871.

The year 867 was the third time Adrian had been elected pope; he had refused the offer in 855 and 858. In 867, however, the electors were riven by disputes caused by the strident policies of Nicholas, and Adrian reluctantly accepted the post as a compromise candidate.

When Lothair died, his brother Emperor Louis II was fighting the Muslims in southern Italy. His uncles, Charles the Bald and Louis the German, took advantage of the situation by seizing all Lothair's lands north of the Alps and leaving Louis only Italy. Adrian tried to intervene on behalf of Louis, arguing in a series of letters that the emperor was entitled to all his father's lands. The letters provoked only hostility and anger, so much so that Adrian had to disown them and blame his secretary, Anastasius, for their blunt wording.

In 869, The Byzantine emperor Basil I called a great council of bishops to discuss, among other things, the situation of the patriarch of Constantinople, Photius, and the ranking of the patriarchs. Adrian sent two envoys to take part, supported by a sizeable retinue that included Anastasius as the representative of Louis II. The meeting, recognized as the Eighth General Council of the Church, went well. The Roman view of Photius (that he should be expelled from office) was upheld. The patriarchs were ranked with Rome first, Constantinople second, then Alexandria, Antioch, and Jerusalem. The more minor matters were also decided in a way acceptable to Adrian. However, the churchmen

The Byzantine emperor Basil I.

also ruled that the newly Christianized Bulgars were to fall under the authority of the Patriarch of Constantinople, not the pope. Eastern prelates hastened to the Bulgars and expelled the Western clerics, causing a new dispute between Eastern and Western churches.

Back in Italy, Holy Roman Emperor Louis II had decided to pay a visit to Prince Adelchis of Benevento. While there, Louis was suddenly attacked and thrown into prison until he took a vow not to seek revenge on Adelchis. Louis did so, then raced to Rome to ask Adrian to release him from the oath. Adrian went further, crowning Louis a second time to restore his imperial prestige. Adrian died a few weeks later.

868

Alfred the Great of Wessex supports Burgred of Mercia against Viking raiders, it is Alfred's first experience of war.

869

The last dated inscription is made at Tikal, one of the final Mayan cities to remain in use.

870

Malta is conquered by Muslims from Sicily.

871

England's Year of Nine Battles. Alfred the Great of Wessex fights nine times against the Vikings, the conflict ends with a fragile peace treaty.

872

The first hospital to be opened in the Muslim world is founded in Cairo.

Born Rome, Italy; date unknown

Parents Father, Gundo; Mother, unknown

Papacy December 14, 872–December 16, 882

Died Rome, Italy; December 16, 882

JOHN VIII The 107th Pope 872–882

John is considered to have been more of a politician than a clergyman and it was probably his political skills that got him elected—Rome was in dire need of them. When Adrian II died, the Muslim Saracens of Sicily had secured a bridgehead in southern Italy and were posing a real threat.

John's first military moves were to build an extension of the walls of Rome to include the Basilica of St. Paul and the residential districts around it. He then ordered the building of a small fleet based at Portus to patrol the seas off the mouth of the Tiber. Clearly this would not be enough, so John began using his political skills to build an alliance of Christian rulers in Italy to face the Saracens. But when Emperor Louis died, the alliance fell apart.

John believed that Charles the Bald, ruler of the western Frank lands, could be persuaded to fight the Saracens, so he and the people of Rome acclaimed Charles to be the next Holy Roman emperor. Charles came to Rome to be crowned on December 29, 875. Charles authorized an enlargement of the Papal States, withdrew the imperial observer from Rome, and promised that papal elections in future would be free of imperial interference. Feeling secure with imperial backing, John then exiled and excommunicated several nobles and clergymen who he believed were conspiring against him, among them Formosus, bishop of Portus.

Unfortunately for John, Charles proved to be uninterested in Italy. When his nephew Carloman arrived to claim the throne of Italy, Charles retreated and died soon after. Carloman made it clear that he expected to be made Holy Roman emperor, but John delayed. Rome was then occupied by Carloman's supporters and John fled to the western Frank lands, then in the process of becoming France. There he crowned as Emperor Charles the Bald's son Louis the Stammerer in September 878. When Louis died the following spring, John chose Charles the Fat, son of Louis the German and so young brother of Carloman. By the time John got back to Rome in 881 he was recognized as arbiter of the imperial title.

Meanwhile, John had also been trying to recruit help from Constantinople against the Saracens but the Byzantine emperor Basil I made it a condition of even receiving papal envoys that the pope had to recognize Photius as patriarch (*see* p.91). This John agreed to do on condition that Photius apologize for his past misdeeds and that Bulgaria be moved from the jurisdiction of Constantinople to that of Rome. When the papal envoys reached Constantinople they found Photius refusing to accept either condition. The council of bishops that followed was skilfully managed. Doctrinal differences between Rome and Constantinople were not mentioned, Photius did not apologize, and the Eastern bishops recognized papal supremacy. As a result there was peace between the Eastern and Western Churches. Most importantly, from John's point of view, Basil sent Byzantine forces to fight the Saracens in Italy.

On December 16, 882, for reasons that have never been satisfactorily explained, Pope John VIII was murdered by members of his own household. He was the first pope known to have been murdered—a sombre and ominous precedent.

874
Start of the ten year Huang Chao Rebellion in China that would lead to millions of deaths and fatally undermine the already weakened Tang Dynasty.

877
The Vikings capture Exeter, England.

878
Battle of Ethandun. Alfred the Great of Wessex decisively defeats the Vikings under Guthrum.

881
Battle of Saucourt-en-Vimeu. Louis III decisively defeats Vikings near the River Somme, an event later commemorated in the poem Ludwigslied.

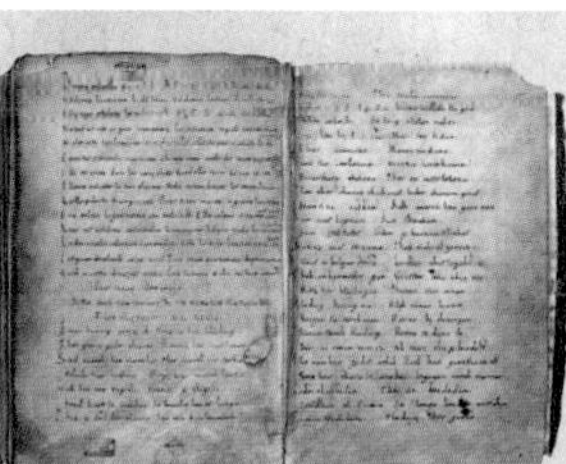

MARINUS I ✠ The 108th Pope 882–884

Born Gallese, Italy; date unknown

Parents Unknown

Papacy December 16, 882–May 15, 884

Died Rome, Italy; May 15, 884

Marinus was already bishop of Cerveteri, making his election as bishop of Rome controversial. It was assumed that bishops were in position for life as early canon law banned a move from one bishopric to another.

This rule seems to have been ignored and may have been an indication that the position of pope was beginning to be seen as special and not bound by the rules governing other bishops.

Marinus was exceptionally talented. When he was just 12 years old, he had moved from his aristocratic home in Tuscany to Rome to work in the papal curia. He was made a deacon by Nicholas I and was sent by Adrian II to be one of the three papal legates at the Fourth Council of Constantinople in 869. While there, Marinus had a bitter exchange of words with the Byzantine emperor Basil I.

As pope, Marinus quickly forgave those exiled by John VIII and released them from the vows they had been obliged to take. In June 883, Emperor Charles the Fat came to Italy, and talks seem to have gone well as Charles ordered that Duke Guy of Spoleto be deprived of his lands for having infringed on papal territories. Though the order was never enforced it served to curb Guy's future actions.

ST. ADRIAN III ✠ The 109th Pope 884–885

Born Rome, Italy; date unknown

Parents Father, Benedict; Mother, unknown

Papacy May 17, 884–July or September, 885

Died Modena, Italy; July or September, 885

A highly controversial pope, Adrian III is also one of the most poorly documented. Nothing is known of his election, but he was clearly a supporter of John VIII and therefore an opponent of Marinus.

In 885, Charles the Fat summoned a great diet—a meeting of nobles and prelates—to discuss the imperial succession. Charles had no legitimate heir and wanted his illegitimate son Bernard to succeed him. Although Church law was against Bernard, Adrian agreed to dethrone any German bishop who opposed Bernard's appointment.

Adrian was less conciliatory in his dealings with the bloody feuds that were wracking the Papal States during his papacy. Details of the disputes within the curia are not known but, almost as soon as he was elected, Adrian ordered the arrest of George of the Aventine, a high-ranking official in the Lateran Palace. The hapless George was convicted of unspecified crimes, for which he was blinded and cast out. Next, Adrian had an unnamed lady from one of Rome's most noble families whipped naked through the streets, again for reasons unknown.

At the monastery of San Cesario sul Penaro, near Modena, Adrian fell suddenly ill and died. It was widely assumed he had been murdered.

883	884	884	885	885
The great monastery of Monte Cassino is captured and pillaged by Muslim Saracens from Sicily.	Traditional date for the conversion of Afghanistan to Islam.	France's Carloman is succeeded by Holy Roman Emperor Charles III (the Fat), son of the late Louis the German.	The Vikings lay siege to Paris but are driven off.	Murder of Godfrith, duke of Frisia, and subsequent campaigns see the Vikings lose control of the Netherlands to the Franks.

STEPHEN V ✣ The 110th Pope 885–891

Born Rome, Italy; date unknown

Parents Father, Hadrian; Mother, unknown

Papacy September 885–September 14, 891

Died Rome, Italy; September 14, 891

Charles the Fat put down a rebellion in 886 but then seemed to lose control of his family, empire, and himself.

At the news of the murder of Adrian III, the clergy and leading nobles met to elect a new pope. It seems they had had enough of the murderous policies of recent popes for they unanimously elected the cardinal priest Stephen, noted for his honesty, sanctity, and simple devotion to duty.

When the Holy Roman emperor Charles the Fat heard the news he was furious. At the time, he was trying to secure his illegitimate son Bernard as his heir and had been relying on the support of Adrian III to win over the German clerics. Charles at once despatched his chancellor Liutprand and a force of soldiers to go to Rome to sound out the new pope and depose him if necessary. Arriving in Rome, Liutprand found the clergy and nobles firmly united behind Stephen. Having secured some sort of promise of papal help for Bernard, Liutprand retired over the Alps to his imperial master.

Stephen had his own problems. The Muslim Saracens from Sicily and North Africa were becoming bolder in raiding Italian coastal towns and were venturing inland. Stephen persuaded the Byzantine emperor Basil I to send warships to patrol Italian waters with some success. When Basil died in 886, Stephen moved quickly to establish friendly relations with the new emperor, Leo VI, and the new patriarch of Constantinople, Leo's brother Stephen I.

Helpful as the Byzantine ships were, Stephen also wanted soldiers to fight on land. He appealed to Charles the Fat, who crossed the Alps in the spring of 886 for talks. Charles promised troops in return for Stephen's support for Bernard. The deal was never completed. In November, Charles was dethroned. Each area of the empire chose its own ruler, and the great Carolingian empire collapsed.

Stephen appealed to Arnulf, king of East Frankia, to send soldiers to Rome, but Arnulf sent only supportive words. Stephen had to swallow his pride and reverse generations of papal policy by turning to native Italian nobles for military help. He chose Duke Guy of Spoleto, who had declared himself king of Italy when Charles was ousted and was busily trying to impose his rule on the other Italian nobles. As the price for his help, Guy demanded that he be crowned emperor in St. Peter's in Rome by Stephen himself. The ceremony took place on 21 February, 891, and thereafter Guy styled himself emperor in all documentation. The title was, however, an empty one as none of the other rulers of what had been Carolingian lands recognized him. Rome was, however, militarily safe.

CONVERSION OF THE SLAVS

Archbishop Methodius had died in April 885 and indicated that he wished the local cleric Goradz to succeed him. Goradz wished to continue using the Slavonic liturgy on the grounds that his Slav congregation could understand it. However, the German bishops wanted the Slavonic liturgy abolished and the Moravian church put under their control. Eager for German help against the Saracens, Stephen ignored Goradz and instead appointed the German Wiching. The Moravians appealed to the patriarch of Constantinople, who agreed to the Slavonic rite in return for allegiance. The subsequent conversion of the Slavs, including all of Russia, was therefore carried out under the auspices and control of Constantinople, not Rome.

886	887	889	890	891
King Alfred the Great of Wessex captures London from the Vikings.	Death of Abu ibn Majah, Muslim scholar who compiled the official hadiths of the Sunni branch of Islam.	In the Iberian Peninsula, Toledo and Coimbra are freed from Muslim rule by uprisings of the local Christian population.	Birth of Olga the Beautiful, later to be the first Christian ruler of Kiev.	The king of Italy Guy of Spoleto is crowned Holy Roman emperor by Pope Stephen V.

FORMOSUS ✠ The 111th Pope 891–896

Born Ostia; date unknown
Parents Unknown
Papacy October 6, 891–April 4, 896
Died Rome, Italy; April 4, 896

Arnulf of Carinthia aided Formosus in the pope's plan to get rid of Guy of Spoleto.

Formosus seems to have come from a noble family and to have entered the papal service at a young age. Intelligent, honest, and personally beyond reproach, he nevertheless acquired many enemies, who would eventually inflict on him the most degrading and macabre of indignities.

Formosus first gained notice when, in 864, he was appointed bishop of Porto—the title was largely ceremonial but provided an income to support men used by the popes for a variety of duties. Formosus was first sent to organize the conversion of the Bulgars. He performed this duty so well that the Bulgars begged for him to be made their permanent bishop, but Pope Nicholas I and Adrian II both refused on the grounds that it was against canon law for a bishop to move from one bishopric to another. Under Adrian II, Formosus returned to Rome where he organized the synod of 869 and other important meetings.

He at first remained in office under John VIII, but by the end of 875 had fallen out with the new pope for reasons unknown. Fearing for his life, Formosus fled the Papal States. John at once used the pretext that Formosus had abandoned his duties to have him deposed as bishop and excommunicated—a sentence that was lifted on condition that he vowed never to return to Rome or to Porto and never to practice as a priest. After John died, Formosus appealed to Marinus I, who absolved him of his vows and reappointed him as bishop of Porto.

When Stephen V died Formosus was elected pope. He thus followed the precedent set by Marinus that the bishop of another see could become bishop of Rome.

The first business facing Formosus was the demand by Guy of Spoleto, king of Italy and emperor, that his son Lambert should be crowned in St. Peter's as co-emperor and joint king. Formosus was reluctant as Guy had been using his dominance in Italy to divert funds from the Papal States. Instead, Formosus favored Berengar of Friuli who also had a claim to the kingdom of Italy. But with Guy and his army in Rome, Formosus had little choice. He crowned Lambert, then sent messages over the Alps to King Arnulf of the Eastern Franks promising to make him emperor if he came to Italy to support Berengar. Arnulf came in the spring of 894, defeated Guy in battle, and was crowned emperor. Guy then died and Arnulf went home, leaving Berengar as king of Italy.

THE CADAVER SYNOD

In January 897, Pope Stephen VI had the rotting corpse of Formosus dug up, dressed in papal robes, and put on trial for the original charges laid against him by John VIII. Stephen himself presided at the trial, known as the Cadaver Synod, found Formosus guilty, and declared him *damnatio memoriae*, "expunged from history." All the decisions, acts, and appointments of Formosus were declared invalid. The body of the dead pope was then thrown into the Tiber to be washed out to sea. Instead, a monk secretly hooked it ashore and hid it.

891
Death of Photius, the controversial former patriarch of Constantinople.

892
England is invaded by the Danes who arrive from the mainland in 330 ships accompanied by their wives and children.

893
The Battle of Benfleet, Essex. The English under Athelred of Mercia defeat a large Viking army, clearing the Thames Estuary for trade, and build a church on the battlefield to celebrate the victory.

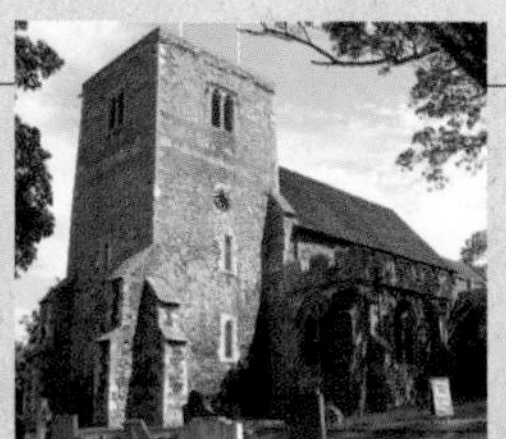

893
King Alfonso III of Leon captures Zamora from the Muslims.

BONIFACE VI ✠ The 112th Pope 896

Born Rome, Italy; date unknown

Parents Father, Hadrian; Mother, unknown

Papacy April 896

Died Rome, Italy, April 896

Little is known about Boniface VI, and what is known for certain is not entirely flattering. He entered the church at a young age and had risen to be a deacon by the time John VIII became pope.

John defrocked Boniface for unspecified immorality but, after the errant Boniface had performed penance, he was reinstated. Boniface rose to be a priest before he was once again thrown out of office for immorality.

When Formosus died (*see* opposite), the people of Rome rioted. The object of their anger seems to have been Farold, the representative of the Holy Roman emperor Arnulf who, it was thought, had secret orders to impose as pope a candidate favored by Arnulf. True or not, the rioting population demanded that Boniface be made pope. Exactly how the subsequent election was conducted is unclear, but Boniface was installed in the Lateran Palace as pope.

Boniface suffered from severe gout and just 15 days after taking office he was dead. Whether this was due to gout or Farold is unclear. In 898, Pope John IX declared that it was uncanonical to elect a man who was not a priest, and ruled Boniface's election invalid. He is, nevertheless, generally counted to have been a genuine pope.

STEPHEN VI  The 113th Pope 896–897

Born Rome, Italy; date unknown

Parents Unknown

Papacy May 22, 896–August 897

Died Rome, Italy; August 897

Stephen VI emerges from the records as one of the most unpleasant men to have sat on St. Peter's throne, though some have suggested that this is more a reflection on the surviving writings than on Stephen himself.

Stephen was consecrated bishop of Anagni by Pope Formosus but, after a major dispute, the two became a bitter enemies. Stephen was elected pope apparently as the leader of a faction in Rome that supported Lambert of Spoleto as king of Italy against Berengar of Friuli. Lambert too had a grudge against the dead Formosus and urged Stephen to exact posthumous revenge, resulting in the Cadaver Synod (*see* opposite). Stephen ruled that those appointed while Formosus was pope had to submit themselves for confirmation in office. Stephen ensured that confirmation was given only to those who condemned Formosus's memory.

It did not take the Romans long to tire of Stephen. A monk had fished Formosus's body out of the Tiber and stories spread that the corpse had miraculous powers. When an earthquake hit Rome and destroyed the Lateran Basilica, the people of Rome took it as a sign of divine anger and rose in rebellion. Stephen was thrown into prison and later strangled.

894

The Holy Roman emperor Guy of Spoleto dies after a three-year reign.

896

Traditional date for the arrival of the Magyar tribes in the Hungarian Plain, the start of the kingdom of Hungary.

896

England's Alfred the Great ends the threat by the Danes to his country.

896

Compilation of the *Musica Enchiriadis* manuscript in France marks the start of polyphonic music notation.

ROMANUS ✠ The 114th Pope 897

Born Gallese, Italy; date unknown
Parents Unknown
Papacy August 897–November 897
Died place unknown; date unknown

After Stephen VI was imprisoned, the Romans elected Romanus, cardinal priest of San Pietro, as his successor. It is not known who was allowed to vote or whether anyone waited until the death of Stephen.

Once Romanus was ensconced in the Lateran Palace, legitimately or otherwise, Patriarch Vitalis of Grado arrived wanting to be granted a pallium. The issue was fraught with political as well as religious and financial issues. Grado lay within the realm of Friuli, home to Berengar who claimed the title of king of Italy in opposition to Lambert of Spoleto whose armies were in control of Rome. In the event, Romanus decided to grant the pallium, though it is not known how much money changed hands.

Another issue related to the bishops of Gerona in Spain and Elne in Rousillon who claimed privileges over monasteries and other church properties within their sees. Again, Romanus gave the bishops what they wanted. After four months, Romanus was persuaded—why, how, and by whom is not known—to become a monk. By the conventions of the time, a king or other ruler could abdicate by becoming a monk and it seems to have been accepted that a pope could do the same.

THEODORE II ✠ The 115th Pope 897

Born Rome, Italy; date unknown
Parents Unknown
Papacy probably November 897
Died Rome, Italy; probably November 897

The succession of Theodore II is shrouded in mystery. Once in power, he made no secret of his support for the dead pope Formosus and his determination to restore the former pontiff's reputation.

Theodore called a synod that countermanded the orders of the infamous Cadaver Synod (*see* p.98). Formosus was cleared of all charges laid against him and the sentence of *damnatio memoriae* was overturned—all the actions and appointments of Formosus were, once again, officially valid. All the bishops and priests who had earlier been ordered to subject themselves to reappointment were told this was no longer necessary. Moreover, those who had been reappointed were told to burn the documents relating to that process in order to demonstrate their acceptance Formosus's rehabilitation.

Theodore ordered that the corpse of Formosus should again be dug up and clad in ceremonial robes. The by now decidedly putrid body was carried in procession to St. Peter's Basilica where it was placed back into the grave from which it had been taken eleven months earlier. Within days of the reburial, Theodore himself was dead. His death was convenient for several in Rome and, yet again, foul play cannot be ruled out.

897

Yahya al-Hadi ila'l-Haqq establishes the rule of imams of the Zaidi branch of Shiite Islam in Yemen. The line of imams will survive for more than a thousand years.

897

The Japanese emperor Uda abdicates at age 30 and is succeeded by his 12-year-old son, who will reign for 33 years as Emperor Daigo.

898

King Odo of France dies and is succeeded by Charles the Simple.

JOHN IX ✠ The 116th Pope 898–900

Born Tivoli, Italy ; date unknown

Parents Unknown

Papacy January 898–January 900

Died Rome, Italy; January 900

Of immediate importance to Rome was the need to sort out the confusions of the past two years and restore some kind of order. John's aim was to find a solution acceptable to as wide a spread of opinion as possible, and to get all persons of influence to agree to it.

Lambert of Spoleto presided over the election of Pope John IX in 898.

John IX's election was as dramatic as any of his predecessors. The sudden death of Theodore II caught his supporters by surprise. The anti-Formosus faction was, however, poised for action. Sergius, bishop of Cerveteri, was in Rome ready for his supporters to rally round and march on the Lateran Palace—the basilica was still in ruins following an earthquake (*see* p.99), but the palace itself was intact. The mob stormed inside, threw out any officials who opposed them, and installed Sergius on the papal throne. Before he could be properly consecrated, however, Sergius found himself facing the serried ranks of an army sent by Emperor Lambert of Spoleto. Sergius was ejected from the Lateran at swordpoint and a fresh election held. With the troops watching and fingering their swords, it was no surprise that the electors chose a man approved of by the emperor.

In an attempt to restore peace, John summoned a synod made up of all Italian bishops to meet in Rome. After some debate, the synod agreed to annul all the findings of the Cadaver Synod (*see* p.98) and to burn the records of its decisions. However, those who had taken part in it were pardoned on condition that they agreed to its annulment and confessed that they had taken part only under duress. Only six men refused, among them Sergius of Cerveteri. The synod also banned the future trial of dead bodies and prohibited the translation of a bishop from one bishopric to another. This act was clearly aimed at ruling Sergius's election invalid, but left the synod with the awkward fact that Formosus himself had been translated in this way. He was declared to have been a special exception. Finally, the synod turned to the thorny issue of who should be recognized as emperor in the west. Formosus had crowned two men as emperor, both of them still alive and claiming to be the true emperor. The synod chose Lambert on the grounds that he had been crowned first, but no doubt were influenced by the fact that he and his army were in Italy while Arnulf was in Germany.

Having convinced the Italian bishops to sign up to his peace plan, John moved to Ravenna where a much larger meeting with a wider guest list and presided over by Emperor Lambert was asked to confirm the decisions. This the new meeting did, but with some additions. It was specified that future papal elections would be held at the request of the senate and people of Rome, with electors limited to the clergy, and that the entire process would be overseen by the legates of the emperor to ensure fair play. Lambert promised to respect the ancient customs and privileges of the bishops of Rome and, in return, John promised to respect Lambert's rights as king of Italy. It was unfortunate that just a few weeks later Lambert was killed in a hunting accident. The carefully agreed arrangement between pope and emperor at once fell apart. John survived him by only three months.

899	899	899	900
Death of Alfred the Great, king of Wessex, who consolidated England around his kngdom, compiled the best laws of earlier kings, and encouraged learning with his own translations of Latin works. He is succeeded by his eldest son Edward the Elder.	Pagan Magyar raiders from Hungary rampage through northern Italy, killing Bishop Azzo of Reggio Emilia.	The Holy Roman emperor Arnulf dies and is succeeded as German king by his six-year-old son Louis.	Greenland is discovered by the Norseman Gunbjorn, who is blown off course while sailing from Norway to Iceland.

The Middle Ages
10th to 13th Centuries

CHAPTER THREE

The Middle Ages saw the papacy at the peak of its influence, power, and wealth. Paganism had been banished from Europe and the rival Christian sects had been expunged or absorbed. Although relations with Eastern Christianity were at times tetchy, the popes held undisputed sway over Christianity across most of Europe. Kings, princes, and even emperors found themselves humbled in the face of the power of faith and the influence of the papacy. The popes even raised armies to attack the rising power of Islam in the Middle East, starting the crusades. The Church was triumphant, and it was the popes who were its undisputed leaders.

BENEDICT IV ✢ The 117th Pope 900–903

Born Rome, Italy; date unknown

Parents Father, Mamolus; Mother, unknown

Papacy Probably May 900–probably August 903

Died Rome, Italy; probably August, 903

Benedict followed John's lead in seeking peace through compromise. In 900, he summoned a synod to meet in the Lateran Palace to deal with unresolved difficulties, including the position of the bishop Argrinus.

Bishop Argrinus of Langres had been installed by Formosus, ousted by Stephen VI, and restored by John IX. The synod confirmed the decision of John. The synod also had to decide on the fate of Count Baldwin II of Flanders who had ordered the murder of Archbishop Fulk of Reims during a dispute over ownership of the Abbey of St. Vaast at Arras. It was decided that Baldwin should be excommunicated.

Benedict then turned his attention to the imperial succession. By this date it was assumed that the pope could confer the title of emperor on whoever he liked. Instead of choosing Berengar, the king of Italy, Benedict turned to Louis of Provence, grandson of Emperor Louis II. In 900, Louis and his allies brushed Berengar aside and Louis was crowned king of Italy and Holy Roman emperor. In 902, however, Berengar drove Louis back to Provence. His foreign policy in ruins, Benedict died in July or August of 903 and was buried outside the front of St. Peter's Basilica.

LEO V  The 118th Pope 903

Born Place unknown; date unknown

Parents Unknown

Papacy August 903–September 903

Died Rome, Italy; date unknown

The reign of Leo V was short, violent, and poorly recorded. When Benedict IV died, the clergy and nobility on the spot chose Leo, an apparently obscure priest of Priapi some 25 miles south of Rome.

Whatever the reason for Leo's sudden elevation to the status of pope, he seems to have settled down to the routine administrative tasks well enough. His first recorded action was to settle a tax dispute with the canons of Bologna, a city in the Papal States. As events were to pan out, this was also his last known action. After only 30 days as pope, Leo was overthrown in a coup organized by the cardinal priest of San Damaso, a man named Christopher. The reasons for the coup are unclear. Christopher appears to have been a partisan of Formosus, just as was Leo. The key difference seems to have been that Christopher came from a Roman family, while Leo had been an outsider. Christopher had Leo thrown into prison, then arranged an election that resulted in himself being created pope. In his day and for centuries afterward, Christopher was considered a genuine pope. More recently, however, the fact that Leo neither abdicated nor died before Christopher's election has meant that Christopher is now seen as an antipope.

900	900	901	902	904
Persian scientist Rhazes distinguishes between smallpox and measles.	The Byzantine Empire begins a major offensive against Muslim forces in Anatolia and Mesopotamia.	Rebel general Zhu Wen captures the Chinese capital Chang'an, marking the start of the final collapse of the Tang Dynasty.	Majorca is conquered by Issam, Emir of Cordoba, marking the end of Byzantine power in the western Mediterranean.	Thessalonika, the second largest city in the Byzantine Empire, is captured by a Muslim army and utterly destroyed.

Born Rome, Italy; date unknown

Parents Unknown

Papacy January 29, 904– April 14, 911

Died Rome, Italy; April 14, 911

SERGIUS III ✦ The 119th Pope 904–911

Sergius III was the Sergius who had been elected pope in 898 but who had been driven out by the pro-Formosus John IX with the military aid of Lambert of Spoleto (*see* p.101). He had since been living in exile, watching events in Rome closely.

In late 903, Sergius allied himself to Theophylactus, the papal treasurer and commander of the militia of Rome. The two men then approached Duke Alberic of Spoleto, who promised military support. In January 904, Sergius marched into Rome at the head of Alberic's army, while the Roman militia stood by and did nothing. The antipope Christopher (*see* opposite) was arrested and thrown into prison alongside Leo. Sergius then declared that no new papal election was needed since he had in fact been pope ever since 898 but had been improperly ousted from office. On January 29, he was finally consecrated in office. Modern historians date his reign from this consecration, but he himself always dated it from his election six years earlier. He then sent orders that both Leo and Christopher should be strangled in their prison cells—declaring that he did so out of pity for their predicament.

Now securely in power, Sergius set about regularizing the situation as he saw it. He began by summoning a synod to meet in Rome. When the various clergy arrived, they found that the soldiers of Alberic were still on hand. The first bishop who objected was beaten so savagely that he nearly died. Cowed, the synod hurriedly ratified everything demanded of them by Sergius. The main decisions of the synod were to declare that Formosus had been illegally elected pope since he was already bishop of Porto at the time. The synod also resurrected the findings of the Cadaver Synod (*see* p.98) and repealed the acts of the two synods held by John IX. The resulting confusion was immense.

Sergius then found himself summoned by the Byzantine emperor Leo VI to rule on the subject of marriage. Lacking a male heir by his first three wives, Leo VI wanted to marry a fourth time. The patriarch of Constantinople, Nicholas I, had ruled this illegal in canon law. Sergius sent envoys to listen to the arguments of both sides then decide in Leo's favor. Nicholas was ousted and the Eastern Church collapsed into an anarchy almost as bad as that in the West.

Sergius completed the rebuilding of the Lateran Basilica, the cathedral church of Rome, which had been destroyed by an earthquake in 897 soon after the ending of the Cadaver Synod, in which Sergius had taken part. Little else is known of his work in Rome. The circumstances of Sergius's death are unclear, but it appears to have been natural.

THEOPHYLACTUS AND THEODORA

Lurking behind Sergius were the immensely rich and powerful families of Theophylactus and his wife Theodora. Theophylactus was the hereditary count of Tusculum, a small town near Rome, who married the equally aristocratic and ruthless Theodora some time around 885. Together they helped engineer the victory of Sergius III and largely controlled that pope's government not least through the seductive powers of their teenage daughter Marozia, who became the lover of Sergius. Some time around 905, Marozia gave birth to Sergius's son, a boy who was named John.

907
The final collapse of the ailing Tang Dynasty in China comes when Emperor Ai is poisoned by the military commander Zhu Wen who declares himself the new emperor. China rapidly fragments into a number of warring states, a period known as the Five Dynasties and Ten Kingdoms.

909
The last inscription with a date is made in Tonina, marking the official end of the Mayan civilization, which had been in decline for decades.

909
Abdullāh al-Mahdī Billah founds the Fatimid Dynasty in North Africa, claiming descent from the Prophet Mohammed by way of his daughter Fatima.

910
Battle of Tettenhall in England sees the joint Wessex-Mercian forces destroy the army of Northumbrian Vikings, killing the joint kings Halfdan and Eowils.

ANASTASIUS III ✠ The 120th Pope 911–913

Born Rome, Italy; date unknown

Parents Unknown

Papacy April 911–June 900

Died Rome, Italy; June 913

nastasius's election was manipulated by the nobleman Theophylactus and his wife Theodora. It is not known which, if any, of the actions of Anastasius were his own and which were dictated by Theophylactus.

It was probably during the reign of Anastasius that Thephylactus was granted the title consul of Rome. The title had not been used for centuries and does not seem to have brought with it any new powers, but its prestige was still immense, being considered second only to that of "Emperor of Rome."

King Berengar of Italy also loomed large in papal affairs. Anastasius granted the request of Berengar that Bishop Ragimbert of Vercelli be given the pallium, and also granted honors to the bishop of Pavia, another city controlled by Berengar. In 912, the patriarch Nicholas I of Constantinople was restored to office. He sent a long and bluntly worded letter to Anastasius condemning the actions of Sergius III that had led to his own removal from office and demanding that Anastasius recant. The reply sent by Anastasius has not survived, but it cannot have been to Nicholas's liking for he removed the pope's name from the list of those for whom prayers were said in Constantinople.

LANDO  The 121st Pope 913–914

Born Fornovo, Italy; date unknown

Parents Father, Taino; Mother, unknown

Papacy August 913–March 914

Died Rome, Italy; March 914

f not much is known about Anastasius III, even less is known about Lando. He is said to have come from an immensely rich Lombard family, which would make him an outsider to Rome.

The term "pornocracy" was coined by later historians to refer to the years of the tenth century when the papacy was in the gift of the nobleman Theophylactus and his family. The word means "rule of the harlots" and was coined by Protestant historians partly to blacken the reputation of the popes. Catholic historians prefer the more neutral term *Saeculum Obscurum*, which mean "Hidden Times," referring to the lack of contemporary written evidence in the papal archives from these years. It may be that his election was a favor by the real ruler of Rome, Theophylactus, to the family of Taino, but this is mere conjecture. The only recorded act of Lando's time in office was his donation of a large sum of money to the cathedral at San Salvatore at Fornovo, which must count as a way of diverting cash from the papal treasury to his home town. The last pope to use his personal name as pope, Lando died after only 6 months and 11 days in office. There is no evidence to suggest foul play.

911	912	912	913	913
The Fatimids, Muslim rulers of North Africa, begin the conquest of Sicily from rival Muslim rulers.	King Ordono of Galicia and Leon conquers Evora from the Muslims in Spain.	Death of Oleg of Novgorod who had united Novgorod and Kiev, founding the Russian state.	The Muslim Fatimid Dynasty of North Africa is defeated in Sicily and in Egypt.	Death of Byzantine emperor Alexander III.

JOHN X ✠ The 122nd Pope 914–928

Born Tossignano, Italy; date unknown

Parents Father, John; Mother, unknown

Papacy March 914–May 928

Died Rome, Italy; 929

Consul Theophylactus chose Archbishop John of Ravenna as the next pope for various reasons: John was close to King Berengar of Italy, he was known to be a consummate diplomat and organizer, and he had been to Rome several times before and had got on well with Theophylactus.

The most immediate task facing the new pope was to deal with the Saracens. The Muslims from North Africa had conquered Sicily many decades earlier and had secured footholds at various places in Italy. The most important of these was at Carigliano, a few miles south of Rome. Several rulers in southern Italy had done deals with the Saracens to save themselves. John now set about using his diplomatic skills to form a grand alliance of Christian Italian rulers against the Saracens. By spring 915, he had succeeded, even gaining the support of Emperor Constantine VII of Constantinople who sent a powerful fleet to aid the campaign. After a lightning offensive, the Saracens were cooped up in their fortress at Garigliano. When it fell in August 915, John himself supervised the killing of all Muslims. The decisive defeat put the Saracens on the defensive and effectively confined them to Sicily. For his part in the campaign, Berengar was crowned emperor.

As part of the arrangement that brought the Byzantine ships to his aid, John had agreed to recognize that the Eastern Church did not allow a person to marry more than three times. He also settled a long-running dispute over who should be bishop of Narbonne and another similar dispute in Louvain.

In 924, Berengar died, followed in less than a year by Theophylactus and Duke Alberic of Spoleto. John made his own brother Peter the new Duke of Spoleto and sent messages to Hugh of Provence, the new king of Italy, seeking friendship. Theophylactus's daughter, Marozia, had meanwhile married Guy, Margrave of Tuscany. She expected to take over her father's role as effective ruler of the Papal States and saw John's actions as a threat to this ambition. She banished Peter from Rome, but allowed him to return when it became clear that King Hugh had too many troubles in Provence to consider taking up power in Italy.

Peter proved to be a wily operator and slowly began to get a grip on power at the cost of Marozia. Unwilling to accept this, Marozia secretly moved a body of her husband's troops into Rome. Waiting until John and Peter were without their customary bodyguard, the troops burst into the Lateran Palace, killed Peter on the spot, and bundled John into his private quarters where he was kept under armed guard while Marozia secured her position. Some weeks later, apparently in May 928, John was persuaded to become a monk and so effectively abdicate as pope. He seems to have died, perhaps murdered on the orders of Marozia, in 929.

THE PORNOCRACY

Understandably, later Church writers condemned the idea that the Church should be controlled by secular hands. It was, however, merely a culmination of a process that had been taking place ever since the pope had become the secular ruler of the Papal States. The popes had welcomed this move as it put the papacy on a sound financial footing and gave them the means to raise an army to defend the holy city against Saracen raiders. An unintended consequence was that the nobles of the Papal States started to demand influence over the way their country was run. The rivalry for power was to lead to the years of the "pornocracy," generally taken to refer to the years 904 to 964.

914	919	920	924	927
Viking settlers found Waterford, now recognized as being the oldest city in Ireland.	Approximate date for the building of Pueblo Bonito, the largest town of the Chaco culture in what is now New Mexico.	Hywel Dda becomes king of Deheubarth. He will later codify traditional Welsh laws into a legal code that will be used for centuries.	Battle of Seven sees the Armenians defeat an invasion by Muslim Arabs.	King Athelstan of Wessex and Mercia is accepted as overlord by all rulers in England, creating a unified Kingdom of England.

LEO VI ✠ The 123rd Pope 928

Born Rome, Italy; date unknown

Parents Father, Christophorus; Mother, unknown

Papacy May 928–probably December 928

Died Rome, Italy; probably December 928

It is thought that Marozia was planning to make her son by Sergius III pope (*see* p.105) and chose Leo because the elderly cardinal priest would not be around for long and would do her bidding in the meantime.

Born into the noble Roman Sanguini family, Leo may well have been related to Marozia but, at any rate, it seems that he did nothing without her approval. By the time Leo took office, Marozia was using the titles of "Senatrix" and "Patricia"—both titles were unprecedented and showed the extent of the woman's power.

The only known act of Leo was his effort to resolve issues in Dalmatia and Croatia. The area had long been in dispute between Rome and Constantinople and local bishops were feuding over rights, responsibilities, and revenues. Leo sort to solve the issue by sending the prestigious pallium to Archbishop John of Spalato (now Split). This, he hoped, would give John sufficient prestige to be able to adjudicate in the many and complex disputes that wracked the region. Within the Church, Leo sought to clarify a number of canon laws, including a ban on castrati—men castrated as boys to preserve their singing voices—from marrying. Leo died peacefully, probably in December 928.

STEPHEN VII ✠ The 124th Pope 928–931

Born Rome, Italy; date unknown

Parents Father, Theodemundus; Mother, unknown

Papacy probably December 928–probably February 931

Died Rome, Italy; probably February 931

Like Leo VI before him, Stephen was chosen as much for his great age as for his background as a member of a Roman noble family. The real ruler of the Papal States was still the noblewoman Marozia (*see* p.105).

It is thought that Marozia was keen to select an elderly pontiff so that her son would not have long to wait before he could be maneuvered into the papal chair. Marozia schemed successfully to get her son elected as Pope John XI, and by her marriage to Duke Alberic I of Spoleto, she founded a long-lasting dynasty. Popes John XII and Benedict VII were both her grandsons. Popes Benedict VIII and John XIX were both her great grandsons. Pope Benedict IX was her great great grandson. Stephen was almost certainly a member of the Gabrielli family, which claimed descent from the emperor Caracalla, who ruled Rome from 198 to 217 and went on to hold a variety of titles including "Prince of Prossedi." The family has included a number of prominent Italian soldiers, statesmen, and clerics, marrying into some of the leading royal families of Europe. However, almost nothing is known about the pontificate of Stephen. Even the date of his death is uncertain.

928	929	929	930
Death of Tomislav, first king of a united Croatia.	Death of King Charles the Simple of France.	Abd-ar-Rahman III of Cordoba proclaims himself Caliph in opposition to the Fatimid ruler Abdul-Lāh al-Mahdī bi'llāh who had similarly assumed the title of Caliph.	Founding of the Althing, the Parliament of Iceland, the oldest Parliament in the world.

JOHN XI ✠ The 125th Pope 931–936

Born Rome, Italy; c.905

Parents Father, Pope Sergius III; Mother, Marozia

Papacy probably February 931–probably January 936

Died Rome, Italy; probably January 936

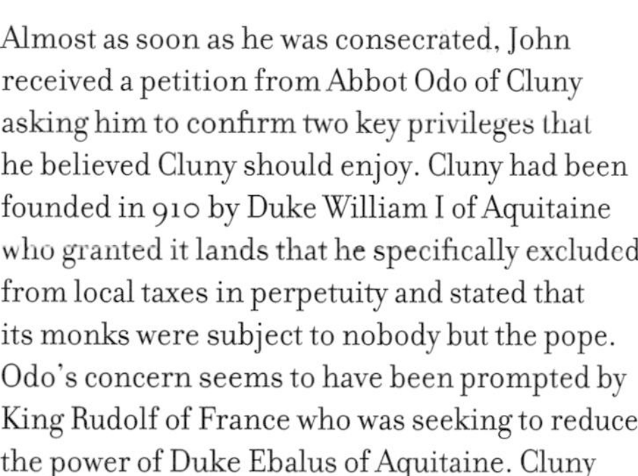

For decades the noblewoman Marozia had been the effective ruler of Rome when she engineered the elevation of her son John to become pope. John was aged about 25 at the time he became pope, having previously been made cardinal priest of Santa Maria in Trastevere.

Almost as soon as he was consecrated, John received a petition from Abbot Odo of Cluny asking him to confirm two key privileges that he believed Cluny should enjoy. Cluny had been founded in 910 by Duke William I of Aquitaine who granted it lands that he specifically excluded from local taxes in perpetuity and stated that its monks were subject to nobody but the pope. Odo's concern seems to have been prompted by King Rudolf of France who was seeking to reduce the power of Duke Ebalus of Aquitaine. Cluny lay in the territories that Rudolf was seeking to strip from Ebalus and Odo thought that Rudolf would not respect the agreement made when the abbey was founded. Although he himself had gained office through exactly the type of secular interference in ecclesiastical matters that Cluny opposed, John lost no time in confirming the privileges of Cluny Abbey.

In early 932 the Byzantine emperor Romanus I asked John if it were proper for him to appoint his 16-year-old son Theophylact to be patriarch of Constantinople. John replied it was and sent two bishops to help in the boy's consecration.

Also in 932, Marozia became a widow for the second time when Margrave Guy of Tuscany died. She decided to marry his half-brother, King Hugh of Italy, who promptly annulled his marriage so that he could agree. The wedding was held in great style in Rome in December 932. At the wedding feast Hugh insulted Marozia's son by her first marriage, Duke Alberic II of Spoleto. Alberic walked out, raised a mob of Romans by inciting them against the supposed rule of the foreigner Hugh, and stormed back into the Castel Sant'Angelo. Hugh's men were killed, though he managed to escape over the walls in ignominious flight. Marozia was thrown into prison and John reduced to a figurehead.

For the rest of his life John was kept firmly under lock and key in the Lateran Palace. He was allowed out to conduct necessary church ceremonies, but all decision-making was in the hands of his younger half-brother Alberic. Marozia is thought to have died in the summer of 936, apparently of natural causes.

POPE'S SON

As the son of Sergius III, John was only the second son of a pope to become pope himself. The other had been Silverius (*see* p.59) who had been the son of Hormisdas. Unlike John, however, Silverius was a legitimate son as Hormisdas had been married to his mother and entered the priesthood only after he was widowed.

Cluny Abbey was intended to have the strictest possible interpretation of the Rule of St. Benedict, to abhor corruption, and to serve as a model for other monasteries.

931	933	933	934
Death of King Harald Fairhair, first ruler of a united Norway.	Henry the Fowler, king of Germany, defeats the Magyars at the Battle of Riade.	Rudolf II of Burgundy reunites all of Burgundy under his rule.	The largest basalt flow in recorded history takes place when the volcano Eldgja erupts in southern Iceland.

LEO VII ✠ The 126th Pope 936–939

Born Rome, Italy; date unknown

Parents Unknown

Papacy January 3, 936–July 13, 939

Died Rome, Italy; July 13, 939

Alberic II of Spoleto took over the titles of senator and patrician and continued controlling the papacy. When John XI died, Alberic's choice fell upon Leo, the cardinal priest of San Sisto.

Alberic was deeply interested in the more spiritual side of monasticism and wanted a pope who shared those interests. Leo was not interested in becoming pope, being perfectly content where he was, but Alberic insisted.

So far as can be discerned from the few records available, Leo spent most of his time in prayer or conducting the various services of the Roman Church. It was Alberic who made the decisions, even those affecting the Church, with Leo being brought out to give his approval to what had already been agreed. Despite this somewhat unedifying process, Leo's reign did see some important ecclesiastical changes. The great reforming monastery of Cluny in France again gained favors, as did the Abbey of Gorze. In 936, Abbot Odo of Cluny was invited to come to Rome to inspect and make recommendations for the reform of monasteries in and around Rome. The main focus of the reform in Rome seems to have been St. Paul Outside the Walls, one of the four major basilicas of the city.

STEPHEN VIII ✠ The 127th Pope 939–942

Born Rome, Italy; date unknown

Parents Unknown

Papacy July 14, 939–October 942

Died Rome, Italy; probably October 942

Like Leo VII before him, Stephen was chosen for the papacy by Alberic II of Spoleto, who was the real ruler of Rome and the Papal States. Indeed, Alberic had by this date acquired the title of "prince of Rome."

Stephen was the cardinal priest of the Church of SS. Silvestro and Martino when Alberic told him that he was going to be pope. It is most likely that he was allowed to carry out his spiritual duties himself, but that all real decisions remained with Alberic. At this time King Louis IV of France was experiencing troubles with rebellious nobles. In 942, Stephen offered to recognize Hugh of Vermandois, son of a leading rebel, as archbishop of Reims if the rebellion ended. This, together with the threat of excommunication, ended the rebellion and secured Louis on his throne.

In the same year, King Hugh of Italy marched on Rome, laying brief and unsuccessful siege to the city as part of his ongoing feud with Alberic. When several bishops were found to be part of a plot to murder Alberic, the outraged prince of Rome blamed Stephen and summoned a synod in Rome. Alberic used the occasion to demonstrate his power and threw Stephen into prison, where the pope died conveniently quickly.

936
Otto I is crowned king of Germany at Aachen. He is later recognized as the founder of the Holy Roman Empire in its medieval form.

937
Battle of Brunanburh sees King Athelstan of England defeat a grand alliance of Irish, Scots, Welsh, and Viking opponents, thus preserving the united English kingdom and securing English dominance over the British Isles.

939
The Christian kingdom of Leon captures Madrid from the Muslim rulers of Spain.

940
Gorm the Old unites the various Danish tribes into a single kingdom of Denmark.

940
Death of Ibn Muqla, renowned Islamic calligrapher.

MARINUS II ✠ The 128th Pope 942–946

Born Rome, Italy; date unknown

Parents Unknown

Papacy October 942–May 946

Died Rome, Italy; May 946

Marinus's time in office was almost completely overshadowed by the powerful secular ruler Duke Alberic II of Spoleto. But, given that his predecessor Stephen VIII had been murdered by Alberic, it is hardly surprising that Marinus chose to keep a low profile.

Other than the facts that he was born in Rome and was serving as cardinal priest of San Ciriaco when he was chosen to be pope, nothing is known for certain about Marinus before he took office. Once installed as pope, he seems to have restricted himself to doing as Alberic wished—even going so far as to put Alberic's name as well as his own on the coins minted in Rome. Marinus is known to have spent money refurbishing several churches in Rome and donated funds to the care of the poor.

On the ecclesiastical front, Marinus took an interest in the great monastery of Monte Cassino. In 944, he ordered Bishop Sico of Capua to restore property to the monastery that he had taken for the use of his diocese, and went on to issue a bull reiterating the ancient privileges and rights of Monte Cassino. In 946, he appointed Archbishop Frederick of Mainz to be papal envoy to Germany with powers to hold synods and to investigate, and punish, irregularities or abuses by clergy or monks in Germany.

As with Marinus I, a later confusion of names meant that for many years Marinus II was counted as being Martin III, with the result that the second Pope Martin was numbered as Martin IV, with consequent misnumbering of later Martins.

DUCHY OF SPOLETO

The powerful duchy of Spoleto that dominated the papacy for so long had its origins in the Lombard invasion of Italy in the mid-sixth century. The Lombards were a Germanic people who conquered nearly all of Italy between 568 and 572. The king established his capital in Pavia while most of the country was divided up into territories, each ruled by a duke dependent on the king. One such duke was resident on the hilltop fortress of Spoleto from at least 576. By the late-eighth century, the duchy extended from the Apennines to the sea and was one of the richer states in Italy. After the Frankish conquest of Italy in the 770s, the status of Spoleto became somewhat ambivalent. The duchy was made a fief of the Church, though it remained outside the Papal States and the Frankish emperor retained the right to confirm a new duke in his possessions. As Frankish influence waned, that of the Church increased, and it was this that brought Spoleto into Roman politics. In the tenth and eleventh centuries the dispute over who should appoint a new duke of Spoleto led to disputes between the papacy and the Holy Roman Empire. In 1198, the papacy gained a de facto control over the duchy of Spoleto that became formalized in 1213 when most of its land was incorporated into the Papal States.

The great monastery of Monte Cassino, southeast of Rome, was established by St. Benedict of Nursia around 530.

942	944	944	945	946
Death of Prince Idwal Foel of Gwynedd in battle against the English allows Hywell Dda of Deheubarth to annex Gwynedd and Powys, making him ruler of all of Wales.	A great storm hits England causing immense damage, including the collapse of 1,500 houses and churches in London alone.	The city of Algiers is founded by Buluggin ibn Ziri.	St. Dunstan becomes Abbot of Glastonbury, England.	The Battle of Baghdad, which saw the almost total destruction of the city, marks the end of the long war between the Emir of Iraq and the Emir of Mosul, with victory going to the Iraqis.

AGAPETUS II ✣ The 129th Pope 946–955

Born Rome, Italy; date unknown

Parents Unknown

Papacy May 10, 946–probably December 955

Died Rome, Italy; probably December 955

Agapetus was chosen by Duke Alberic II of Spoleto, who ruled Rome and the Papal States with an iron hand. Like his immediate predecessors, Agapetus was allowed to do little more than agree with what Alberic wanted and officiate at formal ceremonies.

Again, like his predecessor, Agapetus took an interest in monastic reform. Cluny and Gorze, centers of the movement to reform and strengthen the European monastic movement, were favored. He also summoned monks from Gorze to come to Rome to inject some reforming zeal into the monks of St. Paul Outside the Walls. Leo VII had also tried to reform that basilica, so the problems must have been deep seated.

Agapetus was also asked to adjudicate in a number of foreign disputes, though to what extent the decisions he made were influenced by Alberic is unclear. In June 948, Agapetus sent Bishop Marinus of Tolymatis to preside over the important Synod of Ingelheim, which was called to decide which of two rival claimants should be archbishop of Reims. Since the Reims question was tied up with disputes in France over the extent and nature of royal power, the synod was dealing with temporal as well as ecclesiastical affairs. The synod ruled in favor of Artaud, the protégé of King Louis IV of France and against Hugh of Vermandois who was favored by the rebels opposing an expansion of royal authority. It went further, ordering the rebels to cease opposition to Louis under pain of excommunication. In 949, Agapetus held a synod in Rome that confirmed these decisions.

In 951, the German king Otto I crossed the Alps with a large army to assert his claim to be king of Italy and marry Lothair's beautiful 19-year-old widow, Adelaide, who was also the daughter of King Rudolf of Italy and Burgundy. He then sent messengers to Agapetus to open discussions on whether he could be elevated to the position of emperor. Alberic, however, was wary of Otto's ambition, and sent his men to turn the messengers back with sweet words, but firmness.

In 954, feeling death coming upon him, Alberic summoned a great council of all the nobles and clerics of the Papal States. He asked them to promise that his son Octavianus would follow him as prince of Rome, and would be elected to succeed Agapetus as pope. The first promise was easy to arrange, but the latter was illegal under canon law. Nevertheless, Agapetus readily gave his promise, as did the other churchmen. When Alberic died, Octavianus took up his titles and powers as seculer ruler. Agapetus died a year later and Octavianus moved to enforce the promises made to his father.

The papal basilica of St. Paul Outside the Walls is one of Rome's four ancient basilicas. It was founded by the Roman emperor Constantine I at the burial place of St. Paul.

The German king Otto I gained the support of Agapetus on questions of ecclesiastical organization. The boundaries of the bishoprics of Germany were unclear, and Agapetus came down on the side of proposals put forward by King Otto.

947
Traditional date for the death of Ce Acatl Topiltzin, first ruler of a unified Toltec state in Central America.

948
Traditional date for the founding of the Nri state in West Africa that would survive to the present day.

950
Emir Sayf al-Dawla of Aleppo invades the Byzantine Empire, but is heavily defeated.

954
Erik Bloodaxe, last independent king of York, is killed by Earl Maccus. Thereafter, all England is permanently united under the Wessex dynasty.

JOHN XII ✠ The 130th Pope 955–963

Born probably Rome, 937

Parents Father, Crescentius; Mother, unknown

Papacy December 16, 955–December 4, 963

Died Campagna, May 14, 964

When Agapetus II died, Prince Octavianus of Rome summoned the papal electors and reminded them of their promises to elect him as the next pope. The electors honored those promises and Octavianus renounced his name and took that of John to become Pope John XII.

John's reputation has suffered from the writings of his enemies. According to them he was a drunken seducer of married women, who was addicted to prostitutes and quite unable to appreciate the fine arts. Given that John was only 18 when he became pope, and that he did so merely to bolster his political power, it is more than likely that his conduct fell short of the blameless spiritual ideal of later reformers. On the other hand, he emerges from contemporary documents as a man trying to do his best for the Church in difficult circumstances.

John devoted much time to the Church in Spain. The Christian rulers of northern Spain were at this time starting to drive back the Muslim invaders. The bishops who had reached accommodation with the Muslims were torn between supporting the Christian attack and avoiding Muslim reprisals.

John supported monasteries where the reform movement flourished and sought to ensure that worthy men were appointed to such bishoprics and archbishoprics as fell vacant. The granting of the pallium to St. Dunstan of Canterbury was probably his greatest triumph in this field.

Politically, however, John proved to be as inept as his father had been adept. In 958, he led the armies of Rome and Spoleto on an invasion of Capua and Benevento to force their dukes to hand over areas of land that the papacy claimed as part of the Papal States. The two dukes appealed to Gisulf of Salerno and Berengar of Ivlea who marched to their aid. John fell back to Rome and asked King Otto of Germany, claimant to the kingdom of Italy for help. Otto agreed, but first extracted a promise that he would be crowned emperor.

In the summer of 961, Otto marched into Italy, crushed Berengar, brought the other Italian nobles to heel, and marched on to Rome. On February 2, 962, he was crowned emperor. As soon as Otto left Rome, John contacted Berengar and the Magyars to seek Otto's destruction. When Otto learnt of this treachery, he marched back to Rome. John fled to Tivoli with the papal treasury. Otto summoned a synod that charged John with assorted crimes and pronounced him deposed. An election was quickly held that put Leo VIII on the papal throne. Otto left again in January 964, whereupon John returned with hired mercenaries and drove Leo into exile. Otto once again marched on Rome, but before he arrived John suffered a fatal seizure when in bed with one of his lovers.

The great synod of 962 led to the "Ottonian Privilege": Otto agreed to protect the rights, possessions, and prerogatives of the Catholic Church, including the right of the Romans to elect future popes free of outside interference; John promised that the popes would swear fealty to the emperor and recognize him as overlord of the Papal States.

CONFUSED CHRONOLOGY

The chronology of the popes during the 960s is confused. Some historians put Benedict V after John XII and before Leo VIII, while others put Leo VIII before Benedict V. The dispute centers on the legitimacy of the assorted depositions and elections that took place at this time.

956

An earthquake tumbles the Lighthouse of Alexandria, one of the Seven Wonders of the Ancient World.

958

Didda, famous for her wisdom, becomes ruler of Kashmir where she will hold power for almost 50 years.

960

Foundation of the Chinese Song Dynasty occurs when the military leader Taizu of Song takes over power in the Zhou kingdom and then conquers the other petty kingdoms to reunite China under his rule by 976.

963

The GrandyDuchy of Luxembourg is founded when Siegfried of Ardennes buys the Bock Rock from the Abbey of St. Maximin and builds the castle of Luxembourg on the impregnable site.

BENEDICT V ✠ The 131st Pope 964

Born Rome, Italy; date unknown
Parents Unknown
Papacy May 22, 964–June 23, 964
Died Hamburg, Germany; July 966

enedict had served under John XII and taken part in the synod that deposed him. Despite this, he was allowed to remain a deacon when John returned—an indication both of his goodness and insignificance.

The Romans elected Benedict—despite his lowly status—because he was one of the most educated men in Rome and had a personal life that was utterly blameless. Emperor Otto, however, was determined that Leo should be pope (*see* p.113) and was willing to back up his choice with armed force. The emperor marched on Rome, laid siege, and cut off the city's food supplies. Pope Benedict appeared on the city walls in his formal purple robes and performed the dread ceremony of anathema on the besieging army, which consigned them to eternal damnation unless they lifted the siege. It had no effect.

On June 23, Rome surrendered and opened the gates to Otto. The emperor summoned a new synod, presided over by Leo, which declared Benedict to be a usurper and banished him from Rome, though out of regard for his exemplary life he retained the rank of deacon and was not otherwise punished. Benedict left for Hamburg, where Archbishop Adaldag welcomed him with great honor. He died there just two years later.

LEO VIII  The 132nd Pope 963–965

Born Rome, Italy; date unknown
Parents Father, John; Mother, unknown
Papacy June 23, 964–March 1, 965
Died Rome, Italy; March 1, 96

he chronology of the popes in the 960s is confused with some placing Leo VIII after John XII and other placing Benedict V after John. The point at dispute is the validity of the election of Leo in December 964.

In January 964, Leo was driven out of Rome by supporters of John who refused to accept the sentence of deposition imposed by Otto. John then returned briefly to power. When John died in May 964, the Romans elected Benedict V (*see* above), but Otto returned with his army and captured Rome. A fresh synod was held, which ruled Benedict an antipope. Benedict did not defend himself, but allowed his accusers to remove his papal robes and break the papal scepter over his head. He then went into exile. Leo was now back in undisputed power, but what he did with it is unclear. There are numerous documents bearing his name that grant to Otto and his successors as emperor a wide variety of privileges and powers over the Papal States and the Church in general. These, however, survive only as later copies and it is widely assumed that they were altered and tampered with by imperial clerks in later centuries when the popes and emperors were in bitter dispute over precisely these matters (*see* p.138).

965
Byzantine armies reconquer Cyprus from the Muslims and crush the Emirate of Cilicia, ending Muslim raids on Anatolia.

966
Duke Mieszko of Poland is baptized a Christian, marking the start of the process of converting the Poles from paganism to Christianity.

968
The nomadic Pecheneg tribe of Turks lays siege to Kiev, but is beaten off.

JOHN XIII ✠ The 133rd Pope 965–972

Born Rome, Italy; date unknown

Parents Father, John Episcopus; Mother, unknown

Papacy October 1, 965–September 6, 972

Died Rome, Italy; September 6, 972

When Leo VIII died in March 965, the deposed Benedict V was still alive and in exile. Confusion resulted and several months passed before a new election was held. This resulted in the installation into the Lateran of John XIII, then the bishop of Narni in Umbria.

John was a native Roman and had spent his entire adult life working in the curia. The fact that his election led to no controversy shows that by this date it was accepted that it was proper for a bishop to move from his current see to that of Rome, something that had caused bitter wrangling less than a century before.

It was not long before John ran into trouble. Many Romans resented having to put up with a pope they regarded as an imperial stooge. In December 965, a riot broke out with the malcontents getting the upper hand. John was beaten up, then put under house arrest in a villa outside Rome. At this time, John was supported by the Crescenti, a noble family from the Sabine Hills north of Rome—it has been suggested that John may have been a member of this family.

In the summer of 966, John escaped and got word to Otto, who marched south with an army. On 14 November, John marched into Rome in triumph, with Otto not far behind. Those who had organized John's imprisonment were executed, while the Crescenti were rewarded with lands and lucrative positions in the government of the Papal States. Otto also was rewarded when John raised the bishopric of Magdeburg to the status of an archbishopric. John also crowned Otto's son Emperor Otto II, to rule jointly with his father.

It is clear that John acted mostly with the agreement of the emperor, though it is unclear whether he slavishly followed imperial orders or was merely careful not to antagonize his imperial benefactor. It is known, for instance, that the newly promoted archbishop of Magdeburg was given authority over the bishops of the newly converted Slavs, but that he was not given blanket authority over future converts as Otto had apparently wanted.

John's other promotions had less happy results. He raised both Capua and Benevento to be archbishoprics, moves which annoyed the patriarch of Constantinople who in response raised Otranto to the same status. What threatened to become an ecclesiastical conflict of some importance in southern Italy was checked by Otto's desire for friendship with the Byzantine emperors. In 972, the young Otto II was married to Theophano, niece of John I of Constantinople.

John died just a couple of weeks after Otto had left Italy to return to Germany where various matters required his attention. The absence of the emperor would lead to delay and disputes in agreeing a successor.

At Christmas 967, Pope John XIII crowned Otto's son, also Otto, as Emperor Otto II to rule jointly with his father.

MONASTIC REFORMS

In 972, Archbishop Oswald of York came to Rome to collect a pallium from the hands of John. The trip seems, however, to have been mainly concerned with the reform of the monasteries of Britain. The reform movement born at Cluny had by this date spread widely across France and Germany, and was becoming established in Italy. Britain had as yet remained outside the orbit of the reformers, but Oswald seems to have been keen to import Cluniac practices.

969

The Muslim Fatimid dynasty of North Africa conquers Egypt and founds a new dynastic capital city—Cairo.

970

Eric the Victorious unites the Swedes and becomes the first king of Sweden.

971

At Chichester, England, the body of St. Swithun is moved from its outside tomb to a newly built indoor shrine, an event followed by 40 days of constant rain.

BENEDICT VI ✠ The 134th Pope 973–974

Born Rome, Italy; date unknown

Parents Hildebrand; Mother, unknown

Papacy January 19, 973–probably July 974

Died Rome, Italy; probably July 974

Exactly what happened after the death of John XIII is unclear. The powerful Crescenti family put forward a deacon named Franco, but the imperial representatives of Otto I favored a monk named Benedict, who also enjoyed the support of the reformist faction in the Church.

Although the date of Benedict's election is unknown, it is clear that he delayed his consecration until such time as formal approval could be received from Otto, which arrived in January. Benedict then set about following policies traditionally favored by Otto. For example, he sent a letter confirming that Trier was the oldest see in Germany. He also backed the reformers within the Church, explicitly banning bishops from charging fees for ordinations and consecrations. He also gave privileges to monasteries that were following the reformist lead of Cluny.

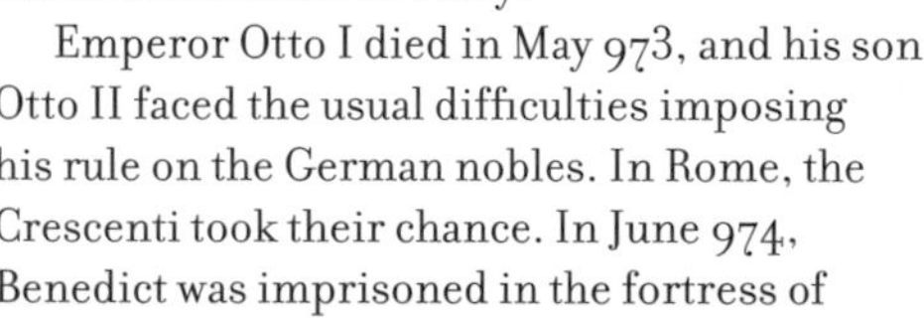

Emperor Otto I died in May 973, and his son Otto II faced the usual difficulties imposing his rule on the German nobles. In Rome, the Crescenti took their chance. In June 974, Benedict was imprisoned in the fortress of Castel Sant'Angelo. Exactly what charges were leveled against him is not recorded. Before he could be brought to trial, Count Sicco of Spoleto, who was Otto's representative in Italy, marched on Rome with an army. Franco, by now enthroned as Boniface VII, sent a priest named Stephen to Benedict's cell to strangle the imprisoned pope. The precise date of the murder is unknown, but it was probably July 974.

In June 974, Benedict was seized by men acting on the instructions of Franco and thrown into prison in the fortress of Castel Sant'Angelo.

ANTIPOPE BONIFACE VII

The deacon Franco who had himself elected as Boniface VII was born in Rome, the son of a nobleman named Ferrucius. Whether he was a member of the Crescenti family or merely allied to them is not known. He also had the support of the Byzantine government, keen to cause trouble for the new Western emperor Otto II and to destabilize the papacy at a time when the patriarch of Constantinople was seeking to extend his influence over the Christians living under Muslim rule in Sicily and southern Italy. Once Benedict had been murdered, Boniface found that public opinion in Rome turned against him. He grabbed as much of the papal treasury as he could take with him and fled to seek sanctuary in a Byzantine-held fortress.

973	973	974	975	976
The Holy Roman emperor Otto I dies, aged 60. He is succeeded by his 18-year-old son Otto II.	Death of St. Ulrich of Augsburg, the German bishop instrumental in spreading the reformist movement to the German Church.	Death of Ratherius the Wanderer of Verona, itinerant Christian preacher who used fables to explain complex theological matters to lay people.	Modern arithmetical notation is introduced into Europe by the Arabs.	Leopold Babenberg becomes Margrave of Austria. His family will rule Austria until 1246.

BENEDICT VII ✠ The 135th Pope 974–983

Born Rome, Italy; date unknown
Parents Unknown
Papacy October 974–July 10, 983
Died Rome, Italy; July 10, 983

With Benedict VI dead and the antipope Boniface VII fled (*see opposite*), Duke Sicco of Spoleto ordered that a new election be held. The victorious candidate was Benedict, bishop of Sutri.

Benedict was a compromise candidate for he was known to favor the reformist policies of the emperor Otto II but was related to both the Crescenti and the Alberti, the two most powerful noble families in the Papal States.

Benedict summoned a synod for the sole purpose of excommunicating the antipope Boniface VII. That done, he set about pursuing the reformist agenda: bishops and monasteries favoring reform were given privileges and the ban on simony was renewed. He loyally implemented policies favored by Otto II, redrawing the boundaries of German dioceses along politically expedient lines. Also, Benedict made Bishop Dietrich of Trier the cardinal priest of Santi Quattro Coronati—the first time a Roman cardinal had not been a local man.

In 980, while Benedict was away, the antipope Boniface VII suddenly reappeared. He summoned his supporters and installed himself in the Lateran Palace. Benedict was unable to return until 981 when Otto II sent him an army.

JOHN XIV ✠ The 136th Pope 983–984

Born Pavia, Italy; date unknown
Parents Unknown
Papacy December 983–August 20, 984
Died Rome, Italy; August 20, 984

The death of Benedict VII found Emperor Otto II in Italy with a large army to fight the Saracens and thus in an ideal position to impose his favored candidate—Peter Canepanova, bishop of Pavia.

Peter arrived in Rome and was consecrated as Pope John XIV without so much as a pretence of an election. A few days later, Otto II arrived in Rome. He had contracted a fever while leading his army against the Muslims and was seriously ill. He received absolution for his sins from John, then passed away in his arms. When rumors reached Italy that Duke Henry II of Bavaria was preparing a coup, the Empress Theophanu abandoned the war against the Muslims and marched the imperial army back to Germany. In April 984, the antipope Boniface VII rode into Rome at the head of an army hired with Byzantine gold. John was thrown into prison and, four months later, he was dead from starvation—the second pope murdered by Boniface. Boniface held sway in Rome for the next 11 months. He died on 20 July, 985, whereupon his body was dragged through the streets of Rome, tied to the statue of the emperor Marcus Aurelius, and brutally mutilated by the mob before being thrown into an unmarked grave.

976	978	979	981	984
The Byzantine coemperor John I Tzimisces dies. The emperor Basil II, now 20, will reign alone until 1025.	The book *Taiping Guangji* is completed in China. The 500 volume book contains 3 million Chinese characters and is composed of about 7,000 stories and anecdotes of Chinese history and mythology.	The city of Brussels is founded as a fortress on an island in the Senne River.	Viking Eric the Red discovers Greenland, then enjoying a much warmer climate than it does today, and leads settlers to the new land.	Chinese engineer Qiao Wei builds the first pound lock on the Grand Canal, allowing boats to move between different water levels more safely.

JOHN XV ✠ The 137th Pope 985–996

Born Rome, Italy; date unknown

Parents Father, Leo; Mother, unknown

Papacy August 985–March 996

Died Rome, Italy; March 996

The powerful Crescenti family took advantage of the imperial absence following the death of Otto II to arrange matters in Rome to their satisfaction. John Crescentius, the head of the family, took the title of patrician of Rome and chose the cardinal priest John of San Vitale to be pope.

John was highly respected within the papal curia and enjoyed a reputation for learning. Nevertheless, he turned out to be greedy both for money and for positions for his own family and the Crescenti. Within only a few weeks of becoming pope, he had fallen out with his own curia and with many churchmen. Despite this, John proved to be a competent pope in his dealings with the Church outside Rome. In January 993, he held a synod that formally canonized Ulrich of Augsburg—after which the papacy would gradually acquire the exclusive right to declare a person to be a saint.

The main action of John's reign was a dispute with the French bishops. Although the point at issue was who should be archbishop of Reims, the real issue was papal authority over the French Church. In 991, King Hugh Capet of France summoned a synod that ousted Archbishop Arnoul of Reims after he had supported the rebellion of Charles of Lorraine. John objected that he alone had the right to dismiss an archbishop, whereupon the French bishops met at Chelles to declare that they had every right to decide matters relating to the French Church without consulting the pope. Not until 995, at the Synod of Mouzon, did John persuade the French to reinstate Arnoul.

Meanwhile, John Crescentius had died and been replaced as patrician of Rome by his brother Crescentius. The new ruler sought to impose his will on ecclesiastical as well as secular matters. John appealed to Emperor Otto III. Otto replied he was on his way, whereupon Crescentius backed down. John died of a fever soon after, sometime in March 996.

CLUNIAC REFORMS

The great abbey of Cluny in Burgundy led a wave of reforms that swept across Europe during the tenth and eleventh centuries. The monks of Cluny devoted themselves to prayer, study, and worship to the exclusion of the manual labor favored by other, older houses. Cluny had beautifully trained choirs, elegantly appointed churches, and fine regalia. The monks of Cluny were able to specialize in ritual and academic activities by hiring staff to do the work in the fields and run the estates on their behalf. This shift meant that Cluny, and the monasteries that followed its lead, were able to attract monks born into noble families who were thus assured of a gentle life once they had taken holy orders. This in turn brought more money to the abbey, allowing the monks to dine on fine food and wear sumptuous clothes.

The Basilica of San Vitale in Rome was built in 400 and consecrated by Pope Innocent I.

986	986	987	988
Al Mansur, Muslim ruler of southern Spain, continues his efforts to conquer the Christian states of Spain by sacking Coimbra, Barcelona, and Leon.	Viking Bjarnni Herjolfsson becomes the first European to sight North America, but he does not land.	Louis V of the Franks dies in May. His death ends the Carolingian dynasty founded by Charlemagne in 800. Hugh Capet comes to power and founds the Capetian dynasty.	Dublin, Ireland, is founded by Viking settlers.

GREGORY V ✢ The 138th Pope 996–999

Born Saxony, Germany; c.972

Parents Father, Duke Otto of Carinthia; Mother, unknown

Papacy May 3, 996–February 18, 999

Died Rome, Italy; February 18, 999

The death of Pope John XV did not deter Emperor Otto III from marching on Rome (*see* opposite). Patrician Crescentius sent messengers to meet Otto and promise abject surrender. Otto chose as his price that the Romans had to elect as pope his cousin Bruno of Saxony.

Bruno was not unworthy of his promotion, being a priest of learning and ability. He hurried to Rome where he was formally elected, and chose the name of Gregory V in tribute to Gregory the Great whom he admired. Otto followed him to Rome and, on May 21, was crowned emperor in St. Peter's, also taking the title of patrician formerly used by Crescentius. By June, Otto was finding the heat of Rome to be oppressive, so he returned to Germany.

In October, Crescentius struck. He led a rebellion of the Romans who were resentful of having a German pope foisted on them. Gregory was driven out of Rome having been stripped of everything except his shirt. He fled to Spoleto where he was given sanctuary. The Duke of Spoleto mustered his army but was unable to capture Rome, so Gregory appealed to Otto. Crescentius, meanwhile, declared the papacy to be vacant and organized a fresh election that installed John XVI. Crescentius took up his former position as patrician with the active support of the Byzantine envoy Leo.

In February 997, Gregory held a synod in Pavia at which he excommunicated Crescentius. It was another year before Otto III could lead an army over the Alps and march on Rome. Otto and Gregory arrived to find the gates of Rome thrown open to them. Crescentius was holed up in the Castel Sant'Angelo with his men, while John had vanished. John was later found hiding in a castle nearby—he was blinded and had his ears and nose cut off before being brought to Rome for trial. Crescentius was not given a trial. When his men surrendered the fortress, he was hanged from the battlements. Gregory then held a synod that declared John deposed and sentenced him to be imprisoned in a monastery.

Firmly installed as pope, Gregory turned to the matter of his authority over the French bishops, which had been left unresolved by John XV. He suspended from office those bishops who had defied John and restored Arnoul as archbishop of Reims. Next, Gregory moved against King Robert II of France who he blamed for the whole affair. Robert had married his cousin Bertha without seeking papal dispensation. Gregory ordered Robert to give up Bertha and, when the king refused, excommunicated him. The dispute was still ongoing when Gregory died of a fever.

ANTIPOPE JOHN XVI

Although a Greek from southern Italy, John was well known to Otto III having been the emperor's childhood tutor. It is likely the Roman nobles, led by Crescentius, elected John in the hope that he would prove acceptable to Otto, though why John accepted elevation to the papacy is unclear. When Otto began his march on Rome, John announced his abdication and fled. After his brutal deposition, John was sent to live in a Roman monastery where he died in 1001.

991
Battle of Maldon sees the English defeated by the Vikings marking the start of renewed Viking raids on England.

996
Niujie Mosque is built in Beijin to serve as center of worship for the growing community of Muslim merchants resident in the Chinese city.

997
The first Christian Magyar duke, Geza, dies and is succeeded by his son Stephen I.

998
St. Volodimir of Rus ritually baptizes his entire kingdom into the Christian faith.

SYLVESTER II ✠ The 139th Pope 999–1003

Born Auvergne, France; c.945
Parents Unknown
Papacy April 2, 999–May 12, 1003
Died Rome, Italy; May 12, 1003

Sylvester II was one of the most intellectually gifted men ever to become pope. So wide-ranging were his interests and so spectacular his career that a later legend credited his gifts to a pact with a female demon. It was because of his distinguished career that Sylvester was chosen to be pope, after which his time in Rome came as something of an anticlimax.

Illustration depicting Pope Sylvester II making a pact with Satan.

Statue of Pope Sylvester in his native Auvergne, France.

Gerbert of Aurillac came from a very poor family but his intelligence was obvious from a young age so he was sent to the monastery of St. Gerald at Aurillac to be educated. When Gerbert was in his early 20s, the monastery was visited by Count Borrell II of Barcelona, who took Gerbert home with him so that he could study mathematics in Spain and come into contact with Arabic learning on the subject.

In Spain, Gerbert came under the care of Bishop Atto of Vic and spent time at the Monastery of Santa Maria de Ripoli. In about 970, Atto was sent by Borrell on a diplomatic mission to Cordoba where he met Al-Hakam II and was given freedom to meet local scholars and scientists, as well as the local Christian bishop who dressed like an Arab and spoke Arabic. Atto returned laden with books and treatises that he passed on to Gerbert. Gerbert had meanwhile visited Rome with Borell. He met John XIII and Emperor Otto I.

In 972, Gerbert moved to Reims at the invitation of Archbishop Adalbero. Gerbert intended to study but soon found himself teaching and then became head of the school at Reims. In 980, he went on a visit to the court of Emperor Otto II and was asked to debate with Otric, head of the cathedral school at Magdeburg. So impressed was the emperor that he invited Gerbert to become Abbot of Bobbio, a large abbey near Genoa. Bobbio was to prove to be a rare failure. He ran into massive administrative problems made worse by the resentment of many Genoans that a foreigner was made abbot of their prime monastery. In 984, he gave up and went back to Reims.

When King Louis V of France died childless, the Carolingian line went extinct. The nobles of France met in a great assembly to elect a new king, and Gerbert joined with his bishop Adalbero in lobbying for Hugh Capet, duke of the Franks and a wealthy landowner in northern France. Hugh was descended from Charlemagne by his paternal grandmother, and from the

999

The Faroe Islands are converted to Christianity by Sigmundur Brestisson, who threatened to behead any pagan who did not convert immediately.

1000

Viking explorer Leif Ericson becomes the first European to land in North America, though the site of his landing is now uncertain.

1000

Death of Hrotsvitha, Saxon nun, poetess, and playwright who is thought to have been the first person in Europe to write a play for 600 years.

1000

The Indian mathematician Sridhara recognizes the importance of the zero.

Gerbert wrote extensively about the armillary sphere, which he used to study the Earth as well as the heavens. His calculation of the position of the equator was exact, while he worked out the Tropic of Cancer to within a degree and the Polar Circle to within three degrees.

Ottonian dynasty through his mother. He was a capable administrator and famed soldier. Hugh was duly elected, founding the Capetian dynasty that would rule France until 1328.

Two years later, Archbishop Adalbero died and it was expected Gerbert would succeed him. Instead, King Hugh chose Arnaul, the illegitimate son of Louis V. When Arnaul was caught plotting with rebels against Hugh, the king summoned a synod that ousted him and installed Gerbert instead. That led to a wrangle with Pope John XV (*see* p.118) over who had the authority to depose and appoint archbishops. In the end, Gerbert was excluded from Reims so he moved to the imperial court, becoming an adviser to Emperor Otto III.

In 998, Otto made Gerbert archbishop of Ravenna, but when Pope Gregory V died a greater prize was on offer. Otto sent word to Rome that he wanted Gerbert elected pope, and the electors obediently did as told. Like Gregory before him, Gerbert decided to change his name in honor of a past pope who he admired. In Gerbert's case, he chose the name Sylvester to honor Sylvester I who had been an adviser to Emperor Constantine the Great.

Sylvester's first move came as something of a surprise. He changed his position on who could appoint, or invest, archbishops. When a candidate for Reims, he had argued that the king had the right to invest; now, he argued that the papacy had the exclusive right and used it to confirm Arnaul in position. In other matters he worked closely with Otto to extend and encourage monastic reforms. In particular, he was keen that monks of a monastery should be free to elect whoever they wanted as abbot. This move set him at odds with many noble families who had donated lands to found or enlarge a monastery on condition that they would choose the abbot. Sylvester also promoted celibacy among the priesthood, something that had been accepted in Rome for centuries but was not widely practiced in northern Europe.

Successful as Sylvester was in dealings outside of Rome, he failed to understand the nuances of the political situation in Rome and the Papal States. Unfortunately for Sylvester, a master of local politics and intrigue was John Crescentius II, son of the Crescentius who had been hanged from the battlements of Castel Sant'Angelo by Otto III. In February 1001, John Crescentius led a rebellion of local nobles that took Sylvester completely by surprise.

Sylvester fled from Rome, asking Otto to come to his aid. The emperor mustered an army at Ravenna and marched south, but before he could reach Rome he fell ill with a fever, probably malaria, and died. Otto was only 21 when he died and had no children. No less than four cousins put themselves forward as his heir, and the Germans had no time to interfere in Italian or Church matters. Sylvester therefore accepted the invitation of John Crescentius to return to Rome as pope, but on the understanding that he would busy himself with ecclesiastical matters only and leave the secular business of running the Papal States to the nobles. Thus did Sylvester spend the rest of his life.

POPE AND SCIENTIST

Before he became Pope Sylvester, Gerbert of Aurillac immersed himself in the wealth of learning from Arab Spain. He used this knowledge to write works on arithmetic, music, geometry, and astronomy that were widely circulated in Europe. He is thought to have written a description of the astrolabe, though this survives only in an anonymous copy. He was also instrumental in popularizing the use of the abacus in Europe. It was much quicker to use the abacus for calculations than cumbersome roman numerals, so within a century of Gerbert adopting it the abacus was widespread across Europe.

1002

The Holy Roman emperor Otto III dies on January 23, aged just 21. He is succeeded as king of the Franks and Bavarians by his cousin Henry, duke of Bavaria.

1002

Danish settlers in England are massacred on St. Brice's Day by order of Ethelred II.

1003

The Viking king Sweyn Forkbeard plunders the English coast in retaliation for the massacre of Danish settlers. The raids will continue almost annually until 1014.

JOHN XVII  The 140th Pope 1003

Born Rome, Italy; date unknown

Parents Father, John Sicco; Mother, unknown

Papacy May 16, 1003–November 6, 1003

Died Rome, Italy; November 6, 1003

Nothing is recorded of the election of John, who had been bishop of Praeneste, though it is assumed that some form of election was held under the watchful eye of the Roman patrician John Crescentius.

John was given the name of John XVII because the Romans at this time held John XVI, who had been put into office by John Crescentius's father, to be a legitimate pope.

As pope, John received a message from Bruno of Querfurt, a missionary in Eastern Europe in the lands of the Kievian Rus. Bruno asked the pope to authorize his companion Benedict to go among the pagan Slavs to convert them to Christianity. John agreed, but it was to prove to be a controversial move since missionaries from Constantinople were already at work. The disputes between Eastern and Western missions would turn violent, with Bruno himself being beheaded in 1009.

Back in Rome, John heard that Otto III's cousin Duke Henry of Bavaria had been crowned king of Germany. John wanted to send a diplomatic message of congratulations, but John Crescentius stepped in to block the move. A few weeks later John XVII died in circumstances that are unclear.

JOHN XVIII The 141st Pope 1003–1009

Born Rapagnano, Italy; date unknown

Parents Father, Leo or Ursus; Mother, Stephania

Papacy December 25, 1003–probably June, 1009

Died Rome, Italy; possibly July 1009

John XVIII was a cardinal priest when elected as pope. His actions show him to be a pope concerned both to foster the reform movement based at Cluny Abbey and to ensure proper conduct by senior clerics.

John's first known act was the restoration of the bishopric of Merseburg in 1004. Also in Germany, John founded the see of Bemberg to act as a missionary center for German monks heading into pagan Eastern Europe—a project dear to the new King Henry II of Germany.

When, in 1007, news reached Rome of a dispute between the abbot of Fleury and the bishops of Orleans and Sens, John reacted strongly. He summoned the two bishops to come to Rome immediately to explain their behavior. When they refused, John sent word to King Robert II of France that unless he forced the bishops either to give way on the dispute or to travel to Rome he would place a ban on France so that no church services could take place.

In the summer of 1009, John became a monk and withdrew into the Basilica of St. Paul Outside the Walls. This was a normal way for a ruler to abdicate. Whether John did so voluntarily is not known, neither is it known for sure how long he lived afterward.

1003	1005	1007	1008	1010
King Stephen of Hungary conquers Transylvania and orders the inhabitants to become Christians.	Brian Boru, high king of Ireland, recognizes the bishop of Armagh as the successor to St. Patrick and grants Armagh supremacy over all other bishops in Ireland.	The city of Shanghai is founded in China.	Domiyat of Cairo is sent to travel by sea to China to open direct trading links between the Fatimid Caliphs and the Song emperors.	Monk Elmer of Malmesbury, England, built a wooden and cloth glider in which he leapt from the monastery tower and glided over 200 metres before crashing and breaking both his legs.

SERGIUS IV ✠ The 142nd Pope 1009–1012

Born Rome, Italy; date unknown

Parents Father, Peter; Mother, unknown

Papacy July 31, 1009–May 12, 1012

Died Rome, Italy; May 12, 1012

Bishop Peter of Albano was known as Buccaporci, meaning "pig-snout," doubtless a reference to his looks. He changed his name to Sergius out of respect for St. Peter rather than as a tribute to an earlier Sergius.

Sergius's first act was to send an announcement of his election to the patriarch of Constantinople. One version of events states that Sergius made a reference to the "filioque" clause of the Nicene Creed considered invalid in Constantinople, thus he is held to have reopened the dispute.

In the autumn of 1009, the Muslim Caliph of Cairo, Al-Hakim, ordered the total destruction of the Church of the Holy Sepulchre in Jerusalem, which marked where Christ had been buried. The destruction was so complete that even the foundations were dug up and the stone carted off for use elsewhere. The act caused shock and anger throughout Christendom. The immediate reaction of Sergius was to try to put together a league of Italian Christian states to drive the Muslims out of Sicily, though the campaign was not totally successful.

Sergius died during a series of riots as the nobles of the Crescenti and Tusculum fought for control of the Papal States, but it is unknown if he was murdered or died of natural causes.

BENEDICT VIII  The 143rd Pope 1012–1024

Born Probably Tusculum; date unknown

Parents Count Gregory of Tusculum; Mother, unknown

Papacy May 18, 1012–April 9, 1024

Died Rome, Italy; April 9, 1024

In the spring of 1012, a bloody power struggle erupted in the Papal States. Out of the chaos, Alberic emerged as head of the Tusculum family, while his brother Theophylact became Pope Benedict VIII.

Benedict's first concern was to aid his brothers in securing a firm grip on power. He then turned his attention to gaining the support of King Henry II of Germany by confirming the privileges of the bishop of Bamberg and appointing Henry's brother Arnold as archbishop of Ravenna. Benedict also accepted various features of the reforming movement centered on the Abbey of Cluny, including that the creed should be sung at mass and that minimum ages be introduced for the holding of Church offices. In February 1014, Henry II came to Rome to be crowned Holy Roman emperor.

Benedict then formed an alliance with Pisa and Genoa, crushing Saracen naval power and liberating Sardinia from Muslim rule. Having imposed papal rule in disputed areas of Tuscany and Campagna, Benedict set about encouraging Norman adventurers who were carving out territories for themselves in southern Italy at the expense of the Saracens and Byzantines. In 1022, Henry returned to Italy to aid the pope.

1011

Egyptian scholar Ibn al-Haytham starts work on his influential *Book of Optics*, which revolutionized the study of light.

1013

The Muslim rulers of southern Spain expel all Jews from their lands.

1020

Construction of the Kandariya Mahadeva Temple is completed in India. At the time it is the largest Hindu temple in the world.

JOHN XIX ✠ The 144th Pope 1024–1032

Born probably Tusculum, Italy; date unknown

Parents Father, Count Gregory of Tusculum; Mother, unknown

Papacy April 19, 1024–October 20, 1032

Died Rome, Italy; October 20, 1032

When Benedict VIII died, his younger brother Romanus, head of the secular government of the Papal States, took his place. The fact that he was not a clergyman and therefore ineligible to stand was brushed aside by his being consecrated a priest after he had won, but before he was enthroned.

Romanus adopted the name of John. Given his entirely secular background, it is not surprising that he proved to have a better grasp of the politics of the papacy than of its spiritual side. This was shown when, within months of taking office, he received a delegation from Patriarch Eustatius of Constantinople. The Byzantines bore lavish gifts for the pope and asked for papal approval for Eustatius to use the title ecumenical patriarch. John was eager for Byzantine help against the Saracens as much as he was to pocket the gifts, so he agreed.

However, other churchmen knew that this was a dangerous title as it implied that the patriarch of Constantinople had absolute authority over all Christians in the Eastern Mediterranean and was of an equal rank to the pope. The protests were loudest from the reformers following the Cluniac program (*see* p.118), which was supported by Holy Roman Emperor Henry II. John changed his mind but kept the gifts, and thus earned the enmity of the Church in Constantinople.

A more straightforward political decision came in 1024 when Henry II of Germany died without a son. The German nobles met quickly and elected Count Conrad of Speyer to be the next king of Germany. Henry's titles of king of Italy and Holy Roman emperor both lay vacant, and John had to decide who to support. The Italian nobles were divided over whether to elect Conrad, or Duke William of Aquitaine. John backed Conrad and instructed all the Italian bishops to do likewise. In the spring of 1026, Conrad was elected and crowned king of Italy in Milan. Conrad then moved south to Rome where John crowned him Holy Roman emperor. It is notable that the earlier agreements of the emperor to protect the Holy See and of the pope to bear fealty to the emperor were not renewed. John proved to be keen to ingratiate himself with Conrad. In April 1027, he obediently issued a bull that raised the archbishop of Aquileia to the rank of patriarch and gave him authority over all the bishops of Italy, saving the bishop of Rome. The move was made as the then archbishop of Aquileia was Poppo, a close friend of Conrad's.

A later account suggests that John was killed when he got caught up in a riot of peasants angered by harsh taxes in the Papal States but the cause of his death is not known for certain.

PETER'S PENCE

When King Cnut of England visited Rome in 1027, an agreement was reached by which papal demands on various monasteries and bishoprics in England would be abandoned in return for "Peter's Pence," a tax of one penny levied on every household in the kingdom on August 1 each year. The tax continued to be paid until the Reformation split England from Rome in 1555.

1024	1026	1028	1031	1034	1035
The Holy Roman emperor Henry II dies, aged 51. He is succeeded by his son Conrad II.	King Cnut of England, Denmark, and Norway begins a pilgrimage to Rome.	The Byzantine emperor Constantine VIII dies, aged 68. Romanus III becomes emperor.	France's Capetian king Robert the Pious dies, aged 61. He is succeeded by his son, who will reign until 1060 as Henry I.	The Pisans capture the port of Annaba in what is now Algeria, the first Christian toehold in Africa for centuries. They hold it for only one year.	Death of Cnut, king of England, Norway, Sweden, and Denmark. After his death his empire splits up.

BENEDICT IX ✦ The 145th Pope 1032–1044

Born probably Tusculum; c.1010

Parents Count Alberic III of Tusculum; Mother, unknown

Papacy October 21, 1032–September 1044 (first term)

Died Grottaferrata, Italy; perhaps 1055

Like Benedict VIII and John XIX, Benedict came from the powerful Tusculum family who ruled the Papal States with an iron hand. The two previous popes had been brothers of Count Alberic III but both died childless so Alberic chose his own son Theophylact to be the next pope.

The youth was aged about 20 and had already been involved in a number of fights, seductions, and alleged rapes as well as extended bouts of heavy drinking and alleged homosexual affairs. Theophylact had no real interest in the papacy, and took the job on only because his father told him to do so. No details have survived of his election, which was organized and no doubt controlled by Count Alberic. His first recorded act as Pope Benedict IX was to hold a drunken party in the Lateran Palace to which some notoriously immoral women were invited.

Benedict was soon confronted by one of the most unusual problems ever to face a pope when certain clerics began preaching that the end of the world was about to arrive. The fear of apocalypse affected not only the clerics, but also the peasants—who already faced famine due to severe weather— and the nobles who ruled them. There was a wave of penitential processions, religious devotion, and mass confessions of sin. In places, the clamor for salvation led to work in the fields being neglected, making only more certain the likely famine. Benedict was called upon to calm nerves, which he did by issuing explanations and exhortations. That, together with the onset of better weather, calmed nerves. The passing of Easter and the anniversary of the Crucifixion without the Earth being destroyed ended the panic.

Benedict proved to be entirely orthodox in his religious policies—perhaps because he left the real work to his curia—and astute in politics.

"A DEMON FROM HELL"

Benedict's contemporary St. Peter Damian of Ravenna wrote that he "feasted on immorality," and Bishop Benno of Piacenza recorded him guilty of "many vile adulteries and murders." The future Pope Victor III, who was in Rome at the time, wrote "...his rapes, murders, and other unspeakable acts. His life as a pope so vile, so foul, so execrable, that I shudder to think of it." Later historians were even less restrained with Ferdinand Gregorovius writing "a demon from hell in the disguise of a priest...occupied the chair of Peter."

In 1037, the Holy Roman emperor Conrad II deposed Archbishop Aribert of Milan who had provoked a rebellion in northern Italy. Benedict did not meekly do as instructed but insisted on investigating the matter first. Nearly a year passed before he announced he would excommunicate Aribert.

In September 1044, a minor incident led to major rioting as mobs rampaged through Rome. The anger of the crowd turned against Benedict, accused of incompetence and greed as well as his established vices of drinking and debauchery. Caught by surprise and with no more wish to become a martyr than he had had to become celibate, Benedict fled from Rome.

Fear of the approaching apocalypse was based on a reading of the Book of Revelations that seemed to promise the Second Coming of Christ would take place a thousand years after His Crucifixion—an event dated to the year 33. The savage winter of 1032/33 only added to the panic.

1036

Muslim Zirid dynasty seeks to establish control of Sicily, but Norman adventurers and local Christians resist them in the early stages of a long war for control of the island.

1039

Foundation of the Abbey of Bec, later to be one of the most influential in northern Europe.

1040

The Weihenstephan Brewery first brews beer—as it has done ever since, making this the oldest brewery in the world.

1042

Edward the Confessor becomes king of England.

SYLVESTER III ✣ The 146th Pope 1045

Born Rome, Italy; c.1000
Parents Unknown
Papacy January 20, 1045–March 10, 1045
Died Sabina, Italy; probably 1063

The man who emerged as pope from the riots of 1044 was the saintly and entirely unambitious Bishop John of Sabina. His surname of Crescenti-Ottaviani shows that he was a member of the powerful Crescenti family, who had controlled the papacy for decades until 1012.

When riots broke out in Rome in 1044, and the mob turned against Benedict IX of the Tusculum family, the rival Crescenti family saw its chance. The Crescenti had its powerbase in the Sabine Hills north of Rome and between 965 and 1012 had ruled Rome and the Papal States. They had been badly depleted in the civil war that engulfed Rome and led to the death of Sergius II, but had not been destroyed entirely. While they had gone along with the rule of the Tusculum family, they had neither forgotten their ambition nor their previous status.

Forming rapid alliances with other local noble families, the Crescenti called a synod of Roman clergy that declared Benedict IX to be deposed. It was some months before order could be restored to Rome and deals done between the various factions but, finally, in January 1045, an election was held to produce a new pope. John had his cathedral seat in Fara Sabina, a small town in the Sabine Hills near Rieti that, in 1006, had been fortified by the addition of an immensely strong castle. His ambition seems to have been limited to the bishopric of Sabina and to leading a quiet, holy life in his diocese. He seems to have been chosen partly for his saintly reputation and partly because he was the only cleric acceptable to the various factions involved in deposing Benedict IX. John adopted the name of Sylvester III, apparently in tribute to Sylvester I. He moved into the Lateran Palace and began clearing up the mess left by Benedict.

No sooner was Sylvester in his new home, however, than word came from Trastevere, downriver on the Tiber from Rome. Benedict IX was back, protected by the armed might of the Tusculum and in no mood to compromise. In February, Benedict announced that he had excommunicated Sylvester. On March 10, having first conducted a diplomatic drive to detach allies from the Crescenti, the Tusculum family struck. Benedict dressed himself in his full papal regalia and led the Tusculum army on a march on Rome. The gates of the city were thrown open and Benedict arrived in triumph, as Sylvester fled back to Fara Sabina and resumed his duties as bishop of Sabina. Although driven from power in Rome, the Crescenti retained their lands and castles in the Sabine Hills. Their military strength meant that Benedict's revenge could not touch Sylvester.

In December 1046, the Synod of Sutri (*see* p.128) declared that Sylvester should become a monk and be unfrocked as a priest, which would have made him ineligible to continue as bishop of Sabina but the sentence was never enforced. It is thought that his successors as pope were content to leave Sylvester to his diocese since he was quite obviously not a threat, having not wanted to become pope in the first place.

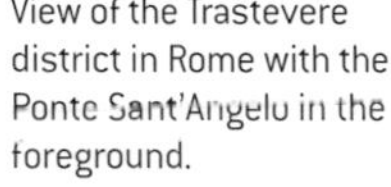

View of the Trastevere district in Rome with the Ponte Sant'Angelo in the foreground.

1045

St. Sigfrid of Sweden dies. A Benedictine monk and bishop, Sigfrid converted King Olof Skötkonung of Sweden to Christianity in 1008.

1045

The Japanese emperor Go-Suzaku dies, aged 36, after a nine-year reign. He is succeeded by his 16-year-old son who will reign until 1068 as the emperor Go-Reizei.

1045

The Lingxiao Pagoda of China is built during the Song Dynasty.

1045

Moveable type printing is developed by Chinese printer Bi Sheng, who used porcelain squares for his type.

BENEDICT IX ✠ The 147th Pope 1045

Born probably Tusculum; c.1010

Parents Count Alberic III of Tusculum; Mother, unknown

Papacy March 10, 1045 to May 1, 1045 (second term)

Died Grottaferrata, Italy; perhaps 1055

In March 1045, the young Pope Benedict IX did his duty by his family by leading their army into Rome and ousting Sylvester III (*see* p.126). In so doing, he introduced one of the more contentious episodes in the Papal Apostolic Succession—the events of 1045 left a rather unholy mess.

Having regained the papacy, Benedict IX then focused all his energy on ridding himself of the title. All he was concerned about in the spring of 1045 was that he had fallen in love and wanted to get married. As pope, he was vowed to chastity, making marriage impossible. He was consequently keen to stop being pope as soon as he could. For several weeks after his return to Rome, Benedict willingly did the business of his family, signing decrees and other acts as instructed.

At some point in April, however, Benedict went to see his godfather, John Gratian, who was priest of the Basilica of St. John by the Latin Gate. Benedict asked if there was a legal way in which he could abdicate. John was a reformist clergyman and, although closely allied to the Tusculum faction, had never approved of the dissolute Benedict being pope. He advised that Benedict could stand down either by becoming a monk or by signing a formal document renouncing his position as pope. Benedict had no wish to become a monk so he opted for the document.

Benedict then raised a difficulty—his only source of income was the papacy. In his hoped-for status as a married nobleman, Benedict would need money. What followed next is unclear, probably because those involved chose to keep the details hidden. The most reasonable reading of available evidence is that Benedict wanted to keep hold of certain papal lands to give him an income once he had stood down. This was a controversial theological and political issue. One reason why the Cluniac reformers (*see* p.118) were firmly in favor of clerical celibacy was that married bishops and priests had used their positions to grant lands and wealth belonging to the Church to their children. For the pope now to give a lead in precisely this sin was out of the question. Instead, Benedict was paid a huge sum in cash to stand down. Those paying the money wanted something in return, and that something was control of the papacy.

TWO-TIME POPE

It has generally been held that a man continues to be pope until either his death or his abdication, since no earthly power can judge the Holy See so, strictly speaking, Sylvester's election was invalid and he was technically a usurper, or antipope. However, Sylvester was of undeniably saintly temperament and it appeared that everyone had acted in good faith because it was only after Sylvester III was elected that Benedict send a message to Rome saying that he did not accept his own deposition and that he considered himself to still be pope. For this reason, the official view of the Catholic Church is that Benedict ceased to be pope when he was deposed, that Sylvester became pope when he was elected and then ceased to be pope when he was in turn deposed, at which point Benedict became pope again. Benedict IX is thus unique in papal records for having legitimately become pope twice.

1045

King Edward the Confessor of England begins the building of Westminster Abbey on an island in marshes beside the Thames to the west of London.

1045

Death of Count Radbot of Habsburg, founder of the Habsburg dynasty that would later come to dominate European politics.

GREGORY VI ✠ The 148th Pope 1045–1046

Born Rome, Italy; date unknown

Parents Father, unknown; Mother, unknown

Papacy May 1, 1045–December 20, 1046

Died Cologne, Germany; probably November 1047

Count Alberic III used his immense influence to ensure that the priest John Gratian succeeded Benedict IX. At the election there was a call from the crowd that John adopt the name Gregory—after the antipope who, in 1012, had been the nominee of the Crescenti, Alberic's bitter rivals.

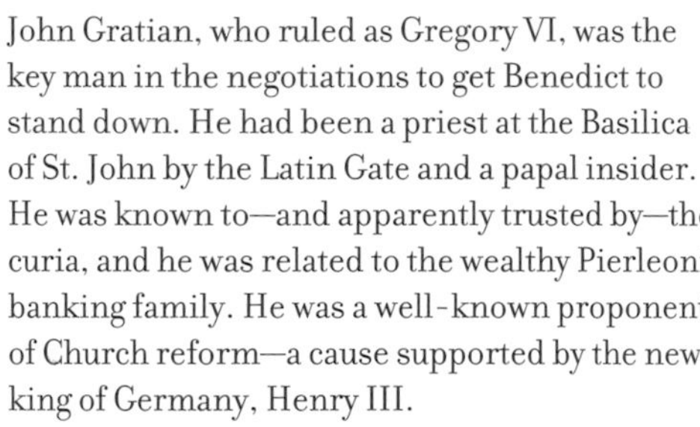

John Gratian, who ruled as Gregory VI, was the key man in the negotiations to get Benedict to stand down. He had been a priest at the Basilica of St. John by the Latin Gate and a papal insider. He was known to—and apparently trusted by—the curia, and he was related to the wealthy Pierleoni banking family. He was a well-known proponent of Church reform—a cause supported by the new king of Germany, Henry III.

When he arrived in the Lateran Palace, Gregory found that the papacy was in a mess. Despite the huge income from the Papal States, lands owned in other countries, and assorted bequests and legacies, the papacy was effectively bankrupt. Gregory was lucky to find among the many clerks in the curia a young man named Hildebrand Bonizi. A blacksmith's son from Sovana in Tuscany, Hildebrand had shown remarkable intelligence at a young age and so had been educated by the local nobility. By 1045, he was a senior financial clerk in the curia. Together, Gregory and Hildebrand set about reforming the papal finances and repairing the years of plundering.

Henry III of Germany before Tivoli in a fifteenth-century manuscript.

Gregory also made a start on supporting the reformers based at Cluny and other monasteries. This won him instant acclaim in all quarters and seemed to set the papacy on a course that would take it away from the control of local nobles. By the late summer, Gregory was being talked about as the best pope for decades. King Henry III of Germany chose this moment to come to Italy to be crowned as Holy Roman emperor.

Sutri, some 50 miles from Rome, provided the venue for Henry III's second synod in December 1045.

As soon as he was over the Alps, Henry began hearing about the murky arrangement by which Benedict had been bribed to abdicate and the financial mess of the papacy. At Pavia, Henry summoned a synod which, among other things, condemned the sin of simony. Gregory hurried north to welcome Henry and the two men got on well. Nevertheless, Henry summoned a second synod to meet on December 20 at Sutri. He summoned not only Gregory VI, but also Sylvester III and Benedict IX. Benedict did not show up. Sylvester did arrive and was promptly told that he was no longer pope. Gregory was then accused of having paid to become pope. In vain did he explain that he had merely contributed to the fund to persuade Benedict to stand aside but that his actual election had been fair. He too was deposed. Henry sent Gregory north to Cologne to live in comfortable house arrest until his death.

1046

Munjong is crowned 11th king of Goryeo (Korea).

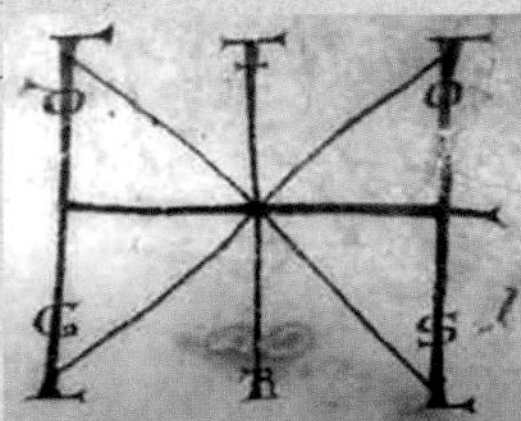

1046

The German king is crowned Holy Roman Emperor Henry III on Christmas Day at Rome by the bishop of Bemberg who he has installed as Pope Clement II.

1046

Pagan backlash in Hungary leads to rioting and the murder of leading Christian missionaries, including St. Gerard Sagredo.

1046

Death of Bishop Oliba of Vic, leading cleric of the Church reform movement in Spain and tireless champion of peace between the Christian rulers in Spain.

Born Homburg, Germany; date unknown

Parents Father, Count Konrad of Morsleben and Hornburg; Mother, Amulrad

Papacy December 24, 1046–October 9, 1047

Died Pesaro, Italy; October 9, 1047

CLEMENT II ✦ The 149th Pope 1046–1047

Bishop Suidger of Bamberg was elected unanimously and took the name Clement II. He was enthroned on Christmas Day and then crowned Henry III as Holy Roman emperor and appointed him patrician of Rome—the title used by the Crescenti and Tusculums to control the city.

The many years of determination by successive popes to assert the primacy of the Holy See of Rome over all others in Christendom meant that the pope could appoint or depose bishops, abbots, archbishops, and others at will. His rulings on matters of doctrine were highly regarded and were usually followed. These powers were not only over ecclesiastical matters, but also impinged on secular concerns right across Europe. By the middle of the eleventh century, the position of the pope had become simply too important to be left to the Romans. Who was pope and how he conducted himself was a matter for all of Western Christendom.

As the most important and powerful secular ruler in Europe, the Holy Roman emperor had more reason than most to be concerned about who was pope and how they behaved. It was for this reason that Henry III had held the Synod of Sutri, in December 1046, which deposed Gregory VI, Sylvester III, and Benedict IX and replaced them with the man who was a friend and confidant and shared his enthusiasm for reform of the Christian Church.

Pope and emperor then set out to impose their authority on southern Italy, with general success though Benevento refused to submit. Back in Rome by the end of February, Clement began the process of reform. He ordered that all bishops had to be investigated in case they had been guilty of simony. Then followed a string of letters and instructions to all corners of Europe encouraging the reform movement. He was assiduous in taking advice from Abbot Odilo of Cluny on various matters. Despite this move toward reform, Clement found time for a bit of old-fashioned favoritism and issued a bull confirming all sorts of privileges on the bishopric of Bamberg.

On October 1, Clement was visiting the Abbey of San Tommaso near Pesaro when he fell ill and later died. His body was embalmed and taken north to be buried in Bamberg Cathedral.

GROWING PAPAL POWER

Bishoprics and abbeys were sometimes large-scale landholders. Those estates owed taxes to the local secular rulers, and very often owed feudal dues as well. The most important feudal duty of any large landholder was to go to war as leader of the levies from the estates. Not many bishops wanted to go to war, though some did, and they usually hired somebody to lead on their behalf. But having command of a sizeable body of armed men meant that a bishop or abbot was also a key political player in his home state. Secular rulers had the power to get rid of any troublesome noble and replace him with someone more reliable, but the increasing power of the papacy meant that a ruler was no longer able to oust a churchman he did not like.

1047

Magnus I dies after 12 years as king of Norway and 5 years as king of Denmark. He is succeeded in Norway by Harald III, who will reign until 1066, and in Denmark by Sweyn II, who will reign until 1075.

1047

Battle of Val es Dunes sees Duke William II of Normandy crush the rebels who had opposed his accession to the ducal title.

1047

Harald Hardrada becomes king of Norway.

BENEDICT IX ✥ The 150th Pope 1047–1048

Born probably Tusculum; c.1010

Parents Count Alberic III of Tusculum; Mother, unknown

Papacy November 8, 1047–July 16, 1048 (third term)

Died Grottaferrata, Italy; perhaps 1056

After being paid a huge sum of money to stand down as pope in May 1045, Benedict IX went to live near the rural town of Frascati, then as now famous for its wine. Nestling in the Alban Hills, Frascati was in the heart of the lands of the Tusculum family of which he was a member.

The Abbey of San Nilo in Grottaferrata, Italy—the town in which Benedict died.

In Frascati, Benedict settled down to the married life he had craved, while his godfather became Pope Gregory VI with the support of the Tusculum clan. When King Henry III of Germany marched across the Alps and into Italy to be crowned Holy Roman emperor, Benedict stayed at home reasoning this was a matter for Gregory to deal with. When Henry summoned a synod at Sutri and demanded Benedict attend, the ex-pope again wisely stayed at home being wary of the consequences. He thus avoided being imprisoned as were Gregory and Sylvester. The installation of a new pope, Clement II, also saw Benedict stay in Frascati now hiding behind the troops of his uncle, Count Alberic III of Tusculum.

But when Clement died suddenly in October 1047, it was time for Benedict to make a move. It seems unlikely that he would willingly have given up the wedded bliss for which he had abandoned the papacy only two years earlier. Much more likely is the fact that Count Alberic was behind the move. Whatever the cause, Benedict was greeted with wild enthusiasm when he rode into Rome on November 8, 1047. The Romans had not enjoyed either being told who to elect by an outsider or the experience of being ruled by a German. They were therefore keen to get a pope who was once again one of them. The clergy and people of Rome flocked to the Lateran to hail Benedict as pope, though whether this event counts as a formal election is unclear. In any case, Benedict was now firmly back in power.

It could not last. Emperor Henry sent orders to his representative in Italy, Margrave Boniface III of Tuscany, that Benedict had to be ousted. Boniface was at first reluctant as he was a friend and ally of Count Alberic, and moreover had some sympathy with the view that the bishop of Rome should be a Roman. After further orders arrived, Boniface finally marched into Rome and told Benedict that he had to retire to Frascati. This Benedict did, ignoring a demand from the next pope, Damasus II, that he should go to Rome to stand trial. He likewise ignored the excommunication that Leo IX imposed on him in 1049 and then lifted in 1055. His subsequent fate is unknown, but he was buried in Grottaferrata and is so presumed to have died there and was certainly dead by the time Pope Stephen IX was elected in 1057.

APOSTOLIC SUCCESSION

The primacy of the bishop of Rome is based on the doctrine of Apostolic Succession. The most important bishoprics are those that were founded by an Apostle of Christ: Rome (St. Peter), Constantinople (St. Andrew), Alexandria (St. Mark), Antioch (St. Peter), Jerusalem (St. James the Just), Etchmiadzin (SS. Bartholomew and Jude), Kerala (St. Thomas), Tewahedo (St. Philip), New Justiana (St. Paul), and Kiev (St. Andrew). Rome has long claimed precedence over the others. The colorful career of Benedict IX threatened to disrupt the succession, so papal historians decided that he was legitimately enthroned as pope on three separate occasions keeping the apostolic succession of Rome intact.

1047

The duchies of Carinthia, Bavaria, and Swabia are restored by the Holy Roman emperor Henry III.

1047

Hungary's Peter Orseolo is overthrown by his cousin Andras, who will reign until 1060 as Andrew I.

1047

The rebel general Leo Tornikios proclaims himself Byzantine emperor and besieges Constantinople. His army is repelled by Constantine IX.

DAMASUS II ✠ The 151st Pope 1048

Born Pidenau, Germany; date unknown

Parents Father, unknown; Mother, unknown

Papacy July 17, 1048–August 9, 1048

Died Palestrina, Italy; August 9, 104

Bishop Poppo of Brixen, as Damasus was when elected, was probably a younger son of a Bavarian noble family. As bishop of Brixen in the Tyrol since 1040, Poppo built up a reputation as a man of formidable intelligence and learning, though being rather touchy about his honor.

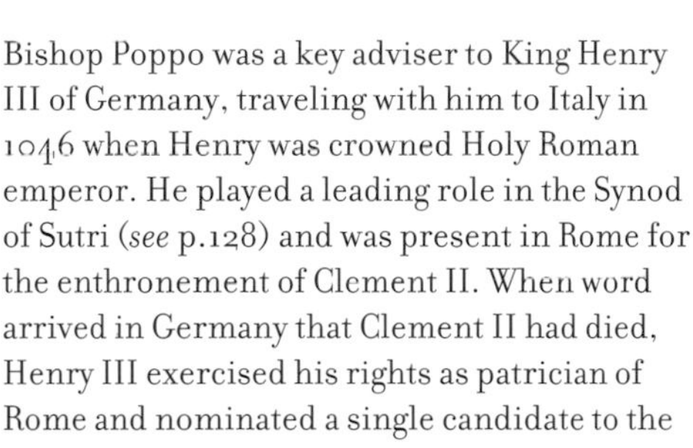

Bishop Poppo was a key adviser to King Henry III of Germany, traveling with him to Italy in 1046 when Henry was crowned Holy Roman emperor. He played a leading role in the Synod of Sutri (*see* p.128) and was present in Rome for the enthronement of Clement II. When word arrived in Germany that Clement II had died, Henry III exercised his rights as patrician of Rome and nominated a single candidate to the Roman clergy for election. After seeking—and ignoring—the advice of Bishop Wazo of Liege, the leading bishop in the Holy Roman Empire, Henry asked Poppo if he would be pope. Poppo agreed and set off with a squad of soldiers and Henry's letter of nomination.

Margrave Boniface III of Tuscany (below) was ordered by Holy Roman Emperor Henry III to march on Rome and secure the bishop of Brixen as the new pope.

Poppo had reached Tuscany when he learned that the former pope Benedict IX had marched into Rome and was back in control of the Lateran Palace. Margrave Boniface III of Tuscany advised Poppo to give up and go home, being in league with Benedict's uncle Count Alberic III of Tusculum. Poppo refused and appealed to Emperor Henry who wrote to Boniface informing him that if he did not march on Rome then an imperial army would come over the Alps to sort things out. Boniface took the none-too-gentle hint that the situation in Rome would not be the only thing to be dealt with by the emperor. He mustered his men for war and took Poppo to Rome. Count Alberic chose to back down and Benedict retired once again to his comfortable home in Frascati.

With the troops of Boniface in the city, the clergy of Rome dutifully elected Poppo on July 17, who thus became yet another German to be elected pope on instruction from the emperor. Poppo took the name of Damasus II, perhaps to honor Damasus I who had encouraged the veneration of martyrs and done much to codify canon law. The first act of Damasus seems to have been to try to get to grips with the appalling state of the papal finances and to understand the febrile state of politics both within the curia and among the nobles of the Papal States. He was hindered in both by a blistering heat wave that struck Rome in later July. Damasus moved, along with as much of the papal court as would make the journey, to Palestrina in the Apennines where the air was cooler. Among those who made the move was Gerhard Brazutus, a member of the financial sector within the curia. Brazutus was a known supporter of Benedict IX and a friend of Hildebrand Bonizi who had moved to Germany with Gregory VI. When Damasus suddenly fell sick with a fever and died, suspicious eyes fell on Brazutus who promptly fled.

1048

City of Oslo is founded by King Harald III of Norway.

1048

King Edward the Confessor of England goes to war against Flanders.

1048

Birth of Omar Khayyám—Persian poet, astronomer, mathematician, and philosopher.

ST. LEO IX ✣ The 152nd Pope 1049–1054

Born Alsace, France; June 21, 1002

Parents Father, Count Hugh of Egisheim; Mother, Heilwig

Papacy February 12, 1049–April 19, 1054

Died Rome, Italy; April 19, 1054

Leo was born Bruno, son of the ruler of the county of Egisheim in what is now the Alsace region of France. As such, he had a privileged upbringing and education in the cathedral school of Toul. In 1025, he took command of the troops from Toul that marched with Conrad II into Italy where Conrad was crowned Holy Roman emperor (*see* p.124).

When Bruno returned to Toul in 1027, he found the bishop had died and that Conrad had appointed him as the replacement. In his new role, Bruno proved to be a relentless reformer, disciplining any clergy who did not follow his lead. This uncompromising stance won him favor with Emperor Henry III who strongly supported the reform agenda.

In early September 1048, messengers came from Italy announcing the death of Damasus II and requesting that Emperor Henry nominate Bishop Halinard of Lyons as the next pope, but Henry wanted Bruno to be pope and summoned a synod. Bruno, wary of the fate of earlier popes forced on an unwilling Rome, stipulated that he would accept only if the Roman clergy and people accepted him willingly.

Before he set out for Rome, Bruno met with Abbot Hugh of Cluny to discuss how best he could use his position as pope to promote the reform agenda. Bruno also collected as part of his entourage Hildebrand Bonizi, the monk who had vainly sought to aid Gregory VI in reforming the finances of the papal curia. Bruno then traveled south and, in February 1049, arrived in Rome on foot and dressed as an ordinary pilgrim—a move designed to emphasize that he came as a penitent sinner before Christ, not as the autocratic agent of an emperor. This act won over the populace and he was unanimously elected as pope, enthroned on February 12, and took the name of Leo IX to emphasize his admiration for the purity of the early Church.

On April 9, Leo summoned a synod to meet where he made a forceful and passionate speech giving his views on reform. He demanded,

THE WARRIOR POPE

When Leo became pope, the Norman adventurers in southern Italy had driven the Muslim Saracens from their strongholds and were preparing to attack the Emirate of Sicily. However, the Normans had also filched lands in southeastern Italy from the Byzantine Empire and were active on the southern borders of the Papal States, staking claims to papal lands. In May 1053, Leo led a papal army into southern Italy to bring the Normans to heel. The Normans were led by Count Humphrey of Apulia, who was appalled at the idea of facing the pope in battle. He sent messages suggesting a number of compromises, but Leo rebuffed him. The armies met at Civitate, near Foggia, on June 18, when Leo's army was crushed. The victorious Count Humphrey threw himself at Leo's feet begging forgiveness. Leo, however, was a prisoner for the next nine months.

Leo's first move as pope was to summon a synod to push forward his reforms. Top of his agenda were the banning of simony and marriage for members of the clergy.

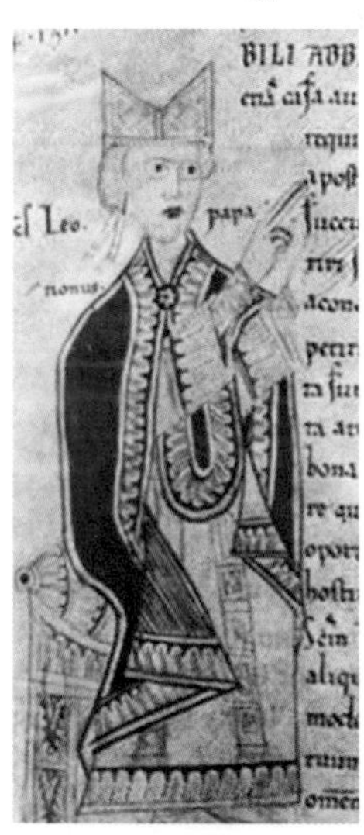

1049
Pisa completes the conquest of Sardinia from the Muslims of southern Spain.

1050
The Byzantine empress Zoë (right) dies, aged 70, and her older sister Theodora is left to rule with the profligate Constantine IX.

1050
The great Viking trading center of Hedeby is destroyed by King Harald Hardrada of Norway during his war with Denmark.

1051
England reaches the brink of civil war between Earl Godwin of Wessex and King Edward the Confessor, but Godwin backs down at the last minute.

THE BLOOD OF CHRIST

In 1052, word reached Rome that the highly respected monk Berengar of Tours was preaching that while Christ's blood and body were present in the wine and bread, they were there only in a spiritual sense and that there was no actual material change. Berengar had been thrown into prison by King Henry I of France but no definitive decision could be reached as to whether or not his views were heretical. The dispute rumbled on throughout Leo's reign.

Norman knights helped to repel the Muslim Saracens but caused problems for Leo by taking land that was claimed by the Church.

and got, the deposition of several bishops who he accused of having bought their way into office. He also demanded that all priests who had been consecrated by those bishops should be unfrocked, but the synod decided that this would unfairly punish worthy priests and decreed penance instead. Undeterred, Leo announced a radical restructuring of the papal curia. Hildebrand was put in charge of the reform, with Abbot Hugh of Cluny, Bishop Halinard of Lyons, and the Parma monk Peter Damiani offering advice and support. Leo's reforms introduced a rather stricter interpretation of financial honesty than that to which the curia had been accustomed. The process took several years but, eventually, the papacy was put on a sound financial footing for the first time in generations. Leo's thirst for reform was not restricted to Rome. Suspecting that clerics a long way from the papal throne might ignore or delay his orders, he set out on a series of journeys to enforce his program. No earlier pope traveled as widely when in office as did Leo, and no earlier pope had so firmly stamped his rule on the Church.

Leo's cataclysmic rift with the Byzantines began innocuously enough. When Leo had visited Spinoto in 1050, he had failed to ask permission of the patriarch of Constantinople in whose jurisdiction the city officially lay. The patriarch of the time, Michael Cerularius, expressed his annoyance. Leo now appointed a cleric named Humbert of Silva Candida to be archbishop of Sicily as a preliminary move for the Norman attack on that island (*see* box). Patriarch Michael was incensed because the island was supposed to be under his supremacy. He reacted by closing down all the Western churches in Constantinople, then he sent a bluntly worded letter to Rome that reopened long dormant disputes and viciously attacked Western ritual practices as heretical.

Leo at first prepared an equally forthright reply, then thought better of it in the face of the need for a united front against Islam. Instead, he sent Humbert to Constantinople as legate to smooth things over. It was a disastrous move. Patriarch Michael insulted Humbert and the papacy, while Humbert responded in savage fashion. While Michael was holding a service in the great cathedral of Hagia Sophia, Humbert strode up to the altar, pushed the protesting clerics aside and declared Michael to be excommunicated. Michael responded by excommunicating Leo.

In a sense it was too late, for by the time of this dramatic confrontation Leo had passed away. But the split between Rome and Constantinople would prove to be permanent and became known as the Great Schism of 1054.

1053

The Norman Empire in southern Italy is founded by the Norseman Robert Guiscard, who takes Benevento from the Byzantines.

1053

Godwin, the earl of Wessex, dies leaving his vast estates to his son Harold Godwinsson, who is related to the royal family through his mother.

1053

Master Japanese sculptor Jocho Busshi creates his masterpiece, the Amida Buddha.

1054

Death of Yaroslav the Wise, prince of Kiev, who had first codified the laws of the Russians.

1054

Normandy is invaded by France's Henry I, who is defeated at Mortemer.

VICTOR II ✠ The 153rd Pope 1055–1057

Born place unknown; 1018

Parents Father, Count Hartwig of Calw; Mother, unknown

Papacy April 13, 1055 to July 28, 1057

Died Arezzo, Italy; July 28, 1057

Eichstätt Cathedral in Bavaria. A combination of family influence and his own formidable administrative skills led Gebhard, the future Pope Victor II, to be made bishop of Eichstätt when he was only 24 years old.

The death of Leo IX meant that Emperor Henry III, as patrician of Rome, once again had to find a candidate for the papacy. He dispensed with asking advice from churchmen and named Bishop Gebhard of Eichstätt who had been born into a noble family from Swabia that had long proved its loyalty.

At a young age, Gebhard had impressed his family with his intellectual abilities, so they put him into the Church. As bishop of Eichstätt, he continued to pursue his family's usual policy of loyalty to the emperor, implementing all Henry's policies without complaint and quickly becoming one of the emperor's most favored advisers.

Gebhard, however, was not too keen to go to Rome. He was not only concerned about the might of the Normans in southern Italy, but also about Duke Godfrey of Lorraine, one of the most powerful nobles in the Holy Roman Empire, who had already clashed with Gebhard over policies of Emperor Henry. In 1054, Godfrey had married Beatrice of Bar, widow of the powerful Margrave Boniface of Tuscany. He was now in Italy, officially safeguarding the inheritance of his Italian stepchildren but also furthering his own ambitions by getting his brother Frederick installed as Chancellor of the Papal States.

Gebhard agreed to go to Rome only after Henry had agreed to lead an imperial army into Italy to settle matters to Gebhard's satisfaction. Taking the name of Victor II, Gebhard went to Rome and was enthroned a year after the death of Leo IX. Two months later he and Henry held a synod at Florence where simony and clerical marriage were declared anathema, along with the alienation of Church property. A number of bishops were deposed for apparent abuses. Henry then moved south, forcing Godfrey to flee back to his own lands. Beatrice of Bar and her children were taken into imperial custody, while Frederick fled Rome to become a monk in Monte Cassino. His promises fulfilled, Henry returned to Germany and left Victor to get on with his job as pope.

Henry, however, could not dispense with Victor's advice completely. In August 1056, he summoned Victor to join him in Bodfeld to discuss various matters. Victor was therefore on the spot when Henry died suddenly at the age of 49, leaving as his heir the five-year-old Henry IV. Victor and the empress Agnes were left as joint regents of the Kingdom of Germany. Victor summoned a great council of the imperial nobles to meet in Cologne in December. There he negotiated reconciliations with Godfrey of Lorraine. With Godfrey now an ally in Italy, Victor knew that Rome was safe from attack by the Normans. He stayed in Germany sorting out various imperial matters before returning over the Alps in the spring of 1057.

In June, the Abbot of Monte Cassino died and the monks elected Frederick, brother of Godfrey to be Abbot. Victor welcomed Frederick to Rome, promoting him to be cardinal priest of San Crisogeno. It was one of Victor's last recorded acts for he died of a sudden fever when visiting Arezzo. His body was embalmed and loaded onto a carriage to take it to Eichstätt. However, the cortege got only as far as Ravenna before it was captured by an armed mob who stole the corpse and buried it in their Church of Santa Maria Rotunda where it remains.

1055

King Ferdinand I of Castile begins a campaign against the Muslims of southern Spain that will lead to extensive conquests and see him recognized as the leader of the Christian kingdoms in Spain.

1055

Theodora becomes empress of Constantinople in her own right. She is the last of the Macedonian dynasty of Byzantium and her death is followed by 30 years of civil war.

1056

The Muslim Fatimid Caliphs expel all Christians from Jerusalem.

1056

Death of Syrian poet Al-Ma'arri, famous for his collection of satirical poems "Unnecessary Necessity".

STEPHEN IX ✠ The 154th Pope 1057–1058

Born Lorraine, France; c.1020

Parents Father, Duke Gothelo of Lorraine; Mother, unknown

Papacy August 2, 1057–March 29, 1058

Died Florence, Italy; March 29, 1058

Stephen had already led a busy career before his election as pope. He had been born Frederick, a younger son of Duke Gozelon of Lorraine, and, like many younger sons who showed intelligence, was sent to the Church. At Liege young Frederick flourished, rising to be an archdeacon.

The death of Pope Victor II left the clergy of Rome in an awkward position. The changes made by the recent German popes meant that the curia and clergy in Rome were dominated by those favoring reform of the Church and the independence of the papacy from the nobles of the Papal States. However, there was currently no Holy Roman emperor and King Henry IV of Germany was only six years old. There was a real and understandable fear that the local nobles might seek to reestablish their grip on the Papal States.

In the circumstances, the clergy sought Frederick's advice as the oldest, wealthiest, and most respected abbey in Italy. Frederick put forward the names of five men who he believed would both favor the cause of reform and would enjoy the support of Godfrey and the German royal family. However, the clergy ignored the advice and elected Frederick himself to be pope. He took the name of Stephen IX as August 2 was the feast day of St. Stephen and moved into the Lateran Palace.

As expected, Pope Stephen IX favored reform. He made the outspoken monk Peter Damiani cardinal bishop of Ostia to allow him to speak authoritatively for reforms. He made Humbert of Silva Candida his chancellor, while Hildebrand Bonizi became his chief adviser. He then issued numerous letters and judgements backing clerical celibacy and, once again, attacking simony and other abuses that plagued the Church.

In 1057, Stephen sent Hildebrand north of the Alps to talk to Empress Agnes, regent for young Henry IV, about a campaign against the Normans in southern Italy planned for the summer of 1058. Stephen himself traveled to Florence in March to discuss the same campaign with his brother Godfrey.

Stephen was already ill and, before leaving Rome, he made the clergy take a solemn vow that if he were to die they would not elect a successor before Hildebrand returned from Germany. In the event, he did die during the trip to Florence, but his succession would not go as smoothly as he had hoped.

When Henry marched on Rome in 1055 to install Victor II as pope, Frederick, the future Pope Stephen IX, retired as a monk to the Abbey of Monte Cassino (below). He was later reconciled to Victor, became abbot, and was then promoted to cardinal priest.

1057

Death of King Macbeth of Scotland in battle. He is succeeded by his stepson Lulach.

1057

Anawrahta of Pagan captures Thanton, unifying the Irrawaddy Valley under his rule and thus founding the state that would become Burma (Myanmar).

1058

Boleslaus II becomes duke of Poland. During his reign he would be the first Polish ruler to mint coins and found monasteries.

1058

Death of St. Alfwold, English monk and bishop of Sherborne, who sought to introduce reformist ideas to England.

NICHOLAS II ✣ The 155th Pope 1058–1061

Born Lorraine, France; c.1010

Parents Father, unknown; Mother, unknown

Papacy December 6, 1058 to July 1061

Died Florence, Italy; July 1061

Nicholas II formed an alliance with the Normans, investing the Norman adventurer Robert Guiscard as duke of Apulia, Calabria, and Sicily.

The disputed succession to Stephen IX—the Germans chose Nicholas II, while the Italians elected the antipope Benedict X—had the crucial effect of leading to new rules relating to the conduct of papal elections that have, with a few amendments, continued to the present day.

When Stephen IX realized that he was dying, he persuaded the Roman clergy to promise that no election would take place until Hildebrand Bonizi returned from Germany (*see* p.135). Scarcely was Stephen in his grave, however, before an election was held. The local nobles Count Gregory of Tusculum and Count Gerard of Galeria had not enjoyed being ruled by German popes and, deciding that the child emperor Henry IV was in no position to intervene, they rounded up the electors and put forward Bishop John Mincius of Velletri.

All the cardinals and senior clergy promptly fled Rome for Siena to await Hildebrand who was gathering support from the powerful Duke Godfrey of Lorraine and Tuscany and the German court. In December 1058, Hildebrand presided over the election in Siena of Gerard of Bourgogne, who took the name Nicholas II.

Backed by the army of Godfrey, Nicholas then marched into Rome while Benedict fled to his family's estates and shut himself up in a castle.

Nicholas promptly held a synod at the Lateran at which he laid down rules for papal elections. He then moved on to other reforms, banning marriage for clergy and issuing strict rules to enforce celibacy. Investiture by laymen was banned, removing the influence of local lords over the clergy in their lands.

In August 1059, Nicholas made a political decision as far reaching as his clerical ones. He sent for the Norman adventurers Richard of Aversa and Robert Guiscard, offering an alliance. The Normans accepted with alacrity. Richard's first service to Nicholas was to storm the castle of Galeria where Benedict was hiding and drag the fugitive ex-pope to Rome where Nicholas had him formally degraded and confined to a monastery. The reformers Peter Damiani and Anselm of Lucca were sent to Milan, where they humbled Archbishop Guido and forced him to accept reforms, including putting aside his live-in girlfriend. Guido then accepted a ring of office from Nicholas, effectively accepting that his initial appointment by the German emperor had been invalid. The Germans were understandably annoyed by the Norman alliance and by the humbling of Guido. Papal ambassadors to the German court were refused entry and a synod of German bishops declared Nicholas incompetent to rule. Nicholas died soon after hearing this news.

PAPAL ELECTION REFORMS

Nicholas's reforms instructed that elections would be held in secret after the death of a pope with only the cardinals taking part. Once the cardinals had chosen a candidate, the other clergy and the people of Rome would be summoned and asked if they agreed. A letter would then be sent to the Holy Roman emperor to ask for his approval. Elections should take place in Rome and preference should be given to Roman candidates, but the cardinals were free to hold their meeting elsewhere and to elect a non-Roman if they wished. Rules for the conduct of the election itself were not written down until 1278, but they seem to have been established by Nicholas.

1058	1059	1060	1063
Antipope Benedict X sends the pallium to Archbishop Stigand of Canterbury, who accepts it and so plunges the English Church into crisis and disputes.	Alp Arslan becomes Sultan of the Turks and at once starts a war against the Byzantine Empire and fellow Muslim leaders that would make the Turks the most powerful force in the Middle East.	Chinese scholar Cai Xiang completes his *Book of Tea*, credited with laying the foundations of the Chinese tea industry.	St. Mark's Basilica in Venice is begun on the site of an earlier church built in 828.

ALEXANDER II ✠ The 156th Pope 1061–1073

Born Milan, Italy; date unknown

Parents Unknown

Papacy September 30, 1061–April 21, 1073

Died Rome, Italy; April 21, 1073

The reformers in Rome followed the rules laid down by Nicholas (*see* p.136), and the cardinals elected the bishop of Lucca as Pope Alexander II. Meanwhile, the Romans sent messengers to Germany to ask Regent Agnes, as patrician of Rome, to nominate a candidate for the papacy.

Regent Agnes chose Peter Cadalus, bishop of Parma, who declared himself Honorius II. In April 1062, Honorius arrived in Rome with an army of mercenaries and drove out the Normans and Alexander. A few weeks later, Duke Godfrey of Lorraine and Tuscany arrived with an army even larger than that of Honorius and took control of Rome himself. He ordered both claimants to return to their home sees until the matter could be sorted out.

Investigations dragged on until May 1064, when a great synod of Italian and German bishops was held at Mantua. Both claimants were summoned, but only Alexander turned up. He took an oath of purgation before Archbishop Anno of Cologne, who had by this point taken over as imperial regent. Alexander was then confirmed as pope, while Honorius was allowed to continue as bishop of Parma (although he never gave up his claim to be pope).

Having finally secured his position as pope, Alexander proved himself to be a ferocious supporter of reform and of holy war. Already, in 1063, he had sent to Robert Guiscard a holy banner, blessed by the pope in St. Peter's, which he was instructed to carry into battle when conquering Sicily from the Muslims. He sent a similar banner to a group of French nobles when they marched into Spain to help the Spanish Christians fight the Muslims there. Both groups were given indulgences to remit their sins, on condition that they cross swords with the Muslims in battle. In 1066, he combined the ideas of holy war and clerical reforms when he granted Duke William of Normandy a papal banner for his invasion of England on condition that, if he won, William was to subject the English Church to the strict reforms that it had to that date avoided.

These reforms were pushed forward at great speed by Alexander. He sent legates to archbishoprics across Europe with instructions to hold local synods to enforce reform. In particular, any clergy suspected of simony (paying a fee to gain office) were to be thoroughly investigated, while any clergy who had been invested into office by a lay person had to undergo a fresh investiture by the papal legate. The latter move was intended to emphasize that only investiture by the pope was valid. The most high-profile victim of the campaign was the bishop of Constance, who was deposed for simony, but many others had to undergo investigation, take oaths of innocence, or undergo fresh investiture.

In 1071, Alexander's campaign led to an open rupture with Holy Roman Emperor Henry IV, now ruling in his own right. Archbishop Guido of Milan died and Henry appointed Godfrey de Castiglione to succeed him. Alexander declared that nobody could appoint or invest an archbishop except the pope and appointed the Milanese priest Attone. Henry sent five men to Rome to discuss the issue, but Alexander refused to see them and excommunicated them. It was his last act before his sudden death.

In March 1065, Holy Roman Emperor Henry IV was declared of age and began to rule in his own right.

1063

A fleet from Pisa captures Palermo, Sicily, from the Muslim emir of Sicily.

1066

King Harold Godwinson of England is killed at the Battle of Hastings, which is won by Duke William of Normandy who thus becomes King William I of England.

1067

The traditional date for the founding of the Russian city of Minsk.

1069

Wang Anshi begins a thorough reform of the governmental system of China aimed at ending corruption, boosting the economy, and improving the army.

1070

Marrakesh is founded as a trading and educational center by local ruler Abu Bakr ibn Umar.

ST. GREGORY VII ✠ The 157th Pope 1073–1085

Born Sovana, Italy; date unknown
Parents Unknown
Papacy April 22, 1073–May 25, 1085
Died Salerno, Italy; May 25, 1085

ope Gregory VII rewrote the rules of the papacy with a single-minded determination that brought him into conflict with kings and emperors across Christendom. In his own lifetime, much of what he sought to achieve ended in failure, but his ideas survived his death and did much to reshape Europe and Western Christianity.

Gregory was born Hildebrand Bonizi, son of an illiterate blacksmith in Savona. At an early age his obvious intelligence won him a place at the school of Santa Maria all'Aventino in Rome. According to one source, a relative of his was abbot of a monastery in Rome at the time. Among his teachers were Lawrence of Amalfi and John Gratian, both keen supporters of the reform movement based at the Abbey of Cluny (*see* p.118). When John Gratian was elected Pope Gregory VI, he made Hildebrand his chaplain and entrusted him with key tasks within the curia, and Gregory VI's deposition on the orders of Emperor Henry III (*see* p.128) seems to have had a profound impact on Hildebrand. He went into exile in Germany with his mentor and, after Gregory died, moved to the Abbey of Cluny. There, Hildebrand's zeal for reform was encouraged and his learning enhanced by Abbot Hugh of Cluny. In 1049, Bruno of Toul was appointed to be pope by a joint German-Italian synod summoned by Henry III. Before leaving for Rome to become Pope Leo IX, Bruno contacted Abbot Hugh for advice on the reformist agenda. Hugh advised him to take Hildebrand with him to Rome as an assistant.

Robert Guiscard is granted the keys to the city of Palermo. Robert was excommunicated by Pope Gregory VII but soon regained papal favor by conquering the Island of Sicily, which had been in the hands of the Muslims.

The following popes, Victor II and Stephen IX, both entrusted important tasks to Hildebrand who, by 1060, was recognized as the most important man in Rome after the pope. Nor was Hildebrand shy of undertaking less intellectual and more brutal tasks. In 1060, he persuaded Duke Richard of Aversa to lend him 300 knights, 2,000 men, and siege equipment, to take Galeria Castle, in which the antipope Benedict X was taking refuge. Richard agreed, so Hildebrand led the small army in the successful siege. Hildebrand then ignored all pleas and appeals to law and dragged the antipope to Rome for summary trial and degradation.

By 1061, Hildebrand held the rank of archdeacon and engineered the election of the reformer Alexander II. The two men co-operated closely in the cause of reform, and it is generally accepted that it was Hildebrand who wrote the rules that restricted participation in future papal elections to the cardinals. When Alexander died, Hildebrand played his part in arranging the funeral. He was at the altar in the Lateran Basilica praying for the soul of the departed Alexander when a shout went up from the back of the funeral congregation, "St. Peter has chosen Hildebrand the archdeacon." Others began shouting, "Hildebrand for pope," and soon the funeral collapsed into chaos. The people of Rome poured out onto the streets to

1073
A reorganization of the English Church makes York subordinate to Canterbury.

1075
The Seljuk Turks capture Jerusalem from the Fatimids.

1075
China invades Vietnam, prompting Vietnamese commander Ly Thuong Kiet to write a refutation of Chinese claims to overlordship that is now considered to be the Vietnamese Declaration of Independence and founding document.

THE INVESTITURE CONTROVERSY

In centuries past, many secular rulers had donated lands to monasteries or bishoprics both for the good of their souls and to set the Christian Church on a sound financial footing. Many of these rulers had made a condition of the gift that they and their successors had the right to choose, or at least approve, who should be bishop or abbot of the institution whenever it fell vacant. Other rulers felt that they had a direct interest in who should be bishop or abbot in their realm as that person would be a major landholder able to wield considerable secular power. Kings were able to appoint or demote noblemen and many felt they had a right to act identically with regard to churchmen who held secular power. The reformers within the Church, however, abhorred this idea. Many bishops and abbots invested into office by secular rulers were pious and effective office holders, but others put the interests of their king above those of the Church. The reformers believed that only the Church should be able to invest churchmen in office. In particular, they believed that only the pope should be able to invest archbishops and bishops.

join demonstrations and marches demanding that Hildebrand be made pope. Later that day, the cardinals met in the Basilica of St. Peter ad Vincula. As the crowds surged around the building and threatened to break in, the cardinals elected Hildebrand to be pope.

Exactly how valid this election was proved controversial. Some alleged that the cardinals had acted out of fear of the crowd. In any case, it quite clearly reversed the procedure laid down in the rules written by Hildebrand himself. The cardinals were meant to choose someone, then ask the people for approval, but now it had been the people who chose and the cardinals who approved. The formal rules were bent in another way when Hildebrand was consecrated and enthroned without waiting for a response to the news of his election from the Holy Roman emperor Henry IV. However, whether the election was technically valid or not, it was accepted by everyone. Hildebrand adopted the papal name Gregory, both in homage to his old benefactor—the reformer Gregory VI—and in admiration of Gregory the Great.

Gregory's first concerns as pope were the activities of the constantly turbulent Normans of southern Italy and the threat posed to the Christian Byzantine Empire by the Muslim Turks. His worries about the Normans were heightened when the papal fief of Benevento was attacked by his supposed ally Robert Guiscard on a spurious pretext. Gregory embarked on a complex web of intrigue and negotiation with Norman rulers that ended when Guiscard was first excommunicated, then brought back into papal favor when he broke the power of the Muslim Emir of Sicily and turned his attentions to the conquest of that island.

The Turkish threat to Constantinople proved more intransigent. At the Battle of Manzikert in 1071, the Turks had wiped out almost the entire Byzantine army and captured Emperor Romanos IV. Vast swathes of prosperous territory were taken over by the Turks, while the Byzantines collapsed in disarray. Gregory established good relations with the new Byzantine emperor Michael VII. He began seeking to persuade European knights to go to Constantinople to fight the Turks. He sought to repeat the successes of Alexander II's program of holy war by consecrating holy banners and offering indulgences for sins to those who took up arms against Islam.

However, Gregory's reign as pope came to be defined by his relations with the Holy Roman emperor Henry IV and what became known as the Investiture Controversy (*see* box). The dispute had been brewing for some decades, but was to come to a head in December 1075.

The issue had already led to a dispute between Alexander II and Henry IV over the successor to Archbishop Guido of Milan, with both pope and emperor appointing a new archbishop. Gregory inherited the dispute, but at first it did not seem to be too serious. Henry IV was busy with a

1076

The Trial of Penenden Heath in Kent decides that ancient English laws take precedence in England over imported Norman customs.

1077

The Byzantine emperor Michael VII abdicates and is succeeded by Nicephorus III Botaniates (right).

1078

King Alfonso VI of Castile captures Coria in his ongoing wars against the Muslims of southern Spain.

Holy Roman Emperor Henry IV leads his army to put down a rebellion in Saxony. Gregory VII's reign as pope came to be defined by his relations with Henry IV and what became known as the Investiture Controversy.

PAPAL INFALLIBILITY

The Catholic doctrine of papal infallibility holds that the pope is incapable of making an error when, in the exercise of his office as shepherd and teacher of all Christians, in virtue of his supreme apostolic authority, he defines a doctrine concerning faith or morals to be held by the whole Church. The doctrine is bound up with the primacy of Rome in the apostolic succession (*see* p.130) and in large part relies on a passage in the Gospel of Luke where Jesus gives St. Peter the task of ensuring the purity and continuance of the Christian faith. The doctrine was not codified in its current form until the First Vatican Council of 1869, but is generally thought to date back to the time of Gregory VII.

rebellion in Saxony and did not want to provoke a split with the papacy. At Nuremburg in 1074 Henry did penance before the papal legates for continuing contact with men excommunicated by Alexander II or Gregory himself, and made vague promises about supporting Gregory's efforts to reform the Church.

By the summer of 1075, however, the Saxon rebellion had been put down and Henry was free to act. He sent an army into northern Italy under Count Eberhard to exact taxes due to him, ensure obedience from his subjects, and to ensure that his nominees were installed into the vacant bishoprics of Fermo and Spoleto as well as Milan. Gregory responded with a furious letter that accused Henry of having broken his promises and being unfit to be king of Germany.

There then took place a murky and bizarre event. On the evening of Christmas Day, Gregory was officiating at a service in Santa Maria Maggiore when a gang of armed men burst in, grabbed him, and bundled him out the door before the astonished congregation could react. The leader of the gang was identified as a nobleman named Cencio Frangipane. A mob quickly formed and stormed the Frangipane residence, liberating Gregory from a locked room and chasing Frangipane out of the city. Gregory accused Henry of being behind the event, but it is far from clear what had really happened nor why.

In any case, Henry was moving fast. On January 24, the Synod of Worms was summoned. The German bishops, many of whom opposed the more extreme reforms, found Gregory guilty of a catalogue of crimes. Henry IV added his own judgment declaring that Gregory was deposed and calling on the clergy and people of Rome to elect a new pope. A second synod was summoned from Henry's other kingdom, Italy, to meet at Piacenza. Only the northern Italian bishops attended, but they too renounced their allegiance to Gregory. Roland of Parma took the decisions of the two synods to Rome, and was almost murdered by the mob for his trouble. The day after hearing the news, Gregory held a solemn ceremony in which he excommunicated Henry, declared him divested of his kingdoms and absolved Henry's subjects from all oaths

1080

King Alfonso VI of Castille accepts Roman liturgy in his kingdom, replacing the ancient Spanish forms of service.

1080

Death of Ísleifur Gissurarson, first bishop of Iceland, while conducting a service in Skalholt.

1081

Battle of Mynydd Carn sees Gruffudd ap Cynan become Prince of Gwynedd, uniting most of Wales under his rule.

and duties to him. It was an astonishing move, but one that Gregory believed he had every right to take. He believed that the pope was God's deputy on Earth and that all others held office only with the permission of the pope.

In northern Italy, support for Henry evaporated almost over night. In Germany, many nobles who had resented the recent centralizations of power under Henry III and Henry IV took the opportunity given by Gregory and rebelled. They invited Gregory to come to Germany to judge their claims. Realizing he had gone too far, Henry rushed to intercept Gregory at Canossa in northern Italy. On January 25, 1077, Henry reached Canossa clad only in a hairshirt. He fell on his knees in prayer before the gates and refused all food until Gregory would see him. When the two met, Henry flung himself to the floor begging forgiveness. Gregory lifted the excommunication, but not the other penalties. Henry rushed back to Germany where he found Rudolf of Swabia claiming his throne. Germany descended into civil war.

By contrast, Gregory achieved almost nothing in France or England. King Phillip I of France and King William I of England were every bit as guilty as Henry IV of appointing bishops and abbots, and ignoring papal instructions. Gregory went so far as to prepare the documents of excommunication and deposition against Phillip, but on hearing that the French nobles were backing their king he desisted. William of England was simply ignored, it being all too obvious that the papacy enjoyed little support there.

Three years later, Rudolf won a small battle over Henry. Hearing the news, Gregory declared that Rudolf was the rightful King of Germany and again excommunicated Henry. This time it was Gregory who had overstepped the mark. The excommunication was too obviously for political purposes and it was ignored. To make matters worse for Gregory, Rudolf then died and the vast majority of German nobles returned their loyalty to Henry.

In June 1080, a synod of German bishops at Brixen declared Gregory deposed and put forward Guibert of Ravenna as the new pope. By 1083, Henry was secure on his throne, and he invaded Italy. In March 1084, Henry marched unopposed into Rome, while Gregory barricaded himself into the Castel Sant'Angelo. Henry offered to recognize Gregory as pope if he in turn crowned Henry as Holy Roman emperor. Gregory refused and again excommunicated Henry.

Henry installed Guibert in the Lateran as Clement III, who then crowned Henry as Holy Roman emperor. Gregory excommunicated Clement and everyone else at the ceremony. A large army of Normans under Robert Guiscard now approached Rome, forcing Henry and Clement to abandon the city. The Norman army proceeded to sack the city, sparking an uprising against Gregory by the Roman people who believed he had betrayed them.

Gregory fled to Monte Cassino, then to Salerno. Feeling that death was close, Gregory lifted the sentences of excommunication on everyone except Henry and Clement.

The tomb of Pope Gregory VII in Salerno Cathedral. He gave orders that his tomb should be engraved with the words "I love justice and hated iniquity, and so I die in exile."

1082	1083	1084
The Buddhist holy writings of the Tripitaka are translated into Korean.	King Alfonso VI of Castile captures Talavera from the Emirate of Cordoba.	St. Bruno of Cologne founds the Carthusian Order of Monks, later also to include nuns, with a set of rules distinct from those of St. Benedict.

VICTOR III ✠ The 158th Pope 1086–1087

Born Benevento, Italy; probably 1026

Parents Father, Prince Landulf V of Benevento; Mother, unknown

Papacy May 24, 1086–September 16, 1087

Died Cassino, Italy; September 16, 1087

Of all the men to have occupied the papal throne, Victor III was probably the most reluctant to take up the office. Given the factional disputes and violence that was wracking the Church at the time this is hardly surprising. Indeed, the majority of Victor's achievements came before he reluctantly ascended the papal throne.

Victor was born Daufari, son of the ruler of Benevento, which was then a papal fief although it lay outside the Papal States proper. His family expected him to make a suitable marriage and to play his part in running the principality, but Daufari preferred a religious life. He entered the Monastery of Santa Sophia in his home town, but later moved to live with some hermits in the mountains before settling in the Monastery of San Nicolo on an island in the Adriatic. At some point he met two monks from the ancient Monastery of Monte Cassino and was so impressed by them that he moved there. By 1057, he was abbot of the dependent house in Capua and was using the name of Desiderius.

At this point, Abbot Frederick of Monte Cassino was elected pope as Stephen IX (*see* p.135). The monks of Monte Cassino elected Desiderius to succeed him as abbot, but Stephen opted to retain his position at Monte Cassino while he was also pope. It was not until 1058 that Desiderius assumed office in Monte Cassino, and soon afterward the new pope Nicholas II made him cardinal priest of Santa Cecilia in Trastevere as well as appointing him the papal vicar, or deputy, to oversee all monasteries in southern Italy.

As abbot of Monte Cassino, Desiderius launched a massive program of renewal, improvement, and reform. He was a keen supporter of the reforms originating at the French Abbey of Cluny (*see* p.118), with their emphasis on clerical purity, Church authority, and lavish embellishments that appealed to noblemen such as himself. His recruitment drive resulted in a large number of new monks joining the monastery, boosting numbers to over 200. Many of these newcomers were drawn from the ranks of the nobility and brought with them handsome bequests of cash, land, or annuities. The money was put to good use by Desiderius, following the precepts of Cluny. The old basilica was torn down and a new one erected in the latest architectural style and dripping with luxurious embellishments. The high altar was given a front of pure beaten gold adorned with jewels and enamels. The main doors were made of bronze adorned with silver panels, and colorful frescoes adorned the walls.

As well as improving the music of the monastery, Desiderius also set about reforming its learning. Rare books and manuscripts were borrowed from far and near to be copied in the monastic scriptorium, on which vast sums were lavished. It was not only Christian works that Desiderius acquired. Ancient pagan writers such as Virgil, Seneca, and Cicero also featured in the growing library of Monte Cassino. The work of improving Monte Cassino inevitably brought Desiderius into contact with the great rulers of southern Italy, among them the turbulent Normans. He was friendly with Robert Guiscard and with Richard of Aversa. Desiderius occasionally acted as a go-between to carry

Apart from issuing letters denouncing him as a usurper who had not been properly elected, Victor and other supporters of reform did nothing at first to remove the antipope Clement. In 1086, however, they ousted Clement with the support of the Normans.

1086

Count Roger I of Sicily captures Syracuse, the last major Muslim stronghold on Sicily.

1086

The Domesday Book is compiled by order of King William I of England to list all landholdings in the kingdom and provide a basis for taxation. The Oath of Salisbury makes English vassals responsible directly to the crown.

1086

Castile's Alfonso VI is defeated at Zallaka by a Muslim army from Africa under Yusuf ibn Tashfin, leader of the fanatical Berber sect (the Almoravids) that has gained dominance in North Africa.

1087

A vast fleet drawn from Genoa and Pisa captures the city of Mahdia in North Africa. The Pisan share of the plunder was used to build the famous Cathedral in Pisa.

VICTOR'S BONES

His body had a rather more adventurous career than most. In 1515, his body was moved to the main abbey church to cater for the large number of visitors coming to Monte Cassino who considered him to have been a man of unusual holiness. The body was moved again to a special Chapel of St. Victor when he was canonized in 1887. In 1943, when war came to Monte Cassino, his body—along with other treasures—was removed to Rome for safe keeping. In February 1944, the ancient abbey was destroyed by American bombing. It was not until 1963 that Victor's body could be moved back to the rebuilt Monte Cassino (left).

messages from Gregory VII to the Normans, even when the two sides were virtually at war.

When Gregory died, the German nominee for the papacy, Clement III was exercising papal authority over western Christendom. The supporters of Gregory and of reform, including Desiderius, met to decide how to respond but failed to reach agreement. Clement, however, was busily getting the bishops of Britain, Germany, and Russia to recognize him as pope. Even 13 cardinals defected and declared their support for him. However, as the anniversary of the death of Gregory VII approached, the reformers decided something had to be done. Backed by the military might of the Normans they marched on Rome, ousted Clement, and declared an election would take place on May 24, 1086. Desiderius was among those who gathered for the election. The cardinals decided to elect Desiderius, much against his wishes, probably because they believed he could keep both the Normans and Emperor Henry IV on side. Desiderius took the name of Victor III.

Just four days after his election and before he was consecrated, a bloody riot broke out in Rome. Abandoned by many of the more extreme reformers, and now confronted by supporters of Clement, Victor announced he was abdicating and went back to Monte Cassino.

In March 1087, Prince Jordan of Capua persuaded Victor to use his authority as papal vicar in southern Italy to convene a synod of bishops and abbots from that area. Other reformers came to the synod, among them Archbishop Hugh of Lyons. Barely had the synod begun than Jordan demanded that Victor take up his duties as pope. Most there agreed, but Hugh of Lyons objected and was promptly excommunicated by the other bishops. Jordan led a march on Rome that secured control of the city and, on May 9, Victor was consecrated in St. Peter's. Again it proved only a short stay as, on May 17, he was forced to flee as Clement attacked and gained control of Rome again.

Once more Victor retired to Monte Cassino but, in June, Countess Matilda of Tuscany captured Rome and invited Victor back once again. By July 1, he was in full control of the city and surroundings and was able to take up residence in the Lateran Palace. In August, he held a synod in his home town of Benevento and the antipope Clement was declared excommunicated.

As the synod drew to a close, Victor fell ill. He had himself carried back to Monte Cassino where he insisted on catching up with the business of the monastery. Even though he was desperately ill, Victor made a string of decisions about the monastery's affairs. Finally, sensing death was approaching, he suggested that Bishop Odo of Ostia should be elected pope in his stead. Three days later he was dead. He was buried in the tomb he had prepared for himself in the abbey's chapter house.

1087

Japanese emperor Shirakawa abdicates and retires to a monastery. His successor Emperor Horikawa carries out the arduous ritual duties, while Shirakawa rules Japan from behind the scenes, initiating the "cloistered rule" era of Japanese history.

1087

William the Conqueror dies in Rouen. He has invaded the French Vexin to retaliate for raids on his territory and sacked and burned the town of Mantes. But when he rides out to survey the ruins he is thrown from his horse and fatally injured.

1087

The Byzantine emperor Alexius I Comnenus is defeated at the Battle of Drystra by heretic Bogomils in Thrace and Bulgaria.

URBAN II ✠ The 159th Pope 1088–1099

Born Lagery, France; c.1042

Parents Unknown

Papacy March 12, 1088–July 29, 1099

Died Rome, Italy; July 29, 1099

Upon election as pope, Urban II at once announced his firm adherence to the reform program (*see* p.118), denounced Clement III as a usurper, and summoned a synod to meet at Melfi in September 1089. At Melfi he repeated the condemnation of lay investiture, clerical marriage, simony, and other abuses that had been opposed so vehemently by Gregory.

On Victor's death the reforming party were still in exile from Rome for the antipope Clement III was in firm control of the city thanks to troops supplied by Henry IV. The majority of cardinals met at Terracina, which was at least the seat of a bishopric in the Papal States, to elect a successor to Victor. Their choice fell on Odo, a staunch supporter of the reforming agenda of Gregory who had been prior at the Abbey of Cluny. Odo adopted the name of Urban II to honor the purity of faith achieved under Urban I.

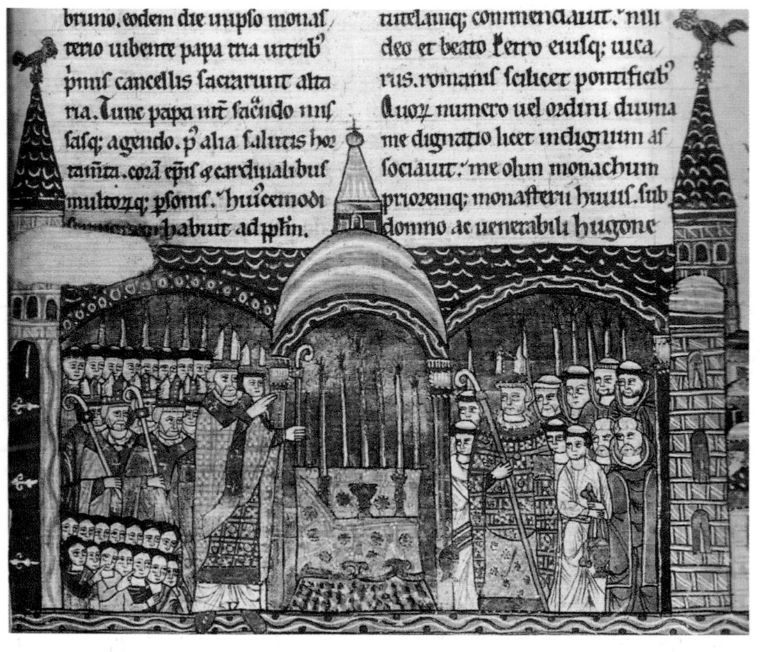

Manuscript depicting Pope Urban II consecrating the altar of the Monastery of Cluny.

Although a staunch supporter of the reform program, it was soon clear that Urban preferred negotiation to confrontation. He recalled the permanent legates who had been sent out by Pope Gregory VII to impose reforms on Europe, softened the penalties laid on those clerics who had been invested by lay lords or who had married, and generally tried to win over opponents by soft words.

Late in 1089, he was confronted by unexpected news from Rome. Clement had held a synod at which he, too, had condemned simony and clerical marriage and supported other elements of the reformist program. Clement had also granted to those cardinals who had given him their support additional privileges. Worried that more cardinals might change sides, Urban matched the privileges and so effectively founded the College of Cardinals.

In 1090, Urban was able to move into Rome, but it was only temporary. That summer Henry IV marched into Italy with a large army, forcing Urban to leave Rome once again. By 1093, however, Henry's campaign was bogged down in northern Italy as Matilda of Tuscany managed to turn the Italian nobles against him. Urban returned to Rome, this time permanently, though clerics loyal to Clement remained in post and forbade him access to various churches. It was not until 1094 that Urban was able to get into the Lateran and the great fortress of Castel Sant'Angelo was closed to him until 1099.

1088

Christian troops capture Tarragona as part of the ongoing campaigns to drive the Muslims out of Spain.

1089

The Abbey of Citeaux, later to become the mother house of the Cistercian Order, is founded in southern France.

1091

Norman nobleman Count Roger of Sicily takes Malta from the Muslims.

THE FIRST CRUSADE

Four separate armies of crusaders left Europe to march on Jerusalem by way of Constantinople, where they were given supplies and guides in return for promises of allegiance, and reached Nicaea in June 1097. That city surrendered to them and at Dorylaeum the crusaders defeated a Turkish army, opening the way through to the Holy Land. The great city of Antioch was captured in June 1098 (right), and Jerusalem fell in July 1099 amid much slaughter. An attempt to drive the crusaders out by the Fatimids of North Africa ended with a great Christian victory at Ascalon in August 1099. The crusaders then established the Kingdom of Jerusalem as a Christian state that would survive, with various setbacks and triumphs, until 1291.

Meanwhile, Urban had been gradually persuading kings and nobles to recognize him as the true pope and abandon Clement. The Normans of southern Italy were with him from the start, and France and Spain came across fairly soon. King William II of England declared that he recognized neither pope and would run the Church in England himself. William recognized Urban only after extracting a number of concessions, one of which was that papal legates could enter England only with the king's permission.

By 1095, only Henry IV was still backing Clement, so Urban decided to hold a series of synods to promote the reformist agenda. The first was held at Piacenza in March 1095. Here Urban abandoned some of his earlier conciliatory moves. All ordinations of priests and bishops by Clement were declared invalid, though those clerics whose appointments were otherwise legitimate were allowed to apply to Urban for ordination. The teachings of Berengar of Tours (*see* p.132) were condemned again. Of importance for the future, Urban received an embassy from the Byzantine emperor Alexius I Comnenus asking for military help against the Muslims. Urban followed recent papal practice by giving indulgences to those who went to help.

In November, he moved to Clermont in France where he held a fresh synod. The same rulings were decreed as at Piacenza, with the addition of the ruling that bishops and priests must not become vassals of secular lords. It was at Clermont that Urban made the greatest decision of his papacy, one that would change the face of the Middle East for centuries. He called on all Christian warriors to rescue Jerusalem from Muslim rule. The response was massive. Those at the synod were fired by fervor for holy war, and carried the message throughout Europe. Soon a vast army was on its way to the Holy Land to fight the Muslims. This was not quite what Emperor Alexius I Comnenus had asked for, he had wanted some European knights to join his army. Now he found a massive force entirely beyond his control coming like an avalanche toward his realm. The First Crusade had begun.

Urban then moved back to Rome where he sought to improve relations with those clerics in southern Italy who followed the rituals of the Eastern Church. Also consuming much of Urban's remaining time was the reformation of the papal curia. Up to this date the bureaucracy of the papacy had been based on that of the ancient Church, with ad-hoc innovations being introduced and sometimes becoming permanent. Under Urban, the curia was thoroughly restructured to reflect contemporary secular practice. Although it has been reformed several times since, the curia of today is substantially based on that created by Urban.

Statue of Pope Urban II. in the Place de la Victoire, Clermont-Ferrand, France.

1091

King Malcolm III of Scotland is defeated in battle and forced to pay feudal homage to King William II of England.

1092

A great storm floods islands off the coast of Kent that then become the Goodwin Sands, exposed only at low tide.

1094

Spanish Christian hero El Cid captures Valencia from the Muslims and begins his rule of the area that will last to his death in 1099.

PASCHAL II ✠ The 160th Pope 1099–1118

Born Bleda, Italy; date unknown

Parents Father, unknown; Mother, unknown

Papacy August 13, 1099–January 21, 1118

Died Rome, Italy; January 21, 1118

The cardinals met just 16 days after the death of Urban II and elected the cardinal priest Ranierius as Paschal II. Paschal ruled for a long time compared to other medieval popes. Much of his reign was spent pushing forward the reforms and seeking better relations with Constantinople.

In 1099, the antipope Clement III, supported by Emperor Henry IV, was still in residence near Rome, but was quickly driven away. When Clement died in September 1100, Paschal was absent from Rome. Clement's supporters infiltrated the city and, at dead of night, met in St. Peter's Basilica to elect a new pope—Theodoric. Apart from his immediate followers, nobody recognized Theodoric—not even Henry IV. He was quickly arrested and sentenced to spend his life in a monastery. Theodoric's remaining supporters then elected a man named Adalbert. He, too, was arrested and confined to a monastery for life.

In 1102, Paschal repeated Urban's condemnations of Henry. In January 1105, Henry IV's son, another Henry, launched a rebellion against his father that quickly attracted the support of disaffected nobles. Paschal gleefully gave the younger Henry his support and, when Henry IV died in March 1106, his son took over as King Henry V of Germany and Italy. Both Henry V and Paschal II expected the other to make concessions and refused to make any compromises themselves. From 1106 to 1110—at successive synods at Gauastealla, Troyes, Benevento, and the Lateran—Paschal repeated the ban on investiture by lay lords, while Henry maintained his right to appoint anyone he wanted.

In 1110, Henry marched into Italy at the head of an army to be crowned King of Italy, though his rule extended only over the northern half of the peninsula. He took advantage of the visit to arrange a meeting with Paschal, resulting in the compromise of Sutri of February 1111. Henry agreed to give up appointing bishops and Paschal agreed to hand over to Henry all lands held by the bishops that involved feudal obligations. The pair then went to Rome where, on February 12, Henry was to be crowned Holy Roman emperor. However, when word of the deal got out, the clergy rioted, inciting the mob to attack the Germans. Henry arrested Paschal and the cardinals and forced them to accompany his retreating army. Henry held the churchmen prisoner until they agreed that he would have the right to veto the investment of any churchman in his realms.

Once Paschal was back in Rome in the summer of 1111 he was so ashamed of what he had done that he offered to abdicate. Instead, his cardinals advised him to repudiate the agreement as having been imposed by force, which he did at the Lateran Synod of 1112. Paschal spent his final years squabbling with the emperor and excommunicating anyone who supported him. His efforts to restore relations with Eastern Christianity foundered when he insisted that the pope be recognized as the senior bishop with authority over all Christians.

Bishop Ivo of Chartres suggested a compromise during the Investiture Crisis, which was taken up in France and England. The bishop was said to owe his position to God, and so was invested by the pope, but to owe his lands to his king, and so he had to swear fealty to the secular lord. This meant that if the bishop or abbot did not fulfil his duties to his king he could be deprived of his lands, but not of his position.

1100 Approximate date for the founding of Cuzco, Peru, later to be the capital of the Inca Empire.

1100 Kaifeng, then capital of China, reaches a population of 1 million people.

1101 King Baldwin of Jerusalem captures Arsuf and Caesarea for the crusaders.

1107 The city of Florence begins to extend its power in Tuscany by taking the nearby town of Monte Orlandi.

1108 The Battle of Ucles sees a victory for the Muslims in Spain over the Christian kingdom of Castile, resulting in the Muslim recapture of swathes of territory.

GELASIUS II ✠ The 161st Pope 1118–1119

Born Gaeta, Italy; c.1061
Parents Unknown
Papacy January 24, 1118–January 29, 1119
Died Cluny, France; January 29, 1119

Pen-and-ink drawing depicting Emperor Henry V visiting his father in prison.

The short reign of Gelasius II was dominated by the Investiture Crisis – the question of who should invest into office a new bishop or abbot—and the resulting disputes with the Holy Roman emperor Henry V and his allies. In fact, much of his life had been dominated by the same dispute.

Gelasius came from the noble Caetani family of Pisa, though which branch is unknown. He entered the great Monastery of Monte Cassino as a boy, becoming a monk there as soon as he was old enough to do so. At some point in the 1080s, he moved to Rome to join the curia, becoming a cardinal in 1088 and chancellor of Rome in 1089. For the next 29 years, he held office as chancellor, overseeing many of the reforms to the papal bureaucracy that have endured to the present day. He joined Paschal II in captivity under Emperor Henry V and loyally supported the pope to the end.

He was elected pope unanimously by the cardinals three days after Paschal died, taking the name of Gelasius II. That night Gelasius was kidnapped by a gang led by Cencio Frangipane, who took the new pope to his fortified home in Rome but was soon confronted by an angry mob led by the city prefect. The abduction was probably an attempt by the local nobles to impose their will on the secular side of the government of the Papal States.

No sooner was Gelasius free from Frangipane than he heard that Henry V was marching on Rome at the head of a large army. Gelasius and the cardinals fled to Gaeta where the consecration of the new pope took place on March 10. From Rome, Henry sent a message demanding that Gelasius return to the city for talks to solve the Investiture Crisis. The pope refused, insisting that he would call a great Council to meet in Milan, in northern Italy, to discuss the issue instead.

Henry V was furious. He announced that Gelasius had been improperly elected and organized a new election at which Archbishop Maurice of Braga was elected as Gregory VIII. In response, Gelasius excommunicated both Henry and Gregory and sent long, tightly argued letters throughout Christendom explaining why he was the legitimate pope. Nobody other than Henry recognized the claims of Gregory, now regarded as an antipope. In June 1118, Henry and Gregory left Rome, and Gelasius tried to return. However, imperial troops were in control of the city and Gelasius fled to France.

In January 1119, Gelasius held a synod at Vienne where he announced that a great council would be held to decide various issues, prominently the Investiture Crisis. He then fell ill and was taken to the Abbey of Cluny, where he died.

NORBERT OF XANTEN

At Saint Gilles, near Nimes, Gelasius made possibly his most far-reaching decision. In audience with the German monk and ascetic, Norbert of Xanten, Gelasius granted permission for Norbert to become an itinerant preacher. This meant that Norbert could preach sermons anywhere he liked without fear of being hounded by the local authorities. Given that Norbert's views on penance and luxury tended to be controversially strict, this was a highly valued gift. Norbert went on to found the famously strict Premonstratensian order of monks.

1110	1112	1118	1118	1118
The crusaders capture Sidon and Beirut.	The margravate of Baden becomes independent of the duchy of Swabia, part of a trend toward fragmentation of the states in Germany.	The crusaders invade Egypt but are defeated.	In Spain, Tarragona and Zaragozza are recaptured from the Muslims by Christian rulers along with the Ebro Valley.	A great fire destroys nearly all of Magdeburg in Germany.

CALLIXTUS II ✠ The 162nd Pope 1119–1124

Born probably Burgundy; c.1064

Parents Father, Count William I of Burgundy; Mother, Countess Stephanie of Burgundy

Papacy February 2, 1119–December 14, 1124

Died Rome, Italy; December 14, 1124

The handful of cardinals in France following the death of Pope Gelasius at Cluny elected a man who they felt was ideally positioned to do a deal with the Holy Roman emperor Henry V. That man was Archbishop Guy of Vienne, who took the name of Callixtus II. Callixtus had been born into one of the most powerful families in Europe.

Callixtus's childhood had been spent at the royal courts of Germany, France, and England where he had got to know not only the kings, but also heirs and numerous nobles. He was on familiar terms with kings and the emperor.

Callixtus was, however, also a fervent reformer. He had been an outspoken supporter of Gregory VII in his disputes with Emperor Henry IV (*see* p.140) and had led the condemnations of Paschal II's abortive agreement with Henry V (*see* p.146). Going further than any pope during the Investiture Crisis, he had denounced lay investiture as a heresy and refused to recognize Henry as emperor. He was also seeking to prove the long-claimed superiority of the bishop of Vienne over the bishop of Arles.

Vienne Cathedral where Callixtus became archbishiop in 1088.

When the other cardinals, who had been left behind in Italy, heard of Callixtus's elevation they approved it, then waited to see what Callixtus would do. Given his previously intransigent stand, what Callixtus did next took everyone by surprise. He contacted Henry and suggested that they send representatives to thrash out a compromise with which both could agree.

After much discussion, the two sides produced a document that they hoped emperor and pope could accept. Callixtus, however, thought that the wording was too vague on certain points, then got distracted trying to patch up a deal between King Henry I of England and his brother Duke Robert II of Normandy. Henry V had meanwhile mustered an army 30,000 strong but had not sent a response to the draft. Assuming the emperor intended to renege on the deal and bully the Church into submission, Callixtus excommunicated him and then set off for Rome.

The journey south turned into a triumphal procession as supporters flocked to cheer Callixtus. When he arrived in Rome it was to find that antipope Gregory had fled to nearby Sutri. He was quickly dragged back to Rome, excommunicated, and imprisoned in a monastery where he lived until around 1143. In fact, Henry had been prepared to recognize Callixtus as pope and to accept any deal that did not impinge on his honor. New messages were exchanged and, in 1122, talks reopened with Bishop Lamberto of Ostia leading the papal delegation.

After weeks of argument at Worms in Germany, the two sides agreed the Concordat of Worms on September 23, 1122. Under this agreement, the clergy of Germany were free

1119

Battles of Ager and Hab. Ilgahzi of Aleppo wipes out the crusader army of Antioch at Ager before being himself crushed at Hab by King Badlwin II of Jerusalem.

1119

The order of the Knights Templar is founded in Jerusalem by French knight Hugues de Payens with the aim of protecting pilgrims on the roads of the Holy Land.

1122

French theologian Peter Abelard writes his ground breaking work *Sic et Non*, which brings logic to bear on Christian beliefs.

Worms cathedral where representatives of the pope and Emperor Henry V agreed the Concordat of Worms.

to elect their own bishops and abbots so long as the elections took place in the presence of the emperor or his representative. The emperor was no longer to invest the new cleric into his position, but he was to invest him with the lands and feudal fiefs that went with the position. The Church had gained free elections, the emperor had maintained his grip on secular privileges. The Investiture Crisis was over—almost.

In March 1123, Callixtus at last convened the great council planned by his predecessor Paschal II at the Lateran in Rome. When he announced the details of the Concordat of Worms there was enormous uproar from stricter supporters of reform. They argued that the lands held by the bishops and abbots belonged to God and that granting the emperor the right to invest bishops with the lands compromised this principle. Callixtus replied that the practice should be tolerated in fact, but not accepted in law. He thus left open the possibility that a future pope might reopen the dispute.

Henry V and the Archbishop Adalbert of Mainz, Germany, who played a key role in opposing Henry V during the Investiture Crisis.

The Lateran Council of 1123 is recognized in the West as the Ninth General Council of the Church since the time of Christ. The scale of the event was vast, with over 900 bishops and abbots attending along with their assorted servants and entourages. As well as ratifying the Concordat, the Council formalized a number of canon laws and other regulations that had been announced by popes at recent synods. These included indulgences for those on crusade against the Muslims, protection for pilgrims, and various disciplinary canon laws

PRIESTLY CELIBACY

The issue of celibacy for clergy came to be an issue in the early days of the reign of Stephen III when clergy were allowed to marry. The scriptural basis for celibacy was drawn primarily from the Gospel of St. Matthew where those serving God were asked to be "eunuchs for the sake of heaven" and from passages in the letters of St. Paul that imply celibacy allows a man to serve God better. As early as the year 300, the Synod of Elvira called on all priests in Spain to be celibate, and other similar summonses followed at regular intervals throughout Christendom. Celibacy finally became mandatory at the First Lateran Council in 1123 under Calixtus II, with slavery being the punishment for any wives or children of priests who did not abandon their spouse. The Reformation of the 16th century saw most Protestant churches abandon clerical celibacy. During the early 21st century there were calls from some Catholic theologians for the issue to be reexamined and discussed.

After the Council broke up, Callixtus returned to an issue that he had pursued before his elevation to the papacy. He decreed that the Bishopric of Vienne was superior to the Bishopric of Arles. Going further, he gave Vienne supremacy over the bishops of Grenoble, Valence, Die, Viviers, Geneva, Maurienne, Tarantaise, Bourges, Narbonne, Bordeaux, Aix, Auch, and Embrun as well. The newly promoted archbishop of Vienne was given the title primate of primates.

Before his death, Callixtus had time to order the restoration of several churches in Rome, most notably Santa Maria in Cosmedin.

1123

The Italian city of Bologna elects consuls to run its internal government, continuing a trend among Italian cities to become effectively independent of the king of Italy.

1123

St. Bartholomew's Hospital, the oldest hospital in Britain, is founded in London.

1124

Arnald becomes the first bishop of Greenland.

1124

Mael Maedoc ua Morgair (St. Malachy) becomes bishop of Down in Ireland and starts to introduce Cluniac reforms to the Irish Church.

HONORIUS II ✠ The 163rd Pope 1124–1130

Born Fiagnano, Italy; date unknown

Parents Unknown

Papacy December 21, 1124–February 13, 1130

Died Rome, Italy; 13 February, 1130

The papal election of 1124 was one of the most dramatic on record, with Honorius coming out the winner only to endure an equally turbulent and mostly unsuccessful papacy. Honorius was born as Lamberto Scannabecchi to a poor family in northern Italy. His intelligence won him an education in the Church and he had risen to be cardinal bishop of Ostia.

The death of Callixtus II was not unexpected, and it would seem that the various factions of cardinals had been laying their plans. Key to those plans were the local Roman nobles, who had their own motives for getting involved. The Frangipani family owned the Colosseum, which they converted into a fortress, and favored the foreign cardinals. The equally wealthy Pierleoni family were based on the Tiber Island.

On December 16, the cardinals gathered in a chapel attached to the Lateran. The discussions were heading toward electing Cardinal Saxo when one cardinal, a friend of the Pierleoni, suggested Cardinal Theobaldo Boccapecci instead. A quick vote produced a majority for Theobaldo, who took the name Celestine II. He was then clad in the papal robes, enthroned, and signaled the traditional *Te Deum* be sung. At this point, the doors were flung open and in rushed a gang of armed men led by Leo Frangipani who bundled Theobaldo from the throne. Cardinal Aymeric then proposed Lamberto for pope. With Frangipani swords at their throats, the cardinals elected Lamberto.

Rioting and bloodshed followed, until Leo Frangipani offered the city prefect a huge bribe, and won over the Pierleoni with promises. Celestine was declared not to have been properly elected as he had not been consecrated and Lamberto was hailed as Pope Honorius II. Unfortunately, Lamberto had in the meantime abdicated to halt the bloodshed. A hurried second election reelected him and he took office.

Celestine, meanwhile, had been carried off to receive medical treatment for the wounds he suffered during the election. He was described by his contemporaries as being elderly and, although he recovered from his wounds, he does not seem to have ever fully regained his health. He went back to being cardinal priest of Santa Anastasia, where he died sometime before the end of 1126. Because he was never consecrated, he is not recognized as being a valid pope. He had, however, been elected and enthroned so he is officially deemed to have been an antipope.

One of Honorius's first actions as pope was to make Aymeric chancellor of the papacy. Together, the two men concentrated on internal Church reforms. Chief among these issues was the drive to raise the moral, spiritual,

THE NEW CARDINALS

The days when the cardinals were simply the local parish priests of Rome were fading; over recent decades there had been a growing tendency for popes to appoint cardinals for their talents or their contacts. By 1124, most cardinals were men from outside Rome—many from outside Italy—who hired a junior cleric to undertake the actual work of being a parish priest in Rome. The future Honorius II was typical of such men. Honorius had been a close adviser to both Gelasius II and Callixtus II and was recognized as a leading figure among the newer, non-Roman cardinals.

1124	1125	1126	1127
Hungary's Stephen II is defeated in battle by the Byzantine emperor John II Comnenus who supports claims to the throne by Bela, who had been blinded by the Hungarian king Coloman.	The Holy Roman emperor Henry V dies at Utrecht, aged 44, having led an expedition against France's Louis VI. He is succeeded by Lothair III.	The Peace of 1126 ends hostilities between John II Comnenus and the Hungarians and Venetians.	Sicily's Roger II claims the Hauteville possessions in Italy as well as overlordship of Capua, but subjects of Apulia resist union with Sicily and are supported by Pope Honorius II who excommunicates Roger and lays claim himself to Norman possessions in southern Italy.

Seal of Emperor Lothair III, who wrote a letter to Honorius formally announcing his election. The letter was couched in terms that later popes took to mean that he had asked Honorius to approve his election.

and educational levels of priests and other clerics.

It was a long, drawn-out process with little by way of dramatic incidents that called for sustained effort and an eye for detail. Honorius promoted to the rank of cardinal men who shared his views on the need for internal improvement.

Honorius believed that the older monastic orders were too concerned with their own affairs to be of much use, and so favored the canons regular—communities of priests usually attached to a cathedral. While monks lived a cloistered life and were generally lay brothers, canons were ordained priests who went out into the community. He also favored new orders that promised to share his agenda. Among these were the Premonstratensians and the Knights Templar, the former an order of unrivaled strictness and austerity while the latter was a military order dedicated to fighting the Muslims.

The older orders do not seem to have taken kindly to the favor being shown elsewhere. The details are obscure but, in 1126, Abbot Pontius of Cluny was suddenly arrested and imprisoned. Shortly afterwards Abbot Oderisius of Monte Cassino was summoned to Rome for an interview with Honorius and at once resigned, presumably not wanting to share the fate of Pontius. What either man had actually done wrong is unclear, the charges of personal extravagance and luxury leveled at Pontius were clearly untrue.

Although Honorius wished to devote his papacy to Church reforms, he was inevitably dragged into political matters. The most important of these came in 1125 when Henry V died without an heir. The thrones of Germany, Italy, and the Holy Roman Empire were all vacant, but there was no shortage of claimants. In Germany, Lothair of Supplinburg and Frederick of Swabia were the leading contenders. Both were rich, powerful men who were descended from the old Carolingian dynasty. In the event the German nobles elected Lothair, who wrote a letter to Honorius formally announcing his election. When Frederick died, his claim was taken up by his brother Conrad who had himself crowned king of Italy by Archbishop Anselm of Milan. Honorius promptly excommunicated both men and declared that Lothair was the true king.

Honorius was asked to judge the disputes between the bishops of Britain as to who had primacy. The archbishop of Canterbury thought he was the head of the Church in all Great Britain, but the Scottish and Welsh bishops objected, as did the archbishop of York. Honorius avoided giving a definitive ruling but instead made William of Canterbury his legate in Britain, assuring him of primacy by virtue of that position.

In 1127, Duke William of Apulia and Calabria died childless. His cousin Roger II of Sicily at once invaded southern Italy and seized both duchies. Honorius had no wish to see the Normans of southern Italy united under one strong leader. He wrote to Roger instructing him to return to Sicily while putting together an alliance of other Norman nobles to oppose Roger. There followed an indecisive campaign of sieges, long marches, and tactical retreats. In the end Aymeric visited Roger and negotiated a deal by which Roger gave up Calabria in return for papal recognition of his rule over Apulia.

In January 1130, Honorius fell ill and it soon became clear that death was approaching. On the orders of Aymeric, Honorius was moved to the monastery of St. Gregory on the Caelian Hill where he was put under armed guard by the Frangipani. His death was kept secret for Aymeric had his own plans for the papacy and did not want the cardinals to interfere.

1127

The order of the Knights Templar, founded in 1120, is recognized and confirmed by Pope Honorius II.

1128

Cistercian monks from Normandy settle in England and begin an extensive program of swamp reclamation, agricultural improvement, and stock breeding.

1129

Sicily's Roger II is recognized as duke at Melfi in September by the barons of Naples, Bari, Capua, Salerno, and the other cities that have resisted him.

INNOCENT II ✢ The 164th Pope 1130–1143

Born Probably Rome, Italy; date unknown
Parents Unknown
Papacy February 14, 113–September 24 1143
Died Rome, Italy; September 24, 1143

Born Gregorio Papareschi, probably in Rome, Innocent II was related to one of the noble families that had their home in the fashionable Trastevere area. In 1116, he became cardinal deacon of San Angelo. His papacy was marked by schism between rival popes representing different camps of reformers. His eventual victory marked a definite shift in Church policies.

Gregorio was part of the mission sent to Germany that concluded the Concordat of Worms (*see* p.148). He also undertook work for Honorius II. When Honorius died on the evening of February 13, 1130, the powerful papal chancellor Aymeric put the body in a temporary grave in the Monastery of St. Gregory in total secrecy and summoned the minority of cardinals who supported the new reform movement that he and Honorius had espoused. They elected Gregorio to be pope and, as dawn broke, the group of cardinals hurried to the Lateran where they enthroned him as Innocent II. Word spread quickly, and the other cardinals met at San Marco where they elected Pietro Pierleoni to be Anacletus II.

Furious negotiations followed, but no agreement could be reached. On February 23 both popes were consecrated. Innocent was consecrated by the bishop of Ostia in Sta Maria Nuova, Anacletus by the bishop of Porto in St. Peter's. It was by this date usual for new popes to be consecrated by the bishops of Ostia and Porto acting together, so neither claimant could say that his consecration was correctly carried out.

A 12th-century mosaic in the Church of Santa Maria in Trastevere, Rome, showing Pope Innocent II (left) next to St. Lawrence. The church, which the pope is depicted holding, was razed by Innocent along with the tomb of his rival Anacletus and rebuilt to enshrine his own tomb instead.

Behind the dispute lay differing views on Church reform. The supporters of Anacletus were the older cardinals and those from Italy who favored the program set out by Gregory VII. They wanted to see a Church separated from secular control that was able to run its own affairs. The younger cardinals, and those from outside Italy, backed Innocent. They wanted to see cooperation with secular rulers while improving the quality of learning and morality in the Church.

Within days, Anacletus had managed to win over to his side nearly everybody in Rome by promising to restore the influence of the people and nobles of Rome in papal elections. He was just as successful in getting the support of the powerful Norman baron Roger of Sicily by recognizing his right to rule Apulia and Calabria as well as Sicily and granting him the title king of Sicily. Innocent fled, sending messengers with his version of events to rally support.

By 1132, the bishops and rulers of Europe had made their decisions. With the exception of Scotland, Aquitaine, and Sicily, they all recognized Innocent as pope. It seems that everyone had had enough of disputes between Church and state and favored the peaceful reforms promised by Innocent. Anacletus proposed a meeting to sort things out, but Innocent declared that Christendom had made its choice. He then declared an anathema on Anacletus. Later historians have followed Innocent, so Anacletus is now regarded as an antipope.

Innocent met Lothair III, king of Germany, and induced him to invade Italy on the promise of

1132

The abbeys of Fountains, Tintern, and Rievaulx are founded in England.

1133

Geoffrey of Monmouth completes his *History of the Kings of Britain*, a highly influential work that was considered to be true at the time, but is now recognized as being a mix of truth, legend, and myth.

1133

Battle of Fraga. King Alfonso I of Aragon is defeated by the Muslim army of the Almoravid dynasty leading to a setback in the Christian campaign to drive the Muslims from Spain.

1134

The Basilica of St. Denis, France, is destroyed by fire. The rebuilding work heralds a new style of architecture—Gothic.

PETER ABELARD

The French Philosopher Peter Abelard has been recognized as one of the most influential thinkers of the Middle Ages. He brought the cold light of logic to bear on Christian theology and on an eclectic mix of writings from pagan antiquity. He is, however, rather better known today for his doomed romance. By 1115, when he became a canon at Notre Dame in Paris, Abelard was the most famous teacher in Europe, attracting hundreds of student to each of his lectures. He then fell desperately in love with a pupil—the beautiful and intelligent Heloise, daughter of his fellow canon Fulbert. The two secretly married and had a son, Astrolabe. Fulbert was furious. He bundled Heloise off to a convent and hired a gang of thugs to castrate Abelard. Abelard then became a monk and devoted himself to study, producing his most mature philosophical work. However, he was accused of heresy by a council at Sens. Abelard set out to appeal to Pope Innocent II, who had confirmed the condemnation. He died en route to Rome.

crowning him Holy Roman emperor. In May 1133, Lothair and Innocent entered Rome in triumph—marred by the fact that Anacletus and his men were barricaded inside St. Peter's and the buildings on the Vatican Hill. Innocent took up residence in the Lateran, crowning Lothair Holy Roman emperor there on June 3.

Lothair then tried to reopen the Investiture Crisis by asking Innocent to grant to him the right to invest bishops and abbots inside his realms. Innocent had no wish to unpick the agreement of the Concordat of Worms, but he knew he had to concede something. He therefore told German bishops that they had to do homage to the emperor for their lands before they could start collecting rents. He also confirmed Lothair in his possession of the vast estates of Countess Matilda of Tuscany, while emphasizing that the pope was overlord of these lands.

Lothair then had to return to Germany to take care of his empire. As soon as he was gone, Anacletus emerged from the Vatican Hill and drove Innocent out of Rome. Taking up residence in Pisa, Innocent set about driving forward his program of reform, which included the condemnation of Peter Abelard (*see* box).

In 1138, news came of the death of Anacletus. His followers quickly elected a replacement, Cardinal Gregorio Conti, who took the title Victor IV. However, Roger of Sicily was already in talks with Innocent and almost nobody recognized the claims of the new antipope. In May, Victor and his supporters made submission to Innocent at Pisa and were pardoned. Once he was firmly back in Rome, however, Innocent held the Second Lateran Council at which he condemned Victor and his supporters, deprived them of their offices and incomes, and threw them out of Rome. Many of Innocent's own supporters were appalled by this breach of promise, but Innocent stood firm.

His intransigence also led to trouble with Roger of Sicily. It was only when Roger marched on Rome, defeated the papal army, and captured Innocent himself that Innocent was induced to honor his promises. At the Treaty of Migniano, Roger was recognized as king of Sicily with power over his mainland estates. Innocent was no more tactful with the people of Rome, who rioted in the summer of 1143. The citizens set up a city government as a rival to the authority of the pope. This Commune of Rome established democratic elections for a senate to rule the city, with Giordano Pierleone elected patrician, or chief official. Innocent just had time to hear this news before his death from fever.

1135

Death of King Henry I of England. The crown his claimed by his daughter Matilda and his nephew Stephen, plunging England into years of civil war and anarchy.

1137

The Zagwe Dynasty takes control of most of Christian Ethiopia, which it will rule until 1270.

1138

Florence becomes self-governing under elected consuls, effectively throwing off rule by the king of Italy, who is also Holy Roman emperor.

1143

Roger of Sicily captures Sfax in North Africa and imposes his overlordship on the emirate of Mahdia.

CELESTINE II ✠ The 165th Pope 1143–1144

Born Citta de Castello, Italy; date unknown

Parents Unknown

Papacy September 26, 1143–March 8, 1144

Died Rome, Italy; March 8, 1144

Celstine was born Guy di Castello in Umbria to parents of the minor nobility. His reign is recognized as one of the least impressive of the medieval period. He failed to achieve almost everything he set out to do, and is notorious for launching the disastrous Second Crusade.

As a youth, Guy had studied under Peter Abelard (*see* p.153) and went on to become a teacher himself. He was already middle aged when he came to Rome to serve Callixtus II. In 1127, he was made cardinal deacon at Santa Maria in Via Lata by Honorius II and promoted to be cardinal priest at San Marco by Innocent II. He shared the reformist program of Honorius and Innocent and was a friend of the powerful papal chancellor Aymeric.

Two days after Innocent's death, Guy was elected by a unanimous vote of the cardinals. His drive for reform found early expression in his launching of a collection for the Knights Templar. He also granted control of the hospital of Saint Mary Teutonicorum to the Knights Hospitaller, another new reformist body of armed monks.

In the political sphere, however, Celestine turned against the policies of his predecessor. He sought agreement with Louis VII of France. An arrangement was reached by which Louis accepted Pierre de la Chartre as archbishop of Bourge, as Innocent had wanted, and in return Celestine lifted the punishments that Innocent had imposed and backed down on some other demands made by Innocent. Having received the warm support of Matilda, widow of Emperor Henry V, Celestine returned the favor by supporting her claim to the throne of England.

In Italy, Celestine decided to challenge the might of King Roger of Sicily. He refused to honor the terms of the Treaty of Migniano agreed between Roger and Innocent. He recognized Roger's rule over Sicily, but not over his mainland dominions. Roger at once mustered his men for war and marched on Benevento, a papal fief outside the Papal States proper. Realizing that his own military resources were not up to the task of defending the Papal States, Celestine at once capitulated and sent messengers to Roger. He died before they could return.

Celestine supported Empress Matilda's claim to the English throne but the blessing did little to help. So chaotic did the civil war become, it was claimed that "God and his angels slept."

The Second Crusade was the first to be led by royalty, with both King Louis VII of France (below) and King Conrad III of Germany marching for the Holy Land. Louis was defeated by the Turks at Cadmus in January 1148. The Crusade ended in a humiliating defeat for the European kings, who were sent scurrying back to Jerusalem with heavy casualties.

1143

Portuguese independence is recognized by Castile in the Treaty of Zamora arranged by the Vatican. Alfonso Henriques is proclaimed king and founds the Portuguese monarchy and Burgundian dynasty.

1143

The Byzantine emperor John II Comnenus dies, aged 55, after a 25-year reign. He is succeeded by his 23-year-old son, who will reign for 37 years as Manuel I Comnenus.

LUCIUS II ✢ The 166th Pope 1144–1145

Born Bologna, Italy; date unknown

Parents Father, Orso Caccianemici; Mother, unknown

Papacy March 12, 1144 – February 15, 1145

Died Rome, Italy; February 15, 1145

Born Gherado Caccianemici, into comfortable circumstances, Lucius came to the papal throne with much promise but was unable to deal with the problems left by his predecessors. He was destined to become one of the few popes to die as a result of wounds suffered in battle.

At a young age, Gherado joined the community of canons at San Frediano in Lucca, at the time recognized as perhaps the most important such house in Italy. He somehow attracted the attention of Pope Honorius II who, in 1124, summoned him to Rome to become cardinal priest of Santa Croce in Gerusalemme. In 1128, he was given the particularly delicate task of being governor of Benevento. The citizens of Benevento had just murdered the previous governor and declared that they wanted self-government under papal suzerainty. Gherado introduced some reforms to placate the rebels.

When the powerful papal chancellor Aymeric died in 1141, Gherado was appointed to succeed him. He was thus ideally placed to take over when Celestine II died. On being elected pope, Gherado adopted the name Lucius II in honor of the pope whose feast day fell on March 5.

Lucius at once found himself confronted with a host of difficulties. Some of these were relatively straightforward. He confirmed the rights of the archbishop of Tours to preside over the bishops of Brittany, rejecting the claims of the bishop of Dol to be independent. He similarly put down the claims of Bishop Bernard of St. David's to be independent of Canterbury. Also in Britain, he confirmed the claimed ancient rights of the Abbey of St. Edmund at Bury St. Edmunds to be free of all secular control, taxes, and duties. He thus laid the basis on which the Abbey came to be one of the richest in all England.

Meanwhile, Alfonso of Portugal had recently won independence from the kingdom of Leon and wanted ecclesiastical freedom for his bishops from the archbishop of Toledo. Lucius refused.

It was, however, the situation in Rome itself that was to prove intractable. For help against the Commune of Rome (*see* p.152), Lucius turned to King Roger II of Sicily. When he had been governor of Benevento, Lucius had known Roger and the two had got on well. Roger, however, was in the midst of a massive overhaul of the administration of his various domains so Lucius turned to King Conrad III of Germany but he, too, was otherwise engaged—dealing with a rebellion by Duke Henry of Saxony.

Lucius therefore called out the militia and feudal array of the Papal States. As Lucius and his army approached, the newly appointed patrician Giordano Pierleoni offered peace if Lucius would accept that within the walls of Rome his status and powers were restricted to those of bishop. Lucius refused out of hand and attacked. Some Roman nobles, notably the Frangipani family, promptly declared for the pope and the papal army streamed into the city. Pierleoni, most of the elected senators, and many citizens retreated to the fortress on top of the Capitoline Hill. From there they launched numerous sorties that turned the Forum into a battlefield. When Lucius launched an attack on the Capitoline he was driven back, being badly wounded by a stone hurled from the battlements. He died a few days later.

Lucius II asked King Conrad III of Germany (below) for help resisting the Commune of Rome but Conrad had his own rebellion to deal with. In the Second Crusade, Conrad marched into Anatolia where he was defeated and wounded by the Turks at Dorylaeum on October 25, 1147.

1144

Geoffrey of Anjou (right), son-in-law of England's late Henry I, becomes duke of Normandy

1144

The murder of William, a 12 year old boy in Norwich, is blamed on local Jews who are said to have carried out the murder for ritual reasons, the first known example of what became known as the Blood Libel.

1144

The crusader state of Edessa falls to Zengi, Muslim atabeg of Mosul.

EUGENE III ✠ The 167th Pope 1145–1153

Born Pisa, Italy; c.1087
Parents Unknown
Papacy February 15, 1145–July 8, 1153
Died Tivoli, Italy; July 8, 1153

The papacy of Eugene III is remembered for his sponsorship of the disastrous Second Crusade launched by Celestine II (*see* p.154), but far more of his time was spent trying to grapple with intractable political issues inside Italy. The last of the popes who loudly promoted reform, his difficulties elsewhere meant he was able to achieve little real change.

Eugene was born as Bernardo Pignatelli in Pisa. His parents were not rich, but seem to have been engaged in trade of some kind. There are indications that his family may have been linked somehow to the rich and noble Paganelli, but the connection, if it existed, is quite obscure. By 1106, he was a canon attached to the cathedral at Pisa and appears in a document of 1115 as a subdeacon there. By 1137, he was Prior of San Zeno, again in Pisa, but then he met Bernard of Clairveaux and left Pisa for Clairveaux, France, where he became a monk of the Cistercian Order and took up its reform agenda with zeal.

In 1140, Innocent II made Bernardo abbot of San Anastasio alle Tre Fontane near Rome with instructions to reform the abbey along Cistercian lines. The abbey was massively renovated and restored at this time, with Bernardo winning a reputation for sanctity and determination.

When Lucius II was killed fighting the forces of the Commune of Rome (*see* p.155), there were 34 cardinals in Rome out of about 40 then in office. They hurriedly retreated to San Cesareo in Palatio and—barely two hours after the death of Lucius—elected Benardo, who took the name Eugene III.

The city of Rome was quite unsafe by next morning, so the cardinals hurried 30 miles north to the Monastery of Farfa where Eugene was consecrated. Unable to return to Rome, he retreated to Viterbo.

Eugene summoned to his aid the militia of the Papal States and King Roger II of Sicily. By Christmas 1145, he was able to take up residence in the Lateran but, within days, his uncompromising stance on who should govern Rome led to fresh trouble with the Commune authorities and he again fled to Viterbo.

He had meanwhile heard of the fall of the crusader county of Edessa to the Muslims. On December 1, 1145, after consulting with Bernard of Clairveaux (*see* box), he sent a bull to King Louis VII of France authorizing him to raise a crusade to go to the Holy Land and fight the Muslims. The usual indulgences were given to those leaving on crusade and other inducements given to Louis. In January 1146, Eugene himself went to France to discuss the crusade with Louis and, in March, he authorized Bernard of Clairveaux to preach the crusade and call for volunteers. Bernard exceeded his instructions by preaching the crusade outside France, winning over King Conrad III of Germany and many of his nobles to the cause. Word of the crusade spread throughout Europe and soon a small army was gathering in England, while another in Spain prepared to renew the assault on the Muslims of southern Spain.

Hildegard of Bingen, a German abbess and philosopher, was called upon to explain her claim to have visions of "the light of God" and some of her writings. An intense correspondence followed, but Hildegard gained the support of Bernard of Clairveaux and so was given permission to continue in office.

1145
Merv in central Asia is estimated to have a population of over 200,000, making it the largest Muslim city and probably the largest city outside China.

1145
Construction of Chartres Cathedral begins.

1147
Traditional date for the founding of Moscow.

1147
The fundamentalist Muslim movement of the Almohads completes its conquest of North Africa west of Egypt and moves into southern Spain.

BERNARD OF CLAIRVEAUX

Bernard was born near Dijon in France, in 1090, to a wealthy noble family. He became a monk at the age of 21 and, just three years later, was sent to found a new house in the Val d'Absinthe. He cleared the dense forest of the area and named the foundation "Claire Vallée," which was soon corrupted to Clairveaux. He became a great champion of orthodoxy within the Church, condemning in forthright terms anything he considered to be heretical. As such, he led the campaign to have the writings of Peter Abelard condemned. His enthusiasm for reading and contemplating the scriptures and for prayer helped to establish *Lectio Divina* as a key activity for monks. His influence was immense and many bishops and rulers sought his advice.

Frederick I concluded the Agreement of Constance with Pope Eugene III.

As the crusaders set off to march to the Holy Land, Eugene pushed ahead with his agenda to reform the Church. He relentlessly championed high-quality learning and moral rectitude among the clergy, being unforgiving to those who fell below his own high standards. Archbishop William of York, for instance, was ousted from office after allegations were made that he had been improperly installed by King Stephen who needed a supportive Church for his civil war against his cousin Matilda.

William was not the only one to suffer. Also subjected to intense study were the writings of the German abbess Hildegard of Bingen and the French philosopher Gilbert de la Porree. Gilbert studied the ancient Greek writers and postulated that the eternal God was a pure being of incomprehensible goodness, while the Trinity was the way that God manifested himself on Earth. He was put on trial for heresy, with Eugene himself presiding and Bernard of Clairveaux acting as prosecutor. It is generally thought that Gilbert defended himself well, but that Bernard's influence over the pope ensured a guilty verdict. Gilbert was given the opportunity to change certain sections of his writings before sentence was passed. This he did, and so was allowed to walk free. Hildegard of Bingen remained in office largely because she gained the support of Bernard of Clairveaux.

Among Eugene's reforms was the reorganization of the Church in Ireland into four archdioceses and his declaration of the doctrine that St. Peter had given to his successors as bishops of Rome supreme authority in all temporal and spiritual matters.

The crushing defeat of the Second Crusade had a profound effect on Eugene and undermined the influence of Bernard of Clairveaux. In 1149, Eugene tried to come to terms with the Commune of Rome. They remained steadfast in their determination that Eugene should have the rights and powers of a bishop, but no more than that. Eugene would not accept any reduction in his absolute powers to rule, so he turned to King Roger of Sicily for help. As in 1145, Roger led an army to Rome and, in December 1149, Eugene again took up residence in the Lateran. Once again, however, Roger did not stay in Rome and, as soon as he was gone, Eugene was driven out again.

Eugene then turned to King Conrad III of Germany. It was arranged that Conrad would lead an army into Italy in 1152, arriving in Rome by the autumn, whereupon he would be crowned Holy Roman emperor by Eugene. The deal fell through when Conrad died in February 1152. The following month his son Frederick Barbarossa was elected king of Germany. Frederick sent a message to Eugene announcing his election and promising to support Eugene. There was some friction as Frederick did not seek papal confirmation of his election, as Eugene thought he should. Eugene replied giving his confirmation, which Frederick thought he did not need.

The spat was soon smoothed over and, in March 1153, pope and king concluded the Agreement of Constance by which Frederick undertook to come to Rome to install Eugene in the Lateran and be crowned Holy Roman emperor. However, before Frederick could muster his army for the long march south, Eugene had died.

1147

Sicily's Roger II takes advantage of the disastrous Second Crusade to seize the Greek islands and attack Athens, Thebes, and Corinth.

1150

The University of Paris (Sorbonne) is founded.

1150

The vat Hindu temple of Angkor Wat is completed at Yasodharapura, capital of the Khmer Empire in what is now Cambodia.

1151

The Anping Bridge is completed at Quanzhou, China. At 1.25 miles long it is the longest in the world and will remain so until 1846.

ANASTASIUS IV ✠ The 168th Pope 1153–1154

Born Rome, Italy; c.1073

Parents Father, Benedictus de Suburra; Mother, unknown

Papacy July 8, 1153–December 3, 1154

Died Rome, Italy; December 3, 1154

Anastasius was already old by the time he became pope, and he was to survive for just over a year. In that time he made remarkable strides in bringing peace to the papacy and its relations with both the secular and ecclesiastical world around it.

Anastasius was born with the name of Corrado into a family of merchants or traders of some kind that may have been related to the far more illustrious Demetri family of nobles. Absolutely nothing is known of the first 41 years of his life, but we do know that, in 1114, he became cardinal priest of Santa Pudenziana. In 1127, he became bishop of Sabina, apparently after he had helped Honorius II deal with the disputed appointment of a new abbot of Farfa. In 1130, he sided with Innocent II against the antipope Anacletus II. While Innocent was absent from Rome, it was Corrado who represented him in and around Italy's capital. He performed a similar duty for Eugene III during the years that he was in exile. During these years, he established and maintained a working relationship with the Commune of Rome and with a large number of nobles and clerics in central and southern Italy. It was probably this, along with his reputation for diplomacy, that ensured the cardinals elected him on the day that Eugene III died.

Immediately after his election, Anastasius took up residence in the Lateran Palace. There was no attempt by the Commune to drive him from Rome and he seems to have enjoyed good relations with the civic authorities. Soon after this, Anastasius began building a new complex close to the Pantheon, another sign of good relations with the Commune.

Anastasius also solved a dispute with King Frederick I of Germany. The Archdiocese of Magdeburg had fallen vacant in the last days of Eugene, and Frederick had expressed a preference for Wichmann von Seeburg, bishop of Naumburg. Eugene had worried that such an open statement by the king of Germany risked reopening the Investiture Crisis and had withheld his permission for Seeburg to take over. Anastasius, however, recognized that Seeburg was a perfectly acceptable person to serve in Magdeburg and sent his approval.

He similarly ended the dispute with England over William of York who had been ousted as archbishop of York by Eugene. It had been alleged that William had been installed when King Stephen had interfered in the election, and that William had paid bribes to electors. It had since become clear that the evidence against William had been exaggerated by local Cistercians because they had wanted their own candidate Henry Murdac, abbot of Fountains Abbey, to be archbishop of York. Eugene, being a Cistercian, had taken their side, ousted William, and installed Murdac. The English Church was understandably annoyed. When Murdac died, Anastasis reinstated William. After William's death, his tomb in York Minster was said to be the focus for several miracles and, in 1227, he was canonized as St. William of York.

In Rome, Anastasius spent lavishly on the Lateran Basilica and Palace. When he died, the ancient sarcophagus traditionally held to have originally been that of the Empress Helena, mother of Constantine the Great, was brought out and reused as his tomb.

The Helena sarcophagus, reused by Anastasius IV, was the only tomb to survive the 14th-century Lateran fires. It is currently housed in the Vatican Museum.

1153

The population of the Maldives Islands convert to Islam.

1153

The Treaty of Wallingford ends the civil war in England between King Stephen and Empress Matilda

1153

The Republic of Genoa sells the city of Tortosa to the Count of Barcelona to stave off bankruptcy.

1154

The Almohads capture Grenada, completing their conquest of Muslim Spain.

1156

The Muslim citizens of Sfax in North Africa drive out the Sicilian occupying force and massacre all Christians in the area.

ADRIAN IV ✠ The 169th Pope 1154–1159

Born Abbots Langley, England; c.1100

Parents Father, Robert Breakspear; Mother, unknown

Papacy December 4, 1154–September 1, 1159

Died Anagni, Italy; September 1, 1159

Adrian IV was born Nicholas Breakspear and was at first educated in St. Albans, England, but his intelligence marked him out for higher things. The only Englishman to have become pope, Adrian had a turbulent papacy that tested his political abilities to breaking point.

In 1150, Breakspear was sent to Scandinavia as papal legate to reorganize the Church there and achieved great success, returning to Rome in 1154 as a very highly regarded individual. No sooner was Breakspear back in Rome than Anastasius IV died. Clearly the man of the moment, he was unanimously elected pope the next day, taking the name Adrian IV. His first move was to contact King Frederick I of Germany to affirm the Agreement of Constance (*see* p.156) and laid an interdict on Rome until such time as the rebellious canon Arnold of Brescia was expelled. This meant that the churches of Rome were closed and that nobody could get married, baptized, take mass, or go to confession—except the terminally ill.

In June 1155, Frederick came to Rome, meeting the pope at nearby Sutri as the situation in Rome was volatile. However, the pope demanded deference from Frederick that he was not inclined to give. Frederick was determined to restore the Holy Roman Empire to the status it had held in the days of Charlemagne, an ambition that involved treating the pope as an equal. When the imperial coronation took place in St. Peter's on June 18, Frederick was furious to discover that Adrian had introduced some innovations that implied that the emperor was subordinate to the pope. Frederick stayed in Rome just long enough to put down a riot and to arrest Arnold of Brescia and hand him over to Adrian for trial. He then marched off to impose his rule on Milan and return to Germany.

Realizing he would get little help from Frederick, Adrian turned to King William I of Sicily. Adrian signed the Treaty of Benevento which recognized William's rule over most of southern Italy in return for an annual cash payment and military help against the Commune. The agreement shocked many cardinals who opposed unifying southern Italy under the rule of any one man who might then be a threat to the Papal States.

In November 1158, Frederick held a council at Roncaglia at which he asserted imperial claims to hold sovereignty over Corsica and northern Italy in terms that Adrian believed infringed papal rights. Adrian began putting together an alliance of Italian cities that resented the reimposition of imperial rule. He then wrote to Frederick threatening to excommunicate him if he did not renounce the claims made at Roncaglia within 40 days. Before Frederick could reply, Adrian was dead.

Anagni Cathedral. Adrian IV threatened to excommunicate Emperor Fredrick I but died at Anagni before the threat could be carried out.

VICAR OF CHRIST

Until the reign of Adrian IV, the only title used consistently by popes was that of "Bishop of Rome." Other epithets and names came and went over the years. One of these was taken up by Adrian and turned into a title that is now classed as the second most important held by popes after Bishop of Rome. The term "Vicar of Christ" was first used of popes in the time of Gregory II. It refers to the section of the Gospel of John, Chapter 21, where Jesus instructs St. Peter to care for His flock in His absence, thus making St. Peter is deputy, *vicarius* in Latin.

1156

The Hogen Rebellion begins in Japan. The civil war that followed would end with the emperors being reduced to a ceremonial role and real power lying in the hands of a succession of samurai warlords.

1157

Albert the Bear becomes margrave of Brandenburg, winning important powers and privileges from Emperor Frederick I that lay the foundations for what would later become the Kingdom of Prussia.

1158

Abbot Raymundo of Fitero appeals for knights to defend his lands around Calatrava from Muslim raiders. The resulting Order of Calatrava would lead the Christian reconquest of Spain from the Muslims.

ALEXANDER III ✠ The 170th Pope 1159–1181

Born Siena, Italy; c.1100

Parents Father, Ranuccio of Bologna; Mother, unknown

Papacy September 7, 1159–August 30, 1181

Died Civita Catellana, Italy; August 30, 1181

The death of Adrian IV left the cardinals divided. A majority elected Orlando of Siena, who took the title Alexander III; a minority elected Ottaviano, who took the title Victor IV. The disputed election was to divide Christendom and the division was to dominate the papacy of Alexander, who was obliged to contend with no fewer than four antipopes (*see* opposite).

Not much is known of Orlando's career until 1150 when he was appointed cardinal deacon of Santi Cosma and Damiano by Eugene III, becoming cardinal priest of St. Mark in 1151 and then Chancellor in 1153. He remained Chancellor under Adrian IV and it would appear to have been Orlando who was the main adviser pushing for an alliance with King William I of Sicily.

At this date, the political situation in Italy was fraught. Sicily and southern Italy had long been contested between the Byzantine Empire and Muslims from North Africa but had recently been united under King William of Sicily, a Norman. Some of the titles he now held had ancient claims to areas of the Papal States. The Byzantines wanted their lands back, while many of the lesser nobility and cities resented William's autocratic rule. In northern Italy, the old Kingdom of Italy that traditionally belonged to the king of Germany in his role as Holy Roman emperor was fragmenting. Many cities and towns had gradually acquired rights to self government that they had extended to become effectively independent. Now Emperor Frederick I Barbarossa was trying to reimpose his rule, leading no less than four invasions of Italy between 1154 and 1174. The Papal States were caught in the middle, their boundaries and legal status disputed by all comers. To make the situation even more complex, Rome itself had elected a Commune that claimed the right of internal self-rule and opposed papal monarchical powers over the city.

Traditionally, the popes had sided with the emperors, relying on German military might to protect the Papal States. The recent decline in imperial power in northern Italy had, however, undermined this policy. Adrian IV had therefore turned to William, who was closer, for military support and had antagonized Frederick by reviving claims to precedence over the emperor. Some cardinals had opposed this policy. At the papal election of 1159, Orlando Bandinelli headed those supporting the pro-Norman policy; Ottaviano of Monticelli led those favoring the imperial alliance. It was quickly clear that neither side would compromise and no unanimity was possible. The division would dominate the pontificate of Alexander III at a time when the papacy was very much in need of unity and strength.

Emperor Frederick I Barbarossa submits to the authority of Pope Alexander.

1163

Norman king William of Sicily loses his last toehold in North Africa to the Almohad Muslims.

1164

The Muslim Almohad rulers of North Africa and Spain sign commercial treaties opening up their ports to Christian merchants based at Pisa, Marseilles, Savnoa, and other cities.

1165

Leipzig obtains a charter from Emperor Frederick Barbarossa, continuing the trend by which cities in Germany gain self-government in return for cash payments and taxes.

1167

Crusaders from Jerusalem invade Egypt, but are defeated.

THE FOUR ANTIPOPES

Victor IV was born nobleman Orlando Bandinelli and was elected by a minority of cardinals on the death of Adrian IV. He was never recognized outside the Holy Roman Empire.

Paschal III was elected on the day of Victor IV's death. Like Victor, he was supported by Holy Roman Emperor Frederick I who led an army into Italy to impose his rule.

Callixtus III was Abbot of Struma when the supporters of Paschal III in Rome elected him to succeed Paschal. Callixtus later abdicated and recognized Alexander, who appointed him governor of Benevento.

Innocent III was set up as pope by the citizens of Rome when they expelled Alexander III in 1179. One of Innocent's supporters was bribed to hand him over, after which he was confined to a monastery.

King Henry II of England disputes with the archbishop of Canterbury. Alexander III backed his archbishop but made frequent efforts to persuade the fiery cleric to compromise or tone down his declarations—without much success.

Riots and fights at once broke out between supporters of the two rivals. Alexander took refuge in the Vatican castle then fled to the castle at Ninfa where he was consecrated on September 20, and where he excommunicated Victor. Emperor Frederick summoned a council to decide the issue, but ensured that he invited only bishops from Germany and Italy. At Pavia, in February 1160, the council declared that Victor was the true pope, whereupon Alexander declared Frederick anathema. Henry II of England and Louis VII of France summoned a council of all other Western bishops at Toulouse in October. That council declared that Alexander was the true pope.

In 1162, Alexander and his cardinals moved to Sens in France to rally support to his cause. After the death of Victor, he returned to Rome in 1165 only to find that Frederick was now backing a new claimant, Paschal III. Alexander opened talks with the Byzantine emperor Manuel I Comnenus. Manuel offered to support Alexander and reunite the Eastern and Western churches under papal dominion in return for being crowned Holy Roman emperor with dominion over all Europe. Those talks came to nothing and, by 1176, Frederick was tiring of the stalemate. Talks opened that led to the Treaty of Venice that confirmed Alexander as pope, but left other issues unresolved.

Alexander had, meanwhile, been wrestling with a major problem in England. King Henry II had fallen out with the archbishop of Canterbury, Thomas Becket. At issue were the rights of the monarch over Church lands and clergy. In 1164, Henry enacted the Constitutions of Clarendon, which aimed to reverse recent concessions to the Church and to limit papal authority over the English Church. Thomas Becket objected and began a bitter dispute that extended to legal challenges, land disputes, tax disputes, and reached into nearly every corner of England. In 1170, Henry lost his temper and launched a vicious tirade that four of his knights took to be an instruction to murder Thomas Becket, which they then did inside Canterbury Cathedral. The sacrilege of this act shocked Europe and allowed Alexander to bring the dispute to a conclusion that greatly favored the papacy.

Back in Rome, after making peace with Frederick, Alexander set about governing the reunited Church. He laid down a rule that, in future papal elections, a two-thirds majority of participating cardinals would count as a victory and that a small minority of cardinals could no longer set up a rival pope. He instructed all cathedrals to run a school to educate boys in the hope they would enter the Church. In March 1179, he held the Second Lateran Council, attended by more than a thousand churchmen from all over Christendom. The council confirmed the standard reformists' demands banning lay investiture, clerical marriage, and the like, but also enforced Alexander's new measures. Shortly afterward new disagreements with the Commune of Rome forced Alexander to flee the city. He died soon after.

1169	1174	1176	1178	1178
Saladin become Sultan of Egypt on behalf of his uncle Nur ad Din, thus starting his rise to power.	A horse race is held at Newmarket, England, on the first known racetrack in Europe of post-Roman times.	First known mechanical clock in Europe is installed at Sens Cathedral, France.	Chinese documents record the discovery of a land in the Pacific named Mu Lan Pi, possibly California.	The Leaning Tower of Pisa begins to lean.

LUCIUS III ✠ The 171st Pope 1181–1185

Born Lucca, Italy; probably c.1097

Parents Father, Orlando; Mother, unknown

Papacy September 1, 1181–November 25, 1185

Died Verona, Italy; November 25, 1185

Lucius was born Ubaldo Allucingoli and became cardinal deacon of San Adriano in 1138. His papacy opened with hopes high that a general political settlement could be reached in the affairs of Italy. It ended with frustration all round and agreement as far off as ever.

Ubaldo was raised to be cardinal bishop of Ostia and Velletri in 1158 and was influential under Alexander III. It was Ubaldo who negotiated the Treaty of Venice between Alexander and the Holy Roman emperor Frederick I Barbarossa, earning the trust of the emperor by his plain dealing. He was described by Thomas Becket as being one of only two cardinals who it was impossible to bribe.

He was elected in Rome, but relations between the pope and the Commune of Rome were so bad that he fled to Velletri to be consecrated. Apart from a few weeks around Christmas 1181, Lucius never returned to Rome again.

The main task facing Lucius on taking office was to tidy up the issues left unresolved by Alexander and Frederick. Protracted and complex talks led to a face-to-face meeting at Verona in October 1184. First on the agenda were the extensive lands left by Countess Matilda of Tuscany, which belonged to the papacy but were administered by the emperor. Both felt the other was cheating somehow, and no deal was found. Frederick wanted clergy ordained by the antipopes of Alexander's reign to be recognized. Lucius at first agreed, then said a church council had to be summoned. Next on the agenda was the disputed election to the bishopric of Trier. Both men favored one candidate, but Lucius refused to confirm the appointment until further investigations were completed. The final issue was that Frederick wanted his eldest son Henry to be crowned co-emperor to secure his succession. Lucius refused, claiming that two men could not be emperor at the same time.

Frederick was exasperated by the apparent indecision, or perhaps subterfuges, of Lucius. He announced that young Henry would marry Constance of Sicily to unite the Holy Roman Empire and the Kingdom of Sicily. He then left Verona to embark on a lengthy campaign to enforce his rule over the recalcitrant cities of northern Italy.

Lucius turned to Church matters, holding a synod as soon as Frederick left. The most pressing issue was what to do about a number of sects in Europe that held beliefs that were not in accordance with orthodoxy as defined in Rome. Most prominent among these were the Cathars of southern France, Paterines of Milan, Waldensians of Lyon, and Arnoldists of Rome. The synod declared the teachings to be heresies and excommunicated those who espoused them. The bull *Ab Abolendum* decreed that those accused of heresy who could not prove themselves innocent were to be punished by the secular authorities. This bull would later be used as the foundation of the Inquisition.

THE CISTERCIANS

By the time of Lucius III the Cistercians were one of the most influential forces within the Church. The order of monks took their name from the Abbey of Citeaux, near Dijon in France. The abbey had been founded, in 1098, by a group of monks wanting to lead a more ascetic life of prayer and labor that was closer to the founding ideals of St. Benedict than was then to be found in other orders. The Cistercians opposed the luxury, flamboyance, and learning of the Cluniac reforms and preferred simple buildings, Bible study, and ascetic piety.

1181

Chinese and Japanese astronomers record what seems to be a temporary and very bright star. It is now thought to have been a supernova, probably 3C58.

1182

A crusader naval raid in the Red Sea led by Raynald of Chatillon lands a small army that reaches the gates of the Muslim holy city of Medina before it is defeated. The Muslims behead all prisoners.

1183

The Byzantine emperor Alexius II Comnenus is strangled by agents of his uncle and co-emperor, who assumes sole power as Andronicus I Comnenus.

URBAN III ✦ The 172nd Pope 1185–1187

Born Cuggiono, Italy; date unknown

Parents Unknown

Papacy November 25, 1185–October 19, 1187

Died Ferrara, Italy; October 19, 1187

When Lucius III died about 18 of the 26 cardinals were in Verona for the council he had summoned. Within hours of his death they had unanimously elected Umberto Crivelli, archbishop of Milan—a known opponent of the Holy Roman emperor Frederick I Barbarossa.

A dispute between pope and emperor was not long in coming. Frederick asked Urban to crown his son Henry as co-emperor and Urban, like Lucius, refused. Frederick decided on the next best thing and had Henry crowned king of Italy by the patriarch of Aquileia. Urban promptly suspended the patriarch, claiming that he should have asked papal permission first.

Urban then denounced the so-called Right of Spoils, by which the emperor took over the management of the secular lands owned by a bishopric or abbey in the interval between a bishop or abbot dying and his replacement being installed. The practice was widespread but Urban chose to condemn it only in the lands of the emperor. Following further disputes and provocations, Frederick responded by sending Henry with an army to lay siege to the pope in Verona and to occupy the Papal States.

Milan Cathedral. Urban was born into Milanese aristocracy. His family was prominent in a move to win independence and suffered badly when Frederick I sacked the city in 1162.

Seeking to foster trouble in Germany, Urban appointed Archbishop Philip of Cologne as papal legate to Germany, knowing that Philip opposed many of the policies of Frederick. At the Diet of Gelnhausen in November 1186, Philip denounced Frederick, but the German bishops and nobles united behind their emperor. Secure at home, Frederick sent messages to Urban seeking a deal. The two men reached an agreement and Frederick sent word to Henry to lift the siege of Verona. However, Urban was merely playing for time. He now laid plans to excommunicate Frederick, setting a date for the ceremony to take place in Verona Cathedral. The citizens of Verona refused to have any part in it and expelled Urban by force.

On the road to Ferrara, Urban heard that the crusaders had been defeated in a great battle at Hattin (*see* box). He suffered a fit from which he never recovered and died a few days later.

THE BATTLE OF HATTIN

In June 1187, Saladin, Muslim ruler of Egypt and Syria, mustered a huge army and laid siege to Tiberias, luring the entire crusader army into marching across the desert from Sephoria to relieve the city. He ambushed the Christians at Hattin on July 4. Almost the entire Christian army was wiped out or captured. Even the True Cross of Jesus Christ was captured.

1184

Canterbury Cathedral is completed in Kent, England, after five years of construction to replace the cathedral in which Thomas Becket was murdered.

1185

Battle of Dan-no-ura is a decisive victory for the Minamoto clan of samurai over the Taira clan in the Japanese Genpei War—a civil war for control of the government.

1186

Serbia becomes independent of the Byzantine Empire.

GREGORY VIII ✠ The 173rd Pope 1187

Born Benevento, Italy; c.1110

Parents Father, Sartorius di Morra; Mother, unknown

Papacy October 21, 1187–December 17, 1187

Died Pisa, Italy; December 17, 1187

The cardinals in Ferrara when Urban III died knew that they could not afford to waste time in electing a new pope. The devastating news of the defeat of the crusaders at the Battle of Hattin (*see* p.163) meant that a new crusade would be needed, and only a pope could summon such a holy war. Alberto de Morro, papal chancellor, won the election.

Alberto had been born into a rich and noble family that assured him of a sound education and a good start in his career in the Church. He became cardinal priest at San Lorenzo in Lucina in 1158. In 1171, Pope Alexander III chose him for a difficult and delicate mission to England following the murder of Archbishop Thomas Becket of Canterbury (*see* p.161). The killing had been prompted by a bitter dispute over the rights of the Church in England, and of the power of the papacy over that Church. Now the contrite Henry wanted to absolve his sins in having inadvertently caused the murder and solve the dispute. Alberto stayed in England for two years, returning with the Compromise of Avranches. This purged Henry of his sins and allowed papal supremacy over the Church in England, though not all the privileges demanded by Becket were agreed. It was widely recognized that Alberto had done a good job, ensuring he was sent as legate on other missions to Portugal and Dalmatia.

In 1178, Alberto was appointed papal chancellor. As chancellor, he codified the form and style of papal documents, establishing a style of writing Latin that later became known as the *stylus gregorianus* in his honor. He also compiled the great *Forma Dicendi*, a collection of papal acts and decrees still in force at the time.

In 1185, Alberto founded a monastery in his home town of Benevento. The rules he wrote were framed clearly in the Cistercian tradition (*see* p.162) of simplicity, austerity, and prayer.

Whether it was this policy or his known good relationship with the Holy Roman emperor Frederick I Barbarossa that ensured his election is unknown. It is probable that, in the wake of the catastrophic defeat at the Battle of Hattin, both were attractions.

As pope, Gregory's first tasks were quite clearly to bring harmony to Christendom and to organize a new crusade to rescue the crusader states after Hattin. Even before his consecration, Gregory had made a start. He wrote to Frederick and his son Henry to end the disputes between them and the papacy. Even the way he started the letter showed he meant business for he addressed Henry as "Emperor Elect," although both Urban III and Lucius III had refused to crown him co-emperor. Gregory went on to approve Frederick's nominee for the archbishopric of Trier, abandoning Folmar who had been appointed by Urban. Frederick responded by sending orders to all his vassals and men in Italy that Gregory should be welcomed and given hospitality wherever he went. Frederick also sent a guard of honor to accompany the pope on his travels.

Gregory declared a holy crusade to go to the Holy Land. He dispatched legates across Christendom to preach the crusade, gather recruits, and organize the campaign. The effort was given added urgency when the news arrived that Jerusalem had fallen to the Muslims on October 2, 1187.

The son of Emperor Frederick I Barbarossa would reign as Emperor Henry VI. It was Gregory VIII who first gave papal blessing to Henry's elevation to imperial power.

1187

A Muslim army led by Egypt's Saladin defeats the Christian forces at the Battle of Cresson on May 1.

1187

Jerusalem is retaken for Islam by Egypt's Saladin who defeats a Christian army at Hattin. The event will inspire Europe's enthusiasm for a Third Crusade, which is proposed by Pope Gregory VIII in the bull *Audita tremendi*.

Gregory VII died in the great port city of Pisa, where he was trying to rally naval support for the crusade.

Gregory himself believed that the disasters in the Holy Land were a judgement of God on the sins of Christendom. He announced that a moral and spiritual renewal was necessary if Islam was to be defeated. Such a program involving all Europe was beyond his power, but Gregory did have authority over the Church and the crusades. He issued a flurry of new edicts on the behavior of the clergy. He banned clergy from gambling or playing games and forbade them from wearing luxurious clothing. Bishops and priests were ordered to spend their time praising God and caring for their flocks. Crusaders were ordered to wear penitential robes, similar to monastic garb; to attend regular divine service; and to be of modest bearing. To further expunge past guilt, Gregory took advantage of a trip to Lucca. He entered the cathedral with a group of men and smashed open the tomb of antipope Victor IV, deemed guilty of having split Christendom. His bones were smashed and thrown out of the church.

So that the papal curia would be free to concentrate on the great task of organizing the crusade, he introduced a number of reforms designed to shift work away from the curia itself. A large number of minor matters were declared ineligible for appeal to Rome and had to be dealt with instead by a local bishop.

Having visited Modena and Parma, Gregory moved on to the great port city of Pisa. His aim was to broker a peace between Pisa and its maritime rival Genoa so that the ports and ships of both would be available to the coming crusade. The effort of the past 55 days had been too much: on December 15, Gregory collapsed, and two days later he was dead.

THE FALL OF JERUSALEM

By 1187 Jerusalem had been a Christian city for nearly a century. The Muslim army led by Sultan Saladin arrived in front of the city on September 20. Saladin had an army of over 20,000 men, while the defending commander, Balian of Ibelin, had about 3,000. For nine days the Muslims attacked with siege towers, showering the walls with arrows. On September 29, a mine dug under the walls was collapsed bringing down a section of walls. Saladin sent his men to storm the breach, but they failed to break through. Balian recognized that defeat was inevitable and rode out under a flag of truce to talk to Saladin, even as a renewed assault on the breach took place. Not until the attack had been driven back did Saladin offer terms. These were so brutal that Balian refused, saying that his men would spend that night destroying all Muslim holy places inside the city before fighting to the death. Saladin moderated his demands. The citizens of the city would be allowed to go free if they could pay a ransom set at 10 bezants for a man, five for a woman, and one for a child—those who could not pay would be sold as slaves. The treasury of the kingdom paid the ransoms of many poor people but, even so, around 7,000 went into slavery.

1187

The Punjab is conquered by Mohammed of Ghor who rules at Ghazni as governor for his brother Ghiyas-ud-Din Mohammed.

1187

In Italy, Verona Cathedral is completed after 48 years of construction

1187

Zen Buddhism arrives in Japan.

CLEMENT III ✠ The 174th Pope 1187–1191

Born Rome, Italy; 1130
Parents Unknown
Papacy December 19, 1187–late March 1191
Died Rome, Italy; late March, 1191

There were only a handful of cardinals in Pisa with Gregory VIII when he died, but they all knew that time was of the essence and elected a new pope within 48 hours. It fell to Clement III to organize the Third Crusade and bring the harmony to Christendom on which that crusade depended.

The cardinals had initially elected Bishop Teobaldo of Ostia to be pope but he did not want the job. A second election took place and Archpriest Paolo Scolari became Pope Clement III.

Pope Gregory VIII had been in talks to bring peace between Pisa and Genoa when he died. Clement took his place and concluded a temporary truce to ensure peace for the coming crusade. He then had to deal with both the Commune of Rome (*see* p.167) and with Holy Roman Emperor Frederick I Barbarossa. He was helped by Leone de Monumento—a Roman senator and a close friend of the emperor.

Agreement was reached with the Commune first. It was agreed that the administration of the city would be handled by the Commune using funds given by the pope. In return, the taxes raised in Rome would be paid directly to the pope and that senators on taking office would swear allegiance to the pope and recognize his sovereignty. Clement entered Rome in February 1188, taking up residence in the Lateran.

A peace deal with Frederick took longer, the final Treaty of Strasbourg not being signed until April 3, 1189. This settled a number of outstanding issues left over from the agreement reached by Gregory. It also formalized the position of the Papal States. Harking back to the original Donation of Pepin agreed by King Pepin of the Franks and Pope Stephen II in 754, the pope was to be the supreme secular ruler of the Papal States, but those states remained a technical part of the Kingdom of Italy—part of the Holy Roman Empire. The pope was thus confirmed as ruler over his extensive domains, though in secular terms he was nominally subject to the emperor. Clement also agreed to crown Frederick's son Henry co-emperor.

All this work came to fruition when the Third Crusade set off for the Holy Land. The Emperor Frederick, King Richard I of England, and King Philip II of France all led their nations to war along with a host of counts, dukes, princes, archdukes, and other nobility. Frederick died on campaign, while Richard and Philip argued incessantly. The crusade did not recapture Jerusalem as had been hoped, but it did solidify crusader control over the coast of the Holy Land and many important cities. Before he left for England, Richard agreed a treaty with Saladin that guaranteed the rights of Christian pilgrims to visit Jerusalem without molestation.

A problem closer to home occurred when King William II of Sicily died without legitimate children. His heiress was Constance of Sicily, married to Emperor Frederick's son, now Henry VI. However, the nobles of Sicily elected William's illegitimate brother Tancred instead. It was not in the interests of the papacy either to antagonize Henry VI, or to have him in undisputed control of all Italy. Clement therefore refused to answer messages from either Tancred or from Henry that demanded his support. In the spring of 1191, Henry led an army south to take his wife's inheritance by force. By then Clement was dead, leaving the problem to his successor.

1188
The advance of Saladin through the Holy Land is halted at the fortress of Krak des Chevaliers by the Knights Hospitallers.

1188
Alfonso IX of Leon convenes in Leon a meeting of nobles, clergy, and town representatives that is later recognized as being the first parliament in Spain.

1189
The crusader fortresses of Montreal and Kerak fall to Saladin. The Battle of Acre ends in a costly crusader victory over Saladin. The Christians then lay siege to Acre, which holds out for two years.

1190
The Holy Roman emperor Frederick I Barbarossa drowns while crossing the Calycadnus River. He is succeeded by his son who will reign until 1197 as Henry VI.

CELESTINE III ✠ The 175th Pope 1191–1198

Born Rome, Italy; c.1106
Parents Unknown
Papacy early April, 1191–January 8, 1198
Died Rome, Italy; January 8, 1198

When Giacinto Bobo was elected as Pope Celestine III, King Henry VI of Germany and Italy was waiting with an army outside Rome demanding to be crowned Holy Roman emperor. Relations with Henry would dominate the entire papacy of Celestine III.

Richard I of England was held prisoner by King Henry VI of Germany.

Eager to maintain good relations with Henry, Celestine crowned him on April 15. Like Clement, however, he avoided committing himself on Henry's disputed right to rule the Kingdom of Sicily. Henry marched on south, but was driven back from the gates of Naples by troops loyal to Tancred, the other claimant. Back in his homeland of Germany, Henry took to claiming the right and privileges that had caused conflicts between earlier popes and emperors. He rejected men elected to be bishops and instead appointed his own men. He also antagonized the pope by holding prisoner King Richard I of England, although as a returning crusader he was technically under the protection of Rome.

In 1194, Tancred died and again Henry marched south. This time he was successful and imposed his rule on southern Italy. Henry now wanted to convert the kingdoms of Germany and Italy from elective monarchies into hereditary kingdoms and asked Celestine to endorse the move. The German nobles and Italian City States were opposed to the idea, and Celestine avoided giving a direct answer. Next, Henry suggested that the Papal States revert to imperial control, with the papacy instead getting a hefty annual cash payment from every bishop. Again, Celestine avoided answering and delayed the matter. In September 1197, Henry died and Germany collapsed into chaos over the succession.

Celestine found his influence over events elsewhere waning. King Philip II of France ignored Celestine's ruling that his first marriage was valid and went ahead with a second wedding. King Richard I of England fell out with the papal legate William of Ely and ignored his advice. Only in Spain did Celestine do well, managing to unite the squabbling Christian rulers of northern Spain against the Muslim foe to the south.

THE COMMUNE OF ROME

In the last days of Pope Innocent II, the leading citizens of Rome declared a Commune to take over many aspects of ruling the city from the pope. In the early months of the reign of Pope Lucius II, these aspirations became a reality but led to decades of conflict between the papacy and the Commune, which generally had the upper hand—often driving the pope into exile.
It was not until the disaster of the Battle of Hattin forced Clement III to agree a compromise that the dispute between pope and Commune ended. Under Celestine III, a new statute was brought in to form a constitution for the Commune that allowed the pope some influence, but little power. Thereafter, with a few intervals, relations between pope and city remained cordial.

1191	1191	1192	1193	1196
On the Third Crusade, Richard I of England defeats Saladin at the Battle of Arsuf.	Two magnificent ancient tombs, claimed to be those of King Arthur and Queen Guinevere, are found at Glastonbury Abbey, England.	Battle of Tarain. Sultan Shahabuddin Muhammad Ghauri of Afghanistan defeats a vast Rajput army, going on to capture Delhi and a vast swathe of northern India. The resulting Sultanate of Delhi persisted to 1857.	Traditional date on which the Aztec people of Central America leave their legendary homeland of Aztlan to migrate south into Mexico.	Riots in London, England, led by Robert Fitz Osborn attack the houses of the rich, but the rioters disperse rather than fight the king's forces. Fitz Osborn is captured in St. Mary le Bow and hanged.

INNOCENT III ✠ The 176th Pope 1198–1216

Born Anagni, Italy; 1160
Parents Father, Count Trasimondo of Segni; Mother, Claricia Scotti
Papacy January 8, 1198–July 16, 1216
Died Perugia, Italy; July 16, 1216

Lotario of Segni was elected pope at the unusually young age of 37. He took the name of Innocent III. Innocent's pontificate has in recent years come to be overshadowed by the crusade he let loose on the Christian sect of the Cathars—an episode that obscured the achievements of the man who many consider to have been the greatest pope of the Middle Ages.

Lotario was born into the minor nobility of the Papal States, a nephew of Pope Clement III. As a youth he went to the great University of Paris, where he studied under Peter of Corbeil. At the age of 30, he was brought to Rome and made cardinal deacon of SS Sergio and Bacco by his uncle. During the papacy of Celestine III he wrote a number of theological and mystical works, including *De miseria humanae conditionis* (On the Misery of the Human Condition), which was copied extensively across Europe and established his reputation as a religious thinker.

Innocent III depicted greeting Otto IV. In fact, the two men were often in conflict and, in 1210, Otto was excommunicated.

On the day that Celestine died, the 21 cardinals in Rome gathered to elect a successor. An innovation at this election was that the votes were cast in writing and then counted by scrutineers who then announced the result to the other cardinals. The first vote produced a clear majority for Cardinal Giovanni di Salerno, but he refused the job. A second vote favored Lotario.

Innocent proclaimed that his main concern was to be the religious war against the Muslims in the Holy Land and in Spain, but more mundane affairs would frequently get in the way. The first of these was the business of ruling the Papal States. Many of the key positions were in the hands of men appointed by the emperors Frederick I and Henry VI, while others were local nobles who resented papal interference. Patiently and carefully, Innocent worked to get these men removed, or he waited until they died and then replaced them with men willing to serve the interests of the Church, not the empire or local nobles. Even the Roman Commune (*see* p.167) was handled so that men favorable to Innocent were in charge. By 1205, Innocent's grip on the Papal States was secure.

When Henry VI had died he had left the Kingdom of Sicily to his four-year-old son Frederick with his wife Constance as regent. Innocent got on well with Constance, persuading her to relinquish special rights the secular rulers of Sicily had over the local churches and, when she died in 1198, taking over as Regent of Sicily and southern Italy.

In 1198, the squabbling rivals for the Kingdom of Germany both appealed to Innocent to decide who should take the throne. At this date Germany was an elective monarchy, with the nobles choosing the next king when the old one died. The senior nobles favored Duke Philip of Swabia, brother of Henry VI. The lesser nobles wanted Otto of Brunswick.

Innocent put off making a decision so that the self-governing cities of northern Italy had time to form the League of San Genesio to oust imperial officials. Otto had meanwhile contacted Innocent and promised to recognize Spoleto and Ancona as part of the Papal States and to waive the emperor's right to seize the personal belongings of any bishop on his death. Otto also had the advantage, from Innocent's point of view, that he had no right to Sicily.

1199
Death of Abu Yusuf Yaqub al-Mansur, probably the greatest of the Almohad caliphs of North Africa and Spain.

1199
England's Richard the Lionheart is mortally wounded by a crossbow bolt while laying siege to the Chalus Castle in Limousin, France. He dies on April 6 and is succeeded by his brother John Lackland.

1206
The various Merkits, Naimans, Mongols, Keraits, Tatars, and Uyghurs tribes of eastern Asia are united under the rule of Temujin, better known by his title of Genghis Khan.

1206
St. Francis of Assisi founds the Order of the Friars Minor.

THE CATHARS

The Christian sect known as the Cathars was ruthlessly exterminated and it is now difficult accurately to assess their beliefs. They appear to have believed that Jesus was a normal human being who was adopted by God as His Son, rather than being a part of the eternal Trinity. They did not hold baptisms, weddings, or other rites, but instead had a single sacrament termed the Consolation, which was performed only once and turned a normal believer into a "Perfect," who was expected to then live an exemplary life of celibacy and vegetarianism. The sect was condemned as heretical and incurred the anger of the Church for setting up a rival organization complete with bishops.

In 1201, Innocent declared that Otto was the legitimate king of Germany, producing a carefully argued document explaining why the pope had the right to make this decision if the German nobles could not agree. Philip then launched a civil war that saw him crush Otto's forces and take Otto prisoner. All seemed settled when, in June 1208, Philip was murdered by Count Otto of Wittelsbach, who had been spurned as a husband by Philip's daughter. Otto of Brunswick was then freed to become undisputed king of Germany.

The situation in Germany seemed settled again but, in 1210, Otto marched into Italy to invade Sicily. Innocent objected and, after being ignored, excommunicated Otto and declared him deposed. Innocent now recognized Frederick, son of Emperor Henry VI, who marched north to Germany and reignited the civil war. The conflict dragged on for the rest of Innocent's life.

King John of England refused to accept Stephen Langton as archbishop of Canterbury and was imposing royal rule over the Church. Innocent backed rebel nobles in their uprising that led to the Magna Carta.

England, too, was in turmoil. Innocent put England under an interdict, making rites such as marriage and baptism impossible, and backed rebel nobles in their uprising that led to the Magna Carta of 1215, which put restrictions on royal power. But when John accepted Langton and made England a fief of the pope, Innocent absolved him of his oath to abide by Magna Carta and excommunicated the barons as rebels. That sparked a civil war that was still raging when John died in 1216. The war ended only when Langton and leading nobleman William Marshal became regents, enacted Magna Carta and sacked John's cronies from government.

In his campaign to purge Christendom of sin and win God's favor for the wars against the Muslims, Innocent sent preachers into southern France where the heretical Catharism was strong. In 1208, the papal legate to the area was killed and Innocent declared a crusade against the Cathars. King Philip II of France took up the idea with enthusiasm to tighten his grip on southern France. French knights poured into the area killing around 20,000 civilians.

The Fourth Crusade was the best equipped so far, being funded by a five percent levy on all Churchmen, but it never fought the Muslims. Instead, it was diverted by a series of accidents and intrigues to fight the Byzantine Empire. In 1204, Constantinople fell to the crusaders, who set up their own emperor and imposed Catholic ritual and theology on the orthodox citizens.

In 1215, Innocent summoned the Fourth Lateran Council, attended by over 1,200 senior clerics. It confirmed many decisions of earlier councils, and pushed the drive to improve the education of the clergy. When the Council ended, Innocent began preparing for another crusade, but died suddenly of a fever at Perugia.

1209

Old London Bridge (actually probably the 6th bridge over the Thames on the site) is completed. It will stand until 1831.

1209

The Mongols under Genghis Khan conquer the Xia state of northern China.

1211

Amatino Manucci, a Florentine merchant, develops double-entry book keeping, which remains the foundation of commercial accountancy into the 21st century.

1214

The Mongols under Genghis Khan conquer the Jin state of northern China, implementing a policy of massacre that sees tens of thousands killed.

HONORIUS III ✠ The 177th Pope 1216–1227

Born Rome, Italy; 1148

Parents Father, Aimerico Savelli; Mother, unknown

Papacy July 18, 1216–March 18, 1227

Died Rome, Italy; March 18, 1227

There were 17 cardinals with Innocent III in Perugia when he died. Two days later they met to elect a new pope but took the unusual step of delegating the election to just two cardinals—Ugolino of Ostia and Guido of Palestrina—possibly to speed up the procedure. They chose Cardinal Cencio Savelli, who took the name Honorius III.

Savelli was a member of a rich and powerful family and seems to have entered the Church at a young age as a canon at Santa Maria Maggiore. In 1193, he became cardinal deacon of Santa Lucia in Silice before Clement III made him Treasurer of the Roman Church. It was here that he performed perhaps his greatest service to the Church. He undertook the monumental task of compiling a complete list of all papal assets that listed by province and diocese all the spiritual and secular institutions that owed duties and payments to the Holy See. The resulting document, *Liber censuum*, ran to 18 hefty volumes and served as the basis for calculating the wealth of the pope up to 1429, by which time it occupied 37 volumes.

Savelli became chancellor of the Church in 1194. Then, in 1198, he became tutor to the child-king Frederick of Sicily. Two years later Innocent III made him cardinal priest of SS. Ioannis and Paul. He was consecrated as pope in Perugia, then traveled to Rome where he was welcomed by cheering crowds.

The main concern of Honorius was to organize a new crusade. He believed that the only man with the talents, power, and wealth to make that a reality was his former pupil, Frederick of Sicily, now king of Germany and Italy. Frederick, though he mouthed support for a crusade, was really more interested in securing his own shaky grip on power and establishing his Hohenstaufen Dynasty on a stable basis. The relationship between Honorius and Frederick—with its evasions, promises, and duplicity—dominated the pontificate.

The defeat of the Fifth Crusade (*see* box) finally brought pope and emperor together in Rome in the autumn of 1220. Frederick promised that he would not unite his Kingdom of Sicily with that of Italy (effectively covering northern Italy) or with that of Germany. He also promised to respect the incorporation of Spoleto and Ancona into the Papal States and to respect the rights of the Church in Sicily. Having apparently secured all papal desires, Honorius crowned Frederick Holy Roman emperor on November 22.

Now enjoying the dignity of emperor, Frederick moved on to the lands of the Kingdom of Sicily in southern Italy. At Capua, he issued the Assizes of Capua that sought to codify and standardize the laws of the various territories. In fact, Frederick used the codification to increase the power of the monarch at the expense of the nobles and cities—a process he would continue in 1231 at Melfi, when he effectively made the kingdom an autocracy with a set of constitutional rules that would endure to 1819. At the same time, Frederick put out feelers to Ancona and Spoleto to test their loyalty to the papacy.

Honorius urged King Louis VIII of France (below) to intensify the war against the Cathars. The city of Avignon held out for months, citing the fact that the city was the property of Emperor Frederick, but Louis was not to be denied. Soon only Toulouse remained unconquered.

1218	1218	1219	1220
The Holy Roman emperor Otto IV dies, aged 36, leaving the German king Frederick II without opposition.	Mongols led by Genghis Khan destroy the Kara Khitan Khanate of central Asia.	The windmill, developed in Europe around 50 BC, is introduced to China.	The building of Salisbury Cathedral begins in England.

THE FIFTH CRUSADE

The Fifth Crusade was launched by Innocent III and took place under Honorius III. Like the Third Crusade, this effort was led by crowned heads who could be trusted to concentrate on the business of fighting the Muslims. The Crusade began in 1217 with King Andrew II of Hungary and Duke Leopold VI of Austria attacking Jerusalem but being driven off. A pact was made with the Seljuk Turks for a combined assault on the Ayyubid Dynasty, with the Turks attacking from Anatolia and the crusaders assaulting Egypt. In 1218, joined by Oliver of Cologne and William of Holland, with a combined German-Dutch-Frisian army, the crusaders captured the port of Damietta in Egypt. The Egyptians offered to swap Jerusalem for Damietta, but the papal legate Pelagius believed the Egyptians were beaten and refused the deal. Disease and famine then struck the crusaders, who tried to march on Cairo but were surrounded and forced to surrender in 1219.

The Dominican order was established by St. Dominic of Guzman to combat heresy though education and theological debate. The order has remained an intellectual force within Christianity and today has over 5,000 members.

Moving to northern Italy in 1225, Frederick summoned a diet of the empire to meet at Cremona. It soon became clear that he wished to repeat the exercise of Capua but this time stripping the cities and nobles of northern Italy of their rights of self-government. Under the leadership of Milan, the cities mobilized for war, forcing Frederick to cancel the diet and appeal to Honorius to broker a compromise deal.

Honorius had meanwhile been busy elsewhere. In 1217, he welcomed Peter of Courtenay, grandson of Louis VI of France, who had been chosen by the leaders of the Westerners in Constantinople to be their new emperor. Hoping that Peter would be able to convert the Easterners to Roman rituals and theology, and to accept papal supremacy, Honorius crowned Peter as emperor of Constantinople in a ceremony in Rome. Peter then set out to claim his crown, but never got there. He was ambushed by Theodore Doukas, the native Byzantine claimant to the imperial title, and thrown into prison where he died.

In 1218, Honorius authorized a new crusade in Spain. All the customary indulgences were given to those campaigning against the Muslims and the bishops of Spain were given instructions to do their best to stop squabbles between the Christian rulers. Sancho II of Portugal, Alfonso IX of León, Ferdinand III of Castile, and James I of Aragon attacked, driving the Almohad Dynasty out of Spain. By 1228, the Muslim territories in Spain had fragmented into a number of local city states that no longer had the power to threaten the Christians.

Honorius urged King Louis VIII of France to intensify the increasingly brutal war against the Cathars (*see* p.168). In 1226, Louis led a royal army into the Cathar region, capturing castles and towns with ease.

Nor did Honorius ignore ecclesiastical affairs. In December 1216, he authorized the Dominican Order; in 1223, the Rule of the Franciscans was approved; and, in 1226, that of the Carmelites. He also granted favors and privileges to the great universities of Paris and Bologna with the aim of raising the level of education in the clergy.

1220	1221	1223	1226
The Mongols capture the cities of Samarkand and Bokhara in central Asia.	The Mongols complete their conquest of Muslim central Asia with the capture of Merv, killing an estimated one million citizens and refugees and sparing only 400 skilled artisans.	Battle of Kalka River. The Mongols defeat the Russians, but do not occupy Russia.	Francis of Assisi dies, aged 44.

GREGORY IX ✠ The 178th Pope 1227–1241

Born Anagni, Italy; date unknown

Parents Father, unknown member of the Segni family; Mother, unknown

Papacy March 19, 1227–August 22, 1241

Died Rome, Italy; August 22, 1241

When Frederick II was crowned Holy Roman emperor in 1220, the cardinal bishop of Ostia, Ugolino Segni, presented him with the symbolic cross of a crusader. But seven years past before Frederick set off on crusade, just weeks after Ugolino had been elected Pope Gregory IX.

Frederick II reached the port of Brindisi with his army but suddenly stopped. Gregory refused to believe the reports that the emperor was dangerously ill and concluded instead that Frederick was delaying yet again. Gregory excommunicated the emperor. Frederick compounded the insult by then getting better and leading the crusade, even though excommunicated, and actually liberating Jerusalem from Muslim rule. Gregory was furious and raised an army to invade the Kingdom of Sicily. Frederick returned from Jerusalem and crushed the papal army. However, at Ceprano in 1230, a peace deal was agreed that saw Frederick withdraw claims on papal territory while Gregory lifted the excommunication. Despite the peace agreement, the two men remained on bad terms and the division was destined to blight Gregory's entire papacy.

Gregory had the satisfaction of seeing the end of the crusade against the Cathar heretics (*see* p.168) when Toulouse surrendered to Louis VIII of France (below). Gregory founded a university at Toulouse, granting it extensive and valuable privileges, so that the teaching of orthodox theology could take place to counter remaining pockets of heresy.

Gregory turned to ecclesiastical matters. In 1228, he made Francis of Assisi a saint, bestowing the same honor on Dominic of Guzman in 1234, thus bestowing new honors on the Franciscan friars and Dominican Order. The Dominicans were given special duties in the suppression of heresy. This involved education and debate, but also persecution.

In 1237, Frederick won the Battle of Cortenuova against the combined armies of the cities of northern Italy. He then systematically began imposing his rule on the cities, stripping them of rights of the self-government they had won in previous decades. The next year he married his son to a high-ranking Sardinian noblewoman and gave him the title "King of Sardinia," even though the island was formally a papal fief.

Although clerics were forbidden from passing sentence of death, Gregory made it possible for the Dominicans to hand obdurate heretics over to secular justice already condemned and recommended for death.

Gregory believed that Frederick would next move against the Papal States and excommunicated him again. Frederick, in turn, declared Gregory unfit to hold office and invaded the Papal States while calling a council of bishops to judge the pope. By the middle of August, the imperial army was camped around the walls of Rome. At this point Gregory died and Frederick retreated.

1227	1228	1229	1230
Genghis Khan dies and is replaced as ruler of the Mongols by his son Tolui.	Sukaphaa establishes the Ahom Dynasty of Assam that will rule the area until 1826.	Holy Roman Emperor Frederick II gains possession of Jerusalem, Bethlehem, Nazareth—a corridor from Jerusalem to the port of Acre for use by Christian plgrims.	Sundiata Keita founds the Mali Dynasty that would spread to rule a vast area of West Africa until 1610 when a civil war broke out and the empire collapsed.

CELESTINE IV ✠ The 179th Pope 1241

Born Milan, Italy; date unknown

Parents Unknown

Papacy October 25, 1241–November 10, 1241

Died Rome, Italy; November 10, 1241

The pontificate of Gregory IX's successor, Celestine IV, was one of the shortest and most dramatic in the history of the papacy. Gregory's sudden death occurred when the imperial army of the Holy Roman emperor Frederick II was laying siege to Rome.

At this date there were only 14 cardinals, ten of whom were in Rome, while two others were prisoners of the emperor. The civilian government of the city was in the hands of the powerful nobleman Matteo Orsini, whose main desire was to get a pope elected quickly so that peace could be made with the emperor.

The cardinals were, however, deeply divided. Four of them—Romano Bonaventura, Rinaldo Conti de Segni, Sinibaldo Fieschi, and Riccardo Annibaldi—wanted to see the emperor humbled and reduced to the status of a papal vassal. Four others—Goffredo da Castiglione, Giovanni Colonna, Robert Somercotes, and Rainiero Capocci—were just as determined to come to terms with the emperor. After protracted wrangling, a ballot produced a majority of six to four for Goffredo da Castiglione over Romano Bonaventura, but this fell short of the two thirds majority required.

Eager for a decision, Orsini got his men to remove tiles from the roof so that the rain could get at the assembled cardinals. When that did not work, he cut the supplies of food to starvation levels and halted the removal of rubbish, even excrement. The days passed by without result, so Orsini ordered his men to urinate down on the cardinals through the broken roof, but still the anti-imperialists refused to back Castiglione. Orsini then sent a message to Frederick explaining the situation.

Frederick retorted that Bonaventura was totally unacceptable, using as his excuse an alleged affair many years before between Bonaventura and Queen Blanche of Castile. In reality, it was Bonaventura's role in the feud between Frederick and Gregory that made him unacceptable. Frederick then questioned the two cardinals being held in his camp. Giacomo da Pecorara snarled defiance and began to excommunicate the emperor, but Oddone di Monferrato declared himself willing to back Castiglione. Frederick sent him to Rome.

By the time Monferrato arrived, however, Somercotes had died. His body had been carried out by Orsini's men, then the doors of the Septizodium were locked again. Castiglione was also dangerously ill, but the arrival of Monferrato tipped the balance and he was elected. The cardinals had been confined for 60 days.

As soon as the result was known, Orsini had the doors opened and conducted the new Celestine IV to the Lateran. On October 28, Celestine was enthroned and three days later conducted a great ceremonial mass in the Lateran. He then excommunicated Orsini for having treated the cardinals so disgracefully. The following day Celestine collapsed and, on November 10, he died. The papal throne was vacant once more.

Matteo Orsini rounded up the cardinals in Rome and bundled them into a dilapidated baronial palace known as the Septizodium. Orsini locked the cardinals in and told them they would not be allowed out until they had elected a new pope.

1232
First recorded use in warfare of rockets with exploding heads by the Chinese defenders at the siege of Kai Feng Fu against Mongol attackers.

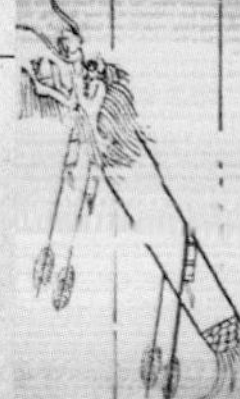

1234
The Jin state of northern China is conquered by the Mongols of Tolui.

1236
The Mongols invade Song China, capturing four of 58 districts in the first year and inflicting a death toll estimated at over one million.

1237
The Mongol Invasion of Europe begins. The four-year campaign will witness the destruction of numerous east European states and mass slaughter of civilians.

1239
Rinderpest first breaks out among European cattle, leading to a massive death toll of livestock. It is thought to have been brought from Asia by Mongol livestock.

INNOCENT IV ✠ The 180th Pope 1243–1254

Born Genoa, Italy; c. 1195
Parents Father, Count Ugo Fieschi of Lavagna; Mother, Brumisan di Grillo
Papacy June 25, 1243–December 7, 1254
Died Naples, Italy; December 7, 1254

Sinibaldo Fieschi had been born into nobility. As Pope Innocent IV, he sought constantly to enhance the prestige of the papacy, which he believed had been entrusted by Christ with both the temporal and spiritual government of humanity. In fact, his single-minded determination and the methods he used ended up lowering the prestige of the papacy.

In 1241, the cardinals had no wish to repeat the terrible conditions experienced during the election of Celestine IV (*see* p.173) so they simply refused to elect a new pope. Instead, they used the election process as a bargaining piece in talks with Emperor Frederick II, whose troops were occupying the Papal States and held Rome itself under conditions of near siege. Frederick, for his part, wanted the sentence of excommunication passed on him by Gregory IX rescinded and a new pope installed who was more sympathetic to the needs of the Empire. It took 18 months before agreement was reached under which Frederick would evacuate the Papal States in return for having his excommunication lifted and a free election could go ahead at Anagni.

Pope Innocent IV had been a brilliant canon lawyer who had led a varied life. He had studied, then taught, at the great university of Bologna before, in 1226, being brought to Rome to be a curia judge hearing clerical disputes. In 1227, he was raised to be cardinal priest of San Lorenzo in Lucina, and became vice chancellor of the Roman Church. In 1235, he went north to become governor of Ancona, where for five years he was able to enjoy the luxurious palace and the reins of power in that wealthy papal fief. In Ancona, Fieschi had much to do with the imperial officials and governors of the kingdom of Italy to the north. He met Frederick on many occasions and the two men had got on well.

Nevertheless, Frederick at least was under no illusions that his personal friendship with the new pope would outweigh the fact that empire and papacy had serious disputes. When he heard that Fieschi had become Innocent IV, Frederick joked that "I have lost the friendship of a cardinal, but made up for it by gaining the hatred of a pope." And so it proved.

For a year Innocent prepared the ground by assiduously and ruthlessly sacking anyone he did not trust implicitly and replacing them with men he did trust, very often relatives of his or old cronies from Ancona. This process caused a degree of disquiet, but Innocent stamped out any protests. He also took personal control of

THE MONGOLS

Innocent's method of attempting to deal with the Mongols was to try to convert them to Christianity. Two letters were sent to "the emperor of the Tatars," since nobody knew who ruled the terrible barbarians. One letter reached the general Guyuk who read it courteously, questioned the messengers, then sent them back with a letter demanding that the pope and all Christians accept the Mongols as rulers or face the consequences. The second letter was handled by the khan Baichu who sent two envoys, Aibeg and Serkis, to meet the pope. The envoys reached Lyons early in 1248 and stayed almost a year. Their message was just as uncompromising as that from Guyuk. Innocent replied that he regretted the khan's refusal to accept the true faith. The envoys returned home, there being no noticeable change in the Mongol policy of slaughtering Christians.

1243
Battle of Kosedag. The Mongols defeat the Seljuq Turks.

1244
In Spain, Janita, Biar, and Altea are captured by the Christians from the Muslims.

1246
Masterpiece of early Gothic architecture La Sainte-Chapelle is completed in Paris.

1246
The Aztecs settle around the Chapultepec hill in the Valley of Mexico, marking the start of the stable settlement of the tribe.

Frederick's son and heir in Sicily, Manfred, accepted papal overlordship as the price of peace.

the cash income from endowments and estates, diverting the money from traditional good works and church renovations for use bribing men into becoming allies.

In June 1244, Innocent fled Rome for France by way of his native Genoa. There he summoned a great Council of churchmen to discuss help for the crusaders, what to do about the Mongols, and "the business of the emperor." The resulting Council of Lyons met in the summer of 1245. Frederick had been summoned to attend but refused to go. Innocent excommunicated and deposed the emperor, released the nobles from their oaths of loyalty to him, and instructed them to find a new king of Germany.

At the Council of Lyon, Emperor Frederick was found guilty of perjury, heresy, sacrilege, and breach of the peace. Innocent solemnly excommunicated him and deposed him as emperor.

Frederick was outraged and summoned lawyers to dispute the pope's right to depose an emperor. But Innocent was moving fast. The archbishops of Cologne and Mainz declared Frederick deposed and hired an army of mercenaries to put Heinrich Raspe on the throne of Germany. To clear the way for Raspe, Innocent's brother-in-law, Orlando de Rossi, was sent to organize the assassination of the emperor. The plot was well advanced when the plotters approached the Count of Caserta, who at once told Frederick. The plotters were caught and slaughtered. Frederick was now in no mood to compromise. His armies crushed those of Raspe, who then died, and marched into northern Italy to destroy the pope's allies and rally waverers. By 1247, Innocent had to fling himself on the mercy of King Louis IX of France.

The tide then turned in Innocent's favor—at least in northern Italy. City after city decided it would rather have a papal master than an imperial one. The war there was still raging when, in 1250, Frederick died after a bout of dysentery. Frederick's son and heir in Sicily, Manfred, accepted papal overlordship. Another son, Conrad, became king of Germany and then marched into Italy to impose his rule there.

Innocent sought to gain support against Conrad by offering the kingdom of Sicily to both Henry III of England and Charles of Anjou. Manfred predictably revolted and raised an army to attack Innocent, who was in Naples at the time. The news reached Innocent just as he fell ill and he died soon after.

THE SEVENTH CRUSADE

The Sixth Crusade had successfully won Jerusalem by diplomacy but, in 1245, it fell again to the Muslims. Most rulers in Europe were uninterested in going on crusade to win it back. Only Louis IX of France responded to Innocent's appeal to go to the Holy Land. Louis sailed to Egypt, intending to crush the Muslims there and secure the country as a base for an assault on the Holy Land. The campaign began well in June with the capture of the port of Damietta, but by November new Muslim armies had gathered and the Christians were in trouble. At the Battle of Fariskur, in March 1250, the French were utterly defeated and Louis captured. He had to pay a huge ransom and promise to leave Egypt forever before he and the surviving crusaders were allowed to leave.

1248
English friar Roger Bacon publishes the recipe for black exploding powder (later known as gunpowder).

1249
The Sukhothai declare themselves independent of the Khmer empire under ruler Pho Khun Si Indrathit, an event now recognized as the birth of Thailand.

1252
The Church of St. Francis is completed at Assisi.

1254
The Mongols defeat the Koreans, taking around 200,000 people into slavery.

ALEXANDER IV The 181st Pope 76–c.92

Born Jenne, Italy; either 1185 or 1199

Parents Father, unknown; Mother, unknown

Papacy December 12, 1254–May 25, 1261

Died Viterbo, Italy; May 25, 1261

Gentle, scholarly, and indecisive, Count Rinaldo of Segni had risen to be bishop of Ostia. He proved to be a pope adept at handling ecclesiastical matters but hopelessly at sea in power politics. His reign as Alexander IV left the Papal States in a financial and political mess.

Alexander had been the cardinal protector of the Franciscan Order and he was soon busy helping John of Parma, head of the Franciscans, establish that Order in new territories. He also backed the Order in a dispute with the University of Paris that ended with Franciscans being licensed to teach in Paris and gaining the right to have theological schools attached to their friaries.

In 1256, Alexander decided that the various disparate groups of hermits needed to be properly organized. He invited representatives to Rome where they adopted a basic set of rules and styled themselves the Augustinian Hermits. Alexander made the hermits free of the control of their local bishops, meaning that they were subject only to the orders of the pope.

As well as regularizing such matters, Alexander turned his attention to correcting the numerous financial irregularities of Innocent IV. The lavish bribes that Innocent had promised as annual payments to assorted foreign magnates were canceled and the money redirected to the curia for good works.

The death of King Conrad IV of Germany, in 1254, had left as his heir his two-year-old son Conradin. In Germany, Duke Louis II of Bavaria was regent for his ancestral lands in Swabia. But the German nobles did not want a child as king. Instead, they held an election, which produced a divided result. The Germans turned to Alexander to choose a king. Alexander prevaricated with the result that the German nobles began to enjoy not having a king and the independence this gave.

In Sicily, Conradin's half-uncle Manfred was regent. Alexander opposed Manfred and excommunicated him in March 1255, offering the crown of Sicily and southern Italy to Edmund, second son of King Henry III of England, for an extortionate price. However, Manfred made himself king of Sicily and, by 1258, had formed a league of north Italian cities opposed to papal influence. In 1261, he even had himself elected to the council that ran the internal affairs of Rome itself. Perhaps wisely, Alexander retreated to Viterbo, where he died.

In 1255, Alexander IV canonized Clare of Assisi, who had founded the Poor Clares, a contemplative order of nuns, in 1212. This gave added respectability and prestige to the order, which then began a rapid expansion.

1255	1258	1258	1262	1264
Mongol campaign against the Muslims of southwestern Asia begins.	The Mongols capture Baghdad, massacre around 200,000 citizens, and burn the city to the ground.	Prince Llywelyn ap Gruffydd becomes ruler of all the lands in Wales not yet taken over by English lords.	The Commonwealth of Iceland accepts King Haakon IV of Norway as ruler, ending three centuries of independence.	Kublai Khan becomes great Khan of the Mongols. Under his rule the more far-flung areas of the vast Mongol Empire begin to become independent.

URBAN IV ✠ The 182nd Pope 1261–1264

Born Troyes, France; c.1195

Parents Father, unknown; Mother, unknown

Papacy August 29, 1261–October 2, 1264

Died Perugia, Italy; October 2, 1264

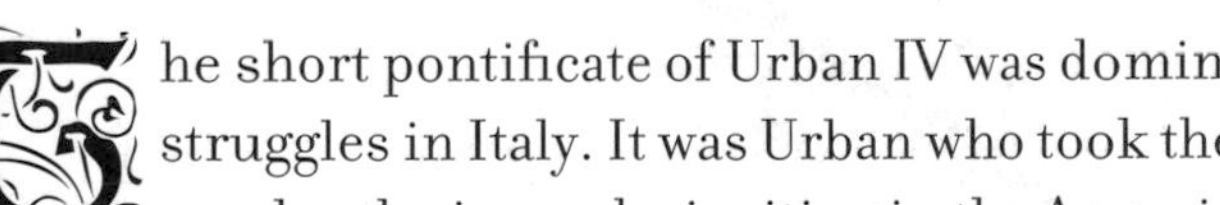

The short pontificate of Urban IV was dominated by the political struggles in Italy. It was Urban who took the fateful step of seeking to resolve the issues by inviting in the Angevin Dynasty.

Jacques Pantaleon was born the son of a cobbler but his intelligence won him a good education at the local cathedral school. By 1245 he was archdeacon of Liege, in which position he attended the Council of Lyons (*see* p.174). In 1252, he became bishop of Verdun and, in 1255, Alexander IV named him patriarch of Jerusalem. Pantaleon was visiting Italy when Alexander died at Viterbo. There were by this date only eight cardinals, after three months of indecision, they elected Pantaleon as Urban IV.

As a Frenchman with no links to any Italian faction or family, Urban had no scruples about inviting Count Charles of Anjou, wealthy and ambitious brother to King Louis IX of France, to come to Italy as king of Sicily. Charles promised to pay 10,000 ounces of gold each year and not to seek to take any lands in northern Italy. The then king of Sicily, Manfred, invaded the Papal States, roused the northern cities against the pope, and fomented riots in Rome that drove Urban into exile where he died.

CLEMENT IV ✠ The 183rd Pope 1265–1268

Born St. Giles sur Rhone, France; c.1195

Parents Father, unknown; Mother, unknown

Papacy February 5, 1265–November 29, 1268

Died Viterbo, Italy; November 29, 1268

Before his death, Urban IV had appointed 16 new cardinals. These cardinals met at Perugia and, after four months of wrangling, elected the only cardinal who was not there—Guy Foulques of Sabina.

Foulques had been married with two children before he was widowed and entered the Church in 1255—rising spectacularly through the ranks. Hearing he had been elected pope and knowing that King Manfred of Sicily had put a price on his head, Guy disguised himself as a monk for the journey to Italy. His first act as Pope Clement IV was to confirm Urban's appointment of Charles of Anjou as the new king of Sicily. Charles reached Rome in May 1265; he defeated and killed Manfred at Benevento in February 1266.

Manfred's death brought his nephew, Duke Conradin of Swabia marching south to exact revenge. Charles took advantage of the German invasion to wring new concessions from Clement before defeating Conradin in the Po Valley in August 1268. The young German count was put on trial on trumped up charges and executed. The move disillusioned Clement who, as a former lawyer, recognized a judicial murder when he saw one. He also realized that Charles was now effectively the master of Italy.

1264

Battle of Lewes sees King Henry III of England defeated by rebel lords and commoners led by Simon de Montfort, Earl of Leicester (right). Montfort institutes a series of government reforms one of which is to invite representatives of commoners to Parliament, formerly reserved for nobles and bishops.

1265

Kublai Khan begins the Mongol invasion of China, capturing Sichuan Province.

1268

The crusader city of Antioch falls to the Muslim Sultan Baibars of Egypt who then sold the entire population into slavery and burned the city to the ground.

1268

Mongol Kublai Khan sends a message to Koreyasu, Shogun of Japan, demanding that Japan recognizes him as overlord and pays tribute. Koreyasu refuses.

GREGORY X ✠ The 184th Pope 1271–1276

Born Piacenza; c.1210

Parents Unknown

Papacy September 1, 1271–January 10, 1276

Died Arezzo, Italy; January 10, 1276

The death of Clement IV was followed by years of procrastination before the election of a non-cardinal, Tebaldo Visconti, who took the name Gregory X. Gregory declared that he was going to devote his papacy to a new and mighty crusade to deliver Jerusalem. In this ambition he failed, but in other regards his was a successful reign that solved many issues.

When Clement IV died in Viterbo the main issue of the day was the unexpectedly aggressive stance of Charles of Anjou, newly created king of Sicily. The aim had been to put southern Italy into the hands of a strong ruler who was entirely unrelated to the Holy Roman emperors who ruled northern Italy. The papacy had long feared a union between the rulers of Sicily and the emperors, who came from the same family. By giving Sicily and southern Italy to Charles this union would be blocked. Unfortunately for the papacy, Charles had quickly won power and influence in northern Italy by opposing the German kings. The papacy found itself with the situation they sought to avoid—a single ruler to north and south of the Papal States

Statue of Charles of Anjou at the Royal Palace of Naples, Italy. Charles, brother of the French king, had been invited to Italy and made king of Sicily by Urban IV.

day. The Orsini cardinal changed sides regularly, but neither faction could get the two-thirds majority needed to elect one of themselves. A

Viterbo Cathedral and papal palace where Pope Clement IV died and where the cardinals met to elect a new pope. The cathedral, in Lazio, Italy, is dedicated to St. Lawrence.

few weeks after voting began, Charles of Anjou arrived with an army.

By the autumn of 1269, no decision had been reached and the cardinals had stopped their daily ballots. The people of Viterbo were by this time fed up with the Angevin army camped outside the walls and the papal curia camped within them. Ranieri Gatti sent armed men to round up the cardinals and locked them into the papal palace with orders to make a decision. As the months passed, Gatti slowly increased the pressure. First, food rations were reduced, then only bread and water was allowed, then the cardinals' servants were removed, then firewood for heat and cooking was banned, then the roof was torn off to allow the rain in. Still no decision was reached, so Charles of Anjou

1271	1272	1272	1273	1273
Marco Polo leaves his native Venice to begin his famous journey to China.	Charles of Anjou, king of Sicily, conquers Albania.	England's Henry III dies at Westminster, aged 65, after a reign of 56 years. He is succeeded by his son Edward I.	The Mongols of Kublai Khan win the key battle of Xiangyang during their invasion of Song China.	The Great Interregnum that has left the Holy Roman Empire without a ruler since 1254 ends September 29 with the election of the count of Hapsburg as German king. He will reign for 18 years as Rudolph I.

GUELF AND GHIBELLINE

For much of the later Middle Ages, politics in northern Italy was dominated by two broad factions: the Guelfs and the Ghibellines. The parties had their origins in the conflicts between the popes and emperors. The Ghibellines favored the control of the Holy Roman Empire in northern Italy; the Guelfs favored the side of the pope and took their name from the Welf dynasty who were rivals of Frederick in Germany. As time passed and the pope-emperor dispute faded, the Guelfs came to favor policies that helped trade and industry, while the Ghibellines supported agriculture and landowners. While both factions were active in most cities, those cities that drew wealth from trade, such as Florence, were ruled by Guelfs and those relying on agriculture by Ghibellines. The factions gradually faded in importance and by about 1550 the terms fell out of use.

Richard of Cornwall was elected as king of Germany in 1256 by four of the seven German Electoral Princes. However, his candidacy was opposed by Alfonso X of Castile who was elected by Saxony, Brandenburg, and Trier.

sent in a message. As a result, a committee of six cardinals was given power to choose.

Tebaldo Visconti was in the Holy Land with Prince Edward of England (later King Edward I) when he heard the news of his election as pope. He at once took ship for Italy, reaching Rome in March 1272. One of his first acts as Pope Gregory X was to issue the bull *Ubi periculum*, which set up new rules for papal elections. These stated that election had to start ten days after the death of the previous pope, in Rome if possible, with the cardinals being locked in until they reached a decision. This was the origin of the conclave.

Setting the launch of a new crusade as the top priority of his papacy, Gregory sent messengers across Europe to prepare the ground, and called a general council of the Church to meet at Lyons in the spring of 1274. By this date, nearly two centuries after the First Crusade, the burning desire in Europe to wage holy war had waned. The Muslims were in retreat and most rulers had other problems to worry about. The kings of France, England, Aragon, and Sicily all agreed to take part, but none with any real enthusiasm.

In 1272, Richard of Cornwall, one of two men who had been elected to be king of Germany, died, while the other, Alfonso of Castile, announced he no longer wanted the troublesome crown. Gregory insisted that a new election be held at once, and the nobles opted for Count Rudolf of Habsburg. Rudolf's main attraction was that he was relatively obscure and was unlikely to have the resources to impose royal rule on his fellow nobles who had recently grown used to being increasingly independent. Gregory met Rudolf and persuaded him to renounce German rights over the Papal States and any residual rights to Sicily. Neither issue was ever again to be seriously contested.

The Second Council of Lyons was attended by representatives of the Byzantine Empire. They reached agreement with the Western bishops over various doctrinal issues and accepted that the pope was superior to the patriarch of Constantinople. Hopes were high that union between Eastern and Western Christendom was close. The Council also confirmed the conclave procedure and passed decrees against a bishop holding two sees at the same time, taking long absences from his see, and against other abuses.

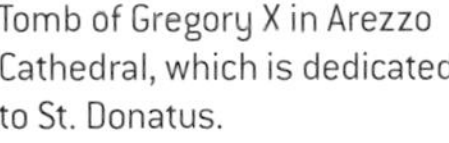

Tomb of Gregory X in Arezzo Cathedral, which is dedicated to St. Donatus.

The Eighth Crusade had meanwhile taken place when King Louis of France attacked Tunis but died in battle. The Ninth Crusade was aimed at the Holy Land but nothing was achieved.

Gregory then went on a lengthy tour of Germany and northern Italy. He had set out to return to Rome but he fell ill and died at Arezzo, in Tuscany.

1274

A Mongol army of 30,000 men sets sail to invade Japan, but the fleet is wrecked by a sudden storm—dubbed the kamikaze (divine wind) by the Japanese.

1275

Marco Polo reaches Xanadu, Mongolia, summer capital of Kublai Khan.

1275

Amsterdam is chartered by the count of Holland Floris IV.

INNOCENT V ✠ The 185th Pope 1276

Born Near Moutiers on the French/Italian border; c.1225

Parents Unknown

Papacy January 21, 1276–June 22, 1276

Died Rome, Italy; June 22, 1276

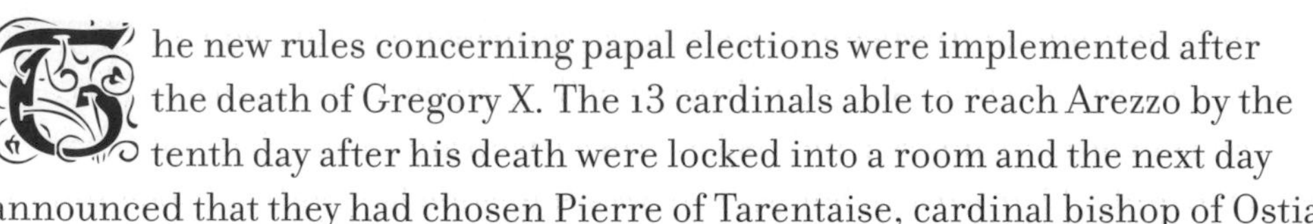

The new rules concerning papal elections were implemented after the death of Gregory X. The 13 cardinals able to reach Arezzo by the tenth day after his death were locked into a room and the next day announced that they had chosen Pierre of Tarentaise, cardinal bishop of Ostia.

Tarentaise had been born in the County of Savoy, part of the Kingdom of Arles. Nothing is known of his family or his youth but we know that, in about 1245, he joined the Dominican Order, probably at Lyons. He then studied in Paris where he met Thomas Aquinas and Albertus Magnus. In 1259, he graduated as Master of Theology and embarked on a career of teaching and writing that would make him famous across Europe. Among his best-known works were commentaries on the letters of St. Paul and a study of the controversial "Sentences" by Peter Lombard, which had been alternately praised and condemned as heretical.

In 1272, Gregory X made Tarentaise archbishop of Lyons, then raised him to Ostia the following year. Tarentaise played a major role in preparing the Second Council of Lyons and preached a famous sermon at the funeral of his fellow theologian Bonaventura in 1274. He then accompanied Pope Gregory on his perambulations through Germany and Italy, being at his side when he died at Arezzo on the journey back to Rome.

Thomas Aquinas (c.1225–1274) was an immensely influential philosopher and theologian. His influence on Western thought is immense, particularly in the areas of ethics, natural law, and metaphysics.

Although he was greatly trusted by Gregory, Tarentaise had clearly disagreed with his policies. As soon as he became Pope Innocent V, he set about reversing many of Gregory's acts. King Rudolf of Germany was rebuffed. Gregory had invited him to Rome to be crowned Holy Roman emperor, but Innocent wrote to him telling him that he would not be welcome until the various disputes about the rival claims of papacy and Empire in the Romagna region of northern Italy had been sorted out.

By contrast, Charles of Anjou, king of Sicily, was treated with great warmth. His election as a senator of Rome was welcomed, and he was confirmed as papal representative in Tuscany. When he seized Corfu, Innocent approved even though Charles's claim was quite unfounded. When Charles began acting on behalf of the Western pretenders to the Byzantine throne, Innocent did nothing to curb his ambitions, even though the papacy was supposed to be supporting a reunion of the Eastern and Western churches. On a more positive note, he did manage to broker a peace deal between Pisa and the Tuscan League of cities.

Regarding the issue of the Eastern Church, Innocent drafted a letter to be sent to the patriarch of Constantinople that included a clause insisting that all Eastern clerics had to take an oath accepting papal authority or be ousted from office. This inflammatory letter was in the hands of the envoy due to take it to Constantinople when Innocent suddenly died.

1276

The Song Dynasty court and at least 750,000 people abandon Hangzhou as the Mongol invasion force draws near.

1276

Augsburg and Ravensburg become Imperial Free Cities, meaning that they enjoy considerable rights of self-government in return for paying taxes direct to the Holy Roman Empire, continuing a trend that by 1400 would see the 200 largest cities in Germany become free.

1276

Emperor Rudolph I outlaws Bohemia's Ottokar the Great, but Ottokar submits to Rudolph who permits him to retain Bohemia and Moravia.

ADRIAN V ✠ The 186th Pope 1276

Born Genoa, Italy; c.1210
Parents Unknown
Papacy July 11, 1276–August 18, 1276
Died Viterbo, Italy; August 18, 1276

Adrian was a partisan of Charles of Anjou, king of Sicily, who was expected to use his position as pope to tirelessly promote the interests of Charles. In the event he died just over a month following his election as pope and before he was able to achieve very much at all.

Although the names of the parents of Ottobuono de Fieschi are unknown, it is certain that his father was part of the famous Fieschi family, the heads of which were the counts of Lavagna in the northwest of Italy. Several sources say that he was a nephew of Pope Innocent IV, but this may simply be a way of saying that he was a close relative of that pope.

The events during the youth of Fieschi cannot be determined with any real accuracy. However, once he became archdeacon of Bologna, in 1244, his career can be followed—although not without ambiguities. In 1247, he went to Piacenza to be head of the cathedral chapter and, in 1248, he moved to Parma to be archdeacon there for a number of years. He is recorded as leaving Parma in 1255, but another source states that he was chancellor of the cathedral at Rheims around the year 1250. Perhaps he left Parma for Rheims and then returned. More confusion is caused by his term as a canon of the cathedral in Paris for a year or so at some obscure date before 1270.

More certainly, Fieschi became cardinal deacon of San Adriano in December 1251, when Innocent IV was pope. In 1262, he was archpriest of the Basilica of Santa Maria Maggiore and, in 1265, he was sent as papal legate to England, serving there throughout the civil wars that were instigated by the baron's revolt under Simon de Montfort, Earl of Leicester. While in England, he codified English canon law in a form that would last until the Protestant Reformation three centuries later.

Fieschi returned to Rome in 1268, whereupon he took up full-time duties in the curia. At some point he met and was impressed by Charles of Anjou, king of Sicily. Throughout his time in the curia, Fieschi worked assiduously to forward the cause of Charles and push aside the interests of his opponents.

When Innocent V died suddenly, both Fieschi and Charles were in Rome. In line with the rules of Gregory X on papal elections, the electoral conclave began 10 days later. The cardinals gathered in the Lateran Basilica under the watchful eyes of Charles and his soldiers. As the days passed without a decision, Charles cut down the amount of food and water allowed into the Lateran until only bread and water went in. Several of the more elderly cardinals had to withdraw due to the heat. After nine days, the cardinals elected Fieschi—a move calculated to please Charles. Fieschi took the name Adrian V.

After a no doubt welcome meal and drink, Adrian summoned the cardinals back to the Lateran. He announced that he was revoking the rules of Gregory that had recently caused them such suffering. He then hurried away from Rome for the cooler climate of Viterbo without waiting to be consecrated or enthroned. A month later he was dead, apparently of exhaustion and heatstroke.

Adrian V was a staunch supporter of Charles of Anjou (below). But Charles's harsh treatment of the cardinals during the election led to Adrian's death from exhaustion shortly after his election as pope.

1276

Death of Italian poet Guido Guinizelli, who founded a new school of literature dealing with secular concerns, including love.

1276

Death of King James the Conqueror of Aragon marks a temporary end to the Christian wars against the Muslims in Spain.

1276

Paper-making reaches Montefano in Italy.

JOHN XXI ✢ The 187th Pope 1276–1277

Born Lisbon, Portugal; c.1210

Parents Unknown

Papacy September 8, 1276–May 20, 1277

Died Viterbo, Italy; May 20, 1277

Pope John XXI gained a reputation as a peacemaker with his efforts to quell wars. His main aim, however, was to launch a new crusade against the Muslims in the Holy Land, and his determination to bring peace across Europe was merely a means to this end.

Born Pedro Juliao in Lisbon, he trained and practiced as a doctor before entering the Church. It has long been assumed that he was the same Pedro from Portugal who lived in Siena in the 1240s and wrote a book of medicine entitled *Thesaurus Pauperum* (Poor Man's Treasury). In recent years this fact, which is not entirely certain, has caused controversy. The book advocates and gives instructions on forms of contraception, which, since 1968, have been considered immoral by the Catholic Church.

Gregory X summoned Juliao to Rome in 1271 to act as Papal physician, but was so impressed by his religious learning that he appointed him archbishop of Braga. Juliao did not have time to take up this new honor for, within weeks, the position of cardinal bishop of Tusculum fell vacant and Gregory appointed him to that position instead.

Cloister of Lisbon Cathedral in Portugal. The original building was completed in the early 13th century.

When Innocent V died, Juliao took part in the conclave that elected Adrian V but does not appear to have been considered a candidate himself. The death of Adrian, however, propelled him forward. His great friend cardinal Giovanni Gaetano led a faction of cardinals that wanted to reassert the political independence of the papacy but, due to his many local enemies (*see* opposite), there was little chance that Gaetano would be elected. Instead, Gaetano suggested Juliao, knowing that he would rather write than attend to the duties of pope.

There was a short confusion when the Mayor of Viterbo locked the cardinals into the cathedral and it had to be explained to him that Adrian had revoked Gregory's election rules (*see* p.178). According to one account, Cardinal Vicedomino de Vicedomini was elected and announced he would be Gregory XI, but he suffered a heart attack and died before the result could be announced. The cardinals then swiftly elected Juliao who took the name John XXI.

John then brokered peace between France and Castile, between Rudolf of Germany and Charles of Anjou, and persuaded the Byzantine Emperor Michael VIII to accept papal authority and a number of doctrinal rulings to which earlier Byzantines had objected. In fact, much of this was the work of Gaetano, who had accurately predicted that the new pope would spend most of his time in his study writing.

On May 18, the ceiling of John's study collapsed on top of him. He died two days later.

POPE JOHN XX

When Pedro Juliao chose the name of John it was well known that the previous pope of that name had been John XIX. However, Pedro did not use the number 20 as he believed that John XIX had miscounted the earlier Johns. The official papal records included John XIV twice, once when he was ruling as pope and again when he was imprisoned by the antipope Boniface VII. Pedro thought this double entry meant two separate Popes named John had followed each other. He therefore counted himself John XXI in order to put right an error that had not, in fact, existed. As a result there has never been a John XX.

1277	1277	1277	1278
Kublai Khan's Mongols invade Burma and defeat Narathihapate at the Battle of Ngasaunggyan. Within ten years, Burma would be crushed and a puppet of the Mongols installed in power.	The Condemnation of Paris sees the University of Paris list and ban 219 propositions. The penalty for teaching any of these was to be immediate excommunication.	The cross of St. George is first recorded being used by an English army as a flag.	The principality of Andorra becomes independent under the joint rule of the counts of Foix and bishops of Urgell.

NICHOLAS III ✠ The 188th Pope 1277–1280

Born Rome, Italy; c.1210
Parents Father, Matteo Rossi; Mother, Perna Gaetani
Papacy November 25, 1277–August 22, 1280
Died Viterbo, Italy; August 22, 1280

Cardinal Giovanni Gaetan had been a powerful figure in the papal government for years. Under John XXI, he had effectively run the papacy. When his turn came to be pope, he survived for only three years but managed to push through a number of important measures.

In many ways, Giovanni Gaetani was the ultimate papal insider. He had been born in Rome to rich and aristocratic parents. His mother belonged to the same family as had Pope Gelasius II and had links to the nobility of Pisa. His father was part of the great Orsini family. The Orsinis had risen to prominence and wealth in the early 11th century and, by the time Giovanni was born, were among the richest families in Rome. He entered the Church at a young age and spent his entire career in Rome. In about 1245, he was made cardinal deacon of St. Nicola in Carcere Tulliano by Pope Innocent IV, after which his rise was steady.

Although Gaetani's family links had undoubtedly helped his career, they also held him back for the Orsinis had many enemies. It was for this reason that he stood aside in the conclave of September 1276. By 1277, the situation had changed. There were now only eight cardinals still living, and one of them was absent in France. Moreover, one of Gaetani's main opponents, Charles of Anjou, King of Sicily, was having troubles of his own.

The cardinals met once each day to cast their votes in Viterbo Cathedral, and for two months Gaetani was ahead by four votes to three, which fell short of the two thirds majority needed. Then the Mayor of Viterbo seized the cardinals and locked them into a room in the town hall. Three weeks later Gaetani was elected and took the name of Nicholas III after the church of which he was cardinal deacon.

Nicholas moved quickly to reduce the influence of Charles of Anjou. When Charles's term as senator of Rome ended, Nicholas persuaded him not to restand. He then stood himself, was elected, and talked the Roman senate into granting him powers that effectively made him dictator of Rome. He redrafted the constitution of the city so that no outsider could hold office, and so that the popes had the right of veto over any decision of the senate. Thereafter, the papal grip on the city was secure until 1870. Nicholas then involved himself with the city states of northern Italy, seeking to bring peace and harmony so that Charles would have neither excuse nor opportunity to meddle there.

Nicholas held talks with King Rudolf Habsburg of Germany, suggesting a radical constitutional change. The kingdom of Germany would be made hereditary in the Habsburg family instead of being elective. At the same time the Holy Roman Empire would be divided into four kingdoms. The scheme never came to fruition, but Nicholas did persuade Rudolf to give up claims to Romagna and Ravenna. Both had been under papal control for years, but now the control was legal.

Meanwhile, Nicholas appointed a large number of new men to positions in the curia and created seven new cardinals. Most of these men were talented and hard working, but three were his nephews. The three were nicknamed the Little Bears—in Italian this is *orsatti* and was a pun on the Orsini family name.

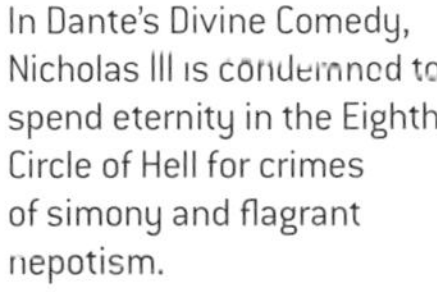

In Dante's Divine Comedy, Nicholas III is condemned to spend eternity in the Eighth Circle of Hell for crimes of simony and flagrant nepotism.

1278	1279	1280	1280
The Battle of Marchfield is the biggest clash of mounted knights in history with an estimated 20,000 knights and 60,000 others involved. The victory of Rudolf Habsburg of Germany over Ottaker of Bohemia effectively gave control of the upper Danube basin to the Habsburg family for the next 600 years.	Battle of Yamen sees the final destruction of the Song Dynasty of China by the Mongol armies of Kublai Khan, who thus becomes Emperor of China and founds the Yuan Dynasty.	The approximate date of the onset of the "Wolf Minimum"—a period of low solar activity that coincides with the cooling of the world's climate for the next three centuries.	Marco Polo visits Hangchow in China, a city of 900,000, which he describes as "beyond doubt, the greatest city in the world."

MARTIN IV ✠ The 189th Pope 1281–1285

Born Meinpincien, France; c.1220

Parents Father, Jean de Brion; Mother, unknown

Papacy February 22, 1281–March 28, 1285

Died Perugia, Italy; March 28, 1285

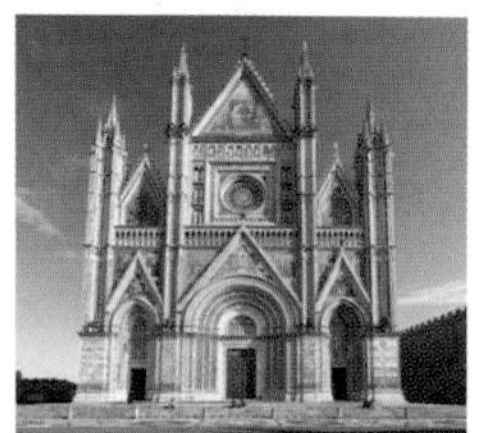

Orvieto Cathedral in Umbria, Italy, where Martin IV was crowned pope in 1281.

Born Simon de Brion into the minor nobility of central France, Martin IV was throughout his reign entirely dependent on Charles of Anjou, king of Sicily, who had manipulated the papal election to get him installed. When Charles fell from power, Martin's own fortunes declined rapidly.

Simon de Brion was archdeacon at Rouen, France, when he then caught the eye of King Louis IX and was moved to be treasurer of the influential church of St. Martin at Tours. The position was not only important in itself but brought Brion into the royal court where he held the additional position of Keeper of the Great Seal and stayed by the king's side.

When Pope Nicholas III died, the cardinals began meeting in Viterbo on September 22, 1280, but were divided over how to deal with Charles of Anjou who was expanding his influence into northern Italy and the Papal States. Most of the Roman and Italian cardinals wanted to oppose him; most of the other cardinals favored compromise. After six months no decision had been reached. Riccardeilo Annibaldi, Mayor of Viterbo and a supporter of Charles, marched armed men into a meeting and arrested three Roman cardinals linked to the Orsini (*see* p.183). The remaining cardinals promptly elected the absent de Brion expecting him to be favorable to a compromise with Charles.

De Brion hurried to Italy, but soon found that the people of Rome wanted nothing to do with him and he was crowned at Orvieto instead. Nevertheless, the Romans were induced to elect the new pope Martin IV to be their sole senator in charge of civil government. Martin promptly passed the office on to Charles of Anjou. Not only was this unconstitutional, but it also set the tone of abject obedience to Charles.

Martin carried out a purge of papal officials, sacking or demoting anyone who had ever expressed opposition to Charles and replacing them with men who could be relied upon to back the king. In November 1281, Martin excommunicated Emperor Michael VIII of Constantinople for no reason other than that Charles was planning an expedition against Constantinople and needed an excuse to act. The move broke the agreement reached under Gregory X to reunify Eastern and Western Christianity.

The situation was thrown into turmoil, in 1282, by the uprising known as the Sicilian Vespers. At the vespers church service at Palermo, a French official began pestering a local married woman, starting a brawl with the husband that ended with the Frenchman dead. The incident set off an uprising against French rule that, in six weeks, saw every Frenchman in Sicily killed. The Sicilian nobles elected a new king, Pedro III of Aragon, who had married the daughter of Manfred—the king who had been killed by Charles of Anjou.

Martin slavishly did as Charles ordered: Pedro was declared excommunicated and his kingdom was confiscated. When that did not work, Martin declared a new crusade to be raised and directed at Aragon, but nobody joined it. Charles died in January 1285, by which time Martin too was ill. He died two months later.

THE MISSING MARTINS

Although he is known as Martin IV, this pope was really Martin II. At the time the official papal records were muddled and referred to the Popes Marinus I and Marinus II as "Martin." When he came to the throne, therefore, Jean de Brion took these two popes to have been Martin II and Martin III, so named himself Martin IV.

1281

A second Mongol invasion fleet bound for Japan is destroyed by a storm, reinforcing the myth that a divine wind (kamikaze) will defend Japan from foreign invasion.

1282

Mongol Invasion of Syria is halted at the Battle of Homs by Sultan Qalawun.

1282

Welsh Prince Dafydd ap Gruffydd attacks Hawarden Castle, sparking the Anglo-Welsh War that will end Welsh independence.

1284

Mongol invasion of Hungary under Nogai Khan is defeated with heavy losses by Ladislaus IV.

HONORIUS IV ✠ The 190th Pope 1285–1287

Born Rome, Italy; probably 1210

Parents Father, Luca Savelli; Mother, unknown

Papacy April 2, 1285–April 3, 1287

Died Rome, Italy; April 3, 1287

Honorius was elected as a candidate who could bridge the divide that had split the cardinals and Papal States in recent years. He aimed to end the conflicts and bring harmony to the papacy, though this process was still incomplete by the time of his death.

Giacomo Savelli was born in Rome to a junior branch of the Savelli family—one of the richest and most ancient families in Rome. When Martin IV died, Savelli was among the 15 cardinals at Perugia who took part in the election. The cardinals met in the papal palace and, as custom dictated, began by casting votes before any discussion took place. It seems to have come as a surprise when 14 of the votes cast were for Savelli—the only one who voted for someone else being Savelli himself. On May 20, he was crowned in St. Peter's in Rome.

As a native Roman, Honorius was welcome in the city in a way recent popes had not been. He eased out the French officials installed by his predecessor and replaced them with Italians from a wide range of backgrounds. He also built himself a magnificent home on the Aventine Hill, handing over the Lateran and Vatican to officials.

Although Roman, Honorius had long been a firm supporter of Charles of Anjou. Now that Charles was dead he wanted to maintain a French presence in southern Italy to balance the German influence in the north. However, the Sicilians had invited Pedro of Aragon to be their new king. Honorius gave King Philip III of France a papal banner to lead a crusade against Aragon, a war the French were keen to fight in any case. The invasion foundered, with both Philip and Pedro dying within weeks of each other.

Pedro left Aragon to his elder son Alfonso and Sicily to his younger son James. James persuaded his prisoner, Charles of Salerno (son of Charles of Anjou), to resign his claim to Sicily and offered to do homage to the pope for the kingdom. Honorius was furious, excommunicated James and told Charles he had no right to resign his crown. He then busied himself with regulating the government of the mainland areas of the kingdom, ostensibly on behalf of Charles of Salerno.

The medieval cathedral of Todi in Perugia, Umbria, Italy. Perugia was the venue for the papal elections of 1285.

In Church affairs, Honorius favored the newer Orders such as the Franciscans and Carmelites. He appointed men from their ranks to bishoprics and granted special privileges to the Orders. Among these was the right to hear confession, something until then reserved to ordained priests.

1285

Sultan Qalawan captures the supposedly impregnable crusader fortress of Margat—a major blow to the Knights Hospitaller.

1285

King Philip III of France imposes new taxes and customs on merchants attending the great fairs at Troyes. Within a few years the fairs have ceased as trade moves to the Low Countries instead.

1285

France's Philip III dies of plague. He is succeeded by his 17-year-old son who will rule for almost 30 years as Philip IV.

1286

King Alexander III of Scotland dies leaving no male heir, ushering in a period of political instability.

NICHOLAS IV ✣ The 191st Pope 1288–1292

Born Lisciano, Italy; September 30, 1227

Parents Unknown

Papacy February 22, 1288–April 4, 1292

Died Rome, Italy; April 4, 1292

The pontificate of Nicholas IV saw the final demise of the crusader states in the Holy Land, though in truth the impulse to fight holy wars had ended decades earlier. Nicholas tried to make up for the loss by sponsoring missionary activity as far afield as China, but much of his time was taken up trying to deal with political events closer to home.

Girolamo Masci, who would become Nicholas IV, was born the son of a humble clerk in the north of the Papal States. At an early age he joined the Franciscan friars and devoted his life to spreading a better understanding of scripture and the importance of Christ to poorer lay people. By 1272, he was in charge of the Franciscans in Dalmatia, and two years later he became Minister General of the entire Order. At the time, the Franciscan Order was riven by disagreement between those who wanted to adhere strictly to the ruling of the founder St. Francis of Assisi that friars should own nothing at all and those who thought friars should be able to own items necessary for their calling—such as clothes, books and food. Masci sought to ease the conflict by declaring that absolute poverty was holy but that friars could reserve for their personal use items without actually owning them. It was a delicate distinction that looked good in writing, but which failed to convince hardline supporters of poverty, known as "spirituals". In 1279, he was brought to Rome by Nicholas III, who made him cardinal priest of Santa Pudenziana and took his advice on the governing of the mendicant orders. Masci was promoted to be cardinal bishop of Palestrina by Martin IV and it was this position he occupied when Honorius IV died.

The spectacular domed ceiling in the Basilica of Santa Maria Maggiore depicts Christ with the Blessed Virgin Mary. The basilica was a particular favorite of Pope Nicholas IV.

Nicholas declared a crusade, but only a handful of knights and soldiers sailed in the papal fleet for Acre. In April 1289, Tripoli fell, followed by Acre (below) in 1291.

As with several recent papal elections, the 16 cardinals had difficulty getting the two thirds majority needed for victory. As the meetings dragged on, nature took a hand. The summer of that year was intensely hot in Rome, and malaria broke out. As the weeks passed, the cardinals began to die. During a three-week period in late summer seven cardinals passed away, while most of the others fell ill. The election was called off until winter.

When the cardinals reassembled in February they found that Masci was not there. He had become absorbed in his duties and was too busy

1288

Mongol-Chinese invasion of Vietnam is defeated at the Battle of Back Dang.

1289

Battle of Campaldino is fought between the Guelph cities of Florence, Lucca, Pistoia, Siena, and Prato against the Ghibbelline city of Arezzo. The Guelph victory secured their grip on Tuscany for decades.

1290

The Ottoman Empire that will rule much of the Mediterranean for the next six centuries is founded by the Byitynian king Osman al-Ghazi, aged 31, leader of the Seljuk Turks.

Pope Nicholas IV gives his blessing to the Dominican monk and missionary Ricoldo de Montecroce. Nicholas organized numerous missions to spread Catholicism around the world.

to turn up to what he expected to be another fruitless round of debate. By now themselves having had enough of the election, the surviving cardinals elected Masci pope on February 15. However, Masci said that he did not want the job and asked the cardinals to choose again. They voted again on February 22 and this time it was a unanimous result for Masci, who now accepted the result and took the name Nicholas IV.

Nicholas's first concern was the perilous position of the Christians in the Holy Land. The crusaders now held only Tripoli, Acre, and a small area of land between. Nicholas declared a crusade, but only a handful of knights and soldiers sailed in the papal fleet for Acre.

In an effort to make up for the failure of military Christianity, Nicholas tried persuasion. He organized numerous missions to go to preach the faith in the Balkans, eastern Europe, and even within the Mongolian Empire. In 1289, he sent a fellow friar Giovanni da Montecorvino to go to China to preach Christianity.

Meanwhile the troubled kingdom of Sicily, which included southern Italy, demanded his attention. He continued recent papal policy of supporting the claims of Charles of Salerno, who held the mainland, against James of Aragon, who ruled Sicily. Nicholas not only crowned Charles King of Sicily in 1289, but also declared the war to be a crusade, and raised Church taxes to fund it. James got the better of the war, however, and a treaty was signed that left the kingdom divided.

Relations with Rudolf of Habsburg, king of Germany, were no more fruitful. Rudolf had been waiting for years to come to Rome to be crowned Holy Roman emperor, but there had always been reasons why the move was inconvenient either to him or to previous popes. Despite the best efforts of both sides, nothing changed and the imperial throne remained empty.

Within the Papal States itself, Nicholas followed recent precedent by appointing as officials local men who he knew he could trust. In Nicholas's case that meant men from the aristocratic Colonna family. His own family was linked to the Colonna in some way, perhaps his father had worked for them. He appointed Pietro Colonna to be a cardinal, while the senatorial elections were manipulated to make Giovanni Colonna sole senator of Rome. This understandably annoyed the other noble families who were denied lucrative and powerful positions. As a result there were intermittent outbreaks of rioting in Rome that sometimes forced Nicholas to reside elsewhere.

PAPAL ART

Nicholas IV established what would become a papal tradition of patronizing artists. He invited Arnolfo di Gambio to come and work in Rome, giving him important commissions. Gambio was followed by Pietro Cavallini and Giacomo Torriti. The three, with others, were put to work to modernize and embellish the basilicas of St. Paul Outside the Walls, the Lateran, and Santa Maria Maggiore. The latter was a particular favorite of Nicholas. When he died, he arranged for his body to buried under the floor—marked by a simple stone. His tomb was later rebuilt in magnificent style and adorned with sculptures.

1290	1291	1291	1292
An earthquake at Chihli in China kills an estimated 100,000.	Squabbling Scottish nobles agree to submit the issue of who should be the next king of Scotland to King Edward I of England.	The Alpine counties of Uri, Schwyz, and Unterwalden unite in a confederation that will slowly grow to become Switzerland.	King Edward I of England chooses John Balliol to be king of Scotland, imposing such harsh conditions that Scotland becomes a vassal of England.

ST. CELESTINE V ✢ The 192nd Pope 1294

Born Molise, Italy; 1209 or 1215

Parents Father, Angelerio; Mother, Maria

Papacy July 5, 1294–December 13, 1294

Died Ferentino, Italy; May 19, 1296

Celestine was undoubtedly a good, holy, and kind man, but he just as surely lacked many of the qualities needed to lead an organization as large as the Catholic Church. He himself recognized this and abdicated—the last pope to stand down from office until the 21st century.

Pietro del Morrone had been born the eleventh child of peasant parents. He was probably a Benedictine monk but he abandoned the cloisters to live alone in a cave on Monte Morrone near Sulmona. His sanctity and simple wisdom became well known, attracting many local people who came to ask his advice. Seeking peace and tranquility, in 1245, Pietro retreated further into the Abruzzi mountains, settling high on the Maiella range. By 1259, Pietro's fame was so widespread that a group of like-minded hermits had settled in the wild hills around his cave and built a small church. In 1263, Pope Urban IV placed the hermits of the Abruzzi hills under the Benedictine Order to give them a measure of organizational respectability. Pietro's fame continued to spread and his visitors included cardinals and nobles, with even Charles of Anjou, king of Sicily, making the trip to see him.

In June 1294, Pietro became frustrated that the cardinals had still not chosen a new pope more than two years after the death of Nicholas IV. He wrote a letter prophesizing that God would send retribution if his Church was left much longer without a leader. When the letter was read out, the cardinals hailed it as a sign from God and promptly elected Pietro.

This was absolutely not what Pietro had wanted, but he gave in to what he, too, saw as the will of God. Under the eyes of Charles of Salerno, Pietro was enthroned and took the name Celestine V. He moved to Naples to take up residence in comfortable rooms supplied by King Charles. However, it was soon obvious that the task of pope was too much for Pietro. He could not speak or read Latin, so business had to be done in Italian. While he happily agreed propositions from the curia, he also did as instructed by Charles with the result that of 12 new cardinals, seven were Frenchmen loyal to Charles. Celestine's memory was failing and he issued contradictory instructions and even appointed more than one man to a vacant position.

When Advent came Celestine decided he had enough and consulted the canon lawyer Cardinal Benedetto Caetani. On December 13, he read out a statement of abdication, dressed himself in his hermit's clothes, and set off to walk back to Monte Morrone. He never got back to his old home. The cardinals worried that he might be used by powerful nobles as an alternative pope, so they had him locked up in comfortable rooms at Ferentino for the rest of his life.

Pietro del Morrone was enthroned as Celestine V in Santa Maria di Collemaggio in Aquila, Italy.

Fresco depicting Pope Celestine V in the Castel Nuovo in Naples, Italy.

1294	1294	1295	1296	1297
The death of Kublai Khan sees the vast Mongol Empire divide into four: The Yuan Dynasty in China, the Golden Horde in Russia, the Chagatai Horde in central Asia, and the Ilkhans of Persia.	England and Portugal agree a treaty of alliance of mutual assistance in case of invasion. It remains in force and is the oldest still active international agreement in the world.	Marco Polo returns to Venice after his extended journey to China and other far-eastern countries.	The Scots rebel against King John Balliol, widely seen as an English puppet, starting the Scottish Wars of Independence.	Genoese nobleman Francesco Grimaldi captures the Castle of Monaco by subterfuge, establishing his family's rule over the castle that continues to this day.

BONIFACE VIII ✠ The 193rd Pope 1294–1303

Born Anagni, Italy; c.1235
Parents Father, unknown; Mother, unknown
Papacy December 24, 1294–October 11, 1303
Died Rome, Italy; October 11, 1303

Intelligent, forceful, and opinionated, Boniface set out to turn the clock back and impose papal rule on secular powers across Europe. Times had changed, however, and the kings and princes were no longer willing to take such pretensions as seriously as had their forebears.

Hommage of Edward I of England to Philip IV of France.

Benedetto Caetani was born into a minor branch of the noble Caetani family of the Papal State, which—fatally for his future—had a long-running dispute with the Colonna family over land ownership. In 1291, he was sent by Nicholas IV on a mission to broker peace between France and England and to formalize the rights of the mendicant orders in France. In thanks, he was made cardinal priest.

In December 1294, Celestine V sought Caetani's advice about his proposed abdication. Caetani drew up what he claimed was a legally valid instrument of abdication, which Celestine then signed. At the subsequent papal conclave, held in Naples, Caetani was elected with a clear majority on the third ballot. Taking the name Boniface VIII, he set out to achieve the papacy's long-standing political aims.

In southern Italy, the papacy had long wanted to see the Kingdom of Sicily reunited under Charles of Salerno. Sicily was in the hands of Frederick, who had been elected by the island's nobles. An attempted invasion by Charles with papal troops was defeated at the Battle of Falconeria in 1299, where Charles's son Philip was taken prisoner. Peace came in 1302, with the Treaty of Caltabellotta, when the kingdom was divided in two with Charles taking the mainland territories and Frederick Sicily. Frederick married Charles's daughter Eleanor and released Philip. All of Boniface's work on Charles's behalf had come to nothing.

In Germany, the papal policy had been to seek a powerful friend as king of Germany who could, if he behaved, be crowned Holy Roman emperor. When King Rudolf of Habsburg died, Boniface favored Adolf of Nassau as the next king, but Rudolf's son Albert raised an army and defeated Adolf at Golheim, in 1298, after which Albert was crowned king of Germany. Boniface had to swallow his pride and recognize Albert as king.

Meanwhile, Boniface had been using his position to settle his family's dispute with the Colonna family. The Colonna retaliated by questioning his role in the abdication of Celestine V and declaring his election invalid. Boniface struck back, deposing the two Colonna cardinals and ordering the destruction of defenses at Colonna castles. When, in 1302, Philip of France imprisoned a bishop for crimes of which he was undoubtedly guilty, Boniface declared that no secular ruler could judge a bishop. He issued the bull *Unam sanctam* declaring that the pope was superior to every secular ruler. Philip took up the Colonna allegations and sent a force of mercenaries to arrest Boniface at Anagni. On September 7, 1303, there were running street battles between the French mercenaries and townsfolk loyal to the pope. Boniface just managed to get away but was injured and died in Rome a few weeks later.

CLERICIS LAICOS

In 1295, King Philip IV of France raised a special tax—including on Church lands—to pay for war against England. In February 1296, Boniface issued a bull banning the move. Philip retaliated by forbidding French churchmen moving money out of the kingdom, which at a stroke cut off a large chunk of papal funds. Boniface eventually backed down.

1297
King Denis of Portugal and King Ferdinand IV of Castile agree the boundaries of Portugal that remain fixed, apart from a minor change in 1801, to this day.

1298
Battle of Falkirk sees an English victory over the Scots, ending the first phase of the Scottish Wars of Independence.

1301
Edward of Caernarfon, son of King Edward I of England, is proclaimed Prince of Wales replacing the native Welsh dynasty. It becomes customary for the eldest son of the English monarch to become Prince of Wales.

1302
De Potestate Regia et Papali by the Dominican friar John of Paris defends the authority of the king over the pope in secular matters.

The Early Modern Period
14th to 16th Centuries

CHAPTER FOUR

From its pinnacle of prestige and wealth in the thirteenth century, the papacy was to fall hard and fast. Undoubtedly, the Great Schism that began in 1378 had much to do with this fall from grace. The sight of two men both claiming to be the only true pope shocked Christendom, but far worse was the political and financial maneuvering that went on around the rival popes. What was supposed to be a religious institution was shown to be as venal as more secular organizations. By the time the schism ended unedifying practices had become so ingrained that many feared the Church was beyond reform. The Reformation, when it came, saw the Church split irrevocably and irreparably.

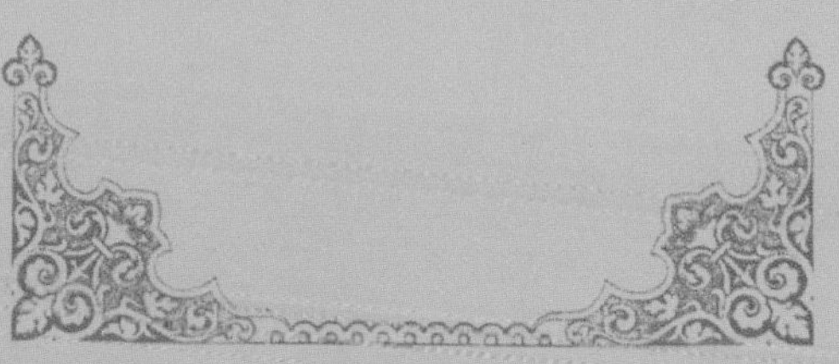

BENEDICT XI ✠ The 194th Pope 1303–1304

Born Treviso, Italy; 1240
Parents Unknown
Papacy October 22, 1303–July 7, 1304
Died Perugia, Italy; July 7, 1304

Born Niccolo Boccasino into a humble family in northern Italy, Benedict XI was perhaps better suited to be a scholar than a pope. Nevertheless he made valiant attempts to solve some of the intractable problems facing the papacy at the start of the fourteenth century. That he failed was more due the strength of opposition than to a lack of effort on his part.

Niccolo Boccasino joined the Dominicans before he reached his twentieth birthday. As a monk he wrote several important studies, including commentaries on the Book of Job and the Book of Revelations, as well as on the Gospel of St. Matthew. He also displayed a talent for organization and, in 1286, was elected head of the order in Lombardy. Ten years later he became master general of the entire order. At this date the Dominicans were undergoing a marked development of mysticism, especially in Lombardy where Boccasino was active. Many Dominicans came to favor an ascetic and contemplative life, though the order was also active against heresy as it led the Inquisition and was authorized to use torture in certain circumstances.

As master general, Boccasino tirelessly championed the cause of Pope Boniface VIII. He instructed the Dominicans to champion the legitimacy of Boniface's election and forbade any Dominican even to discuss the idea that Boniface may have been elected improperly. In thanks, Boniface brought Boccasino to Rome as cardinal in 1298 and, two years later, raised him to be cardinal bishop of Ostia. In 1301, Boccasino was sent to Hungary to champion Charles Robert in the disputed succession to the crown. Although Charles Robert had a respectable claim, Boniface supported him because he was grandson to the papal ally King Charles II of Naples. Boccasino was ultimately unsuccessful, but his skilful work was recognized.

Philip IV of France tried to control the French clergy in order to strengthen the monarchy, which led to conflict with the papacy.

When Boniface died, Boccasino was among the cardinals who went into conclave. His humble birth and origins outside Rome or France meant he was thought to be neutral in the various disputes then raging. He was elected on the first ballot and took the name Benedict to honor the birth name of Boniface.

Benedict's first move was to deal with the noble Colonna family with whom Boniface had been feuding. He offered the Colonna a compromise by which he absolved them of all charges and lifted the sentences of excommunication, but did not restore all the properties confiscated by Boniface. Nor were the two Colonna cardinals restored to office. The Colonna accepted reluctantly, but the anti-Colonna families were so incensed that they rioted in Rome, forcing Benedict to move to Perugia.

Elsewhere in Italy his efforts were equally mixed. King Frederick III of Sicily had taken advantage of the weakened state of the papacy to

1303	1303	1303	1303
Scottish victory at the small-scale Battle of Roslin puts fresh heart into those fighting for independence from England.	The defeat of the Byzantines at the Battle of Dimbos confirms Ottoman rule over most of Anatolia.	France returns Gascony to England's Edward I.	The merchant's charter is granted by England's King Edward I, allowing foreign merchants free entry with their goods and free departure with goods they have bought or failed to sell (with the exception of wine). Edward's policy will endure for nearly two centuries.

The Tomb of Benedict XI with sculptures by the master Giovanni Pisano, whose naturalistic works are held to prefigure the Renaissance.

Frederick III of Sicily stopped paying tribute to the papacy until he was forcefully reminded of his duties by Benedict XI.

stop paying the tribute that, since Sicily was a papal fief, was due annually. Benedict forcefully reminded him of his status and his obligations, and the unpaid money was handed over. In Florence and Tuscany he sought to dampen down the feuding between the increasingly wealthy and important merchants and the old aristocracy who were seeing their wealth and power gradually diminish. His efforts were determined but ultimately futile.

The increasingly ambitious King Philip IV of France was especially difficult to handle. He was continuing his feud with Boniface beyond the grave, demanding that the election of the dead pontiff be declared invalid (*see* p.189). Benedict opposed that as it would nullify the actions and decisions of Boniface, but at the same time he wanted to end the dispute with France. In March 1304, French envoys arrived in Rome to deliver to Benedict Philip's congratulations on his election and to listen to any announcements the new pope might wish to make. Benedict took the hint and released Philip from all the censures that Boniface had imposed on him during their dispute. The French envoys withdrew, nevertheless Philip did not rescind his call for Boniface's humiliation.

Instead Philip sent William de Nogaret, the French government official who had organized the attack on Boniface, as envoy to Rome to demand general absolution for all those who had supported Philip in his dispute with Boniface. Benedict refused to meet Nogaret, but he withdrew Boniface's bull *Clericis laicos*, which had banned Philip from raising taxes on Church property and which had begun the dispute in the first place. Philip finally dropped his demand to disgrace Boniface. Benedict then issued the general absolution, but with the proviso that it did not include Nogaret. Nogaret responded with abject apologies, mixed with accusations against Boniface.

Benedict had meanwhile been dealing with internal Church business. He appointed three new cardinals, all Dominicans, and took great care to make no decisions without consulting the cardinals. He lifted the ban on Franciscans and other mendicant orders preaching and hearing confession, but he imposed harsh penalties on the more extreme Franciscans—the "spirituals" who advocated that the Church should own no property. When the highly respected Arnold of Villanova spoke out in favor of the spirituals, he was put in prison without trial.

On June 7, Benedict suddenly announced that Nogaret should be put on trial in Rome and would face excommunication if he did not turn up. Philip was aghast and began preparing for a new conflict with the papacy. But before the deadline for Nogaret to arrive had run out Benedict had died of a severe attack of dysentery.

At the time it was widely rumored that a papal servant had been bribed by Nogaret to poison Benedict. Nogaret was probably innocent, but he did his cause no good by loudly proclaiming that Benedict's death was an act of God and a vindication of his own position.

Benedict's body had meanwhile been buried in the Basilica of San Domenico in Perugia. Miracles were soon being reported at the tomb. Benedict was beatified by Clement XII in 1736 with his feast day fixed on July 7, the anniversary of his death.

1303

The weight system of pounds and ounces is standardized in England, following the practice of merchants of the Hanseatic League when measuring wool.

1304

Sultan Ala-ud-din Khilji of Delhi conquers Gujarat. His subsequent love affair with Rani Padmini, queen of Chittor, would become legendary and form the basis of the epic poem *Padmavat*.

1304

Florentine artist Giotto di Bondone, generally regarded as the founder of modern painting, is commissioned to decorate Padua's Arena Chapel.

CLEMENT V ✣ The 195th Pope 1305–1314

Born Villandraut, France; 1264
Parents Unknown
Papacy June 5, 1305–April 20, 1314
Died Roquemaure, France; April 20, 1314

With hindsight it can be seen that the pontificate of Clement V was one of the more important of the medieval period. At the time, however, it did not seem to be that way. He was initially chosen as a compromise candidate and appeared to be merely marking time until the Church found a more dynamic pope.

Bertrand de Got was born into the nobility of Aquitaine and entered the Church at an early age. Although he was ethnically French, Aquitaine at this date was a possession of the English crown. As a young man he went to Orleans to study canon law before moving on to the great university at Bologna. He then returned to his native Aquitaine to become a canon at the Cathedral of Bordeaux. From there he moved to Lyon to be deputy to his brother the archbishop. In 1295, he became bishop of Saint-Bertrand-de-Comminges. Although this post was something of a sinecure, de Got raised money to embellish and enlarge the cathedral. With only light duties but a comfortable income, de Got was free to undertake other missions. He went on a diplomatic mission to France and did much work at the French court. Finally, in 1297, he became archbishop of Bordeaux and it was there that he learned that he had been elected pope.

Saint-Bertrand-de-Comminges, Aquitaine, where Bertrand de Got served as bishop before he became Pope Clement V.

The conclave that led to de Got's election as Clement V was a fractious one. When Benedict XI died he was in the midst of a bitter dispute with King Philip IV of France, who was supported by the powerful Colonna family in Rome. The enemies of the Colonna, the Orsini, ensured that two Colonna cardinals who had been demoted by Benedict did not take part in the conclave. That left 15 cardinals, of whom five were French and favored an accommodation with Philip and the rest were divided as to the way forward. After 11 months of stalemate, the name of de Got was put forward. He was known as a supporter of Benedict, but was friendly with the French court.

Having elected de Got, the cardinals invited him to join them in Perugia, but he replied inviting them to meet him in Lyons. It was in Lyons that he was crowned Pope Clement V, and there that he created ten new cardinals. Among these were four men who were his relatives and five more who were French, and he also restored the Colonna cardinals. The French faction clearly now had the upper hand.

Philip had hurried to Lyons to be present at the coronation. He at once began pressing the new pope to condemn the deceased Pope Boniface VIII, with whom he had had a feud (*see* p.189). Philip wanted Boniface's election declared invalid, his acts declared void, and his body dug up and burned. Clement promised to summon a synod to deal with the matter as soon as he got to Rome and, in the meantime, gave Philip permission to tax Church lands in France for the next five years.

Instead of going to Rome, Clement moved to Poitiers, back in Aquitaine, then to Toulouse,

1306	1307	1307	1308	1311
France and England expel vast numbers of Jews, stripping them of their possessions.	England's Edward I dies on July 7, aged 68, while preparing to join battle with Scotland's Robert the Bruce. He is succeeded by his son who reigns as Edward II.	The Knights Hospitaller conquer Rhodes, which they will retain until 1522.	The Muslim Sultanate of Rum breaks up into a number of small Turkish states.	Notre Dame Cathedral at Reims, a masterpiece of Gothic architecture, is completed after 99 years of construction.

King Philip IV of France made it his mission to destroy the Knights Templar, many of whom were tortured and burned in the early 14th century.

back to Poitiers, and so to Bordeaux before going back to Poitiers. During these journeys, Clement dealt with a number of issues. In 1306, he excommunicated Robert the Bruce (the future king of Scotland) for the murder of John Comyn inside Dumfries Cathedral, and he deposed two Scottish bishops who had supported him. He also began a process of denuding the papal treasury to enrich his family and friends. By the end of his reign the papacy would be almost bankrupt, in itself a remarkable fact. Also, in 1306, he suspended Robert of Winchelsea as archbishop of Canterbury because of a dispute over taxes, restoring him, in 1308, when the dispute was settled. He also issued a definitive ruling on the disputed crown of Hungary that put Charles Robert on the throne.

When King Albert of Germany died, Clement avoided siding with Philip IV's brother Charles of Valois (below) and instead recognized as valid the election of Henry of Luxembourg, who was crowned Holy Roman emperor in Rome by three bishops in 1312.

In his government of the Church, Clement was an enthusiastic centralizer and took every opportunity to remove decisions from local bodies and move them to Rome—especially when it came to appointing new bishops.

In 1307, Clement received letters written by Giovanni de Montecorvino in China (*see* p.189). Montecorvino described the success of his mission to date, having made some 6,000 converts to Christianity among the Mongols and Chinese and having established churches in China and in India. He had bought 150 boys, training them in Latin and teaching them to help with the ritual of Mass and to sing in choirs. Also, he had learned to speak Mongolian and had translated the New Testament into the language. Clement was delighted. He chose seven Franciscans, consecrated ten bishops, and sent them off on the long journey to join Montecorvino. In the event only three got to China, but they consecrated Montecorvino archbishop of Peking. The Church in China survived until 1369 when the newly established Ming Dynasty expelled them as being an unwanted foreign influence.

On October 13, 1307, hundreds of Knights Templar were arrested in France on order of King Philip. They were accused of heresy, bizarre sexual practices, and dishonesty, though it is now thought likely that Philip merely wanted their wealth. The Templars were, indeed, a wealthy order, but they were also vulnerable. The order had been founded to protect Christians in the Holy Land, but the crusader states were a thing of the past. Several Templars were tortured until they confessed, then the confessions sent to Clement. Philip demanded that the pope abolish the order, but Clement decided to summon a council at Vienne to decide the fate of the Templars. When the council met it sided with the Templars, but Clement abolished the order anyway. He ordered that the assets of the Templars be handed over to the Knights Hospitallers. Philip eventually gave the Templar lands to the Hospitallers, but not before he had stripped them of everything of value.

In 1309, Clement took what is perhaps his best known decision—he accepted an invitation to stay at the Dominican Monastery at Avignon. At the time Avignon was a fief of the Kingdom of Naples, thus being an island of non-French territory wholly enclosed within the Kingdom of France. He spent the last six years of his life there.

1311

The completion of the spire of Lincoln Cathedral, in England. At a height of 525 feet, it is the tallest building in the world, surpassing the Great Pyramid of Giza. The spire collapses in a storm in 1549 and is never rebuilt.

1312

The Canary Islands are discovered by Genoese mariner Lancelotto Malucello. The islands had been known to the Romans, but knowledge of them was forgotten after the fall of Rome.

1313

The Holy Roman emperor Henry VII dies at Buonconvento near Siena, Italy, on August 24.

1314

Battle of Bannockburn. The Scots under Robert the Bruce defeat the English army of King Edward II and so regain Scottish independence.

JOHN XXII ✠ The 196th Pope 1315–1334

Born Cahors, France; 1244
Parents Unknown
Papacy August 7, 1315–December 4, 1334
Died Avignon, France; December 4, 1334

It was John XXII who established the papacy firmly in Avignon, where it would remain for the next forty years. His papacy was marked by a theological dispute over the Beatific Vision, with John taking a position that was later judged to be heretical.

The death of Clement V precipitated a crisis in the college of cardinals. The election began peacefully enough, with the cardinals retiring to the bishop's palace at Carpentras. However, factions soon formed. The Italians wanted the papacy to return to Rome, the French wanted it to stay in France, and the relatives of Clement wanted to hang on to their lucrative positions. A few days after the election began, a column of tough mercenaries arrived—hired by the family of Clement—and the Italian and French cardinals fled. It would be nearly two years before the cardinals met again. They were virtually forced to meet in Lyon by Count Philip of Poitiers, who became King Philip V of France. After protracted squabbling Cardinal Jacques d'Euse was elected as John XXII.

The issue of the Beatific Vision was of rising importance at this time. John belonged to the party that held that when a person died their soul waited until the end of time brought the Last Judgement, whereupon they would be consigned to Heaven (where they met God and so enjoyed the Beatific Vision), Hell, or Purgatory. Others believed that when a person died in grace with God they went straight to Heaven. A key point was that if saints went straight to Heaven they could intercede with God for humans still on Earth, whereas if they did not there was no point praying to them. The majority of theologians favored the view that souls went straight to Heaven, but John preached against this throughout his time as pope.

A theological dispute with more practical import was over whether Christ and the disciples had owned anything of their own or not. John believed they had, but the Franciscans believed they had not. In 1323, John declared the Franciscans to be heretics, and it took until 1325 before most of them changed their views. A minority, however, refused and fled for protection to King Louis IV of Germany.

In 1327, Louis came to Italy to be crowned king of Italy in Milan then marched on to Rome where he was crowned Holy Roman emperor. There he declared John to be deposed on the grounds of heresy and, in 1328, he set up one of the Franciscans, Pietro Rainalducci, to be "Pope" Nicholas V. Nicholas did not relish his role and soon fled to Avignon to gain the pardon of John. Louis responded by summoning the nobles of Germany who issued the Declaration of Rhense. This held that once the majority of the nobles entitled to vote had declared for a candidate to be king of Germany he automatically became Holy Roman emperor as well without needing to await coronation by the pope. It was a decisive split between the empire and the papacy.

John was, meanwhile, continuing his predecessor's policy of favoring Gascons and Frenchmen. Nearly every new cardinal was French and John showered lucrative positions on his relatives and friends. He was, however, an able and shrewd administrator who kept the papacy solvent and well ordered.

King Louis IV of Germany was already at loggerheads with John over the respective rights of royal and Papal authority in Italy. He then took up the cause of the minority Franciscans who the pope had condemned as heretics in 1323.

1316	1325	1327	1330	1333
A cold, damp summer causes extensive crop failures across Europe, leading to what was dubbed "The Great Famine," in which hundreds of thousands died. The crops failed again in 1321.	The wandering Aztec tribes settle on the island of Tenochtitlan in Lake Texcoco, an event later recognized as the start of the Aztec Empire.	King Edward II of England is deposed and murdered by his wife Isabella and her lover Roger Mortimer, who then set up the young Edward III to be their puppet ruler.	Edward III of England overthrows his mother, establishing himself on the throne.	Battle of Halidon Hill sees Edward III of England crush a Scottish army near the disputed border town of Berwick. The battle sees the first massed use of volleys of longbow arrows, a tactic soon dubbed "arrowstorm."

BENEDICT XII ✠ The 197th Pope 1334–1342

Born probably Saverdun, France; c.1280

Parents Unknown

Papacy December 20, 1334–April 25, 1342

Died Avignon, France; April 25, 1342

Benedict XII devoted much time to theological debate, where he managed to settle several disputes, and sought to halt many of the abuses that had arisen in papal government. However, he proved less adept at diplomacy and politics.

Jacques Fournier, who would become Benedict XII, entered the Cistercian monastery of Boulbonne in southwestern France around 1295 and graduated as a master of theology from Paris in about 1310. In 1317, he became bishop of Parniers before becoming bishop of Mirepoix in 1326. He was a skilled member of the Inquisition, being able to trap suspects into confessions, though being rather less inclined than others to send heretics to be burned at the stake. His success saw him promoted to cardinal priest of Santa Prisca by John XXII in 1327. His election was speedy and smooth in a conclave that lasted only a few days.

Benedict failed to broker a deal between Edward III of England (above) and Philip VI of France. The two nations went to war in 1337.

As pope, Benedict moved quickly to settle the dispute over the Beatific Vision, declaring that souls go straight to Heaven after death. Just as swiftly he sought to stamp out the corruption that had grown rife in the curia. He halted many of the informal payments that were draining the papal treasury, ensured proper record-keeping of decisions (to stop bribes being taken to alter decisions after they had been made), and forced those issuing indulgences to stick to the rules.

Benedict also sought to enforce a strict observance of the rules on the monastic and mendicant orders. The luxury of life in some monasteries had become notorious, and many monks became "vagabonds," meaning they roamed from one monastery to another without permission or apparent purpose. Benedict set up a system of regular inspections of such institutions. Vagabonds were ordered back to their home monastery and forbidden to leave without the permission of their superiors.

Benedict himself retained his simple monk's habit throughout his life and led a life of frugal simplicity. He promoted no relatives, nor did his friends do well out of the papacy. There were rumors that he drank too much, but these mostly came from men who had suffered from his clamp down on corruption.

His position in Avignon meant that Benedict often came under pressure from King Philip VI of France. Benedict's efforts to heal the breach with Holy Roman Emperor Louis IV were close to completion when Philip stepped in and stopped further talks. Louis eventually became frustrated and, in 1338, summoned an imperial diet that approved the document *Fidem Catholicam*, which declared that the authority of the Holy Roman emperor came direct from God, not via the papacy. Three years later he went further with the *Licet Iuris*, which laid down rules for the election of future emperors in which the pope played no part.

Benedict also failed to broker a deal between France and England due to Philip's insistence that he toe the French line, and war broke out between the two kingdoms in 1337. Benedict made efforts to move to Rome, undertaking an expensive renovation of the Lateran and of St. Peter's in preparation for his arrival. However, the outbreak of war in Italy between various city states and the desire of most cardinals to remain in France kept him where he was.

1335	1335	1337	1338	1340
Carinthia and Carniola are given to Duke Otto the Merry of Austria, remaining in Habsburg hands to 1918.	The Mongol state of Ilkhan, based around Persia, fragments after the death of ruler Abu Said without an heir.	The first good harvest in China for four years ends a famine that is thought to have killed around 6 million people.	A French fleet sacks Portsmouth in the first major action of the Hundred Years War between England and France.	The Battle of Sluys sees the entire French fleet destroyed or captured by the English fleet.

CLEMENT VI ✠ The 198th Pope 1342–1352

Born Maumont, France; 1291

Parents Father, Lord Guillaume Roger of Rosier; Mother, unknown

Papacy May 7, 1342–December 6, 1352

Died Avignon, France; December 6, 1352

Clement made the papacy's residence in Avignon more or less permanent and sought to end disagreements with the Holy Roman Empire. However, his papacy was overshadowed by the arrival in Europe of the terrible disease of the Black Death.

Born as Pierre Roger, son of one of the richest minor lords in France, he became abbot of the prestigious Benedictine Abbey of Fecamp in 1326 and was archbishop of Rouen by 1330. By this time he was also chancellor of France, displaying a ferocious skill for administrative efficiency. He became a cardinal in 1338. His election was one of the fastest on record, being completed on the first ballot "by divine inspiration alone."

Once installed as pope, Clement set out to enjoy himself, famously declaring "My predecessors did not know how to be pope." His reputation for lavish hospitality and impressive parties soon became legendary. Clement was a great lover of the arts and of music in particular. He brought many musicians and artists to Avignon, among them the poet and composer Philippe de Vitry. His easygoing nature allowed many of the abuses that Benedict XII had sought to eradicate to return to the Curia.

In 1348 he bought Avignon from its owner, Queen Joanna of Naples, and began the building of the great papal palace, effectively signalling the end of an intention to return to Rome. In 1347, the Romans rejected papal rule and set up a dictator named Cola di Rienzo, who introduced radical ideas of democracy. Clement moved to have him overthrown, but it was not until the Romans turned against him in 1354 that Rienzo fell and was killed.

In 1347 a terrifying new disease struck Constantinople, having come from Asia.

Burying plague victims. Around 80 percent of those who caught the disease died within five days. Overall, around a third of the population of a village would be killed..

Sufferers had extremely painful swellings in the groin and armpits, and black blotches on the skin. The Black Death reached Italy in January 1347, then spread rapidly across Europe. The massive depopulation led to panic, some blamed the Jews, gypsies, or friars, launching riots and massacres. Clement issued numerous proclamations attempting to protect such minorities. Others blamed the general sin of humanity, and sought to extirpate those sins by religious practices. The flagellants were the most famous of these groups, forming processions, and whipping themselves until the blood flowed. Nothing served to stem the disease, and up to 100 million people died in Europe in just four years.

The death of Emperor Louis IV allowed Clement to make peace with the new emperor Charles IV (below). However, Charles did not repudiate his predecessor's declarations of independence from the papacy.

1344	1345	1346	1347	1349
Three large Florentine banks—Compagnia dei Bardi, the Peruzzi, and the Acciaiuoli—all go bankrupt as economic conditions worsen across Europe.	The Miracle of the Host occurs in Amsterdam—an event that is still commemorated with a civil procession.	The Battle of Crecy sees England's Edward III defeat Philip VI of France using massed volleys of long arrows. The vast death toll, especially among the nobility, shocks Europe.	The Black Death arrives in Europe. About a third of the population is killed by the disease, which returns at intervals for the next three centuries to continue to take a toll.	An earthquake in Rome causes widespread damage, including the partial collapse of the Colosseum leaving it as it stands today.

INNOCENT VI ✠ The 199th Pope 1352–1362

Born Les Monts, France; probably 1295

Parents Father, Lord Adhemar Aubert de Montel-de-Gelat; Mother, unknown

Papacy 18 December, 1352–12 September, 1362

Died Avignon, France; 12 September, 1362

The Battle of Poitiers, 1356, was an overwhelming English victory against France, with King John II of France taken prisoner.

Weak, indecisive, and physically frail, Innocent VI nevertheless built a reputation for honesty, justice, and mercy. He came to the papal throne with high hopes but a succession of disputes and emergencies caused him to fritter away his time so that he achieved little.

Born as Etienne Aubert, a member of the minor French nobility, he became bishop of Noyon in 1338, bishop of Clermont in 1340, and cardinal bishop of Ostia in 1352, just weeks before the conclave met to elect a successor to Clement VI.

The conclave met in the papal palace in Avignon and almost at once there was a move to reach a remarkable agreement. In recent decades power within the Church had become increasingly centralized into the hands of the papacy. The popes had long ruled as sovereign lords, which many saw as not only tantamount to a dictatorship over the Church, but also as a weakness since one man could not hope to supervise properly the multifaceted activities of the Church. Instead, it was thought by some that power should be diffused among the cardinals, making the pope little more than simply most important of the cardinals. In the conclave of 1352 the cardinals agreed that a wide range of papal decisions had to be agreed by a vote of the cardinals before they became valid and that the cardinals could summon the pope to a meeting to question him about his decisions and activities. All cardinals signed this agreement before the election was allowed to proceed.

After only two days of deliberations, the cardinals elected Aubert, who took the name Innocent VI. At first Innocent stuck to the agreement made in the conclave, but soon lost patience with his cardinals. He declared the agreement legally invalid and began ruling as autocratically as his predecessors.

Innocent wanted to move the papacy back to Rome and to this end set about bringing order to Italy. He sent the vigorous Spanish cardinal Gil de Albornoz to quell the squabbling nobles and so reimpose papal rule over the Papal States. It proved to be a herculean task requiring the building of alliances, fighting of battles, and the making of treaties. It took Albornoz until 1360 to gain an insecure control of the Papal States.

Meanwhile, Innocent had been pursuing a campaign of his own to reform the papal curia and bureaucracy. He sought to stamp out corruption, root out favoritism, and end abuses arising from poor record keeping. His success was impressive, but only partial. The reforms did mean that less of the papal treasury disappeared into corruption but, instead, it went to fund Albornoz's campaign. By 1361, Innocent was almost bankrupt. It was only by selling off art treasures that Innocent avoided financial catastrophe.

The war between England and France was brought starkly to Innocent's attention when a wandering band of mercenaries arrived outside Avignon, blockaded the city, and demanded a large cash payment to go away. Emissaries from the warring kingdoms came to Avignon and, in 1360, a peace treaty was agreed to last the next ten years. He was less successful in attempts to end a war between Aragon and Castile, a situation complicated by the fact that King Peter of Castile was in dispute with Innocent over which if his three marriages was the valid one.

1352	1354	1355	1356	1359
Zug, Glarus, and Bern join the Swiss confederation.	The cities of Kallipolis and Didymoteicho are captured from the Byzantine Empire by the Ottoman Turks.	Charles IV is crowned Holy Roman emperor in Rome by the bishop of Ostia with papal permission.	The Golden Bull issured by the Holy Roman emperor Charles IV fixes the form and place of the imperial election, transforming the empire from a monarchy into an aristocratic federation that will last for 450 years.	Defeat by the Ottoman Turks forces Byzantine emperor John V to cede so much territory that his rule is confined to little more than the city of Constantinople.

URBAN V ✠ The 200th Pope 1362–1370

Born Grisac, France; 1310

Parents Father, William de Grimoard, Lord of Bellegarde; Mother, Amphélise de Montferrand

Papacy September 28, 1362–December 19, 1370

Died Avignon, France; December 19, 1370

Urban V, born William de Grimoard into the minor nobility of France, was the last pope to consider seriously a crusade against the Muslims in the Holy Land. He made determined efforts to get a military campaign of some kind together, but troubles closer to home got in the way.

William de Grimoard was in Florence when he received a message from Avignon telling him that Innocent had died and that the cardinals in conclave were deadlocked. The message asked de Grimoard to return to Avignon at once as the cardinals wanted to seek his advice. He got to Avignon in November to find that the message had been a ruse—he had been elected pope on September 28 but the cardinals had kept the news quiet in case he was attacked en route.

Taking the title Urban V, the new pope announced that he was to continue the efforts of Innocent to reimpose papal rule in Italy and stamp out corruption inside the curia. These were but means to an end. His ultimate aims, of which he made no secret, were to return the papacy to Rome and launch a great crusade.

The efforts to rid the curia of corruption and favoritism proved to be a drawn out affair and, while Urban made progress, he failed to achieve his aims completely. His time was not entirely wasted, however: the money that became available was used to fund scholarships for 1,000 students at various universities across Europe and to found or preserve colleges at Toulouse, Montpellier, Quézac, Bédouès, and Ispagnac.

In the ongoing Italian conflicts, Urban backed Cardinal Albornoz, but the papal army was quite unable to defeat Bernabò Visconti, Lord of Milan. Urban declared the war against Milan to be a crusade, allowing him to divert funds earmarked to fight the Muslims. Urban excommunicated Visconti, who forced the papal legate who brought the bull to Milan to eat it, lead seal and all, before he was allowed to leave.

Bernabò Visconti, Lord of Milan, took Bologna and refused to hand it back to the Papal States.

Urban was ultimately forced to agree a peace treaty with the Lord of Milan (above) that involved handing Milan a huge payment in return for Bologna.

The long-awaited crusade against the Muslims finally got under way in 1365 when an alliance of Cyprus, Rhodes, and Venice sent a joint fleet to attack Alexandria, which was captured and looted. The crusaders were soon faced by a huge Egyptian army and retreated to Cyprus. The following year an army from Savoy captured Emona and Gallipoli from the Ottoman Turks. The lands were held for ten years before they were recaptured. The expeditions were the last efforts of Christian crusading against the Muslims.

In 1367, Urban moved to Rome but several cities rebelled against papal rule and few of the cardinals joined him. In 1370, he went back to Avignon, where he died.

1363	1363	1368	1368
One of the largest naval battles in history takes place at Lake Poyang when the Han fleet of 140 ships and 650,000 men is catastrophically defeated by the Ming fleet of over 100 ships and 200,000 men.	Philip the Bold become duke of Burgundy, later launching a bid for independence from France.	Tamerlaine (Timur) becomes Emir of Samarkand.	The Ming Dynastry of China is founded by Zhu Yuanzhang after his rebel Red Turban movement drives the Mongol Yuan Dynasty out of China.

GREGORY XI ✢ The 201st Pope 1370–1378

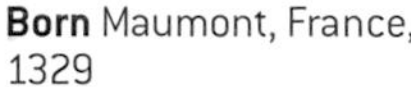

Born Maumont, France, 1329

Parents Father, Guillaume de Beaufort; Mother, Marie du Chambon

Papacy December 30 1370–March 27, 1378

Died Rome, Italy; March 27, 1378

Saint Catherine of Siena depicted exchanging her heart with Christ.

Gregory XI, who was born into a family of wealthy nobles, is famous for returning the papacy to Rome from Avignon, but the return home was not entirely enjoyable. In his own time, Gregory was perhaps better known for his enthusiastic suppression of heresy.

Not only was Pierre Roger de Beaufort, who was to become Gregory XI, from a wealthy family, he was also the nephew of a pope: Clement VI. By the age of eleven he was a canon in Paris and just eight years later he was a cardinal deacon. He then set off for Perugia where he was educated in canon law and established a reputation for piety, mysticism, and terrible health problems.

When Urban V died, the 18 cardinals in Avignon gathered at the papal palace to elect a successor. On the very first ballot Beaufort got the two thirds majority necessary. He made a show of refusing the honor but was careful not to be too forceful before accepting. He took the name Gregory XI and announced his intention of returning the papacy to Rome as well as mouthing the conventional ambitions of launching a crusade and restoring unity with Eastern Christianity.

Nothing could be achieved with an empty treasury, however, so Gregory began by borrowing some money and zealously collecting all funds due to the papacy. England and France were again at war as the Hundred Years War entered a new phase, and Gregory expended much effort in a fruitless effort to broker peace. In Italy, Milan was occupying the Romagna and invading Savoy, so Gregory sought to put together a league of Italian states against Milan but, by 1375, had to admit failure and make peace.

The terms of the peace deal caused Florence to throw off its allegiance to the pope and soon most of the Papal States were in rebellion. A large army of mercenaries was hired to put down the revolt, which it did with a bloody violence that earned Gregory few friends. Nevertheless, Gregory moved to Rome in 1377 and took up residence in the Vatican. He was encouraged by the holy Catherine of Siena, later to be canonized, but she became annoyed at Gregory's insistence on harsh peace terms to be imposed on the rebellious cities. The cities themselves also objected and rebellion broke out afresh. It was the unexpected peace overtures of Bernabò Visconti, Lord of Milan, that ensured that a peace conference was organized for March 1378. Gregory instructed his representatives that peace must be achieved, but before his orders could be carried out he had died.

THE INQUISITION

In his own day Gregory XI was famous for his merciless hounding of heretics and enthusiastic support for the Inquisition. The Inquiry into Heretical Perversity, as the organization for enforcing orthodox belief was known, had originated in a series of temporary ecclesiastical courts in southern France in the twelfth century to identify and punish those guilty of the Cathar heresy (*see* p.168). In 1229, the courts were made permanent and put under the authority of the Dominicans based in Rome. The Spanish inquisition was founded in 1434 and quickly became infamous for its ruthless methods and punishments. It eased its investigations after about 1650 but continued until 1834. The papal Inquisition underwent several changes over the years. It is today known as the Congregation for the Doctrine of the Faith and is concerned with issuing rulings on matters of doctrine or morals.

1371

Battle of Maritsa. The Ottoman Turks invade Serbia, defeating the Serb army and wiping out nearly all the Serb nobles, after which large areas of the Balkans fall to the Turks.

1371

Hongwu of the Ming Dynasty begins a census of China that records a population of 59,873,305 people liable for tax. However some categories of people are excluded, so the total population is thought to have been around 75 million.

1373

The city of Phnom Penh, Cambodia, is founded.

1377

The "Bad Parliament" meets in England and, under royal pressure, introduces a number of new taxes and relaxes controls introduced to reduce corruption in royal government.

URBAN VI ✠ The 202nd Pope 1378–1389

Born Itri, Italy; 1318
Parents Unknown
Papacy April 8, 1378–October 15, 1389
Died Rome, Italy; October 15, 1389

Bartolomeo Prignano was appointed archbishop of Bari, Italy, in 1377 and became pope a year later. It was during his reign as Urban VI that the Great Western Schism began, and this has understandably marred the memory of his pontificate. While the schism was not entirely his fault, Urban's attitude and behavior certainly did his cause no good.

When Gregory XI died crowds poured out on to the streets of Rome. They were in bellicose mood, determined that the papacy should remain in Rome and on no account be moved back to Avignon. They demanded that the next pope should be "a Roman, or at least an Italian." As the mobs thronged the streets, the 16 cardinals in Rome gathered in the old St. Peter's Basilica to begin the election. That evening the city officials went to St. Peter's to tell the cardinals that they could not guarantee order on the streets or safety for the cardinals if they allowed the election to drag on. To make the point, a crowd surged into the basilica and refused to leave. It was not until the next day that the church was cleared and the election could begin. The mob, however, was demonstrating loudly outside. Scared for their lives, the cardinals with one exception voted for Bartolomeo Prignano who was Italian, but had lived for years in France and was in Rome at the time. Since he was not a cardinal he was not present, so messengers were sent to summon him. Realizing the election was over, the mob burst into St. Peter's and found Cardinal Francesco Tebaldeschi holding the papal insignia. Assuming this elderly Roman was the new pope, the mob went wild with joy. It was not until the next day that the news broke that Prignano was pope as Urban VI.

Urban was a devout and austere monk and at once made it clear that he expected his lead to be followed by the entire Church, especially the cardinals. He declared that the financial problems of the Church could be solved if all cardinals, archbishops, and bishops lived lives of ascetic austerity, all corruption ended, and secular engagement came to an end. He set about imposing this new regime with enthusiasm that bordered on mania. One by one the cardinals withdrew from Rome, meeting at Anagni. They decided that the new regime was unacceptable and sent messengers to Rome urging Urban to modify his tone. Urban refused in truculence and, on August 2, the cardinals formally declared his election invalid on the grounds that they had acted out of fear of the mob, not according to their consciences. Urban, they said, was deposed. On September 20, a new election was held and Cardinal Robert of Geneva was elected as Clement VII.

Each pope excommunicated the other, then sent letters to the bishops and crowned heads of Europe demanding recognition and the payment of papal dues. France, Burgundy, Savoy, Naples, and Scotland declared for Clement; England, Germany, Italy, and central Europe for Urban. The Spanish kingdoms remained neutral. Western Christendom was divided and the Great Western Schism had begun.

Once the split was in the open, Urban behaved with a bizarre mixture of skill and foolishness. He began by appointing 29 new cardinals, taking care to choose men well

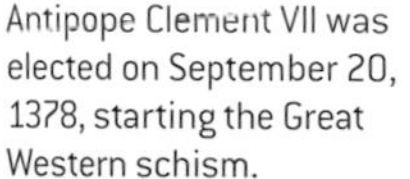

Antipope Clement VII was elected on September 20, 1378, starting the Great Western schism.

1378

The Holy Roman emperor Charles IV divides his lands among his three sons and dies at Prague on November 29, aged 62.

1378

In England, the priest John Wycliffe calls for a major reform of the Church with papal authority being condemned in favor of each person establishing his own relationship with God based on reading the Bible, translated into English. His followers, the Lollards, would later be hailed as early precursers of the Protestant Reformation.

1381

The Peasants Revolt in England sees large sections of the kingdom rise in a rebellion fueled by demands for social reforms and discontent with heavy taxation. The revolt is put down and its leaders executed, but reforms later take place.

Queen Joanna of Naples initially supported Pope Urban VI, but she later switched her allegiance and declared for Clement VII in Avignon.

thought of in the nations that supported him, thus consolidating his adherents. He then secured all of Rome and hired mercenaries who, at the Battle of Marion in April 1379, crushed Clement's supporters in Italy.

Clement retreated to Naples but hostility there drove him out and he moved to Avignon to occupy the papal palace under the protection of King Charles V of France. There he established a court and began organizing a curia and network of supporters as if he were the real pope. His efforts came to little, however, as Urban continued to rally support to his cause and used mercenaries to dominate Italy. Later papal historians have judged that Urban was properly elected and have held that Clement was, therefore, an antipope.

With victory almost in his grasp, Urban then seemed to lose his sense. He was rude and dismissive to his powerful ally Queen Joanna of Naples, who then declared for Clement. In turn, Urban declared her excommunicated and deposed, giving the crown to her cousin Charles of Durazzo. Charles came to Rome in 1381 to be crowned by Urban. In return for a promise to make Urban's favorite nephew ruler of Capua, Caserta, Aversa, Nocera, and Amalfi, Charles was given lavish funding to hire soldiers. He marched into southern Italy and murdered Joanna. By 1384, however, Urban had fallen out with Charles over a succession of minor issues. Charles approached six cardinals to see if Urban's autocratic rule could be tempered by a council of cardinals. When Urban heard of the move he arrested the six cardinals and had them hideously tortured to death. Five more cardinals vanished without trace.

Urban hired a new army and invaded Naples, precipitating an indecisive war. By October 1388 Urban had run out of money, whereupon the mercenaries abandoned him. He had also run out of friends and retreated to the Vatican fortress. On the way to the Vatican he fell off his mule and sustained serious injuries. He barricaded himself inside the Vatican but died a few weeks later. Whether he died of injuries from his fall or from poison is disputed.

The old Romanesque-style cathedral in Bari, Puglia, Italy, where Urban VI had been appointed archbishop.

1381

Tamerlaine begins his conquest of Persia, which would be completed by 1387. He initiates a program of building towers made from the decapitated heads of those who oppose him. After the fall of Isfahan he has 28 towers made of 1,500 heads each.

1386

Venice conquers Corfu, beginning an expansion into the eastern Mediterranean.

1387

The Battle of Otterburn sees the Scottish commander James Douglas killed and the English commander Harry Hotspur Percy captured. It is considered a Scottish victory.

BONIFACE IX ✠ The 203rd Pope 1389–1404

Born Naples, Italy; c.1350

Parents Father, Baron Casarano; Mother, unknown

Papacy November 2, 1389–October 1, 1404

Died Rome, Italy; October 1, 1404

Clever, genial, and unscrupulous, Boniface IX was determined to prove that he was the legitimate pope. His entire pontificate was devoted to establishing his recognition throughout Christendom, an ambition in which Boniface failed utterly. His tenure as pope left the papacy in a state of bankruptcy and the Church even more divided.

Not very much is known of the early life of Piero Tomacelli. He was born a son of the baron of Casarano, who despite his title was desperately poor. Young Tomacelli did not attend a regular school and throughout his life his lack of learning would be a target for ridicule by his opponents. He was, however, a gifted orator and famous preacher. Urban VI made Tomacelli a cardinal when all the existing cardinals decamped to France at the start of the Great Western Schism and, in 1385, he was promoted to cardinal priest of Santa Anastasia.

When Urban died the cardinals in Rome made no move to reach an accommodation with the rival pope, Clement VII. The dispute was so bitter that they believed he would depose them all, deprive them of their lucrative incomes, and very possibly have them thrown in prison. Instead, they held a quick election and made one of their own, Tomacelli, pope. Because papal historians have ruled that the election of Urban VI was valid, it follows that Boniface IX was his legitimate successor while Clement remains an antipope.

The port of Naples is one of the largest Italian seaports. In the early years of Boniface's reign, it was the scene of a bloody power struggle between the rival popes who each backed a different candidate to rule this important papal fief.

As soon as Clement heard of Boniface's election he excommunicated the new pope, who returned the favor instantly. These formalities over, the two men claiming to be pope launched into an intense campaign to unseat each other.

The initial field of conflict was the Kingdom of Naples. As Naples was a papal fief, the pope had the right to decide on a new ruler in the case of a disputed succession. Clement was backing Louis of Anjou, while Boniface now backed Ladislas, son of Charles of Durazzo. Neither claimant was able to gain an advantage and war engulfed all of southern Italy. Boniface kept Ladislas supplied with plenty of money and thousands of mercenaries. Slowly the weight of numbers began to tell and, in July 1400, Ladislas was secure on his throne. He celebrated his formal entry into Naples by giving orders for the murder of a string of local noblemen.

In September 1394, Clement died and there were hopes that some sort of a compromise might be reached with Boniface. King Charles VI of France urged them to delay electing a successor until messages could be sent to Boniface asking if a deal were possible, but the cardinals refused and promptly elected Spanish cardinal Pedro de Luna to be Benedict XIII, now also considered an antipope. Hearing of the French king's move, Boniface now made a generous offer to Benedict, which was turned down. In 1397, a council of French bishops

1391	1391	1392	1394
Tamerlaine defeats the Mongol Golden Horde at the Battle of the Kondurcha River. He installs a puppet ruler of the Golden Horde.	Earl Henry of Orkney conquers the Shetland and Faroe Islands.	Go Komatsu becomes the 100th emperor of Japan, reuniting the country after a period of anarchy.	King Charles VI expels all Jews from France.

Statue of Benedict XIII (r.1394–1417) in Peniscola, Spain, where the antipope spent the last six years of his life. Benedict put up a determined resistance to the rule of Boniface IX.

voted to recognize Boniface, and King Charles agreed. An army was sent to blockade Avignon to force Benedict to give way.

In northern Italy, Boniface followed a policy of compromise. He recognized the status quo in most cases, asking only for declarations of support in return. In the Papal States he was more forceful but no less tactful. Armies led by his brothers moved through the states to impose his rule, offering lenient terms to those who accepted papal authority at once but being tougher on those who delayed. Viterbo held out, and was crushed by an army led by Boniface himself.

In Rome itself Boniface had fluctuating fortunes. At first he was popular, but his increasingly heavy taxation began to cause resentment. In 1398, it was discovered that several leading members of the Roman city government were conspiring with Clement's successor Benedict XIII. Boniface at once dismissed all the city officials and, instead of allowing new elections, appointed men to office himself. Democracy in Rome was now effectively dead as the city officials were henceforth appointed by the pope.

In March 1403, Benedict escaped from Avignon and set about rallying support to his cause once again. He declared that he would abdicate immediately should Boniface die or abdicate, whereupon a fresh election could be held with all cardinals of both popes taking part. In September 1404, having talked the French Church around to his point of view, Benedict went on an embassy to Rome asking Boniface to give a similar pledge and so end the schism. Boniface refused, but then started coming under pressure from his supporters to give way. He died still defiant.

The Church that Boniface left was not only hopelessly divided, it was morally and financially bankrupt. The huge cost of paying for mercenaries had emptied the papal treasury. Boniface not only had to continue paying the soldiers, but also needed to find cash to hand out bribes in northern Italy and to courtiers in countries across Europe. To get the money, he embarked on a program of corruption that scandalized even his supporters. Positions and offices were sold openly, irrespective of the qualities of those taking up office. The papacy owned a vast number of benefices, usually in the form of parcels of land the rents of which were settled on a person for life in return for services rendered to the Church. Whenever one of these fell vacant, Boniface auctioned it off for cash. The work of the Church suffered accordingly as benefices intended to support charitable or educational work went instead to secular hands. Worst of all, in the view of contemporaries, was his sale of indulgences. An indulgence was the recognition by the pope that a person who confessed their sins had done some form of good work for God that, in part or in full, atoned for those sins and reduced the punishment that might be expected. Boniface declared that giving money to the pope counted as a good work and so could be used to acquire an indulgence. Whether the person had confessed or not was immaterial, simply handing over the cash was enough.

1394	1395	1396	1398
The Sultanate of Delhi enters a 20 year period of civil war after the death of Sultan Mahmud II.	Gian Visconti buys the title of duke from the Holy Roman emperor, making his rule over Milan hereditary.	The Cursade of Nicopolis advances along the Danube, pillaging and killing under the leadership of the Hungarian king Sigismund who is supported by both the Roman and the Avignon popes.	Tamerlaine invades northern India, sacking Delhi and massacring an estimated 500,000 Hindus.

INNOCENT VII ✠ The 204th Pope 1404–1406

Born Sulmona, Italy; 1336
Parents Unknown
Papacy October 17, 1404–November 6, 1406
Died Rome, Italy; November 6, 1406

Born Cosimo Gentile de' Migliorati into a respectable merchant family, Pope Innocent was a pious man and a patron of the arts. Nevertheless, his short reign saw murder, mayhem, and violence on a large scale, with the Great Western Schism remaining as entrenched as ever.

When Boniface died, envoys from the rival pope Benedict XIII urged the cardinals in Rome to delay an election. Benedict had already promised to abdicate when Boniface died, so that all the cardinals could elect a new pope to unify Europe. The leading citizens of Rome also urged delay, and many of Boniface's foreign supporters were known to favor a deal with Benedict.

The cardinals retired to discuss what to do and emerged nine days later to announce that they had elected Migliorati as Pope Innocent VII. The news sparked an immediate riot in Rome. King Ladislas of Naples marched into the city with an army to impose order. He exploited the crisis to extract concessions from Innocent and to move his troops into key fortresses belonging to the Papal States.

Word came from King Rupert of Germany that an end to the schism had to be found. In response to this and other pressure Innocent summoned a council of bishops who supported his papacy to meet in Rome in November 1405.

The coronation of King Charles VI of France.

Soon afterward Innocent's nephew Ludovico Migliorati, a mercenary commander, brought his army to Rome to help his uncle. Innocent made Ludovico a cardinal, following the by now established practice that a pope would promote relatives and friends to the rank of cardinal to support him in his work.

In August 1405, the citizens of Rome again began urging an end to the schism and objecting to heavy taxes. Ludovico invited 11 leading citizens to his house, where he had them all murdered. Rome erupted into riots and when an armed mob stormed the Vatican, Innocent, the cardinals, and other churchmen fled to Viterbo, leaving 30 papal servants dead behind them. Again, Ladislas of Naples marched in to restore order and, again, he extracted concessions.

By January 1406, Rome was quiet once more so Innocent and the cardinals returned. Innocent granted Ludovico the title of Marquis and made him Count of Fermo with extensive lands to govern, and tax. Ladislas kept his troops in Rome, most notably in the Castel Sant'Angelo, which had been thoroughly modernized. Innocent had to excommunicate the Neapolitan king before he pulled his men out, after which the ban was lifted and Ladislas was promoted to be Standard Bearer of the Church.

The long-delayed council could not be put off much longer as Charles VI of France had added his voice to those demanding it should take place, so Innocent announced that he would be summoning his bishops to Rome in the immediate future. At this point, Innocent suddenly collapsed and died. Foul play was suspected but never proved.

1404
Flanders, Zeeland, and Holland are inundated by St. Elizabeth's Flood, which kills thousands.

1405
First record of whiskey being made in Ireland.

1405
Death of Tamerlaine while leading an army to invade China. It is thought that his career of conquest across Asia led to the deaths of about 17 million people, around five percent of the total world population at the time. His empire fragmented soon after his death.

1406
Dick Whittington is elected Lord Mayor of London for the first time. He would later be elected three more times.

GREGORY XII ✦ The 205th Pope 1406–1415

Born Venice, Italy; 1325
Parents Unknown
Papacy November 30, 1406–July 4, 1415
Died Recanati, Italy; October 18, 1417

The pontificate of Gregory XII, former cardinal priest of San Marco Angelo Correr, is notable chiefly for the way in which it ended, bringing to a close the Great Western Schism that had wracked European Christendom and undermined the moral authority of the Church.

When the cardinals went into conclave following the death of Innocent VII, the first thing they did was to all agree that, if elected, they would create no new cardinals except to replace one who died and would abdicate if the rival pope Benedict XIII should die or abdicate. After 12 days of deliberation, Correr emerged as the winner and took the title of Gregory XII.

By this date all of Europe had had enough of the schism between rival popes- many believed that it was being maintained simply because the men involved were personally ambitious. Gregory's first move was to announce he wanted to meet Benedict. He send a delegation to his rival to arrange the terms of the meeting and, after prolonged bickering, it was agreed in April that Benedict and Gregory, each accompanied by their cardinals and a small force of soldiers, would meet at Savona on November 1, 1407.

Both sides set to work planning negotiating tactics. King Ladislas of Naples, however, feared that Gregory would agree that he would be ousted and replaced by a rival favored by Benedict. He invaded the Papal States, stopping only when he was flung back from the gates of Florence. Under pressure from Ladislas, Gregory first postponed the meeting with Benedict and then canceled it.

Gregory's cardinals were furious and constantly urged him to seek a compromise with Benedict. To outmaneuver them, Gregory created four new cardinals, two of them his nephews. At this point, most of the old cardinals fled to Pisa, from where they sent Gregory a letter, copied widely to others, declaring it was time to end the schism. At Livorno, the rebel cardinals were met by cardinals who had abandoned Benedict. After talks, the now united cardinals announced that they were summoning a council of clerics to meet at Pisa in March 1409. Everyone of substance was invited to attend to solve the problem of the Schism.

The Council of Pisa was well attended, though neither Benedict nor Gregory either attended or sent representatives. On 5 June, the council announced that both men claiming to be pope were deposed on grounds of being heretics and the holy see was declared vacant. The cardinals in Pisa then went into conclave and elected Pietro Philarghi to be Pope Alexander V. Neither Gregory nor Benedict agreed to stand down, so the main result of the Council of Pisa was that there were now three popes.

Despite the apparent failure at Pisa, the schism was almost over. Support drained away from Gregory, who was soon left with the support of only a few towns in Italy, and from Benedict, who ended up ruling only the island fortress of Peniscola off the east coast of Spain. Alexander V died in 1410 and was replaced by John XXIII, both now considered antipopes.

King Sigismund of Germany now summoned a new council. This time its authority was widely recognized and everyone except the three popes agreed to abide by its decision. It met in Constance.

Antipope John XXIII (r.1410–1415) called the Council of Constance, under the instructions of King Sigismund of Germany.

1407

Ming Dynasty China, having finally defeated the remnants of the Yuan Dynasty in Mongolia, begins to expand by conquering Vietnam.

1410

The Teutonic Knights are crushed by a joint Polish-Lithuanian army in the Battle of Grunwald (or Tannenburg). The Teutonic Order then entered a decline from which it never recovered.

1415

The Battle of Agincourt sees a crushing victory by England over France, after which King Henry V of England marries Catherine, daughter of Charles VI of France, and is recognized as heir to the French throne.

MARTIN V ✠ The 206th Pope 1417–1431

Born Gennazano, Italy; 1368

Parents Father, Agapito Colonna; Mother, Caterina Conti

Papacy November 11, 1417–February 20, 1431

Died Rome, Italy; February 20, 1431

The reign of Martin V began at the Council of Constance—a meeting with overwhelming authority to sort out the problems afflicting European Christianity and which ended the Great Western Schism. It did not, however, end many of the abuses and scandals that had grown during the Schism and that would later contribute to the Protestant Reformation.

The Council began by defining its right to adjudicate in Church matters. On April 6, 1415, it declared itself "Legitimately assembled in the holy Spirit, constituting a general council and representing the Catholic church militant, it has power immediately from Christ; and that everyone of whatever state or dignity, even papal, is bound to obey it in those matters which pertain to the faith, the eradication of the said schism and the general reform of the said church of God in head and members."

With that taken care of, the most pressing problem was the Great Schism, the fact that there were three different men claiming to be the legitimate pope: Gregory XII, Benedict XIII, and John XXIII. The schism had begun under Urban VI (*see* p.202) and had persisted for more than 30 years despite the deaths of nearly everyone involved in the original disputes. While those in the higher reaches of the various factions within the Church held the differences to be important, most others believed the split was based largely on personal enmities and ambitions and that it was doing great harm to the prestige of the Church. The main impetus to summon the Council of Constance had come from secular rulers, primarily Sigismund of Germany, Holy Roman emperor, who attended most of the sessions. He did not have the authority to summon clerics to attend, however, so he had used John XXIII to summon the great council.

Later Church historians have decided that in the original dispute, Urban VI had been in the right. This meant that he was the real pope while his opponent Clement VII was not genuine and so is termed an antipope. It follows that the successors of Urban VI were genuine; those who followed Clement were not. Thus, by the time of the Council of Constance, it was Gregory XII who was the genuine pope, while Benedict and John were antipopes. The fact that it was John who summoned the Council means that, in strictly legalistic terms, the Council was invalid. At the time, however, everyone wanted to get the situation sorted out and recognized the legitimacy of the Council.

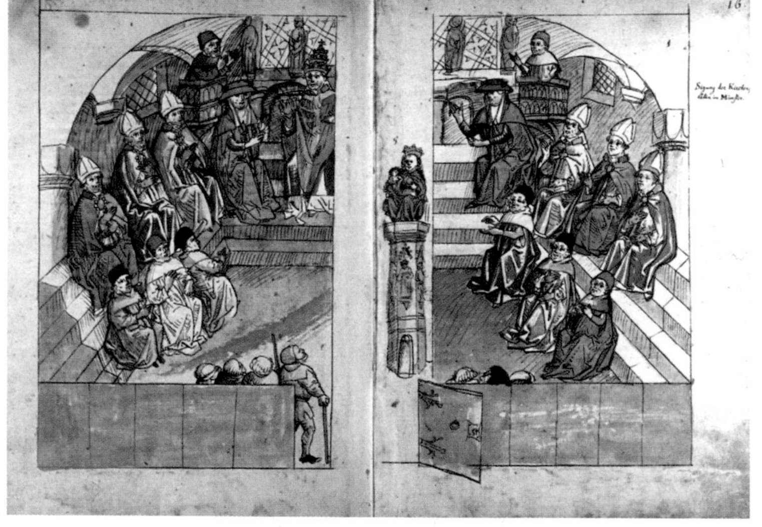

The great Council of Constance opened on November 16, 1414, and lasted, with breaks, until April 22, 1418. It was attended by 29 cardinals, 100 "learned doctors of law and divinity," 134 abbots, and 183 bishops and archbishops.

1417	1418	1427	1428
King Henry V of England starts to use English in official correspondence, replacing French.	The Portuguese begin the colonization of the Madeira Islands.	Diego de Silvas of Portugal discovers the Azores.	The Aztec Triple Alliance is agreed between three Aztec cities—Tenochtitlán, Texcoco, and Tlacopán—unifying the various Aztec states that cover the Valley of Mexico.

HUSSITES

The Great Schism and the squabbling it entailed greatly lowered the prestige of the papacy. In central Europe the Czech priest Jan Hus led the discontent. In 1412, he began arguing that selling indulgences for cash was wrong, that popes should not fight wars, and that the Christian faith depended on the Bible, not on the teachings of the Church. His followers went further, stating that the papacy was a fraudulent mob of sinners and criminals. Hus was given safe conduct by Holy Roman Emperor Sigismund to attend the Council at Constance to press his case for reform. However, the archbishop of Constance engineered his capture and put him on trial for heresy, after which he was burnt at the stake. The execution sparked the Hussite Wars that engulfed much of central Europe for the next 20 years. The Hussite Church, based on the teachings of Hus and his followers survived and still functions in the Czech Republic.

After some discussion, the Council decided that the best solution would be for all three "popes" to abdicate. Then the Council could elect a successor who would be recognized by all of Europe. John XXIII, having convoked the Council in the first place and being on the spot, was the first to be approached. He agreed to abdicate, but only if the Council first confirmed the decisions of the Council of Pisa (*see* p.207). This would have ruled out Gregory and Benedict, making him the sole legitimate pope. Realizing this might have given him authority over themselves, the Council refused.

That night John disguised himself as a groom and slipped out of Constance. He rode hard to Freiburg where he sought sanctuary. The Council sent soldiers after him who prised him away from Freiburg and dragged him back to Constance. There the Council put him on trial for perjury and simony, found him guilty, and deposed him as pope. He was handed over to Ludwig of Bavaria who locked John up in strict if comfortable imprisonment. Three years later, John escaped and went to Italy where he humbled himself in front of Martin and was rewarded with the position of bishop of Tusculum.

Image depicting Antipope John XXIII who fled from the Council of Constance, only to be captured at Freiburg. He was taken back to Constance and deposed as pope.

Next to be dealt with was Gregory. He sent Cardinal Dominici of Ragusa and Prince Charles of Malatesta as his legates. They stated that Gregory was willing to abdicate if he were allowed to remain a bishop for life and if they, his legates, closed and then reopened the Council to ensure it was meeting under his authority, not that of John whom Gregory regarded as a usurper. The Council agreed. On July 4, Ragusa and Malatesta closed the Council, reopened it, and read out the already signed letter of abdication from Gregory. Gregory then took up his new position as cardinal bishop of Porto and went into honored retirement.

Finally, the council turned to Benedict. He refused to even consider abdicating, condemned the Council as having no authority, and appointed four more cardinals. He could not be touched in his impregnable fortress of Peniscola, and so was simply ignored. He lived on until 1423.

The Council then elected as the new pope Cardinal Oddo Colonna, who took the name of Martin V. What the Church most needed now was a period of calm, which is what Martin provided. He put together a new curia made up of men who had served all three predecessors and set about restoring the papacy. He slowly reimposed papal ruler over the Papal States, winning the Battle of L'Aquila in 1424 and overcoming Bologna in 1429. This process cost money, however, so Martin did little to halt the various financial abuses that had been begun by Boniface IX and which had done so much to undermine the moral authority of the papacy.

In 1431 he summoned another great council to meet in Basle, but he died before it convened.

1428	1429	1430
Florence's Church of San Lorenzo is completed by Filippo Brunelleschi after seven years of construction.	Peasant girl Joan of Arc announces that she has heard the voices of saints urging her to rid France of English soldiers. She leads a successful relief expedition that lifts the siege of Orleans and is hailed a heroine by the French.	The Order of the Golden Fleece is founded by Duke Philip III of Burgundy to celebrate his marriage to Isabella of Portugal. It will later become the most coveted order of chivalry in Europe and still exists today.

EUGENE IV ✠ The 207th Pope 1431–1447

Born Venice, Italy; 1383
Parents Unknown
Papacy March 3, 1431–February 23, 1447
Died Rome, Italy; February 23, 1447

Eugene was a devout and temperate man, but his papacy was beset by troubles caused by a changing world. He was born Gabrielle Condulmer into a wealthy family and was a relative of Pope Gregory XII. The defining issue of his papacy was the conflict with the Council of Basle over which body had ultimate authority over the Church: Council or pope.

The Basilica of Santa Maria in Trastevere is one of the oldest churches in Rome.

As a teenager, Gabrielle Condulmer entered the body of canons on the island of San Giorgio in the Venetian Lagoon. There he devoted himself to study and prayer until he was summoned by Gregory XII, in 1411, to be bishop of Siena. The Sienese, however, wanted a local man and, since Gregory needed their support during the Great Schism, he gave way. Condulmer instead went to Rome to be papal treasurer and cardinal priest of San Clemente. He stayed in Rome to serve Martin V after the Great Schism ended, who moved him to Santa Maria in Trastevere. He was to serve as governor of Ancona and of Bologna under Martin, performing both duties well.

When Martin died, the 14 cardinals in Rome met in St. Peter's and, before starting the election, signed a solemn capitulation. This bound whichever of them won to share half of all papal revenues with the cardinals, to seek the consent of a majority of cardinals on any important issue, and to recognize the decisions of the Council of Basle, due to meet soon. On the first ballot, Condulmer gained the necessary two thirds majority and was acclaimed unanimously. He then issued a solemn bull confirming the capitulation, which he then ignored for the rest of his reign.

Eugene's first concern was to get back the vast lands that Martin V had granted to members of his Colonna family of Roman nobles. Some of these lands were let on agreements that could be rescinded easily enough but others were more difficult to deal with. In the end Eugene had to hire condottieri to wrest the lands back from the Colonna. All this took time, cost money, and alienated significant sections of the Italian nobility who looked upon the papacy as a source of money and favors that they had a right to enjoy.

Eugene aimed to reunite the Eastern Christians with those of the West. With Constantinople threatened ever more seriously by the Muslim Ottoman Turks, the prospect of a reunited Christendom became increasingly likely. Byzantine emperor John VIII Palaeologus agreed to a deal in 1439 that recognized the primacy of the pope over the patriarch of Constantinople, agreed to the papal views on purgatory, the origin of the Holy Spirit, and other matters. The agreement would turn out to be only temporary due to a lack of good will on both sides, but it did spur Eugene on to make contact with the Coptic Christians of Egypt, the Nestorians of Mesopotamia, and other detached Christian groups in the East. No formal agreement was ever reached with these

1431

Joan of Arc is burned at the stake in the Old Market Square of Rouen on 30 May.

1433

The Ming Dynasty of China decides to abandon ambitions to trade with or colonize distant regions and largely disbands its large warfleet. This creates a naval power vacuum in the Indian Ocean, which will later be filled by European fleets.

1434

African slaves introduced into Portugal by a caravel returning from the southern continent are the first of millions that will be exported in the next four centuries.

1436

The great dome of Florence Cathedral is completed. Designed by Filippo Brunelleschi it was the largest unsupported octagonal dome in the world.

congregations, but at least amicable relations were established.

Meanwhile, the Council of Basle had gathered, on July 23, 1431, under Cardinal Giuliano Cesarini. The turn out was disappointing, and those who did turn up did not seem to be well disposed toward Eugene. On December 18 Eugene sent a bull that dissolved the Council and ordered that a new one was to meet in Bologna, safely inside Papal territory, in the summer of 1433. The prelates in Basle refused to disperse, repeated the decisions of the Council of Constance (*see* p.208) that a General Council was superior to the pope, and summoned Eugene to come to Basle to explain himself.

Milan chose this moment to invade Tuscany and the Papal States, while the Colonna launched a rebellion in Rome to set up a republic. Eugene fled in his old monk's habit and took refuge in Bologna. There he hired Francesco Sforza, the finest condottiero of his time, and launched a reinvasion of the Papal States. The war with Milan and the Colonna proved to be long and arduous. It would be 1443 before Eugene could return to Rome.

Byzantine emperor John VIII Paleologus agreed to a deal in 1439 that recognized the primacy of the pope over the patriarch of Constantinople.

In 1438, Eugene convened a new Council to meet at Ferrara. The majority of prelates met there, and Eugene excommunicated those still in Basle. In June 1439, the Basle Council responded by declaring Eugene to be a heretic and to be deposed as pope. In his place they elected Duke Amadeus VIII of Savoy to be Felix V. The Council had passed a number of reform canons intended to reduce the power of the papacy over archbishops and bishops. These were adopted in France and Germany but, although the prelates and nobles were keen to diminish the powers of the papacy, there was no appetite for a new schism. Felix failed to gain significant support. As his hopes faded, so too did those of the Council, which soon broke up.

As he lay on his deathbed, Eugene bitterly regretted ever having left his monastic cell.

CONDOTTIERI

From about 1350 to around 1550, warfare in Italy was dominated by the condottieri—small armies of professional mercenaries who undertook to fight for whichever government was willing to pay them. The condottieri emerged when cities such as Florence, Venice, and Genoa grew to be enormously wealthy through trade and industry, but lacked the big populations of larger states from which to recruit armies. The condottieri usually had long-term contracts with a state, agreeing to fight for a city for a set number of years and each year to field an army of an agreed size in return for an annual payment. When the contract ended a condottiero was free to find another employer, and the state to find another mercenary army. The mercenaries were highly skilled in the arts of war and when necessity demanded were able to fight hard and long. More often, however, they preferred to avoid fighting and sought to win a campaign by maneuver, protracted sieges, or bribery. Decline set in around 1500 with the French invasion of Italy, which brought a large, single army into play against the disunited Italian city states. By 1550, most Italian soldiers of talent were fighting for rich masters outside of Italy.

1437	1438	1440	1442	1445
The Holy Roman emperor Sigismund dies on Dec 9, aged 69, and the house of Luxemburg becomes extinct.	Pachacuti becomes ruler of the Inca of Cuzco, later going on to expand his state massively by a series of conquests and alliances.	England's Eton School is founded by Henry VI. It will become the largest of the ancient English public schools.	Austria's Hapsburg archduke Frederick V is crowned German emperor at Aix-la-Chapelle. He will reign as Frederick IV until 1493.	The Portuguese set up their first permanent trading post in Africa, at Arguin, in what is now Mauretania.

NICHOLAS V ✠ The 208th Pope 1447–1455

Born Sarzana, Italy; November 15, 1397

Parents Unknown

Papacy March 6, 1447–March 24, 1455

Died Rome, Italy; March 24, 1455

Nicholas V, born Tommaso Parentucelli, opened his papacy with declarations of ambitious intentions. He was to achieve much of what he set out to do, but many aims went unfulfilled and events to the East would cast a dark shadow over the final months of his life.

In December 1446, Parentucelli became cardinal priest of Santa Susanna and just two months later entered the conclave on the death of Eugene IV—notable for a dispute that broke out between the cardinals and nobles of Rome. For centuries it had been traditional that the nobles guarded the conclave, and on many occasions they had been free to come and go carrying messages to cardinals. This time the cardinals objected and expelled the nobles. In future, only cardinals would be allowed to be present during debate and voting.

Parentucelli took the name Nicholas V and declared his aims to be the restoration of the glory of Rome, the peace of the Church, and the civilization of men. His aim of restoring Rome cost a lot of money, but it was one that he came close to achieving. He hired the finest artists of his day, including Fra Angelico, to adorn the many churches and palaces that he rebuilt or renovated. Scholars and academics also flocked to Rome to enjoy his patronage, greatly raising the standard of education among curia officials.

Peace for the Church was achieved by ending the schism with antipope Felix V and what was left of the Basle Council. Past differences were put aside and pensions handed to those who could not be restored to their former positions. The Papal States war came to an end as patient diplomacy and a willingness to compromise on realities while being firm on principle brought recalcitrant nobles and cities back to papal allegiance.

THE LAST ANTIPOPES

When antipope Benedict XIII died in May 1423, he made the four cardinals with him promise to elect a successor and not to submit to Martin V. They therefore elected Gil Sanches Munoz to be Clement VIII. When he was told that he would get no support from Aragon, Clement gracefully abdicated, solemnly entered conclave with his cardinals and elected Martin V as pope, which he already was. Martin made Clement bishop of Majorca. Meanwhile, another cardinal, Jean Carrier, declared that Munoz's election had been invalid and declared a priest, Bernard Garnier, to be Pope Benedict XIV. Carrier and Garnier went into hiding and their subsequent fate is unknown. There were to be no more antipopes.

When Nicholas crowned Frederick III of Germany Holy Roman emperor in St. Peter's, on March 19, 1452, all seemed set fair for pope and papacy. Then, in June 1453, came news that Constantinople—the great bastion of Christendom in the East—had fallen to the forces of the Muslim Ottoman Turks. All Europe went into shock. Nicholas was by now crippled with gout. He was unable to rise to the challenge, he knew it, and fell into depression. His last months were unhappy ones.

1447	1448	1449	1451
The Spanish Inquisition is founded as a separate organization.	King Christopher of Denmark, Norway, and Sweden dies without an heir, after which the three countries separate.	The French capture Rouen from the English, continuing a process of French successes in a grinding war of sieges and attrition that will end with the English being driven from France.	The Lodi dynasty takes over the Muslim Delhi sultanate in northern India.

CALLIXTUS III ✠ The 209 Pope 1455–1458

Born La Torreta, Spain; December 31, 1378

Parents Father, Domingo de Borja; Mother, Francina Llancol

Papacy April 8, 1455–August 6, 1458

Died Rome, Italy; August 6, 1458

Contemporaries thought Callixtus to be a weak and ineffectual man, and a pope of little merit. This was mostly due to his advanced age and poor health when he became pope. In fact, his papacy proved to be significant in more ways than one.

Alfonso de Borja was born the son of a small landholder whose claims to a noble background were not taken very seriously by his fellows. The family did have enough money to allow Alfonso to study law at Lerida, after which he earned a comfortable living. He caught the eye of King Alfonso V of Aragon, who made him the confidential royal secretary charged with dealing with private matters. In 1429, he was sent to advise antipope Clement VIII privately that Alfonso's support was about to be withdrawn and that he had better agree terms with Pope Nicholas V. Nicholas was so pleased that he at once made Borja bishop of Valencia, one of the richest sees in Spain, even though he had no background in the Church.

Borja was promoted again when he persuaded Alfonso to stop supporting the Council of Basle. This time he was taken to Rome to be cardinal priest of SS Quatro Coronati. There he spent the next 12 years studying and undertaking tasks in the curia without attracting much attention to himself. It was this very reticence that assured his election. The conclave of 1455 was divided between supporters of Prospero Colonna and John Bessarion, neither of whom could stand the other but both of whom were friendly with Borja. After four days Borja was elected and took the name Callixtus III.

As pope he proved to be determined to do everything he could to stop the Turkish advance into the Balkans. He stopped the massive building and artistic programs of Nicholas V, putting the money into equipping an army to relieve Belgrade, then under siege by an army of over 100,000 Turks. He also imposed a special tax on Church lands, which caused resentment in France and Germany. The effort seemed worthwhile, however, for the Turks were thrown back from Belgrade then defeated at the Battle of Lesbos in 1457. Callixtus ordered that all church bells in Europe should be rung at noon to celebrate the victory. This could be seen as the last success of the crusading movement, though it was more a triumph of funding and supply than of mobilizing armies.

In 1456, Callixtus reopened the case of the French heroine Joan of Arc, who had been convicted of heresy and witchcraft in 1431 and burned at the stake. Her innocence was declared and the conviction overturned. She would eventually be canonized in 1920.

In Rome, Callixtus followed the by now traditional papal policy of promoting family and friends who could be trusted into positions of influence, but he took the process further than most. Within months, there was not an important fortress in the Papal States that did not have a Spanish commander. He brought three nephews from Spain. Pedro Luis was made Duke of Spoleto and given command of the mighty Castle Sant-Angelo. Luis de Mila was made a cardinal and given key tasks in the curia. Rodrigo Borja was likewise made a cardinal and raised to be vice chancellor of the curia.

Callixtus III diverted funds from building and artistic programs in Rome to equip an army to relieve Belgrade, which was under siege by the Turks.

1455

The Gutenberg Bible, the first book to be printed with moveable type in Europe, is produced in Mainz by Johannes Gutenberg.

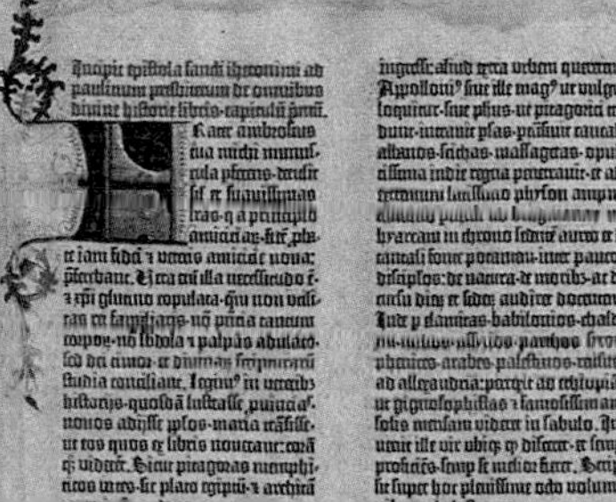

1455

The Battle of St. Albans marks the outbreak of the civil wars known as the Wars of the Roses fought between two branches of the Plantagenet dynasty.

1458

Portuguese mariner Luis Cadamosto discovers the Cape Verde Islands.

PIUS II ✠ The 210th Pope 1458–1464

Born Corsignano, Italy; October 18, 1405

Parents Father, Silvio Piccolomini; Mother, Vitoria

Papacy August 19, 1458–August 15, 1464

Died Ancona, Italy; August 15, 1464

Pius II has the distinction of being the only pope to have written a complete autobiography (and the only pope known to have written an erotic novel), just part of a prodigious literary output both before and after he became pope. His papacy, by contrast, was undistinguished.

Before he became a priest at the age of 41, Enea Piccolomini led what might be kindly termed a colorful life. He traveled widely, earning a reputation as a fine scholar and serial seducer. He worked for the Council of Basle, producing tracts that opposed Eugene IV in no uncertain terms, for which he was made secretary to antipope Felix V. In 1442, he abandoned Felix to work for King Frederick III of Germany. But, in 1445, he suffered a serious illness and underwent a religious epiphany that convinced him that his true calling was as a priest.

Abandoning his employer, lover, and children he took holy orders and by 1447 was bishop of Trieste. In 1450, he became bishop of Siena, the diocese where he had been born, and, in 1456, Callixtus III made him a cardinal. The conclave of 1458 became notorious for flagrant bribery by Guillaume d'Estouteville, who nevertheless failed to get the two thirds majority. Piccolomini was then elected after the Italian cardinals decided to vote for him en bloc. Taking the name Pius II, he at once declared a crusade and summoned a Council at Mantua. The meeting failed to reach any serious agreement, but papal financial help did go to those nobles fighting the Turks in the Balkans, with the Wallachian Vlad Dracula being particularly successful, at least for a time.

Pius devoted a lot of time to his home area around Siena. Catherine of Siena was proclaimed a saint in July 1461 to the great joy of local citizens. He also set about completely rebuilding his home town of Corsignano, which he renamed Pienza. The resulting hilltop fortress town was equipped with a cathedral, three palaces and beautifully laid out streets.

In southern Italy, a war broke out after Alfonso I of Aragon and Naples died without a legitimate heir. He left Naples to his illegitimate son Ferdinand, but the crown was also claimed by Duke Rene of Anjou. Rene was not only duke of Anjou but also count of Provence, count of Piedmont, duke of Bar, duke of Lorraine, and father-in-law to King Henry VI of England. Pius had no wish to have such a powerful man established in Italy, so he pronounced in favor of Ferdinand. The move alienated King Charles VII of France who confirmed the decrees of the Council of Basle (*see* p.210), which had reduced papal power over the French Church.

Pius also had problems in Germany where disquiet about papal corruption and irregular practices was growing. Pius himself wanted to curb the abuses, but his need for money and troubles in Naples caused him to overlook the need for reform and, instead, seek to stave off criticisms. In June 1464, Pius announced that he was going on crusade himself to fight the Turks in the Balkans—an effort to shame the kings of Europe into sending serious help. It came to nothing when Pius died at Ancona a few weeks later.

Pius II completely rebuilt his home town of Corsignano, which he renamed Pienza. The top humanist architects Bernardo Gambarelli and Leon Battista Alberti were hired for the project. Pius used the town as a rural retreat from the pressures of Rome. The town is now a UNESCO World Heritage Site.

1461

The first phase of the Wars of the Roses in England ends at the Battle of Towton, possibly the largest battle fought in England with an estimated 60,000 men involved of whom 20,000 are killed. Edward, duke of York, becomes King Edward IV, overthrowing Henry VI who is imprisoned.

1461

Trebizond, the last outpost of the Byzantines after the fall of Constantinople in 1453, surrenders to Ottoman Sultan Mehmet II.

1463

Bosnia and Herzegovina in the Balkans come under the rule of Sultan Mehmet II of the Ottoman Turks.

1466

The Incas of South America conquer the extensive Chimu State, adding a large area of fertile coastal lands to their empire.

PAUL II ✠ The 211th Pope 1464–1471

Born Venice, Italy; February 1417

Parents Unknown

Papacy August 30, 1464–July 26, 1471

Died Rome, Italy; July 26, 1471

Pietro Barbo was the nephew of Pope Eugene IV and was cardinal priest of San Marco. Paul's papacy is often described as being dominated by the wars against the Turks and disputes with the French Church. For contemporaries, however, it was a time of parties and public festivities.

When Pius II died the 19 cardinals present in Rome retired to the Vatican to elect a successor. They agreed between themselves that whoever won had to be bound to five promises: to call a general council of bishops within three years, to continue the war against the Ottoman Turks, to stay in Rome unless permitted to leave by the cardinals, to promote only one relative to be a cardinal, and to have no more than 24 cardinals (and not to promote anyone to be a cardinal without the consent of the existing cardinals).

On the very first ballot Barbo was elected pope. He began his reign as he meant to continue by summoning tailors to design new papal robes of astonishing magnificence and instructing the civic authorities to plan a carnival of unrivaled showiness. For the rest of his reign, the people of Rome enjoyed a succession of carnivals and festivities.

To fund the war against the Muslim Turks, Paul turned to the alum mines of Tolfa, discovered in 1461. Alum was essential for dying wool, and Tolfa was the only source of the mineral that did not lie in Muslim hands. The virtual monopoly the pope enjoyed on alum meant that a vast flow of funds poured into Rome. Impressive though the alum income was, it was not enough. Paul imposed a tax on the benefices that had been sold by recent popes, meaning that at least some of that money returned to the papacy. He did not, however, end all the financial abuses and scandals that beset the papacy at this time. The effort to reverse the rulings of Basle involved Paul in constant discussions and conflicts with King Louis XI of France. His relations with Holy Roman Emperor Frederick III were much better, though that did not mean the German Church paid much more than the French.

The cardinal's residence in San Marco, Venice, which was transformed by Pietro Barbo, later Pope Paul II, into a sumptuous palace, now the Palazzo di Venezia.

Large sums of money were sent to the Balkans to fund the wars against the Turks. George Skanderbeg of Albania was the most competent of the leaders in this war, along with Matthias Corvinus, king of Hungary. It was unfortunate that the other great warrior was George Podebrady, king of Bohemia, who held Hussite views (*see* p.208) and so was detested by Paul. On the other hand, Paul was able to bring Persia into the war against the Turks. Paul sought to bring the Russian Church under papal guidance, but his plans came to nothing. He died of a heart attack in 1471.

George Skanderbeg of Albania was the most compent of the leaders in the wars against the Turks.

1466	1467	1468	1469	1470
The Kingdom of Georgia, which has been in long-term decline since the Mongol Wars, finally collapses and fragments into a number of petty states.	Charles the Bold (to his friends) or Charles the Terrible (to his enemies) becomes Duke of Burgundy and launches a bid to make his wealthy domains independent of France.	The Orkneys transfer from Norway to Scotland as the dowry of Princess Margaret who marries King James III of Scotland.	The expanding Songhai Empire of West Africa annexes the rich trading city of Timbuktu.	The second phase of the Wars of the Roses in England breaks out when the earl of Warwick rebels against King Edward IV, only to be killed along with most Lancastrian lords in 1471.

SIXTUS IV ✠ The 212th Pope 1471–1484

Born Celle, Italy; July 21, 1414

Parents Father, Leonardo della Rovere; Mother, Luchina Monleoni

Papacy August 9, 1471–August 12, 1484

Died Rome, Italy; August 12, 1484

The first of the great Renaissance popes, famed for building the Sistine Chapel within the Vatican between 1477 and 1480, Sixtus IV was ruthless and unscrupulous. He plunged the papacy into wars and adventures it could not afford, spent lavishly on the arts, and turned a blind eye to ecclesiastical abuses.

Francesco della Rovere was born into a poor family near Genoa and at an early age he joined the Franciscans, both facts that would influence his later life. He studied at Bologna and at Padua, later lecturing at both universities and elsewhere. He specialized in philosophy and theology, but was also a fiery preacher and able administrator. Among the rarified works he produced was a treatise *On the Blood of Christ*, helping to give him a reputation for unworldly piety that he did not fully deserve. He rose to be head of the Franciscans in Liguria, and then of the order as a whole in 1464. Three years later he was brought to Rome by Paul II who made him Cardinal of San Pietro in Vincoli.

When Paul died suddenly, a number of cardinals were absent from Rome, giving the Italian cardinals a working majority for first time in decades. There then followed determined lobbying by Cardinal Rodrigo Borgia in favor of Rovere and promises of lavish gifts by Rovere's secretary and nephew Pietro Riario. On the third day of the conclave Rovere achieved the necessary two thirds majority but, unusually, the other cardinals did not then change their votes to make it a unanimous decision.

Sixtus inherited from Paul promises to help the wars against the Turks in the Balkans. Rather than raise funds to help men on the spot, Sixtus decided to build a papal fleet to take the war to the Turks. Together with a Venetian fleet, the papal forces landed in Asia Minor to capture, loot, and burn the cities of Smyrna, Foca, and Cesme. Thereafter, the fleet was employed fruitlessly in the Adriatic and Aegean achieving little. When the Turks captured Otranto in Italy itself, Sixtus sent his fleet to drive them out, but it failed. The Turks left of their own accord when Sultan Mehmet II died and his successor Bayezid II lost interest in the venture.

In ecclesiastical matters, Sixtus favored the veneration of the Virgin Mary. In 1476, he approved the Feast of the Conception of the Blessed Virgin Mary, though he stopped short of calling it the Immaculate Conception as the doctrine that the Virgin Mary had been free of original sin was not yet widely accepted in Europe. He also greatly favored his own Franciscan Order and granted it numerous

The Sistine Chapel ceiling was painted by Michelangelo between 1508 and 1512.

1472

Portuguese explorer João Vaz Corte-Real discovers the island of Bacalao in the Atlantic. His description is so vague that later mariners were unable to find it again. It is now thought he may have reached Newfoundland.

1473

Aztec ruler Axayacatl conquers the city of Tlatelolco, converting what had been a tribal alliance into an Aztec autocracy and starting the rise of the Aztec Empire.

Michelangelo sketched this drawing of the execution of Bernardo Baroncelli following the Pazzi Conspiracy in 1478, which plotted the murder of the Medici rulers of Florence.

privileges, though he failed to end a split within the Order on the issue of collective poverty.

Of rather more concern to Sixtus was the secular status of the papacy, and a desire to lead his family away from its habitual poverty. Pietro Riario, who had aided his rise to the papacy, and another young nephew named Giuliano della Rovere, were created cardinals along with four other relatives and almost thirty men linked to the Rovere family in some way. Scores of other relatives came to Rome from Liguria and to all of them Sixtus gave jobs and lucrative incomes. This was nothing new to the papacy for many popes had chosen to give jobs to relatives whom they could trust to follow orders. What was new was the sheer number of relatives being given jobs and the fact that many of them were grossly incompetent and yet retained their positions.

If Sixtus spent money on his family, he also spent it on Rome. His chief aim was to turn Rome into a fully modern city. He built the first bridge over the Tiber in a thousand years, the Ponte Sisto, and built a new road running direct from the Vatican fortress to the Castel Sant'Angelo fortress. Dozens of other streets were widened by the demolition of intruding buildings and sweeping away porticoes and gateways. He also undertook a systematic repaving of every street in Rome, something not done for so long that the city archives had no record that it had ever been done.

As a patron of the arts and learning, Sixtus also reorganized the papal library and papal museums, starting them on the course that would lead them to become among the greatest museums of the world. He built the Sistine Chapel as well as other churches and hired the finest artists to adorn them with paintings and sculptures. The talented Florentine Antonio del Pollaiolo was hired to produce a magnificent bronze tomb for Sixtus, inaugurating a program of lavish tombs to be followed by several later popes.

In an effort to enlarge and consolidate the Papal States, Sixtus engaged in a succession of wars and intrigues. Although he was quick to threaten or to use ecclesiastical sanctions, his behavior was little different from that of other rulers and soon the Papal States were just one player in the Italian political scene.

In 1478, Sixtus was told in advance of a plot by members of the Pazzi family to murder Lorenzo and Giuliano Medici, the rulers of Florence. The Pazzi Conspiracy spread far beyond Florence to Milan and other cities that stood to gain from a fall in Medici wealth. Sixtus was interested because he had bought from Milan the town of Imola, even though the Milanese claim was not universally accepted and the Medici had a claim themselves. The Medici brothers were to be murdered during Mass at Florence cathedral, with the conspirators striking when the archbishop lifted the host. In the event, only Giuliano was killed, though Lorenzo was seriously injured, and the citizens of Florence rallied to the Medici cause.

When the role of Sixtus in the conspiracy was revealed, Florence declared war and invaded the Papal States. Sixtus then persuaded Venice to attack Ferrara, an ally of Florence, but failed to honor his promises to help Venice when Naples invaded the Papal States to aid Ferrara. The wars ended in 1484 with the Treaty of Bagnolo. Sixtus gained virtually nothing. When the terms of the treaty were read out to him in Rome he flew into an ungovernable rage, ranting and shouting through the night. Next morning he suffered a heart attack and died.

1474

Venice inaugurates the first patent system to allow inventors to have exclusive use of their inventions for a set period of time.

1477

Charles the Bold of Burgundy is killed by Duke Rene of Lorraine at the Battle of Nancy, his extensive lands then start to fragment.

1482

Ivan III declares that Russia is independent of the Mongol Empire and refuses to pay the usual tribute.

INNOCENT VIII ✠ The 213th Pope 1484–1492

Born Genoa, Italy; 1432

Parents Father, Arano Cybo; Mother, Teodorina de Mari

Papacy August 29, 1484–July 25, 1492

Died Rome, Italy; July 25, 1492

Witch trials in Germany where thousands of innocent people were tortured and executed by the Inquisition.

Affable, genial, and indecisive, Innocent VIII inherited a papacy that was virtually bankrupt. He made little effort to improve the financial situation, nor to curb the ecclesiastical abuses that were increasingly undermining the moral authority of not just the papacy, but also of the Church as a whole.

Giovanni Battista Cybo came from a cosmopolitan family. His father, Arano, had been a senator in Rome during the 1450s, later moving on to Naples. Young Cybo spent a rather dissolute youth, fathering several illegitimate children by different women, and studying at Padua and Rome. It was in Rome that he caught the eye of Cardinal Calandnini, half brother to Pope Nicholas V. The Cardinal employed him and persuaded Cybo to become a priest to further his chances of promotion within the Church. To what extent Cybo curbed his lifestyle on entering the Church is unclear, but he does at least seem not to have fathered any more children.

In 1467 he became bishop of Savona and, in 1472, of Molfetta. In neither position did Cybo do much diocesan work, instead taking the money and hiring staff to do his work while he remained mostly in Rome working for cardinals and for Sixtus IV. In 1473, Sixtus made him a cardinal and for the next 20 years Cybo worked hard in the curia and on papal business but without attracting much attention.

Sixtus had created so many cardinals from relatives and friends that 32 cardinals were eligible to vote, though seven were absent from Rome at the time of his death. Those who took part in the conclave were equally split on whether to continue fighting wars to enlarge the Papal States or whether to accept peace on unfavorable terms. The factions were complicated by rivalries between the Roman nobles of the Orsini and Colonna families and by the personal ambitions of several cardinals. It was when Cybo formed an alliance with Giuliano della Rovere that a breakthrough came. Cybo would be pope, Rovere the power behind the throne.

On being elected Cybo took the name of Innocent VIII and set about solving what he saw as the most urgent problem, the effective bankruptcy of the papacy. Unable to regain papal income from churches in other states and with the Papal States not yielding enough rents and taxes to cover the shortfall, Innocent began selling positions within the Church that brought with them comfortable incomes. When he ran out of those, he invented titles and offices that had no reality but that sounded good and sold those as well.

Not all the profitable positions were sold. Innocent's two surviving illegitimate sons were brought to Rome and well cared for. One of them, Franschetto, was married to the illegitimate daughter of Lorenzo de Medici of Florence. Lorenzo's son Giovanni was made a cardinal, despite being only 13 years old. The Florentine alliance that this produced gave Innocent a reliable partner in northern Italy and kept the ambitions of other northern states in check.

A money-making venture even more unusual came his way in 1489 when the Ottoman prince

1485

In the English civil war known as the War of the Roses King Richard III is killed at the Battle of Bosworth by his rival Henry Tudor who then becomes King Henry VII.

1485

First outbreak of a disease known as the English Sweat occurs in London. Symptoms included high fever, profuse sweating, and sudden death. Later outbreaks came in 1502, 1507, 1517, and 1528, sometimes spreading to Europe. The disease has not be identified by modern doctors.

1486

The first giraffe seen in Europe for 1,200 years arrives in Florence as a gift to Lorenzo de Medici from Sultan Qaitbay of Egypt (right).

Ferdinand II of Aragon and Queen Isabella I of Castlille were given the right to use the title "Catholic Majesty" after capturing Grenada from the Muslims.

Jem was captured by Pierre d'Aubusson, Grand Master of the Knights Hospitaller on Rhodes. Innocent created d'Aubusson a cardinal in return for Jem being sent to Rome. Innocent knew that Jem had sought to oust Sultan Bayezid II from the Ottoman throne, so he sent a message to Bayezid asking how much he would pay to ensure that Jem remained in Rome and did not return home to create trouble. Thereafter Innocent was paid 40,000 golden ducats each year from Bayezid, plus the immediate gift of the Holy Lance. This relic was believed to have been the lance used to pierce the side of Christ as he was crucified. It had been captured by the Ottomans in the fall of Constantinople in 1453.

Savona Cathedral. Sixtus had been made bishop of Savona in 1467.

The huge inflow of money did little to alleviate the financial state of the papacy for Innocent found himself with new bills to pay. In 1485, King Ferdinand I of Naples withheld payment of the tribute he owed to Rome as his kingdom was a fief of the pope. A rebellion of Neapolitan nobles gave Innocent a pretext and he invaded the southern kingdom. The invasion was a disaster and a hasty peace was patched up in 1486. Innocent was determined on revenge, however, so when Ferdinand again failed to pay his tribute Innocent declared him excommunicated and deposed. He gave the throne instead to the ousted Angevin branch of the Neapolitan royal family. Since the direct Angevin line had died out, that meant giving the throne to King Charles VIII of France. Charles had problems of his own and so did not at once march on Naples, but the move would dominate events in Italy for the next half century.

In the meantime, Innocent was taking other decisions that would have repercussions he never imagined. In Germany, the Inquisition was finding itself taking on an increasing number of accusations of witchcraft. Inquisitors Heinrich Kramer and Jacobus Sprenger consulted Innocent who responded with the bull *Summis desiderantes*. This equated witchcraft with devil worship and thus brought the hunting and punishment of witchcraft within the remit of the Inquisition. Kramer then wrote the book *Malleus Maleficarum*, which explained how witches could be detected and laid the ground for the massive spate of witch trials that followed. Pope Alexander VI ruled that the *Malleus Maleficarum* was based on faulty logic, but by then it was too late. Over the next 150 years about 40,000 people would be executed as witches in Germany and central Europe.

In the spring of 1492, news came from Spain that Grenada, the last Muslim city in the Iberian Peninsula, had been captured by King Ferdinand II of Aragon and Queen Isabella I of Castile. Innocent was delighted and gave the royal pair the right to use the title "Catholic Majesty." It was to be his last act before he entered his final illness.

1487

Malaga is captured by Christian forces of Ferdinand of Aragon. The entire Muslim population is then sold into slavery.

1488

Portuguese mariner Bartolomeu Diaz rounds the southern tip of Africa at the Cape of Good Hope.

1489

Childless Queen Catherine of Cyprus sells her kingdom to Venice and retires to estates owned by Venice in northern Italy. Cyprus remains Venetian for 80 years until conquered by the Turks.

1491

Marriage of Anne of Brittany to King Charles VIII of France unites the two realms and ends a thousand years of Breton independence.

ALEXANDER VI ✠ The 214th Pope 1492–1503

Born Jativa, Spain; January 1, 1431

Parents Father, Jofre Llancol i Escriva; Mother, Isabel de Borja

Papacy August 11, 1492 to August 18, 1503

Died Rome, August 18, 1503

One of the most famous of all popes, Alexander VI continued the tradition set by his immediate predecessors of neglecting Church duties in favor of a career as a sovereign prince engaged in the power politics of Italy. As vice chancellor of the Holy See, he had embezzled a vast fortune and was one of the richest men in Rome.

Rodrigo de Borja y Borja, better known as Rodrigo Borgia, was born near Valencia, where his mother's brother was bishop. The family had owned land in the area for generations, but had more recently fallen on relatively hard times. Fortunately for them, Bishop Alfonso was willing to divert diocesan funds to his relatives to enable them to enjoy a better standard of living. When Bishop Alfonso became Pope Callixtus III, in 1455, the family's fortunes increased enormously, as did those of Rodrigo.

Young Rodrigo first went to study in Bologna, then in 1456 moved to Rome where his uncle made him a cardinal deacon and gave him a number of well paid offices. In the months that followed Rodrigo was made bishop of a number of sees and abbot of a number of abbeys. He did not do any of the actual work himself, of course, but instead took the income and used a fraction of it to hire a poor but talented underling to act as his deputy. In 1457, he was made Vice Chancellor of the Holy See, which was not only well paid but also powerful. He was to hold the position for over 30 years, maintaining his grip as much through intrigue as through talent.

Painting by John Collier: *A Glass of Wine with Cesare Borgia*. From left: Cesare Borgia, Lucrezia, Pope Alexander, and a young nobleman holding an empty glass. The shifty glance from the pope and Lucretia's cold gaze heighten the sense of intrigue. The wine is almost certainly poisoned.

During those years Borgia rarely missed an opportunity to divert funds or lands into his own hands and became so wealthy that he was believed to be the second richest man in Rome. He also lived openly with his mistress, Vannozza dei Cattani, who came from a noble family and who bore him four children: Giovanni, Cesare, Lucrezia and Goffredo. Three other children—Girolama, Isabella and Pedro-Luiz—were born to other mistresses. Around 1485, he separated from Vannozza and moved the equally noble Giulia Farnese into his palace instead. She bore him only one child, Laura, born in 1492.

When Innocent VIII died 23 cardinals were in Rome and went to the Sistine Chapel for the conclave, the first to be held there. The first three ballots failed to produce a result. Borgia then decided the time was ripe for some bribery. Cardinal Ascanio Sforza was offered the office of Vice-Chancellor, the Palazzo

1492	1492	1493	1495	1496
The first Papal conclave held at the Sistine chapel.	Columbus reaches the new world.	Genoese mariner employed by Spain returns from a voyage in the Atlantic to announce that he had reached islands off the coast of China, though in fact he had reached the Caribbean.	The world's first dry dock is built at Portsmouth by command of King Henry VII for the use of the English Royal Navy.	Bartholomew Columbus, brother of Christopher, founds a colony at Santo Domingo, which is still inhabited and thus the oldest European settlement in the Americas.

Despite having gained the papacy by such disreputable means, Alexander at first made a good impression. He was the first pope for some time who refused to take bribes when dispensing justice and instead handed down judgement based solely on the law and the facts of the case. He also swiftly imposed order on the more turbulent nobles and gangs of the Papal States and promised to do the same to the disordered state of the curia and Church more widely.

It quickly became clear, however, that Alexander VI's main concern was to look after his children. The sheer scale of his ambition for his family took some years to become clear, but the early signs were there for those willing to see them. In 1494, he made Cesare, his favorite son, a cardinal at the age of 18 and settled on him a number of highly profitable bishoprics, none of which Cesare visited. Also raised to the rank of cardinal was Alessandro Farnese, brother of Giulia.

Alexander's eldest son Juan was meanwhile made papal standard bearer and captain general of the Church, or commander-in-chief of the papal army. He was also made governor of St. Peter's, a position which brought with it a heavy income, and was married to Maria de Luna, a Spanish noblewoman whose dowry included the Duchy of Gandia. In 1497, he was given Benevento. This prosperous duchy was usually ruled by a governor appointed by the pope, but Alexander named his nephew Juan "Duke of Benevento," with the implication that the duchy was to be hereditary in Juan's family and would owe only a small tribute to future popes.

Lucrezia Borgia was treated with equal generosity. She was arguably the most intelligent of the Borgias, and certainly Alexander trusted her implicitly. When he was away from Rome he frequently left Lucrezia in charge, something that scandalized the traditionally-male curia. As a young girl,

The Borgia Apartments are a suite of six monumental rooms in the Apostolic Palace that were adapted for person use by Alexander VI.

The Room of the Sibyls in the Borgia Apartments is lavishly decorated with frescoes of prophets and sibyls.

Borgia, the Castle of Nepi, the bishopric of Erlau and a cash downpayment of four mule-loads of silver. Cardinal Giambattista Orsini got the fortified towns of Monticelli and Soriano, the legation of the Marches, and the bishopric of Cartagena. The other cardinals were less influential, and so cheaper. Cardinal Colonna was given the abbey of Subiaco, Cardinal Savelli got Civita Castellana and the bishopric of Majorca, Cardinal Pallavicini received the bishopric of Pamplona, Cardinal Michiel, the see of Porto, and the others an assortment of benefices and cash payments. Exactly how much cash changed hands in all is unknown as Borgia's first action on becoming Pope Alexander VI was to impound the financial accounts of the papacy.

1497

The Wars of the Roses in England end when Yorkist pretender Perkin Warbeck (right) is captured by the forces of King Henry VII after a failed rebellion.

1498

Leonardo da Vinci paints *The Last Supper* in Milan.

1498

Portuguese mariner Vasco da Gama reaches India after sailing round the south of Africa and effectively frees Europe from dependence on Venetian middlemen in the spice trade.

Girolamo Savonarola was a Dominican friar and preacher who led a frenetic campaign for Church reform and the repentance of sins. He is notorious for his bonfires of the vanities in which he encouraged the destruction of objects deemed to be "occasions of sin," including books and artworks. He was excommunicated by Pope Alexander VI and burned at the stake for heresy in Florence's Piazza della Signoria.

Lucrezia was engaged twice to wealthy Spanish noblemen only to have these called off when her father became pope. Her first marriage, at the age of 13, was to Giovanni Sforza, Lord of Pesaro and a relative of the rulers of Milan. The political value of that marriage soon waned, so Alexander declared it had not been consummated, bought Sforza off, and annulled the marriage.

In 1498, Lucrezia married the Neapolitan lord Alfonso of Aragon, and had a son, but Alfonso was murdered two years later. The murder was rumored to have been carried out by Cesare, who had just allied himself with France against Naples. In 1502, she married again to Alfonso d'Este, Duke of Ferrara, and very soon embarked on an affair with her brother in law. By one or other of the Este brothers she had six children, including Ercole who became Duke of Ferrara in 1534.

Goffredo, the youngest son, was married to Sancia of Aragon, daughter of King Alfonso II of Naples, who granted him the Principality of Squillace. Even though Sancia died, Goffredo kept his principality as a vassal of Naples. He married again, had four children, and remained on his lands to his death in 1518.

In 1494, King Charles VIII of France marched into Italy with a large army to take up the Kingdom of Naples given to him by Innocent VIII. Alexander at first opposed the French king as he did not want such a powerful ruler in Naples. Alexander even sought help from Bayezid II, Sultan of the Ottoman Turks, but in the end he had to evacuate Rome to the French, who went on to occupy Naples. Alexander then set about putting together a league of north Italian states to oppose the French. In 1495, they narrowly defeated the French army at Fornovo and forced Charles to retreat to France.

Cesare went to France in 1500 to meet the new French king, Louis XII, returning with a French alliance, the French title of "Duke of Velentinois," and a French bride. With French troops, Cesare then attacked the lords of the Romagna, traditionally a part of the Papal States but more recently semi-independent. Following the lead of Giovanni in Benevento, Alexander now set up Cesare as Lord of the Romagna, apparently as the new hereditary ruler who would owe only light tribute to the papacy.

The curia had followed the lead of the Borgias and had become even more corrupt and venal than it already was. Discontent with the papacy was spreading and becoming more serious. In Florence the friar Savonarola led a populist uprising that temporarily drove the Medici from power and began a process of religious reforms that, if carried to Rome, would have created havoc. Fortunately for Alexander, Savonarola was overthrown in 1498 and the Medici returned to power.

The apparent rise to permanent power of the Borgia had by now seriously alarmed the local nobility. The Orsini and the Colonna, long the bitterest of rivals, now united, hired an army and marched on Rome in the autumn of 1502. Cesare defeated them then, under pretence of a truce, seized and murdered the ringleaders. In Rome, Alexander had Cardinal Orsini murdered, and arrested all his relatives who did not escape in time.

In August 1503, Cesare was preparing a military campaign against the remaining recalcitrant Roman nobles when he and Alexander went to dinner with Cardinal Adriano da Corneto. That night both the Borgias fell seriously ill. Five days later Alexander was dead. Cesare was prostrated for weeks, but eventually recovered. It was announced that the two men had gone down with malaria, but a rumor soon went about that one of their servants had been ordered to poison Corneto, but had put the poison on the wrong plates.

1498	1498	1499	1499
Christopher Colombus makes a third voyage to the New World, this time with six ships and discovers Trinidad.	France's Charles VIII dies, aged 27, as he prepares for a new invasion of Italy. He is succeeded by his cousin who will reign as Louis XII.	Louis XII of France gains Venetian support for his claims to Milan and invades Italy.	Venice's campanile is completed in the Piazza San Marco after three years of construction.

PIUS III ✠ The 215th Pope 1503

Born Siena, Italy; May 29, 1439
Parents Unknown
Papacy September 22, 1503–October 18, 1503
Died Rome, Italy; October 18, 1503

After the papacy of Alexander VI it was thought that almost anyone would be an improvement. The Church, the curia, and the papacy all needed reforms, but in the event Pius III proved a bitter disappointment, though this was not his fault.

Francesco Todeschini was born in Siena and, through his mother, was related to Pope Pius II. Pius II raised the bishopric of Siena to be an Archbishopric and when it fell vacant in 1460 appointed young Francesco to be Archbishop of Siena, even though he was not a priest. Later that year Francesco moved to Rome to become cardinal deacon of St. Eustachio. He fell out with Alexander VI when he spoke out against making Alexander's son the duke of Benevento. He argued, probably correctly, that this was an attempt to alienate the prosperous lands of Benevento from papal control.

The papal conclave that followed the death of Alexander was dominated by one man who was not there—Cesare Borgia. Alexander's son, was known to be highly ambitious, ruthlessly violent, and in command of the papal army. He was also very sick and unable to apply pressure in the way he had intended to do when his father died. Nevertheless, everyone was worried about what Cesare Borgia might do when he recovered.

The conclave was split into various factions. The French wanted Cardinal Georges d'Amboise, but the Italians feared he might move the papacy back to Avignon. The Spanish did not want a French pope either, but nor did they want to back the leading Italian, Cardinal Giuliano della Rovere. On the first ballot d'Amboise got 13 votes, Rovere 15 and the remaining four cardinals voted for Francesco. Both main candidates realized they could not win themselves but, seeing that Francesco was ill, calculated that he would not last long and another conclave would take place soon. Francesco who was elected on the second ballot and took the name Pius III to honor his uncle.

Less than a month later, Pius III died and a new conclave began.

HUMANISM

A growing intellectual movement in the early 16th century was Humanism. This movement sought to discover, study ,and propagate ancient texts from both Christian and pagan writers. They wanted to improve and correct standard texts that had often been copied many times by hand, with inevitable mistakes creeping in. They were generally held to be interested in the subjects of grammar, rhetoric, poetry, moral philosophy, and history. Gradually the range of studies widened to include aspects of science and technology that went along with the artistic changes that would lead to the Renaissance. After 1500 some Humanists turned their techniques on the Bible, discovering as they did so that the versions used in Europe were in some ways different from the earliest versions now becoming available.

When Alexander VI was elected, Francesco Todeschini moved Pius II's library out of Rome to Siena where he paid for a new library to be built adjacent to the cathedral.

1503
Christopher Columbus discovers Panama on his fourth voyage to the New World.

1503
Leonardo da Vinci begins his great mural The Battle of Anghiari for Florence's Palazzo della Signoria.

1503
England's Canterbury Cathedral is completed after 436 years of construction.

1503
France's Louis XII abandons claims to Naples following the breakup of his alliance with Ferdinand of Aragon.

JULIUS II ✣ The 216th Pope 1503–1513

Born Alibssola, Italy; December 5, 1453
Parents Unknown
Papacy November 1, 1503–February 21, 1513
Died Rome, Italy; February 21, 1513

Ruthless, violent, and artistic, Julius II is famed for bringing to Rome Michelangelo, Raphael, and Bramante. He had a very clear sense of where he wanted the papacy to go and how he wanted to take it there. It was unfortunate for him that a large number of people wanted the Church to go in a quite different direction altogether.

Giuliano della Rovere was born to parents in relatively poor circumstances and was educated to go into trade—his schooling being financed by his wealthy uncle Francesco della Rovere. But when Giuliano was 18 years old his uncle became Pope Sixtus IV and everything changed. As was then traditional, Sixtus brought to Rome a number of friends and relatives on whom he could rely and gave them jobs and incomes. Among these was young Giuliano, who was made bishop of Carpentras to give him an income and cardinal priest of San Pietro in Vincoli to give him authority and power. He never looked back.

One of Giuliano's activities proved to be the gathering of ecclesiastical offices, bringing ever larger sums of money flowing into his hands. In 1480, he went to France as legate in order to broker a deal between Louis XI of France and Maximilian I of Austria over the vast inheritance of Duke Charles the Bold of Burgundy, to which both men had a claim. His success in this tricky task, dealing with two awkward men, marked him out as a talented diplomat for the future. He continued to be a prominent papal servant under Innocent VIII, but a rivalry with another powerful cardinal, Rodrigo Borgia, was growing steadily.

Michelangelo produced the vast paintings on the ceiling and east wall of the Sistine Chapel for Julius and started work on an immense tomb that was never finished

When Borgia became pope as Alexander VI in 1492, Giuliano quickly (and no doubt correctly) became convinced that he had been marked down for assassination and fled to France where he was welcomed at the court of King Charles VIII, no friend of the new pope. Giuliano did his best to persuade Charles to investigate the blatant bribery that had won Alexander the papal throne (*see* p.220), but Charles had other matters

Following the death of Alexander VI, that pope's son Cesare Borgia (above) was seem as a major threat to Julius's plans.

1504

Ferdinand of Aragon completes his conquest of Naples with the surrender of French forces at Gaeta in January.

1504

The Treaty of Blois brings peace between France and the German king Maximilian I.

1504

Castile's Isabella the Catholic dies in November, aged 53, after a 30-year reign in which she has financed the voyages of Christopher Colombus and persecuted non-Catholics with the Inquisition.

1504

Zahir-ud-din Muhammad Babur (Babur) becomes ruler of Kabul beginning his career of conquest. He was a descendent of Tamerlane through his father and of Genghis Khan through his mother.

Michelangelo's spectacular sculpture of Moses for the Tomb of Julius II.

to deal with. So long as Alexander was Pope, Giuliano remained in exile, often in hiding.

When Alexander died, Giuliano hurried to Rome and arrived in time for the conclave. Having been absent for years he did not hope to win the vote himself, so backed Pius III thinking he would live only a few years during which time Giuliano himself could build up support for his own bid. In the event Pius died within days and another conclave was held. This time Giuliano worked quickly. He made promises to the large numbers of French and Spanish cardinals, then offered gifts to the Italians. He was elected on the first ballot and took the name Julius II.

Julius believed that the best way to secure the future for the papacy was to make the Papal States the largest and richest state in an Italy free of foreign intervention. That would, he thought, secure the papal income and enable the pope to take religious decisions without fearing

1505

Sri Lanka (Ceylon) is discovered by the Portuguese off the southeast coast of India.

1506

Chistopher Colombus dies in obscurity at Valladolid on May 21, aged 55, still believing he has found and outlying part of Asia

1507

Leonardo da Vinci paints the *Mona Lisa*.

1507

The Diet of Constance recognizes the unity of the Holy Roman Empire and founds the Imperial Chamber.

Julius was a friend and patron of the great Renaissance artist Raphael. Raphael painted a sublime portrait of Julius in 1511, just two years before the pope died of a fever.

secular repercussions. This aim meant Julius had to confront two formidable enemies: Cesare Borgia and King Louis XII of France.

Borgia was tackled first. He was misled by promises of support and friendship but, as soon as he went into action as leader of the papal army, he found Julius withheld crucial supplies. He was captured by Gian Baglioni, Lord of Perugia, and thrown into prison. Julius then stripped him of all titles and lands, taking them back to the Papal States, and arranged for him to be imprisoned in Spain. The power of the Borgias was broken.

Julius wanted to drive France from Italy, but the fractious Italian states did not all agree this was a good idea. He began by allying himself with France against Venice, driving the Venetians out of the Romagna. In 1506, he himself led the papal army on a campaign to subdue Perugia and Bologna, forcing their lords to accept papal sovereignty. Two years later he was at war with Venice again, this time defeating them utterly and seizing Rimini and Faenza as well as regaining control of church incomes. He then recognized Ferdinand of Aragon as king of Naples, which caused a breach with France. The French ally Ferrara was attacked in 1510, but it was a diversion to clear the way for his army to take Modena and Mirandola. Venice now joined the Spanish-Papal alliance to drive the French out of northern Italy, an aim achieved by the end of 1512. Julius took Parma, Piacenza, and Reggio Emilia into the much enlarged Papal States. His political ambitions for the papacy had been largely achieved, though Spain retained an interest in Naples.

Julius II commissioned Bramante (below) to design an entirely new St. Peter's Basilica, Julius having decided that the old one was so dilapidated that it was beyond repair and needed replacing.

In ecclesiastical matters, Julius was traditionally orthodox and carried out routine tasks with efficiency. It was Julius who gave Prince Henry of England (later Henry VIII) dispensation to marry his brother's widow Catherine of Aragon and thereby stored up a host of future troubles. More positively, Julius organized the first bishoprics in the Americas and sought to crack down on the sort of simony that had given his great rival, Alexander VI, the papal throne. He also sought, less successfully, to regain papal control over the various ecclesiastical incomes that since the Basle Council had been kept by bishops.

PLURALISM

Many bishoprics and abbacies brought with them a sizeable income. This was intended to provide the incumbent with the funds necessary to care for his flock, fund scholarships, and carry out other religious or charitable works. The rules were lax to give the office holder maximum flexibility about how to best spend the money. Unfortunately this meant that an office holder could also spend the money on himself. This made the wealthier positions highly sought after by men who took the money, then hired a deputy to do the actual work. The holding of more than one office, and hiring men to carry out the duties, was known as pluralism and it was banned by a succession of Council and papal edicts. By the time of Julius, however, it was possible to gain papal dispensation that made pluralism possible. It was routine for cardinals to be bishop of dozens of sees and abbot of dozens of abbeys simply to gain the incomes. Pluralism was one of those practices that was widely practiced and accepted in Rome but which was causing increasing resentment in the wider Christian community.

1508

The German king Maximilian assumes the title of Holy Roman Emperor Elect, a position that is confirmed by Pope Julius II.

1509

England's Henry VII dies after a reign of nearly 24 years. He is succeeded by his 17-year-old son who will reign for almost four decades as Henry VIII.

1513

French forces in Italy are heavily defeated at Novora by England's Henry VIII and Holy Roman Emperor Maximilian. The allies force Louis XII to give up Milan.

Michelangelo's spectacular and controversial painting of The Last Judgement on the altar wall of the Sistine Chapel.

LEO X ✠ The 217th Pope 1513–1521

Born Florence, Italy; December 11, 1475

Parents Father, Lorenzo de Medici; Mother, Clarice Orsini

Papacy March 11, 1513–December 1, 1521

Died Rome, Italy; December 1, 1521

Educated, sophisticated, and notoriously devious, Leo X was a member of the powerful Medici family of Florence. As pope, he was determined to continue the political aims of Julius II, while enriching his own family as much as possible. It was, however, his financial measures that were to have the greatest long-term impact on the papacy.

The fabulously wealthy and powerful Medici family of Florence dominated trade, finance, and government in their native city. When they decided that they needed to influence the Church as well, they chose seven-year-old Giovanni de Medici, second son of Lorenzo the Magnificent, for the task. His hair was tonsured and he was given benefices and appointments as he grew and was educated. His education was dominated by Humanism (*see* page 223) before, in 1479, he began studying theology and canon law at Pisa University. Already a cardinal deacon from the age of 13, Giovanni became a cardinal priest at the age of 17.

Most of the following years were spent traveling in France, Germany, and the Low Countries. He went back to Rome in 1500 under Alexander VI where he showed a great interest in, and appreciation of, the artistic wonders of the Renaissance. Under Julius II, Giovanni decided that it was safe to take an interest in papal politics, and soon became an enthusiastic supporter of the pope's aim to enlarge the Papal States and drive foreign powers out of Italy. He was papal legate to Bologna in 1511 and led the Papal army, without much success, in 1512. His dedication to Rome was thereafter tempered by demands on his time from Florence, of which he was effective ruler for some years.

At the conclave of 1513, the anti-bribery rules of Julius II held sway. Instead, the cardinals agreed that whoever won would pay each of the other cardinals 1,500 ducats to make up for the lost bribes. The voting that followed is among the most famous on record, with most younger cardinals favoring Giovanni de Medici and most older ones favoring Raffaele Riario, who had gained distinction as a diplomat during the reign of Alexander VI. However, most cardinals wanted to disguise which of these two they supported and so decided to support a nonentity with no chance of winning for their first ballot. By sheer chance, 13 opted for Cardinal Serra i Cau, an elderly old scholar of no real talent. This gave Medici and Riario such a shock that they got together to do

Francis I was a monarch of the House of Valois who ruled France from 1515 until his death in 1547. He succeeded his cousin Louis XII, who died without a male heir.

1513

King James IV of Scotland invades England in support of his French ally, but is defeated and killed, along with most of the Scottish nobility, at the Battle of Flodden.

1513

Spanish explorer Vasco Núñez de Balboa climbs a mountain in central America and becomes the first European to see the Pacific Ocean.

1516

Bavaria introduces the Reinheitsgebot law to control the purity of beer, which remains in force.

The great Renaissance artist Titian painted this portrait of Holy Roman Emperor Charles V. Charles reigned as emperor from 1519 until he abdicated in 1555.

a deal before anything silly happened. Medici became Pope Leo X while Riario was loaded with honors and benefices.

Within weeks of becoming pope, Leo learned that Venice had allied itself with France and was marching against Milan while France attacked Naples. He promptly joined the League of Mechlin alongside the Holy Roman Empire, Spain, and England to fight France. In June, France was routed at the Battle of Novara, at which Swiss mercenary pikemen in dense formation defeated the famous French cavalry. Louis XII of France retreated from Italy, but three years later his successor, Francis I, returned and won a victory at Marignano, at which the French artillery decimated the Swiss pikemen who had wreaked havoc at Navara.

The Swiss then signed an "Eternal Peace" with France on surprisingly lenient terms that would last until the fall of the Kingdom of France in the French Revolution. Francis offered Leo a similarly generous peace, and Leo took it. Parma and Piacenza had to be given up and the king of France confirmed as duke of Milan, but Florence was left intact for the Medici. The papacy got back all the lucrative lands and income lost in the Council of Basle but had to hand to the king of France the right to appoint bishops and other clerics. Like the Swiss arrangement, it would endure until the French Revolution of 1789.

With France securely in Italy, but apparently content with their gains, Leo felt free to deal with other enemies. In 1516, he attacked Urbino ostensibly to return the city to papal control but, in fact, to win it for his nephew Lorenzo de Medici. The war was won, but at a fearful cost that almost bankrupted the papacy. When Emperor Maximilian died there was no obvious heir, and Leo threw himself into complex diplomacy to try to win maximum advantage for the papacy from the disputed succession. At first he backed Frederick of Saxony, then Francis of France, before finally settling on Charles of Spain, who was duly elected as Holy Roman Emperor Charles V in 1521.

In the meantime, a faction among the cardinals had become exasperated by his lavish spending and tortuous diplomacy. In 1517, they hatched a plot to poison Leo, but the plan was betrayed to Leo. He had the ringleader, Cardinal Alfonso Petrucci, strangled and several others thrown into prison. Leo then appointed 31 new cardinals so as to surround himself with men whose loyalty he could trust.

1517

Sultan Selim I of the Ottoman Turks invades Egypt, defeats the Mamluk Dynasty, and proclaims himself Caliph.

1518

The Dancing Plague of Strasbourg. Frau Troffea begins dancing the streets of Strasbourg, soon joined by others until over 400 people are dancing constantly, day and night. Around 50 eventually die of heart attacks, exhaustion, and dehydration. It is now thought to have been a form of mass hysteria.

1519

Spanish soldier and explorer Hernan Cortes lands in Mexico. By the end of the year he and his men have marched to Tenochtitlan to meet Montezuma, ruler of the Aztec Empire.

The financial crisis facing the papacy was, by 1516, becoming desperate. Several of the new cardinals in 1517 had simply bought their new positions for enormous cash donations, and the usual selling of benefices and positions to the highest bidder brought in more money. But the continuing drain of constructing St. Peter's Basilica proved to be the greatest problem. At this point Leo was approached by Archbishop Albert of Magdeburg, who was himself heavily in debt. Albert wanted permission to sell indulgences in Germany. Leo agreed, on condition that half the money raised be sent to Rome to fund the building work on St. Peter's.

When the sale of indulgences reached Wittenberg it enraged an Augustinian monk name Martin Luther. Luther nailed a paper on which he had written 95 theses to the door of the local Church. These attacked the indulgences along with other papal rulings and privileges. Luther's ideas caused a minor fuss locally but it was more than a year before an account of the 95 Theses reached Leo. He told the head of the Augustinian Order to get Luther to drop the subject. When that did not work Leo asked the local secular ruler, Frederick of Saxony, to arrest Luther. Frederick, however, was still smarting from the way Leo had betrayed him over the imperial succession and refused. Leo then sent a bull, *Exsurge Domine*, to Germany condemning Luther's teachings but Luther simply burned it in public. Leo then excommunicated Luther, hoping that would settle the matter.

Martin Luther (1483–1546). Engraved by C.E. Wagstaff.

1520

Battle of Otumpa. Spanish adventurer Hernan Cortes with local allies defeats the main Aztec army.

1520

King Christian II of Denmark invades Sweden promising a free pardon to any opponents who recognize him as lawful sovereign. After his victory he breaks his promise and executes over 400 Swedish nobles and clergy, an event known as the Stockholm Bloodbath.

1521

Cuauhtémoc, ruler of the Aztec Empire, surrenders to Hernan Cortes. He is later executed and his empire taken over by Spain.

ADRIAN VI ✢ The 218th Pope 1522–1523

Born Utrecht, Netherlands, March 2 1459

Parents Father, Florensz Boeyens van Utrecht; Mother, Gertrude

Papacy January 9, 1522 to September 14, 1523

Died September 14, 1523

Suleiman the Magnificent of the Ottoman empire.

The first pope to recognize the gravity of the threats from Luther in Germany and the Turks in the Balkans, Adrian VI strived to mobilize forces to meet both but was held back by vested interests that eventually overwhelmed him.

That conclave following the death of Leo X proved to be a long one. Due to the large number of cardinals appointed by Leo X, 36 of the 39 cardinals who took part were Italian and several had close links to the Medici family. Cardinal Giulio de'Medici could count on the support of 17 cardinals, but most others opposed him as they did not want to risk the papacy becoming seen as hereditary. The English Cardinal Wolsey also had significant support, aided by 100,000 golden ducats sent by King Henry VIII. King Francis I of France countered by sending a million gold ecu coins to secure the election of a Frenchman. By January 9 it was clear a deadlock had been reached. Cardinal Medici then suggested they should think about cardinals not present and suggested Adrian.

Arriving in Rome, Adrian announced his two main priorities were to deal with the religious unrest in Germany and the advance of Islam under Caliph Suleiman the Magnificent in the Balkans. He sought to achieve the former by both arguing against Luther's theological points and by tackling the corruptions and shady practices that were mobilizing the nobles and common people to support Luther. However, the cardinals objected to the way he gave benefices to be used for their true purpose instead of handing them out to senior clergy as rewards for service. Nor did the Roman population like the way that funds were diverted from beautifying Rome—and thus employing Romans—to be spent in the areas where the funds had been raised. Obstacles were thrown in the way of reforms and little was achieved.

The Siege of Rhodes, in 1522, united the major monarchs behind an effort to stop the spread of Islam.

Adrian caught Cardinal Francesco Solderini plotting with Francis I of France to undermine nobles in northern Italy and extend French influence at the expense of the Papal States. Adrian had Solderini arrested and thrown into prison. Francis at once abandoned the campaign against the Turks and instead mustered his army to invade northern Italy. Emperor Charles V mobilized to come to the aid of the pope and Henry VIII of England prepared to see who would offer him the best deal.

Frustrated, exhausted, and sick, Adrian retired to his private chambers were he succumbed, apparently to the heat.

1522

Vittoria returns to Spain, thus becoming the first ship in history to have circumnavigated the world.

1522

Portuguese mariner Cristovao de Mendonca sights land after being blown off course en route to Malacca. The position is poorly recorded, but this may have been the first European sighting of Australia.

1523

Martin Luther publishes his translation of the Bible in German.

CLEMENT VII ✢ The 219th Pope 1523–1534

Born Florence, Italy; May 26, 1478

Parents Father, Giuliano de Medici; Mother, Fioretta Gorini

Papacy November 19, 1523–September 25, 1534

Died Rome, Italy; September 25, 1534

Gifted, talented and popular in so many ways, Clement VII proved himself to be hopelessly unable to understand the very serious issues facing the Church, still less to be able to do anything constructive to deal with them. His pontificate ultimately became little more than a catalogue of missed opportunities and at least one disaster—the Sack of Rome in 1527.

Giulio de'Medici might have been thought to have had a good start in life, being born into one of the richest and most powerful families in Europe. But his father was murdered a month before he was born and his mother died shortly afterward, leaving him an orphan—and an illegitimate one at that. He was, nevertheless, cared for by his grandfather Lorenzo the Magnificent and earmarked for the Church. He joined the Knights of Rhodes and was given some clerical benefices that afforded him a useful income. When his cousin became Leo X he was raised to be bishop of Worcester, archbishop of Florence, and then cardinal. He moved to Rome where he became vice chancellor and is believed to have been largely responsible for the foreign policy of Leo X.

Henry VIII of England had been a powerful ally of the papacy until Clement VII refused to annul his marriage to Catherine of Aragon. The dispute led to the creation of the Church of England and Henry's excommunication.

When Adrian VI died the conclave was delayed to give the French cardinals time to arrive—King Francis I was at that moment leading an army in northern Italy and nobody wanting to offend him. A total of 27 votes was needed to gain the two thirds majority, and Cardinal Wolsey from England was an early leader with 22 votes on 11 October, but he failed to build on this early lead. The daily voting then continued with Wolsey losing votes and the cardinals shifting positions frequently until the Roman nobles led by the Colonna family switched to supporting Medici and he had the necessary majority and took the name of Clement VII.

By the time Clement came to the throne, previous papal foreign policies had led to Italy becoming a battleground between the French and the Holy Roman Empire. Clement's main aims were to safeguard the Papal States for the papacy and Florence for the Medici, both of which would be helped by being on the winning side. King Francis I of France recaptured Milan and convinced Clement that he would win the war. The Papal States accordingly became allied to France and Venice.

Then, in February 1525, Francis was surprised and surrounded at Pavia by an imperial army. Some 90 percent of the French army was killed or captured, with Francis himself being among the prisoners. The French seemed crushed, so Clement abandoned his allies and joined Emperor Charles V. Unknown to his allies, however, Charles had run out of money and was virtually bankrupt. Eager to get peace, Charles signed the Treaty of Madrid with Francis, gaining Flanders, Artois, and Burgundy, while Francis surrendered all his claims in Italy. The former duke of Milan, Francesco Sforza, was restored to power.

Francis was released but was aware of Charles's weakness so he repudiated the treaty as having been forced on him and again attacked. Fearing Charles's apparent strength, Clement absolved Francis from his oaths and

1524

Explorer Giovanni da Verrazzano enters what will later be named New York Bay and becomes the first European to see Manhattan.

1526

Central Asian monarch Babur invades northern India, occupies Delhi and founds the Mughal dynasty that will rule most of India until the 19th century.

1526

The Battle of Mohacs sees Turkish Caliph Suleiman the Magnificent defeat and kill King Louis II of Hungary, after which most of Hungary and adjacent lands fall to Turkish rule.

A 17th-century depiction of The Sack of Rome of 1527 by Johannes Lingelbach. The city was sacked with great brutality. Anything of value that could be found was stolen, almost a thousand militiamen who surrendered were butchered along with around 10,000 civilians, and rape was widespread.

threw the papal army into a French alliance. It was a disaster. Charles hired a huge mercenary army, including many Germans who were supporters of Martin Luther's call for reform of the Church. They easily defeated the French in Italy but it then emerged that Charles did not have any money to pay the army, which promptly mutinied. Nearby towns were sacked, then the army headed for Rome.

On May 6, 1527, the imperial army reached Rome and launched an immediate assault on the walls. The city militia were overwhelmed and the Germans surged into Rome. Clement himself was in the Vatican and taken by surprise. His personal guard of Swiss mercenaries hurried to fight a rearguard action while he fled to the Castel Sant'Angelo—of the 190 guards only 42 reached the fortress with Clement.

The sack of Rome ended the Roman Renaissance. The population of the city is thought to have been around 55,000 in 1520, but was only 10,000 in 1530. Charles was deeply embarrassed by the episode, though that did not stop him from imposing a harsh peace on Clement. Nor was Venice shy of annexing from the Papal States the disputed cities of Ravenna and Cervia.

Amid all this political maneuvering and military campaigning, other pressing problems facing the Church got ignored. The followers of Martin Luther had begun by calling for reform of the Church but now were talking about setting up new institutions free of the papacy. In 1526, the imperial diet at Speyer refused to impose papal punishments on the protestors and reformers. Many seeking reform inside the Church urged Clement to summon a General Council of all the bishops, abbots, and leading clerics to discuss how to tackle the scandals while defeating the separatists. There may yet have been time to solve the issues within the existing Church structures but Clement refused to believe the situation was so serious and no council took place.

Even worse, he flung loyal Catholics into the arms of the reformers. When Henry VIII of England wanted his marriage to Catherine of Aragon annulled, Clement first agreed, then delayed, then flatly refused. When Henry went ahead anyway, Clement declared him to be excommunicated. Henry at once separated the English Church from the papacy, declaring that he himself was now head of the Church in England. The break between king and pope opened the way for reformers to take control of the Church of England.

In September 1534, Clement fell seriously ill after eating a dish of mushrooms, one of which is presumed to have been of a poisonous variety. Whether this was simply a terrible accident by the cook or a deliberate act of poisoning has never been ascertained.

As might be expected of a member of the Medici family, Clement proved to be a patron of the arts. Raphael, Cellini, and Michelangelo were all given commissions, while the construction of the new St. Peter's continued. It was Clement who commissioned Michelangelo to paint the huge *Last Supper* fresco in the Sistine Chapel, though he did not live to see its completion. He was also interested in history, commissioning Francesco Guicciardini and Niccolo Machiavelli to produce works.

1530

The Knights Hospitaller are given Malta as a base by Holy Roman Emperor Charles V.

1532

Spanish soldier Francisco Pizarro invades the Inca Empire, captures the ruler Atahualpa, and extracts a ransom of gold estimated to be worth at modern prices around $150 million. He later kills Atahualpa anyway.

1532

Nicolaus Copernicus completes work on his book *De Revolutionibus Orbium Coelestium*, which states that the Earth orbits around the Sun. He circulates copies privately to trusted friends and colleagues but refuses to publish it for fear of the reaction it might provoke.

PAUL III ✠ The 220th Pope 1534–1549

Born Canino, Italy; February 29, 1468
Parents Father, Pier Luigi Farnese; Mother, Giovanna Caetani
Papacy October 13, 1534–November 10, 1549
Died Rome, Italy; November 10, 1549

By temperament Paul III was real Renaissance man, favoring arts and learning while exploiting the benefits of office to line the pockets of his own family. He was not, however, blind to the problems facing the papacy and, although he himself did nothing radical, his actions served to lay the groundwork for the changes to the Catholic Church that were to come.

Paul's father came from a famous family of condottieri (*see* p.210) though he himself saw no military action. His mother came from the great Caetani family of which Pope Boniface VIII had been a member. The youthful Alessandro Farnese thus grew up well connected, wealthy, and well educated. He studied at Rome, Florence, and Pisa before moving to Rome and rising to be papal treasurer and cardinal deacon by 1493. His links to the papacy increased when his sister became the mistress of Pope Alexander VI, whereupon he was nicknamed "Cardinal Petticoat." His high status continued under Clement VII, a tribute to his many gifts, and he gathered to himself a large number of lucrative benefices and positions.

When Clement VII died in 1534, Farnese was one of the 35 cardinals who went into conclave, another 11 being absent from Rome. As the conclave began on October 11 he was already the favorite. King Francis I of France was known to favor him, while Emperor Charles V did not object to him. That left only the Italian cardinals who wanted an Italian cardinal, led by Ippolito de'Medici, undecided. The first full day of conclave saw de'Medici declare for Farnese, so it came as no surprise when the next day he was elected unanimously except for his own vote.

One of his first concerns was to repair the damage of the Sack of Rome (*see* p.232). He hired Michelangelo to rebuild the buildings on top of the Capitoline Hill, making the great bronze statue of Emperor Marcus Aurelius the centerpiece, and to continue the rebuilding of St. Peter's Basilica. Michelangelo was also commissioned to complete two frescoes—the *Crucifixion of St. Peter* and the *Conversion of St. Paul*—in the Pauline Chapel of the Vatican. Like several previous popes he lavished money on his tomb, by Guglielmo della Porta, and portraits of himself, by Titian.

Funds were, however, short and much of them went not on buildings of artistic merit, but on those of military functionality. The Vatican fortress was redesigned as were many of the castles and fortresses that dotted the Papal States. Although he prepared carefully for war, Paul was determined to achieve peace. He steered clear of alliances and assiduously avoided conflict.

PAPABILI

By the time of Paul III the term papabili was being used to describe those cardinals entering conclave who were considered to have a chance of being elected. Betting in Rome was rife during conclaves, with details leaked by servants being eagerly snapped up by betters wanting to have an edge in the keenly fought battle for advantage. In more recent years, the flow of information from the conclave has become increasingly rare as the secrecy was tightened up. These days, speculation surrounding the papabili is based exclusively on information gained before the conclave begins.

1534
The Reformation is established in England by the Act of Supremacy, which appoints the king as the head of the Church of England.

1535
Sir Thomas More is executed for refusing to acknowledge King Henry VIII as head of the Church in England.

1536
The Incas under Manco Inca Yupanqui rebel against Spanish rule, setting up an independent state in the remote forests of lowland Peru near Vilacampa.

Ottavio Farnese (1524–1586) reigned as Duke of Parma and Piacenza from 1547 and Duke of Castro from 1545 until his death.

The only war in which Paul was interested was that being fought against the Turks in the Balkans. For some years the Turks had been on the advance, conquering Christian state after Christian state. In 1529, the armies of Suleiman the Magnificent had reached Vienna, laying siege to that city for a month before they retreated. Paul was instrumental in getting the fractious Hungarian nobles to elect Ferdinand Habsburg of Austria to be their king. It was hoped that the powerful Habsburgs could defeat the Turks, but the war ended in a brutal stalemate.

Meanwhile, the growing tide of Protestantism meant that large areas of Europe were leaving the Roman Church to set up new institutions that owed no allegiance and no tribute to the pope. This was not only a serious blow to the unity of Christendom in the face of the Turkish threat, but also a financial setback for the popes. Paul announced that he would hold a Great Council of the entire Church in Mantua in 1537, then moved it to Vicenza in 1538. A vexed issue was whether clerics supporting what was becoming called the Protestant faith should be invited. Ultimately, Paul decided that they would not be welcome. The Council eventually met at Trent in 1545, with Paul dying before its work was complete.

He had, however, taken some steps of his own. He appointed a number of brilliant new cardinals dedicated to reform, including Reginald Pole, Marcello Cervini, and Giovanni Carafa. He used these men to serve on a commission to investigate the state of the Church. The report in 1537 was hard-headed and brutally frank, laying bear the many problems that needed setting right.

In 1540, he issued the bull *Regimini militantis Ecclesiae*, which approved the establishment of the Society of Jesus, better known as the Jesuits. The Jesuits would later lead the reform movement, championing conversion, education, and theology as the route to renewal. Other bodies approved by Paul included the Theatines, Barnabites, and Ursulines.

Less successful were his dealings with the touchy King Henry VIII of England. He confirmed the excommunication of the king by Clement VII and went further by placing England under an interdict. This ban on church services was less effective than it might have been since the English clergy simply ignored it and carried on as before. His efforts to get the continental powers to tackle England failed completely.

Quite apart from these moves, Farnese continued one papal tradition by using his position to enhance the wealth and prestige of his family. In 1534, he made both his grandsons cardinals when they were aged only 14 and 16. His son Pierluigi was made Duke of Parma and Piacenza. Although these cities remained within the Papal States, Pierluigi was made their hereditary ruler subject only to paying tribute to the papacy. The emperor Charles V had his eye on the duchies partly because he wanted to unite them with his own Milan, but also because Pierluigi's son Ottavio was married to his own illegitimate daughter Margaret. In 1547, Pierluigi was murdered by nobles from Parma in protest at his harsh taxes. The news devastated Paul, but Charles V accepted Ottavio as the next ruler of Parma if Piacenza passed to Milan. Mollified, Paul accepted. The emotional upset had, however, broken his health and he slipped into an illness from which he did not recover.

1540

Waltham Abbey, the last monastic house in England, is closed down by order of King Henry VIII as part of his reformation of the Church in England.

1542

Spanish Explorer Hernando de Soto becomes the first European to see the Mississippi River.

1547

England's Henry VIII dies, aged 55, of syphilis and cirrhosis of the liver. He is succeeded by his son Edward VI.

1547

France's Francis I dies, aged 52, and is succeeded by his son Henry II.

JULIUS III ✠ The 221st Pope 1550–1555

Born Rome, Italy; 10 September, 1487

Parents Unknown

Papacy February 8, 1550–March 23, 1555

Died Rome, Italy; March 23, 1555

Julius III was able to draw a clear and distinct line between his public life as pope—where he was hardworking and open to reform—and his private life of debauched laziness. Others failed to see the distinction and the blurring of the lines did much damage to the papacy.

Giovanni Maria Ciocchi del Monte studied law in Perugia and Siena before returning to Rome to serve as chamberlain to Pope Julius II. In 1511, he became archbishop of Siponto, moving to Pavia in 1520. In 1534, Paul III made him vice-legate in Bologna, a position that called for great tact, and then two years later made him cardinal priest. In 1543, he became cardinal bishop of Palestrina. Paul sent him to open the Council of Trent, a cause to which he appeared committed.

In 1547, he was visiting Piacenza when he became hopelessly infatuated with a 13-year-old boy named Innocenzo who was working as a junior servant in the household of the city's governor. Giovanni took Innocenzo into his service, officially as the keeper of his pet monkey, and when a paid job became available handed it to the boy.

The death of Paul III precipitated a long conclave during which the future of the Council of Trent dominated religious topics, while the rivalry between Henry II of France and Emperor Charles V dominated the politics. The cardinals were divided between factions favoring and opposing reform and those favoring or opposing France. Englishman Reginald Pole missed being elected by a single vote before Giovanni del Monte won as a neutral candidate acceptable to all sides after more than two months of conclave.

One of Julius III's first actions was to raise young Innocenzo to the rank of cardinal and gave him lucrative benefices. At first, Julius sought to justify this move by making Innocenzo his secretary, but the duties were beyond the boy and were given to a deputy while Innocenzo loafed about with the pope. Together Julius and Innocenzo enjoyed parties, hunting, the theatre, and other less reputable activities.

Meanwhile, there was work to be done. Julius reassembled the Council of Trent in May 1551. When some Protestants were allowed to attend in an unofficial capacity, King Henry II of France withdrew the French bishops and abbots. The remaining clerics did make efforts to introduce reforms. Pluralism (*see* p.224) was brought under some sort of control, monastic discipline was tightened up, and attempts were even made to reform the curia. On doctrinal issues, limited efforts at compromise were made on issues such as original sin and the sacraments, but opposing views were more firmly entrenched there than on organizational matters. In April 1552, the Council broke up, supposedly for a short break, but as events turned out it never reassembled.

In 1553, England's Protestant king Edward VI, son of Henry VIII, died aged only 15 and was succeeded by his elder sister Mary. Julius rejoiced that such a large Protestant country should return to the Catholic fold and sent Reginald Pole as legate with wide-ranging powers to supervise the restoration of papal authority. Hoping to repeat the success in Germany, Julius sent Cardinal Morone as legate to Germany. Julius would die before he learned of the ultimate failure of both missions.

Henry II of France was determined to suppress the Protestant Reformation even as the Huguenots became an increasingly large minority during his 12-year reign.

1550

The vast silver mines of Potosi are discovered in Spanish America, massively increasing the wealth of Spain, and ultimately devaluing silver.

1551

Ottoman Turks invade and conquer the Mediterranean island of Gozo. Before abandoning the island they carry off the entire population of 6,000 to be sold as slaves.

1551

The University of San Marco is established at Lima, Peru, the oldest university in the Americas.

MARCELLUS II ✣ The 222nd Pope 1555

Born Montefano, Italy; May 6, 1501

Parents Father, Ricardo Cervini; Mother, unknown

Papacy April 9, 1555–May 1, 1555

Died Rome, Italy; May 1, 1555

The first pope who fully understood the need for reform in the 16th century, Marcellus II began his papacy with a whirlwind of activity and action. However, very little of his good work and good intentions amounted to anything significant, as he died just 22 days into his papacy.

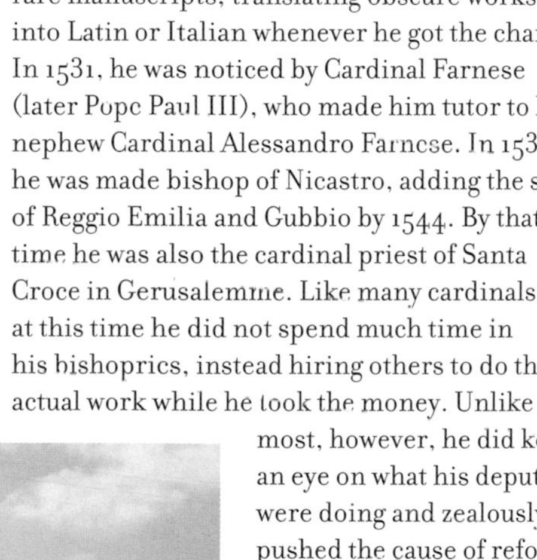

Marcello Cervini had a passion for books and rare manuscripts, translating obscure works into Latin or Italian whenever he got the chance. In 1531, he was noticed by Cardinal Farnese (later Pope Paul III), who made him tutor to his nephew Cardinal Alessandro Farnese. In 1539, he was made bishop of Nicastro, adding the sees of Reggio Emilia and Gubbio by 1544. By that time he was also the cardinal priest of Santa Croce in Gerusalemme. Like many cardinals at this time he did not spend much time in his bishoprics, instead hiring others to do the actual work while he took the money. Unlike most, however, he did keep an eye on what his deputies were doing and zealously pushed the cause of reform. The freedom that the incomes gave him meant he could be sent on diplomatic missions to France and Germany, being legate to Emperor Charles V in 1543.

In 1548, he was given the task of reorganizing the papal library, a job he relished. That task was still unfinished when Julius III came to the throne and Cervini fell out of favor. When Julius died, Cervini hurried to Rome to take part in the conclave, determined to ensure the election of someone who supported the reform agenda.

The conclave began on 5 April with the 37 cardinals taking part divided into three factions. The French cardinals faced the German cardinals, while the Italians were divided. It was soon obvious that neither the French nor the Germans would get their man elected, so the French suggested Cervini and, after some hesitation, the German faction agreed, with the Italians then falling into line. He was consecrated as Marcellus II later that day.

From the moment he was consecrated, Marcellus showed that he was serious about reforms. The coronation was frugal in the extreme, and many members of the papal court were dismissed or sent to carry out more practical tasks in the curia. The pile of petitions asking for favors was waved aside while petitions for justice were brought forward and dealt with impartially and without any bribes being taken or favoritism shown. Perhaps most shocking for contemporaries was the fact that he issued an instruction banning any member of his family from entering the city of Rome. Clearly nepotism was at an end. Next he announced that he was going to produce a comprehensive bull of reform. To this end he issued orders that all the documents about reform prepared for Julius III, but then brushed aside, should be brought to him.

Before the great reform bull could be issues, however, Marcellus suffered a stroke and died.

Gubbio Cathedral. Cervini led the group of cardinals who criticized the laziness and frivolity of Julius III. Julius made his displeasure very clear, so Cervini retreated to his see of Gubbio.

1551	1555	1555	1555
Forty-two articles that will be the basis of the Anglican Protestant Church are published by England's archbishop of Canterbury Thomas Cranmer.	The Sultanate of Adal which has dominated the Horn of Africa for nearly two centuries suddenly collapses into chaos.	The Treaty of Augsburg ends a period of religious wars in the German states by compromising on differences between Catholics and Protestants.	Michelangelo completes his sculpture Pietà. The work for the Duomo at Florence has taken him five years to complete.

PAUL IV ✠ The 223rd Pope 1555–1559

Born Capriglia Ipirna, Italy; June 28, 1476

Parents Father, Giovanni Antonio Carafa; Mother, Vittoria Camponeschi

Papacy May 23, 1555–August 18, 1559

Died Rome, Italy; August 18, 1559

Passionately devoted to the reform of the Church, Paul IV was never able to understand why others might take a different view. In particular he hated those who left the Church, condemning them as heretics to unpleasant fates.

Giampietro Carafa was born into a junior branch of a noble family from Naples that was related to a leading Portuguese family and grew up with a deep distrust of the Habsburg dynasty and its ambitions. At a young age he moved to Rome to join the household of his uncle, Cardinal Oliviero Carafa. By 1505, he was bishop of Chieti and, in 1518, he rose to be archbishop of Brindisi and, like most high-ranking clerics, collected a number of other sees to add to his income, hiring deputies to do the actual work.

That changed in 1524 when Adrian VI asked Giampietro to look into the need for reform within the Church. The investigation did not lead to much, but Giampietro became so convinced of the urgency of the problems that he first introduced reforms to his sees, then resigned from them to avoid pluralism (*see* p.224). He was created cardinal priest of San Pancrazio and archbishop of Naples in 1536, whereupon he became the recognized leader of the reform movement in Rome.

He supported the election of the reformist Marcellus in April 1555, and when that pope died after less than a month in office he was quickly elected to follow him. Carafa took the name of Paul IV and was hailed by reformers as the pope who was needed to reunite European Christendom around a reformed Church. However, it was not to be.

Taking the traditional view that he could trust only his own kin, Paul's nephew Carlo Carafa was raised to be a cardinal and effectively put in charge of papal foreign policy. Another nephew was given command of the papal army and a third took over the papal Swiss Guard. Together those three followed an anti-Habsburg line that led Paul into an alliance with France against Spain. Paul deprived Philip II of Spain of the Neapolitan crown, a papal fief, and awaited the arrival of a French army to mount a joint invasion. The French never arrived for it was crushed at the Battle of St. Quentin in the Low Countries. The Spanish army in Naples then occupied the entire Papal States almost without a fight. Paul was granted generous terms for peace and turned on his relatives who were dismissed from office and banished from Rome.

Paul's reform policies included banning pluralism and forcing bishops to live in their sees, reinforcing the rules on monastic orders, and rewriting the missal. Other than his nephew, Paul appointed only men of the highest character and abilities to be cardinals. However, his efforts were blighted by his own intolerance. Those who questioned his reforms or who left the Church were seen as heretics and thrown into prison for the attentions of the Inquisition. The Jews of Italy were forced to live in ghettoes while wearing distinctive clothes. In 1557, he published the Index of Forbidden Books.

His intolerance and ascetic nature combined to make him unpopular in Rome. When he died a mob destroyed his statue and ransacked the offices of the Inquisition.

1555

Queen Mary I of England begins a program of executing Protestants who refuse to recant when clergyman John Rogers is burned at the stake in Smithfield, London.

1556

The great Shaanxi Earthquake strikes China killing an estimated 860,000 people, making this the deadliest earthquake in history.

1557

Tsar Ivan the Terrible of Russia conquers Astrakhan taking control of the Volga River. His use of the title "Tsar" (Caesar) reveals his imperial ambitions and rivals that of the Holy Roman emperor.

1558

English Queen Mary I dies. Mary's re-establishment of Roman Catholicism is reversed after her death by her half-sister and successor Elizabeth I who will reign for 44 years.

PIUS IV ✠ The 224th Pope 1559–1565

Born Milan, Italy; March 31, 1499
Parents Unknown
Papacy December 25, 1559–December 9, 1565
Died Rome, Italy; December 9, 1565

Pius IV reconvened the Council of Trent and brought it to a successful conclusion. He also continued to patronize Michelangelo and other great artists. However, his wider efforts to encourage reform within the Church and bring Protestants back to allegiance to Rome were to end in failure.

Giovanni Angelo Medici was only distantly related to the more famous de'Medici family that ruled Florence. In 1549, he became a cardinal but fell out with Paul IV over the new pope's anti-Habsburg policies. When Paul died, Medici took part in a conclave that was divided between those favoring a pro-Habsburg policy and those wanting closer ties to France. The balance of power was held by cardinals appointed by Paul, including his nephew Carlo Carafa who blocked anyone who would not promise him amnesty for his various crimes. When Medici gave that promise, Carafa backed him, but as soon as he was safely in the Vatican as Pius IV, he executed Carafa, along with his brother and several supporters. The move shocked Rome, but was followed by the release of many of Paul's prisoners and a slackening of the repressive nature of the regime of Paul.

Pius reconvened the Council of Trent in January 1562 and ran until December 1563. Many bishops were keen to evade the requirement to live in their diocese, while there was much disagreement over how far to agree concessions to the Protestants. In the end, the Council refined doctrine, giving some ground to Protestant views, but firmly decreed that the Church under the pope was the final arbiter on issues of faith and backed some contentious issues such as indulgences, veneration of the Virgin Mary, and veneration of relics.

Pius refrained from excommunicating Queen Elizabeth I of England in the hope that she would return allegiance to Rome in return for concessions. In France, however, he took a hard line, encouraging King Charles IX to take the most repressive measures against the Huguenots.

Pius built the Porta Pia and the road, Via Pia, that leads to it. Santa Maria degli Angeli was carved out of the ancient Baths of Diocletian by Michelangelo.

In Rome, Pius continued to patronize the finest artists, employing Michelangelo to rework the northern defenses of Rome. For his own use, Pius commissioned Pirro Ligorio to build the Villa Pia in the grounds of the Vatican, the interior decorations being completed by Federico Barocci, Federico Zuccari, and Santi di Tito. Despite this, the general levels of spending in Rome were drastically cut as taxes rose. This prompted a plot to murder Pius led by Cardinal Benedetto Accolti, who was under suspicion of having embezzled money intended to help the wars against the Turks. The plot was crushed, but Pius died a few months later anyway.

1560
The overwhelming Turkish naval victory at the Battle of Djerba over a combined fleet of Christian powers gives them control of the eastern Mediterranean.

1560
The first tulip bulbs are brought to the Netherlands from Turkey.

1560
Scotland officially breaks with Rome to become a Protestant country.

1565
At the Battle of Talikota, the large Hindu Vijayanagara empire is defeated by the Muslim rulers of the Deccan ending independent Hindu power in India.

1565
The Great Siege of Malta takes place when a large Ottoman army attacks the Knights Hospitallers on Malta. The siege is eventually driven off after huge losses on both sides.

ST. PIUS V ✠ The 225th Pope 1566–1572

Born Bosco, Italy; January 17, 1504

Parents Unknown

Papacy January 7, 1566–May 1, 1572

Died Rome, Italy; May 1, 1572

Pius was concerned with orthodoxy of belief as well as with correcting abuses within the Church. He took a strong line with both and at times seemed determined to make everyone else follow his own strict lifestyle. He was canonized once the importance of his work in promoting the Counter-Reformation was recognized.

Michele Ghislieri was born into poverty in the hills northwest of Milan. He followed his family trade as a shepherd until, at the age of 14, he presented himself at a local Dominican friary and was admitted to the Order. He was sent to study at Bologna and, in 1528, was ordained a priest within the Dominicans. He spent the next 16 years lecturing in law at Pavia, during which time he wrote a treatise putting forward 30 Propositions establishing the primacy of the pope and condemning the teachings of Protestantism as heresy.

In 1570, Pope Pius V excommunicated Queen Elizabeth I of England and released her subjects from their oaths and loyalty to her.

Largely because of his treatise, Michele was appointed head of the Inquisition in Como and Bergamo. He was so zealous in seeking out heretical views and investigating those alleged to hold them that he won the favor of the famously orthodox cardinal Giampietro Carafa. Carafa sent Michele to Rome with letters of introduction to Pope Julius III, which were so persuasive that he was appointed to the central Roman Inquisition. In 1555, Carafa became Pope Paul IV and almost at once made Michele Bishop of Nepi and Sutrui, raising him to the rank of cardinal in 1557. In 1558, Michele achieved his dearest wish when he was appointed to be head of the Roman Inquisition in 1558. His personal piety was never in doubt, nor was his zeal to promote orthodox belief. His severity as Inquisitor General lost him favor under Pius IV, who moved him to be bishop of Mondovi back in the area where he had grown up.

When Pius IV died, Michele traveled back to Rome to join the conclave. The conclave was interrupted by the Christmas festivities, so it was not until January 7, 1566, that a result was achieved and Michele became pope as Pius V.

He began his drive to reform and improve the Church immediately on taking office. He forced bishops and priests to reside in the areas for which they had responsibility and curbed pluralism (*see* p.224) even more than before. He banned the practice of investing lands within the Papal States as feudal fiefs. This practice had long been used by popes to give lands belonging to the papacy to their relatives in return for a nominal tribute. As each fief fell vacant it would revert to the papacy, bringing with it increased flows of taxes, rents, and other incomes. Thus Pius ensured the gradual enrichment of the papacy without alienating any of the powerful men who currently held the fiefs. To reduce expenditure he cut the size of the papal court.

1566

The Siege of Szigetvar ends with a Turkish victory over the Croat defenders, but Caliph Suleiman the Magnficent dies during the siege.

1567

Catholic Mary, Queen of Scots, is forced to abdicate by her Protestant subjects who then crown her one-year-old son as King James VI. Mary later goes to England to seek support from her cousin Queen Elizabeth I but is put under house arrest.

Pius began a process of investigating the religious Orders. He ruthlessly closed down or reformed any houses that fell below the standards expected and, in 1571, closed the entire Order of Humiliati with their 94 monasteries being sold and the proceeds donated to charity. When one leading Humiliati tried to murder Pius's agent the entire leadership of the Order was executed.

Parishes and dioceses within the Papal States and Naples were visited by papal staff to ensure orthodox teaching and high standards of ritual and learning among the clergy. Pius himself undertook the visitations within Rome, making him the first bishop of Rome for generations to take his local pastoral duties seriously.

Following the decisions of the Council of Trent, Pius reformed the liturgy to be used in churches. Up until this time many dioceses and even parishes had their own forms of liturgy, some of which were ancient but others of which were developing. The concern was that Protestant rites might creep into Catholic rituals, so a uniform liturgy was decided upon. Knowing that opposition could be expected in some areas, Pius decreed that local variations more than 200 years old could be retained as optional forms of ritual.

Pius also led a campaign to eradicate heresy. Seven French bishops were accused of favoring Protestantism and dismissed from office. In 1570, he issued the bull *Regnans in Excelsis*, which excommunicated Queen Elizabeth I of England and released her subjects from their oaths and loyalty to her. She responded by ending the tolerance for Catholic worship in private and enforced attendance at Protestant churches.

Pius's relationship with Holy Roman Emperor Maximillian II was almost as difficult due to the emperor tolerating Protestants in his realms, though in truth he was not strong enough to do anything about them. Pius even came close to falling out with his closest ally, King Philip II of Spain, when Philip exercised what he saw as his rights over the Church in Spain.

Pius did manage to sponsor the formation of the Holy League, composed of the Papal States, Spain, Naples, Sicily, Venice, Genoa, Tuscany, Savoy, Parma, Urbino, and the Knights of Malta. The League was formed after Cyprus fell to the Ottoman Turks in 1570. The next year its fleet utterly destroyed the Turkish fleet at the Battle of Lepanto, ending forever Muslim control of the Mediterranean.

On the evening after the battle, Pius fell into a trance in his private rooms. When he awoke he declared that he had seen a vision of the Turkish fleet sinking and that he believed a great battle had been fought and won. News of the victory arrived a few days later, confirming his vision.

Pius V died in the spring of 1572, whereupon it was found that under his fine papal vestments he had continued to wear the rough habit of the Dominicans. On the centenary of his death, he was beatified, then canonized in 1712.

COUNTER-REFORMATION

The pontificate of Pius V is recognized as the start of the Counter-Reformation. Although given urgency by the rise of Protestantism, the drive to reform the Church had begun earlier. The movement had four main strands: the growth of new religious orders; the glorification of God through art and ritual; the ending of corruption and other scandals; and associated political changes. The Counter Reformation effectively stopped the spread of Protestantism beyond the areas it already dominated and rejuvenated the Catholic Church. However, it failed to bring Protestants back within the Catholic faith in any numbers and so must be counted as having been only a partial success.

1568

The Eighty Years War breaks out as the mostly Protestant provinces of the Netherlands seek independence from the Catholic Philip II of Spain. Seven of the 17 provinces gain independence, but the fighting continues intermittently until 1648.

1569

German cartographer Gerardus Mercator first uses Mercator's projection in drawing a world map. It soon becomes the standard projection used on charts and maps.

1570

The Whitechapel Bell Foundry is started, it remains in business as the oldest manufacturing company in Britain.

GREGORY XIII ✠ The 226th Pope 1572–1585

Born Bologna, Italy; January 7, 1507

Parents Father, Cristoforo Boncompagni; Mother, Angela Marescalchi

Papacy May 14, 1572–April 10, 1585

Died Rome, Italy; April 10, 1585

Gregory XIII is best known for having introduced the Gregorian Calendar, the most widely used calendar in the world today. However, he himself believed that his greatest achievement was to extend the Catholic faith to remote areas of Asia. He is also notorious for helping to fund the Catholic League, which was aimed at destroying Protestantism in France.

Gregory was born as Ugo Boncompagni, fourth son of a reasonably prosperous merchant in the thriving, intellectual hothouse that was 16th-century Bologna. He attended the local university and graduated in law in 1531 before spending the next eight years lecturing. Among his students were Church leaders such as Cardinals Alexander Farnese, Reginald Pole, and Charles Borromeo. At this stage in his life, he was neither very religious nor overly concerned with Church matters—as witness the fact that he kept a mistress by whom he had a son.

In 1535, he went to Rome to work for Pope Paul III who employed him in a range of legal offices. However, it was Pius IV who raised him to be cardinal priest of San Sisto Vecchio, in which capacity he attended the Council of Trent. Pius then sent Boncompagni to Spain to investigate allegations about the bishop of Toledo. While there, he met King Philip II with whom he forged a lasting friendship.

The St. Bartholomew's Day Massacre resulted in at least 3,000 deaths.

Boncompagni was back in Rome when Pius V died and so entered the conclave along with 52 other cardinals. As the conclave began it was known that the cardinals were divided between supporters of Cardinals Farnese and Medici, and it was expected to be a long process. However, King Philip II of Spain sent a message that he would accept neither of the leading contenders. The surprised cardinals spent most of the first day trying to decide on a compromise candidate, and on the second day settled on Boncompagni, who took the name Gregory XIII in honor of Gregory I.

Gregory had undergone a religious conversion since his days in Bologna. He now held an earnest and orthodox faith, believing that in recent decades the Church had failed its flock. Without dwelling on past mistakes, Gregory set out to ensure that in future the Church would be staffed by professional, highly educated staff at all levels. He entirely reorganized the Roman College, later renamed the Gregorian College, to train priests. He also established the English College, the German College, the Greek College, the Maronite College, and the Armenian College. The costs were enormous, but could be afforded through the increased flow of revenues from the Papal States secured by Pius V. The colleges would, within a few years, be producing a steady flow of dedicated and competent clergy. The German and English colleges sent priests to their homelands to battle Protestantism. The colleges also produced priests to go out to convert people in newly discovered lands in the Americas, East Indies, Philippines, and Japan.

Alongside the colleges, Gregory reorganized the nunciatures, the small number of

1572

The last remaining independent Inca state, Vilcabamba, is conquered by Spanish conquistadores.

1572

Italian mathematician Rafael Bombelli successfully defines imaginary numbers for the first time.

1575

The Raid of the Redeswire is the last armed conflict between England and Scotland, though only a few hundred men were involved.

The Catholic Mary Queen of Scots was accused of plotting against her cousin Elizabeth I of England and was executed in 1587.

permanent diplomatic missions maintained by the papacy. These had previously been diplomatic missions representing the papacy to local secular rulers. They now became instruments of reform imposing papal edicts on the local clergy. In addition to those already existing, Gregory opened new nunciatures at Cologne, Lucerne, and Graz. Of especial importance was the requirement that bishops and priests had to live in their diocese or parish, a rule to which Gregory allowed very few exceptions.

Within the curia, Gregory made one reform of great importance to the future. He took the role of secretary intimus, the pope's private office manager, and massively enhanced its importance and duties to the point where its holder effectively ran the political and diplomatic activities of the papacy. Under the title of Cardinal Secretary of State the office continues to wield enormous power to this day. For this important post Gregory chose Tolomeo Gallio who was to remain an important figure in Rome until his death in 1607.

In his international dealings, Gregory had mixed fortunes. Poland was won to the Catholic cause permanently, but talks with the Russians broke down and that country and its dominions remained Orthodox. He set up a special German Congregation of cardinals, which was given funds and powers to use in expanding the Catholic faith in the Holy Roman Empire. In the Netherlands, papal diplomacy caused the alliance of 17 provinces to split when several southern provinces abandoned their bid for independence from rule by King Philip II of Spain. The division proved to be permanent with the seven northern, Protestant provinces today forming the Netherlands and the southern provinces forming Belgium.

In dealing with Protestant England and Scotland, Gregory sought to persuade the Catholic Irish to invade Britain in conjunction with a Spanish army from the Low Countries. The plan miscarried in 1578. Thereafter Gregory gave funds and resources to a succession of plots to assassinate Queen Elizabeth of England and replace her with her cousin the Catholic Mary Queen of Scots. These plots served only to harden the measures taken by the English government against Catholics, especially priests, and would ultimately prove fatal for Mary.

In France Gregory sent funds and help to the Catholic League, a grouping of French nobles formed in 1576 that aimed to destroy Protestantism. That move came as the kingdom descended into civil war. There had been earlier conflicts and battles between Catholics and Protestants, though such confrontations were sometimes as much political and dynastic as they were religious. The most notorious of these events had been the St. Bartholomew's Day Massacre of 1572. The leaders of the Huguenot Protestants were in Paris to see their leader, Henry of Navarre married to Margaret, sister to King Charles IX. Amid intense tension a group of Catholic nobles plotted to murder a handful of leading Huguenots. They struck on August 23, whereupon the people of Paris began a general massacre of Huguenots that lasted three days and left 3,000 dead. As news of the massacre spread, Catholics elsewhere turned to violence and as many as 10,000 other Protestants may have been killed. When he heard the news, Gregory ordered a *Te Deum* to be sung in thanks and struck a medal. Civil war broke out again in France.

1577

English mariner Francis Drake leaves England with a small fleet of ships that he will take into the Pacific to plunder Spanish colonies and ships. It is the start of an unofficial naval war between England and Spain while those kingdoms remain officially at peace.

1582

The Gregorian Calendar is introduced, though at first only Catholic countries adopt it. It corrects a discrepancy between the Julian Calendar of Julius Caesar and the actual movement of the Earth, which amounted to 3 days every 400 years.

1585

England's Elizabeth breaks with Spain and sends troops to aid the Lowlanders in their struggle against the Spanish.

SIXTUS V ✠ The 227th Pope 1585–1590

Born Grottammare, Italy; December 13, 1520

Parents Unknown

Papacy April 24, 1585–August 27, 1590

Died Rome, Italy; August 27, 1590

Born Felice Peretti, Sixtus was a ruthless man who did not scruple to impose his will on his fellow men whenever he felt he was in the right—which was most of the time.

Although unpopular with the public, Peretti was admired and popular among his fellow cardinals, so his election as Pope Sixtus V in April 1585 surprised the public, but not curia insiders. Recognizing that the Reformation had robbed the papacy of vast funds in Protestant nations, Sixtus decided that the revenue from the Papal States had to be boosted. He hunted down brigands without mercy, hanging over a thousand of them in his first year in power. With order assured he set about draining marshes, encouraging the silk industry, and promoting the cause of small farmers. Fiscal reforms meant that taxation was fair and equitable, encouraging enterprise that supplied higher tax returns. Expenditure was meanwhile slashed. The result was that by 1587 he was one of the richest princes in Europe. His reform of the curia involved establishing 15 permanent offices, each overseen by a committee of cardinals chosen by himself. This stripped cardinals he did not care for of all power.

URBAN VII ✠ The 228th Pope 1590

Born Rome, Italy, August 4, 1521

Parents Baron Castagna; Mother, unknown

Papacy September 15, 1590–September 27, 1590

Died Rome, Italy; September 27, 1590

Pious, hardworking, and popular, Urban VII came to the papal throne amid high hopes that he would push forward the cause of reform and push back the Protestantism that had divided Europe. It was not to be.

Giambattista Castagna became a cardinal in 1583. Although he at first opposed the election of Sixtus V, Castagna was reconciled to the new pope and remained in charge of Bologna. The conclave of 1590 was attended by 67 cardinals, and all but 15 of them were Italian. Castagna was a popular candidate and was quickly elected on a promise of continuing reform and took the name Urban VII.

Once pope, Urban confirmed in office the men who had served Sixtus and declared his determination to continue the reforms. He also took the opportunity to ban a pet hate of his: smoking tobacco was prohibited inside churches. In this Urban was well ahead of his time. Tobacco had been introduced to Europe from North America only a dozen years before.

The day after his election, Urban went down with malaria. Despite his healthy constitution he died just 12 days later. Urban therefore holds the dubious distinction of being the shortest reigning pope of all time.

1596

Toyotomi Hideyoshi becomes shogun of Japan, introducing reforms to society and government that would shape Japan into the 19th century.

1587

English settlers arrive on Roanoke Island, now in North Carolina, to establish the first permanent English colony in the New World, though it would be abandoned by 1590 in mysterious circumstances.

1588

The Spanish Armada sets sail from Spain to invade England after the execution of Catholic Mary Queen of Scots by Protestant Queen Elizabeth I. After an epic running battle in the English Channel, the Armada limps back to Spain with heavy losses.

1589

Henry III of France dies and the throne passes to Protestant Henry of Navarre, but many French Catholics refuse to accept him as king and civil war continues.

GREGORY XIV ✠ The 229th Pope 1590–1591

Born Somma Lombardo, Italy; February 11, 1535

Parents Father, Francesco Sfondrati,; Mother, Anna Visconti

Papacy December 5, 1590–October 16, 1591

Died Rome, Italy; October 16, 1591

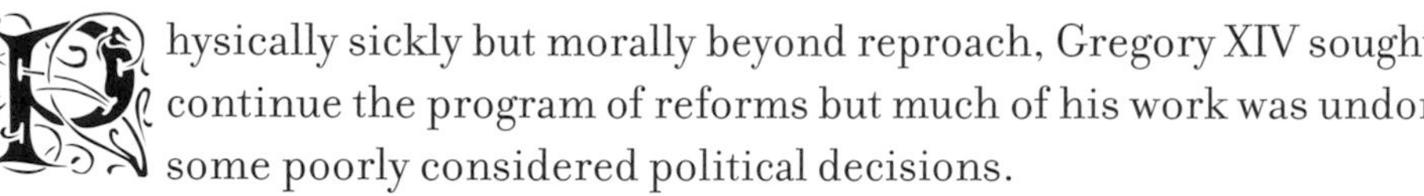

Physically sickly but morally beyond reproach, Gregory XIV sought to continue the program of reforms but much of his work was undone by some poorly considered political decisions.

Niccolo Sfondrati was born into one of the wealthiest families in the Duchy of Milan and became cardinal of Santa Cecilia in 1583.

The conclave that followed the death of Urban VII lasted two months before King Philip II of Spain sent in a list of seven cardinals with instructions the conclave had to choose one of them. Sfondrati's was the last name on the list, but nobody objected to him so he was chosen. On being told the news he burst into tears and cried "God forgive you. What have you done?"

Once pope he continued with reforms, though at a slower pace than before. Painfully aware he lacked experience in politics, Gregory brought in his 29-year-old nephew Paolo Sfondrati who decided to involve the papacy in the civil war in France. Hatching an alliance with Philip II of Spain, Sfondrati sent a papal army to France to fight against the Protestant heir to the throne Henry of Navarre. The foreign intervention actually undermined the Catholic cause as most Frenchmen detested a Spanish-Italian invasion.

INNOCENT IX ✠ The 230th Pope 1591

Born Bologna, Italy; July 20, 1519

Parents Unknown

Papacy October 29, 1591–December 30, 1591

Died Rome, Italy; December 30, 1591

Giovanni Antonio Fachinetti was one of the leading churchmen of his day. It was hoped his undoubted administrative talents would help the papacy, but in the event in had barely started before he died.

When Gregory XIV died, Philip II of Spain sent to the conclave a list of names and instructed the cardinals to choose a candidate off the list. It is thought Fachinetti was chosen because his failing health made him the least objectionable to those who opposed to a pro-Spanish policy.

Taking the name Innocent IX, the new pope declared himself fully behind the controversial decision of Gregory XIV to intervene in the French civil war. The papal army was at this date marching to Rouen to lift the siege of the city by the Protestant forces of Henry of Navarre. Funds were short, so Innocent had to send a large sum of money north to keep the army in the field. That brought home to him just how expensive war was, so he began a thorough study of the papal finances. On November 8, he announced changes to the papal financial system with the establishment of a permanent treasury in Castel Sant'Angelo the main feature. It is known that he had other plans to reform the curia but died before he could put them into effect.

1590

1590 The siege of Paris brings hunger and malnutrition that leads to the death of 13,000 in the city.

1591

The Rialto Bridge in Venice is completed, the first bridge ever built across the Grand Canal.

1591

The Songhai Empire of West Africa collapses into more than a dozen warring states after being defeated by Judar Pasha of Morocco at the Battle of Tondibi.

CLEMENT VIII ✠ The 231st Pope 1592–1605

Born Fano, Italy; February 24, 1535

Parents Father, Aldobrandini; Mother, unknown

Papacy January 30, 1592–March 5, 1605

Died Rome, Italy; March 5, 1605

Dedicated, hardworking, and pious, Clement VIII was born Ippolito Aldobrandini. Renowned as an effective, if sometimes ruthless, administrator, Clement might have been a great pope were it not for the series of illnesses that sapped his strength and forced him time and again to put off decisions that urgently needed making.

Ippolito Aldobrandini was born in Fano, but his family came from Florence having been driven into exile by the hostility of the Medici family. Cardinal Alessandro Farnese paid for his education at Padua, Bologna, and Perugia from where he graduated. In the 1550s, he moved to Rome where he was noticed by Pope Pius V who gave him a succession of positions in the papal service before, in 1569, making him auditor of the papal judicial system. In 1571, he was a junior member of a diplomatic mission to France, but did not achieve much.

By securing the succession of Sigismund III of Poland, Aldobrandini helped to bring peace to that country.

Gregory XIII did not give much work to Aldobrandini, though it is not clear why, but Sixtus V did. In 1580, Aldobrandini became a priest and thereafter his rise through the ranks was swift. In 1585, he gained the highly influential position of datary, making him responsible for recommending to the pope who should fill benefices and other positions that were in the gift of the pope. Previous holders had taken the chance to become rich taking bribes, but Aldobrandini remained honest. He became a cardinal priest of San Pancrazio in the same year he took over as Datary. Three years later he went to Poland as legate to try to stop the outbreak of a civil war over the disputed succession to the crown. He managed to persuade Maximillian of Habsburg to give up his claim in favor of Sigismund III and so brought peace.

At the conclave of January 1592 to elect a successor to Innocent IX, King Philip II of Spain again let it be known that he would want the cardinals to select one of a group of men he favored. Of these, Philip's favorite was Giulio Santori. Voting began on 11 January, with one ballot each day. In every vote except one Santori got the most votes, but never the two thirds majority required. On January 29, Cardinal Montalto withdrew his candidacy and declared for Aldobrandini. The other candidates then followed suit being keen to block Santori. On January 30, Aldobrandini was elected and took the name of Clement VIII.

Clement was himself devout. He made confession regularly, led an austere life, and frequently heard mass. Every month he left off papal business to walk on foot around Rome to visit the seven pilgrimage churches and to pray at each. The idea of visiting these seven churches was new, having been introduced by St. Philip Neri only a few years before. St. Philip had devoted much time to helping pilgrims visiting Rome, making it easier for them to find

1592

Japan invades the Korean peninsula, starting a seven year war that would see China taking the Korean side and will end with stalemate.

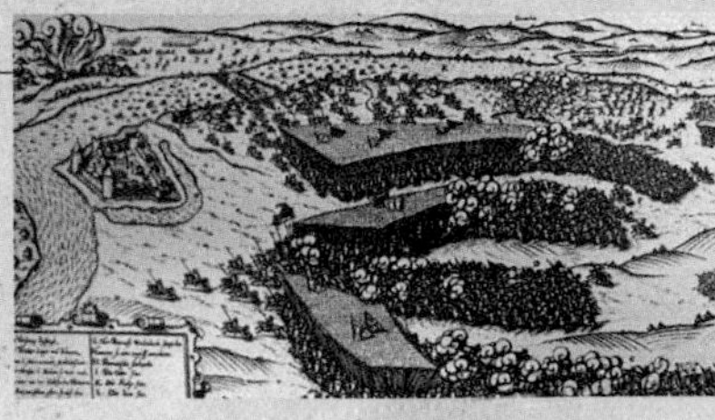

1593

The Ottoman Turks invade Croatia, triggering the Long War between Habsburgs and Ottomans that would last to 1603 and end with the borders roughly where they had begun.

1595

First known performance of a Shakespeare play: Richard II.

lodgings and to find the place of veneration they wished to visit. His innovation of a tour of seven churches in one day was aimed at those pilgrims who had come to Rome without wishing to venerate any one saint in particular. The seven churches were the four patriarchal basilicas of St. Peter's, St. John Lateran, St. Paul Outside the Walls, and Santa Maria Maggiore, plus St. Lawrence Outside the Walls, the Basilica of the Holy Cross in Jerusalem, and the Shrine of Our Lady of Divine Love.

Clement continued to insist on the precepts of the Council of Trent being introduced and was firm on any who demurred. He believed that the monastic orders had not yet been thoroughly reformed and issued a series of edicts to ensure that they were. In 1592, he issued an updated version of the Vulgate Bible, taking into account all the latest developments in biblical scholarship. This "Clementine Bible" remained the authoritative edition in the Catholic Church until the 20th century. Revised editions of the missal, breviary, and pontifical followed. He also revised the Index of Forbidden Books, adding a large number by Jewish writers.

However, Clement was prepared to be flexible when necessary. In 1596, he agreed that Orthodox converts to Catholicism in Poland could keep aspects of their liturgy.

Perhaps the most pressing political problem facing the papacy was the civil war in France. Clement decided to reverse previous policy and come to an accommodation with Henry of Navarre. Although a Protestant throughout his life, Henry had recently become a Catholic and was now accepted by nearly all of his kingdom as King Henry IV. Quite how genuine the conversion might be was open to question. Henry himself had quipped "Paris is worth a mass." But Clement was keen for peace and he had to accept the Edict of Nantes, which granted freedom of worship to the Protestant Huguenots in France but, in return, guaranteed Henry's enduring friendship.

Henry of Navarre was king of France from 1589 to 1610. The first French monarch of the House of Bourbon, he led Protestant forces against the royal army.

When the Este dynasty died out, Henry was instrumental in getting their fief of Ferrara to revert to the papacy rather than passing to some remote cousin, as the Spanish wanted. It proved to be a momentous break between the papacy and Spain. Henceforth, Spanish influence would diminish rapidly.

In 1593, Clement reverted to practice common before the reform movement by promoting two nephews—Cinzio and Pietro—to the rank of cardinal. Then, a few years later, he brought in a grand nephew as a cardinal even though he was only 14 years old.

1597

Christianity is banned in Japan.

1600

The East India Company is founded in England.

1603

Queen Elizabeth I of England dies and is succeeded by King James VI of Scotland, who becomes James I of England and unites the two realms as the United Kingdom.

The Modern Period
17th to 21st Centuries

CHAPTER FIVE

With the upheavals of the Reformation and religious wars behind it, the papacy began to seek a new role and position within Christendom. Although they continued to assert their primacy with undiminished eloquence, the popes came to accept that other Christian denominations were here to stay and sought to establish a working relationship with them pending the day when Christianity could be reunited under the guidance of the bishops of Rome. By the 21st Century, the papacy had lost its temporal power but still sought to give a moral and spiritual lead in Christian countries whenever possible, though sometimes that led the Church into controversy and disputes.

LEO XI  The 232rd Pope 1605

Born Florence, Italy; June 2, 1535

Parents Father, Ottaviano de Medici; Mother, Francesca Salviati

Papacy April 1, 1605–April 27, 1605

Died Rome, Italy; April 27, 1605

Leo earmarked generous funds to be sent to the Holy Roman Emperor Rudolf II (above) to be employed in the continuing war against the Ottoman Turks.

Leo XI died before he could achieve very much as pope, but he had already achieved a good deal as both a servant of the papacy and as a clergyman. Even so, his short reign marked a decisive break with Spain as Leo was elected against the wishes of Philip II.

It is not clear quite how Alessandro Ottaviano de'Medici was related to the branch of the Medici family ruling Florence, but the link was close enough for him to enjoy the favor of his wealthy relatives. By his mother he was also related to Pope Leo X. Alessandro himself wanted to become a priest, but his parents refused and instead got him a job in the Florentine government. Duke Cosimo I of Florence was impressed enough by young Alessandro to make him ambassador to Rome, a position he held for 15 years. In 1573, Gregory XIII made him bishop of Pistoia, but only a year later the archbishopric of Florence fell vacant and Alessandro was moved there. As Archbishop, Alessandro proved to be a supporter of reform who introduced all the rules agreed at the Council of Trent.

After nine years in Florence he moved back to Rome to become cardinal priest of Santi Quirico e Giulitta. As cardinal he promoted the cause of reform and worked closely with the Dominicans to root out heresy.

The Basilica di Santa Maria del Fiore was begun in 1296 in the Gothic style to the design of Arnolfo di Cambio and completed structurally in 1436 with the dome engineered by Filippo Brunelleschi.

From 1596 to 1598, he was papal legate to France and is generally credited with persuading Clement VIII to accept Henry of Navarre, a former Protestant, as king of France. In France, Medici found that his main task was restoring and enforcing some kind of order on the Catholic Church there, where the recent Wars of Religion had wreaked havoc.

In 1600, he was promoted to be cardinal bishop of Albano and two years later was moved to Palestrina, the position he held when the conclave met to elect a successor to Clement VIII. As before, King Philip II of Spain sent a list of cardinals who he supported. Under Clement, however, Spanish influence had reduced so the cardinals felt emboldened to ignore the list completely. Medici was not on the list, but he was elected anyway, probably owing his election to the enthusiastic support of French cardinals.

After his election, Leo XI went to the Lateran plan its redecoration, and while there caught a severe chill. The following week was a whirlwind of activity. He found funds to allow a tax cut in the Papal States, which made him immediately popular in Rome. Among the other matters to get his early attention was a dispute between the bishops and the Jesuits in Spain and the system of voting in conclave. However, his cold was getting worse and before long he was confined to his chambers. He never left, dying just 27 days after being elected.

1606	1606	1607	1611
Dutch sea captain Willem Janszoon makes the first confirmed sighting of Australia by a European.	The English colony of Virginia is granted its first Charter.	The Flight of the Earls. Irish Catholic nationalists the earl of Tyrone and earl of Tyrconnell flee Ireland to avoid arrest by the English.	The Authorized King James Version of the Bible is published in England.

PAUL V ✠ The 233rd Pope 1605–1621

Born Rome, Italy; September 17, 1552

Parents Father, Marcantonio Borghese; Mother, unknown

Papacy May 16, 1605–January 28, 1621

Died Rome, Italy; January 28, 1621

A strange mixture of modern opinions and old fashioned views, Paul V struggled to accept the new reality that Europe was now divided not by a traditional schism of the Church but by division into quite separate Churches. For his family, he as generous as any of the Renaissance popes.

Camillo Borghese was born into the noble Borghese family of Siena, although his lawyer father had moved to Rome some years earlier. When Leo XI died, Borghese was barely known outside of Rome—a fact that helped get him elected as most of the papabili were disapproved of by some faction or monarch.

Taking the name of Paul V, he began by declaring that the rules of the Council of Trent would be firmly applied. Several bishops were in Rome using some pretext or other to be away from their dioceses and close to the seat of ecclesiastical power. Paul summoned them all to an audience, then told them bluntly that they were unwelcome in Rome and had to go home.

The first crisis of Paul's reign came from an unexpected direction. Venice passed a new law forbidding the building of new churches and the granting of land to the Church without permission of the Doge. It then put two priests in front of a secular court on criminal charges. Paul's legal mind was affronted, for canon law held that clerics should be tried in ecclesiastical courts. On December 10, 1605, he demanded the two priests be set free, but Venice refused. He excommunicated the senate of Venice and put the state under an interdict. When Venice threatened to become a Protestant state, King Henry IV of France stepped in to broker a deal. The priests were released, but the laws remained in place.

The next crisis began in England where a group of Catholics tried to murder King James I in the Gunpowder Plot. The government asked English Catholics to take an oath of loyalty to James that included a clause denying the pope's right to depose kings. Paul reacted with a treatise declaring that he did have such a right.

Guy Fawkes and his fellow conspirators in the Gunpowder Plot that was hatched to kill the English king James I.

In Rome, Paul undertook one project of great importance. He repaired the aquaduct built by Trajan in 109 that brought water from Lake Bracciano, 25 miles north of the city, and that had recently become blocked. Not content with merely patching it up, Paul stripped the aquaduct down and rebuilt it in its entirety. The water was fed to numerous fountains in the city, from which the population drew their domestic water supply.

For his family, Paul proved to be as assiduously generous as any of the Renaissance popes. By the time of his death the Borghese were among the richest families in the Papal States. His nephew, Cardinal Scipione Borghese, became rich enough to build the fabulous Villa Borghese.

Paul's insistence that popes had the right to depose kings alienated the new French King Louis XIII. A breach between the papacy and France on the issue was narrowly avoided in 1613.

1613	1616	1618	1620
Algonquian princess Pocahontas converts to Christianity and takes the name "Rebecca."	In England, the traditional figure of Father Winter is renamed Father Christmas for a pageant organized by Ben Johnson for King James I.	The Defenestration of Prague. Angry Protestant noblemen hurl representatives of Catholic emperor Ferdinand II out of a window—an event that leads to the Thirty Years War.	The voyage of the Mayflower carrying Puritan colonists to North America.

GREGORY XV  The 234th Pope 1621–1623

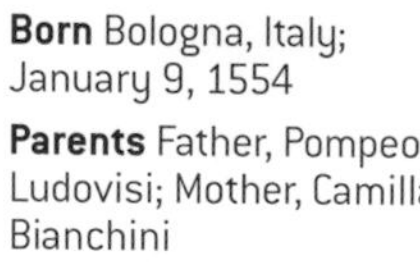

Born Bologna, Italy; January 9, 1554

Parents Father, Pompeo Ludovisi; Mother, Camilla Bianchini

Papacy February 9, 1621–July 8, 1623

Died Rome, Italy; July 8, 1623

Pope Gregory XV was the first pope to have been educated by the Jesuits. He believed that the role of the papacy was to maintain the unity of the Catholic powers so that they could push back the tide of Protestantism that seemed to have been brought to a halt in recent years.

When the 51 cardinals in Rome entered conclave on 8 February, Alessandro Ludovisi was not considered a serious candidate. However, he was well respected by most and objected to by none. He was elected on the second day of the conclave and took the name Gregory XV. However, he was frail and unwell, so he turned to Cardinal Borghese, nephew of Paul V, and to his own nephew Ludovico Ludovisi, who he made a cardinal. Together, the trio ran the papacy for the next two years.

One of Gregory's first actions came in response to widespread criticism of how recent conclaves had been run. To stop outside influences being brought to bear, the conclaves would in future be held behind locked doors with only the cardinals being present and no voting would take place until after the doors were closed. Voting would be by secret written ballot, a process intended to stop cardinals influencing each other unduly. These new rules have remained in force ever since.

Gregory's other important reform was to establish the Sacred Congregation for the Propagation of the Faith in 1622. This body was headed by a committee of cardinals and was in charge of missionary work in both heathen lands and Protestant states. The new organization had a troubled start as until now missionary work had been under the control of secular rulers who did not want to see papal officials interfering, but it soon developed into a powerful organization.

Protestant king Gustavus Adolphus of Sweden won the Battle of Breitenfeld. A legendary tactician, he was the greatest military commander in the Thirty Years War.

The Thirty Years War had begun in 1618 and by the time Gregory took the papal throne was in full swing. The war was a complex conflict that pitched Catholic states against Protestant, but also saw war between those states backing the Habsburg Dynasty against the Bourbons. The fighting devastated Germany and central Europe with entire towns laid waste and some regions suffering a depopulation of 50 percent as the armies looted, raped, and murdered their way across the countryside. Gregory channeled funds to the Catholic League of Holy Roman Emperor Ferdinand II of the Habsburg Dynasty and rejoiced when Protestantism was bloodily expunged from Bohemia.

Medallion depicting the profile of Gregory XV's nephew Ludovico Ludovisi.

1621	1621	1624	1626	1629	1630
The Tamblot Uprising in the Philippines is inspired by a pagan revival against Christianity. It will be violently put down by 1622.	The English settlers of Plymouth Colony sign a peace treaty with Massasoit of the Wampanoags.	Cardinal Richelieu becomes First Minister of France.	Dutch merchant Peter Minuit buys Manhattan Island from the local tribe for trade goods valued at 60 guilders (about 24 US dollars).	Two survivors of the wreck of the Dutch merchant ship *Batavia* opt to stay on shore rather than seek safety in a boat. They thus become the first European settlers in Australia. They are never seen again.	English settlers in North America are shown how to make popcorn by local Quadequine.

URBAN VIII ✠ The 235th Pope 1623–1644

Born Florence, Italy; April 5, 1568

Parents Father, Antonio Barberini; Mother, Camilla Barbadoro

Papacy August 6, 1623–July 29, 1644

Died Rome, Italy; July 29, 1644

Authoritarian, secretive, and competent, Urban VIII made a number of contentious decisions that would have reverberations in the papacy and the wider world for decades to come. Crucially, he withdrew funds for the Catholic army of the Holy Roman emperor Ferdinand II.

Maffeo Berberini was born into a wealthy family that could trace their noble Tuscan pedigree back at least seven centuries. Berberini decided on a career in the law, not the commerce that had made his family's fortune, and studied at Pisa and Rome. When he graduated, he began his career in papal service rising quickly to become governor of Fano in 1592. In 1601, he was sent on a routine mission to France, but got on so well with King Henry IV that he stayed in France and became nuncio in Paris.

Clement VIII made him bishop of Nazareth, an empty title as that town was in the hands of the Turks, but Paul V later made him cardinal priest of San Pietro in Montorio before giving him the real diocese of Spoleto in 1608. In Spoleto, Maffeo proved to be an avid reformer, and to be keen to spend his fabulous wealth on beautifying the town and its churches.

When Gregory XV died there were 54 cardinals in Rome. The following conclave was free of foreign influence and, after 18 days, chose Maffeo, who took the name Urban VIII.

The most immediate issue facing Urban was the Thirty Years War, in which King Gustavus Adolphus of Sweden had intervened to help the Protestants. He chose not to continue to pay for the Catholic army of Holy Roman Emperor Ferdinand II as he was worried about the growth of Habsburg power in Italy. When Duke Vincenzo II of Mantua died without an heir, Urban again snubbed Ferdinand by backing the French claimant, the duke Charles of Nevers who was accepted as Duke of Mantua in 1631. When France joined the Thirty Years War, in 1635, it was in opposition to the Habsburgs and with papal blessing.

When Odoardo Farnese, Duke of the papal fief of Castro, failed to pay his annual tribute in 1641, Urban took the drastic step of depriving him of his lands and titles. Farnese formed an alliance with Venice, Modena, and Tuscany, then invaded the Papal States to deliver a crushing defeat on the papal army. When Urban saw the terms of the peace he had to sign, he fainted.

Within Rome, Urban spent lavishly beautifying the city and improving its defenses. The Castel Sant'Angelo and the new fortress of Castelfranco were given new artillery and bastions. He also spent vast sums to enrich his own family. A brother and two nephews were made cardinals with large incomes while other family members were put into the curia with permission to milk Church funds to their own benefit.

ST. PETER'S BASILICA

Urban VIII consecrated the new Basilica of St. Peter on November 18, 1626. The vast church was 730 feet long, 500 feet wide, and had taken 120 years to build. Even when it was consecrated the building was not completely finished, and various alterations and additions have been made since. Urban hired Gianlorenzo Bernini to complete the internal details, ensuring that the interior of St. Peter's became one of the first and greatest of the Baroque churches of Rome. In 1667, Bernini was to add the great piazza in front of the basilica.

1631	1633	1637	1642	1644
The Sack of Magdeburg in the Thirty Years War shocks Europe and leads to moves to codify warfare to make it less barbaric. At least 20,000 civilians are known to have been killed.	Galileo Galilei is convicted of heresy in Rome for teaching that the Earth orbits about the Sun.	The warship *Sovereign of the Seas* is launched at Woolwich, England. The first ship to carry more than 100 cannon, she will remain in service for 60 years.	Outbreak of civil war in England between King Charles I and his Parliament. The war will later spread to Scotland and Ireland.	The Ming Dynasty in China ends as the country collapses into civil war and foreign invaders sweep down from the north. The northern invaders will found the Qing Dynasty that will survive to 1912.

INNOCENT X ✣ The 236th Pope 1644–1655

Born Rome, Italy; May 6, 1574

Parents Father, Camillo Pamfili; Mother, Flaminia de Bubalis

Papacy September 15 1644–January 7, 1655

Died Rome, Italy; January 7 1655

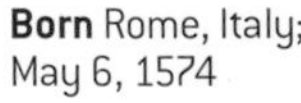

Innocent X was an able politician and fine connoisseur of art, who commissioned the great Diego Velázquez to paint his portrait. What might have been an outstanding papal reign was held back by constant shortages of money and internal disagreements.

Giambetta Pamfili was a papal insider all his life, never straying from papal employment and rarely leaving the Papal States. Like his uncle Giralamo Pamfili, he joined the curia as a lawyer and rose steadily until, in 1625, he served on the staff of Cardinal Francesco Barberini, nephew of Urban VIII, on a diplomatic mission to Spain where he formed a life-long attachment with the Spanish court. Urban raised him to cardinal priest of Sant'Eusebio in 1629.

At some point in his career Pamfili conceived an intense hatred for Urban and his family despite the fact that they had helped his career. This feeling was exacerbated during the conclave following Urban's death when the Barberini hired mercenaries and brought them to Rome to intimidate cardinals into voting for their preferred candidate, Giulio Sacchetti. The conclave saw furious politicking and bribery. Pamfili emerged victorious.

His first move as Pope Innocent X was to launch an attack on the Barberini. That they had helped themselves to vast amounts of money from the Church was no secret, and Innocent lost no time in confiscating all their property and hauling them in front of a commission investigating corruption. Cardinal Mazarin, First Minister of France, stepped in to save the lives of men who had served France well in the past.

Innocent's next move was to lavish gifts and positions on his own relatives. One of these, the widow of his elder brother, was to become notorious. Donna Olimpia Maidalchini was made Princess of San Martino and given a host of lucrative sinecures. She became the pope's chief advisor, moving into his palace and causing gossip about the true nature of their relationship. Her son, Camillo Pamphili, was made a cardinal as were her nephew and cousin.

Innocent did at least limit the number of worthless relatives he raised to high office, preferring to rely on men of talent. Of these the most obviously gifted was Cardinal Fabio Chigi. In 1648, Chigi was sent to represent the papacy in the negotiations that ended the Thirty Years War with the Peace of Westphalia.

Innocent devoted much care to the missions in far flung areas of the globe that were converting heathens to Christianity. The Philippines and China missions both benefited from his attentions. Less happy was his venture into theology. In 1640, Cornelius Jansen had published a study of St. Augustine's teaching on grace and free will that put especial emphasis on faith. The validity of these ideas was hotly debated. Innocent tried to end the debate by condemning Jansen's five central propositions as being heretical, but the arguments he advanced convinced nobody.

By common consent one of the world's supreme masterpieces of portraiture, Velázquez's painting did not at first please the sitter, who described it as "too true."

1645

The turning point in the English Civil War comes at the Battle of Naseby where Parliamentarian Oliver Cromwell defeats King Charles I in a set-piece battle.

1648

The Treaty of Westphalia, actually a series of related and interlocking treaties, ends the Thirty Years War. The Treaty set the political map of Europe that would last to the French Revolution.

1649

King Charles I of England, Scotland and Ireland is beheaded having been found guilty of treason by a tribunal set up by the English Parliament. England becomes a republic. Scotland invites Charles's son, also Charles, to be king.

1650

Charles II arrives in Scotland to claim his kingdom, but is defeated by English armies at the battles of Dunbar and Worcester. He flees abroad having hidden up an oak tree from enemy troopers.

ALEXANDER VII ✠ The 237th Pope 1655–1667

Born Siena, Italy; February 13, 1599

Parents Father, Flavio Chigi; Mother, unknown

Papacy April 7, 1655–May 22, 1667

Died Rome, Italy; May 22, 1667

A deeply scholarly man and an accomplished poet, Alexander VII published works anonymously when pope. His papacy was, however, dominated by relations with France, which culminated in a dispute with Louis XIV that took the Papal States to the brink of war.

The conclave to replace Innocent opened with no obvious leading contender and the cardinals hopelessly divided into a mass of competing and overlapping factions. The secretary of state Fabio Chigi was elected as Alexander VII after a marathon 80-day conclave when the younger cardinals lost patience and demanded an immediate decision, settling on Chigi as the senior cardinal they objected to least.

The conclave began Alexander's troubles for the French never forgave him for having blocked their candidate Giulio Cesare Sacchetti. Cardinal Mazarin, First Minister of France, threw the power and wealth of France behind the junior branches of the Este and Farnese families who were claiming that the papal fiefs their families had held in the past should be restored to them. Mazarin's death in 1661 did nothing to ease the tension.

When a group of boisterous mercenaries in the pay of Alexander shouted abuse at the French ambassador in Rome, King Louis XIV expelled the nuncio in Paris, occupied Avignon and other papal lands in France, and began to mobilize to invade the Papal States. The following Treaty of Pisa, in 1664, brought peace but at the price of Louis gaining the right to appoint anyone he liked to bishoprics and abbacies in France.

More productively, Alexander ended he disputes with Venice that dated back to Paul V and, in 1658, helped to get his old friend Leopold of Austria elected to be Holy Roman Emperor.

In 1656, Alexander stepped in to the theological dispute over the writings of Jansen (*see* p.254). He repeated Innocent's condemnation of Jansen in more convincing terms and insisted that all clergy had to sign a document supporting this position. He also spoke out on Probabilism, the proposition that in difficult moral choices it is permissible to follow a doctrine that is probable even if the opposite is more probable. The Jesuits supported the doctrine, but Alexander opposed it. He stopped short of outright condemnation, instead issuing guidance that seemed to contradict Probabilism.

Alexander's approach to nepotism was restrained. He gave his relatives lucrative positions and well paid jobs, but gave them no real influence over papal affairs.

Bernini's equestrian statue of King Louis XIV in the courtyard of the Louvre Museum in Paris, France.

1654
Parliamentarian general Oliver Cromwell becomes Lord Protector of England, Scotland, and Ireland with powers that are almost dictatorial.

1656
The pendulum clock is invented by Dutch mathematician Christiaan Huygens.

1658
The Taj Mahal is completed in Agra, India.

1660
After the death of Lord Protector Oliver Cromwell, King Charles II returns to Britain to claim the crowns of England, Scotland, and Ireland.

1662
The world's first public bus service opens in Paris.

CLEMENT IX ✠ The 238th Pope 1667–1669

Born Pistoia, Italy; January 28, 1600
Parents Unknown
Papacy June 20, 1667–December 9, 1669
Died Rome, Italy; December 9, 1669

Clement IX took a name associated with peace-making and, indeed, he spent much of his short pontificate ending disputes and quelling crises. When he did seek to make war in an effort to halt the Ottoman invasion of Crete, the intervention ended in disaster.

In 1644, Urban VIII made Giulio Rospigliosi Archbishop of Tarsus, an empty title, and sent him as nuncio to Spain. In 1653, he returned to Rome to become governor of the city before, in 1657, becoming cardinal and taking over papal foreign policy. He managed the difficult task of retaining the good will of both France and Spain, a feat which made him the leading candidate in the conclave of 1667. It nevertheless took 18 days to persuade the 64 cardinals to give him a two thirds majority.

His first task as peacemaker was to end the war between France and Spain, which had begun in 1667 when Louis XIV claimed the Duchies of Limburg and Brabant. The resulting Peace of Aachen was signed in May 1668 and was widely thought to be favorable to Louis, leaving as it did key border fortresses in French hands.

In February 1668, Clement helped the Portuguese gain Spanish recognition of their independence. That allowed him to appoint bishops to the Portuguese sees—something the Spanish had forbidden. The Portuguese Church was thus brought back to order.

Clement then had to turn his attention to the thorny issue of Jansenism. Both Alexander VII and Innocent X had condemned the five central propositions put forward by Cornelius Jansen in his studies of the writings of St. Augustine concerning free will and divine grace. Jansen himself was long dead, but his supporters refused to accept the papal condemnation and continued to look for loopholes. In February 1669, Clement accepted assurances from four French Jansenist bishops that they accepted orthodox teaching, though they avoided accepting the condemnation of Jansen.

Fortifications of Candia (now Heraklion) in Crete. The fortress town fell to the Ottoman Turks in September 1669.

As pope, Clement indulged his love of the arts. He hired Bernini to carve the angels on the Ponte Sant'Angelo and to finish off the facade of St. Peter's. Unlike many popes, he refused to give his relatives lucrative state positions.

The Ottoman Turks had been gradually taking over Crete and, by 1668, only the fortress town of Candia still held out. It was garrisoned by Venetian troops and now Venice appealed to Clement to put together an alliance to save it from the Ottomans. The expedition began well with French, Spanish, and Venetian ships, but bickering among the commanders paralysed the campaign and, in September 1669, Candia fell to the Turks. Clement collapsed when he heard the news and died a few months later.

1668

British buccaneer Henry Morgan leads a mixed force of raiders to capture the city of Panama, loot it, and burn it to the ground.

1668

The British East India Company gains ownership of Bombay, henceforth one of the main centers of British rule in India.

1668

The world's first reflecting telescope is produced by English scientist Isaac Newton.

1670

The Hudson's Bay Company is founded in England to trade with Canada. At first trading in furs, it later turned to retail and is still in business.

CLEMENT X ✢ The 239th Pope 1670–1676

Born Rome, Italy; July 13 1590

Parents Father, Lorenzo Altieri; Mother, Victoria Delphini

Papacy April 29, 1670–July 22, 1676

Died Rome, Italy; July 22, 1676

Clement X was already old when he became pope and many thought that he would be weak. In the face of much pressure, he sought to maintain the papacy's traditional privileges and powers, and became notable for the number of saints he canonized.

Emilio Altieri was born into a rich and noble family. He studied law in Rome, gaining his doctorate in 1611 and practicing law for 13 years before he became a priest and entered papal service. He spent three years in Poland on the staff of the nuncio, then spent 27 years as bishop of Camerino. In 1669, Clement IX made the 79 year old Altieri a cardinal, apparently in thanks for long service to the Church.

Altieri thus entered the conclave of 1669 with no hopes of being elected pope. The 62 cardinals in conclave could not, however, agree on a successor. After nearly five months they agreed to choose an elderly cardinal as the next pope in the expectation that before too long there would another election. They chose Altieri, who took the name of Clement X to honor the pope who had raised him to cardinal.

Clement X was well aware of his physical frailty and was daunted by the long hours of concentration needed to deal with the papal workload. He therefore chose for high office Cardinal Paluzzi degli Albertoni. Paluzzi's nephew had married Altieri's neice, so the two were linked by marriage and had got on well in the past. Paluzzi used the excuse of Clement's undoubted frailty to restrict access to the pope. Only those whom he favored or who handed over bribes were allowed to see Clement, and he almost certainly held back documents he did not want the pope to see. While Clement himself did not give his family undue wealth or office, Paluzzi did.

In 1672, the Turks invaded Poland and Clement's old friends appealed to him for help. Clement was unable to put together an old-style crusade, but did send funds to aid the leading Polish general John Sobieski. The Turks were crushed and, when King Michael died in 1674, Sobieski was elected King of Poland.

Clement's dealings with Louis XIV of France were less successful. Louis told Clement that he was intending to invade the Protestant Netherlands to restore the true faith, and so gained Papal support. Spain launched objections on the grounds that the Netherlands were really Spanish property, but Clement ignored them. Louis attacked in 1674, but his first move was to annex Austrian-owned Franche Comte. Clement realized Louis was set on aggrandizing France and sent legates to try to broker peace, but Louis ignored them.

In 1675, Louis announced that the King of France had the absolute right to appoint anyone he liked to ecclesiastical office, and to the administer vacant positions. Clement was still considering how to react to the flagrant attack on papal power when he died.

General John Sobieski was elected as king of Poland in 1674 after he successfully defended his country against Turkish invaders.

1672

The Eastern Orthodox Church holds the Synod of Jerusalem to discuss, and finally condemn, the theological ideas of the European Reformation.

1674

Father Jacques Marquette founds a mission to convert the Iroquois people. The station grows steadily and is now the city of Chicago.

1675

Outbreak of King Philip's War, fought between British colonists in North America and the Wampanoag, Nipmuck, Podunk, Narragansett, and Nashaway peoples. After four years fighting, the war ends with the virtual extermination of the native tribes.

INNOCENT XI ✠ The 240th Pope 1676–1689

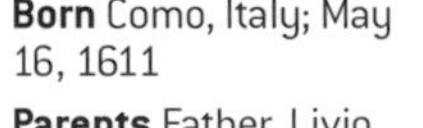

Born Como, Italy; May 16, 1611

Parents Father, Livio Odescalchi; Mother, Paola Castelli Giovanelli

Papacy September 21, 1676 to August 12, 1689

Died Rome, Italy; August 12, 1689

Innocent XI is widely recognized as having been the outstanding pope of the 17th century. At a time when papal power and influence was on the wane, he managed to stand firm and left the papacy in a far better condition than he found it. Innocent initiated the Holy League in defense of Vienna, which was being besieged by the Ottoman Turks.

The Odescalchi were among the lower nobility of northern Italy when Benedetto was born, but they were more famous for the success they had in commerce than for their ancient lineage. At the age of 15, Benedetto left home to work in a bank in Genoa, but he soon left to study law in Rome and, in 1639, entered papal service. He rose rapidly as his legal and financial talents were recognized and put to work. Innocent X made him a cardinal in 1645, and five years later he became Bishop of Novara. He had already earned a reputation for personal piety, and in Novara astonished the locals not only by his austere lifestyle, but also by the way he spent nearly the entire episcopal income on caring for the poor. In 1654, poor health made him return to Rome where he spent his days in quiet study and occasional forays into curia duties.

The Battle of Vienna in 1683 was a turning point in the history of Europe, as the Ottoman Turks were defeated by a Christian alliance organized by Pope Innocent XI.

Benedetto had been briefly considered for election in the conclave of 1670, but the French cardinals had been instructed by King Louis XIV to veto his candidacy because he was considered to be too friendly to the Spanish. Benedetto himself expected the veto to be repeated but, as the 67 cardinals gathered in conclave, it was revealed that no such veto had come from Paris. Nevertheless the first ballot revealed no fewer than 14 cardinals getting votes, and a long conclave was expected. So it proved.

By mid September, most cardinals were abstaining—waiting to see if any of the four candidates left in contention gained an advantage. On September 21, Benedetto was suddenly surrounded by a group of the abstaining cardinals who hailed him as pope and fell to their knees kissing his ring. The other cardinals followed suit. Benedetto was taken by surprise. He declared that he would not accept office unless the cardinals swore to uphold a 14-point plan for reform of the Church that had been under discussion. They agreed, so he took the name of Innocent XI to honor the pope who had raised him to be cardinal.

When he became pope, Innocent inherited a dispute with Louis XIV of France, who had claimed to have the absolute right to appoint candidates to ecclesiastical office. Innocent began by forcefully telling Louis that he had no such right. Louis responded by summoning a council of French clergy, which obediently passed the Four Gallican Articles. These stated that the pope had authority in spiritual matters, not secular; that the pope was subject to canon law; that the pope's authority was subject to General Councils; and that, while the pope may advise in matters of faith, it was up to bishops and others in authority to interpret that advice.

1678

In England, Titus Oates makes allegations of a widespread Catholic conspiracy to overthrow the government. The allegations would be believed for the next three years, leading to the execution of 15 men and the banning Catholics from Parliament.

1680

The Great Comet is seen. Now designated C/1680 V1 it was so bright it could be seen in daytime and had a tail that stretch half way across the night sky.

EXPOSICION
ASTRONOMICA
DE EL COMETA,

1681

The dodo goes extinct.

Guy Tachard, with Siamese envoys, translating a letter from king Narai of Siam to Pope Innocent XI in December 1688.

Innocent reacted to this blatant threat to the powers of the papacy by refusing to appoint anyone to any senior French positions that fell vacant—with the result that, by 1688, a total of 35 sees had no bishop.

Louis tried to mollify Innocent by passing increasingly strict laws against the French Protestants, or Huguenots, but Innocent actually objected to Louis's use of violence. In 1687, Innocent refused to accept a new French ambassador to Rome and, in January 1688, wrote Louis a confidential note telling him that he was about to be excommunicated.

The final break came over the archbishopric of Cologne, which was not only a rich diocese but also an influential semi-independent state within the Holy Roman Empire. There were two candidates in the election of 1688, one French the other German. Louis supported the Frenchman, but as it happened neither man got the required two thirds majority. The electors deferred to Innocent, who chose the German. Louis reacted by occupying Avignon and other papal territories within France. The dispute was still ongoing when Innocent died.

King Louis XIV of France continued to clash with the papacy during the reign of Innocent XI and invaded papal territory in France.

Intractable as the French problem was, it was not the only issue confronting Innocent. In 1683 King Charles II of Britain died, leaving the throne to his Catholic brother James II. Innocent rejoiced that Catholics in England, Scotland, and Ireland would no longer be persecuted. But soon Innocent became uneasy. James began to pursue a policy of restoring Catholicism as the state religion and of making himself an absolute monarch in imitation of Louis XIV. The exact nature of the letters sent from Innocent to James is unclear, but certainly Innocent wanted James to moderate his policies. James, however, pushed ahead and, in 1688, was ousted from his thrones by what became known as the Glorious Revolution. Even worse, from Innocent's point of view, the new British monarchs were the staunchly Protestant William and Mary.

Disturbing as these events were, the great crisis for Innocent came in the Balkans. For three years it had been clear that the Ottoman Turks had been preparing for a major military campaign. In March 1683, Mehmet IV launched his army of 150,000 men and 130 cannon against the city of Vienna. Innocent realized the great importance of the campaign. If Vienna fell, all of central Europe would be open to the Turks. He worked to persuade the monarchs of Europe that the Turkish threat was so great that they must put aside their own differences.

Poland, Lithuania, the Holy Roman Empire, Bavaria, Saxony, Franconia, Hungary, and Swabia responded. On September 11, as Vienna was on the point of surrender, the 80,000-strong allied army swept down on the Turks. After an exhausting 12 hour battle the Christians were triumphant while 60,000 Turks were dead or taken prisoner. Never again would the Ottomans be able to mount such a large expedition and soon the Turkish Empire was in decline. European Christianity was safe. It was Innocent's greatest success.

1681

In England, Titus Oates is unmasked as a fraud who had invented the tale of a Catholic plot. He is sentence to be whipped through the streets of London five days a year for the remainder of his life.

1684

The Great Frost. For the first three months of the year, most of northern Europe remains beneath freezing even at mid-day. The sea off Kent is frozen for up to 2 miles from the coast.

1686

New York City receives its first charter.

ALEXANDER VIII  The 241st Pope 1689–1691

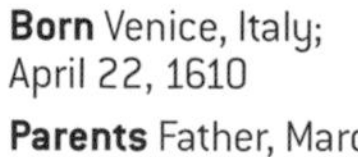

Born Venice, Italy; April 22, 1610

Parents Father, Marco Ottoboni; Mother, unknown

Papacy October 6, 1689–February 1, 1691

Died Rome, Italy; February 1, 1691

Pietro Ottoboni was born into a wealthy Venetian merchant family that had recently been ennobled. His father was grand chancellor of Venice and other relatives held senior government positions. He graduated in law then went to Rome and joined the papal service.

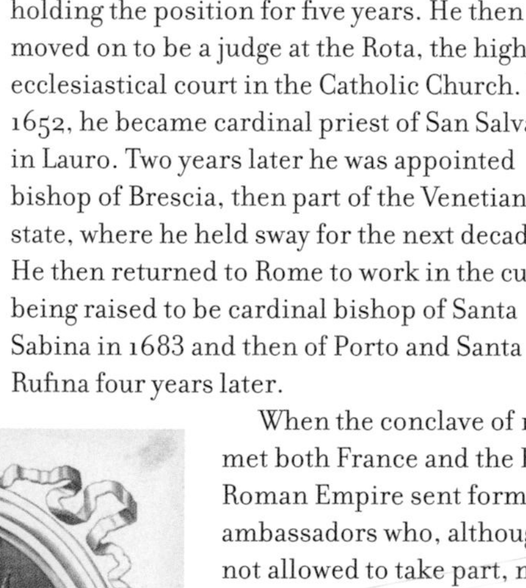

Ottoboni's rise was rapid, serving in turn as governor of Terni, Rieti, and Spoleto before becoming governor of Rome itself in 1638 and holding the position for five years. He then moved on to be a judge at the Rota, the highest ecclesiastical court in the Catholic Church. In 1652, he became cardinal priest of San Salvatore in Lauro. Two years later he was appointed bishop of Brescia, then part of the Venetian state, where he held sway for the next decade. He then returned to Rome to work in the curia, being raised to be cardinal bishop of Santa Sabina in 1683 and then of Porto and Santa Rufina four years later.

When the conclave of 1689 met both France and the Holy Roman Empire sent formal ambassadors who, although not allowed to take part, made it their business to represent the views of their monarchs. The innovation would last for some years. In fact, the Italian and Spanish cardinals had already decided that they wanted Ottoboni to be pope and when the French agreed the Germans fell into line. Ottoboni was elected and took the name of Alexander VIII.

Alexander's first task was to try to heal the breach with Louis XIV of France. Both men wanted to come to an agreement. Louis restored Avignon and the other papal possessions, while Alexander accepted the ambassador rejected by Innocent XI and raised to the rank of cardinal nominations from Louis. But when Louis put forward to be a bishop a man central to the adoption of the Four Gallican Articles (*see* p.258), Alexander vetoed him and the dispute broke out afresh.

Although the Ottoman Turks had been driven back from the gates of Vienna with heavy loss (*see* p.258), they still ruled large Christian populations in the Balkans. Alexander removed from the Holy Roman Empire and Poland the subsidies that Innocent had sent them to pay for their armies to campaign against the Turks. Instead, he sent the money to his native Venice to pay for a fleet to take the war to the coastal regions of the Ottoman Empire. Emperor Leopold I was understandably annoyed and relations between papacy and empire cooled.

In Rome, Alexander cut several taxes and threw lavish public entertainments, which assured his popularity. Unlike recent popes, he returned to the practice of nepotism, raising a nephew to be cardinal and giving dozens of other relatives highly paid and influential positions in both the Church and the government of the Papal States. He was also an assiduous defender of orthodox faith. He firmly condemned two propositions popular with the Jesuits concerning "philosophic sin," an act that was morally bad but not offensive to God.

Leopold I was the Holy Roman emperor, king of Hungary, and king of Bohemia. Relations between the emperor and papacy cooled markedly during the reign of Pope Alexander VIII.

1689

The Boston Revolt. The citizens of Boston, Massachusetts, rise against unpopular governor Edmund Andros and force his removal from office.

1689

The Jacobite Rising of '89 sees several Highland clans of Scotland rebel in support of exiled King James VII of Scotland. They are led by the charismatic Viscount John of Dundee, but the rising collapses after his death in battle.

1689

Tsar Peter the Great orders the construction of the Great Siberian Road from Moscow to Peking. Delays, cost escalation, and wars slow construction so that the road takes more than a century to complete.

INNOCENT XII ✠ The 242nd Pope 1691–1700

Born Spinassola, Italy, March 13, 1615

Parents Unknown

Papacy July 12, 1691–September 27, 1700

Died Rome, Italy; September 27, 1700

Statue of Charles II of Spain in Madrid. Charles was the last Habsburg ruler of Spain.

At a time when the papacy's fortunes were declining in terms of influence and of wealth, Innocent XII introduced much needed reforms to enable the papacy to face a changing world, often against the wishes of those in the Church who refused to accept reality.

Antonio Pignatelli, archbishop of Naples, took part in the conclave of 1689 but was not a candidate. He was not seriously considered when the 1691 conclave began either. However, after five months of deadlock between the factions of cardinals, the people of Rome began noisy protests, so the elderly Pignatelli was chosen as a compromise and took the name Innocent XII to honor the pope who raised him to be a cardinal.

Innocent recognized at once that the papacy could no longer rely on a steady flow of funds from across Europe. The Reformation had blocked many income streams, and even Catholic monarchs were finding ways to keep Church money within their own borders. Innocent tackled the growing financial crisis by both cutting expenditure and boosting income from the Papal States. He enlarged and modernized the port facilities at Nettuno and Civitavecchia to boost trade, which could be taxed, and drastically reduced the costs of the papal court.

Innocent also moved to reduce corruption, though the cost-benefit balance of this was open to doubt. On the one hand, he established new rules that forbade himself and future popes from giving jobs to relatives, although he did allow one relative to be made a cardinal to act as the pope's personal helper. Numerous jobs that carried lucrative salaries but non-existent duties were axed. On the other hand, he forbade jobs to be sold, which reduced papal income. Many cardinals and curia officials refused to accept the measures were needed, but Innocent pushed them through.

The dispute with France that Innocent inherited was brought to a messy conclusion in 1693. Louis XIV of France had tried to conquer the Palatinate on France's eastern border, but had been faced by a Grand Alliance of Britain, Spain, Austria, Portugal, the Holy Roman Empire, and a host of smaller states. Needing support wherever he could find it, Louis agreed to revoke the Gallican Articles (*see* p.258), ratify episcopal appointments made by the papacy, and to back down on a host of other issues. Innocent, on the other hand, had to accept that, in future, the king of France would appoint bishops and archbishops.

A sign of the diminishing prestige of the papacy came when no papal legate was invited to attend the peace negotiations between France and the Grand Alliance. Innocent sent one anyway and was thus able to get inserted into the Treaty of Ryswick a clause guaranteeing freedom of worship to Catholics in Protestant realms in Germany.

In 1699, the heir to King Charles II of Spain suddenly died. Among the assorted cousins who declared that they were now the heir were Charles of Austria of the Habsburg Dynasty and Philip of Anjou, a grandson of Louis XIV of France. After some thought, Innocent declared for Philip, whereupon Charles II appointed Philip his heir.

1691	1692	1692	1694	1697
China conquers Mongolia.	The Salem Witch Trials take place in the British colony of Massachusetts, during which 19 people were hanged.	The Massacre of Glencoe sees the Campbell Clan use an order of King William III as an excuse to slaughter their rivals the MacDonalds of Glencoe. In all 38 were killed, with another 40 or so dying of exposure as they fled into the winter snows.	The Bank of England is founded. It is the first central state bank in the modern sense of the word and later forms the model for all such banks.	French author and folklorist Charles Perrault publishes his collection of fairy stories that includes classics as *Sleeping Beauty* and *Little Red Riding Hood*.

CLEMENT XI  The 243rd Pope 1700–1721

Born Urbino, Italy; July 23, 1649

Parents Father, Annibale Albini; Mother, unknown

Papacy November 23, 1700–March 19, 1721

Died Rome, Italy; March 19, 1721

The weaknesses of the papacy against which Innocent XII had warned were cruelly exposed during the reign of Clement XI. The pontiff in part redeemed his time by hard work, personal piety, and a keen awareness of what was possible for him to achieve but, in truth, his attempts at wielding political influence in a rapidly changing world were largely ignored.

Giovanni Francesco Albani was born into a family of minor nobility with a long history of distinguished military service for both the papacy and anyone who would pay them. He himself had more interest in law and philosophy, being educated in Rome at the academy of the exiled Queen Christina of Sweden. He joined the curia as soon as his education was complete and rose steadily. In the 1680s he served as governor of Rieti, then of his native Urbino. Alexander VIII made him cardinal deacon of S. Maria in Aquiro in 1690.

Philip V of Spain was the grandson of Louis XIV of France.

One of the last acts of Innocent XII had been to declare for Philip of Anjou, the French claimant for the Spanish crown. It was clear that other European states would oppose the move, probably by war. Knowing that the various monarchs would want a new pope who favored their position, the cardinals gathering for conclave feared they would come under pressure from their home governments. They thus decided to act quickly, abandoning factions and intrigues to appoint a man not closely identified to any faction and possessed of charm and tact. They chose Albani.

In other circumstance the fact that Albani was not a priest, still less a bishop, would have ruled him out, but not with a major European war imminent. He was hurriedly ordained a priest, celebrated his first mass a couple of hours later, and the next day declared to be a bishop, swiftly followed by his consecration as pope under the name Clement XI.

War was, indeed, approaching fast. Most European powers wanted to stop the aggressive King Louis XIV of the Bourbon dynasty putting his grandson on to the throne of Spain. Holy Roman Emperor Leopold I of the Habsburgs had his own candidate, his younger son Charles. Other possible candidates were brushed aside as the various states and monarchs of Europe declared for either Philip or Charles.

In the event, Philip got to Spain first and was acknowledged as their monarch by the Spanish nobles. Clement XI wrote to the two claimants offering to mediate, but was ignored. In 1701, Elector Frederick III of Prussia declared himself to be a king, a move that needed papal sanction. Clement wrote asking him to justify his claim but, again, was ignored. The monarchs of Europe had other concerns for, in the summer of 1701, an Austrian army led by Eugene of Savoy

1701

In Britain Jethro Tull invents a machine to place seeds in holes drilled in the soil. This seed drill starts the agricultural revolution that massively increases the amount of food that can be grown.

1703

The Great Storm. A powerful storm sweeps across northern France and southern England killing an estimated 8,000 people.

1704

The Battle of Blenheim sees an Anglo-Austrian army under the Duke of Marlborough decisively defeat a Franco-Bavarian army.

marched into Milan, which was then a Spanish possession, to enforce the rule of Charles. The Spanish garrison put up a token resistance, but the first shots had been fired. Within months France and Spain were at war with Britain, the Netherlands, Savoy, the Holy Roman Empire, most German states, and Portugal. Saxony later joined France. For the next 13 years war raged across much of Europe.

Clement soon found himself put into an awkward corner. Sicily and Naples were papal fiefs that for many years had been self-governing kingdoms within the Spanish empire. Philip and Charles both demanded that Clement appoint them king of Sicily and king of Naples. Clement delayed making a decision and kept the kingdoms under his own eye. In 1709, a large army loyal to Charles marched south from Austria, overran the Papal States, conquered Naples, and marched on Rome itself. Clement was told that unless he immediately gave Naples and Sicily to Charles and recognized Charles as King of Spain the German troops would be let loose to pillage and plunder Rome. Clement accepted the inevitable and declared for Charles, though under protest.

The Italian campaign was but one among several successful campaigns being carried out for Charles Habsburg. By 1713, France and Spain were financially exhausted and militarily defeated. The belligerents met in Utrecht to negotiate peace. Clement was not invited to attend the talks, nor was his legate treated with much respect. The papacy was becoming irrelevant to European diplomacy.

The resulting Treaty of Utrecht was a blow to Clement. Philip was allowed to remain king of Spain, but on condition he lost all his European possessions outside Spain itself. In the resulting carve up of territories, Clement was ignored and his overlordship of various Italian lands simply brushed aside. Sicily was given to Savoy and Naples to Austria without Clement being consulted, while Parma and Piacenza went to the Farnese dynasty. In 1715, Clement published a bull which clearly set out his rights to these territories and annulled the provisions of the Treaty of Utrecht. Nobody paid the slightest bit of attention.

Although the papacy had effectively lost all political and diplomatic power, it was still highly regarded in religious matters. Clement was called upon to settle two major disputes. In 1705, the old issue of the five propositions of Cornelius Jansen (*see* p.254) erupted again when the Sorbonne University in Paris declared that it was possible to condemn the five propositions without condemning the writings of Jansen in which they occurred. Clement contradicted the Sorbonne in 1708 and, in 1713, issued the bull *Unigenitus* in which he forthrightly condemned the writings of Pasquier Quesnel, the leading supporter of Jansenist ideas.

The second religious issue concerned the Chinese Rites. Jesuit missionaries active in China allowed converts to Christianity to continue to make offerings to ancestral spirits and to the Chinese emperor as well as to join in popular festivals celebrating the sage Confucius. However, Dominican missionaries in China viewed these activities as pagan worship and idolatry. The Dominicans asked Clement for a ruling. In 1715, he issued the bull *Ex illa die*, which banned Christians from taking part in the Chinese Rites. When the news reached China the Emperor Kangxi banned all Christian missionaries from his domains.

In 1708, Clement made the Feast of the Immaculate Conception of the Blessed Virgin Mary obligatory, though he stopped short of making the teaching on which it was based Catholic dogma.

Ancestor worship by Christians in China, which was championed by the sage Confucius, was banned by Clement XI. In response, the Chinese emperor banned all Christian missionaries from his domains.

1707

England and Scotland, which have had the same monarch since 1603, formally unite into a single state.

1709

In England, Abraham Derby successfully produces cast iron using coke instead of the more expensive charcoal. The price of iron plummets, making possible the later industrial revolution.

1717

First known attack by the pirate Edward Teach, who would later gain fame by his nickname Blackbeard.

1720

The South Sea Bubble stock market crash occurs in Britain, reducing hundreds to poverty.

INNOCENT XIII ✠ The 244th Pope 1721–1724

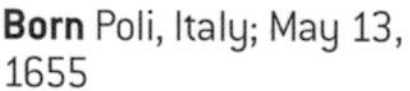

Born Poli, Italy; May 13, 1655

Parents Father, Duke Carlo of Poli; Mother, unknown

Papacy May 8, 1721–March 7, 1724

Died Rome, Italy; March 7, 1724

Innocent made his main mission as pontiff reducing tensions with the Catholic powers left over from the War of the Spanish Succession, though he was not shy of increasing tensions with Protestant monarchs, notably King George I of Great Britain.

The family from which Michelangelo dei Conti sprang had already provided two popes—Gregory IX and Alexander IV—as well as numerous officials in the curia and other papal servants. He himself decided on a Church career when still young and first attracted notice as nuncio to Switzerland in 1695, moving to Portugal in 1698 where he stayed for the next nine years. In 1706, he became cardinal priest of Santi Quirico e Giulitta, taking the see of Osimo. He was moved to Viterbo in 1712 and returned to Rome in 1719.

The conclave of 1721 was widely expected to elect Fabrizio Paolucci. However, Cardinal Althan announced that Emperor Charles VI vetoed Paolucci. The veto had no legal force but the views of major monarchs were routinely taken into account at conclaves, so Paolucci was forced to withdraw. After five weeks, Conti was elected as Innocent XIII.

Within days, Innocent made peace with Charles VI by officially endorsing his takeover of Naples and Sicily, both papal fiefs that were in the gift of the pope. In 1722, tension with Charles rose again when Charles pressured the childless Antonio Farnese, Duke of Parma and Piacenza, to make the Bourbon Spanish prince Don Carlos his heir, instead of handing his lands back to the pope as should have occurred.

Innocent soon learned that the Jesuits had not complied with Clement's instructions regarding integrating local pagan customs into Christian life, an issue known as Chinese Rites (*see* p.265).

Osimo Cathedral. In 1706, Clement XI made Conti cardinal priest of Santi Quirico e Giulitta, giving him the see of Osimo.

He banned the Jesuits from accepting new members until they obeyed papal instructions. He also confirmed Clement's bull *Unigenitus*, condemning the teachings of Jansen (*see* p.254) and wrote to King Louis XV of France asking him to take action against seven French bishops who persisted in supporting the banned teachings.

The crown of Britain at this point had recently passed to King George I of Hanover. The British Parliament had chosen George because of his Protestant religion and willingness to accept the democratic constitution of the country, passing over the claims of James Stuart, a Catholic who favored absolute monarchy. Innocent declared that James was more closely related to the former monarch, Anne, and so should be king of Britain. He gave James a good income and encouraged him to seek support among Catholic monarchs for a bid for power.

The tomb of Cardinal Guillaume Dubois in the Church of St. Roch, Paris. Innocent XII built bridges with France by raising Dubois to the rank of cardinal. Dubois had been refused the honor by Clement XI on account of his well known corrupt activity.

1721	1722	1725
Peter the Great replaces his ancestral title of Tsar of Russia with the new title Tsar of all the Russias, thus founding the Russian Empire and claiming ownership over all areas where Russian is spoken.	Death of Emperor Kangxi of China's Qing Dynasty after a reign of 61 years, the longest in Chinese history.	A boy aged about 10 is found living wild in woods near Hamelin. He runs on all fours, eats berries and small animals, and speaks no language. Dubbed "Peter the Wild Boy" he proved to be mentally handicapped but lived another 60 years.

BENEDICT XIII ✠ The 245th Pope 1724–1730

Born Gravina, Italy; February 2, 1650

Parents Father, Duke Fernando Orsini of Gravina; Mother, Giovanna Frangipani della Tolfa

Papacy May 29, 1724–February 21, 1730

Died Rome, Italy; February 21, 1730

Simple, pious, and dedicated to the Church, Benedict XIII worked relentlessly for the good of his flock and his city, but his inability to recognize duplicity in others, most notably his secretary Niccolo Coscia, led him into scandals and disasters.

Pietro Francesco Orsini was born the eldest son and heir of the powerful Neapolitan nobleman Fernando of Gravina, a member of the ancient Orsini family of Rome. From birth he was groomed to take over his father's titles and estates, so it came as a shock to the Orisini when he announced as a teenager that he wanted to become a Benedictine monk. After furious arguments, Pietro got his way and entered the Order under the name of Vincenzo Maria.

In 1672, Clement X raised Vincenzo to be cardinal priest of San Sisto, but Vincenzo refused. Clement then talked to the head of the Benedictines who ordered Vincenzo to accept. Vincenzo was then sent to be bishop of Manfredonia before, in 1686, being promoted to be archbishop of Benevento. In that town Vincenzo found happiness, devoting himself to pastoral care and the writing of theological tracts. He left most of the administration of the archdiocese to his secretary, the talented, clever, but dishonest Niccolo Coscia.

The conclave of 1724 was, as was usual at this date, split. After more than two months the cardinals compromised by choosing an elderly cardinal not linked to any faction and so elected Vincenzo. Once again, Vincenzo refused his elevation, giving way only when ordered to do so by the head of the Benedictines and on being told he could remain archbishop of Benevento. He took the name Benedict XIV, but changed it to Benedict XIII on realizing that the previous Benedict XIII had been an antipope.

As had been his habit in Benevento, Benedict left the administration to Niccolo Coscia, who was promoted to be a cardinal to better fit him for his elevated duties in Rome. That left Benedict free to deal with what he saw as the more important pastoral duties of the bishop of Rome. He consecrated new altars and chapels with zeal, visited the sick, administered the sacraments, and taught students. He spent much effort cutting back on papal ritual, encouraging the cardinals to do likewise, and frequently launched diatribes against cardinals who wore expensive clothes or cut their beards in fashionable styles.

Meanwhile Coscia, just as he had in Benevento, set about diverting Church funds into his own hands and those of his family. As each senior position in the curia fell vacant, Coscia brought henchmen from Benevento to fill them. He even persuaded Benedict to make a relative Secretary of State over the protests of the cardinals. Coscia also took bribes, often of astonishing size. Duke Victor Amadeus II of Savoy and Sardinia, for instance, handed over a fortune in gold in 1725 to be granted the title "King of Sardinia," the later kings of Italy taking their royal status from him.

Circumstances conspired so that Benedict had the job of appointing 139 bishops during his time as pope. As a consequence, around 90 percent of all bishops in the Catholic Church today can trace their episcopal lineage back to Benedict XIII.

1726

Muhammad bin Saud establishes the Saudi dynasty by taking over the government of al-Diriyah.

1728

The Battle of Palkhed sees the Maratha ruler Baji Rao I defeat the Mughal Nizam-ul-Mulk, effectively ending Mughal rule in southern India though lip service is still paid to Mughal sovereignty.

1729

In North America, Baltimore is founded.

CLEMENT XII ✠ The 246th Pope 1730–1740

Born Florence, Italy; April 7, 1652

Parents Father, Marquis Bartolomeo Corsini of Casigliano; Mother, Isabella Strozzi

Papacy July 12, 1730–February 6, 1740

Died February 6, 1740

Already aged 78 when he came to the papal throne, Clement found that his years in power were dominated by financial problems. The situation was not helped by his insistence on continuing the papal tradition of beautifying Rome with elaborate, and expensive, building works.

Lorenzo Corsini was born into wealth and privilege to a Florentine noble family that prided itself on its artistic taste and patronage. For ten years he was papal treasurer, allowing him to see at first hand the parlous state of the papal finances. In 1706, he became cardinal priest of San Pietro in Vincoli and later was promoted to be cardinal bishop of Frascati.

Corsini was considered as a possible pope at the conclaves of 1721 and 1724, and was again in 1730. This time he was successful, though not before the conclave had dragged on for five months and almost half the cardinals had been put forward as candidates.

Taking the name of Clement XII, Corsini's first move was to order the arrest of Niccolo Coscia, the corrupt official who had effectively run the papacy under Benedict XIII. Found guilty of corruption, Coscia was sentenced to ten years in prison but persuaded Clement to commute the sentence to a fine and was soon at large. Clement's second act was to promote to the rank of cardinal his nephew Neri Corsini. Fears that this heralded a return to the bad old days of nepotism proved ill founded as no other members of the Corsini family were given important jobs.

Clement's most important task was to tackle the financial problems of the papacy. He placed restrictions on the export of valuables, imposed taxes on imports, introduced a state lottery, and began printing paper money. A more practical measure was to turn Ancona into a free port to encourage trade and commerce. He also restricted the incomes of the cardinals and other officials. However, nothing could make up for the decline in revenues reaching Rome from other Catholic countries. Also, he spent an enormous amount on improvements to Rome: the facade of St. John Lateran is his work, as is the magnificent Trevi Fountain.

On the international stage, Clement was ignored by the great powers. In 1737, the direct line of the Medici, Grand Dukes of Tuscany, died out. It should have been up to the pope to decide on the fate of Tuscany, but Spain, France, and Austria instead agreed it should go to Francis Stephen who had lost his duchy in the War of the Polish Succession.

In ecclesiastical matters, Clement supported the ban on Chinese Rites (*see* p.263) and condemned freemasonry, but otherwise took little action.

The Trevi Fountain was commissioned by Clement XII.

1732

The British colony of Georgia is founded in North America.

1735

British meteorologist George Hadley publishes a treatise that explains how the trade winds operate, and lays the ground for later understanding of global weather systems.

1737

An earthquake in Calcutta, India, kills an estimated 300,000—the second-largest earthquake toll in history.

1738

British religious leader John Wesley undergoes a religious experience that leads him to found the Methodist movement.

BENEDICT XIV  The 247th Pope 1740–1758

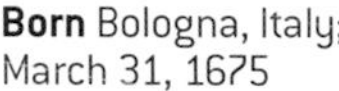

Born Bologna, Italy; March 31, 1675

Parents Father, Marcello Lambertini; Mother, Lucretia Bulgarini

Papacy August 17, 1740–May 3, 1758

Died Rome, Italy; May 3, 1758

In some ways the first of the modern popes, Benedict XIV used his long papacy to introduce a wide range of necessary reforms, accepted the world as it was, and settled many of the disputes in which the papacy had become embroiled.

Prospero Lorenzo Lambertini was born into a junior branch of a noble family, but one without much money. He was sent to Rome to be educated in law and theology, showing great academic talent and a deep interest in history. From college he moved straight into the curia. In 1708, he became Promoter of the Faith, a position he held for the next 19 years. His task was to test the claims of candidates for sainthood, the job being informally known as "Devil's Advocate." Annoyed by the lax standards of applications and past decisions, Lambertini wrote a treatise setting out guidance on good practice that remains the basis of the process of canonization to this day.

In 1727, Lambertini became archbishop of Ancona and cardinal priest of Santa Croce in Gerusalemme (below) the following year. In 1731, he became Archbishop of Bologna, his home town.

When the conclave of 1740 began Lambertini, like everyone else, expected Pietro Ottoboni to be elected Pope, but Ottoboni died just days after the conclave began. For the next six months, the cardinals remained unable to reach a decision, fearing to offend one or other of the great Catholic monarchs. They chose Lambertini as he had never traveled outside Italy and so could not have given offence to any foreign ruler.

Like his immediate predecessors, Benedict faced serious financial problems. He slashed the papal military budget, not only cutting the armed forces but also allowing key fortresses to fall into decay. He continued the process of reducing the number and salaries of papal servants and officials.

Keen to get on good terms with the Catholic monarchs of Europe, Benedict agreed concordats with the rulers of Spain, Portugal, Austria, Sardinia, Sicily, and Milan. He signed away many rights, including that of appointing bishops. He was widely criticized in the Church for this but was merely being realistic by accepting the power of absolute monarchs over their national Churches rather than alienating them.

In 1740, the Holy Roman emperor Charles VI died leaving as his heir his 13-year-old daughter Maria Theresa. There followed a dispute as to whether a woman could inherit the imperial crown, with different nations taking positions based on politics rather than the justice of the cause. Benedict announced that in his view Maria Theresa could inherit her father's lands, but not his title. The war ended in 1748 with total victory for Maria Theresa.

In Church matters, Benedict worked to raise the standards of education and morality among the clergy. He issued a wide range of bulls and encyclicals that generally emphasized traditional teachings, though usually in moderate terms. His combination of firmness and tolerance won him the respect of all, even of Protestants.

1741	1742	1742	1745	1748	1755
The New York Slave Rebellion began with a number of fires, apparently started by slaves.	Robert Walpole, Prime Minister of Britain, is ousted from office over allegations of election rigging.	George Handel's *Messiah* receives its premiere in Dublin, Ireland.	Charles Edward Stuart (Bonnie Prince Charlie), pretender to the British throne leads the Jacobite rebellion.	The ruins of Pompeii are discovered.	Lisbon, Portugal, is destroyed by a violent earthquake that kills 90,000 people.

CLEMENT XIII ✠ The 248th Pope 1758–1769

Born Venice, Italy; March 7, 1693
Parents Father, Giambattista Rezzonico; Mother, unknown
Papacy July 6, 1758–February 2, 1769
Died Rome, Italy; February 2, 1769

Born Carlo della Torre Rezzonico into an extremely wealthy Venetian family, Clement XIII came to the papal throne determined to raise the standards of clerical education, to enforce orthodoxy, and to care for the poor. Instead, almost his entire papacy was taken up with bitter disputes over the Jesuits and associated matters.

Carlo della Torre Rezzonico's family had made its fortune in commerce and had only recently been ennobled. He studied law at Bologna, but then went to Rome to be trained in diplomacy before entering the curia in 1716. He served in various legal offices for the papacy in the years that followed and, in 1737, became cardinal deacon of San Nicola in Carcere. Six years later, Rezzonico was appointed bishop of Padua, where he remained until his elevation to the papacy in 1758. In Padua, he set out to be a pastoral bishop: visiting every parish in his diocese; reorganizing the seminary; and pouring funds into caring for the poor, sick, and unfortunate.

Elected to the papacy after a lengthy conclave, Rezzonico took the name Clement XIII and was at once confronted by a crisis over the Jesuits. The Marquis of Pombal, chief minister of Portugal, accused the Jesuits of illegal trading, being involved in a plot to murder the king, and inciting rebellions in the Americas. Without waiting for any sort of a trial or investigation, Pombal had all assets of the Society of Jesus confiscated in Portugal and her colonies, arrested all Jesuits in Portuguese domains, and shipped them to the Papal States. Clement protested forcefully, as a result of which the Portuguese cut off diplomatic relations with the papacy.

In 1764, the French similarly abolished the Jesuits by royal decree, confiscated their property, and expelled them en masse. In response, Clement produced a well researched and emotionally charged treatise defending the Jesuits and their works but it was ignored. He also authorized the mass and office of the Sacred Heart, something for which the Jesuits had been lobbying for a long time.

In 1767, Spain, Sicily, and Naples abolished the Jesuits, followed by Parma in 1768. The various Bourbon monarchies were now united against the Jesuits. Clement continued to fulminate against the high-handed action of the monarchs, so France invaded Avignon and Naples occupied Benevento.

In 1769, the Bourbons demanded that Clement disband the Society of Jesus altogether. Clement was furious and summoned a special tribunal to meet in Rome to support his views.

INDEX OF FORBIDDEN BOOKS

The *Index Librorum Prohibitorum*, as it was formally know, was a list of books that the Catholic Church decreed either contained theological errors or encouraged immoral behavior. The Index was first put together on the instructions of Pope Paul IV in 1559. It was subsequently updated several times. The Index was abolished by Pope Paul VI in 1966. Although the vast majority of books that were put on the Index were theological in nature, several scientific works were also banned. Most notoriously these included the works of Kepler and Copernicus, which stated that the Earth orbited the Sun and that the Earth was not the center of the Solar System.

1758

Halley's Comet returns as predicted by Edmond Halley in 1705, confirming that comets orbit the Sun.

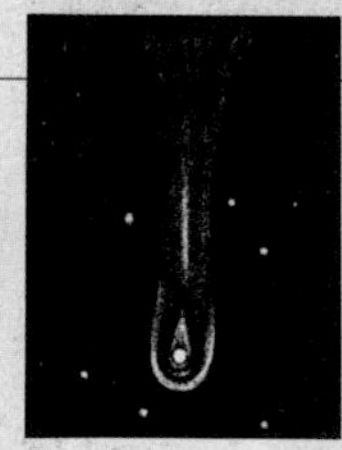

1761

The Bridgewater Canal is opened to freight traffic in England beginning a mass program of canal construction that will revolutionize inland transport.

Padua Cathedral. As bishop of Padua, the future Pope Clement XIII had poured funds into caring for the poor and sick of his parish.

However, the day before it was due to meet he had a seizure and died.

Outside the disputes of the Jesuits, Clement sought to continue in Rome his program of improvements that he had implemented in Padua. He found that the papacy lacked the money to do everything he wanted, but he did support scholarship and the arts whenever he could. Clement took a firm line on unorthodox teachings, adding several books to the Index of banned books and producing the bull *Christianae Reipublicae* protesting that the faithful should "detest books which contain elements shocking to the reader; which are contrary to faith, religion, and good morals."

Clement also denounced what was becoming known as Febronianism. Named after a writer calling himself Justinus Febronius—in reality Johan Hontheim, the bishop of Trier—the movement put forward the idea that the pope was subservient to a general council of bishops and that he was merely the most senior of the bishops. The purpose was to increase the autonomy of the German bishops.

Clement's fame rests these days not so much on his achievements in office, but on a fairly minor decision that he made—he ordered that all the ancient sculptures in the Vatican museums must have their private parts covered up by stone fig leaves.

1763

The British Mariner's Guide by English astronomer Nevil Maskelyne revolutionizes navigation.

1765

The British Parliament passes the Stamp Act, imposing direct taxation on the American colonies in place of the previous system of indirect revenue.

1767

English mariner Samuel Wallis is the first European to sight Tahiti, but he does not land.

CLEMENT XIV ✠ The 249th Pope 1769–1774

Born Sant' Arcangelo, Italy; October 31, 1705
Parents Father, Lorenzo; Mother, unknown
Papacy May 19, 1769–September 22, 1774
Died Rome, Italy; September 22, 1774

Clement XIV brought the papacy to a low point, being bullied by secular rulers into disbanding the Jesuits and accepting humiliating terms from the king of Naples. Given the weakness of the Church however, he probably had little choice. Dealings with King Louis XV of France were especially problematic for Clement.

Giovanni Vincenzo Antonio Ganganelli was born in the humblest of circumstances in a rural backwater in southern Italy. At the age of 17 he joined the Franciscan friars and, after gaining a doctorate of theology, spent years lecturing in theology to his fellow Franciscans and writing on the subject. He moved to Rome in 1740 to enter the curia and became a cardinal in 1759. Under Clement XIII he became gradually estranged from the pope and came to oppose his policy of confronting the Bourbon monarchs over the Jesuit controversy.

When Clement died, the resulting conclave was dominated by the issue of the Jesuits (*see* p.268). The kings of Spain and France invoked their traditional, but informal, rights of veto by letting it be known that no less than 23 of the 47 cardinals would not be accepted. Two Spanish cardinals, Solis and La Cerda, further declared that only a cardinal who signed a written promise to disband the Jesuits would be acceptable. The bulk of the cardinals objected furiously, forcing Solis and La Cerda to accept a verbal promise instead. Ganganelli was asked to give the promise, replying evasively that there would be great advantages if the Jesuits were suppressed. That was good enough for the Spanish, and he was then elected after a conclave that had lasted three months.

Taking the name Clement XIV, the new pope announced that he was going to solve the Jesuit issue. Instead of immediately disbanding the order, however, Clement began investigating the accusations against it to see if there was

When Maria Theresa of Austria told Clement the Jesuits no longer had her support he gave up his attempts to modernize the Jesuits order and disbanded it in 1773.

THE ENLIGHTENMENT

During the later 17th century a movement began in Europe that began to question the accepted norms of society, including religion. What became known as the Enlightenment sought to base all aspects of life on rational enquiry. The movement affected forms of government, literature, and science, but the papacy was most concerned with the new questioning of Christianity. Some thinkers sought to return Christianity to its biblical roots and undertook textual criticism of the sacred works. Others sought to remove religion from politics by giving religious authority to the papacy. The swirl of conflicting ideas reached its zenith in the late 18th century when some advocated removing religion entirely.

1770

The Boston Massacre. Five colonial civilians are killed by British soldiers during a demonstration in Boston, Massachusetts.

1772

The First Partition of Poland. Large areas of the Kingdom of Poland are annexed by Russia, Prussia, and Austria.

The tomb of Pope Clement XIV by Antonio Canova in Santi Apostoli, Rome.

any room for compromise through reform or the removal of individuals. In 1773, however, the Bourbon monarchies told him bluntly to disband the Jesuits or have all relations between Rome and their realms broken off.

On August 16, 1773, the order disbanding the Jesuits was issued. Prussia and Russia alone refused to implement it.

The capitulation by Clement brought immediate benefits to the papacy. The French restored to him Avignon and other possessions, while Naples evacuated Benevento.

Modern historians see the suppression of the Jesuit order as the result of a series of political, economic, and social conflicts rather than a theological controversy. It can also be seen as a manifestation of the burgeoning secularism nurtured by the Enlightenment and culminating with the anti-clericalism of the French Revolution. Somewhat ironically, the suppression was also quite clearly an attempt by European monarchs to gain control of revenues and trade that were previously dominated by the Society of Jesus. Whatever the causes, the resulting damage to missionary activity overseas and to the school system in Europe, particularly for the poor, was immense.

King Louis XV of France then opened up a new dispute by setting up a commission to investigate the state of the monastic orders in France. Many abbeys were immensely rich and not a few were exempt from paying taxes to the monarch. Louis closed down the Crandmont, Celestine, and Camaldolese houses in 1773 and imposed strict conditions on the orders he allowed to remain operational. Clement had proved powerless to protect the monasteries.

Clement took the bold step of removing official papal support for the exiled Catholic Stuart dynasty of Britain, though he did not go so far as to recognize the Protestant Hanoverians who had taken their place. For the first time in generations a papal nuncio was welcomed to Britain and the brother of King George III visited Rome, though in an unofficial capacity. Pressure on Catholics in Britain began to ease as a result.

1773

British mariner James Cook becomes the first European explorer to go south of the Antarctic Circle as part of his Second Voyage to the Pacific.

1773

The Boston Tea Party. Colonists in Boston Massachusetts dress as Indians to destroy a cargo of tea in protest at a tax on tea.

PIUS VI ✠ The 250th Pope 1775–1799

Born Casena, Italy; December 25, 1717

Parents Father, Angelo Braschi; Mother, unknown

Papacy February 15, 1775–August 29, 1799

Died Valence, France; August 29, 1799

Pius VI had the misfortune to face the upheavals of the French Revolution that continued practically throughout his entire pontificate, and which spread quickly to Italy. He faced the troubles calmly and set an example for other priests to follow. Ultimately imprisoned in exile, he nevertheless did much to ensure the survival of the papacy.

Giovanni Braschi was born into modest circumstances, but his father was related to the powerful Braschi family of nobles so he gained a good education and a letter of introduction to Cardinal Antonito Ruffo, who employed him as a secretary. Braschi soon proved his worth and, in 1740, acted as Ruffo's assistant in the lengthy conclave that followed the death of Clement XII. Ruffo then became bishop of Ostia and Braschi moved to the service of Benedict XIV whom he served as private secretary. In 1758, he became a priest and was appointed by Clement XIII to be papal treasurer. Clement XIV made him a cardinal in 1773. Throughout this time Braschi had gained a reputation for hard work and efficiency without taking sides in any of the disputes within the Church.

When Clement XIV died, the controversies surrounding the Jesuits was at its height. As one of the few cardinals not known to have firm views on the matter, Braschi could gather the support of both factions. He was elected after 134 days of conclave and took the name of Pius VI to honor Pius V.

On the immediate issue of the Jesuits, Pius chose inactivity as his policy. The decree of Clement disbanding the organization was allowed to stand, but he made no efforts to enforce it. However, the discontent against the Jesuits in Europe was merely part of a rising tide of dissatisfaction with the privileged status of the Church in many countries.

King Ferdinand IV of Sicily was the first to make an open move. He declared that his kingdom was no longer a feudal fief of the papacy, refused to pay his tribute, and then announced that in future he would appoint bishops in his realm. The feudal obligation was something of a medieval anachronism by this date, but Pius objected all the same. More tellingly, he refused to confirm in office any bishops appointed by King Ferdinand.

Next to act was the Holy Roman emperor Joseph II. By stages, he set about creating a system that in Germany was dubbed "Josephism." This system ostensibly recognized the rights of the Catholic Church but, in reality, stripped the papacy of all power in imperial lands. Church appointments were to be made by the emperor, who also supervised how Church lands and benefices were administered. Total toleration and freedom of worship was given to Protestants of all denominations. All that was left to the pope was the right to issue statements and edicts on religious and moral matters, but he had no official status or force. In 1781, Joseph closed down a number of monasteries and other religious institutions, and he transferred those that were left from papal authority to the control of the local bishops. In 1786, the papal nuncio was sent back to Rome on the grounds that Germany no longer needed such a figure.

In 1786, Josephism was implemented much closer to home, in Tuscany, and elements of the

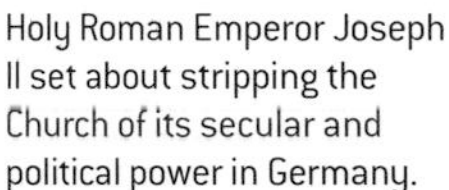

Holy Roman Emperor Joseph II set about stripping the Church of its secular and political power in Germany.

1775

Battle of Lexington in Massachusetts signals the outbreak of the American Revolution.

1776

American Declaration of Independence is signed by representatives of 13 British colonies in North America.

1779

British engineer Abraham Derby III builds an iron bridge over the Severn River in Shropshire—the first such bridge in the world.

1783

Great Britain acknowledges the independence of the United States of America.

Louis XVI of France was executed by guillotine in 1792 during the French Revolution.

program were taken up by other Catholic monarchs.

However, it was the French Revolution that was really to test Pius. In July 1790, the Revolutionary Government in Paris passed its Constitution of the Clergy. This reorganized the Church hierarchy, made priests salaried staff of the state and required all priests and bishops to take an oath of loyalty to the French State. Pius reacted firmly. He declared that no priest could take oaths of loyalty to two different masters, declared secular ordinations to be sacrilegious, and suspended all priests who took the required oath. France reacted by annexing Avignon and other papal enclaves in France and cutting off diplomatic relations with the Holy See. The French Church proceeded to split between those members of the clergy who did and those who did not take the secular oath.

In 1792, Pius welcomed to Rome a number of high-profile aristocratic refugees from France. In April of that year France declared war on Austria, then executed Louis XVI in September. Prussia joined the war against France, as did Britain, Spain, Portugal, Sardinia, the Netherlands, and even the Ottoman Turks. Pius took the papal states into this grand alliance, the First Coalition, and made hostile speeches against republicanism and revolution.

During the Reign of Terror in France, a period of virtual mob rule from 1793 to 1794, between 16,000 and 40,000 people were killed.

By 1795, however, it was clear that the war was going badly for the Coalition. Spain made peace with France and urged Pius to do likewise, but he refused. The following year a French army under a talented young general named Napoleon Bonaparte invaded northern Italy. Sardinia was crushed and the Austrians driven out. Bonaparte set up a number of small republics with constitutions based on that of France. He then sent a letter to Rome peremptorily ordering Pius to expel the French nobles and accept the Constitution of the Clergy. Pius refused. Bonaparte invaded the Papal States and, in 1797, forced Pius to agree the Peace of Tolentino. This confiscated the Romagna from the Papal States, imposed a huge fine on the papacy, and allowed the French to carry off any art treasures they liked—a provision Bonaparte enforced with enthusiasm.

In 1798, the French general left to observe Pius VI was killed in a riot. The French invaded again to exact revenge. This time the pope was dethroned and a Roman Republic set up on the French model. Pius was moved to Florence where he was cut off from the outside world with only his personal servants allowed access, plus the occasional visit by the nuncio to Tuscany.

In 1799, a Second Coalition went to war with France. Fearing a rescue attempt, the French moved Pius over the Alps to Valence and locked him in the citadel. He bore his sufferings with fortitude and dignity—and some cunning. He left firm instructions that no French priest who had sworn loyalty to the French State could bury him, while the French would not allow any priests who had not done so to enter the country. The burial caused a political and diplomatic row just as Pius had intended.

Crucially, Pius also left instructions that would ensure a new pope would be elected following his death, when the French and other revolutionaries had hoped that by imprisoning the pope and occupying Rome they had destroyed the papacy forever.

1783	1788	1789	1792
The Mongolfier Brothers demonstrate their hot air balloon in Paris, France.	First fleet of settlers, including some convicts, arrives in Australia from Britain.	In France, the Third Estate—the "representatives of the people"—declare themselves to be a National Assembly and remove the right of veto to new laws from the nobility and clergy, an event recognized as the start of the French Revolution.	Execution of King Louis XVI of France by the revolutionaries.

PIUS VII ✠ The 251st Pope 1800–1823

Born Cesena, Italy; August 14, 1742
Parents Father, Count Scipione Chiaramonti; Mother, Giovanna
Papacy March 14, 1800–July 20, 1823
Died Rome, Italy; July 20, 1823

It was Pius VII who steered the papacy through the difficult turmoil of the Napoleonic Wars, re-established the Papal States, and sought to restore papal authority over the Catholic Church. Following a dispute with Napoleon Bonaparte, he was imprisoned in exile but remained resolute. When Pius died the papacy was more respected than it had been for decades.

The instructions left by Pius VI meant that a conclave to elect a new pope could take place. The French revolutionaries had hoped that by stripping Pius VI of all his temporal powers and occupying Rome they had destroyed the papacy forever, but the cardinals were determined that this should not be allowed to happen. Pius decreed that the senior cardinal could hold the conclave at a place and time of his choosing with however many cardinals were able to get there.

The closest place to Rome where the cardinals could meet with any safety was Venice, then under the protection of Austrian troops. The conclave was therefore held in the chapel of the San Giorgio Monastery on one of the smaller and more remote Venetian islands. Cardinal Ercole Consalvi was elected with an overwhelming majority, but Emperor Joseph II had already sent a secret note vetoing him. Cardinal Gardil was elected next, but he too was unacceptable to the Austrians. Finally, after four months, Cardinal Barnaba Luigi Chiaramonti was elected. Since the cardinals had none of the papal possessions with them he had to be crowned with a papier-mâché tiara.

Napoleon Bonaparte became emperor of France in 1804.

The new pope took the name Pius VII to show continuity with Pius VI. He had been born a son of Count Chiaramonti and was distantly related to the Braschi family of Pius VI. He had entered the Benedictine Order at the age of 14 and became a teacher within that order. In 1782, Pius VI made him bishop of Tivoli and then, in 1785, moved him to be bishop of Imola, at the same time creating him cardinal priest of the Basilica of St. Calixtus.

When the French revolutionary army invaded Italy he stayed at his post in Imola and made a speech, a key passage of which ran "Christian virtue makes men good democrats. Equality is not an idea of philosophers but of Christ...and I do not believe that the Catholic religion is against democracy." His sentiments were respected on all sides, but the French soldiers looted his palace anyway.

When he became pope, Pius VII showed a determination to heal breaches within the Church by making Cardinal Consalvi his secretary of state. His first priority was to reach some sort of accommodation with Revolutionary France. In 1801, he agreed a Concordat with Napoleon, which restored Pius to Rome to rule over smaller Papal States and allowed Catholicism to function in France once again. Two years later, a similar agreement was reached with the Italian republics. In 1804, Pius attended the coronation of Napoleon as emperor of the French.

1801
First modern census is undertaken in Britain, which is revealed to have a total population of 8.9 million with 700,000 living in London.

1805
Battle of Austerlitz, at which Emperor Napoleon of France crushes a joint Austrian-Russian army and cements French hegemony over Europe.

1805
Battle of Trafalgar, at which Admiral Horatio Nelson of Britain destroys a joint Franco-Spanish fleet and renders an invasion of Britain by Napoleon impossible.

1808
In Britain, engineer Richard Trevithick builds the "Catch Me Who Can"—a steam locomotive that runs on rails pulling passenger carriages, the first successful steam train.

The Congress of Vienna in 1814 was called to peacefully settle many issues arising from the French Revolutionary Wars and the dissolution of the Holy Roman Empire.

One of Pius's greatest triumphs was to lure to Rome Canova, a sculpture of genius, who brought in his wake a host of talented pupils and imitators willing to work for reduced fees to gain experience.

Two years later, Emperor Napoleon demanded that the pope agree to support the total ban on trade with Britain. Pius responded that he believed his role was to be neutral in wars between Christian countries. Napoleon responded by invading states and, in 1809, annexing all the Papal States. Pius was then arrested and put into prison at Savona, in northern Italy, where he was allowed only a handful of personal servants and virtually no contact with the outside world. In 1812, Pius was moved to Fontainbleau in France and held under worse conditions. In 1813, a sick and exhausted Pius agreed to a treaty thrust in front of him by Napoleon that robbed the pope of the Papal States and authority over the Church. Within weeks, Pius recanted and refused to sign, whereupon he was sent back to Savona.

In March 1814, as his enemies marched on Paris, Napoleon released Pius who traveled back to Rome to recover from his long imprisonment. Too feeble to go himself, Pius sent Consalvi to attend the Congress of Vienna at which the victorious allies were redrawing the map of Europe. The Holy Roman Empire was gone. Joseph II was now emperor of Austria with only a vague authority over the German states, now drastically reduced in number. Consalvi found that the prestige of Pius was high and sympathy for him was widespread. He was therefore able to secure the return to the papacy of the Papal States almost in their entirety.

In the years that followed, Pius was able to reach agreements with most of the states in Europe over the status of the Catholic faith. These ranged from freedom of worship to official recognition and although most involved Pius accepting terms that would have been unthinkable a century earlier, they did at least ensure that the relationship between papacy and the Church was settled.

Within the Papal States, Pius sought to modernize the archaic administrative arrangements by introducing some facets of the French revolutionary model. In particular, he wanted to change the financial and economic policies in order to encourage new industries and prosperity so as to give the papacy a solid financial foundation and improve the lot of the population. He sought to promote officials on merit, ending centuries when the administration of the Papal States was in the hands of nobles and high-ranking clergy.

Most of these reforms and agreements were really the work of Consalvi, for Pius was always more interested in the religious aspects of the papacy. Among his early actions after returning to Rome was to revive the Society of Jesus, having earlier assented to the continuation of Jesuit activity in Russia where it had never been suppressed. He preached strongly against the doctrine of Indifferentism, which held that all paths to God are equally valid so no one branch of Christianity is superior to another. The concept had arisen in some countries as priests and Catholic lay people sought to come to terms with the revolutionary principles from France.

In 1814, he found Rome badly damaged. Within the limited financial resources at his disposal, Pius set about restoring the Churches, bridges, and other monuments of his city.

1812

War of 1812. Britain and the USA fight a short war, which ends with both sides claiming victory.

1815

Battle of Waterloo, at which Emperor Napoleon of France is finally defeated by Britain's Wellington and Prussia's Blucher, and is thereafter sent into exile.

1819

The SS Savannah becomes the first steamship to cross the Atlantic.

1823

The first electromagnet is devised by English physicist William Sturgeon.

LEO XII ✢ The 252nd Pope 1823–1829

Born Castello della Genga, Italy; August 22, 1760
Parents Father, Giralamo Conte della Genga; Mother, Maria Luisa Periberti
Papacy September 28, 1823–February 10, 1829
Died Rome, Italy; February 10, 1829

Leo XII represented a decisive turning back of the clock by the Catholic Church. His election was secured by cardinals to whom the principles and ideas of the French Revolution were anathema, and he put their policies into practice.

Leo was born with the impressive name of Annibale Francesco Clemente Melchiore Girolamo Nicola Sermattei della Genga and had a noble lineage every bit as long and imposing. His family had a tradition of service to the papacy, being based near Ancona in the Papal States. He became a priest at the age of 23 and, almost at once, was appointed private secretary to Pius VI. His noble blood, good contacts, and intelligence marked him out for higher things. He became titular archbishop of Tyre in 1793 and, as such, was sent on a string of diplomatic missions to German states.

When Pius died the conservative cardinals, nicknamed the *zelanti*, mobilized quickly behind Genga who was elected as Leo XII after a conclave lasting only a month.

Leo at once dismissed Consalvi from all his posts and began reversing the more modern policies of Pius VII. Officials in the Papal States who were neither from the nobility nor ranked highly in the Church were sacked or eased from office. Policies favoring the landowners were introduced, stifling industrialization and alienating those in society who were frozen out of the new regime.

In foreign policy Leo similarly sought to turn the clock back. The Kingdom of Sicily had been replaced by the Kingdom of the Two Sicilies, which included Sicily and most of southern Italy. Leo persuaded King Ferdinand to accept feudal-fief status for the mainland part of his realm, though this was a merely token arrangement. Leo also acted aggressively in other areas, eschewing Pius's conciliatory approach and robustly negotiating concordats with Hanover, the Netherlands, and elsewhere that were beneficial to the papacy but at the cost of ill will. In 1830, he broke new ground for a pope by reaching an agreement with the Caliph of the Ottoman Turks that allowed more freedom of worship for Catholics in Turkish domains.

In Britain Leo's efforts to gain improved freedoms for Catholics were rebuffed by a government unwilling to take orders from foreigners. Nevertheless, the movement for reforms within Britain was gaining strength and the Catholic Relief Act was passed under the Duke of Wellington a month after Leo's death.

Leo was deeply interested in the purity of religion and theology. He added books to the Index of banned works, condemned tolerance of Protestantism in Catholic countries, and forcefully attacked Indifferentism and freemasonry. His most constructive efforts may have been his determination to raise the standards of education and spiritual fervor among the clergy and in religious houses. Nevertheless, Leo XII's reign was generally regarded as a backward step in papal history that achieved little other than to annoy anyone who did not share his zelantist views.

In 1829, the passage of Catholic emancipation in Britain under the Duke of Wellington ended a highly controversial struggle and was an important landmark in British history.

1823
Congress of Central American countries declares absolute independence from Spain, Mexico, and other states.

1824
In Vienna, Ludwig van Beethoven premieres his Symphony No.9, widely regarded as his finest work.

1826
The Spanish Inquisition imposes its last penalties on those deemed to be heretics.

1827
The Greek War of Independence ends with Turkey recognizing a small independent Greek state in the southern part of what is now Greece.

1828
Hungarian engineer Anyos Jedlik invents an early form of electric motor.

PIUS VIII ✠ The 253rd Pope 1829–1830

Born Cingoli, Italy; November 20, 1761

Parents Father, Count Ottavio Castiglioni; Mother, Sanzia Ghislieri

Papacy March 31, 1829–November 30, 1830

Died Rome, Italy; November 30, 1830

Pius VIII adopted the name Pius in homage to Pius VII, whose policies he intended to follow. His short papacy achieved much but he suffered from a very painful and distressing chronic illness, and his reign as pope ended tragically early.

At the conclave of 1829, Francesco Saverio Castiglione emerged as a leading candidate as a moderate modernizer acceptable to the conservatives, but his obvious ill health seemed to rule him out. However, neither the conservative *zelanti* nor the reformist *politicanti* could gain a two thirds majority so, after 35 days of stalemate, Castiglioni was elected.

Pius VIII began by issuing a letter in which he set out what he expected to be the main themes of his papacy: a renewal of faith in Christian countries by opposing Indifferentism, freemasonry, and other fashionable nostrums inimical to Christianity. The first crisis came from Germany on the issue of marriages between Catholic and Protestants. Pius established the principle that for such a marriage to be valid there must be a prior undertaking that any children would be brought up in the Catholic faith. The German government, however, wanted the faith of the father to be given priority. Pius compromised by allowing a priest to witness, but not conduct, a marriage where the pledge had not been given.

In the spring and summer of 1830 revolutions broke out in Belgium, France, Poland, and Switzerland. The risings were generally in favor of liberal reforms against authoritarian governments. Pius expressed support for the reforms but not for the violence that accompanied them. He recognized the new king Louis Philippe of France and, against the advice of the curia, bestowed on him the title traditional to French monarchy: "Most Christian Majesty."

Plaque commemorating the July Revolution in France, which saw the overthrow of King Charles X, the French Bourbon monarch, and the ascent of his cousin Louis-Philippe.

Further afield, Pius was able to appoint a Catholic archbishop of Constantinople to minister to the needs of Catholics in the Ottoman Empire. The move was the result of prolonged negotiations with the Muslim government of the Ottomans over the previous two papal reigns. In the United States of America, Pius was gratified by the holding of the First Provincial Council of the Catholic Church in the USA. Meeting in Baltimore, the Council recognized the authority of Rome and passed measures that would strengthen the ties between the Holy See and its churches in the USA.

Pope Pius had not enjoyed good health for some years and spent much of his papacy confined to the Vatican. He died after only 20 months in office.

1829

Britain founds the Swan River Colony, soon to be renamed Perth in Western Australia, thus claiming all of Australia.

1929

In Britain, Robert Peel founds the London Metropolitan Police, the first modern police force in the world.

1830

The Liverpool and Manchester Railway opens, the first railway linking two cities carrying paying passengers on a regular timetable operated by steam locomotives.

1830

In the USA, Joseph Smith publishes the Book of Mormon, thus founding the Church of Jesus Christ of Latter Day Saints, known informally as the Mormons.

GREGORY XVI + The 254th Pope 1831–1846

Born Belluno, Italy; September 18, 1765

Parents Father, Giovanni Battista Cappellari; Mother, Giulia Cesa-Pagani

Papacy February 2, 1831–June 1, 1846

Died Rome, Italy; June 1, 1846

The defining event in the life of Pope Gregory XVI came thirty years before he became pope when he witnessed the violence, bloodshed, and upheavals unleashed by the French Revolution. He spent most of his papacy resisting reforms to the papal government, even allowing French troops into Rome to maintain public order.

Bartolomeo Alberto Cappellari was born into the minor nobility of Venice. At the age of 18 he joined the Benedictine Order, choosing the strict Camaldolese branch that ran San Michele on the island of Murano in the Venetian lagoon. He stayed there for the next decade, becoming a professor of philosophy and science and being ordained a priest. He moved to Rome in 1795 to work for the Benedictines.

In 1799, as the ideals and violence of the French Revolution swept across Europe, Cappelari wrote and published a treatise entitled "The Triumph of the Holy See and the Church against the Attacks of the Innovators." It was a no-holds barred condemnation of the new ideas and the bloodshed they had unleashed while praising the Catholic Church and upholding the papal temporal rule of the Papal States. The pamphlet made him a marked man, so he had to flee Rome to take shelter back on Murano where he was safeguarded by Austrian soldiers.

Gregory was anti-revolutionary in every sense. Even the burgeoning Industrial Revolution filled him with horror. When a Frenchman described to him a chemin de fer (railroad), Gregory retorted that it was a "chemin d'enfer" (road to hell) and he refused permission for any railways to be built in the Papal States.

He returned to Rome when the French left in 1814 and busied himself with organizing and supporting missionary work outside Europe. He held the position of abbot at the Monastery of San Gregorio in Rome and was made a cardinal in 1826, but he remained largely unknown outside the curia and missionary circles. At the conclave of 1830, the Spanish cardinals arrived with a veto from King Ferdinand VII blocking the popular cardinal Giacomo Giustiniani. Since most of the cardinals at the conclave had wanted Giustiniani to be pope the subsequent voting was at first complex and fractious. Not until 50 days and 82 ballots had passed did the cardinals turn their support to Cappelari, who won on the 83rd ballot. Since then no conclave has lasted more than six days and 14 ballots.

At the time he was elected, Cappelari was not yet a bishop so he had to be hurriedly consecrated such—the last pope not to have reached that rank before being elected. He took the name of Gregory to honor the monastery of which he was abbot.

On a personal level, Gregory was affable, generous, and warm hearted. He had a deep interest in art and culture, founding the Egyptian and Etruscan Museums in Rome and sponsoring archaeological digs. On the other hand, he viewed all requests for democratic or clerical reforms as a first step on the slippery slope to bloody revolution and viewed them with a profound horror.

No sooner was Gregory in the Vatican than he received a delegation of citizens asking him to consider granting a constitution with a minor

1831	1832	1835	1837
Belgium becomes independent of the Netherlands.	Cholera strikes Europe, killing 3,000 in London alone.	Texas declares itself independent of Mexico, and ten years later it will join the USA.	Samuel Morse patents the telegraph.

Frederick William III of Prussia had a serious disagreement with the papacy on the issue of Prussian marriages. He even went so far as to imprison an archbishop who insisted on following the pope's orders.

role for an assembly elected by male citizens of the Papal States. Gregory was horrified, viewing this once again as an early sign of violent revolution. He refused point blank and, when rioting began, called on Emperor Ferdinand I of Austria to send troops to help him. Once order was restored the Austrians left, but riots broke out again so they came back, along with a detachment of French troops. They were to stay for the next seven years as Gregory turned down any effort to reform his government.

Ferdinand I of Austria helped Gregory maintain order in the Papal States by supplying troops.

Gregory was meanwhile equally forthright in slapping down theological ideas that might disturb the established order. Freedom of conscience, freedom of speech, freedom of the press, and the separation of church and state were all condemned in blunt language that left no room for doubt or compromise.

While Gregory campaigned furiously in Russia for Tsar Nicholas I to grant freedoms to his Catholic subjects in Poland, he condemned the Polish uprising of 1831 that was sparked by those very issues. He similarly discouraged priests in Ireland from getting involved in any political activity as demands for home rule began to grow.

The issue of Prussian marriages resurfaced (*see* p.277) in 1832. Gregory firmly repeated the decision made by Pius, but King Frederick William III would not back down. The affair would drag on until a new king, Frederick William IV, came to the throne in 1840. The new king allowed Gregory to have his way on mixed marriages and guaranteed free episcopal elections so long as the pope did not seek to interfere either.

The one area where Gregory did encourage innovation, change, and action was in missionary work. In India, China, and Africa he championed the conversion of locals and the regularization of the Church hierarchy at the earliest possible opportunity. In all, he established 70 new dioceses and sent out 200 missionary bishops. Nor did he neglect the growing Catholic population of the Americas. He established four new dioceses in Canada and ten in the USA to minister to the settlers pushing out to farm new lands to the west of the established colonies.

In South America, he established a new policy of talking to the governments that actually ruled the countries, not those that claimed the legitimate right to do so. In effect, this meant recognizing the new republics and ignoring the colonial claims of Spain and Portugal. This allowed Gregory to appoint bishops and archbishops to South America, ending a rather chaotic situation that had persisted for some years. It did, however, alienate the monarchs of Spain and Portugal who both introduced controls and restrictions on the Catholic Church.

It was perhaps as well that Gregory died when he did. Within two years Europe would be swept by revolutions and the Papal States would not be immune.

1841

In Britain, Thomas Cook organizes a day trip by rail with all transport and meals included—the world's first package holiday.

1843

The world's first Christmas cards are sold by Thomas Cole in London.

1846

Potato blight is first seen in Ireland, the start of the Great Irish Famine that will kill around one million people and cause as many to emigrate.

PIUS IX ✠ The 255th Pope 1846–1878

Born Senigalia, Italy; May 13, 1792

Parents Father, Girolamo dei conti Ferretti; Mother, unknown

Papacy June 16, 1846–February 7, 1878

Died Rome, Italy; February 7, 1878

Pope Pius IX's reign of 32 years is the longest in the history of the papacy. Politically his papacy was close to a disaster and he was the last pope to rule as sovereign of the Papal States, which were incorporated into the Kingdom of Italy in 1870. Spiritually, however, his papacy was a triumph. By the time he died, he had effectively created the modern papacy.

Giovanni Maria Mastai-Ferrati was born into the minor nobility of the Papal States to a family with a long tradition of papal service. His family wanted him to join the papal army, so, in 1815, he volunteered for the Papal Noble Guard, a heavy cavalry regiment that escorted the pope when he traveled. However, his epilepsy caused him to be dismissed whereupon Pius VII arranged for him to take up theological studies. Mastai-Ferrati was ordained a priest in 1819 and, after a series of appointments and with his epilepsy gone, he rose to be archbishop of Spoleto in 1827 and cardinal by 1840.

In the conclave of 1846, the key issue turned out to be the governance of the Papal States. The conservative *zelanti* wanted to see a continuation of the traditional absolutist rule, while reformers wanted some democracy. On the first ballot *zelanti* Luigi Lambruschini received a majority, but not a two thirds majority. On the fourth ballot, Mastai-Ferrati did achieve the necessary majority being a supporter of modest reforms and so acceptable to both factions. He took the name Pius IX. The next day, Cardinal Karl Kajetan Gaisruck, the archbishop of Milan, arrived with a veto from Emperor Ferdinand I of Austria blocking Mastai-Ferrati, but it was too late.

Pius began by announcing an amnesty for political prisoners. He then set about reforming the government of the Papal States. He announced that the pope would remain monarch of the Papal States since the income they gave was essential to preserving papal independence and neutrality. Within that monarchy, however, he set up democratically elected local councils, including one for Rome.

In 1848, a series of revolutions swept across Europe. In Italy, Sicily broke from Naples; Naples rose and demanded democracy; while in Milan, Venice, and other northern cities, protestors demanding democracy and freedom from Austrian rule drove out Austrian officials and soldiers. Clearly the Austrians would soon mount an invasion to restore their rule, so other Italian states mobilized for war. Piedmont, Tuscany, and Sicily all sent armies north to aid Milan and Venice. The local councils in the Papal States all demanded that the papal army march as well. Pius refused and ordered the army into barracks.

The subsequent defeat of the Italian states was blamed on Pius. In November, riots broke out and the papal Prime Minister Pellegrino Rossi was murdered. Fearing he would be next, Pius fled in disguise to Gaeta in the Kingdom of the Two Sicilies. From there he attempted to run the Papal States but, in February 1849, a Roman Republic was declared. Pius appealed for help. President Napoleon of France (soon to be Emperor Napoleon III) responded by sending an army to invade the Papal States, capture Rome, and reimpose papal rule.

On December 8, 1854, Pius pronounced on the Immaculate Conception of the Blessed Virgin Mary, declaring that Mary had been preserved from sin from the moment of her conception.

1846	1850	1852	1853	1853
The planet Nepture is observed for the first time by German astronomers Johann Gottfried Galle and Heinrich Louis d'Arrest in the place it was predicted to be by the British astronomer John Couch Adams.	The Taiping, or Heavenly Kingdom, Rebellion begins in China. It will last 14 years and cost the lives of 20 million people before the Qing Dynastry put it down.	Great Ormond Street Hospital, the world's first hospital specifically for children, opens in London.	Potato chips (or crisps) are invented by chef George Crum at Saratoga Springs resort, New York, when a customer complains the fried potatoes are too thick.	The Crimean War begins. At first between Russia and Turkey, the war will later see Britain and France joining Turkey to halt Russian expansion in the Balkans.

The breach in the ancient walls of Rome following the Siege of 1870 when Pius retreated to the Vatican.

In April 1850, Pius returned to Rome to find a sullen population. The French soldiers stayed and Pius abolished the local councils, returning to autocratic rule, albeit one with many reformist policies. In 1860, Sicily and Naples again rose in rebellion, this time ousting King Francis II and uniting with the Kingdom of Piedmont under a new democratic constitution. Neapolitan troops from the south and Piedmontese troops from the north invaded the Papal States, which were also united to Piedmont in a new Kingdom of Italy.

Pius was now left with only Rome and the surrounding Lazio District. He protested furiously, but to no avail. In 1870, France went to war with Germany and Napoleon withdrew his troops from Rome. The Italians struck at once, attacking the city and breaking through the ancient walls on September 20, 1870. Ordering the Papal army to surrender after a token resistance, Pius retreated to the Vatican, which he never left.

In the theological field Pius was much more successful than in the political arena. On December 8, 1854, he pronounced on the Immaculate Conception of the Blessed Virgin Mary, declaring that Mary had been preserved from sin from the moment of her conception. This proved to be a definitive move by the papacy and was hugely popular through the Catholic world.

His second important pronouncement came in 1864 when he affirmed that the papacy was under no obligation to alter its teachings to match the demands of secular society, which both established the autonomy of the Church and closed the door on reforms.

In 1869, Pius summoned the First Vatican Council, considered to be the 20th general council of the Church. The council reached a number of decisions on faith, doctrine, and the role of the papacy, but the most important was its decision to affirm papal infallibility. The idea had been developing for a long time, but now it was clearly stated that the pope is preserved from the possibility of error when he defines a doctrine concerning faith or morals to be held by the whole Church.

The Council also moved forward the policy of centralization of power within the Church. As bishops increasingly lost control of the wealth, lands, and political power that they had once held, the states in which they operated began to lose interest in them. This, together with improvements in transport and communication, made it possible for the pope to exercise more and more control over the widespread Church. This provoked the German Chancellor to launch the *Kulturkampf*, an effort to drive Catholicism out of German culture. The monastic orders were driven out and 1,800 priests imprisoned.

In an effort to repair the financial damage to the papacy by the loss of the Papal States Pius reintroduced the old idea of Peter's Pence—a special collection in churches held once a year. It continues to this day, bringing in around $70 million a year.

Throughout his time as pope, Pius sought to revive the spirituality and religious fervor of the clergy and laity. This is probably his greatest legacy as it was the devotion of the people and clergy that allowed the Church to survive.

1854	1857	1859	1860	1861	1866	1870
Eureka Stockade battle takes place in Australia between miners and government soldiers.	Indian regiments across a large area of northern India rise in rebellion against British rule. The rising will last two years.	Charles Darwin publishes *On the Origin of Species*, putting forward the Theory of Evolution.	World's first known sound recording is made by Frenchman Edouard-Leon Scott de Martinville.	American Civil War breaks out as the southern states break away to form the Confederacy.	The British colonies in North America join to form Canada.	Outbreak of the Franco-Prussian War, which will last to 1871 and end with the defeat of France.

LEO XIII ✠ The 256th Pope 1878–1903

Born Carpineto Romano; Italy, 1810

Parents Father, Count Lodovico Pecci; Mother, Anna Prosperi-Buzi

Papacy February 20, 1878–July 20, 1903

Died Rome, Italy; July 20, 1903

Leo XIII was the oldest pope, at 93, and achieved the third longest pontificate after Pius IX and John Paul II. His reign saw determined efforts to adapt the papacy to the modern world. He built many bridges between the papacy and secular powers and even took some tentative steps toward reconciliation with his "lost brothers"—the Protestants.

Giacchino Vincenzo Pecci was born near Rome during the French occupation of the Papal States. As a boy he showed himself to be a brilliant scholar and, at the age of 14, he moved to the Roman College. Wanting to enter papal service, he was ordained a priest in 1837 and was at once appointed governor of Benevento, then governor of Perugia four years later. In both places, he proved himself to be a highly capable administrator who stood no nonsense from subordinates. In 1843, he was granted the titular archbishopric of Damietta, then sent on diplomatic missions to Germany, Britain, and France. These went well but, in 1846, he was expelled from Belgium after injudiciously expressing an opinion on a political dispute over education policy.

Back in Italy, Pecci became bishop of Perugia and, in 1853, a cardinal. When Perugia was annexed from the Papal States to the new Kingdom of Italy he protested vociferously and objected strongly to the secular legislation that the move brought to his diocese. Nevertheless, he knew reality when he saw it and, from 1874 onward, sought to find an accommodation with the new authorities that did not undermine his Catholic teachings.

When Pius IX died, Pecci arrived at the conclave with a reputation for being able to work with the Kingdom of Italy. The necessity of dealing with the new Italy was forced upon the cardinals from the start of the conclave. It had been traditional to hold the conclave in the Quirinal Palace, but that building was now the official Roman residence of the king of Italy and so was unavailable. Instead, the cardinals met in the Sistine Chapel at the Vatican.

As expected, it was the question of relations between Church and state that dominated the conclave. In the first two ballots Pecci was the leader but lacked the two thirds majority needed to win. On the third ballot nobody else stood and Pecci was elected, taking the name of Leo XIII. He was, at the time, 68 years old and in frail health. Nobody could have expected him to reign for 25 years.

The same issue of Church-state relations arose immediately when royal troops stopped the new pope from blessing the crowd from the loggia of St. Peter's and, instead, insisted that he be crowned inside the Sistine Chapel. The government feared a riot of papal supporters if he appeared in public.

Leo set out to restore a measure of cordiality to relations with secular authorities. This bore fruit in 1886 when Germany eased its anti-Catholic legislation and called off the *Kulturkampf*, which had been designed to eradicate Catholic influence on public life.

In 1881, Tsar Alexander II of Russia was assassinated. Leo at once sent a message to the new Tsar, Alexander III, in which he pledged the Catholic Church to the maintenance of order and asked the Tsar to respect the dignity of his

Leo enjoyed improved relations with Russia following the assassination of Tsar Alexander II who was succeeded by Alexander III (below).

1878	1879	1881	1883	1888
Bulgaria, Romania, Montenegro, and Serbia become independent of the Ottoman Empire.	German engineer Karl Benz produces the first working automobile powered by an internal combustion engine.	American outlaw Billy the Kid is shot dead by Sheriff Pat Garrett near Fort Sumner.	Indonesian volcano Krakatoa erupts with what is thought to have been the most powerful volcanic explosion in recorded history. Around 40,000 people are killed by the blast and subsequent tsunami.	The serial killer known as Jack the Ripper murders and mutilates at least five (possibly eight) women in London in a three month reign of terror. He is never caught.

Leo died aged 93. He chose not to be buried in St. Peter's, but in St. John Lateran—his cathedral church as bishop of Rome.

Catholic subjects. Fearing revolution, the Tsar welcomed the move and relations improved. Leo also set about establishing good relations with France, Britain, Brazil, and the USA—though in the last country he was rather unfairly dragged into a dispute over state schooling.

However, the political and diplomatic aspects of Leo's pontificate were dominated by the issue of the Papal States. The loss of those territories had badly affected the papal finances, and this had undermined the ability of the pope to act in an independent and neutral manner. Like Pius IX before him, Leo remained inside the Vatican, refusing to leave as this would involve him with the secular authorities he refused to recognize. The hostility of the Italian governments that confiscated Church lands and properties only made the situation worse. Leo banned Catholics from holding office in the Italian state, though whether this achieved anything productive is unclear.

The Altare della Patria (Altar of the Fatherland) in Rome was built in honor of Victor Emmanuel, the first king of a unified Italy.

Leo sought to regularize and consolidate the massive spread of the Catholic faith in recent decades. He established 248 new sees, 48 vicariates, and 2 patriarchates, most of them in Africa, India, and the Far East. He even managed to reestablish sees in North Africa that had not seen them since the Muslim invasions more than a thousand years earlier. He tentatively sought to deal with Protestantism, referring to Protestants as "lost brothers" instead of "heretics." However, he rejected a suggested federation of denominations as undermining what he saw as the true universal and Catholic Church led by himself.

His personal faith was deep and conservative. He wrote no less than 11 encyclicals on the Blessed Virgin Mary and the rosary. He also laid emphasis on the study of scripture. In the year 1900, he opened up new areas of theological thought when he asked a group of theologians to investigate the possibility of using the jubilee year of 1900 to formally dedicate the entire world to the Sacred Heart of Jesus. Several Catholic orders and institutions had already dedicated themselves in this way, but Leo was worried about the implications of dedicating non-Christians to the Sacred Heart of Jesus. The theologians produced a report stating it was acceptable, so Leo went ahead, and made June the Month of the Sacred Heart.

In his management of the Church, Leo continued the program of centralization begun by Pius IX. Again, it was improving means of transport and communication that largely made this possible, but Leo played his part by moving orders and congregations to Rome. He also intervened in the appointment of bishops.

But Leo had no closed mind. He opened up the Papal Archives to non-Catholic scholars for the first time and encouraged Catholic historians to devote themselves to the truth rather than slavishly supporting papal actions in past centuries. He was also known for his sense of humor and ability to connect with even the humblest of the faithful. At one audience, he was chatting to a man who told the pope that he had attended the last audience given by Pius IX before his death. Leo grinned and replied, "If I had known that you were so dangerous to popes, I would have postponed this audience."

1889

The Coca-Cola Company is founded.

1898

The Spanish-American War lasts 4 months, costs around 60,000 lives, and ends with Cuba and the Philippines gaining independence from Spain.

1899

War breaks out between Britain and the Boer Republics of southern Africa. The war will last three years, cost around 100,000 lives and end with the Boer republics being annexed by Britain.

1900

The Boxer Rebellion breaks out in China when the Society of Harmonious Fists launched a rebellion aimed at expelling Christian missionaries and foreign businessmen from China. The rebellion cost about 150,000 lives.

ST. PIUS X ✠ The 257th Pope 1903–1914

Born Riese, Italy; June 2, 1835

Parents Father, Giovanni Battista Sarto; Mother, Margarita Sanson

Papacy August 4, 1903–August 20, 1914

Died Rome, Italy; August 20, 1914

Of humble origins, Pius X was a contradiction of a pope. Personally conservative, he nevertheless introduced some important reforms. Respectful of authority, he still overturned the imperial veto. Uninterested in politics, he nevertheless facilitated a move by Catholicism into Italian politics.

It would be difficult for a man to have a more humble birth than that of Giuseppe Melchiorre Sarto. He was born in the small rural village of Riese in Venetia. His father was the village postman, while his mother took in needlework to help make ends meet. He went to the local village school before, at the age of 15, transferring to the seminary at Padua—the nearest town of any size. He was ordained in 1858 and took up a position as a rural curate, waiting eight years before he was able to become a priest at Salzano, another rural community in Venetia.

Mantua Cathedral. The town had suffered during the 1866 war between Italy and Austria, which had wrested the area out of Austrian hands.

It was in 1875, when he moved to Treviso to be chancellor, that Sarto was first noticed by anyone other than his parishioners. In Treviso, he also served as spiritual director of the seminary. From there he was promoted to be bishop of Mantua. The diocese was financially poor and suffered a lack of resources in all forms. Sarto had never attained a doctorate from a university and had to be given special dispensation by Leo XIII before he could become bishop. In due course, he would become the last pope not to have a doctorate.

In Mantua, Bishop Sarto worked wonders. He revitalized the spiritual life of the diocese and restored the finances. In 1893, Leo XIII promoted him again to be patriarch of Venice and cardinal priest of San Bernardo alle Terme. As when he was curate, priest, and vicar, Archbishop Sarto concentrated on the pastoral care of his flock. He expressed no views on other matters, though he did discreetly encourage local Catholics to oppose Socialism.

When Leo died, Sarto journeyed to Rome for the conclave along with 61 other cardinals. Only Patrick Moran, Archbishop of Sydney, Australia, did not make it to Rome in time. In itself this was a telling detail of how the Catholic Church was changing. That said, 38 of the 62 cardinals were Italian.

The cardinals had to decide if the next pope would continue Leo's attempts to move the Church into step with the modern world or

1903

The first Tour de France bicycle race is held.

1905

Battle of Tsushima. A Russian fleet of 28 ships is almost wiped out by a Japanese fleet of 52 ships, the first time a major European power has been defeated by an Asian country for 500 years.

1907

Retired British army officer Robert Baden-Powell founds the Boy Scouts.

1908

The Tunguska Event. A fireball is seen in the sky over Siberia, followed by a massive blast that flattened around 850 square miles of forest. It is now thought to have been caused by a comet colliding with Earth.

MODERNISM

Pius was faced by a theological dispute over what became known as Modernism. This movement took various forms but at its heart was the belief that dogma can change over time not only in terms of how the truth is expressed, but also in terms of what the truth actually is. Pius viewed this idea with alarm. He recognized that it meant that the beliefs of the Church were no longer fixed on the basis of what Jesus Christ had preached but could be altered to fit in with whatever a group of people wanted. Ultimately, it would undermine the very meaning of Christianity. Pius condemned it as a heresy and forced all clergy to take an oath repudiating the idea.

return to Pius IX's view that the Church should not bow to contemporary fashions. The leading papabile was Mariano Rampolle, secretary of state to Leo XIII. During the eighteenth century the custom had become established that the three great Catholic monarchs—the kings of Spain and France and the emperor of Austria—had the right to veto a cardinal they did not want to be pope. That power had not been exercised for a century, the last time it had been tried was in 1846, but the Austrian cardinal arrived too late to do so. Now Cardinal Jan Puzyna suddenly announced that Emperor Franz Joseph of Austria was vetoing Rampolle. There was instant uproar. The cardinals were outraged that a secular ruler should try to interfere in Church matters. Feelings ran high.

Even so, when the votes were counted Rampolle failed to be elected. Instead, after just four days, the conclave elected Sarto. His reputation was of a conservative, but one with the common touch and a heavy helping of common sense. Within hours of his election, Sarto had taken three decisions. First, he took the name of Pius X to honor Pius IX. Second, he formally abolished the veto and ruled that any cardinal who announced such a veto would be immediately excommunicated. Third, he gave his inaugural blessing inside St. Peter's, not outside, to symbolize his refusal to accept the Kingdom of Italy's right to rule Rome.

The tomb of St. Pius X in St. Peter's, Rome, sculpted by Pier Enrico Astorri.

Like Leo and Pius before him, Pius X resolutely refused to accept the annexation of the Papal States by the Kingdom of Italy. However, he did give to bishops the right to relax the prohibition on Catholics taking part in political life depending on local circumstances—a measure that was widely taken to mean if there were otherwise a possibility that Socialists might win elections. In France, Pius saw the state confiscate vast amounts of Church property. He refused any compromises that might have saved some of the property and was similarly forthright in his condemnation of the separation of Church and State in Portugal in 1911. In 1910, US President Theodore Roosevelt was visiting Italy and an audience was arranged with Pius. But on hearing that Roosevelt had that morning spoken at a Methodist chapel, Pius at once canceled the audience. The move caused offence in the USA, but Pius paid no attention.

Pius may have been conservative, but he recognized that the changed situation of the Church required internal changes. The curia was massively reorganized with all offices relating to the Papal States and other obsolete matters eliminated. The aims and purposes of the different offices were redefined to recognize new duties, and the numbers of employees drastically reduced. He also ordered a thorough revision of the canon law, insisting on a uniform set of laws across all of the Catholic faith. The liturgy too was overhauled, and Pius made a determined effort to promote Gregorian chants over the elaborate church music of recent centuries.

The outbreak of the First World War badly affected Pius, who suffered a heart attack and died a few days later.

Stories of miracles performed by Pius were current during his lifetime. Other reports were made about his tomb, to which a huge number of pilgrims came, very soon after his death. He was beatified in 1951, and canonized in 1954.

1908

The Hoover Company starts manufacturing vacuum cleaners.

1912

The British luxury liner RMS Titanic sinks after hitting an iceberg at a cost of 1,519 lives.

1912

First Balkan War sees an alliance of Serbia, Montenegro, Bulgaria, and Greece defeat the Ottoman Empire, annexing and partitioning almost all the European territories of the Ottomans.

1914

Charlie Chaplin appears in his first movie: *Making a Living*.

1914

First World War starts when the Austro-Hungarian empire invades Serbia.

BENEDICT XV ✠ The 258th Pope 1914–1922

Born Genoa, Italy; November 21, 1854

Parents Father, Marchese Giuseppe della Chiesa; Mother, Marchesa Giovanna Migliorati

Papacy September 3, 1914–January 22, 1922

Died Rome, Italy; January 22, 1922

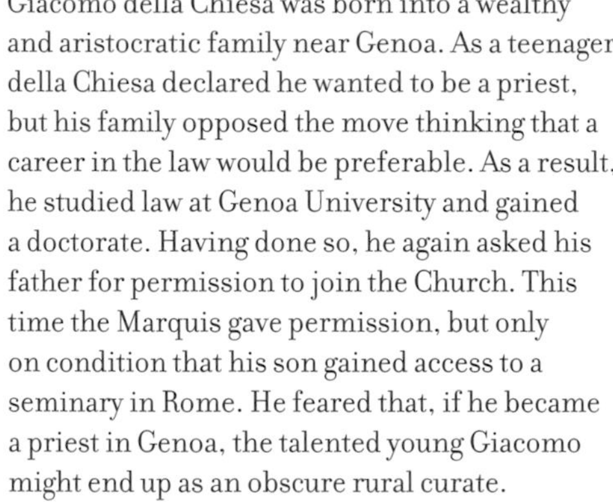

The ponitificate of Benedict XV was dominated by World War I and the terrible human tragedies it brought in its wake. In August 1917, he offered a "Peace Note" to the warring powers to try to bring about the cessation of hostilities. By skilful diplomacy and adroit interventions Benedict managed to do much good and to improve the standing of the papacy.

Giacomo della Chiesa was born into a wealthy and aristocratic family near Genoa. As a teenager della Chiesa declared he wanted to be a priest, but his family opposed the move thinking that a career in the law would be preferable. As a result, he studied law at Genoa University and gained a doctorate. Having done so, he again asked his father for permission to join the Church. This time the Marquis gave permission, but only on condition that his son gained access to a seminary in Rome. He feared that, if he became a priest in Genoa, the talented young Giacomo might end up as an obscure rural curate.

Kaiser Wilhelm II, emperor of Germany, photographed in 1888.

Accordingly, della Chiesa moved to Rome and studied at the Capranica College and Gregorian University. After ordination in 1878, he spent four years as a junior official in the papal diplomatic service and then, in 1873, became secretary to Mariano Rampolle, nuncio to Spain. After 14 years in Spain, Rampolle became a cardinal and papal Secretary of State. Della Chiesa moved to Rome with him. When Rompelle was dismissed as Secretary of State by the incoming Pope Pius X, della Chiesa was moved out of the curia to become archbishop of Bologna. It was not until May 1914 that della Chiesa became a cardinal and three months later he joined the conclave to elect a successor to Pius.

The conclave took place just a few days after a general war had broken out between the major European powers—a conflict that would become World War I. The cardinals were divided as to whether to choose a pope likely to be able to cope with the war or one with a more theological focus. In the end, they opted for della Chiesa because of his established skills as a diplomat and contacts in foreign governments.

Taking the name of Benedict XV, the new pope made a vain appeal for peace before setting his mind to the more practical task of limiting the suffering of the peoples affected by the war. After much soul-searching, Benedict decided to stay neutral in the conflict. Although he had very real fears that a victory for the Allies might see Orthodox Russia moving into central Europe and imposing its faith there, he could not side against Catholic France.

Instead, he used his neutral stance to talk to both sides, even though many diplomats suspected, unfairly, that he favored the other side. Benedict set up an office in the Vatican that was dedicated to transmitting letters between prisoners of war and their families at home. He also persuaded Switzerland to accept soldiers suffering from tuberculosis, no matter which country they came from—clear mountain air being then considered necessary to alleviate the disease.

In 1917, Benedict decided to make another appeal for peace. He sent a letter to all combatant states setting forth a Seven Point Plan for peace with justice. This called for, among other things, a return to pre-war borders and a panel of international diplomats

1914
The First World War spreads to include Germany and Austria-Hungary against Britain, France, Russia, and Belgium.

1915
The Ottoman Empire joins the First World War on the side of Germany and Austro-Hungary.

1916
Romania joins the First World War on the side of Russia, France, and Britain.

1916
The battles of Verdun and the Somme on the Western Front between them claim about 1.3 million lives.

Trench warfare during World War I, which cost the lives of approximately 14 million.

to examine rival claims on territory. Britain, Bulgaria, and Austria-Hungary welcomed the note as the basis for peace talks, but France and Germany rejected it. Russia then collapsed into revolution and civil war, after which Benedict's idea was forgotten.

When peace finally came, Italy demanded that the pope be excluded from the talks and the other Allies agreed. Disappointed, Benedict instead set about making contact with the governments of the new European countries born out of the Versailles Treaty. Poland, Czechoslovakia, Hungary, Austria, and Yugoslavia all needed attention, as did the already established countries. By 1922, the number of countries with a diplomatic embassy in the Vatican had doubled from the number in 1914. Benedict wondered if the collapse of the Tsarist regime in Russia might open the way for union between the Catholic and Orthodox Churches, but the brutally anti-Christian regime of the Communist leader Lenin made this impossible.

Tsar Nicholas II of Russia, photographed in 1898.

The new political map of Europe caused enormous problems in the missionary field. Missionaries who had been sent out to convert locals in a colony of one country found themselves working in a colony belonging to another state of which they might not have been a national. Benedict's solution would prove to have far-reaching results. He told missionaries, and in particular bishops in new dioceses, to concentrate their efforts on caring for the souls of their charges and to ignore the needs or demands of colonial authorities. They were also instructed to make great efforts to educate and ordain local priests drawn from the native populations. As a result, he was hailed as "the Pope of the Missions." The long term results of this drive on the Catholic Church cannot be overstated.

Meanwhile, what had become known as the Roman Question demanded his attention. In 1870, the Kingdom of Italy had invaded and annexed Rome and the remaining Papal States. This move had had a profound impact on papal finances and was deemed illegal by Benedict and his predecessors. By 1918, it was clear that Italy was not going to be persuaded to hand the Papal States back—though Kaiser Wilhelm II of Germany had promised to return them if Benedict came out in support of Germany in the war, an offer Benedict wisely declined.

Benedict concluded that it was time to try to seek a settlement that would give honor to both the pope and to Italy. He put out diplomatic feelers and, although nothing definite was agreed, he did establish contact and begin discussions.

In 1921, at the age of just 67, Benedict went down with influenza. That developed into pneumonia and, soon after the new year of 1922, he passed away.

1917

The USA joins the World War I on the side of Russia, France, Romania, and Britain.

1917

The Russian Revolution sparks a civil war that ends with the Bolshevik Communists in power in Russia.

1918

World War I ends with the defeat of Germany, the Ottoman Empire, and Austro-Hungary. The map of Europe is redrawn with several small countries becoming independent.

1921

Albert Einstein wins the Nobel Prize for Science.

PIUS XI ✠ The 259th Pope 1922–1939

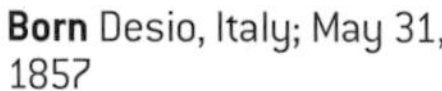

Born Desio, Italy; May 31, 1857

Parents Father, Francis Galli; Mother, Teresa Galli

Papacy February 6, 1922–February 10, 1939

Died Rome, Italy; February 10, 1939

Pius came to the papal throne as a scholar determined to seek compromise and peaceful relations whenever possible. It was his misfortune to have to deal with others who refused compromise or peace in return. Nevertheless, it was during his papacy that the Lateran Treaty was signed between the Kingdom of Italy and the Holy See.

Ambrogio Damiano Achile Ratti was born into a prosperous middle-class family, his father being the manager of a silk-spinning mill. At the time he was born, his native village of Desio, near Milan, was part of the Habsburg Empire but became part of the Kingdom of Italy in 1861. In 1879, he was ordained in the Lateran and embarked on a career as a Christian scholar. He gained three separate doctorates from the Gregorian University, then joined the seminary at Padua as a professor and, in 1888, took over the care of the great Ambrosian Library in Milan. In his spare time Ratti went climbing in the Alps and wrote a number of academic works.

After 23 years as Librarian in Milan, Ratti moved to the Vatican Library. Pope Benedict XV noticed Ratti's language and diplomatic skills and sent him to Poland in 1919 with the title of archbishop of Lepanto. When the Soviet Russians invaded Poland and advanced on Warsaw, Ratti was the only foreign diplomat who did not flee the guns. After the Russians were driven back, Ratti tried to open communication with Lenin's Communist regime to alleviate the sufferings of Catholics persecuted by the atheist Soviets, but with little success. When a plebiscite was announced in Silesia to decide if the region should join Poland or Germany, Ratti declared that Catholic clergy should be neutral—a stance that led to his being asked to leave Poland.

Back in Rome, Ratti was appointed archbishop of Milan and cardinal. A year later he entered the conclave to find a replacement to Benedict XV. The four non-European cardinals all set off for Rome, but none got there in time to take part. The conclave was split between conservatives and liberals. After five days and 14 ballots the 53 cardinals present elected Ratti, a moderate conservative. He took the name Pius XI. One of his first acts was the change the rules to allow cardinals from beyond Europe time to reach Rome for a conclave.

Pius adopted the motto of "Christ's Peace in Christ's Kingdom," proclaiming that he wanted to see the Church active in society, not standing apart from it. In the political sphere, Pius saw his main task as improving relations between the Catholic Church and secular governments to improve the conditions of Catholics and priests.

No relationship with a secular government could be more important than that with Italy. Since 1871, when the Italian government had annexed Rome and the Papal States, the popes had remained inside the vast 16th-century Vatican fortress because to step outside would be to acknowledge Italian rule. Pius took the first step in reaching an agreement minutes after being elected. He gave his first public blessing from the loggia of St. Peter's, facing out toward the City of Rome, not facing in to the basilica as his predecessors had done. Even so, it would take until February 1929 before a

Map showing the limits of the Vatican State as defined by the Lateran Treaty of 1929 between the Kingdom of Italy and the Holy See.

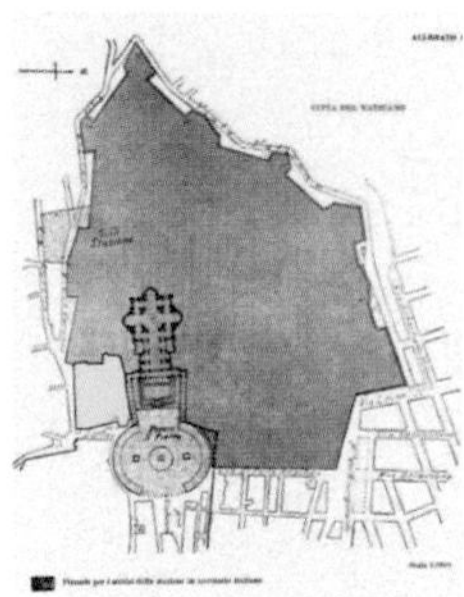

1926

The world's first pedestrian crossing over a road marked by black and white stripes on the road surface is built in the UK.

1928

The world's first all sound feature movie, *The Perfect Crime*, is made in Hollywood by FBO Pictures.

1929

The Wall Street Crash precipitates the Great Depression when millions were unemployed and economic stagnation affected the world.

Mussolini (left) and Adolf Hitler in Berlin, September 1937. In the same year, Pope Pius denounced the Nazi regime as anti-Christian.

final agreement was reached.

The Lateran Treaty of 1929 established the Vatican as a fully independent city state located wholly within the Kingdom of Italy. The Kingdom of Italy paid a large cash sum to compensate the papacy for the loss of the Papal States. Furthermore, a large number of basilicas, cathedrals, and other clerical buildings throughout Italy were given a status akin to that of foreign embassies, exempting them from state taxes and other regulations. Catholicism was made the state religion of Italy and, in return, the papacy lifted its prohibition on Catholics taking part in political life with the Kingdom. Both Italy and the Vatican have generally abided by the Treaty since. Successful concordats with numerous other countries followed.

With two states, Pius failed to establish good relations. The first was the openly atheist Soviet regime in Russia that confiscated Church property, persecuted Catholics, and refused to open relations with the Vatican. The second was Nazi Germany. In 1933, a concordat was agreed with the new Nazi regime of Adolf Hitler, but it soon became clear that Hitler intended to abide by the provisions only when it suited him to do so. In 1937, Pius declared the Nazi regime to be anti-Christian and denounced it without reservation.

Under Joseph Stalin's atheist regime, tens of thousands of priests, monks, and nuns were persecuted and killed. Over 100,000 were shot during the purges of 1937–1938.

In the religious sphere, Pius was passionately committed to spreading the faith of Catholic Christianity. He instructed every religious order to take part in missionary work, with the result that the number of active missionaries doubled. He founded a faculty of missionology at the Gregorian University to boost the movement further. In 1926, he took a momentous step when he personally consecrated six Chinese bishops. The move was controversial for it had to this point been accepted that locals could rise only to the rank of priest, with bishops coming from Europe. Pius followed the move by consecrating a Japanese bishop in 1927 and approving a huge increase in the number of native priests in India, Africa, and Asia.

His views on ecumenicalism were more mixed. He approved talks between Catholics and Anglicans on matters of faith, but was wary of the moves to combine all Protestant denominations. In 1928, he forcefully repeated the Catholic view that Christ's Church was an indivisible whole under the guidance of the pope as St. Peter's successor and could not be a union of independent Churches.

Pius was not, however, averse to change. In 1931, he founded the Vatican Radio, which still broadcasts, to be the voice of the Vatican. A TV station was to be added in the 1990s. He also founded the Pontifical Academy of Sciences to promote the advance of science, with particular reference to how scientific advances interact with Christian faith. Archaeology was greatly encouraged as was astronomy.

On November 25, 1938, Pius suffered two heart attacks from which he never fully recovered. He thereafter remained largely in his chambers and, by February 1939, it was clear he was dying. Those close to him gathered round and heard his final words: "My soul parts from you all in peace."

1933

Adolf Hitler becomes Chancellor of Germany.

1935

Radar (then called Radio Direction Finding) is invented in the UK.

1936

Outbreak of the Spanish Civil War. The conflict will last three years, cost half a million lives, and end with fascist dictator Francisco Franco as ruler of Spain.

1937

Japan invades China achieving early victories, including the capture of Shanghai and Nanking, though the war would by 1939 become stalemated due to the vast hinterland of China.

PIUS XII ✠ The 260th Pope 1939–1958

Born Rome, Italy; March 2, 1876

Parents Father, Filippo Pacelli; Mother, Virginia Graziosi

Papacy March 2, 1939–October 9, 1958

Died Rome, Italy; October 9, 1958

Elected as the shadows of war spread once again across Europe, Pius knew that his main tasks would be peace and reconciliation. To these ends he worked consistently throughout his reign, choosing as his coat of arms a dove of peace holding an olive branch perched on a mountain. His hopes for international peace were, however, to be dashed.

To outward appearances, the background of the future Pius XII was as traditional, even old fashioned, as it was possible to get. He was born in Rome to the Pacelli family, a branch of the old Roman nobility that had remained steadfastly loyal to the papacy when Rome fell to the Kingdom of Italy in 1871. His father, grandfather, brother, and several cousins all worked for the papacy. His future career was effectively chosen from the start.

Although his father sent young Eugenio Maria Giuseppe Giovanni Pacelli to a state school, the teenager chose the Gregorian University for his further education and was ordained a priest in 1899, after which he entered papal service and spent 12 years helping Cardinal Gasparri fully revise and codify canon law. Pacelli was chosen for the delicate task of being nuncio to the Kingdom of Bavaria, then part of the German empire and fighting World War I. Although he worked hard, he failed to get the Germans to agree to Benedict XV's 1917 peace plan. Pacelli remained in Bavaria after the war and, in 1924, was able to agree a concordat with the new Republic of Bavaria regarding Church-State relations. He negotiated a similar, though less favorable, agreement with the Republic of Prussia in 1929.

In 1930, Pacelli returned to Rome be created a cardinal and given the job of secretary of state. In this role he negotiated concordats with Austria and with Germany, when he took at face value the promises made by Adolf Hitler. He undertook an arduous succession of foreign visits, including to Britain, the USA, France, and Hungary.

When Pius XI died in February 1939 it was already clear that a European war was likely. As a seasoned and generally successful diplomat, Pacelli was considered a leading papabille, although there was also a move to elect a non-Italian with Karl Schulte of Munich being the man most talked about. In the event, Pacelli received exactly the required two thirds majority of votes on the second ballot. However, he was well aware of the gravity of the international situation and wanted to be confident that he had the backing of the Church, so he asked for a third ballot and this time was elected unanimously, except for his own vote which went elsewhere.

On May 3, Pius began diplomatic moves proposing that a general European conference be held to identify and negotiate all outstanding differences. He was rebuffed by Hitler and Stalin. On August 24, as Hitler was ramping up the diplomatic pressure on Poland, Pius spoke on Vatican Radio urging all leaders to avoid war. Two weeks later, Germany invaded Poland. Even so, Pius did not give up trying. It was not until Italy declared war on Britain and France in June 1940 that he finally despaired of peace and turned instead to trying to ameliorate the effects of what had become World War II.

In 1950, Pius defined the dogma relating to the Assumption, declaring that the Virgin Mary "having completed the course of her earthly life, was assumed body and soul into heavenly glory." Four years later, he returned to the subject of the Virgin to discuss her royal status, but chose to leave undefined her role in redemption and mediation.

1939

Germany invades Poland, which is supported by Britain and France, thus starting World War II. Poland surrenders after six weeks.

1940

Germany conquers Denmark, Norway, Belgium, Netherlands, Luxembourg, and France. Britain refuses to surrender. Italy declares war on Britain.

1941

Germany invades the Soviet Union. Japan attacks the USA at Pearl Harbor and Britain in Malaya.

1943

Germany is defeated at Stalingrad, Japan is defeated in the Solomons—both turning points in World War II.

Russian Jews await selection at Auschwitz. Vatican Radio first alerted the world to the fact that Jews were being rounded up and shipped off to unknown destinations.

Following the lead of Pope Benedict XV in World War I, Pius adopted a neutral stance. At Christmas 1939, he had laid down the principles on which peace could be achieved, and he consistently pushed the belligerents to accept them. A system for putting prisoners of war in touch with their families at home was established, processing more than 10 million letters and reports by the end of the war. When, in 1943, the Allies demanded unconditional surrender, Pius spoke out against the proposal, believing that this would only strengthen Hitler's grip on the German military. When the Germans occupied Rome in September 1943, Pius denied them entrance to the Vatican and continued to harbor a number of refugees behind the Vatican walls.

An atomic bomb destroys the city of Nagasaki, Japan, on August 9, 1945.

There has been some criticism since the war alleging that Pius did not do enough to oppose the murderous Nazi regime. His denunciations of both Nazi and Soviet atrocities were always couched in diplomatic language. His reticence may well have been influenced by the fact that for most of the war he was living in the Vatican, entirely surrounded by Fascist Italy. If he had spoken out too strongly, Pius may well have found his state invaded and himself arrested, and so unable to do anything at all. Nevertheless, it was the Vatican Radio that first alerted the world to the fact that Jews were being rounded up and shipped off to unknown destinations—in fact to extermination camps—and the papacy did much to try to help vast numbers of individuals.

After the war, Pius continued to concentrate on humanitarian causes. He maintained a neutral stance in the developing Cold War just as he had during the recent real war.

From his youth, Pius had been devoted to the Virgin Mary and took up the cause of Our Lady of Fatima, perhaps influenced by the fact that the first vision at Fatima took place on the same day that he was made an archbishop. In 1952, he dedicated the people of Russia to the immaculate heart of Mary, telling Stalin "The Gates of Hell will never prevail, where she offers her protection."

Pius created more cardinals than any previous pope, a total of 56. The move had a profound effect on the balance of the global Church. For the first time, Italians were in a minority. Conversely, Pius reduced the role of the college of cardinals, preferring to rely on officials and advisers. The number of dioceses also went up, from 1,696 to 2,048. Pius was also an assiduous canonizer of saints, raising 33 people to sainthood, among them Pope Pius X.

In 1954, Pius suffered a severe infection, after which his health was never as robust as it had been. He avoided long ceremonies and preferred to sit when before he might have stood. He continued with his duties however, and in one of his last acts raised a young Polish priest, Karol Wojtyla (later Pope John Paul II), to be a bishop. Pius died in 1958 of heart failure. His funeral was attended by a vast crowd, many of them Romans come to bury "their" pope.

1945	1946	1952	1954	1956
World War II ends with the surrender of Germany and Japan. The war lasted six years and cost about 60 million lives.	Britain's Winston Churchill accuses the Soviet Union of building an Iron Curtain to cut off Communist countries from the rest of the world, later recognized as the start of the Cold War.	The world's first transistor hearing aid transforms life for millions of the hard of hearing.	The BBC broadcasts the world's first regular television news broadcast.	The Hungarian Uprising sees the Hungarian government attempt to shake off Communist control, but the Soviet Union invades and reimposes Communism by force. About 20,000 are killed.

JOHN XXIII ✠ The 261st Pope 1958–1963

Born Sotto il Monte, Italy; November 25, 1881

Parents Father, Giovanni Battista Roncalli; Mother, Marianna Giulia Mazzolla

Papacy October 28, 1958–June 3, 1963

Died Rome, Italy; June 3, 1963

Warm, kind, and of peasant stock, John XXIII declared on his election that he wanted to be "a good shepherd to the Catholic flock." This aim very quickly became the central hallmark of his pontificate, though he is better remembered for having summoned the Second Vatican Council and taking the bold step of inviting non-Catholics to attend.

Angelo Giuseppe Roncalli was the third of 13 children born to a poor peasant family in a tiny village near Bergamo in northern Italy. He went to the local school, then to the seminary in Bergamo, before winning a scholarship to the San Apollinare Institute in Rome. He graduated as a Doctor of Theology in 1904 and became secretary to Bishop Radini-Tedeshci of Bergamo, a post he held for nine years. During these years, he also lectured in diocesan history at the seminary where he himself had been educated.

In 1915, Italy joined World War I to try to gain territory from the Habsburg Empire and young Roncalli was called up. He spent the war working in military hospitals. In 1921, he became national director of the Congregation for the Propagation of the Faith. He had meanwhile become interested in St. Charles Borromeo, who had been Archbishop of Milan from 1564 to 1584 and a leading early figure in the Counter-Reformation. Roncalli wrote a number of papers on St. Charles, the researches for which took him to the Ambrosian Library in Milan where he met Achille Ratti.

When Ratti became Pope Pius XI he made Roncalli titular archbishop of Areopolis and sent him on a series of diplomatic missions to Turkey, Greece, and Bulgaria. He established friendly relations with figures in both the Turkish government and in the Greek Orthodox Church. He remained in the Balkans during World War II as apostolic delegate to Turkey and Greece. With Greece under Italo-German occupation and Turkey friendly to the Axis, Roncalli maintained the strict papal neutrality. But when he became aware of the mass murder of Jews by the Germans, he decided to take a hand. He arranged passage through Turkey, or on ships passing through Turkish waters, to Palestine for large numbers of Jews. He persuaded King Boris of Bulgaria to allow Jewish Bulgarians to leave for Palestine before the Germans rounded them up, and he arranged for the Jews kept at Jasenovac Concentration Camp in Yugoslavia to be released.

THE SECOND VATICAN COUNCIL

John's reign is best known for the summoning of the Second Vatican Council, sometimes called "Vatican II," which he himself ascribed to the inspiration of the Holy Spirit. The aim of the Council was to be a second Pentecost to rejuvenate the Church with improved teaching, discipline, and organization. John shocked many cardinals by inviting observers from 18 non-Catholic denominations to attend. Preparations were begun in 1960 and the Council opened in St. Peter's Basilica on October 11, 1962. After opening the Council, John himself did not attend the sessions, although he did intervene when the members were unable to agree among themselves—most notably on the schema on revelation. On December 8, 1962, he formally closed the first session and announced the second session would open in nine months time.

1958

The European Economic Community (EEC) is founded.

1959

The world's first nuclear-powered ship is launched, US Navy cruiser USS *Long Beach*.

1959

The Cuban Revolution ends after a six-year struggle, with Communist leader Fidel Castro replacing the regime of Fulgencio Batista.

Pope John XXIII had a special interest in St. Charles Borromeo who had been a leading figure in the Counter-Reformation.

In 1944, he was appointed papal nuncio to the newly liberated France. His official task was to seek an arrangement with the new French government on the financing of church schools and other administrative matters, but his time was consumed by the tricky issue of dealing with those bishops who were accused of, to one extent or another, collaborating with the Germans. In 1952, he moved to be the papal observer at UNESCO (United Nations Educational, Scientific and Cultural Organization). The following year he was made patriarch of Venice, proving himself to be an energetic and proactive pastoralist who dispensed with formality whenever he felt it got in the way of his duties.

When Pius XII died there was an immediate discussion about Giovanni Montini, archbishop of Milan. Montini was not a cardinal, but he was highly respected and popular. Some commentators felt he should be pope, but others felt that the tradition of electing a cardinal was now too strong. In fact, Montini did gain votes in the conclave, but most votes went to cardinals. When it was announced that 77-year-old Roncalli had been elected most people saw him as being a caretaker pope, but he himself saw no such limitations to his reign.

Roncalli chose the name of John to honor the disciple, his own father, and the church where he had been baptized. There was then an immediate discussion as to whether John XXIII of the 15th century had been a pope or an antipope. Roncalli himself solved the issue by declaring that he was John XXIII, at once relegating the 15th-century John to antipope status.

The Russian president Nikita Khrushchev was impressed by the pope's knowledge of the Soviet Union.

Building on his invitation to other Christian denominations to attend the Second Vatican Council (*see* box), John received Archbishop John Fisher, head of the Anglican Church, to the Vatican and exchanged friendly messages with other Christian leaders, among them Patriarch Athenagoras of Constantinople.

John's main concern was, however, pastoral. In January 1960, he held a synod of the clergy of Rome in St. John Lateran, the first on record. The aim was to rejuvenate faith within the city itself. He also produced works that called on clerics to pronounce truth in a spirit of love, and that sent greetings to non-Catholic Christians calling them "separated brethren and sons." In 1963, he broke new ground by calling for world peace to be built on foundations of human rights and responsibilities and asking richer countries to aid the poorer ones.

During the Cuban Missile Crisis of 1962, he urged caution on both the USA and the Soviet Union and offered to act as intermediary. The offer was turned down, but both sides were impressed by the pope's humanity and grasp of a complex situation. He also made pronouncements that drew a distinction between Marxist ideology and the actions of Communist regimes. His knowledge of Communism impressed President Khrushchev of the Soviet Union, who sent his son-in-law to the Vatican in 1963.

Within the Vatican, John was renowned for his good humor and shrewdness. He was also more willing to delegate authority than his recent predecessors, pushing decision-making out to lower ranks including to bishops. He also relaxed some of the ceremonial of the papal court when he felt this would help with his primary task.

In September 1962, he was diagnosed with inoperable stomach cancer. He remained able to do his duties until just a week before his death.

1961
Soviet Cosmonaut Yuri Gagarin becomes the first man in space.

1962
The Beatles release their first record "Love Me Do."

1962
US military advisers start arriving in South Vietnam to aid the South Vietnamese counter insurgency from the Communist North Vietnam.

1962
Telstar, the world's first communications satellite, is launched into orbit.

PAUL VI — The 262th Pope 1963–1978

Born Concesio, Italy; September 26, 1897
Parents Father, Giorgio Montini; Mother, Giudetta Alghisi
Papacy June 21, 1963–August 6, 1978
Died Castel Gandolfo, Italy; August 6, 1978

When he was elected pope, Giovanni Montini chose the name Paul to represent his outward-looking mission to the world. Throughout his pontificate Paul sought to make this mission a reality, though not always with great success due to the views of others. The day after his election, Paul announced that the Second Vatican Council would continue as planned.

Giovanni Battista Montini was born the son of a prosperous lawyer who had become a member of the Italian Parliament. The main influence on his early days was, however, his mother. Giudetta was born into the Alghisi family of local minor nobility and had a profoundly deep piety. Giovanni was a sickly child who spent much time at home, where he formed a strong bond with his mother. It was from her that he acquired his legendary love of books.

In 1954, Montini was appointed archbishop of Milan—a daunting post for the sprawling archdiocese contained 1,000 churches, 2,500 ordained priests, and 3.5 million people. The area had, moreover, been fought over during World War II and suffered much from aerial bombing. The industrial economy was fractured by trade disputes, Communist infiltration, and grinding poverty. When Montini arrived in Milan, his staff were amazed and concerned to find that he was accompanied by 90 crates of books, but their fears that he would prove to be an academic without the common touch were soon dispelled as Montini threw himself into the task of reviving his archdiocese. In November 1957, for example, he undertook an exhausting schedule that saw him visit every parish in Milan. He also made a point of meeting every priest in his archdiocese. Montini came to the conclusion that society had become so secularized that Western Europe should be treated as a non-Christian continent that needed to be converted. He used a wide range of tactics and devices to achieve this, including a massive poster campaign in 1957, and selecting 500 priests to go to factories, hotels, offices, hospitals, and town squares to preach and mix with the people. These novel tactics did not please everyone in the Church and met with only mixed success, but at least Montini was facing up to a problem that others denied existed.

John XXIII died in 1963 and Montini entered the conclave as the man most people expected to be elected. A rumor later circulated that the traditionalist Cardinal Giuseppe Siri, archbishop of Genoa, was elected with the necessary two-thirds majority on the second ballot but refused to become pope. The rumor has never been corroborated and Siri himself has refused to comment. Be that as it may, Montini was elected on the sixth ballot and took the name of Paul.

The day after his election Paul announced that Vatican II would continue as planned. He felt himself bound by the decisions of the Council and spent much of the rest of his pontificate seeking to implement its often controversial decisions. One of the most far

Paul reconvened the Second Vatican Council on September 29, 1963. That session lasted until December, with the third session lasting from September to November 1964 and the fourth session continuing from September to December 1965.

1963
Assassination of US President John F. Kennedy.

1968
The Prague Spring—an effort by the Czechoslovak government to ease repressive aspects of the Communist regime is halted by a Soviet invasion.

1969
Neil Armstrong becomes the first man on the moon as he emerges from the lunar module of spacecraft Apollo 11.

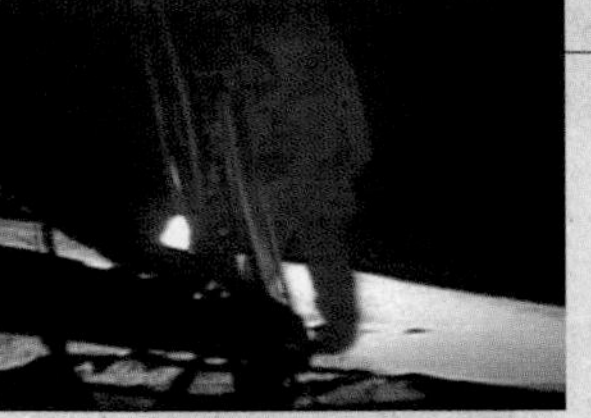

1972
The Munich Olympics are disrupted by an attack by the Black September Palestinian terrorist group that ends with 17 dead, including 12 hostages and five terrorists.

Opposition to the decisions of Vatican II, particularly those affecting the liturgy, was led by the French archbishop Marcel Lefebvre. The dispute came to a head in 1976 when Paul held talks with Lefebvre seeking a way forward, but Lefebvre refused to compromise.

In March 1978, former Italian Prime Minister and a friend of Pope Paul's, Aldo Moro, was kidnapped and later murdered by a Communist terrorist group, the Red Brigade. The murder was a severe blow to Paul, who conducted the funeral mass for his old friend.

reaching reforms was for the liturgy and the mass to be conducted in the vernacular language of the country where a church stood. Latin remained the official language of the master version, but the services were to be conducted in the local language. The Bible also was to be used primarily in the local vernacular, though the Latin version remained the official Bible of the Church. The role of bishops was to be enhanced with all the bishops of the Church forming a college, akin to the college of cardinals, supervised by the pope. Vatican II also held out a hand to other denominations for, while it reinforced the belief that the Catholic Church was the only true Church, it conceded that "many elements of sanctification and of truth are found outside."

Opposition to the decisions of Vatican II were led by Archbishop Marcel Lefebvre who refused to compromise and Paul eventually suspended him as a priest. Despite this dispute, Paul was successful in winning over most of the Catholic Church to the program of Vatican II.

Paul set a new trend in foreign travel. In 1964 he began with a pilgrimage to the Holy Land, holding a meeting with Patriarch Athenagoras of Constantinople in Jerusalem. Later in 1964 he flew to India to take part in the International Eucharistic Conference, also visiting New York, Istanbul, Uganda, Sardinia, Switzerland, and the Philippines, where he narrowly escaped being assassinated.

In 1967 and 1968, Paul produced two encyclicals that would enrage liberals and cause great controversy outside the ranks of the Catholic faithful. The first of these was *Sacerdotalis Caelibatus*, in which he reiterated the discipline that priests had to remain celibate. The document defended celibacy as an ideal state and a long established practice of special importance. However, Paul also recognized that some men find the demands of priestly celibacy too difficult and allowed bishops to permit men to leave the priesthood in certain circumstances.

The second controversial encyclical was *Humanae Vitae*. In this Paul reiterated the traditional Church teaching on marriage and put down in writing what had long been taught, that artificial birth control was condemned. The reaction to this pronouncement was mixed, but the controversy really began when World Bank President Robert McNamara announced, in 1968, that countries that permitted birth control would get preferential access to funds. That launched the debate into the political sphere where it was picked up by feminists, liberals, and others who favored contraception, many of whom were not Catholics. The debate over *Humanae Vitae* continues to this day.

Although Paul made great efforts to improve relations with other denominations, holding talks with the leaders of the Anglican and Orthodox faiths, he recognized that his true task was with the Catholic faith. In 1970, he canonized 40 English and Welsh Catholics who had died for their faith at the hands of the Protestant government in the 16th and 17th centuries, an act hardly calculated to improve relations with Protestants.

Paul sought to make the college of cardinals more representative of the wider Catholic Church. He raised the number of cardinals from 80 to 136, with many of the newcomers being from outside Europe, in particular from Africa and Latin America.

On May 9, 1978, the Red Brigade murdered Paul's friend and former Italian prime minister Aldo Moro. The murder was a severe blow to Paul, who conducted the funeral mass. Falling sick, Paul retreated to Castel Gandolfo, site of the papal summer palace on the shores of Lake Albano. There his sickness turned to a fever, which proved to be fatal.

1974
US President Richard Nixon is forced to resign as a result of the Watergate scandal.

1975
The Vietnam War ends with the conquest of South Vietnam by North Vietnam to form one single Communist Vietnam.

1975
Laos and Cambodia become Communist countries having been invaded by North Vietnamese troops.

1976
The Tanghshan Earthquake kills an estimated 700,000 in China.

JOHN PAUL I ✠ The 263rd Pope 1978

Born Canale d'Agordo, Italy; October 17, 1912

Parents Father, Giovanni Luciani; Mother, Bortola Tancon

Papacy August 26, 1978–September 28, 1978

Died Rome, Italy; September 28, 1978

Pope John Paul I's birthplace at Canale d'Agordo, Italy.

Albino Luciani was ordained on July 7, 1935.

The "Smiling Pope," as John Paul I quickly became known due to his cheerful demeanor, came to the papal throne full of promise and good will, but he was not to have the time to fulfil his ambitions—at just 33 days, his reign as pope is among the shortest in history and resulted in the most recent "Year of Three Popes."

Albino Luciani was born in a small mountain village in northern Italy within the Patriarchate of Venice. He was the eldest of four children born into a poor working-class family. His father was a bricklayer who was often away from home looking for work in the big Italian cities or over the border in Switzerland, so Luciani was brought up largely by his mother. Both his parents were socialists, with his father being an outspoken supporter of far-left policies that he urged on his workmates.

Young Luciani attended a local school before moving on to Belluno Seminary where he was found to be very boisterous. An attempt to join the Jesuits was blocked by the seminary's rector, so Luciani decided to become a priest instead. After completing his military service he was ordained on July 7 1935. He moved to Rome to gain a doctorate from the Gregorian University, then returned to his home village as a curate. Late in 1937 he became vice rector at the Belluno Seminary. He taught there for the next ten years, covering a variety of subjects and also served as vicar-general to the bishop of Belluno. He also, in 1949, was in charge of catechisms at the Belluno eucharistic conference. During these years Luciani was noteworthy among Italian clerics for his contacts with left-wing politicians, even maintaining a good working relationship with local branches of the Communist Party.

In 1958, Pope John XXIII made Luciani bishop of Vittorio Veneto, a small industrial town to the north of Venice. Over the next 11 years Luciani concentrated on his pastoral role and built up an extensive grass-roots ministry that reached out to all levels of society within his diocese. During the Second Vatican Council he played a minor background role on doctrinal matters. His reputation among fellow clergy was influenced by his doctrinal work, but it was primarily his flair for pastoral work that meant that he became Patriarch of Venice when that position fell vacant in 1969.

As Patriarch of Venice, Luciani continued to concentrate on pastoral work. He dispensed with a good deal of the traditional ceremonial and ritual associated with his new position, and encouraged his clergy to sell surplus church plate to raise funds for good works.

He published a book entitled *Illustrissimi*, which proved to be very popular. It was a series of letters written to historical figures or characters from Italian fiction (such as Pinocchio) each of which made a serious moral point couched in humorous and whimsical terms. The book, and other writings, revealed Luciani to be traditional in terms of theology and morals but to be fully aware that humans are not perfect. It also revealed a capacity for forgiveness and understanding.

Behind the scenes Luciani was, however, changing. In 1972, he became Vice President of the Italian Conference of Bishops, a position

1978

President Zia becomes President of Pakistan.

1978

Air India Flight 855, a Boeing 747, crashes into the Arabia Sea as a result of pilot error. All 213 passengers die.

1978

The Camp David Peace Accords are signed by Egypt and Israel.

1978

Louise Brown, the world's first "test-tube baby" is born.

John Paul I with future pope John Paul II.

that greatly increased his profile and fame within the Church. In 1973, he became cardinal priest of San Marco. Although he retained his generally left-wing views –he proposed that wealthy dioceses in the West should donate one percent of their income to poorer dioceses in the Third World—he gradually cut his links to formal left-wing groups. In 1975, he went so far as to state that Communism was incompatible with Christianity. The statement might have been unremarkable coming from other clerics, but from Luciani it marked a shift in attitude.

When Paul VI died in 1978, Luciani was largely unknown outside Italy, but his profile within the Church meant that those in the know considered him to be one of the four leading papabilli. Due to the advent of jet air travel even the most distant cardinal was able to get to Rome in time for the conclave, so no fewer than 111 cardinals took part in the traditional mass in St. Peter's before moving into the Sistine Chapel, the doors to which were then locked.

The four men considered papabilli were Cardinal Siri of Genoa, Cardinal Ursi of Naples, and Cardinal Benelli of Florence. The electors soon agreed that what they needed was a pastoral figure with limited links to the curia and papal establishment. It was thought that an Italian was preferable due to the important role of the papacy in Italian public life. Although the proceedings of the conclave are secret, it is thought that Siri was ahead in the first two ballots with Luciani second. The other candidates then dropped out, allowing Luciani to come first in the third ballot and to achieve the necessary two thirds majority on the fourth ballot.

Inside the Sistine Chapel, meanwhile, Luciani was formally asked if he accepted the result. He replied "May God forgive you for what you have done," then he accepted and declared his name would be John Paul to honor his two immediate predecessors. Cardinals took this as a sign he would steer a moderate course between the liberal pope John XXIII and the traditionalist pope Paul VI.

As the cardinals poured out of the conclave their excitement was clear. Several declared that they had chosen "God's candidate" and the feeling that divine inspiration had guided the vote became widespread. At a press conference John Paul I kept nearly a thousand journalists spellbound with his charm and good humor. He dispensed with the formal five hour coronation and instead was simply invested with the pallium as bishop of Rome.

Three weeks later on Friday, September 29, his housekeeper, Sister Vincenza, noticed that John Paul had not touched the early morning coffee she had left outside his bedroom door, as usual. She knocked, got no reply, and looked in. John Paul was sitting upright in bed, dead. He had apparently died of a heart attack the previous evening. Subsequent conspiracy theories alleging that he was murdered appear to be unfounded.

The sudden death of such a popular figure came as a great shock, and necessitated a second conclave in less than two months.

When the ballot papers of the fourth ballot in 1978 were burned no straw was added, so the smoke was white to indicate Paul's election. But then several cardinals burned their notes, some of which were on poor quality paper than burned with a dark gray smoke. This led to much consternation among the crowd outside who could not decide if the smoke was white or black.

1978

Double Eagle Two becomes the first manned balloon to cross the Atlantic.

1978

The United Nations observes an "international day of solidarity with the Palestinian people." It is boycotted by several countries, including the USA.

1978

Spain becomes a democracy after 40 years of dictatorship.

1978

Bulgarian defector Georgi Markov is murdered in London having been stabbed by a poisoned umbrella by the Bulgarian secret service.

JOHN PAUL II  The 264th Pope 1978–2005

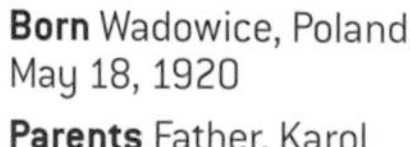

Born Wadowice, Poland; May 18, 1920

Parents Father, Karol Wojtyła; Mother, Emilia Kaczorowska

Papacy October 16, 1978–April 2, 2005

Died Rome, Italy; April 2, 2005

John Paul II was the first non-Italian pope since 1523 and the first Slav pope ever. He was a charismatic figure, widely held to have been the most influential pope of the twentieth century. He generally steered a moderate course in Church affairs despite his own firmly traditionalist views, he traveled widely and reached out to other Christian denominations.

Karol Wojtyla was born to a retired army lieutenant and his wife in Wadowice, an industrial town in Poland. His mother died when he was a young boy, so he was brought up primarily by his father, who supported his family of three children on his modest pension. After attending the local primary school, Wojtyla moved on to secondary school where he proved to be a popular and charismatic pupil. He excelled at sports, especially football and canoeing (he took up his famous hobby of skiing later), and showed a flair for poetry and acting. In 1938, the family moved to Krakow where Wojtyla entered the Jagiellonian University, the premier university in Poland. He studied Polish Literature and became a leading light in the university's amateur dramatics society as well as gaining attention for his poetry.

Wojtyla's life changed forever in September 1939 when Nazi Germany invaded and conquered Poland. The Germans closed down Jagiellonian University and began conscripting all able-bodied males who did not have a job to be taken to Germany to be used as slave labor. To avoid this fate, Wojtyla took a succession of laboring jobs in a quarry, a chemical factory, and a restaurant. The students and lecturers of the university secretly kept some lessons going, with Wojtyla even managing to keep the amateur dramatic society together.

The German occupation of Poland was notoriously brutal and bloody, with around six million civilians, some 20 percent of the population being killed. The capital city of Warsaw was almost completely destroyed, factories were stripped of anything useful and the countryside laid waste. It was during these hard years that Wojtyla turned to religion and began feeling the call to be a priest.

In January 1945, the Germans retreated from Krakow as the Soviet Russians advanced. Amid the chaos Wojtyla and fellow students reoccupied the ruined university buildings and began the task of clearing the rubble and patching up what could be saved. Wojtyla found a 14-year-old Jewish girl, Edith Zierer, unconscious on a railway platform. He carried her to a warm place and stayed with her until she could find somewhere safe. She later credited him with saving her life.

The birthplace of Pope John Paul II in the industrial city Wadowice, in southern Poland.

Wedding portrait of John Paul's parents: Karol and Emilia Wojtyla.

1979

Soviet Union invades Afghanistan to prop up an ailing Communist regime. Ten years later the Soviets will withdraw having lost about 18,000 men.

1980

Ronald Reagan is elected to be President of the USA inaugurating a radical program of economic reforms and reduction of government spending.

1980

The Polish trades union Solidarnosc (Solidarity) is founded under Lech Walesa. The union is later credited with having brought about the collapse of Communism in Poland.

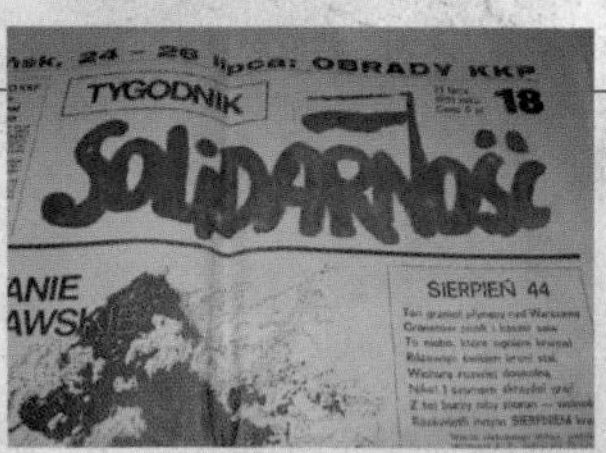

After 1999, John Paul's health began to decline. He continued with his travels, but now went about in a converted vehicle—dubbed the Popemobile.

The Soviet occupation of Poland proved to be almost as unpleasant as that of the Nazis. In some areas, the incoming Russians arrested anyone with a phone on the grounds that they must be bourgeois capitalists and so unsympathetic to a Communist takeover. That takeover came in 1946 when the Soviet secret police murdered hundreds of non-Communist politicians and imprisoned 150,000 suspected opponents, after which the Polish Parliament banned all political parties except the Communist Worker's Party. Elections were held in 1947 at which only Communists were allowed to stand as candidates. In Krakow, where Wojtyla lived, only 16 percent of voters voted for the Communist candidates, the others spoilt their ballot papers in protest. It made no difference and the Communist government took office, backed by Russian tanks.

Wojtyla, meanwhile, had graduated in theology and had published his first collection of poems, *Song of the Hidden God*. In November 1946, he was ordained a priest by Cardinal Adam Sapieha, archbishop of Krakow. As the Communist noose tightened, Sapieha sent Wojtyla to Rome to study at the Pontifical University where he obtained his doctorate in theology in 1948. He then went back to Poland to serve as parish priest in Niegowice near Krakow. In 1952, he began lecturing in social ethics at Krakow Seminary, a position he held for six years. He then returned to Jagiellonian University to study philosophy, writing a thesis in 1960 on Max Scheler. As professor of ethics at Lublin, he was acknowledged as one of Poland's leading thinkers and academics.

In 1958, Pius XII made Wojtyla titular bishop of Ombi and auxilliary bishop in Krakow. Five years later he was promoted to be archbishop of Krakow, a position he held for the next 15 years. He proved to be an implacable but shrewd opponent of the repressive Communist regime in Poland. However, he was wise enough to avoid needlessly provocative actions and became a consummate politician at a time when this could be a dangerous activity. In 1970, for instance, he quashed plans to mark the 50th anniversary of the Polish victory in the Polish-Russian war of 1920 knowing that the Soviets would react violently.

When it came to internal Church matters, Wojtyla was becoming an internationally known figure. In 1960, he wrote a pastoral guide, *Love and Responsibility*, for his clergy on various issues of sexuality and morality that was distributed widely outside Poland. He took an active part in the Second Vatican Council, attending all four sessions. He made two important contributions: the first was to argue fiercely, and successfully, that the Catholic Church should allow other denominations and religions the same level of tolerance and freedom that it asked for itself; the second was to contribute to the teaching on the proper relationship between God and humans.

Wojtyla proved to be an effective and tireless worker for the implementation of the decisions of Vatican II. In his own archdiocese he won over reluctant clergy, while in Rome he joined several bodies devoted to the cause of Vatican II. In 1967, he was created cardinal priest of San Cesareo in Palatio. The following year he saw his *Love and Responsibility* used as the basis for the famous encyclical of Paul VI *Humanae Vitae*.

His work for the Church took him on several visits outside Poland. These excited the suspicions of the Communist government, especially his visits to the USA. He was, nevertheless, able to work with his superior Cardinal Stefan Wyszynski to persuade the

1982

Argentina invades the Falkland Islands, which belong to the UK but are claimed by Argentina, precipitating the Falklands War. The war lasts six months and ends with the British reoccupation of the islands at a cost of about 1,000 dead.

1986

Soviet Leader Mikhail Gorbachev begins a program of limited economic and political reforms in the Soviet Union. The program becomes known as perestroika.

1990

The Berlin Wall is opened as Communist regimes in Eastern Europe collapse.

John Paul made frequent pilgrimages to the Calvary Sanctuary in Kalwaria Zebrzydowska, near to the town of his birth. During a visit in 2002 he said, "This place wondrously helps the heart and mind to gain deeper insight into the mystery of that bond which united the suffering Savior and his co-suffering mother."

government to recognize the Catholic Church and allow it some measure of freedom.

In 1978, Karol Wojtyla traveled to Rome along with 110 other cardinals to elect a successor to John Paul I. It was widely assumed that either Cardinal Siri of Genoa or Cardinal Benelli of Florence would be elected, since both men had garnered many votes at the previous conclave before John Paul was elected. The proceedings within a conclave are secret, but enough subsequently came out for it to be clear that for the first day of the conclave Siri and Benelli were leading the ballot, but neither could get the two thirds majority needed. Wojtyla is thought to have voted for Benelli. It was only on the second day that the non-European cardinals began looking for another candidate and gradually gathered around Wojtyla. On the third day and the eighth ballot Wojtyla was elected. When formally asked if he would accept the position of pope he replied: "With obedience in faith to Christ, my Lord, and with trust in the Mother of Christ and the Church, in spite of great difficulties, I accept."

There then followed some confusion among the public. An Italian newsreader heard that Wojtyla had been elected and exclaimed "Polacco" (The Pole) but many people thought he had said "Polacci," the name of an Italian cardinal and assumed that he had been elected. Eventually, at 7.15pm, Wojtyla appeared on the balcony of St. Peter's as Pope John Paul II and all became clear. He had adopted the name of his immediate predecessor out of respect.

John Paul's "pilgrimages," as his travels became known, had several purposes. First, he believed that it was the duty of a pope to show himself to his flock, by which he meant the worldwide Catholic population, not just the city of which he was bishop, and that jet air travel at last made this possible. Second, he wanted to put into practice the theory of collegiality that had in theory governed the pope's relationship with his bishops but which had not ever been a reality. Third, he wanted to demonstrate the global mission of the Christian Church that he led. Finally, he wanted to advance the cause of ecumenicalism by meeting and talking to the leaders of other Christian churches.

In 1979, he went to Turkey to meet Patriarch Demetrios of Constantinople. They each attended services held by the other but did not take communion together. In 1982, John Paul visited Britain—the first pope ever to do so—where he met Queen Elizabeth II in her role as head of the Church of England. John Paul went further than previous Popes, referring to the Anglican faith as "our beloved sister Church." The subsequent decision by the Anglicans to admit women to the priesthood disappointed him greatly. He then allowed Anglican priests to transfer to become Catholic priests even if they were married.

In 1999, the pope visited Romania to hold talks with the Romanian Orthodox clergy—the first time since the great schism of 1054 that a pope had visited an Orthodox country. Two years later he was in Greece for talks with the Greek Orthodox Church.

It was not just to other Christian denominations that John Paul extended the hand of friendship. In 2001, he visited Damascus and entered the Umayyad Mosque, formerly a Byzantine Christian church where

1990

The Gulf War sees a coalition of Arab states supported by the USA, Britain, and others drive Iraqi occupation forces out of Kuwait.

1992

The Maastricht Treaty changes the European Economic Community into the European Union.

1998

The Good Friday Agreement brings to an end 20 years of terrorist violence in Northern Ireland.

Hundreds of candles were lit in honor of Pope John Paul II following a mass to commemorate the second anniversary of his death.

John the Baptist is thought to be buried. While there he kissed the Koran, later holding talks with leading Islamic figures. Judaism was reached out to by a visit to Israel, including the Yad Vashem monument and Western Wall. John Paul has also held talks with the Dalai Lama, a Buddhist leader.

On one of his many famous "pilgrimages," John Paul went to Fatima in Portugal where a vision of the Virgin Mary had taken place in 1917. He also visited, Holland, Ireland, Papua New Guinea, USA, Haiti, Egypt, Syria, and 119 other countries. On January 15, 1995, he went to Manila in the Philippines and attended World Youth Day, during which he offered mass to a vast open-air crowd estimated at numbering over 5 million people—the largest ever gathering of Christians.

Perhaps John Paul's most significant visits were those to Eastern Europe in the 1980s. The area was then under the boot of repressive Communist regimes largely controlled by Soviet Russia. He made repeated calls for improvement to human rights, an end to political repression, and freedom for religion but, politically astute as he was, stopped short of calling for an end to Communism. He left that work to those he inspired.

In Poland, the trades union Solidarity marshalled opposition to Communism and eventually secured the fall of the Communist regime. Solidarity leader Lech Walesa said, "Before his pontificate, the world was divided into blocs. Nobody knew how to get rid of Communism. In Warsaw, in 1979, he simply said: 'Do not be afraid'." By the end of 1989, popular agitation against Communist repression, largely inspired by John Paul, combined with the economic and military meltdown in the Soviet Union, led to the sudden collapse of Communism across Europe.

In theological matters, John Paul continued to espouse the traditionalist teachings he had followed as archbishop of Krakow. He reaffirmed the teachings of the Church on sex, marriage, homosexuality, and abortion during a visit to the USA in 1980. He also firmly reinforced the orthodox teachings on doctrine and Christology, summoning a Dutch professor to Rome to explain his apparently heterodox views and banning a German professor from teaching Catholic theology who espoused euthanasia.

On May 13, 1981, as he entered St. Peter's Square to speak to a crowd, John Paul was shot by Mehmet Ali Agca, a Turkish member of the fascist Gray Wolves group. The pope suffered multiple wounds to his abdominal cavity. A five-hour operation followed, and John Paul made a slow recovery. The motives behind the attack have never been entirely clear and some believe that the Soviet Union was behind the assassination attempt. In 1995, a plot by the Islamist terrorist group Al Qaeda to kill the pope using a suicide bomber dressed as a priest was uncovered and foiled in the Philippines.

In 2001, John Paul was diagnosed with Parkinson's disease, though this was not made public until 2003. In February 2005, he contracted severe influenza and never fully recovered. His final words: "Allow me to depart to the house of the Father."

Pilgrims listen to the mass during the beatification of Pope John Paul II on May 1, 2011 in Rome.

2001

The 9/11 Attacks see hijacked aircraft crashed into targets in the USA by Islamist terrorists belonging to Al Qaeda. In all, 2,996 people are killed. US President George Bush launches his War on Terror in reaction.

2003

Invasion of Iraq by USA and allies leads to the overthrow of President Hussein, followed by a prolonged period of insurgency.

2004

The Civil Partnership Act in the United Kingdom, giving same-sex couples rights and responsibilities identical to civil marriage. The first civil partnership is registered in 2005.

BENEDICT XVI ✠ The 265th Pope 2005–2013

Born Marktl, Germany; April 16, 1927

Parents Father, Joseph Ratzinger; Mother, Maria Ratzinger

Papacy April 19, 2005–February 28, 2013

The background of Benedict XVI as a conservative theologian of daunting intelligence won him the nickname of "God's rotweiller" long before he became pope. His pontificate was characterized by an emphasis on traditionalist doctrine, values, and rituals. However, his resignation marked a dramatic break with established procedure that shocked the Catholic Church.

Joseph Ratzinger was born in the small Bavarian village of Marktl very close to the Austrian border. His family was respectable, but far from rich. His father was a police officer, while his great uncle had been a member of the Bavarian parliament in the late 19th century. When he was five years old, Ratzinger was chosen to be among a group of children welcoming Cardinal Michael von Faulhaber to the village. Impressed by the cardinal's clothes, Ratzinger announced he wanted to be a cardinal when he grew up. Nobody took him seriously.

Ratzinger's childhood was troubled by the rise of Adolf Hitler's Nazi Party to totalitarian power in Germany. Although the more brutal aspects of the regime did not reach the remote village of Marktl, Ratzinger was forced to join the Hitler Youth. In 1943, at the age of 16, Ratzinger was conscripted into the local anti-aircraft force as a boy soldier. Two years later he was moved to the infantry, but his unit collapsed due to a lack of supplies and orders as the Allies launched their final offensives into Germany. Ratzinger was captured and became a prisoner of war. He was, however, of such a young age and junior rank that he was released as soon as the war was over and resumed his education within a few weeks.

Schulstrasse 11, Merktl, Germany—the birthplace of Pope Benedict.

Having decided, along with his brother, to become a priest, Ratzinger went to the university in Munich. He was ordained on June 29, 1951, and two years later completed his dissertation on St. Augustine. He then studied St. Bonaventure to acquire his professorship in 1957, obtaining a post at the University of Freising, Bavaria. For the next 26 years, Ratzinger pursued an academic career of incident and prestige.

Over the years, Ratzinger served as a professor in Bonn, Munster, Tubingen, and Regensburg. He produced papers and articles that reflected an eclectic range of views. Although of generally traditionalist views, for instance in declaring Socialism to be inconsistent with Christianity, he did at times espouse liberal ideas as when he wrote that the pope had a duty to listen to different opinions before reaching a decision, and questioning if the papal authority should be absolute in all circumstances. From 1962 to 1965 he served as a theological consultant at the Second Vatican Council, a role which brought him to the notice of churchmen from many different countries.

On March 24, 1977, Ratzinger was unexpectedly appointed archbishop of Munich and Friesing by Pope Paul VI. Up to this point Ratzinger had had virtually no pastoral experience at all, highly regarded as he was in academic circles. A few months later he was raised to the rank of cardinal Priest of Santa Maria Consolatrice al Tiburtino.

2005

Hurricane Katrina strikes the USA leaving 1,836 dead and devastating New Orleans.

2006

Twitter is launched.

2006

The Chinese River Dolphin goes extinct.

2007

Harry Potter and the Deathly Hallows is released to become the fastest selling book in history, with 11 million copies sold in the first 24 hours.

2008

World-wide banking "credit crunch" takes hold as the Northern Rock bank in the UK goes under.

Pope Benedict during a visit to Great Britain in 2013.

In 1982, Ratzinger moved to Rome to head the Congregation for the Doctrine of the Faith, in charge of doctrine, a position he was given by John Paul II. As effective head of doctrine, Ratzinger robustly defended and restated traditionalist dogma on a range of issues. Several of these issues were those that liberals within secular society believed should be shown greater tolerance, such as homosexuality and birth control. Although many of these commentators were not Catholic, they attacked the pronouncements of Ratzinger as being out of date and objectionable.

Another controversial move came in 2001 when Ratzinger restated the traditional view that allegations made against priests should in the first instance be investigated privately by the Church, with civil authorities being brought in only if the Church believed that a criminal act had taken place. This was no more than restating an established code but there were accusations that it had permitted a cover up of sexual abuse carried out by some priests.

In 1997, at the age of 70, Ratzinger asked John Paul II to release him from his duties and allow him to take up the less strenuous task of librarian in the Vatican Archives, but the pope refused. It was therefore as one of the longest serving cardinals and most senior figures in the curia that Ratzinger entered the conclave to choose a successor to John Paul II.

Munich Cathedral. Joseph Ratzinger was made archbishop of Munich and Friesing by Pope Paul VI.

The conclave of 2005 was attended by 115 cardinals from 50 countries, with another 58 cardinals being excluded from the conclave as they were over 80 years old. At the age of 78, Ratzinger was one of the oldest attending. Given the great length of the reign of John Paul II, only two cardinals attending had not been appointed by him and therefore had any experience of how papal elections were conducted, Ratzinger being one of these veterans. The 2005 conclave was to be different in another way. Instead of being locked permanently into the Sistine Chapel and adjacent rooms for the entire conclave, the cardinals were locked in only during the daytime hours of discussion and voting. In the evening, they were given bedchambers elsewhere in the Vatican, though contact with the outside world was forbidden along with newspapers, radios, and televisions.

Events within conclave are secret, but enough hints and anecdotes have emerged to make it clear that on the first vote Cardinals Carlo Martini, Camillo Ruini and Joseph Ratzinger established early leads. Black smoke, signifying no result emerged from the chimney of the Sistine. Next day a second ballot likewise did not give a result, though Ratzinger was this time well ahead of the other two. On the third ballot, Ratzinger narrowly achieved the two thirds majority needed, but he wanted to be certain he had the backing of the Church so he asked for another ballot to confirm the result. This fourth ballot took place after lunch on the second day and produced an overwhelming vote for Ratzinger.

At 3.50 pm, the ballot papers were put into the stove and set alight without the straw that

2009

Greenland becomes independent of Denmark.

2009

Scientists discover a 4.4 million year old skull of Ardithipithecus, the oldest known ancestor of humans.

2010

The sculpture *L'Homme qui marche I* by Alberto Giacometti sells in London for £65 million ($103.7 million), setting a new world record for a work of art sold at auction.

2010

Researchers at CERN trap 38 antihydrogen atoms for a sixth of a second, marking the first time in history that humans have trapped antimatter.

2010

An earthquake in Haiti kills an estimated 316,000 people.

Upon his election as pope, Joseph Ratzinger took the name of Benedict XVI to honor both Benedict XV, pope during World War I, and St. Benedict who established the Benedictine Order of monasteries.

would have created black smoke. The resulting white smoke was supposed to emerge overhead to announce that a new pope had been elected. Instead, a gust of wind blew the smoke back into the Sistine Chapel and it was left to the bells of St. Peter's to announce the news.

Early in his reign, Benedict sought to set the tone. At his inaugural mass he dispensed with the lengthy process by which every cardinal kneeled to submit to the new papal authority. Instead, he chose 12 people representative of the Catholic Church—a priest, a married couple, a child, a monk, and so forth—to greet him in the name of the Church. He also selected an open-topped car as his official vehicle. Both were moves intended to signal a new informality and a closer relationship with the Catholic worshippers. Benedict announced that he would continue precedents set by John Paul II, such as baptizing infants born in Rome in the Sistine Chapel, that emphasized his pastoral role as bishop of Rome. Finally, he sought to honor his predecessor by starting the process of beatification that was being urged upon him before the customary five years had elapsed after the death of the person to be beatified. Within a few weeks he began a program of changes to the curia intended to make it more flexible and efficient.

Within six weeks of becoming pope, Benedict turned to what he described as "the central problem of our faith today." This was Relativism, the liberal idea that no moral value was absolute but everything must be seen in the context of its time and place. This was close to the later 19th-century heresy dubbed "Modernism" (*see* p.284), which held that even the most basic truths of Christianity should change to reflect changes in secular society. Benedict condemned relativism saying that "recognizing nothing as definitive, it leaves as the ultimate criterion only the self with its desires. And under the semblance of freedom it becomes a prison for each one, for it separates people from one another, locking each person into his or her own ego." He thus earned the enmity of the liberals who promoted an acceptance of abortion, divorce, and homosexuality in the secular world and objected to a faith that opposed such ideas.

In 2007, Benedict issued a ruling on the ritual of Mass. From 1570 to 1969 the usual form of Mass within the Catholic Church had been the Tridentine Mass, drawn up by the Council of Trent to supersede a large number of local rituals and variants. After the Second Vatican Council a revision of the ritual was undertaken that resulted in the Mass of Paul VI, introduced in 1969. The old Tridentine Mass could be performed only with special permission of a bishop, but Benedict changed this so that a congregation could request that their priest use the old form of mass, and it was up to the priest to decide.

Other older traditions that Benedict revived related to papal dress. He wore the red shoes discarded by John Paul II and the broad-brimmed red hat that kept the summer sun off his head and the wool-lined red skullcap that kept him warm in winter. He also favored more elaborately embroidered vestments, and different versions of the cape, or mozetta, than

2010

In Iceland the volcano Eyjafjallajökull erupts causing massive air-traffic disruption across Europe.

2011

The Tunisian Government resigns, the first of several regimes to fall as a result of mass popular demonstrations in the "Arab Spring."

2011

Prince William, Duke of Cambridge, married Catherine Middleton at Westminster Abbey in London watched live on television by an estimated 2 billion people.

Pope Benedict XVI delivering his Christmas *Urbi Et Orbi* blessing from the balcony of St. Peter's Basilica on Christmas Day, 2008 in Vatican City. He warned that the world was heading toward ruin if selfishness prevails over solidarity during tough economic times for both rich and poor nations.

his immediate predecessors. These moves were part of his drive to revive the link between the papacy and the arts, seeing beauty as a path to lead worshipers to an understanding of the sacred.

Benedict continued the efforts made by John Paul II to open and maintain dialogue with other faiths. He welcomed Rowan Williams, Archbishop of Canterbury, to Rome and issued a joint declaration. At the same time, he reiterated the traditional Catholic view that Christ appointed Peter to lead his Church and that the popes are the heirs of Peter.

His relations with non-Christian faiths was subject to misunderstanding. Some Jews objected when, in 2009, he lifted the excommunication of Richard Williamson. The excommunication had been imposed due to a dispute over clerical investiture and was lifted when that dispute was settled. However, Williamson had meanwhile made statements that questioned if Adolf Hitler had ordered the extermination of millions of Jews. When this was reported to Benedict he suspended Williamson as a bishop.

In 2006, Benedict made a speech in which he quoted a document written in 1391 that criticized Islam. Some Muslims thought that the quote had been part of the speech expressing Benedict's own views and reacted angrily. Two years later Benedict hosted a Catholic-Muslim Seminar in Rome, which passed off well and was held to be an important step forward in Christian-Muslim relations.

Benedict sought to continue John Paul II's apostolic pilgrimages to foreign lands. He has visited Germany twice, the USA, Brazil, Turkey, Australia, Angola, Cameroon, Jordan, Israel, and a number of other countries. These trips were not as frequent as those by John Paul, with Benedict preferring to perform his pastoral role in Rome and welcome visitors at the Vatican.

Although there were no attempts to murder him, Benedict was the center of a number of security scares. The most dramatic of these came on Christmas Eve, 2009, inside St. Peter's. A woman leapt over a barrier, sprang on the pope, and dragged him to the ground along with Roger Etchegaray, the vice dean. Etchegaray suffered a broken hip, but the pope was uninjured. Apparently, the woman had merely wanted to give the pope a message and had got carried away.

Throughout his pontificate, Benedict wore a pacemaker fitted to his heart due to a minor age-related heart problem. On February 11, 2013, Benedict unexpectedly announced that he would be abdicating as pope on February 28. He stated that the decision had been taken due to his advanced age, deteriorating strength, and the heavy demands of being pope. The Vatican later announced that, after his abdication took effect, Benedict would leave for the papal summer residence at Castel Gandolfo while a conclave was held to elect his successor. He would then retire to the Mater Ecclesiae, a small monastery located inside the Vatican City State.

News of Pope Benedict's resignation, the first pontiff to do so in nearly 600 years, reverberated through the world's media. Benedict retired to a small monastery to lead a life of prayer.

2012

A power cut in India leaves 500 million people temporarily without electricity.

2013

A meteor explodes over the Russian city of Chelyabinsk, injuring over 1,100 people and damaging more than 100 buildings.

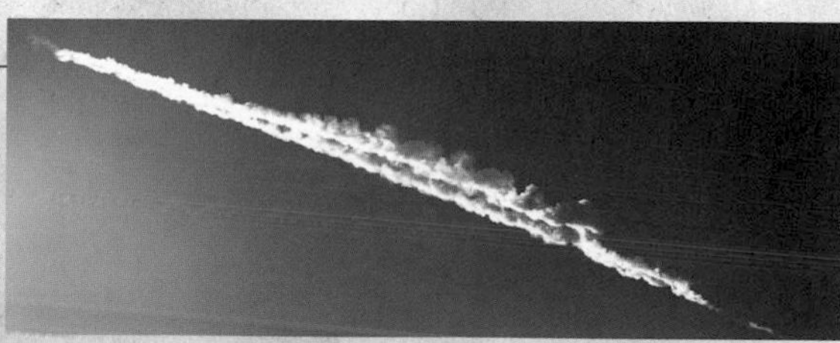

FRANCIS I ✠ The 266th Pope 2013–

Born Buenos Airès, Argentina; December 17, 1936

Parents Father, Mario José Bergoglio; Mother, Regina María Sívori

Papacy March 13, 2013 to present

Born Jorge Mario Bergoglio, Pope Francis is the eldest of five children of an Italian railway worker and his wife who had moved to Argentina to escape the rise of Fascism in Italy. Pope Francis has already marked his papacy with a degree of simplicity and humility unusual among those who occupy the throne of St. Peter.

Bergoglio grew up a fan of his local football club and with an interest in science. He left school with a diploma in chemistry and worked for several years in industry before deciding to enter the local seminary in 1955. He then entered the Society of Jesus and became a Jesuit on March 12, 1960. After some years as a teacher, Bergoglio was ordained a priest in 1969 and studied to become a professor of theology.

By 1973 he was the provincial superior of the Jesuits in Argentina and, in 1979, moved to become the rector of the Faculty of San Miguel. He later spent time in Germany where he was influenced by the painting *Mary, Untier of Knots* painted by Johann Schmidner in about 1700. Bergoglio took a copy of the painting back to Argentina with him. He then served as the spiritual director to the Jesuits in Argentina.

In 1992, Bergoglio became auxiliary bishop of Buenos Aires with the title "Bishop of Auca," and five years later rose to be archbishop of Buenos Aires. At this time he adopted as his motto *Miserando atque eligendo*, meaning "lowly but chosen," a reference to the medieval English scholar Bede's commentary on St. Matthew. He set in motion a reorganization of the parishes of the archdiocese and began a determined drive to move the Church into the poorest slums of the city. The number of priests working the slums doubled in the next five years.

In 2001, Bergoglio was created a cardinal by Pope John Paul II—as cardinal priest of San Roberto Bellamino, the church in Rome served by the Jesuits. He took up the post of Secretary to the Synod of Bishops, which greatly raised his profile outside Latin America. By the time of the 2005 Conclave he had established a firm reputation as a cleric who was open to new ideas and always willing to talk to dissenters, while himself being firmly rooted in traditional teachings and beliefs. His simple lifestyle was well known. He lived in a small flat and cooked his own meals rather than taking up residence in the grand palace of the archbishop of Buenos Aires. It has been reported that at the 2005 Conclave he gathered up to 40 votes at one ballot, but he does not seem to have been a serious contender to be pope then.

Pope Francis during the mass celebrating his installation in the Vatican in March 2013.

2013

The "Iron Lady" Margaret Thatcher dies at the age of 87. She was Britain's first female prime minister and a controversial leader both loved and loathed for her uncompromising character.

2013

Mass protests follow the collapse of an eight-storey factory building in Bangladesh that results in the death of more than a thousand workers.

Pope Francis quickly gained a reputation for his good humor and ready smile. He has reached out to people of all religions, and even to atheists, saying, "Just do good, and we shall find a meeting point."

Since the fall of the dictatorship in Argentina in the 1980s, Bergoglio has sought to engage with politicians without becoming linked to any particular political party. He has sought to encourage the government to retain Catholic teachings in the country's legal code—opposing the legalization of abortion and same-sex marriage, for instance. As archbishop of Buenos Aires he had responsibility for the Eastern Catholics in the area, a task in which he showed a keen understanding of the doctrines and liturgy of his charges.

When Benedict XV announced his retirement, Bergoglio traveled to Rome to take part in his second conclave. His name was not mentioned as one likely to be elected, the media preferring to talk about Christoph Schönborn of Austria, Odilo Scherer of Brazil, Luis Antonio Tagle of the Philippines, Peter Turkson of Ghana, Marc Ouellet of Canada, Péter ErdĐ of Hungary, and Angelo Scola of Italy. Francis Arinze of Nigeria was also considered to be papabile, but as he was aged over 80 he was not taken seriously.

On the first day of the conclave there was one ballot and on the second day three more followed with no result being achieved and black smoke issuing from the Sistine Chapel. Unknown to those outside, the fourth ballot had seen Bergoglio almost achieve the two thirds majority needed. At the fight ballot the cardinals voted overwhelmingly for Bergoglio.

Bergoglio decided to take the name Francis, which had never before been used by a pope. This may have represented a break with the past, but it soon emerged that he took the name in honor of St. Francis of Assisi and of Francis Xavier. The inauguration service followed six days later amid much ceremony at which the new pope struck a humble note.

As pope, Francis has continued with many of the features of his time as archbishop. He continued to celebrate Maundy Thursday by washing the feet of the poor—in 2013, the feet of 12 prisoners in Casal del Marmo prison. In his Easter homily, Francis called for more efforts to be made to secure peace, for Christians to shun greed and corruption, and to preserve God's creation by respecting the environment.

Francis has also begun to make efforts to secure good relationships with other faiths, including with Judaism and Islam as well as other Christian denomination. These resulted in a large number of invitations for Francis to visit countries outside Italy. Although he was aged 76 at the time of his election and has only one lung due to an attack of pneumonia at the age of 21, he is in good health and is, apparently, looking forward to an active papacy.

Pope Francis chose his papal name to honor St. Francis of Assisi, the saint who embraced poverty and sought to imitate the life of Christ and the first person to receive the stigmata. He is the patron saint of animals and the environment.

2013

Syria, in the grip of civil war, accuses Israel of declaring war after Israel's "pre-emptive" missile strikes.

2013

Tensions increase on the Korean Peninsula as North Korea declares that Tokyo will be the first target in an "inevitable nuclear war."

2013

CO2 levels in Earth's atmosphere reach "new danger zone" of 400 parts per million, levels not seen in more than three million years of Earth's history.

Papal Bulls
and Teachings

CHAPTER SIX

Uniquely among the great institutions of the world, the papacy has archives of written documents dating back nearly two millennia. Preserved in the vast Vatican Library are more than 75,000 unique codices containing letters, bulls, encyclicals, canon law, and a host of other key ecclesiastical documents. Reproduced here are a few of the more important documents written by or issued by popes over the years, including the Definition of Faith, issued by the Council of Chalcedon in 451; *Decet Romanum Pontificum*, the papal bull excommunicating Martin Luther in 1521; and *In Supremo Apostolatus*, from 1839, condemning the slave trade.

COUNCIL OF CHALCEDON

POPE LEO I DEFINES THE NATURE OF CHRIST—451

LETTER OF POPE LEO I

to Flavian, bishop of Constantinople, about Eutyches

Surprised as we were at the late arrival of your charity's letter, we read it and examined the account of what the bishops had done. We now see what scandal against the integrity of the faith had reared its head among you. What had previously been kept secret now became clearly revealed to us. Eutyches, who was considered a man of honour because he had the title of priest, is shown to be very rash and extremely ignorant. What the prophet said can be applied to him: He did not want to understand and do good: he plotted evil in his bed. What can be worse than to have an irreligious mind and to pay no heed to those who are wiser and more learned? The people who fall into this folly are those in whom knowledge of the truth is blocked by a kind of dimness. They do not refer to

- the sayings of the prophets, nor to
- the letters of the apostles, nor even to
- the authoritative words of the gospels,

but to themselves. By not being pupils of the truth, they turn out to be masters of error. A man who has not the most elementary understanding even of the creed itself can have learnt nothing from the sacred texts of the New and Old Testaments. This old man has not yet taken to heart what is pronounced by every baptismal candidate the world over!

He had no idea how he ought to think about the incarnation of the Word of God; and he had no desire to acquire the light of understanding by working through the length and breadth of the holy scriptures. So at least he should have listened carefully and accepted the common and undivided creed by which the whole body of the faithful confess that they believe in

1. God the Father almighty and in
2. Jesus Christ his only Son, our Lord,
3. who was born of the holy Spirit and the virgin Mary.

These three statements wreck the tricks of nearly every heretic. When God is believed to be both almighty and Father, the Son is clearly proved to be co-eternal with him, in no way different from the Father, since he was born God from God, almighty from the Almighty, co-eternal from the Eternal, not later in time, not lower in power, not unlike in glory, not distinct in being. The same eternal, only-begotten of the eternal begetter was born of the holy Spirit and the virgin Mary. His birth in time in no way subtracts from or adds to that divine and eternal birth of his: but its whole purpose is to restore humanity, who had been deceived, so that it might defeat death and, by its power, destroy the devil who held the power of death. Overcoming the originator of sin and death would be beyond us, had not he whom sin could not defile, nor could death hold down, taken up our nature and made it his own. He was conceived from the holy Spirit inside the womb of the virgin mother. Her virginity was as untouched in giving him birth as it was in conceiving him. But if it was beyond Eutyches to derive sound understanding from this, the purest source of the Christian faith, because the brightness of manifest truth had been darkened by his own peculiar blindness, then he should have subjected himself to the teaching of the gospels. When Matthew says, The book of the generation of Jesus Christ, son of David, son of Abraham, Eutyches should have looked up the further development in the apostolic preaching. When he read in the letter to the Romans, Paul, the servant of Christ Jesus, called to be an apostle, set apart for God's gospel, which he had formerly promised through his prophets in the holy writings which refer to his Son, who was made for him of David's seed according to the flesh, he should have paid deep and devout attention to the prophetic texts. And when he discovered God making the promise to Abraham that in your seed shall all nations be blessed, he should have followed the apostle, in order to eliminate any doubt about the identity of this seed, when he says, The promises were spoken to Abraham and his seed . He does not say "to his seeds"—as if referring to a multiplicity—but to a single one, "and to thy seed " which is Christ. His inward ear should also have heard Isaiah preaching Behold, a virgin will receive in the womb and will bear a son, and they will call his name Emmanuel, which is translated "God is with us". With faith he should have read the same prophet's words, A child is born to us, a son is given to us. His power is on his shoulders. They will call his name "Angel of great counsel, mighty God, prince of peace, father of the world to come". Then he would not deceive people by saying that the Word was made flesh in the sense that he emerged from the virgin's womb having a human form but not having the reality of his mother's body.

Or was it perhaps that he thought that our lord Jesus Christ did not have our nature because the angel who was sent to the blessed Mary said, The holy Spirit will come upon you and the power of the most High will overshadow you, and so that which will be born holy out of you will be called Son of God, as if it was because the conception by the virgin was worked by God that the flesh of the one conceived did not share the nature of her who conceived it? But uniquely wondrous and wondrously unique as that act of generation was, it is not to be understood as though the proper character of its kind was taken away by the sheer novelty of its creation. It was the holy Spirit that made the virgin pregnant, but the reality of the body derived from body. As Wisdom built a house for herself, the Word was made flesh and dwelt amongst us: that is, in that flesh which he derived from human kind and which he animated with the spirit of a rational life.

So the proper character of both natures was maintained and came together in a single person. Lowliness was taken up by majesty, weakness by strength, mortality by eternity. To pay off the debt of our state, invulnerable nature was united to a nature that could suffer; so that in a way that corresponded to the remedies we needed, one and the same mediator between God and humanity the man Christ Jesus, could both on the one hand die and on the other be incapable of death. Thus was true God born in the undiminished and perfect nature of a true man, complete in what is his and complete in what is ours. By "ours" we mean what the Creator established in us from the beginning and what he took upon himself to restore. There was in the Saviour no trace of the things which the Deceiver brought upon us, and to which deceived humanity gave admittance. His subjection to human weaknesses in common with us did not mean that he shared our sins. He took on the form of a servant without the defilement of sin, thereby enhancing the human and not diminishing the divine. For that self-emptying whereby the Invisible rendered himself visible, and the Creator and Lord of all things chose to join the ranks of mortals, spelled no failure of power: it was an act of merciful favour. So the one who retained the form of God when he made humanity, was made man in the form of a servant. Each nature kept its proper character without loss; and just as the form of God does not take away the form of a servant, so the form of a servant does not detract from the form of God.

It was the devil's boast that humanity had been deceived by his trickery and so had lost the gifts God had given it; and that it had been stripped of the endowment of immortality and so was subject to the harsh sentence of death. He also boasted that, sunk as he was in evil, he himself derived some consolation from having a partner in crime; and that God had been forced by the principle of justice to alter his verdict on humanity, which he had created in such an honourable state. All this called for the realisation of a secret plan whereby the unalterable God, whose will is indistinguishable from his goodness, might bring the original realisation of his kindness towards us to completion by means of a more hidden mystery, and whereby humanity, which had been led into a state of sin by the craftiness of the devil, might be prevented from perishing contrary to the purpose of God.

So without leaving his Father's glory behind, the Son of God comes down from his heavenly throne and enters the depths of our world, born in an unprecedented order by an unprecedented kind of birth. In an unprecedented order, because one who is invisible at his own level was made visible at ours. The ungraspable willed to be grasped. Whilst remaining pre-existent, he begins to exist in time. The Lord of the universe veiled his measureless majesty and took on a servant's form. The God who knew no suffering did not despise becoming a suffering man, and, deathless as he is, to be subject to the laws of death. By an unprecedented kind of birth, because it was inviolable virginity which supplied the material flesh without experiencing sexual desire. What was taken from the mother of the Lord was the nature without the guilt. And the fact that the birth was miraculous does not imply that in the lord Jesus Christ, born from the virgin's womb, the nature is different from ours. The same one is true God and true man.

There is nothing unreal about this oneness, since both the lowliness of the man and the grandeur of the divinity are in mutual relation. As God is not changed by showing mercy, neither is humanity devoured by the dignity received. The activity of each form is what is proper to it in communion with the other: that is, the Word performs what belongs to the Word, and the flesh accomplishes what belongs to the flesh. One of these performs brilliant miracles the other sustains acts of violence. As the Word does not lose its glory which is equal to that of the Father, so neither does the flesh leave the nature of its kind behind. We must say this again and again: one and the same is truly Son of God and truly son of man. God, by the fact that in the beginning was the Word, and the Word was with God, and the Word was God; man, by the fact that the Word was made flesh and dwelt among us. God, by the fact that all things were made through him, and nothing was made without him, man, by the fact that he was made of a woman, made under the law. The birth of flesh reveals human nature; birth from a virgin is a proof of divine power. A lowly cradle manifests the infancy of the child; angels' voices announce the greatness of the most High. Herod evilly strives to kill one who was like a human being at the earliest stage the Magi rejoice to adore on bended knee one who is the Lord of all. And when he came to be baptised by his precursor John, the Father's voice spoke thunder from heaven, to ensure that he did not go unnoticed because the divinity was concealed by the veil of flesh: This is my beloved Son, in whom I am well pleased. Accordingly, the same one whom the devil craftily tempts as a man, the angels dutifully wait on as God. Hunger, thirst, weariness, sleep are patently human. But to satisfy five thousand people with five loaves; to dispense living water to the Samaritan woman, a drink of which will stop her being thirsty ever again; to walk on the surface of the sea with feet that do not sink; to rebuke the storm and level the mounting waves; there can be no doubt these are divine.

So, if I may pass over many instances, it does not belong to the same nature to weep out of deep-felt pity for a dead friend, and to call him back to life again at the word of command, once the mound had been removed from the four-day old grave; or to hang on the cross and, with day changed into night, to make the elements tremble; or to be pierced by nails and to open the gates of paradise for the believing thief. Likewise, it does not belong to the same nature to say I and the Father are one, and to say The Father is greater than I. For although there is in the Lord Jesus Christ a single person who is of God and of man, the insults shared by both have their source in one thing, and the glory that is shared in another. For it is from us that he gets a humanity which is less than the Father; it is from the Father that he gets a divinity which is equal to the Father.

So it is on account of this oneness of the person, which must be understood in both natures, that we both read that the son of man came down from heaven, when the Son of God took flesh from the virgin from whom he was born, and again that the Son of God is said to have been crucified and buried, since he suffered these things not in the divinity itself whereby the Only-begotten is co-eternal and consubstantial with the Father, but in the weakness of the human nature. That is why in the creed, too, we all confess that the only-begotten Son of God was crucified and was buried, following what the apostle said, If they had known, they would never have crucified the Lord of majesty.

And when our Lord and Saviour himself was questioning his disciples and instructing their faith, he says, Who do people say I, the son of man, am? And when they had displayed a variety of other people's opinions, he says, Who do you say I am ? —in other words, I who am the son of man and whom you behold in the form of a servant and in real flesh: Who do you say I am? Whereupon the blessed Peter, inspired by God and making a confession that would benefit all future peoples, says, You are the Christ, the Son of the living God. He thoroughly deserved to be declared "blessed" by the Lord. He derived the stability of both his goodness and his name from the original Rock, for when the Father revealed it to him, he confessed that the same one is both the Son of God and also the Christ. Accepting one of these truths without the other was no help to salvation; and to have believed that the Lord Jesus Christ was either only God and not man, or solely man and not God, was equally dangerous.

After the Lord's resurrection—which was certainly the resurrection of a real body, since the one brought back to life is none other than the one who had been crucified and had died—the whole point of the forty-day delay was to make our faith completely sound and to cleanse it of all darkness. Hence he talked to his disciples and lived and ate with them, and let himself be touched attentively and carefully by those who were in the grip of doubt; he would go in among his disciples when the doors were locked, and impart the holy Spirit by breathing on them, and open up the secrets of the holy scriptures after enlightening their understanding; again, he would point out the wound in his side, the holes made by the nails, and all the signs of the suffering he had just recently undergone, saying, Look at my hands and feet—it is I. Feel and see, because a spirit does not have flesh and bones as you see that I have. All this was so that it would be recognised that the proper character of the divine and of the human nature went on existing inseparable in him; and so that we would realise that the Word is not the same thing as the flesh, but in such a way that we would confess belief in the one Son of God as being both Word and flesh. This Eutyches must be judged to be extremely destitute of this mystery of the faith. Neither the humility of the mortal life nor the glory of the resurrection has made him recognise our nature in the only-begotten of God. Nor has even the statement of the blessed apostle and evangelist John put fear into him: Every spirit which confesses that Jesus Christ came in the flesh is from God, and every spirit which puts Jesus asunder is not from God, and this is Antichrist. But what does putting Jesus as under consist in if not in separating his human nature from him, and in voiding, through the most barefaced fictions, the one mystery by which we have been saved? Once in the dark about the nature of Christ's body, it follows that the same blindness leads him into raving folly about his suffering too. If he does not think that the Lord's cross was unreal and if he has no doubt that the suffering undergone for the world's salvation was real, then let him acknowledge the flesh of the one whose death he believes in. And let him not deny that a man whom he knows to have been subject to suffering had our kind of body, for to deny the reality of the flesh is also to deny the bodily suffering. So if he accepts the Christian faith and does not turn a deaf ear to the preaching of the gospel, let him consider what nature it was that hung, pierced with nails, on the wood of the cross. With the side of the crucified one laid open by the soldier's spear, let him identify the source from which blood and water flowed, to bathe the church of God with both font and cup.

Let him heed what the blessed apostle Peter preaches, that sanctification by the Spirit is effected by the sprinkling of Christ's blood; and let him not skip over the same apostle's words, knowing that you have been redeemed from the empty way of life you inherited from your fathers, not with corruptible gold and silver but by the precious blood of Jesus Christ, as of a lamb without stain or spot. Nor should he withstand the testimony of blessed John the apostle: and the blood of Jesus, the Son of God, purifies us from every sin; and again, This is the victory which conquers the world, our faith. Who is there who conquers the world save one who believes that Jesus is the Son of God ? It is he, Jesus Christ who has come through water and blood, not in water only, but in water and blood. And because the Spirit is truth, it is the Spirit who testifies. For there are three who give testimony—Spirit and water and blood. And the three are one. In other words, the Spirit of sanctification and the blood of redemption and the water of baptism. These three are one and remain indivisible. None of them is separable from its link with the others. The reason is that it is by this faith that the catholic church lives and grows, by believing that neither the humanity is without true divinity nor the divinity without true humanity.

When you cross-examined Eutyches and he replied, "I confess that our Lord was of two natures before the union, but I confess one nature after the union", I am amazed that such an absurd and corrupt declaration of faith was not very severely censured by the judges; and that an extremely foolish statement was disregarded, as if nothing whatever offensive had been heard. It is just as wicked to say that the only-begotten Son of God was of two natures before the incarnation as it is abominable to claim that there was a single nature in him after the Word was made flesh. Eutyches must not suppose that what he said was either correct or tolerable just because no clear statement of yours refuted it. So we remind you, dearest brother, of your charity's responsibility to see to it that if through God's merciful inspiration the case is ever settled, the rash and ignorant fellow is also purged of what is blighting his mind. As the minutes have made clear, he made a good start at abandoning his opinion when, under pressure from your statement, he professed to say what he had not previously said, and to find satisfaction in the faith to which he had previously been a stranger. But when he had refused to be party to the anathematising of his wicked doctrine, your fraternity would have realised that he was persisting in his false belief and that he deserved a verdict of condemnation. If he is honestly and suitably sorry about this, and acknowledges even at this late stage how rightly episcopal authority was set in motion, or if, to make full amends, he condemns every wrong thought he had by word of mouth and by his actual signature, then no amount of mercy towards one who has reformed is excessive. Our Lord, the true and good shepherd who laid down his life for his sheep, and who came not to destroy but to save the souls of men and women, wants us to be imitators of his goodness, so that whilst justice represses sinners, mercy does not reject the converted. The defence of the true faith is never so productive as when false opinion is condemned even by its adherents.

In place of ourself, we have arranged for our brothers, Bishop Julius and the priest Renatus of the church of St Clement, and also my son, the deacon Hilary, to ensure a good and faithful conclusion to the whole case. To their company we have added our notary Dulcitius, of proven loyalty to us. We trust that with God's help he who has fallen into error might condemn the wickedness of his own mind and find salvation.

God keep you safe, dearest brother.

Definition of the Faith

Christ is "acknowledged in two natures" by the Council of Chalcedon

The sacred and great and universal synod by God's grace and by decree of your most religious and Christ-loving emperors Valentinian Augustus and Marcian Augustus assembled in Chalcedon, metropolis of the province of Bithynia, in the shrine of the saintly and triumphant martyr Euphemia, issues the following decrees.

In establishing his disciples in the knowledge of the faith, our lord and saviour Christ said: "My peace I give you, my peace I leave to you"', so that no one should disagree with his neighbour regarding religious doctrines but that the proclamation of the truth would be uniformly presented. But the evil one never stops trying to smother the seeds of religion with his own tares and is for ever inventing some novelty or other against the truth; so the Master, exercising his usual care for the human race, roused this religious and most faithful emperor to zealous action, and summoned to himself the leaders of the priesthood from everywhere, so that through the working of the grace of Christ, the master of all of us, every injurious falsehood might be staved off from the sheep of Christ and they might be fattened on fresh growths of the truth.

This is in fact what we have done. We have driven off erroneous doctrines by our collective resolution and we have renewed the unerring creed of the fathers. We have proclaimed to all the creed of the 318; and we have made our own those fathers who accepted this agreed statement of religion

• the 150 who later met in great Constantinople and themselves set their seal to the same creed.

Therefore, whilst we also stand by

• the decisions and all the formulas relating to the creed from the sacred synod which took place formerly at Ephesus, whose leaders of most holy memory were Celestine of Rome and Cyril of Alexandria we decree that

• pre-eminence belongs to the exposition of the right and spotless creed of the 318 saintly and blessed fathers who were assembled at Nicaea when Constantine of pious memory was emperor: and that

• those decrees also remain in force which were issued in Constantinople by the 150 holy fathers in order to destroy the heresies then rife and to confirm this same catholic and apostolic creed.

• The creed of the 318 fathers at Nicaea.

• And the same of the 150 saintly fathers assembled in Constantinople.

This wise and saving creed, the gift of divine grace, was sufficient for a perfect understanding and establishment of religion. For its teaching about the Father and the Son and the holy Spirit is complete, and it sets out the Lord's becoming human to those who faithfully accept it.

But there are those who are trying to ruin the proclamation of the truth, and through their private heresies they have spawned novel formulas:

• some by daring to corrupt the mystery of the Lord's economy on our behalf, and refusing to apply the word "God-bearer" to the Virgin; and

• others by introducing a confusion and mixture, and mindlessly imagining that there is a single nature of the flesh and the divinity, and fantastically supposing that in the confusion the divine nature of the Only-begotten is passible.

Therefore this sacred and great and universal synod, now in session, in its desire to exclude all their tricks against the truth, and teaching what has been unshakeable in the proclamation from the beginning,

• decrees that the creed of the 318 fathers is, above all else, to remain inviolate. And because of those who oppose the holy Spirit, it

• ratifies the teaching about the being of the holy Spirit handed down by the 150 saintly fathers who met some time later in the imperial city

• the teaching they made known to all,

• not introducing anything left out by their predecessors, but clarifying their ideas about the holy Spirit by the use of scriptural testimonies against those who were trying to do away with his sovereignty.

And because of those who are attempting to corrupt the mystery of the economy and are shamelessly and foolishly asserting that he who was born of the holy virgin Mary was a mere man, it has accepted

• the synodical letters of the blessed Cyril, (already accepted by the Council of Ephesus) pastor of the church in Alexandria, to Nestorius and to the Orientals, as being well-suited to refuting Nestorius's mad folly and to providing an interpretation for those who in their religious zeal might desire understanding of the saving creed.

To these it has suitably added, against false believers and for the establishment of orthodox doctrines

• the letter of the primate of greatest and older Rome, the

most blessed and most saintly Archbishop Leo, written to the sainted Archbishop Flavian to put down Eutyches's evil-mindedness, because it is in agreement with great Peter's confession and represents a support we have in common.

It is opposed to those who attempt to tear apart the mystery of the economy into a duality of sons; and

• it expels from the assembly of the priests those who dare to say that the divinity of the Only-begotten is passible, and

• it stands opposed to those who imagine a mixture or confusion between the two natures of Christ; and

• it expels those who have the mad idea that the servant-form he took from us is of a heavenly or some other kind of being; and

• it anathematises those who concoct two natures of the Lord before the union but imagine a single one after the union.

So, following the saintly fathers, we all with one voice teach the confession of one and the same Son, our Lord Jesus Christ: the same perfect in divinity and perfect in humanity, the same truly God and truly man, of a rational soul and a body; consubstantial with the Father as regards his divinity, and the same consubstantial with us as regards his humanity; like us in all respects except for sin; begotten before the ages from the Father as regards his divinity, and in the last days the same for us and for our salvation from Mary, the virgin God-bearer as regards his humanity; one and the same Christ, Son, Lord, only-begotten, acknowledged in two natures which undergo no confusion, no change, no division, no separation; at no point was the difference between the natures taken away through the union, but rather the property of both natures is preserved and comes together into a single person and a single subsistent being; he is not parted or divided into two persons, but is one and the same only-begotten Son, God, Word, Lord Jesus Christ, just as the prophets taught from the beginning about him, and as the Lord Jesus Christ himself instructed us, and as the creed of the fathers handed it down to us.

Since we have formulated these things with all possible accuracy and attention, the sacred and universal synod decreed that no one is permitted to produce, or even to write down or compose, any other creed or to think or teach otherwise. As for those who dare either to compose another creed or even to promulgate or teach or hand down another creed for those who wish to convert to a recognition of the truth from Hellenism or from Judaism, or from any kind of heresy at all: if they be bishops or clerics, the bishops are to be deposed from the episcopacy and the clerics from the clergy; if they be monks or layfolk, they are to be anathematised.

LIFE IN A MONASTERY

POPE GREGORY I'S ACCOUNT OF LIFE IN A MONASTERY—C.585

There was in my monastery a certain monk, Justus by name, skilled in medicinal arts. . . . When he knew that his end was at hand, he made known to Copiosus, his brother in the flesh, how that he had three gold pieces hidden away. Copiosus, of course, could not conceal this from the brethren. He sought carefully, and examined all his brother's drugs, until he found the three gold pieces hidden away among the medicines. When he told me this great calamity that concerned a brother who had lived in common with us, I could hardly hear it with calmness. For the rule of our monastery was always that the brothers should live in common and own nothing individually.

Then, stricken with great grief, I began to think what I could do to cleanse the dying man, and how I should make his sins a warning to the living brethren. Accordingly, having summoned Pretiosus, the superintendent of the monastery, I commanded him to see that none of the brothers visited the dying man, who was not to hear any words of consolation. If in the hour of death he asked for the brethren, then his own brother in the flesh was to tell him how he was hated by the brethren because he had concealed money; so that at death remorse for his guilt might pierce his heart and cleanse him from the sin he had committed.

When he was dead his body was not placed with the bodies of the brethren, but a grave was dug in the dung pit, and his body was flung down into it, and the three pieces of gold he had left were cast upon him, while all together cried, 'Thy money perish with thee ! ' . . .

When thirty days had passed after his death, my heart began to have compassion on my dead brother, and to ponder prayers with deep grief, and to seek what remedy there might be for him. Then I called before me Pretiosus, superintendent of the monastery, and said sadly: 'It is a long time that our brother who died has been tormented by fire, and we ought to have charity toward him, and aid him so far as we can, that he may be delivered. Go, therefore, and for thirty successive days from this day offer sacrifices for him. See to it that no day is allowed to pass on which the salvation-bringing mass (hostia) is not offered up for his absolution.' He departed forthwith and obeyed my words.

We, however, were busy with other things, and did not count the days as they rolled by. But lo ! the brother who had died appeared by night to a certain brother, even to Copiosus, his brother in the flesh. When Copiosus saw him he asked him, saying, 'What is it, brother? How art thou?' To which he answered: 'Up to this time I have been in torment; but now all is well with me, because today I have received the communion.' This Copiosus straightway reported to the brethren in the monastery.

Then the brethren carefully reckoned the days, and it was the very day on which the thirtieth oblation was made for him. Copiosus did not know what the brethren were doing for his dead brother, and the brethren did not know that Copiosus had seen him; yet at one and the same time he learned what they had done and they learned what he bad seen, and the vision and the sacrifice harmonized. So the fact was plainly shown forth how that the brother who had died had escaped punishment through the salvation-giving mass.

BOOK OF PASTORAL CARE

TREATISE ON THE RESPONSIBILITIES OF THE CLERGY BY POPE GREGORY I—C.590

The conduct of a prelate ought so far to be superior to the conduct of the people as the life of a shepherd is accustomed to exalt him above the flock. For one whose position is such that the people are called his flock ought anxiously to consider how great a necessity is laid upon him to maintain uprightness. It is necessary, then, that in thought he should be pure, in action firm; discreet in keeping silence; profitable in speech; a near neighbor to every one in sympathy; exalted above all in contemplation; a familiar friend of good livers through humility, unbending against the vices of evil-doers through zeal for righteousness; not relaxing in his care for what is inward by reason of being occupied in outward things, nor neglecting to provide for outward things in his anxiety for what is inward.

The pastor should always be pure in thought, inasmuch as no impurity ought to pollute him who has undertaken the office of wiping away the stains of pollution in the hearts of others also; for the hand that would cleanse from dirt must needs be clean, lest, being itself sordid with clinging mire, it soil all the more whatever it touches. The pastor should always be a leader in action, that by his living he may point out the way of life to those who are put under him, and that the flock, which follows the voice and manners of the shepherd, may learn how to walk rather through example than through words. For he who is required by the necessity of his position to speak the highest things is compelled by the same necessity to do the highest things. For that voice more readily penetrates the hearer's heart, which the speaker's life commends, since what he commands by speaking he helps the doing by showing.

The pastor should be discreet in keeping silence, profitable in speech; lest he either utter what ought to be suppressed or suppress what he ought to utter. For, as incautious speaking leads into error, so indiscreet silence leaves in error those who might have been instructed. The pastor ought also to understand how commonly vices pass themselves off as virtues. For often niggardliness excuses itself under the name of frugality, and on the other hand extravagance conceals itself under the name of liberality. Often inordinate carelessness is believed to be loving-kindness, and unbridled wrath is accounted the virtue of spiritual zeal. Often hasty action is taken for promptness, and tardiness for the deliberation of seriousness. Whence it is necessary for the pastor of souls to distinguish with vigilant care and vices between virtues and vices, lest stinginess get possession of his heart while he exults in seeming frugality in expenditure; or, while anything is recklessly wasted, he glory in being, as it were, compassionately liberal; or, in overlooking what he ought to have smitten, he draw on those that are under him to eternal punishment; or, in mercilessly smiting an offense, he himself offend more grievously; or, by rashly anticipating, mar what might have been done properly and gravely; or, by putting off the merit of a good action, change it to something worse.

Since, then, we have shown what manner of man the pastor ought to be, let us now set forth after what manner he should teach. For, as long before us Gregory Nazianzen, of reverend memory, has taught, one and the same exhortation does not suit all, inasmuch as all are not bound together by similarity of character. For the things that profit some often hurt others; seeing that also, for the most part, herbs which nourish some animals are fatal to others; and the gentle hissing that quiets horses incites whelps; and the medicine which abates one disease aggravates another; and the food which invigorates the life of the strong kills little children. Therefore, according to the quality of the hearers ought the discourse of teachers to be fashioned, so as to suit all and each for their several needs, and yet never deviate from the art of common edification. For what are the intent minds of hearers but, so to speak, a kind of harp, which the skillful player, in order to produce a tune possessing harmony, strikes in various ways? And for this reason the strings render back a melodious sound, because they are struck indeed with one quill, but not with one kind of stroke. Whence every teacher also, that he may edify all in the one virtue of charity, ought to touch the hearts of his hearers out of one doctrine, but not with one and the same exhortation.

Differently to be admonished are these that follow:

Men and women.

The poor and the rich.

The joyful and the sad.

Prelates and subordinates.

Servants and masters.

The wise of this world and the dull.

The impudent and the bashful.

The forward and the faint-hearted.

The impatient and the patient.

The kindly disposed and the envious.

The simple and the insincere.

The whole and the sick.

Those who fear scourges, and therefore live innocently; and those who have grown so hard in iniquity as not to be corrected even by scourges.

The too silent, and those who spend time in much speaking.

The slothful and the hasty.

The meek and the passionate.

The humble and the haughty.

The obstinate and the fickle.

The gluttonous and the abstinent.

Those who mercifully give of their own, and those who would fain seize what belongs to others.

Those who neither seize the things of others nor are bountiful with their own; and those who both give away the things they have, and yet cease not to seize the things of others.

Those who are at variance, and those who are at peace.

Lovers of strife and peacemakers.

Those who understand not aright the words of sacred law; and those who understand them indeed aright, but speak them without humility.

Those who, though able to preach worthily, are afraid through excessive humility; and those whom imperfection or age debars from preaching, and yet rashness impels to it....

Differently to be admonished are the wise of this world and the dull. For the wise are to be admonished that they leave off knowing what they know; the dull also are to be admonished that they seek to know what they know not. In the former this thing first, that they think themselves wise, is to be overcome; in the latter, whatsoever is already known of heavenly wisdom is to be built up; since, being in no wise proud, they have, as it were, prepared their hearts for supporting a building. With those we should labor that they become more wisely foolish, leave foolish wisdom, and learn the wise foolishness of God: to these we should preach that from what is accounted foolishness they should pass, as from a nearer neighborhood, to true wisdom.

But in the midst of these things we are brought back by the earnest desire of charity to what we have already said above; that every preacher should give forth a sound more by his deeds than by his words, and rather by good living imprint footsteps for men to follow than by speaking show them the way to walk in. For that cock, too, whom the Lord in his manner of speech takes to represent a good preacher, when he is now preparing to crow, first shakes his wings, and by smiting himself makes himself more awake; since it is surely necessary that those who give utterance to words of holy preaching should first be well awake in earnestness of good living, lest they arouse others with their voice while themselves torpid in performance; that they should first shake themselves up by lofty deeds, and then make others solicitous for good living; that they should first smite themselves with the wings of their thoughts; that whatsoever in themselves is unprofitably torpid they should discover by anxious investigation, and correct by strict self-discipline, and then at length set in order the life of others by speaking; that they should take heed to punish their own faults by bewailings, and then denounce what calls for punishment in others; and that, before they give voice to words of exhortation, they should proclaim in their deeds all that they are about to speak.

COUNCIL OF CLERMONT

POPE URBAN II URGES CHRISTIANS TO RECOVER PALESTINE FROM THE MUSLIMS—1095

Most beloved brethren: Urged by necessity, I, Urban, by the permission of God chief bishop and prelate over the whole world, have come into these parts as an ambassador with a divine admonition to you, the servants of God. I hoped to find you as faithful and as zealous in the service of God as I had supposed you to be. But if there is in you any deformity or crookedness contrary to God's law, with divine help I will do my best to remove it. For God has put you as stewards over his family to minister to it. Happy indeed will you be if he finds you faithful in your stewardship. You are called shepherds; see that you do not act as hirelings. But be true shepherds, with your crooks always in your hands. Do not go to sleep, but guard on all sides the flock committed to you. For if through your carelessness or negligence a wolf carries away one of your sheep, you will surely lose the reward laid up for you with God. And after you have been bitterly scourged with remorse for your faults-, you will be fiercely overwhelmed in hell, the abode of death. For according to the gospel you are the salt of the earth (Matt. 5:13). But if you fall short in your duty, how, it may be asked, can it be salted? O how great the need of salting! It is indeed necessary for you to correct with the salt of wisdom this foolish people which is so devoted to the pleasures of this -world, lest the Lord, when He may wish to speak to them, find them putrefied by their sins unsalted and stinking. For if He, shall find worms, that is, sins, In them, because you have been negligent in your duty, He will command them as worthless to be thrown into the abyss of unclean things. And because you cannot restore to Him His great loss, He will surely condemn you and drive you from His loving presence. But the man who applies this salt should be prudent, provident, modest, learned, peaceable, watchful, pious, just, equitable, and pure. For how can the ignorant teach others? How can the licentious make others modest? And how can the impure make others pure? If anyone hates peace, how can he make others peaceable ? Or if anyone has soiled his hands with baseness, how can he cleanse the impurities of another? We read also that if the blind lead the blind, both will fall into the ditch (Matt. 15:14). But first correct yourselves, in order that, free from blame , you may be able to correct those who are subject to you. If you wish to be the friends of God, gladly do the things which you know will please Him. You must especially let all matters that pertain to the church be controlled by the law of the church. And be careful that simony does not take root among you, lest both those who buy and those who sell (church offices) be beaten with the scourges of the Lord through narrow streets and driven into the place of destruction and confusion. Keep the church and the clergy in all its grades entirely free from the secular power. See that the tithes that belong to God are faithfully paid from all the produce of the land; let them not be sold or withheld. If anyone seizes a bishop let him be treated as an outlaw. If anyone seizes or robs monks, or clergymen, or nuns, or their servants, or pilgrims, or merchants, let him be anathema (that is, cursed). Let robbers and incendiaries and all their accomplices be expelled from the church and anthematized. If a man who does not give a part of his goods as alms is punished with the damnation of hell, how should he be punished who robs another of his goods? For thus it happened to the rich man in the gospel (Luke 16:19); he was not punished because he had stolen the goods of another, but because he had not used well the things which were his.

"You have seen for a long time the great disorder in the world caused by these crimes. It is so bad in some of your provinces, I am told, and you are so weak in the administration of justice, that one can hardly go along the road by day or night without being attacked by robbers; and whether at home or abroad one is in danger of being despoiled either by force or fraud. Therefore it is necessary to reenact the truce, as it is commonly called, which was proclaimed a long time ago by our holy fathers. I exhort and demand that you, each, try hard to have the truce kept in your diocese. And if anyone shall be led by his cupidity or arrogance to break this truce, by the authority of God and with the sanction of this council he shall be anathematized."

After these and various other matters had been attended to, all who were present, clergy and people, gave thanks to God and agreed to the pope's proposition. They all faithfully promised to keep the decrees. Then the pope said that in another part of the world Christianity was suffering from a state of affairs that was worse than the one just mentioned. He continued:

"Although, O sons of God, you have promised more firmly than ever to keep the peace among yourselves and to preserve the rights of the church, there remains still an important work for you to do. Freshly quickened by the divine correction, you must apply the strength of your righteousness to another matter which concerns you as well as God. For your brethren who live in the east are in urgent need of your help, and you must hasten to give them the aid which has often been promised them. For, as the most of you have heard, the Turks and Arabs have attacked them and have conquered the territory of Romania (the Greek empire) as far west as the shore of the Mediterranean and the Hellespont, which is called the Arm of St. George. They have occupied more and more of the lands of those Christians, and have overcome them in seven battles. They have killed and captured many, and have destroyed the churches and devastated the empire. If you permit them to continue thus for awhile with impurity, the faithful of God will be much more widely attacked by them. On this account I, or rather the Lord, beseech you as Christ's heralds to publish this everywhere and to persuade all people of whatever rank, foot-soldiers and knights, poor and rich, to carry aid promptly to those Christians and to destroy that vile race from the lands of our friends. I say this to those who are present, it meant also for those who are absent. Moreover, Christ commands it.

"All who die by the way, whether by land or by sea, or in battle against the pagans, shall have immediate remission of sins. This I grant them through the power of God with which I am invested. O what a disgrace if such a despised and base race, which worships demons, should conquer a people which has the faith of omnipotent God and is made glorious with the name of Christ! With what reproaches will the Lord overwhelm us if you do not aid those who, with us, profess the Christian religion! Let those who have been accustomed unjustly to wage private warfare against the faithful now go against the infidels and end with victory this war which should have been begun long ago. Let those who for a long time, have been robbers, now become knights. Let those who have been fighting against their brothers and relatives now fight in a proper way against the barbarians. Let those who have been serving as mercenaries for small pay now obtain the eternal reward. Let those who have been wearing themselves out in both body and soul now work for a double honor. Behold! on this side will be the sorrowful and poor, on that, the rich; on this side, the enemies of the Lord, on that, his friends. Let those who go not put off the journey, but rent their lands and collect money for their expenses; and as soon as winter is over and spring comes, let hem eagerly set out on the way with God as their guide."

CONCORDAT OF WORMS

AGREEMENT BETWEEN THE POPE AND THE HOLY ROMAN EMPEROR—1122

Privilege of Pope

Calixtus II

I, bishop Calixtus, servant of the servants of God, do grant to thee beloved son, Henry-by the grace of God august emperor of the Romans-that the elections of the bishops and abbots of the German kingdom, who belong to the kingdom, shall take place in thy presence, without simony and without any violence; so that if any discord shall arise between the parties concerned, thou, by the counsel or judgment of the metropolitan and the co-provincials, may'st give consent and aid to the party which has the more right. The one elected, moreover, without any exaction may receive the regalia from thee through the lance, and shall do unto thee for these what he rightfully should. But he who is consecrated in the other parts of the empire (i.e. Burgundy and Italy) shall, within six months, and without any exaction, receive the regalia from thee through the lance, and shall do unto thee for these what he rightfully should. Excepting all things which are known to belong to the Roman church. Concerning matters, however, in which thou dost make complaint to me, and dost demand aid, I, according to the duty of my office, will furnish aid to thee. I give unto thee true peace, and to all who are or have been on thy side in the time of this discord.

Edict of the Emperor

Henry V

In the name of the holy and indivisible Trinity, I, Henry, by the grace of God august emperor of the Romans, for the love of God and of the holy Roman church and of our master pope Calixtus, and for the healing of my soul, do remit to God, and to the holy apostles of God, Peter and Paul, and to the holy catholic church, all investiture through ring and staff; and do grant that in all the churches that are in my kingdom or empire there may be canonical election and free consecration. All the possessions and regalia of St. Peter which, from the beginning of this discord unto this day, whether in the time of my father or also in mine, have been abstracted, and which I hold: I restore to that same holy Roman church. As to those things, moreover, which I do not hold, I will faithfully aid in their restoration. As to the possessions also of all other churches and princes, and of all other lay and clerical persons which have been lost in that war: according to the counsel of the princes, or according to justice, I will restore the things that I hold; and of those things which I do not hold I will faithfully aid in the restoration. And I grant true peace to our master pope Calixtus, and to the holy Roman church, and to all those who are or have been on its side. And in matters where the holy Roman church shall demand aid I will grant it; and in matters concerning which it shall make complaint to me I will duly grant to it justice.

BULL LAUDABILITER

POPE ADRIAN IV GRANTS KING HENRY II CONTROL OVER THE CHURCH IN IRELAND—1155

Adrian, Bishop, servant of the servants of God, to his dearest son in Christ, the illustrious King of the English, greeting and apostolical benediction.

Your Majesty quite laudably and profitably considers how to extend the glory of your name on earth and increase the reward of eternal happiness in Heaven, when, as a Catholic Prince, you propose to extend the limits of the Church, to announce the truth of the Christian faith to ignorant and barbarous nations, and to root out the weeds of vice from the field of the Lord ; and the more effectually to accomplish this you implore the counsel and favour of the Apostolic See. In which matter we are confident that the higher your aim, and the greater the discretion with which you proceed, the happier, with God's help, will be your success; because those things that originate in the ardour of faith and the love of religion are always wont to arrive at a good issue and end.

Certainly Hibernia and all the islands upon which Christ the Sun of Justice has shone, and which have accepted the doctrines of the Christian faith, of right belong, as your Highness doth acknowledge, to blessed Peter and the Holy Roman Church. Wherefore we the more willingly sow in them a faithful plantation and a seed pleasing to God, in as much as we know by internal examination that it will be strictly required of us. You have signified to us, dearest son in Christ, that you desire to enter the island of Hibernia to subject that people to laws, and to root out therefrom the weeds of vice; also that you desire to pay from every house an annual pension ,of one penny to blessed Peter, and to preserve ,the rights of the churches of that land inviolate and whole.

We, therefore, regarding with due favour your pious and laudable desire, and according a gracious assent to your petition, deem it pleasing and acceptable that, for the purpose of extending the limits of the Church, checking the torrent of wickedness, reforming evil manners, sowing seeds of virtue, and increasing the Christian religion, you should enter that island and execute whatever shall be conducive to the honour of God and the salvation of that land. And let the people of that land receive you honourably and reverence you as lord, the rights of the churches remaining indisputably inviolate and whole, and the annual pension of one penny from every house being reserved to blessed Peter and the Holy Roman Church.

If, therefore, you will carry to completion what with a mind so disposed you have conceived, study to form that people to good morals, and, as well by yourself as by those whom you shall find qualified for the purpose by faith, word, and conduct, so act that the Church may be adorned, that the religion of the Christian faith may be planted and may increase; and let all that concerns the honour of God and the salvation of souls be ordered in such manner that you may deserve to obtain from God a plentiful, everlasting reward, and on earth succeed in acquiring a name glorious for ages.

FOURTH LATERAN COUNCIL

THE CANONS OF THE FOURTH LATERAN COUNCIL CONVOKED AND PRESIDED OVER BY POPE INNOCENT III—1215

CANON 1

We firmly believe and openly confess that there is only one true God, eternal and immense, omnipotent, unchangeable, incomprehensible, and ineffable, Father, Son, and Holy Ghost; three Persons indeed but one essense, substance, or nature absolutely simple; the Father (proceeding) from no one, but the Son from the Father only, and the Holy Ghost equally from both, always without beginning and end. The Father begetting, the Son begotten, and the Holy Ghost proceeding; consubstantial and coequal, co-omnipotent and coeternal, the one principle of the universe, Creator of all things invisible and visible, spiritual and corporeal, who from the beginning of time and by His omnipotent power made from nothing creatures both spiritual and corporeal, angelic, namely, and mundane, and then human, as it were, common, composed of spirit and body. The devil and the other demons were indeed created by God good by nature but they became bad through themselves; man, however, sinned at the suggestion of the devil. This Holy Trinity in its common essense undivided and in personal properties divided, through Moses, the holy prophets, and other servants gave to the human race at the most opportune intervals of time the doctrine of salvation. And finally, Jesus Christ, the only begotten Son of God made flesh by the entire Trinity, conceived with the co-operation of the Holy Ghost of Mary ever Virgin, made true man, composed of a rational soul and human flesh, one Person in two natures, pointed out more clearly the way of life. Who according to His divinity is immortal and impassable, according to His humanity was made passable and mortal, suffered on the cross for the salvation of the human race, and being dead descended into hell, rose from the dead, and ascended into heaven. But He descended in soul, arose in flesh, and ascended equally in both; He will come at the end of the world to judge the living and the dead and will render to the reprobate and to the elect according to their works. Who all shall rise with their own bodies which they now have that they may receive according to their merits, whether good or bad, the latter eternal punishment with the devil, the former eternal glory with Christ.

There is one Universal Church of the faithful, outside of which there is absolutely no salvation. In which there is the same priest and sacrifice, Jesus Christ, whose body and blood are truly contained in the sacrament of the altar under the forms of bread and wine; the bread being changed (transsubstantiatio) by divine power into the body, and the wine into the blood, so that to realize the mystery of unity we may receive of Him what He has received of us. And this sacrament no one can effect except the priest who has been duly ordained in accordance with the keys of the Church, which Jesus Christ Himself gave to the Apostles and their successors.

But the sacrament of baptism, which by the invocation of each Person of the Trinity, namely of the Father, Son, and Holy Ghost, is effected in water, duly conferred on children and adults in the form prescribed by the Church by anyone whatsoever, leads to salvation. And should anyone after the reception of baptism have fallen into sin, by true repentance he can always be restored. Not only virgins and those practicing chastity, but also those united in marriage, through the right faith and through works pleasing to God, can merit eternal salvation.

CANON 2

We condemn, therefore, and reprobate the book or tract which Abott Joachim published against Master Peter Lombard concerning the unity or essense of the Trinity, calling him heretical and insane because he said in his Sentences that the Father, Son, and Holy Ghost are some supreme entity in which there is no begetting, no begotten, and no proceeding. Whence he asserts that he (Peter Lombard) attributed to God not so much a trinity as a quaternity, namely, three Persons and that common essense as a fourth, clearly protesting that there is no entity that is Father, Son, and Holy Ghost, neither is it essense or substance or nature, though he concedes that the Father, Son, and Holy Ghost are one essense, one substance, and one nature. But he says that such a unity is not a true and proper (propriam) unity, but rather a collective one or one by way of similitude, as many men are called one people and many faithful one Church, according to the words: "The multitude of believers had but one heart and one soul" (Acts 4: 32); and, "He who is joined to the Lord, is one spirit" (I Cor. 6: I7); similarly, "He that planteth and he that watereth, are one" (I Cor- 3: 8); and, "So we being many, are one body in Christ" (Rom. 12: 5). Again in the Book of Kings (Ruth): "My people and thy people are one" (Ruth I: i6). To strengthen this teaching he cites that most important word which Christ spoke concerning the faithful in the Gospel: will, Father, that they may be one, as we also are one, that they may be made perfect in one" (John I7: 22 f.). For the faithful of Christ, he says, are not one in the sense that they are some one thing that is common to all, but in the sense that they constitute one Church by reason of the unity of the Catholic faith and one kingdom by reason of the union of indissoluble charity, as we read in the canonical Epistle of St. John: "There are three who give testimony in heaven, the Father, the Word, and the Holy Ghost; nd these three are one" (I John 5: 7). And immediately it is added: "And there are three who give testimony on earth, the spirit, the water, and the blood; and these three are one" (I John 5: 8), as it is found in some codices.

But we, with the approval of the holy and general council, believe and confess with Peter (Lombard) that there is one supreme entity, incomprehensible and ineffable, which is truly Father, Son, and Holy Ghost, together (simul) three persons and each one of them singly. And thus in God there is only trinity, not quaternity, because each of the three persons is that entity, namely, substance, essense, or divine nature, which alone is the principle of the universe and besides which there is no other. And that entity is not the one begetting or the one begotten or the one proceeding, but it is the Father who begets, the Son who is begotten, and the Holy Ghost proceeds, in order that there may be distinctions in the Persons who unity in the nature. Though, therefore, the Father is one (being), and the Son is another, and the Holy Ghost is another, yet they are not different (non tamen aliud); but that which is the Father that is the Son and the Holy Ghost, absolutely the same, since according to the Orthodox and Catholic faith they are believed to be consubstantial. For the Father begetting the Son from eternity imparted to Him His own substance, as He Himself testifies: "That which my father hath given me, is greater than all" (John IO: 29). And it cannot- be said that He gave to Him a part of His substance and retained a part for Himself, since the substance of the Father is indivisible, that is, absolutely simple. But neither can it be said that Father in begetting transferred His substance to the Son, as if gave it to the Son without retaining it for Himself, otherwise He would cease to be a substance. It is evident, therefore, that the Son in being begotten received without any diminution the substance of the Father and thus the Father and Son as well as the Holy Ghost proceeding from both are the same entity. When therefore the Truth prays to the Father for the faithful, saying: "I will that they be one in us, even as we are one" (John 7: 22), this term "one" is understood first for the faithful, as implying a union of charity in grace, then for the divine persons, as implying a unity of identity in nature; as the Truth says in another place: "Be you perfect, as your heavenly Father is perfect" (Matt. 5: 48); as if He would say more clearly: be perfect by the perfection of grace as your heavenly Father is perfect by the perfection of nature, namely, each in his own way, because between the Creator and the creature there cannot be a likeness so great that the unlikeness is not greater.

If therefore anyone presume to defend or approve the teaching of the aforesaid Joachim on this point, let him be repressed by all as a heretic.

In this, however, we do not wish to derogate in anything from the monastery of Flora, which Joachim himself founded, since therein is both the regular life and salutary observance, but chiefly because the same Joachim ordered that his writings be submitted to us to be approved or corrected by the judgment of the Apostolic See, dictating a letter which he subscribed with his own hand, in which he firmly confesses that he holds that faith which the Roman Church holds, which by the will of God is the mother and mistress of all the faithful. We also reprobate and condemn the perverse teaching of he impious Amaury (Almaricus, Amalricus) de Bene, whose mind the father of lies has so darkened that his teaching is to be regarded not so much heretical as insane.

CANON 3

We excommunicate and anathematize every heresy that raises against the holy, orthodox and Catholic faith which we have above explained; condemning all heretics under whatever names they may be known, for while they have different faces they are nevertheless bound to each other by their tails, since in all of them vanity is a common element. Those condemned, being handed over to the secular rulers of their bailiffs, let them be abandoned, to be punished with due justice, clerics being first degraded from their orders. As to the property of the condemned, if they are laymen, let it be confiscated; if clerics, let it be applied to the churches from which they received revenues. But those who are only suspected, due consideration being given to the nature of the suspicion and the character of the person, unless they prove their innocence by a proper defense, let them be anathematized and avoided by all r-intil they have made suitable satisfaction; but if they have been under excommunication for one year, then let them be condemned as heretics. Secular authorities, whatever office they may hold, shall be admonished and induced and if necessary compelled by ecclesiastical censure, that as they wish to be esteemed and numbered among the faithful, so for the defense of the faith they ought publicly to take an oath that they will strive in good faith and to the best of their ability to exterminate in the territories subject to their jurisdiction all heretics pointed out by the Church; so that whenever anyone shall have assumed authority, whether spiritual or temporal, let him be bound to confirm this decree by oath. But if a temporal ruler, after having been requested and admonished by the Church, should neglect to cleanse his territory of this heretical foulness, let him be excommunicated by the metropolitan and the other bishops of the province. If he refuses to make satisfaction within a year, let the matter be made known to the supreme pontiff, that he may declare the ruler's vassals absolved from their allegiance and may offer the territory to be ruled lay Catholics, who on the extermination of the heretics may possess it without hindrance and preserve it in the purity of faith; the right, however, of the chief ruler is to be respected as long as he offers no obstacle in this matter and permits freedom of action. The same law is to be observed in regard to those who have no chief rulers (that is, are independent). Catholics who have girded themselves with the cross for the extermination of the heretics, shall enjoy the indulgences and privileges granted to those who go in defense of the Holy Land.

We decree that those who give credence to the teachings of the heretics, as well as those who receive, defend, and patronize them, are excommunicated; and we firmly declare that after any one of them has been branded with excommunication, if he has deliberately failed to make satisfaction within a year, let him incur ipso jure the stigma of infamy and let him not be admitted to public offices or deliberations, and let him not take part in the election of others to such offices or use his right to give testimony in a court of law. Let him also be intestable, that he may not have the free exercise of making a will, and let him be deprived of the right of inheritance. Let no one be urged to give an account to him in any matter, but let him be urged to give an account to others. If perchance he be a judge, let his decisions have no force, nor let any cause be brought to his attention. If he be an advocate, let his assistance by no means be sought. If a notary, let the instruments drawn up by him be considered worthless, for, the author being condemned, let them enjoy a similar fate. In all similar cases we command that the same be observed. If, however, he be a cleric, let him be deposed from every office and benefice, that the greater the fault the graver may be the punishment inflicted.

If any refuse to avoid such after they have been ostracized by the Church, let them be excommunicated till they have made suitable satisfaction. Clerics shall not give the sacraments of the Church to such pestilential people, nor shall they presume to give them Christian burial, or to receive their alms or offerings; otherwise they shall be deprived of their office, to which they may not be restored without a special indult of the Apostolic See. Similarly, all regulars, on whom also this punishment may be imposed, let their privileges be nullified in that diocese in which they have presumed to perpetrate such excesses.

But since some, under "the appearance of godliness, but denying the power thereof," as the Apostle says (II Tim. 3: 5), arrogate to themselves the authority to preach, as the same Apostle says: "How shall they preach unless they be sent?" (Rom. 10:15), all those prohibited or not sent, who, without the authority of the Apostolic See or of the Catholic bishop of the locality, shall presume to usurp the office of preaching either publicly or privately, shall be excommunicated and unless they amend, and the sooner the better, they shall be visited with a further suitable penalty.

We add, moreover, that every archbishop or bishop should himself or through his archdeacon or some other suitable persons, twice or at least once a year make the rounds of his diocese in which report has it that heretics dwell, and there compel three or more men of good character or, if it should be deemed advisable, the entire neighborhood, to swear that if anyone know of the presence there of heretics or others holding secret assemblies, or differing from the common way of the faithful in faith and morals, they will make them known to the bishop. The latter shall then call together before him those accused, who, if they do not purge themselves of the matter of which they are accused, or if after the rejection of their error they lapse into their former wickedness, shall be canonically punished. But if any of them by damnable obstinacy should disapprove of the oath and should perchance be unwilling to swear, from this very fact let them be regarded as heretics.

We wish, therefore, and in virtue of obedience strictly command, that to carry out these instructions effectively the bishops exercise throughout their dioceses a scrupulous vigilance if they wish to escape canonical punishment.

If from sufficient evidence it is apparent that a bishop is negligent or remiss in cleansing his diocese of the ferment of heretical wickedness, let him be deposed from the episcopal office and let another, who will and can confound heretical depravity, be substituted.

CANON 4

Summary. Those baptized by the Latins must not be rebaptized by the Greeks.

Text. Though we wish to favor and honor the Greeks who in our days are returning to the obedience of the Apostolic See by permitting them to retain their customs and rites in so far as the interests of God allow us, in those things, however, that are a danger to souls and derogatory to ecclesiastical propriety, we neither wish nor ought to submit to them. After the Church of the Greeks with some of her accomplices and supporters had severed herself from the obedience of the Apostolic See, to such an extent did the Greeks begin hating the Latins that among other things which they impiously committed derogatory to the Latins was this, that when Latin priests had celebrated upon their altars, they would not offer the sacrifice upon those altars till the altars had first been washed, as if by this they had been defiled. Also, those baptized by the Latins the Greeks rashly presume to rebaptize, and even till now, as we understand, there are some who do not hesitate to do this. Desirous, therefore, of removing such scandal from the Church of God, and advised by the holy council, we strictly command that they do not presume to do such things in the future, but conform themselves as obedient children to the Holy Roman Church, their mother, that there may be "one fold and one shepherd." If anyone shall presume to act contrary to this, let him be excommunicated and deposed from every office and ecclesiastical benefice.

CANON 5

Summary. The council approves the existing order of the patriarchal sees and affirm, three of their privileges: their bishops may confer the pallium and may have the cross borne before them, and appeals may be taken to them.

Text. Renewing the ancient privileges of the patriarchal sees, we decree with the approval of the holy and ecumenical council, that after the Roman Church, which by the will of God holds over all others pre-eminence of ordinary power as the mother and mistress of all the faithful, that of Constantinople shall hold first place, that of Alexandria second, that of Antioch third, and that of Jerusalem fourth, the dignity proper to each to be observed; so that after their bishops have received from the Roman pontiff the pallium, which is the distinguishing mark of the plenitude of the pontifical office, and have taken the oath of fidelity and obedience to him, they may also lawfully bestow the pallium upon their suffragans, receiving from them the canonical profession of faith for themselves, and for the Roman Church the pledge of obedience. They may have the standard of the cross borne before them everywhere, except in the city of Rome and wherever the supreme pontiff or his legate wearing the insignia of Apostolic dignity is present. In all provinces subject to their jurisdiction appeals may be taken to them when necessary, saving the appeals directed to the Apostolic See, which must be humbly respected.

CANON 6

SUMMARY Provincial synod, for the correction of abuses and the enforcement of canonical enactments must be held annually. To ensure this, reliable persons are to be appointed who will investigate such thin as need correction.

Text. In accordance with the ancient provisions of the holy Fathers, the metropolitans must not neglect to hold with their suffragans the annual provincial synods. In these they should be actuated with a genuine fear of God in correcting abuses and reforming morals, especially the morals of the clergy, familiarizing themselves anew with the canonical rules, particularly those that are enacted in this general council, that they may enforce their observance by imposing due punishment on transgressors. That this may be done more effectively, let them appoint in each and every diocese prudent and upright persons, who throughout the entire year shall informally and without any jurisdiction diligently investigate such things as need correction or reform and faithfully present them to the metropolitan, suffragans, and others in the following synod, so that they may give prudent consideration to these and other matters as circumstances demand; and in reference to those things that they decree, let them enforce observance, publishing the decisions in the episcopal synods to be held annually in each diocese. Whoever shall neglect to comply with this salutary statute, let him be suspended from his office and benefits till it shall please his superior to restore him.

CANON 8

SUMMARY: Reports of serious irregularities by prelates and inferior clerics must be investigated bv the superior. The accused must be given occasion to defend himself and, ii-found 'guilty, must be punished accordingly.

Text:. How and when a prelate ought to proceed in the inquiry and punishment of the excesses of subjects (that is, of clerics), is clearly deduced from the authority of the New and Old Testaments, from which the canonical decrees were afterward drawn, as we have long since clearly pointed out and now with the approval of the holy council confirm. For we read in the Gospel that the steward who was accused to his master of wasting his goods, heard him say: "How is it that I hear this of thee? Give an account of thy stewardship, for now thou canst be steward no longer" (Luke i6: 2). And in Genesis the Lord said: "I will go down and see whether they have done according to the cry that is come to me" (Gen. i8: 2i). From these authorities it is clearly proved that not only when a subject (that is, a cleric of a lower rank) but also when a prelate is guilty of excesses and these should come to the ears of the superior through complaint and report, not indeed from spiteful and slanderous persons, but from those who are prudent and upright persons, and not only once but often, he must in the presence of the seniors of the church carefully inquire into the truth of such reports, so that if they prove to be true, the guilty party may be duly punished without the superior being both accuser and judge in the matter. But, while this is to be observed in regard to subjects, the observance must be stricter in reference to prelates, who are, as it were, a ,target for the arrow. Because they cannot please all, since by their very office they are bound not only to rebuke but also at times to loose and bind, they frequently incur the hatred of many and are subject to insidious attacks. The holy fathers, therefore, wisely decreed that accusations against prelates must be accepted with great reserve lest, the pillars being shattered, the edifice itself fall unless proper precaution be exercised by which recourse not only to false but also malicious incrimination is precluded. They wished so to protect prelates that on the one hand they might not be unjustly accused, and on the other hand that they might be on their guard, lest they should become haughtily delinquent; finding a suitable remedy for each disease in the provision that a criminal accusation which calls for a diminutio capitis, that is, degradation, is by no means to be accepted, nisi legitima praecedat inscriptio. But when anyone shall have been accused on account of his excesses, so that the reports and whisperings arising therefrom cannot any longer be ignored without scandal or tolerated without danger, then steps, inspired not by hatred but by charity, must be taken without scruple toward an inquiry and punishment of his excesses. If it is a question of a grave offense, though not one that calls for a degradatio ab ordine, the accused must be deprived absolutely of all administrative authority, which is in accordance with the teaching of the Gospel, namely, that the steward who cannot render a proper account of his office as steward be deprived of his stewardship. He about whom inquiry is to be made must be present, unless he absents himself through stubbornness; and the matter to be investigated must be made known to him, that he may have opportunity to defend himself. Not only the testimony of the witnesses but also their names must be made known to him, that he may be aware who testified against him and what was their testimony; and finally, legitimate exceptions and replications must be admitted, lest by the suppression of names and by the exclusion of exceptions the boldness of the defamer and the false witness be encouraged. The diligence of the prelate in correcting the excesses of his subjects ought to be in proportion to the blameworthiness of allowing the offense to go unpunished. Against such offenders, to say nothing of those who are guilty of notorious crimes, there can be a threefold course of procedure, namely, by accusation, by denunciation, and by inquiry, in all of which, however, proper precaution must be exercised lest perchance by undue haste grave detriment should result. The accusation must be preceded by the legitima inscriptio, denunciation by the caritativa admonitio, and the inquiry by the clamosa insinuatio (diffamatio); such moderation to be always used that the forma sententiae be governed by the forma judicii. The foregoing, however, does not apply to regular clerics, who, when a reason exists, can be removed from their charges more easily and expeditiously.

CANON 9

SUMMARY: In cities and dioceses where there are people of different languages, the bishop must provide suitable priests to minister to them. If necessity requires, let him appoint a vicar who shall be responsible to him. There may not, however, be two bishops in -the same diocese.

Text: Since in many places within the same city and diocese

there are people of different languages having one faith but various rites and customs, we strictly command that the bishops of these cities and dioceses provide suitable men who will, according to the different rites and languages, celebrate the divine offices for them, administer the sacraments of the Church and instruct them by word and example. But we absolutely forbid that one and the same city or diocese have more than one bishop, one body, as it were, with several heads, which is a monstrosity. But if by reason of the aforesaid conditions an urgent necessity should arise, let the bishop of the locality after due deliberation appoint a prelate acceptable to those races, who shall act as vicar in the aforesaid matters and be subject to him all things. If anyone shall act otherwise, let him consider himself excommunicated; and if even then he will not amend, let him be deposed from every ecclesiastical ministry, and if need be, let the secular arm be employed, that such insolence may be curbed.

CANON 13

SUMMARY: The founding of new religious orders is forbidden. New monasteries must accept a rule already approved. A monk may not reside in different monasteries nor may one abbot preside over several monasteries.

Text. Lest too great a diversity of religious orders lead to grave confusion in the Church of God, we strictly forbid anyone in the future to found a new order, but whoever should wish to enter an order, let him choose one already approved. Similarly, he who would wish to found a new monastery, must accept a rule already proved. We forbid also anyone to presume to be a monk in different monasteries (that is, belong to different monasteries), or that one abbot preside over several monasteries.

CANON 14

SUMMARY: Clerics, especially those in sacred orders, shall live chastely and virtuously. Anyone suspended for incontinency who presumes to celebrate the divine mysteries shall be forever deposed.

Text: That the morals and general conduct of clerics may be better let all strive to live chastely and virtuously, particularly those in sacred orders, guarding against every vice of desire, especially that on account of which the anger of God came from heaven upon the children of unbelief, so that in the sight of Almighty God they may perform their duties with a pure heart and chaste body. But lest the facility to obtain pardon be an incentive to do wrong, we decree that whoever shall be found to indulge in the vice of incontinence, shall, in proportion to the gravity of his sin, be punished in accordance with the canonical statutes, which we command to be strictly and rigorously observed, so that he whom divine fear does not restrain from evil, may at least be withheld from sin by a temporal penalty. If therefore anyone suspended for this reason shall presume to celebrate the divine mysteries, let him not only be deprived of his ecclesiastical benefices but for this twofold offense let him be forever deposed. Prelates who dare support such in their iniquities, especially in view of money or other temporal advantages, shall be subject to a like punishment. But if those. who according to the practice of their country have not renounced the conjugal bond, fall by the vice of impurity, they are to be punished more severely, since they can use matrimony lawfully.

CANON 15

SUMMARY Clerics, who after being warned do not abstain from drunkenness, shall be suspended from their office and benefice.

Text. All clerics shall carefully abstain from drunkenness. Wherefore, let them accommodate the wine to themselves, and themselves to the wine. Nor shall anyone be encouraged to drink, for drunkenness banishes reason and incites to lust. We decree, therefore, that that abuse be absolutely abolished by which in some localities the drinkers bind themselves suo modo to an equal portion of drink and he in their judgment is the hero of the day who out drinks the others. Should anyone be culpable in this matter, unless he heeds the warning of the superior and makes suitable satisfaction, let him be suspended from his benefice or office.

We forbid hunting and fowling to all clerics; wherefore, let them not presume to keep dogs and birds for these purposes.

CANON 16

SUMMARY Clerics are not to engage in secular pursuits, attend unbecoming exhibitions, visit taverns, or play games of chance. Their clothing must be in keeping with their dignity.

Text. Clerics shall not hold secular offices or engage in secular and, above all, dishonest pursuits. They shall not attend the performances of mimics and buffoons, or theatrical representations. They shall not visit taverns except in case of necessity, namely, when on a journey. They are forbidden to play games of chance or be present at them. They must have a becoming crown and tonsure and apply themselves diligently to the study of the divine offices and other useful subjects. Their garments must be worn clasped at the top and neither too short nor too long. They are not to use red or green garments or curiously sewed together gloves, or beak-shaped shoes or gilded bridles, saddles, pectoral ornaments (for horses), spurs, or anything else indicative of superfluity. At the divine office in the church they are not to wear cappas with long sleeves, and priests and dignitaries may not wear them elsewhere except in case of danger when circumstances should require a change of outer garments. Buckles may under no condition be worn, nor sashes having ornaments of gold or silver, nor rings, unless it be in keeping with the dignity of their office. All bishops must use in public and in the church outer garments made of linen, except those who are monks, in which case they must wear the habit of their order; in public they must not appear with open mantles, but these must be clasped either on the back of the neck or on the bosom.

CANON 17

SUMMARY. Prelates and clerics are commanded in virtue of obedience to celebrate diligently and devoutly the diurnal and nocturnal offices.

Text: It is a matter for regret that there are some minor clerics and even prelates who spend half of the night in banqueting and in unlawful gossip, not to mention other abuses, and in giving the remainder to sleep. They are scarcely awakened by the diurnal concerts of the birds. Then they hasten through matins in a hurried and careless manner. There are others who say mass scarcely four times a year and, what is worse, do not even attend mass, and when they are present they are engaged outside in conversation with lay people to escape the silence of the choir; so that, while they readily lend their ears to unbecoming talk, they regard with utter indifference things that are divine. These and all similar things, therefore, ,we absolutely forbid under penalty of suspension, and strictly command in virtue of obedience that they celebrate diligently and devoutly the diurnal and nocturnal offices so far as God gives them strength.

CANON 21

SUMMARY Everyone who has attained the age of reason is bound to confess his sins at least once a year to his own parish pastor with his permission to another, and to receive the Eucharist at least at Easter. A priest who reveals a sin confided to him in confession is to be deposed and relegated to a monastery for the remainder of his life.

Text. All the faithful of both sexes shall after they have reached the age of discretion faithfully confess all their sins at least once a year to their own (parish) priest and perform to the best of their ability the penance imposed, receiving reverently at least at Easter the sacrament of the Eucharist, unless perchance at the advice of their own priest they may for a good reason abstain for a time from its reception; otherwise they shall be cut off from the Church (excommunicated) during life and deprived of Christian burial in death. Wherefore, let this salutary decree be published frequently in the churches, that no one may find in the plea of ignorance a shadow of excuse. But if anyone for a good reason should wish to confess his sins to another priest, let him first seek and obtain permission from his own (parish) priest, since otherwise he (the other priest) cannot loose or bind him.

Let the priest be discreet and cautious that he may pour wine and oil into the wounds of the one injured after the manner of a skilful physician, carefully inquiring into the circumstances of the sinner and the sin, from the nature of which he may understand what kind of advice to give and what remedy to apply, making use of different experiments to heal the sick one. But let him exercise the greatest precaution that he does not in any degree by word, sign, or any other manner make known the sinner, but should he need more prudent counsel, let him seek it cautiously without any mention of the person. He who dares to reveal a sin confided to him in the tribunal of penance, we decree that he be not only deposed from the sacerdotal office but also relegated to a monastery of strict observance to do penance for the remainder of his life.

CANON 22

SUMMARY Physicians of the body called to the bedside of the sick shall before all advise them to call for the physician of souls, so that, spiritual health being restored, bodily health will follow.

Text. Since bodily infirmity is sometimes caused by sin, the Lord saying to the sick man whom he had healed: "Go and sin no more, lest some worse thing happen to thee" (John 5: 14), we declare in the present decree and strictly command that when physicians of the body are called to the bedside of the sick, before all else they admonish them to call for the physician of souls, so that after spiritual health has been restored to them, the application of bodily medicine may be of greater benefit, for the cause being removed the effect will pass away. We publish this decree for the reason that some, when they are sick and are advised by the physician in the course of the sickness to attend to the salvation of their soul, give up all hope and yield more easily to the danger of death. If any .physician shall transgress this decree after it has been published by bishops, let him be cut off (arceatur) from the Church till he has made suitable satisfaction for his transgression. And since the soul id far more precious than the body, we forbid under penalty of anathema that a physician advise a patient to have recourse to sinful means for the recovery of bodily health

CANON 23

SUMMARY: If those to whom it Pertains neglect to elect a bishop for a cathedral within three months, then this duty devolves upon the next immediate superior. If he neglects to do so within three months, he shall be punished.

That the ravenous wolf may not invade the Lord's flock that is without a pastor, that a widowed church may not suffer grave loss in its properties, that danger to soul may be averted, and that provision may be made for the security of the churches, we decree that a cathedral or regular church must not be without a bishop for more than three months. If within this time an election has not been held by those to whom it pertains, though there was no impediment, the electors lose their right of voting, and the right to appoint devolves upon the next immediate superior. Let the one upon whom this right to appoint devolves, having God before his eyes, not delay more than three months to provide canonically and with the advice of the chapter and other prudent men the widowed church with a suitable pastor, if he wishes to escape canonical punishment. This pastor is to be chosen from the widowed church itself, or from another in case a suitable one is not found therein.

CANON 68

SUMMARY: Jews and Saracens of both sexes in every Christian province must be distinguished from the Christian by a difference of dress. On Passion Sunday and the last three days of Holy Week they may not appear in public.

Text: In some provinces a difference in dress distinguishes the Jews or Saracens from the Christians, but in certain others such a confusion has grown up that they cannot be distinguished by any difference. Thus it happens at times that through error Christians have relations with the women of Jews or Saracens, and Jews and Saracens with Christian women. Therefore, that they may not, under pretext of error of this sort, excuse themselves in the future for the excesses of such prohibited intercourse, we decree that such Jews and Saracens of both sexes in every Christian province and at all times shall be marked off in the eyes of the public from other peoples through the character of their dress. Particularly, since it may be read in the writings of Moses (Numbers 15:37-41), that this very law has been enjoined upon them.

Moreover, during the last three days before Easter and especially on Good Friday, they shall not go forth in public at all, for the reason that some of them on these very days, as we hear, do not blush to go forth better dressed and are not afraid to mock the Christians who maintain the memory of the most holy Passion by wearing signs of mourning.

This, however, we forbid most severely, that any one should presume at all to break forth in insult to the Redeemer. And since we ought not to ignore any insult to Him who blotted out our disgraceful deeds, we command that such impudent fellows be checked by the secular princes by imposing them proper punishment so that they shall not at all presume to blaspheme Him who was crucified for us.

(Note by Schroeder: In 581 the Synod of Macon enacted in canon 14 that from Thursday in Holy Week until Easter Sunday, Jews may not in accordance with a decision of King Childebert appear in the streets and in public places. Mansi, IX, 934; Hefele-Leclercq, III, 204. In 1227 the Synod of Narbonne in canon 3 ruled: "That Jews may be distinguished from others, we decree and emphatically command that in the center of the breast (of their garments) they shall wear an oval badge, the measure of one finger in width and one half a palm in height. We forbid them moreover, to work publicly on Sundays and on festivals. And lest they scandalize Christians or be scandalized by Christians, we wish and ordain that during Holy Week they shall not leave their houses at all except in case of urgent necessity, and the prelates shall during that week especially have them guarded from vexation by the Christians." Mansi, XXIII, 22; Hefele-Leclercq V 1453. Many decrees similar to these in content were issued by synods before and after this Lateran Council. Hefele-Leclercq, V and VI; Grayzel, The Church and the Jews in the XIIIth Century, Philadelphia, 1933.)

CANON 69

Summary. Jews are not to be given public offices. Anyone instrumental in doing this is to be punished. A Jewish official is to be denied all intercourse with Christians.

Text. Since it is absurd that a blasphemer of Christ exercise authority over Christians, we on account of the boldness of transgressors renew in this general council what the Synod of Toledo (589) wisely enacted in this matter, prohibiting Jews from being given preference in the matter of public offices, since in such capacity they are most troublesome to the Christians. But if anyone should commit such an office to them, let him, after previous warning, be restrained by such punishment as seems proper by the provincial synod which we command to be celebrated every year. The official, however, shall be denied the commercial and other intercourse of the Christians, till in the judgment of the bishop all that he acquired from the Christians from the time he assumed office be restored for the needs of the Christian poor, and the office that he irreverently assumed let him lose with shame. The same we extend also to pagans. (Mansi, IX, 995; Hefele-Leclercq, III, 7.27. This canon 14 of Toledo was frequently renewed.)

EA EST IN FOVENDIS

INNOCENT III AGAINST UNAUTHORIZED PREACHING—ISSUED AT THE LATERAN COUNCIL

Discretion should be preserved, and careful consideration should be employed, by the prelates of the Church in fostering virtues and rooting out vices, so that they are neither harmed either by a thicket of thorns growing among the grain, nor is the wheat picked out along with bthe seeds of the cockle.(2) In cutting away and also in curing the bodies of the sick, the diligence of the eye should thus precede the duty of the hand, and the finger should come before the sword, so that, if the branding iron is used incautiously, it does not both leave the weak parts uncured and also weaken the healthy parts: because the more it should be preserved more diligently in weaker minds, the more we know that the mind is more worthy than the body and spiritual things should be put before worldly things.

Although our venerable brother the bishop of Metz previously explained in his letter that both in the diocese and in the city of Metz not a small multitude, exerting themselves towards a certain French translation of the divine books, also dared to discuss among themselves in secret meetings, rejecting the company of others and standing firm against the priests trying to correct them, whose simplicity they mock, confident in the expertise of their own translation, the matter, which has not been put on trial, does not immediately stir us towards vengeance, but we ourselves, paying attention to this more diligently, have taken care to send an apostolic letter about this matter to everyone established both in the city and in the diocese of Metz, which you can plainly see from an inspection of its contents.

To the same bishop and chapter of Metz we have given orders to inquire carefully about the truth, who was the author of that translation, what was the intention of the translator, what is the faith of those using it, what is the cause of teaching it, if those using it venerate the apostolic See and honour the Catholic Church; so that having been instructed by their letter about these and other things which are necessary for more fully investigating the truth, we might understand more fully and plainly what ought to be done about them. Recently however the same bishop explained to us in his letter that some of them, whom he had noted as notorious in his previous letter, refuse to obey the apostolic command; while some of them privately, and some of them publicly, say that they should obey God alone; they do not cease even from their secret meetings, and although they have been forbidden to do so, they do not fear to usurp for themselves the duty of preaching in secret, although they are sent by no one; they reject people dissimilar to themselves and still insist on using that same translation, and they assert that they will pay no attention to either the bishop or their metropolitan, nor even to us, if we should decree that it should be abolished.

Although such people seem to deserve to be chastised about this, because they carry out meetings in secret, usurp the duty of preaching, despise the simplicity of priests and reject the company of those who do not accept their aforementioned translation; lest we seem to do anything sudden, we command and order through this apostolic letter that, at your discretion, in which we have full confidence, you should approach the city of Metz together, assemble before you, with the bishop, men who are knowledgeable in such matters, and those who adhere to the aforementioned translation, and if possible, after removing the obstacle of appeal, and supported by apostolic authority, you should correct what might be reprehensible in them. But if perhaps they do not wish to accept your correction, you should more diligently inquire the truth about those chapters which, as we told you above, were explained in the letter which we had sent to the bishop, and you should explain more fully what you find through your legate and letter; so that when you have become more certain, we may proceed as far as the matter should proceed.

Since the business of the Church is disturbed in this

matter, and the cause of the Christian faith is questioned, we wish and command that you are studious and prompt in carrying out the command of the apostolic see with the highest diligence and caution. To this end, if you find that M. Crispinus the priest and his associate R. are guilty of these things which the aforementioned bishop thought they should be accused of, you should punish them according to canon law and deny their appeal. Otherwise, you should not delay, with ample warning and with whatever strictness is convenient, to compel the same bishop to relax the punishment, if perhaps he has inflicted any punishment on them, since they did not propose in our presence to do anything against him or the clergy. But if all three of you cannot take part in carrying put these things, they may nevertheless be carried out by two of you.

Issued at the Lateran, on the fifth day before the Ides of December

CUM NON SOLUM

FROM POPE INNOCENT IV TO THE RULER OF THE MONGOLS—1245

Since not only men but also irrational animals and even the very elements of the world machine have been connected by a certain unity of natural affinity on the model of the heavenly spirits, whose hosts God the creator of the universe has established in the unending stability of a peaceful order, we are strongly compelled — not without cause — to be astonished that you, as we have heard, having invaded so many regions of the Christians as well as those of other peoples, laid waste to these with a terrible devastation; and that up to this time you, not ceasing to send pillaging bands in your continuous anger into further regions, with the restraint of natural reason broken and making no exception for age or sex, you have raged against all indifferently with the sword of your anger.

We therefore, desiring to live together by the example of the Pacific King in the unity of peace under the fear of God, warn, request, and advise your unity intently: desist completely from further attacks of this kind and especially from the persecution of Christians, and through the satisfaction of a fitting penance placate the anger of Divine Majesty which on account of so many and such great offenses you most certainly have provoked through these incitements. You ought not accordingly take up the audacity of ravaging further, because, as the sword of your power rages against others, the all-powerful Lord has so far permitted diverse nations to be laid low before you; but He in our age frequently passes over chastening the proud until the right time, so that if they neglect to become humble of their own accord, He may not hesitate to punish their wickedness in time and may exact more serious retribution in the future.

And behold, a chosen son Brother I. and his colleagues the bearers of letters, men conspicuous in religion, distinguished by honesty, and gifted with knowledge of the Holy Scripture, we have led to you concerning this matter. I ask you to receive these men generously and treat honorably as you would us by trusting them in those things they will say to you from us and holding fruitful conversation with them about the things mentioned above and especially those matters pertaining to peace. Tell us fully through these brothers what has moved you to the extermination of other peoples and what further you intend; and look after these in their coming and going through a secure conduct and other necessary things, so that they may return safe to our presence.

UNAM SANCTAM

POPE BONIFACE VIII ON THE UNITY OF THE CATHOLIC CHURCH—1302

Urged by faith, we are obliged to believe and to maintain that the Church is one, holy, catholic, and also apostolic. We believe in her firmly and we confess with simplicity that outside of her there is neither salvation nor the remission of sins, as the Spouse in the Canticles (Sgs 6:8) proclaims: 'One is my dove, my perfect one. She is the only one, the chosen of her who bore her,' and she represents one sole mystical body whose Head is Christ and the head of Christ is God (1 Cor 11:3). In her then is one Lord, one faith, one baptism (Eph 4:5). There had been at the time of the deluge only one ark of Noah, prefiguring the one Church, which ark, having been finished to a single cubit, had only one pilot and guide, i.e., Noah, and we read that, outside of this ark, all that subsisted on the earth was destroyed.

We venerate this Church as one, the Lord having said by the mouth of the prophet: 'Deliver, O God, my soul from the sword and my only one from the hand of the dog.' (Ps 21:20) He has prayed for his soul, that is for himself, heart and body; and this body, that is to say, the Church, He has called one because of the unity of the Spouse, of the faith, of the sacraments, and of the charity of the Church. This is the tunic of the Lord, the seamless tunic, which was not rent but which was cast by lot (Jn 19:23-24). Therefore, of the one and only Church there is one body and one head, not two heads like a monster; that is, Christ and the Vicar of Christ, Peter and the successor of Peter, since the Lord speaking to Peter Himself said: 'Feed my sheep' (Jn 21:17), meaning, my sheep in general, not these, nor those in particular, whence we understand that He entrusted all to him (Peter). Therefore, if the Greeks or others should say that they are not confided to Peter and to his successors, they must confess not being the sheep of Christ, since Our Lord says in John 'there is one sheepfold and one shepherd.' We are informed by the texts of the gospels that in this Church and in its power are two swords; namely, the spiritual and the temporal. For when the Apostles say: 'Behold, here are two swords' (Lk 22:38) that is to say, in the Church, since the Apostles were speaking, the Lord did not reply that there were too many, but sufficient. Certainly the one who denies that the temporal sword is in the power of Peter has not listened well to the word of the Lord commanding: 'Put up thy sword into thy scabbard' (Mt 26:52). Both, therefore, are in the power of the Church, that is to say, the spiritual and the material sword, but the former is to be administered _for_ the Church but the latter by the Church; the former in the hands of the priest; the latter by the hands of kings and soldiers, but at the will and sufferance of the priest.

However, one sword ought to be subordinated to the other and temporal authority, subjected to spiritual power. For since the Apostle said: 'There is no power except from God and the things that are, are ordained of God' (Rom 13:1-2), but they would not be ordained if one sword were not subordinated to the other and if the inferior one, as it were, were not led upwards by the other.

For, according to the Blessed Dionysius, it is a law of the divinity that the lowest things reach the highest place by intermediaries. Then, according to the order of the universe, all things are not led back to order equally and immediately, but the lowest by the intermediary, and the inferior by the superior. Hence we must recognize the more clearly that spiritual power surpasses in dignity and in nobility any temporal power whatever, as spiritual things surpass the temporal. This we see very clearly also by the payment, benediction, and consecration of the tithes, but the acceptance of power itself and by the government even of things. For with truth as our witness, it belongs to spiritual power to establish the terrestrial power and to pass judgement if it has not been good. Thus is accomplished the prophecy of Jeremias concerning the Church and the ecclesiastical power: 'Behold to-day I have placed you over nations, and over kingdoms' and the rest. Therefore, if the terrestrial power err, it will be judged by the spiritual power; but if a minor spiritual power err, it will be judged by a superior spiritual power; but if the highest power of all err, it can be judged only by God, and not by man, according to the testimony of the Apostle: 'The spiritual man judgeth of all things and he himself is judged by no man' (1 Cor 2:15). This authority, however, (though it has been given to man and is exercised by man), is not human but rather divine, granted to Peter by a divine word and reaffirmed to him (Peter) and his successors by the One Whom Peter confessed, the Lord saying to Peter himself, 'Whatsoever you shall bind on earth, shall be bound also in Heaven' etc., (Mt 16:19). Therefore whoever resists this power thus ordained by God, resists the ordinance of God (Rom 13:2), unless he invent like Manicheus two beginnings, which is false and judged by us heretical, since according to the testimony of Moses, it is not in the beginnings but in the beginning that God created heaven and earth (Gen 1:1). Furthermore, we declare, we proclaim, we define that it is absolutely necessary for salvation that every human creature be subject to the Roman Pontiff.

SUBLIMIS DEI

POPE PAUL III BANS THE ENSLAVEMENT OF INDIGENOUS AMERICANS—1458

To all faithful Christians to whom this writing may come, health in Christ our Lord and the apostolic benediction.

The sublime God so loved the human race that He created man in such wise that he might participate, not only in the good that other creatures enjoy, but endowed him with capacity to attain to the inaccessible and invisible Supreme Good and behold it face to face; and since man, according to the testimony of the sacred scriptures, has been created to enjoy eternal life and happiness, which none may obtain save through faith in our Lord Jesus Christ, it is necessary that he should possess the nature and faculties enabling him to receive that faith; and that whoever is thus endowed should be capable of receiving that same faith. Nor is it credible that any one should possess so little understanding as to desire the faith and yet be destitute of the most necessary faculty to enable him to receive it. Hence Christ, who is the Truth itself, that has never failed and can never fail, said to the preachers of the faith whom He chose for that office 'Go ye and teach all nations.' He said all, without exception, for all are capable of receiving the doctrines of the faith.

The enemy of the human race, who opposes all good deeds in order to bring men to destruction, beholding and envying this, invented a means never before heard of, by which he might hinder the preaching of God's word of Salvation to the people: he inspired his satellites who, to please him, have not hesitated to publish abroad that the Indians of the West and the South, and other people of whom We have recent knowledge should be treated as dumb brutes created for our service, pretending that they are incapable of receiving the Catholic Faith.

We, who, though unworthy, exercise on earth the power of our Lord and seek with all our might to bring those sheep of His flock who are outside into the fold committed to our charge, consider, however, that the Indians are truly men and that they are not only capable of understanding the Catholic Faith but, according to our information, they desire exceedingly to receive it. Desiring to provide ample remedy for these evils, We define and declare by these Our letters, or by any translation thereof signed by any notary public and sealed with the seal of any ecclesiastical dignitary, to which the same credit shall be given as to the originals, that, notwithstanding whatever may have been or may be said to the contrary, the said Indians and all other people who may later be discovered by Christians, are by no means to be deprived of their liberty or the possession of their property, even though they be outside the faith of Jesus Christ; and that they may and should, freely and legitimately, enjoy their liberty and the possession of their property; nor should they be in any way enslaved; should the contrary happen, it shall be null and have no effect. By virtue of Our apostolic authority We define and declare by these present letters, or by any translation thereof signed by any notary public and sealed with the seal of any ecclesiastical dignitary, which shall thus command the same obedience as the originals, that the said Indians and other peoples should be converted to the faith of Jesus Christ by preaching the word of God and by the example of good and holy living.

(Dated: May 29, 1537)

DECET ROMANUM PONTIFICEM

POPE LEO X EXCOMMUNICATES MARTIN LUTHER—1521

PREAMBLE: Through the power given him from God, the Roman Pontiff has been appointed to administer spiritual and temporal punishments as each case severally deserves. The purpose of this is the repression of the wicked designs of misguided men, who have been so captivated by the debased impulse of their evil purposes as to forget the fear of the Lord, to set aside with contempt canonical decrees and apostolic commandments, and to dare to formulate new and false dogmas and to introduce the evil of schism into the Church of God—or to support, help and adhere to such schismatics, who make it their business to cleave asunder the seamless robe of our Redeemer and the unity of the orthodox faith. Hence it befits the Pontiff, lest the vessel of Peter appear to sail without pilot or oarsman, to take severe measures against such men and their followers, and by multiplying punitive measures and by other suitable remedies to see to it that these same overbearing men, devoted as they are to purposes of evil, along with their adherents, should not deceive the multitude of the simple by their lies and their deceitful devices, nor drag them along to share their own error and ruination, contaminating them with what amounts to a contagious disease. It also befits the Pontiff, having condemned the schismatics, to ensure their still greater confounding by publicly showing and openly declaring to all faithful Christians how formidable are the censures and punishments to which such guilt can lead; to the end that by such public declaration they themselves may return, in confusion and remorse, to their true selves, making an unqualified withdrawal from the prohibited conversation, fellowship and (above all) obedience to such accursed excommunicates; by this means they may escape divine vengeance and any degree of participation in their damnation.

I (Here the Pope recounts his previous Bull Exsurge Domine and continues)

II We have been informed that after this previous missive had been exhibited in public and the interval or intervals it prescribed had elapsed (60 days)—and we hereby give solemn notice to all faithful Christians that these intervals have and are elapsed—many of those who had followed the errors of Martin took cognisance of our missive and its warnings and injunctions; the spirit of a saner counsel brought them back to themselves, they confessed their errors and abjured the heresy at our instance, and by returning to the true Catholic faith obtained the blessing of absolution with which the self-same messengers had been empowered; and in several states and localities of the said Germany the books and writings of the said Martin were publicly burned, as we had enjoined.

Nevertheless Martin himself—and it gives us grievous sorrow and perplexity to say this—the slave of a depraved mind, has scorned to revoke his errors within the prescribed interval and to send us word of such revocation, or to come to us himself; nay, like a stone of stumbling, he has feared not to write and preach worse things than before against us and this Holy See and the Catholic faith, and to lead others on to do the same.

He has now been declared a heretic; and so also others,

whatever their authority and rank, who have cared nought of their own salvation but publicly and in all men's eyes become followers of Martin's pernicious and heretical sect, and given him openly and publicly their help, counsel and favour, encouraging him in their midst in his disobedience and obstinacy, or hindering the publication of our said missive: such men have incurred the punishments set out in that missive, and are to be treated rightfully as heretics and avoided by all faithful Christians, as the Apostle says (Titus iii. 10-11).

III. Our purpose is that such men should rightfully be ranked with Martin and other accursed heretics and excommunicates, and that even as they have ranged themselves with the obstinacy in sinning of the said Martin, they shall likewise share his punishments and his name, by bearing with them everywhere the title "Lutheran" and the punishments it incurs.

Our previous instructions were so clear and so effectively publicised and we shall adhere so strictly to our present decrees and declarations, that they will lack no proof, warning or citation.

Our decrees which follow are passed against Martin and others who follow him in the obstinacy of his depraved and damnable purpose, as also against those who defend and protect him with a military bodyguard, and do not fear to support him with their own resources or in any other way, and have and do presume to offer and afford help, counsel and favour toward him. All their names, surnames and rank—however lofty and dazzling their dignity may be—we wish to be taken as included in these decrees with the same effect as if they were individually listed and could be so listed in their publication, which must be furthered with an energy to match their contents.

On all these we decree the sentences of excommunication, of anathema, of our perpetual condemnation and interdict; of privation of dignities, honours and property on them and their descendants, and of declared unfitness for such possessions; of the confiscation of their goods and of the crime of treason; and these and the other sentences, censures and punishments which are inflicted by canon law on heretics and are set out in our aforesaid missive, we decree to have fallen on all these men to their damnation.

IV We add to our present declaration, by our Apostolic authority, that states, territories, camps, towns and places in which these men have temporarily lived or chanced to visit, along with their possessions cities which house cathedrals and metropolitans, monasteries and other religious and sacred places, privileged or unprivileged—one and all are placed under our ecclesiastical interdict, while this interdict lasts, no pretext of Apostolic Indulgence (except in cases the law allows, and even there, as it were, with the doors shut and those under excommunication and interdict excluded) shall avail to allow the celebration of mass and the other divine offices. We prescribe and enjoin that the men in question are everywhere to be denounced publicly as excommunicated, accursed, condemned, interdicted, deprived of possessions and incapable of owning them. They are to be strictly shunned by all faithful Christians.

V We would make known to all the small store that Martin, his followers and the other rebels have set on God and his Church by their obstinate and shameless temerity. We would protect the herd from one infectious animal, lest its infection spread to the healthy ones. Hence we lay the following injunction on each and every patriarch, archbishop, bishop, on the prelates of patriarchal, metropolitan, cathedral and collegiate churches, and on the religious of every Order—even the mendicants—privileged or unprivileged, wherever they may be stationed: that in the strength of their vow of obedience and on pain of the sentence of excommunication, they shall, if so required in the execution of these presents, publicly announce and cause to be announced by others in their churches, that this same Martin and the rest are excommunicate, accursed, condemned, heretics, hardened, interdicted, deprived of possessions and incapable of owning them, and so listed in the enforcement of these presents. Three days will be given: we pronounce canonical warning and allow one day's notice on the first, another on the second, but on the third peremptory and final execution of our order. This shall take place on a Sunday or some other festival, when a large congregation assembles for worship. The banner of the cross shall be raised, the bells rung, the candles lit and after a time extinguished, cast on the ground and trampled under foot, and the stones shall be cast forth three times, and the other ceremonies observed which are usual in such cases. The faithful Christians, one and all, shall be enjoined strictly to shun these men.

We would occasion still greater confounding on the said Martin and the other heretics we have mentioned, and on their adherents, followers and partisans: hence, on the strength of their vow of obedience we enjoin each and every patriarch, archbishop and all other prelates, that even as they were appointed on the authority of Jerome to allay schisms, so now in the present crisis, as their office obliges them, they shall make themselves a wall of defence for their Christian people. They shall not keep silence like dumb dogs that cannot bark, but incessantly cry and lift up their voice, preaching and causing to be preached the word of God and the truth of the Catholic faith against the damnable articles and heretics aforesaid.

VI To each and every rector of the parish churches, to the rectors of all the Orders, even the mendicants, privileged or unprivileged, we enjoin in the same terms, on the strength of their vow of obedience, that appointed by the Lord as they are to be like clouds, they shall sprinkle spiritual showers on the people of God, and have no fear in giving the widest publicity to the condemnation of the aforesaid articles, as their office obliges them. It is written that perfect love casteth out fear. Let each and every one of you take up the burden of such a meritorious duty with complete devotion; show yourselves so punctilious in its execution, so zealous and eager in word and deed, that from your labours, by the favour of divine grace, the hoped-for harvest will come in, and that through your devotion you will not only earn that crown of glory which is the due recompense of all who promote religious causes, but also attain from us and the said Holy See the unbounded commendation that your proved diligence will deserve.

VII However, since it would be difficult to deliver the present missive, with its declarations and announcements, to Martin and the other declared excommunicates in person, because of the strength of their faction, our wish is that the public nailing of this missive on the doors of two cathedrals—either both metropolitan, or one cathedral and one metropolitan of the churches in the said Germany—by a messenger of ours in those places, shall have such binding force that Martin and the others we have declared shall be shown to be condemned at every point as decisively as if the missive had been personally made known and presented to them.

VIII It would also be difficult to transmit this missive to every single place where its publication might be necessary. Hence our wish and authoritative decree is that copies of it, sealed by some ecclesiastical prelate or by one of our aforesaid messengers, and countersigned by the hand of some public notary, should everywhere bear the same authority as the production and exhibition of the original itself.

IX No obstacle is afforded to our wishes by the Apostolic constitutions and orders, or by anything in our aforesaid earlier missive which we do not wish to stand in the way, or by any other pronouncements to the contrary.

X No one whatsoever may infringe this our written decision, declaration, precept, injunction, assignation, will, decree; or rashly contravene it. Should anyone dare to attempt such a thing, let him know that he will incur the wrath of Almighty God and of the blessed Apostles Peter and Paul.

Written at St. Peter's, Rome, on the 3rd January 1521, during the eighth year of our pontificate.

TRIDENTINE CREED

CREED OF POPE PIUS IV FROM THE TEACHINGS OF THE COUNCIL OF TRENT—1565

✠ I, N, with a firm faith believe and profess each and everything which is contained in the Creed which the Holy Roman Church maketh use of. To wit:

I believe in one God, The Father Almighty, Maker of heaven and earth, and of all things visible and invisible. And in one Lord, Jesus Christ, the Only-begotten Son of God. Born of the Father before all ages. God of God, Light of Light, true God of true God. Begotten, not made, of one substance with the Father. By whom all things were made. Who for us men and for our salvation came down from heaven. And became incarnate by the Holy Spirit of the Virgin Mary: and was made man. He was also crucified for us, suffered under Pontius Pilate, and was buried. And on the third day He rose again according to the Scriptures. He ascended into heaven and sits at the right hand of the Father. He will come again in glory to judge the living and the dead and His kingdom will have no end. And in the Holy Spirit, the Lord and Giver of life, Who proceeds from the Father and the Son. Who together with the Father and the Son is adored and glorified, and who spoke through the prophets. And one holy, Catholic and Apostolic Church. I confess one baptism for the forgiveness of sins and I await the resurrection of the dead and the life of the world to come. Amen.

I most steadfastly admit and embrace Apostolical and ecclesiastical traditions, and all other observances and constitutions of the Church.

I also admit the Holy Scripture according to that sense which our holy mother the Church hath held, and doth hold, to whom it belongeth to judge of the true sense and interpretations of the Scriptures. Neither will I ever take and interpret them otherwise than according to the unanimous consent of the Fathers.

I also profess that there are truly and properly Seven Sacraments of the New Law, instituted by Jesus Christ our Lord, and necessary for the salvation of mankind, though not all for every one; to wit, Baptism, Confirmation, Eucharist, Penance, Extreme Unction, Holy Orders, and Matrimony; and that they confer grace; and that of these, Baptism, Confirmation, and Holy Orders cannot be reiterated without sacrilege.

I also receive and admit the received and approved ceremonies of the Catholic Church in the solemn administration of the aforesaid sacraments.

I embrace and receive all and every one of the things which have been defined and declared in the holy Council of Trent concerning original sin and justification.

I profess, likewise, that in the Mass there is offered to God a true, proper, and propitiatory sacrifice for the living and the dead; and that in the most holy sacrament of the Eucharist there is truly, really, and substantially, the Body and Blood, together with the soul and divinity, of our Lord Jesus Christ; and that there is made a conversion of the whole substance of the bread into the Body, and of the whole substance of the wine into the Blood, which conversion the Catholic Church calls Transubstantiation. I also confess that under either kind alone Christ is received whole and entire, and a true sacrament.

I constantly hold that there is a Purgatory, and that the souls therein detained are helped by the suffrages of the faithful. Likewise, that the saints, reigning together with Christ, are to be honored and invoked, and that they offer prayers to God for us, and that their relics are to be venerated.

I most firmly assert that the images of Christ, of the Mother of God, ever virgin, and also of other Saints, ought to be had and retained, and that due honor and veneration is to be given them.

I also affirm that the power of indulgences was left by Christ in the Church, and that the use of them is most wholesome to Christian people.

I acknowledge the Holy Catholic Apostolic Roman Church as the mother and mistress of all churches; and I promise true obedience to the Bishop of Rome, successor to St.

Peter, Prince of the Apostles, and Vicar of Jesus Christ. I likewise undoubtedly receive and profess all other things delivered, defined, and declared by the sacred Canons, and general Councils, and particularly by the holy Council of Trent, and by the ecumenical Council of the Vatican, particularly concerning the primacy of the Roman Pontiff and his infallible teaching. I condemn, reject, and anathematize all things contrary thereto, and all heresies which the Church hath condemned, rejected, and anathematized.

This true Catholic faith, outside of which no one can be saved, which I now freely profess and to which I truly adhere, inviolate and with firm constancy until the last breath of life, I do so profess and swear to maintain with the help of God. And I shall strive, as far as possible, that this same faith shall be held, taught, and professed by all those over whom I have charge. I N. do so pledge, promise, and swear, so help me God and these Holy Gospels.

CONSUEVERUNT ROMANI

POPE PIUS V'S LITANY OF THE BLESSED VIRGIN MARY—1569

The Roman Pontiffs, and the other Holy Fathers, our predecessors, when they were pressed in upon by temporal or spiritual wars, or troubled by other trials, in order that they might more easily escape from these, and having achieved tranquillity, might quietly and fervently be free to devote themselves to God, were wont to implore the divine assistance, through supplications or Litanies to call forth the support of the saints, and with David to lift up their eyes unto the Mountains, trusting with firm hope that thence would they receive aid.

1. Prompted by their example, and, as is piously believed, by the Holy Ghost, the inspired Blessed founder of the Order of Friars Preachers, (whose institutes and rule we ourselves expressly professed when we were in minor orders), in circumstances similar to those in which we now find ourselves, when parts of France and of Italy were unhappily troubled by the heresy of the Albegenses, which blinded so many of the worldly that they were raging most savagely against the priests of the Lord and the clergy, raised his eyes up unto heaven, unto that mountain of the Glorious Virgin Mary, loving Mother of God. For she by her seed has crushed the head of the twisted serpent, and has alone destroyed all heresies, and by the blessed fruit of her womb has saved a world condemned by the fall of our first parent. From her, without human hand, was that stone cut, which, struck by wood, poured forth the abundantly flowing waters of graces. And so Dominic looked to that simple way of praying and beseeching God, accessible to all and wholly pious, which is called the Rosary, or Psalter of the Blessed Virgin Mary, in which the same most Blessed Virgin is venerated by the angelic greeting repeated one hundred and fifty times, that is, according to the number of the Davidic Psalter, and by the Lord's Prayer with each decade. Interposed with these prayers are certain meditations showing forth the entire life of Our Lord Jesus Christ, thus completing the method of prayer devised by the by the Fathers of the Holy Roman Church. This same method St. Dominic propagated, and it was, spread by the Friars of Blessed Dominic, namely, of the aforementioned Order, and accepted by not a few of the people. Christ's faithful, inflamed by these prayers, began immediately to be changed into new men. The darkness of heresy began to be dispelled, and the light of the Catholic Faith to be revealed. Sodalities for this form of prayer began to be instituted in many places by the Friars of the same Order, legitimately deputed to this work by their Superiors, and confreres began to be enrolled together.

2. Following the example of our predecessors, seeing that the Church militant, which God has placed in our hands, in these our times is tossed this way and that by so many

heresies, and is grievously troubled troubled and afflicted by so many wars, and by the deprave morals of men, we also raise our eyes, weeping but full of hope, unto that same mountain, whence every aid comes forth, and we encourage and admonish each member of Christ's faithful to do likewise in the Lord.

(Pius goes on to confirm the indults, indulgences, etc., which his predecessors had granted to those who pray the Rosary, and to explicitate several of these indulgences.)

Given at Rome at St. Peter's, under the Fisherman's ring, 17 September 1569, in the fourth year of our Pontificate.

✠ V. Lord, have mercy on us. R. Christ, have mercy on us. V. Lord, have mercy on us. Christ, hear us. R. Christ, graciously hear us.

God, the Father of Heaven, have mercy on us. God the Son, Redeemer of the world, have mercy on us. God the Holy Ghost, have mercy on us. Holy Trinity, one God, have mercy on us.

Holy Mary, pray for us. Holy Mother of God, pray for us. Holy Virgin of virgins, pray for us. Mother of Christ, pray for us. Mother of divine grace, pray for us. Mother most pure, pray for us. Mother most chaste, pray for us. Mother inviolate, pray for us. Mother undefiled, pray for us. Mother most amiable, pray for us. Mother most admirable, pray for us. Mother of our Creator, pray for us. Mother of our Saviour, pray for us. Virgin most prudent, pray for us. Virgin most venerable, pray for us. Virgin most renowned, pray for us. Virgin most powerful, pray for us. Virgin most merciful, pray for us. Virgin most faithful, pray for us. Mirror of justice, pray for us. Seat of wisdom, pray for us. Cause of our joy, pray for us. Spiritual vessel, pray for us. Vessel of honor, pray for us. Singular vessel of devotion, pray for us. Mystical rose, pray for us. Tower of David, pray for us. Tower of ivory, pray for us. House of gold, pray for us. Ark of the covenant, pray for us. Gate of heaven, pray for us. Morning star, pray for us. Health of the sick, pray for us. Refuge of sinners, pray for us. Comforter of the afflicted, pray for us. Help of Christians, pray for us. Queen of Angels, pray for us. Queen of Patriarchs, pray for us. Queen of Prophets, pray for us. Queen of Apostles, pray for us. Queen of Martyrs, pray for us. Queen of Confessors, pray for us. Queen of Virgins, pray for us. Queen of all Saints, pray for us. Queen conceived without original sin, pray for us. Queen of the most holy Rosary, pray for us.

V. Lamb of God, who take away the sins of the world, R. Spare us, O Lord. V. Lamb of God, who take away the sins of the world, R. Graciously hear us, O Lord! V. Lamb of God, who take away the sins of the world, R. Have mercy on us.

V. Pray for us, O holy Mother of God. R. That we may be made worthy of the promises of Christ.

Let us pray. Pour forth, we beseech You, O Lord, Thy grace into our hearts; that as we have known the Incarnation of Christ Thy Son by the message of an angel, so, by His Passion and cross, we may be brought to the glory of His Resurrection; through the same Christ our Lord. Amen.

V. May the divine assistance remain always with us. R. Amen.

We fly to thy patronage, O holy mother of God. Despise not our petitions in our necessities; but deliver us from all dangers, O ever glorious and blessed Virgin.

SOLLICITUDO PASTORALIS

POPE INNOCENT XI ON THE OBSERVANCE OF THE RULE OF ST. FRANCIS OF ASSISI—1679

✠ 1. The pastoral solicitude of office, by which We preside over the governing of the catholic Church spread throughout the whole globe by divine disposition, urges and impels Us to attend to fostering and preserving the Orders of men religious instituted by this holy See with wise piety for the glory of the Omnipotent God and the salvation of souls, and refulgent in the Church of God on account of their great merits in their holy and primeval regulations, and in keeping them safe and fortifying them from those things hurtful, which could extinguish and relax the spirit and rigor of the original conscientiousness, and in providing for their blessed advancement in the way of the mandates of the Lord, as much as is conceded Us from on high. And also since (as We understand them) in the many general chapters of the Order of Friars Minor of St. Francis by the name of the Observance, and recently in that of Vallisoletanus, which was celebrated in the year 1670, it has been declared and protested by the unanimous consent of all the friars who were heard, that until now from none of the precepts of the rule of the Friars Minor (whether they are called "the Friars Minor of the body of the Observance", or "the Observants", or "the Reformed", or "the Discalced", or "the Recollects," have they been dispensed, nor has the body of the Observance itself ever introduced or admitted any dispensation in the rule, but rather have they willed according to their strength, favored as they are by Divine aid, to observe it purely according to the declarations of the Supreme Pontiffs, admitted and received by the Friars Observants or of the Observance in their collection of general statutes, for those of the Cismontane in 1663, and for those of the Utramontane in 1621, and by the Reformed, Discalced and the Recollects in their respective particular constitutions: 2. We, for greater firmness of protestation, and so that in the aforementioned Order the condition and rule of the Friars Minor be observed, and that the pretext for transgressing it be taken away from individual friars, approving and confirming in order the very same protestation and declaration of these things expressed above, by Our own decision and from certain knowledge and Our mature deliberation, and from the plenitude of apostolic power, for the sake of retaining the present things We declare that all and each friar of the body of the Observance of the said Order to be bound in conscience to observe the rule of the Friars Minor of St. Francis and the precepts set forth and enumerated by Nicholas III of blessed memory and Clement V, Our predecessors as Roman Pontiffs according to the norm of the respective aforesaid constitutions, and significantly, besides the precepts which do not so frequently occur to be bound even to the recitation of the Divine Office, to the precept in the rule on fasting, unless necessity excuses them, to going about without footwear, this is without anything that might cover the foot, of whatever material it might be, unless true necessity confirmed by a prelate be present, to not go horseback riding, unless infirmity or necessity proven by the judgement of the superiors excuses them, to cheapness in clothing according to the aforesaid respective constitutions, to not using more pieces of clothing than those which are prescribed by the rule, namely one tunic with a capuche and another without a capuche, a cord and breeches; for any kind of whatever clothing beyond the aforesaid (excepting the mantle which is licit from the beginning of religious life), such as undergarments or shirts; sweat bands, little tunics, and the like, are against the rule, unless true necessity excusing from the precept and approved by the prelate be present; lastly to be bound to the capital precept of the religion of the Friars Minor concerning not receiving money through themselves or through an interposed person, for the Friars Minor of the body of the Observance can have the use of other necessary things, but not the dominion (thereof), of money, however, neither the dominion nor the use; and hence the handling of whatever coins, or money, which is not purely natural, or which is in any manner civil (currency), is entirely prohibited to the Friars Minor Observants or of the Observance; and besides each and every dispensation, concession and custom, if it is ascertained to be against the aforesaid things among the body of the Observance of the aforesaid Order, alike in change, knowledge, deliberation and fullness of power, for the sake of retaining these present things, We revoke, nullify, void, and annul, and both in their force and effect We thoroughly and entirely revoke, and We determine and declare them to be revoked, nullified, voided, and nothings, both in their force and effect thoroughly and entirely empty and to be so forever. Equally, however, declaring those things which are not prohibited by the aforesaid things in the said Order (concerning) the apostolic syndics, since their use is not a dispensation from the rule, but a means provided by Our predecessors the Roman Pontiffs for the purer observance thereof, or syndics of the same kind chosen according to the constitution prescribed by Nicholas III and Clement V the aforementioned predecessors, or according to the disposition of the constitutions restored by Martin IV and Martin V and Paul IV equally Our predecessors, just as their use among each family, congregation, reform, or province of the aforesaid respective Order had been received. 3. Likewise so that in entering religion one wills to undertake each obligation, he be fully informed, we establish that no one is to be received to the regular habit in the same Order, unless he be fully informed beforehand concerning the aforesaid precepts of the rule which oblige in conscience, and that with this previous notification he wills to undergo probation; nor is anyone to be admitted to regular profession, unless he be examined beforehand concerning his understanding of the rule and its precepts according to the aforesaid things, and then a protestation be made by him before the whole community, to (the effect) that he is obliged by profession to the observance of the rule with all its precepts just now enumerated and expressed, and this protestation be received, and he make profession under it. 4. So that the example of the prelates or superiors truly be a more efficacious means of observing the aforesaid things, We therefore likewise establish that no one be able to be chosen a prelate or superior in the aforesaid Order, who does not follow the common life of observance, that is, he who frequently rides horseback, or has a sickness, by which he is excused from the obligation of going about on foot, who uses undergarments or shirts or linens upon himself or on his bed, who goes about with shoes, who does not observe the fasts of the Church or of the rule, who has been seen at anytime handling money, unless he has mended his ways for at least three years now, who notably is defective in attending the community choir, refectory, and other places, as is prescribed in his constitutions. I judge that the election of such a one, who in all the aforementioned things does not follow the common life, must be nullified by the prelate or general superior, after having learnt the information in the external forum, for the sake of his conscience, without the harshness of a sentence, but with the counsel and assent of three friars, who are or have been provincials or at least provincial definitors; nevertheless upon the consciences of these same, lest either one who observes the common life be expelled, or one who does not observe it be confirmed, We place the responsibility. 5. Lastly, so that every occasion of trespassing the precept of not handling coins or money be born away, We enjoin each and every prelate or superior of the said Order in virtue of holy obedience, and under the penalty of the deprivation of their office, to permit no religious of the same Order to have the administration of lands, of returns, or of whatever other things, moveable or immovable, to whomsoever the dominion belong, and significantly that to none of the religious of this kind of Order be permitted the administration of the temporal goods of any monastery of women religious under whatever pretext or name, namely, as administrators, syndics, agents, tenants, superintendents, steward, or any other imaginable. 6. Concluding this present letter and whatever things which must be contained in it, even for (the sake of) that which the superiors and friars of the aforesaid Order, and whatever others exist, of whatever status, grade, order, preeminence or dignity, or others worthy of specific and individual mention and reference, who having or in any manner alleging to have an interest in the aforementioned things, do not consent to them, or to those things which have been spoken of, cited and heard, and to the matter (at hand), on account of which this present letter has been issued, as if they have not been sufficiently adduced, verified, and justified, or for whatever other reason, even however verified, legitimate and privileged a case, appearance, pretext or point, even those contained in the body of law, even the irregular, the most irregular and entirely injurious, not at any time vitiated by subreption or obreption or nullity, or by Our intention or the consent of those who have interest, or for whatever other purpose, even however great and substantial and unconsidered and unthinkable, and on account of lacking individual reference to thus be noted, impugned, infringed, retracted, modified, refuted, called into controversy, or reduced to the terms of law or of the statutes or constitutions of the said Order, or to be understood or accomplished contrary to those things by the opening of the mouth, by complete restitution, or whatever other remedy of law, of fact or of favor, or having accomplished, whether anything in a judicial procedure or outside thereof has even been conceded or decreed by a (legal) motion, equal in knowledge or plenitude of power, or even if in any manner one be able to command it himself; but so that this present letter remain and be forever firm, valid, and efficacious, and to procure and obtain its own plenary and integral effects, and by this, to which it pertains and will pertain in whatever time, in all things and through all things to be observed and fulfilled inviolably and resolutely, and in such a manner that it is not be judged even otherwise in the aforementioned things, and thus by whatever judges, ordinary or delegated, even by the auditors of the causes of the apostolic palace, or by the cardinals of the Holy Roman Church, even by legates a latere and by nuncios of the Apostolic See, or by whatever others who exercise or will exercise whatever preeminence and power, when it has been brought before them and for the sake of whosoever by whatever other faculty and authority in judging and interceding, it be judged and defined to pertain to themselves, and happen to be tried as void and vain (if such is contrary to this letter) by whomsoever, of whatever authority, knowingly or unknowingly. 7. Not withstanding the aforesaid things, and, as much as is needful, Our rule and that of the apostolic chancery concerning not removing a law that has already been granted, and concerning other apostolic laws, and those set forth in universal, and provincial and synodal councils, general or special, in constitutions or ordination, and besides those of the said Order, and of its congregations, reforms, provinces and convents and of whatever other (division), or by others of whatever kind, even having been sworn, by apostolic confirmation, or of whatever other firmness of strength, in statutes, usages, compositions and customs, even immemorial, also by privileges, indults and apostolic letters to the same Order, and its superiors, friars, and persons whatsoever, under whatever tenor and form of words, and even with whatever derogations of this to be derogated, or by other more efficacious, most efficacious and unusual passages, and by those things which would void them, and by other decrees in general or in special, even by a (legal) motion, equal in knowledge and plenitude of power, and others in consistory and in any way conceded contrary to the aforementioned things and of however many confirmed, approved, and renewed vicissitudes; to which each and every, even if for the sufficient derogation of those things and their tenor, special, specific, expressed and individual, and word for word, not even by general indeed important passages, the mention or whatever other expression used or some other exquisite form that would approach this, their tenor being of this kind, having respectively the form, case and occasions to the present letter expressed, most exactly observed and specified fully and sufficiently, those other things which would perdure in their strength, to effect the aforesaid things, with this change alone, We especially and expressly derogate and will to be derogated and in all other contrary things of whatever kind. 8. We also will that when there has been a transferal of the present letter, or its copy, even printed, subscribed to by the hand of any notary public, and sealed with the seal of a person established in ecclesiastical dignity, it be held with exactly the same trust in whatever place as much in court as outside of it, which it should hold by this very same present document even if they should be exhibited or shown (in public). Given at Rome, at St. Peter's, under the ring of the Fisherman, on the 20th day of November, 1679, the fourth year of Our Pontificate.

UNIVERSAL PRAYER

FOR ALL THINGS NECESSARY TO SALVATION, ATTRIBUTED TO POPE CLEMENT XI —1721

✠ O my God, I believe in Thee: do Thou strengthen my faith. All my hopes are in Thee; do Thou secure them. I love Thee; teach me to love Thee daily more and more. I am sorry that I have offended Thee; do Thou increase my sorrow.

I adore Thee as my first beginning; I aspire after Thee as my last end. I give Thee thanks as my constant benefactor; I call upon Thee as my sovereign protector.

Vouchsafe, O my God, to conduct me by Thy wisdom, to restrain me by Thy justice, to comfort me by Thy mercy, to defend me by Thy power.

To Thee I desire to consecrate all my thoughts, words, actions, and sufferings; that henceforward I may think of Thee, speak of Thee, refer all my actions to thy greater glory, and suffer willingly whatever Thou shalt appoint.

Lord, I desire that in all things Thy will may be done, because it is Thy will, and in the manner that Thou willest.

I beg of Thee to enlighten my understanding, to inflame my will, to purify my body, and to sanctify my soul.

Give me strength, O my God, to expiate my offences, to overcome my temptations, to subdue my passions, and to acquire the virtues proper for my state.

Fill my heart with tender affection for Thy goodness, hatred of my faults, love of my neighbor, and contempt of the world.

Let me always remember to be submissive to my superiors, courteous to my inferiors, faithful to my friends, and charitable to my enemies.

Assist me to overcome sensuality by mortification, avarice by almsdeeds, anger by meekness, and tepidity by devotion.

O my God, make me prudent in my undertakings, courageous in dangers, patient in affliction, and humble in prosperity.

Grant that I may be ever attentive at my prayers, temperate at my meals, diligent in my employments, and constant in my resolutions.

Let my conscience be ever upright and pure, my exterior modest, my conversation edifying, and my deportment regular.

Assist me, that I may continually labor to overcome nature, to correspond with Thy grace, to keep Thy commandments, and to work out my salvation,

Discover to me, O my God, the nothingness of this world, the greatness of heaven, the shortness of time, and the length of eternity.

Grant that I may prepare for death; that may fear Thy judgments, escape hell, and in the end obtain heaven; through Jesus Christ our Lord. Amen.

IN EMINENTI

AN EDICT ON FREEMASONRY BY CLEMENT XII—1738

CLEMENT, BISHOP, Servant of the Servants of God to all the faithful, Salutation, and Apostolic Benediction. Since the divine clemency has placed Us, Whose merits are not equal to the task, in the high watch-tower of the Apostolate with the duty of pastoral care confided to Us, We have turned Our attention, as far as it has been granted Us from on high, with unceasing care to those things through which the integrity of Orthodox Religion is kept from errors and vices by preventing their entry, and by which the dangers of disturbance in the most troubled times are repelled from the whole Catholic World. Now it has come to Our ears, and common gossip has made clear, that certain Societies, Companies, Assemblies, Meetings, Congregations or Conventicles called in the popular tongue Liberi Muratori or Francs Massons or by other names according to the various languages, are spreading far and wide and daily growing in strength; and men of any Religion or sect, satisfied with the appearance of natural probity, are joined together, according to their laws and the statutes laid down for them, by a strict and unbreakable bond which obliges them, both by an oath upon the Holy Bible and by a host of grievous punishment, to an inviolable silence about all that they do in secret together. But it is in the nature of crime to betray itself and to show itself by its attendant clamor. Thus these aforesaid Societies or Conventicles have caused in the minds of the faithful the greatest suspicion, and all prudent and upright men have passed the same judgment on them as being depraved and perverted. For if they were not doing evil they would not have so great a hatred of the light. Indeed, this rumor has grown to such proportions that in several countries these societies have been forbidden by the civil authorities as being against the public security, and for some time past have appeared to be prudently eliminated. Therefore, bearing in mind the great harm which is often caused by such Societies or Conventicles not only to the peace of the temporal state but also to the well-being of souls, and realizing that they do not hold by either civil or canonical sanctions; and since We are taught by the divine word that it is the part of faithful servant and of the master of the Lord's household to watch day and night lest such men as these break into the household like thieves, and like foxes seek to destroy the vineyard; in fact, to prevent the hearts of the simple being perverted, and the innocent secretly wounded by their arrows, and to block that broad road which could be opened to the uncorrected commission of sin and for the other just and reasonable motives known to Us; We therefore, having taken counsel of some of Our Venerable Brothers among the Cardinals of the Holy Roman Church, and also of Our own accord and with certain knowledge and mature deliberations, with the plenitude of the Apostolic power do hereby determine and have decreed that these same Societies, Companies, Assemblies, Meetings, Congregations, or Conventicles of Liberi Muratori or Francs Massons, or whatever other name they may go by, are to be condemned and prohibited, and by Our present Constitution, valid for ever, We do condemn and prohibit them. Wherefore We command most strictly and in virtue of holy obedience, all the faithful of whatever state, grade, condition, order, dignity or pre-eminence, whether clerical or lay, secular or regular, even those who are entitled to specific and individual mention, that none, under any pretext or for any reason, shall dare or presume to enter, propagate or support these aforesaid societies of Liberi Muratori or Francs Massons, or however else they are called, or to receive them in their houses or dwellings or to hide them, be enrolled among them, joined to them, be present with them, give power or permission for them to meet elsewhere, to help them in any way, to give them in any way advice, encouragement or support either openly or in secret, directly or indirectly, on their own or through others; nor are they to urge others or tell them, incite or persuade them to be enrolled in such societies or to be counted among their number, or to be present or to assist them in any way; but they must stay completely clear of such Societies, Companies, Assemblies, Meetings, Congregations or Conventicles, under pain of excommunication for all the above mentioned people, which is incurred by the very deed without any declaration being required, and from which no one can obtain the benefit of absolution, other than at the hour of death, except through Ourselves or the Roman Pontiff of the time. Moreover, We desire and command that both Bishops and prelates, and other local ordinaries, as well as inquisitors for heresy, shall investigate and proceed against transgressors of whatever state, grade, condition, order dignity or pre-eminence they may be; and they are to pursue and punish them with condign penalties as being most suspect of heresy. To each and all of these We give and grant the free faculty of calling upon the aid of the secular arm, should the need arise, for investigating and proceeding against those same transgressors and for pursuing and punishing them with condign penalties. Given at Rome, at Saint Mary Mayor, in the year 1738 of Our Lord.

CHRISTIANAE REIPUBLICAE

POPE CLEMENT XIII ON THE DANGERS OF ANTI-CHRISTIAN WRITINGS—1766

To Our Venerable Brothers, all Patriarchs, Primates, Metropolitans, Archbishops, and Bishops Who Enjoy Grace and Communion with the Apostolic See.

Venerable Brothers, Greetings and Apostolic Blessing.

The well-being of the Christian community which has been entrusted to Us by the Prince of shepherds and the Guardian of souls requires Us to see to it that the unaccustomed and offensive licentiousness of books which has emerged from hiding to cause ruin and desolation does not become more destructive as it triumphantly spreads abroad. The distortion of this hateful error and the boldness of the enemy has so increased, especially at this time, in sowing weeds among the wheat either in word or in writing that unless We lay the scythe to the root and bind up the bad plants in bundles to burn, it will not be long before the growing thorns of evil attempt to choke the seedlings of the Lord Sabaoth. For accursed men who have given themselves over to myths and who do not uphold the stronghold of Sion from all sides vomit the poison of serpents from their hearts for the ruin of the Christian people by the contagious plague of books which almost overwhelms us. They pollute the pure waters of belief and destroy the foundations of religion.

They are abominable in their activity. Secretly sitting in ambush, they draw arrows out of the quiver which they shoot at the righteous in the dark. They have not restrained their impious minds from anything divine, holy, and consecrated by the oldest religion of all time; rather in their attack they have sharpened their tongues like a sword. They have run first of all against God in their pride. Armed with a thick neck, they have strengthened themselves against the Almighty. They raise again from the ashes the absurdities of the impious which have been destroyed so often. They deny God even though He makes Himself known everywhere and comes before their eyes daily, not because of the dullness of their mind, but only on the urging of their depraved will. Or else they represent God Himself as lazy and indolent. They do not respect His providence nor do they fear His justice. They preach with a detestable and insane freedom of thought that the origin and nature of our soul is mortal although it was created in the image of the supreme creator little lower than the angels. Whether they think matter has been created or foolishly imagine that it is eternal and independent of the causes, they consider that nothing else exists in this universe. Or else if they are forced to admit that spirit exists with matter, they exclude the soul from the spirit's heavenly nature. They are unwilling to understand that in this very weakness of which we are formed something spiritual and incorruptible abides in us. By its power we know, act, will, look to the future, attend to the present, and remember the past.

On the other hand, there are others who, even if they judge correctly that the fog of earthly reasonings should be dispelled and the smoke of worldly wisdom should be driven from the eye of enlightened faith, still dare to examine with human measures the hidden mysteries of faith which surpass all understanding. Having become investigators of greatness, they are not afraid of being overwhelmed by its glory. They ridicule the faith of simple people. They lay open the mysteries of God. They rashly discourse on questions concerning the highest matters. The bold mind of the enquirer takes everything for itself, examines everything, reserves nothing for faith, and deprives faith of merit by seeking proof for it in human reason.

Should we not also be angry with those who use the most wicked indecency of word and example to corrupt pure and strict morals by mortal sin, who recommend to the minds of the unwary an accursed license of living, and who cause an extreme loss of faith? Then consider how they sprinkle their writings with a certain refined splendor, a seductive pleasantness of speech and allurement so as to penetrate more easily into the readers' minds and infect them more deeply with the poison of their error. Thus they will give the snake's poison in the cup of Babylon to the unwary who are seduced and blinded by their smooth speech and so do not recognize the poison that kills them. Finally, who can avoid deep sadness when he sees the bitter enemy exceed the bounds of modesty and due respect and attack with the publication of outrageous books now in open battle, now in dissimulated combat the very See of Peter which the strong redeemer of Jacob has placed as an iron column and as a bronze wall against the leaders of darkness. Perhaps they are led on by the desperate thought that if they shatter the head of the Church, they will be able more freely to tear to pieces its members.

2. Therefore since the Holy Spirit has made you bishops to govern the Church of God and has taught you concerning the unique sacrament of human salvation, We cannot neglect our duty in the face of these evil books. We must arouse the enthusiasm of your devotion so that you, who are called to share in Our pastoral concern join together to oppose this evil with all energy possible. It is necessary to fight bitterly, as the situation requires, and to eradicate with all our strength the deadly destruction caused by such books. The substance of the error will never be removed unless the criminal elements of wickedness burn in the fire and perish. Since you have been constituted stewards of the mysteries of God and armed with His strength to destroy their defenses, exert yourselves to keep the sheep entrusted to you and redeemed by the blood of Christ at a safe distance from these poisoned pastures. For if it is necessary to avoid the company of evildoers because their words encourage impiety and their speech acts like a cancer, what desolation the plague of their books can cause! Well and cunningly written these books are always with us and forever within our reach. They travel with us, stay at home with us, and enter bedrooms which would be shut to their evil and deception.

Since you have been constituted ministers of Christ for the nations, in order to make holy his Gospel, exert yourselves and do everything in your power both by word and example to cut down the shoots of falsehood. Block up the corrupt springs of vice. Sound the trumpet in case as their leader you have to account for the souls who are lost. Act according to the position you hold, according to the rank with which you are vested, and according to the authority which you have received from the Lord. In addition, as nobody could or should avoid sharing in this sadness and insofar as there is one common reason for everyone to grieve and to help in this great crisis of faith and religion, call to your aid when it is necessary the time-honored piety of Catholic leaders. Explain the cause of the Church's sorrow and arouse its beloved sons who have always served it well on many occasions to bring their help. Since they do not carry the sword without cause, urge them with the united authority of state and of priesthood, to vigorously rout those accursed men who fight against the armies of Israel.

It is principally your duty to stand as a wall so that no foundation can be laid other than the one that is already laid. Watch over the most holy deposit of faith to whose protection you committed yourselves on oath at your solemn consecration. Reveal to the faithful the wolves which are demolishing the Lord's vineyard. They should be warned not to allow themselves to be ensnared by the splendid writing of certain authors in order to halt the diffusion of error by cunning and wicked men. In a word, they should detest books which contain elements shocking to the reader; which are contrary to faith, religion, and good morals; and which lack an atmosphere of Christian virtue. We manifest to you Our great happiness in this matter that most of you, following the apostolic customs and energetically defending the laws of the Church, have shown yourselves zealous and watchful in order to avert this pestilence and have not allowed the simple people to sleep soundly with serpents. Certainly We who are distressed and distracted by Our concern for all the churches and for the salvation of the Christian people, are unsparing of Our efforts, and We promise you assistance too in your own grave danger. Meanwhile, We will not cease to ask God with deep humility to grant you help from His holy place to deflect the cunning of the insidious enemy and to entirely fulfill the duties of your ministry. As a pledge of the desired outcome, we lovingly impart Our apostolic blessing to you and your flock.

Given in Rome in St. Mary Major's on the 25th day of November in the year 1766, the ninth year of Our pontificate.

TRADITI HUMILITATI

POPE PIUS VIII ON THE PROGRAM FOR HIS PONTIFICATE—1829

To Our Venerable Brothers, Patriarchs, Primates, Archbishops, and Bishops.

Venerable Brothers, Greetings and Apostolic Benediction.

According to the custom of Our ancestors, We are about to assume Our pontificate in the church of the Lateran. This office has been granted to Us, even though We are humble and unworthy. We open Our heart with joy to you, venerable brothers, whom God has given to Us as helpers in the conduct of so great an administration. We are pleased to let you know the intimate sentiments of Our will. We also think it helpful to communicate those things from which the Christian cause may benefit. For the duty of Our office is not only to feed, rule, and direct the lambs, namely the Christian people, but also the sheep, that is the clergy.

2. We rejoice and praise Christ, who raised up shepherds for the safekeeping of His flock. These shepherds vigilantly lead their flocks so as not to lose even one of those they have received from the Father. For We know well, venerable brothers, your unshakeable faith, your zeal for religion, your sanctity of life, and your singular prudence. Co-workers such as you make Us happy and confident. This pleasant situation encourages Us when We fear because of the great responsibility of Our office, and it refreshes and strengthens Us when We feel overwhelmed by so many serious concerns. We shall not detain you with a long sermon to remind you what things are required to perform sacred duties well, what the canons prescribe lest anyone depart from vigilance over his flock, and what attention ought to be given in preparing and accepting ministers. Rather We call upon God the Savior that He may protect you with His omnipresent divinity and bless your activities and endeavors with happy success.

3. Although God may console Us with you, We are

nonetheless sad. This is due to the numberless errors and the teachings of perverse doctrines which, no longer secretly and clandestinely but openly and vigorously, attack the Catholic faith. You know how evil men have raised the standard of revolt against religion through philosophy (of which they proclaim themselves doctors) and through empty fallacies devised according to natural reason. In the first place, the Roman See is assailed and the bonds of unity are, every day, being severed. The authority of the Church is weakened and the protectors of things sacred are snatched away and held in contempt. The holy precepts are despised, the celebration of divine offices is ridiculed, and the worship of God is cursed by the sinner.(1) All things which concern religion are relegated to the fables of old women and the superstitions of priests. Truly lions have roared in Israel.(2) With tears We say: "Truly they have conspired against the Lord and against His Christ." Truly the impious have said: "Raze it, raze it down to its foundations."(3)

4. Among these heresies belongs that foul contrivance of the sophists of this age who do not admit any difference among the different professions of faith and who think that the portal of eternal salvation opens for all from any religion. They, therefore, label with the stigma of levity and stupidity those who, having abandoned the religion which they learned, embrace another of any kind, even Catholicism. This is certainly a monstrous impiety which assigns the same praise and the mark of the just and upright man to truth and to error, to virtue and to vice, to goodness and to turpitude. Indeed this deadly idea concerning the lack of difference among religions is refuted even by the light of natural reason. We are assured of this because the various religions do not often agree among themselves. If one is true, the other must be false; there can be no society of darkness with light. Against these experienced sophists the people must be taught that the profession of the Catholic faith is uniquely true, as the apostle proclaims: one Lord, one faith, one baptism.(4) Jerome used to say it this way: he who eats the lamb outside this house will perish as did those during the flood who were not with Noah in the ark.(5) Indeed, no other name than the name of Jesus is given to men, by which they may be saved.(6) He who believes shall be saved; he who does not believe shall be condemned.(7)

5. We must also be wary of those who publish the Bible with new interpretations contrary to the Church's laws. They skillfully distort the meaning by their own interpretation. They print the Bibles in the vernacular and, absorbing an incredible expense, offer them free even to the uneducated. Furthermore, the Bibles are rarely without perverse little inserts to insure that the reader imbibes their lethal poison instead of the saving water of salvation. Long ago the Apostolic See warned about this serious hazard to the faith and drew up a list of the authors of these pernicious notions. The rules of this Index were published by the Council of Trent;(8) the ordinance required that translations of the Bible into the vernacular not be permitted without the approval of the Apostolic See and further required that they be published with commentaries from the Fathers. The sacred Synod of Trent had decreed(9) in order to restrain impudent characters, that no one, relying on his own prudence in matters of faith and of conduct which concerns Christian doctrine, might twist the sacred Scriptures to his own opinion, or to an opinion contrary to that of the Church or the popes. Though such machinations against the Catholic faith had been assailed long ago by these canonical proscriptions, Our recent predecessors made a special effort to check these spreading evils.(10) With these arms may you too strive to fight the battles of the Lord which endanger the sacred teachings, lest this deadly virus spread in your flock.

6. When this corruption has been abolished, then eradicate those secret societies of factious men who, completely opposed to God and to princes, are wholly dedicated to bringing about the fall of the Church, the destruction of kingdoms, and disorder in the whole world. Having cast off the restraints of true religion, they prepare the way for shameful crimes. Indeed, because they concealed their societies, they aroused suspicion of their evil intent. Afterwards this evil intention broke forth, about to assail

the sacred and the civil orders. Hence the supreme pontiffs, Our predecessors, Clement XII, Benedict XIV, Pius VII, Leo XII,(11) repeatedly condemned with anathema that kind of secret society. Our predecessors condemned them in apostolic letters; We confirm those commands and order that they be observed exactly. In this matter We shall be diligent lest the Church and the state suffer harm from the machinations of such sects. With your help We strenuously take up the mission of destroying the strongholds which the putrid impiety of evil men sets up.

7. We want you to know of another secret society organized not so long ago for the corruption of young people who are taught in the gymnasia and the lycea. Its cunning purpose is to engage evil teachers to lead the students along the paths of Baal by teaching them un-Christian doctrines. The perpetrators know well that the students' minds and morals are molded by the precepts of the teachers. Its influence is already so persuasive that all fear of religion has been lost, all discipline of morals has been abandoned, the sanctity of pure doctrine has been contested, and the rights of the sacred and of the civil powers have been trampled upon. Nor are they ashamed of any disgraceful crime OT error. We can truly say with Leo the Great that for them "Law is prevarication; religion, the devil; sacrifice, disgrace."(12) Drive these evils from your dioceses. Strive to assign not only learned, but also good men to train our youth.

8. Also watch the seminaries more diligently. The fathers of Trent made you responsible for their administration.(13) From them must come forth men well instructed both in Christian and ecclesiastical discipline and in the principles of sound doctrine. Such men may then distinguish themselves for their piety and their teaching. Thus, their ministry will be a witness, even to those outside the Church and they will be able to refute those who have strayed from the path of justice. Be very careful in choosing the seminarians since the salvation of the people principally depends on good pastors. Nothing contributes more to the ruin of souls than impious, weak, or uninformed clerics.

9. The heretics have disseminated pestilential books everywhere, by which the teachings of the impious spread, much as a cancer.(14) To counteract this most deadly pest, spare no labor. Be admonished by the words of Pius VII: "May they consider only that kind of food to be healthy to which the voice and authority of Peter has sent them. May they choose such food and nourish themselves with it. May they judge that food from which Peter's voice calls them away to be entirely harmful and pestiferous. May they quickly shrink away from it, and never permit themselves to be caught by its appearance and perverted by its allurements."(15)

10. We also want you to imbue your flock with reverence for the sanctity of marriage so that they may never do anything to detract from the dignity of this sacrament. They should do nothing that might be unbecoming to this spotless union nor anything that might cause doubt about the perpetuity of the bond of matrimony. This goal will be accomplished if the Christian people are accurately taught that the sacrament of matrimony ought to be governed not so much by human law as by divine law and that it ought to be counted among sacred, not earthly, concerns. Thus, it is wholly subject to the Church. Formerly marriage had no other purpose than that of bringing children into the world. But now it has been raised to the dignity of a sacrament by Christ the Lord and enriched with heavenly gifts. Now its purpose is not so much to generate offspring as to educate children for God and for religion. This increases the number of worshippers of the true divinity. It is agreed that the union of marriage signifies the perpetual and sublime union of Christ with His Church; as a result, the close union of husband and wife is a sacrament, that is, a sacred sign of the immortal love of Christ for His spouse. Therefore, teach the people what is sanctioned and what is condemned by the rules of the Church and the decrees of the Councils.(16) Also explain those things which pertain to the essence of the sacrament. Then they will be able to accomplish those things and will not dare to attempt what the Church detests. We ask this earnestly of you because of your love of religion.

11. You know now what causes Our present grief. There are also other things, no less serious, which it would take too long to recount here, but which you know well. Shall We hold back Our voice when the Christian cause is in such great need? Shall We be restrained by human arguments? Shall We suffer in silence the rending of the seamless robe of Christ the Savior, which even the soldiers who crucified Him did not dare to rend? Let it never happen that We be found lacking in zealous pastoral care for Our flock, beset as it is by serious dangers. We know you will do even more than We ask, and that you will cherish, augment, and defend the faith by means of teachings, counsel, work, and zeal.

12. With many ardent prayers We ask that, with God restoring the penitence of Israel, holy religion may flourish everywhere. We also ask that the true happiness of the people may continue undisturbed, and that God may always protect the pastor of His earthly flock and nourish him. May the powerful princes of the nations, with their generous spirits, favor Our cares and endeavors. With God's help, may they continue vigorously to promote the prosperity and safety of the Church, which is afflicted by so many evils.

13. Let us ask these things humbly of Mary, the holy Mother of God. We confess that she alone has overcome all heresies and We salute her with gratitude on this day, the anniversary of Our predecessor, Pius VII's, restoration to the city of Rome after he had suffered many adversities. Let us ask these things of Peter, the Prince of the Apostles, and of his coapostle Paul. With Christ's consent, may these two apostles grant that We, firmly established on the rock of the Church's confession, suffer no disturbing circumstances. From Christ Himself We humbly ask the gifts of grace, peace, and joy for you and for the flock entrusted to you. As a pledge of Our affection We lovingly impart the apostolic benediction.

Given in Rome, at St. Peter's, May 24, 1829, the first year of Our pontificate.

IN SUPREMO APOSTOLATUS

POPE GREGORY XVI CONDEMNS THE SLAVE TRADE—1839

Placed at the summit of the Apostolic power and, although lacking in merits, holding the place of Jesus Christ, the Son of God, Who, being made Man through utmost Charity, deigned to die for the Redemption of the World, We have judged that it belonged to Our pastoral solicitude to exert Ourselves to turn away the Faithful from the inhuman slave trade in Negroes and all other men. Assuredly, since there was spread abroad, first of all amongst the Christians, the light of the Gospel, these miserable people, who in such great numbers, and chiefly through the effects of wars, fell into very cruel slavery, experienced an alleviation of their lot. Inspired in fact by the Divine Spirit, the Apostles, it is true, exhorted the slaves themselves to obey their masters, according to the flesh, as though obeying Christ, and sincerely to accomplish the Will of God; but they ordered the masters to act well towards slaves, to give them what was just and equitable, and to abstain from menaces, knowing that the common Master both of themselves and of the slaves is in Heaven, and that with Him there is no distinction of persons.

But as the law of the Gospel universally and earnestly enjoined a sincere charity towards all, and considering that Our Lord Jesus Christ had declared that He considered as done or refused to Himself everything kind and merciful done or refused to the small and needy, it naturally follows, not only that Christians should regard as their brothers their slaves and, above all, their Christian slaves, but that they should be more inclined to set free those who merited it; which it was the custom to do chiefly upon the occasion of the Easter Feast as Gregory of Nyssa tells us. There were not lacking Christians, who, moved by an ardent charity 'cast themselves into bondage in order to redeem others,' many instances of which our predecessor, Clement I, of very holy memory, declares to have come to his knowledge. In the process of time, the fog of pagan superstition being more completely dissipated and the manners of barbarous people having been softened, thanks to Faith operating by Charity, it at last comes about that, since several centuries, there are no more slaves in the greater number of Christian nations. But - We say with profound sorrow - there were to be found afterwards among the Faithful men who, shamefully blinded by the desire of sordid gain, in lonely and distant countries, did not hesitate to reduce to slavery Indians, negroes and other wretched peoples, or else, by instituting or developing the trade in those who had been made slaves by others, to favour their unworthy practice. Certainly many Roman Pontiffs of glorious memory, Our Predecessors, did not fail, according to the duties of their charge, to blame severely this way of acting as dangerous for the spiritual welfare of those engaged in the traffic and a shame to the Christian name; they foresaw that as a result of this, the infidel peoples would be more and more strengthened in their hatred of the true Religion.

It is at these practices that are aimed the Letter Apostolic of Paul III, given on May 29, 1537, under the seal of the Fisherman, and addressed to the Cardinal Archbishop of Toledo, and afterwards another Letter, more detailed, addressed by Urban VIII on April 22, 1639 to the Collector Jurium of the Apostolic Chamber of Portugal. In the latter are severely and particularly condemned those who should dare 'to reduce to slavery the Indians of the Eastern and Southern Indies,' to sell them, buy them, exchange them or give them, separate them from their wives and children, despoil them of their goods and properties, conduct or transport them into other regions, or deprive them of liberty in any way whatsoever, retain them in servitude, or lend counsel, succour, favour and co-operation to those so acting, under no matter what pretext or excuse, or who proclaim and teach that this way of acting is allowable and co-operate in any manner whatever in the practices indicated.

Benedict XIV confirmed and renewed the penalties of the Popes above mentioned in a new Apostolic Letter addressed on December 20, 1741, to the Bishops of Brazil and some other regions, in which he stimulated, to the same end, the solicitude of the Governors themselves. Another of Our Predecessors, anterior to Benedict XIV, Pius II, as during his life the power of the Portuguese was extending itself over New Guinea, sent on October 7, 1462, to a Bishop who was leaving for that country, a Letter in which he not only gives the Bishop himself the means of exercising there the sacred ministry with more fruit, but on the same occasion, addresses grave warnings with regard to Christians who should reduce neophytes to slavery.

In our time Pius VII, moved by the same religious and charitable spirit as his Predecessors, intervened zealously with those in possession of power to secure that the slave trade should at least cease amongst the Christians. The penalties imposed and the care given by Our Predecessors contributed in no small measure, with the help of God, to protect the Indians and the other people mentioned against the cruelty of the invaders or the cupidity of Christian merchants, without however carrying success to such a point that the Holy See could rejoice over the complete success of its efforts in this direction; for the slave trade, although it has diminished in more than one district, is still practiced by numerous Christians. This is why, desiring to remove such a shame from all the Christian nations, having fully reflected over the whole question and having taken the advice of many of Our Venerable Brothers the Cardinals of the Holy Roman Church, and walking in the footsteps of Our Predecessors, We warn and adjure earnestly in the Lord faithful Christians of every condition that no one in the future dare to vex anyone, despoil him of his possessions, reduce to servitude, or lend aid and favour to those who give themselves up to these practices, or exercise that inhuman traffic by which the Blacks, as if they were not men but rather animals, having been brought into servitude, in no matter what way, are, without any distinction, in contempt of the rights of justice and humanity, bought, sold, and devoted sometimes to the hardest labour. Further, in the hope of gain, propositions of purchase being made to the first owners of the Blacks, dissensions and almost perpetual conflicts are aroused in these regions.

We reprove, then, by virtue of Our Apostolic Authority, all the practices abovementioned as absolutely unworthy of the Christian name. By the same Authority We prohibit and strictly forbid any Ecclesiastic or lay person from presuming to defend as permissible this traffic in Blacks under no matter what pretext or excuse, or from publishing or teaching in any manner whatsoever, in public or privately, opinions contrary to what We have set forth in this Apostolic Letter.

RESPICIENTES

POPE PIUS IX PROTESTS AGAINST THE TAKING OF THE PAPAL STATES—1870

ENCYCLICAL OF POPE

Pius IX protesting the taking of the Pontifical StatesNovember 1, 1870

To All Patriarchs, Primates, Archbishops, Bishops, and other Ordinaries having Favor and Communion with the Apostolic See.

Venerable Brothers, Greetings and Apostolic Benediction.

As We look back on all the things which for many years the government of Piedmont has undertaken in order to overthrow the civil rule which God granted Our Apostolic See, We are moved by profound sorrow. God's purpose in providing the successors of St. Peter with temporal jurisdiction was to enable them to perform their spiritual duties in complete freedom and security. This government, by force and contrary to all divine law, has finally executed the plan it has long considered: the sacrilegious invasion of Our dear City and the cities We continued to rule after the previous occupation. We, prostrate before God, cry out using the words of the prophet: "Therefore do I weep and my eyes run down with water, because the Comforter, the Relief of my soul, is far from me. My children are desolate because the enemy hath prevailed."1

History of the War

2. We have already narrated the history of this evil war to the Catholic world. We did this in addresses, in encyclicals, and in short letters. The short letters were issued at various times, namely November 1, 1850; January 22 and July 26, 1855; June 18 and 28 and September 26, 1859; and January 19, 1860. Our encyclical was released March 26, 1860, and the addresses took place September 28, 1860; March 18 and September 30, 1861; and September 20, October 17, and November 14, 1867. This series of documents reveals and confirms that serious injuries were perpetrated by the government of Piedmont even before the seizure of Our ecclesiastical sovereignty. Such injuries were inflicted by the enacting of laws contrary to the natural, divine, and ecclesiastical order. That government also subjected ministers, religious communities, and even bishops to degrading ill-treatment. It violated its solemn agreements with Us by resolutely denying the inviolable rights of the very agreements it had confirmed. At the same time the government indicated that it wanted to enter into new agreements with Us. These documents demonstrate by what arts and with what sly and disgraceful machinations this same government oppressed the rights of the Apostolic See; they also indicate the efforts We made to check its increasing audacity and to vindicate the cause of the Church.

3. In 1859 the cities of Emilia were stirred up to rebellion by the Piedmontese, who supplied propaganda, conspirators, arms, and money. Not much later, a plebiscite was feigned by announcing a popular election and stealing the votes. By that deceit Our provinces situated in that region were torn from Our paternal rule; the opposition of the faithful proved vain. The following year this same government used deceitful pretexts to launch an unexpected attack, in order to wrest Our provinces located in Picenum, Umbria, and Our patrimony from Our rule. The enemy surrounded Our soldiers and a band of volunteer Catholic youth. Such a sudden attack was not at all anticipated. Our army fought fearlessly for its faith, but was put down in a bloody battle. Everyone knows the extraordinary impudence and hypocrisy of this government. To minimize the odium of this sacrilegious usurpation, they boasted that they invaded these provinces to restore the principles of moral order there. But in fact they spread every kind of false doctrine; they gave free reign to cupidity and impiety; they inflicted undeserved penalties on the bishops and other clerics, even jailing them and permitting them to suffer public insults. Meanwhile, they let persecutors and those who did not even spare the dignity of the Supreme Pontiff go unpunished.

4. In the performance of Our duties, We have always refused the repeated offers and commands to betray Our office shamefully, either by surrendering the rights and possessions of the Church, or by entering a wicked compact with the usurpers. We also opposed these crimes against human and divine law with solemn protestations lodged before both God and man. We declared that the authors of these crimes and their partisans have incurred ecclesiastical censure, and whenever necessary We censured them again with the same sanctions. The previously mentioned government has nevertheless persisted in its contumacy and its schemes. It attempted to stir up rebellion in Our remaining provinces, especially in Rome, by sending in instigators and by all kinds of arts. But these attempts did not go according to plan because of the unshaken fidelity of Our soldiers and because of the love and zeal of Our people, who supported Us.

Enemy Defeated

5. Finally that turbulent storm erupted against Us in the autumn of 1867, when divisions of wicked men attacked Our borders and Our City. They received assistance from the Piedmontese and were inflamed with wrath and crime. A number of them had already secretly infiltrated the City. Because of their arms, along with their cruel and violent nature, We and Our subjects feared painful and bloody treatment. But Our merciful God by the strenuous resistance of Our troops and the assistance of the French legions, returned their ineffectual attacks.

Reputation of the City

6. The piety and zeal of you and your faithful people for Us, manifested by your charity, have consoled Us in the midst of so much grief. With strength from God We never relax Our concern in safeguarding the temporal welfare of Our subjects. People from all nations visit Our City. They note Our public tranquility and security, Our finest arts and sciences, and the confidence and good will of Our people for Us. These visitors stream into Our City at all times, but especially during the many masses and solemn feasts which We celebrate.

Another Attack

7. Just now when Our people were enjoying a state of peace, the King of Piedmont and his government seized the opportunity presented by a war between the two most powerful nations of Europe. They made an agreement with one of the warring nations that they would preserve the present state of ecclesiastical or spiritual authority of the Church and would not permit it to be violated by factious individuals. They decreed that they would, however, invade and subject to their own power the lands which remained under Our temporal authority and Our See itself. What was the purpose of this hostile invasion,

and what causes were presented? Everyone knows what the king discussed in his September 8 letter, which was addressed to us and delivered by his own spokesman. With fallacious sophistries of word and thought he proferred the images of a loving son and of a loyal Catholic and pretended to have the cause of public order, of the pontificate itself, and of Our person at heart. Under these pretenses he asked that We not consider the loss of Our temporal power as a criminal act, but that We surrender that power willingly. He asked Us to trust in his empty promises by which the desires of the Italian people could be reconciled with the freedom and the supreme spiritual authority of the Roman Pontiff.

Rejection of Proposals

8. For Our part We could not help but be astonished at his means of concealing the violence soon to be inflicted on Us. Nor could We help but pity the lot of this same king; driven by unjust counsels, he daily inflicts new wounds on the Church. Because of his reverence for man rather than God, he does not believe that the King of kings and Lord of lords reigns in heaven "who shows no partiality nor does He fear greatness, because He Himself made the great as well as the small . . . but for the powerful a rigorous scrutiny impends."[2] However concerning his proposals, We knew there was no time for delay. Obeying the laws of Our office and conscience, We followed the example of Our predecessors, particularly Pius VII whose problems were much like Our own. We borrow his words here:

"Let us recall with St. Ambrose 'the saintly man Naboth who owned a vineyard and was petitioned by a royal demand to give up his vineyard, so that the king, after cutting down the vines, might sow lowly vegetables. Naboth answered him: "Be it far from me to surrender the inheritance of my predecessors".'[3] We judged that there was far less right for Us to give up so ancient and sacred an inheritance (namely the temporal power of this Holy See, held by the Roman Pontiffs for many centuries). Nor could We tacitly consent that someone occupy Our City and destroy its holy form of government, bequeathed by Jesus Christ to His Church and ordered according to the sacred canons which were inspired by the Holy Spirit. It would be replaced by a system opposed not only to the sacred canons, but also to the precepts of the Gospel. Then, as is customary, a new order of things would be introduced which would tend to associate and confuse all sects and superstitions with the Catholic Church.

"'Naboth defended his vineyard with his own blood.'[4] Similarly, could We restrain Ourselves -- no matter what might happen to Us -- from defending the rights and possessions of the Holy Roman Church when We had sworn to defend the same to the best of Our ability? Could We refuse to protect the freedom of the Apostolic See which is so closely joined with the freedom and welfare of the whole Church? In truth these events demonstrate how necessary this temporal rule is for protecting the safe and free exercise of the pope's spiritual power, which was divinely given to him."[5]

Occupation of the City

9. Therefore clinging to the observations which We had declared in Our addresses, We reproved the king's unjust demands in Our reply to him and We showed that Our bitter pain was joined with paternal charity, which cares even for those sons who imitate the rebellious Absalom. However before We sent this letter, his army occupied Our cities, which until then were untouched and peaceful; the soldiers on guard were easily dispersed when they attempted to resist. Shortly thereafter dawned that unlucky day, September 20, when this City, the Seat of the Prince of the Apostles, the Center of the Catholic religion, and the refuge of all nations, was occupied by many thousands of armed men. It is deplorable to Us that after the walls were breached and fear of the enemy's dreadful missiles spread on all sides, the City was taken at the king's command who, a little before, had professed his filial affection for Us and his fidelity to religion. What could be more lamentable for Us and for all good people than that dread day? After the troops entered the

City, which was already filled with a multitude of foreign agitators, We saw public order immediately disturbed and overturned; We saw the dignity and sanctity of the pontificate impiously attacked; We saw Our faithful soldiers subjected to abuse of every kind; We saw unbridled license and wantonness reigning where a short time before the filial love of children who desire to comfort a common spiritual Parent in his grief had shone forth.

Resultant Evils

10. From that day forward We have seen with Our own eyes events which cannot be recalled without indignation by all good people: Wicked books filled with lies, infamy, and impiety; are offered for sale and disseminated widely; numerous magazines are published each day to corrupt minds and upright laws, to show contempt for religion, and to rouse public opinion against Us and this Apostolic See. In addition, filthy and shameful pictures and other things of this kind are published in which sacred things and persons are derided and exposed to public ridicule. Honors and memorials have been decreed for those convicted of grave crimes, while clerics have been repeatedly and wrongfully harassed, some even wounded by beatings from traitors. Some religious houses were subjected to unjust search and Our Quirinal houses were violated. A cardinal who had his See there was violently forced to flee, while other clerics of Our domestic staff were denied the use of the Quirinal houses and badgered. Laws and decrees were issued which obviously injure and destroy the freedom, immunity, properties, and rights of the Church of God. These evils will spread still more widely unless God intervenes. We, in the meantime, are prevented from bringing any cure because of Our condition. Every day We are violently reminded of Our captivity and of Our lost liberty. They declare with lying words that freedom has been left for Us in the exercise of Our apostolic ministry, and the usurping government boasts that it desires to strengthen this liberty with the necessary precautions, as they call them.

11. We must mention here the monstrous crime which you are certainly aware of. They made use of a ludicrous type of plebiscite in the provinces stolen from Us. As if the properties and rights of the apostolic See, long considered sacred and inviolable, might now be called into question, and as if the censures which are called down upon these violators might be loosened and the robbery which We have suffered might be made legitimate. Those who are accustomed to rejoice in evil events were not ashamed to carry rebellion and contempt for ecclesiastical censures through the cities of Italy on this occasion as in a triumphal procession. But the true feelings of the majority of the Italian people are impeded. Their religion, devotion, and confidence in Us and the Holy Church have been restrained in many ways so that these sentiments cannot flow forth freely.

Papal Protests *against Usurpations*

12. We have been placed by God to rule and govern the whole house of Israel and appointed as the protector of religion, justice, and the rights of the Church. If We remained silent, We could be accused before God and the Church of having consented to these perverse disturbances. We therefore renew and confirm what We have solemnly declared already in the addresses, encyclicals, and short letters cited above, and most recently a protest which Our cardinal in charge of public affairs made in Our name and at Our order on September 20. This protest was delivered to the ambassadors, ministers, and representatives of foreign nations who remained with Us and the Holy See. We now again solemnly declare to you that We are determined to retain all the dominions of this Holy See and its rights whole, entire, and unviolated, and to transmit them to Our successors. We declare all usurpations to be unjust, violent, null, and void. We announce now that any acts committed by Our enemies and invaders to confirm these usurpations–either at the present time or in the future – are condemned by Us and null and invalid. Furthermore, We protest before God and the whole Catholic world that while

detained in such captivity, We are unable to exercise Our supreme pastoral authority safely, expediently, and freely. Finally, We obey the admonition of St. Paul: "For what has justice in common with iniquity? Or what fellowship has light with darkness? What harmony is there between Christ and Belial?"6 We declare openly, mindful of Our office and of Our oath, that We will never assent to a conciliation or an agreement which in any way may destroy or diminish Our rights and therefore those of God and the Holy See. In like manner We confess that for the Church of Christ We are prepared, with the help of divine grace, to drink to the dregs that cup which the Lord first deigned to drink for her. We will never accept and obey unjust demands which are presented to Us. And indeed as Our predecessor Pius VII said: "To do violence to this highest power of the Apostolic See, to disjoin its temporal authority from its spiritual power, to disassociate, separate by force and cut off the duties of Pastor and Prince, is nothing less than to overturn and destroy the work of God. It is nothing less then to attempt to inflict the greatest damage on religion and to deprive it of its most effective defense. Then the highest Ruler of the Church would be unable to offer help to the Catholics spread all over the earth, who request his help and support because of his spiritual power."7

EXCOMMUNICATION *for Usurpers*

13. Our warnings, admonitions, and expostulations had no effect; therefore by Our own authority and that of God and of the Apostles Peter and Paul, We declare to you and to the whole Church that any who have invaded or usurped Our provinces or Our beloved City (as well as those commanding these things and their partisans, helpers, advisers, and followers) have incurred excommunication and the other censures and ecclesiastical penalties imposed by the sacred canons, Apostolic Constitutions, and decrees of Trent (Sess. 22, c. 11 de Reform.) following the form and duration expressed in Our apostolic letter of March 26, 1860.

HOPE THAT USURPERS *Will Reforrn*

14. But mindful that We hold His place on earth who came to seek and save what was lost. We desire nothing more than that the wandering sons, returning to Us, may be embraced with paternal charity. We humbly beseech God, that He may be with Us and help Us. May He also be with His Church, reflecting on the eternal damnation which they pile up for themselves and fearing His justice, may strive to please Him before the Judgment Day. With their wicked schemes abandoned, may they alleviate the groans of Holy Mother Church and Our own grief.

15. But that We may obtain these blessings from the divine clemency, We earnestly request, venerable brothers, that you and your faithful flocks join your fervent prayers with Ours. Then all of us together shall approach the throne of grace and mercy, using as intercessors the Immaculate Virgin Mary, Mother of God, and the blessed Apostles Peter and Paul. "The Church of God from its beginning up to the present time was often in tribulation, and was often delivered. Her voice is: 'Often have they fought against me from my youth, but have not prevailed against me. On my back sinners have wrought havoc; they lengthened their iniquity.' Neither does the Lord now permit the rod of the wicked to rest over the lot of the just. The hand of the Lord has not been shortened, nor made incapable of salvation. Without a doubt He will now deliver His spouse whom He redeemed with His blood, endowed with His spirit, adorned with heavenly gifts, and enriched with terrestrial wealth."8

16. Meanwhile, We pray with all Our soul that you may be showered with the gifts of heavenly graces, venerable brothers, and that all the clergy and the lay faithful entrusted by God to your care may share in these gifts. As a pledge of Our special love, We affectionately impart the apostolic benediction to you and to Our beloved sons. Given in Rome at St. Peter's, November 1, 1870, the 25th year of Our Pontificate.

SAEPE VENERABILES FRATRES

POPE PIUS IX ON THANKSGIVING FOR TWENTY-FIVE YEARS OF PONTIFICATE—1871

To Our Venerable Brothers the Patriarchs, Archbishops, Bishops and all Local Ordinaries of the Catholic World Who are in Loving Communion with the Apostolic See.

Venerable Brothers, We give You Greeting and Our Apostolic Blessing.

Often, venerable brothers, in the course of Our long pontificate, We have addressed you and let you know how pleased We were to receive proof of your devotion and love for Us and this Apostolic See which the God of mercies has inspired in you and in the faithful entrusted to your care. Certainly when the enemies of God began to invade His civil realm in order to defeat Jesus Christ and His Church, the Christian people and yourselves, never stopped beseeching God "Whom winds and seas obey" to calm the storm. You never stopped reiterating the testimonies of your love and performing every service which could console Us in Our affliction. But after Our city was taken and We were delivered into the hands of Our attackers, you and your people redoubled your prayers, and with frequent denunciations, you affirmed the sacred rights of religion and justice which are being trodden down with unbelievable effrontery.

RECORD LENGTH *of Papacy*

2. We have reached the twenty-fifth year of Our papacy, an unusual event which has never before occurred in the succession of Roman pontiffs since the days of St. Peter. You have been so joyful for Us, and you have shown so clearly the vigorous life which everywhere inspires the Christian family, that We have been deeply touched. By joining Our prayers to Yours, We have gained new strength to await with greater confidence the full and complete triumph of the Church.

RESPONSE OF THE *Faithful*

3. Thronging crowds everywhere filled the holy churches to pray for Us. All over the world the faithful attended in very great numbers to give thanks to God for the lengthy Papacy conferred on Us, and to request urgently from Him the victory of the Church. Our sorrow and anxieties were not only relieved but turned into joy, We felt, by the congratulation, obedience, and prayers manifested in your letters, and by the arrival of great numbers of people here from all parts of the world. Among these, many were remarkable for nobility of birth or their ecclesiastical or civil rank, but they were still more remarkable for their faith. They all assembled here from widely scattered places and joined in loving action with many of the citizens of this city and the occupied provinces. They wanted to face the same dangers and insults to which We are subjected, in order to give personal witness to their own religious feelings for Us and to the feelings of their fellow-citizens. They also wanted to present Us with scrolls to which many hundreds of thousands of the faithful of every race had put their own names in sharp disapproval of the invasion of Our realm, demanding its restitution on compelling grounds of religion, justice, and even of politics.

GIFTS FOR THE FAITHFUL

4. On this occasion too the poor as well as the rich made an unusually large contribution to offset Our recent lack of resources. We also received many kinds of remarkable gifts, a splendid tribute of Christian art and invention which was very well suited to aid Our twofold spiritual and royal power granted by God to Us. We received in addition an abundant and fine supply of sacred vestments and utensils so that We could everywhere

remedy the poverty and need of so many churches. It was assuredly a wonderful spectacle of Catholic unity and plainly showed that although the universal Church is spread throughout the whole world and composed of peoples with different customs, talents, and pursuits, it is still inspired by the one spirit of God. The more madly impiety persecutes and oppresses it, and the more cunningly it attempts to deprive the Church of all human aid, the more wonderfully God strengthens the Church.

5. Great and ardent thanks be then to Him Who, while giving glory to His own name, lifts the hopes of the afflicted to certain triumph by the very effective demonstration of His power and might. But while We refer these gifts to the Giver of all good things, We feel the greatest gratitude at the same time towards those who showed themselves instruments of the divine Providence and gave Us lavishly the service of their aid, consolation, obedience, devotion, and love. Lifting Our eyes and hands to heaven, We offer to the Lord everything of this kind that Our sons sent Us in His Name. We urgently beseech Him soon to grant their united prayers for the liberty of this Holy See, the victory of the Church, and the peace of the world. In this way, He can return generous thanks, since We are unable to do so, to each one in heaven and on earth.

6. We would like to thank each person individually, but the very abundance of services offered from every side in goods, letters, and words obviously prevents Us. So We ask you to reveal and proclaim Our feelings to your clergy and people with eloquence. Exhort them all however to persevere firmly with you in confident prayer: for since Scripture assures us that the urgent prayer of the just man passes through the clouds and does not depart until the most High beholds, and since Christ has promised the He will be present where even two are joined in agreement in His name and that the heavenly father will do whatever they request then, all the more should the universal Church at last, by unceasing and united prayer, obtain the sight of the powers of hell crushed, the efforts of human wickedness scattered and destroyed, and peace and justice brought back to the earth.

7. Strive to achieve the closest unity among yourselves so as to advance in full phalanx against the enemies of God who are still attacking the Church with novel stratagems. Although the Church cannot be destroyed by any force, unite in order to withstand their onset and rout their ranks with greater ease and effect. This is what We greatly desire and strive to obtain; this is what We wholeheartedly pray for you and the entire Catholic family. In the meantime, as an augury of that desired event and of God's favor, and as a sure witness of Our particular benevolence and gratitude, We lovingly bestow from Our heart on each one of you, venerable brothers, and on the clergy and all the people committed to your separate care, Our Apostolic blessing.

Given at Rome in St. Peter's on the 5th day of August the feast of St. Mary on the Esquiline in the year of the Lord 1871 in the 26th year of Our Pontificate.

LAMENTABILI SANE

POPE PIUS X CONDEMNS THE ERRORS OF THE MODERNISTS—1907

With truly lamentable results, our age, casting aside all restraint in its search for the ultimate causes of things, frequently pursues novelties so ardently that it rejects the legacy of the human race. Thus it falls into very serious errors, which are even more serious when they concern sacred authority, the interpretation of Sacred Scripture, and the principal mysteries of Faith. The fact that many Catholic writers also go beyond the limits determined by the Fathers and the Church herself is extremely regrettable. In the name of higher knowledge and historical research (they say), they are looking for that progress of dogmas which is, in reality, nothing but the corruption of dogmas.

These errors are being daily spread among the faithful. Lest they captivate the faithful's minds and corrupt the purity of their faith, His Holiness, Pius X, by Divine Providence, Pope, has decided that the chief errors should be noted and condemned by the Office of this Holy Roman and Universal Inquisition.

Therefore, after a very diligent investigation and consultation with the Reverend Consultors, the Most Eminent and Reverend Lord Cardinals, the General Inquisitors in matters of faith and morals have judged the following propositions to be condemned and proscribed. In fact, by this general decree, they are condemned and proscribed.

1. The ecclesiastical law which prescribes that books concerning the Divine Scriptures are subject to previous examination does not apply to critical scholars and students of scientific exegesis of the Old and New Testament.
2. The Church's interpretation of the Sacred Books is by no means to be rejected; nevertheless, it is subject to the more accurate judgment and correction of the exegetes.
3. From the ecclesiastical judgments and censures passed against free and more scientific exegesis, one can conclude that the Faith the Church proposes contradicts history and that Catholic teaching cannot really be reconciled with the true origins of the Christian religion.
4. Even by dogmatic definitions the Church's magisterium cannot determine the genuine sense of the Sacred Scriptures.
5. Since the deposit of Faith contains only revealed truths, the Church has no right to pass judgment on the assertions of the human sciences.
6. The "Church learning" and the "Church teaching" collaborate in such a way in defining truths that it only remains for the "Church teaching" to sanction the opinions of the "Church learning."
7. In proscribing errors, the Church cannot demand any internal assent from the faithful by which the judgments she issues are to be embraced.
8. They are free from all blame who treat lightly the condemnations passed by the Sacred Congregation of the Index or by the Roman Congregations.
9. They display excessive simplicity or ignorance who believe that God is really the author of the Sacred Scriptures.
10. The inspiration of the books of the Old Testament consists in this: The Israelite writers handed down religious doctrines under a peculiar aspect which was either little or not at all known to the Gentiles.
11. Divine inspiration does not extend to all of Sacred Scriptures so that it renders its parts, each and every one, free from every error.
12. If he wishes to apply himself usefully to Biblical studies, the exegete must first put aside all preconceived opinions about the supernatural origin of Sacred Scripture and interpret it the same as any other merely human document.
13. The Evangelists themselves, as well as the Christians of the second and third generation, artificially arranged the evangelical parables. In such a way they explained the scanty fruit of the preaching of Christ among the Jews.
14. In many narrations the Evangelists recorded, not so much things that are true, as things which, even though

false, they judged to be more profitable for their readers.
15. Until the time the canon was defined and constituted, the Gospels were increased by additions and corrections. Therefore there remained in them only a faint and uncertain trace of the doctrine of Christ.
16. The narrations of John are not properly history, but a mystical contemplation of the Gospel. The discourses contained in his Gospel are theological meditations, lacking historical truth concerning the mystery of salvation.
17. The fourth Gospel exaggerated miracles not only in order that the extraordinary might stand out but also in order that it might become more suitable for showing forth the work and glory of the Word Incarnate.
18. John claims for himself the quality of witness concerning Christ. In reality, however, he is only a distinguished witness of the Christian life, or of the life of Christ in the Church at the close of the first century.
19. Heterodox exegetes have expressed the true sense of the Scriptures more faithfully than Catholic exegetes.
20. Revelation could be nothing else than the consciousness man acquired of his revelation to God.
21. Revelation, constituting the object of the Catholic faith, was not completed with the Apostles.
22. The dogmas the Church holds out as revealed are not truths which have fallen from heaven. They are an interpretation of religious facts which the human mind has acquired by laborious effort.
23. Opposition may, and actually does, exist between the facts narrated in Sacred Scripture and the Church's dogmas which rest on them. Thus the critic may reject as false facts the Church holds as most certain.
24. The exegete who constructs premises from which it follows that dogmas are historically false or doubtful is not to be reproved as long as he does not directly deny the dogmas themselves .
25. The assent of faith ultimately rests on a mass of probabilities .
26. The dogmas of the Faith are to be held only according to their practical sense; that is to say, as preceptive norms of conduct and not as norms of believing.
27. The divinity of Jesus Christ is not proved from the Gospels. It is a dogma which the Christian conscience has derived from the notion of the Messias.
28. While He was exercising His ministry, Jesus did not speak with the object of teaching He was the Messias, nor did His miracles tend to prove it.
29. It is permissible to grant that the Christ of history is far inferior to the Christ Who is the object of faith.
30 In all the evangelical texts the name "Son of God" is equivalent only to that of "Messias." It does not in the least way signify that Christ is the true and natural Son of God.
31. The doctrine concerning Christ taught by Paul, John, and the Councils of Nicea, Ephesus and Chalcedon is not that which Jesus taught but that which the Christian conscience conceived concerning Jesus.
32. It is impossible to reconcile the natural sense of the Gospel texts with the sense taught by our theologians concerning the conscience and the infallible knowledge of Jesus Christ.
33 Everyone who is not led by preconceived opinions can readily see that either Jesus professed an error concerning the immediate Messianic coming or the greater part of His doctrine as contained in the Gospels is destitute of authenticity.
34. The critics can ascribe to Christ a knowledge without limits only on a hypothesis which cannot be historically conceived and which is repugnant to the moral sense. That hypothesis is that Christ as man possessed the knowledge of God and yet was unwilling to communicate the knowledge of a great many things to His disciples and posterity.
35. Christ did not always possess the consciousness of His Messianic dignity.
36. The Resurrection of the Savior is not properly a fact of the historical order. It is a fact of merely the supernatural order (neither demonstrated nor demonstrable) which the Christian conscience gradually derived from other facts.
37. In the beginning, faith in the Resurrection of Christ was not so much in the fact itself of the Resurrection as in the immortal life of Christ with God.
38. The doctrine of the expiatory death of Christ is Pauline and not evangelical.

39. The opinions concerning the origin of the Sacraments which the Fathers of Trent held and which certainly influenced their dogmatic canons are very different from those which now rightly exist among historians who examine Christianity .

40. The Sacraments have their origin in the fact that the Apostles and their successors, swayed and moved by circumstances and events, interpreted some idea and intention of Christ.

41. The Sacraments are intended merely to recall to man's mind the ever-beneficent presence of the Creator.

42. The Christian community imposed the necessity of Baptism, adopted it as a necessary rite, and added to it the obligation of the Christian profession.

43. The practice of administering Baptism to infants was a disciplinary evolution, which became one of the causes why the Sacrament was divided into two, namely, Baptism and Penance.

44. There is nothing to prove that the rite of the Sacrament of Confirmation was employed by the Apostles. The formal distinction of the two Sacraments of Baptism and Confirmation does not pertain to the history of primitive Christianity.

45. Not everything which Paul narrates concerning the institution of the Eucharist (I Cor. 11:23-25) is to be taken historically.

46. In the primitive Church the concept of the Christian sinner reconciled by the authority of the Church did not exist. Only very slowly did the Church accustom herself to this concept. As a matter of fact, even after Penance was recognized as an institution of the Church, it was not called a Sacrament since it would be held as a disgraceful Sacrament.

47. The words of the Lord, "Receive the Holy Spirit; whose sins you shall forgive, they are forgiven them; and whose sins you shall retain, they are retained" (John 20:22-23), in no way refer to the Sacrament of Penance, in spite of what it pleased the Fathers of Trent to say.

48. In his Epistle (Ch. 5:14-15) James did not intend to promulgate a Sacrament of Christ but only commend a pious custom. If in this custom he happens to distinguish a means of grace, it is not in that rigorous manner in which it was taken by the theologians who laid down the notion and number of the Sacraments.

49. When the Christian supper gradually assumed the nature of a liturgical action those who customarily presided over the supper acquired the sacerdotal character.

50. The elders who fulfilled the office of watching over the gatherings of the faithful were instituted by the Apostles as priests or bishops to provide for the necessary ordering of the increasing communities and not properly for the perpetuation of the Apostolic mission and power.

51. It is impossible that Matrimony could have become a Sacrament of the new law until later in the Church since it was necessary that a full theological explication of the doctrine of grace and the Sacraments should first take place before Matrimony should be held as a Sacrament.

52. It was far from the mind of Christ to found a Church as a society which would continue on earth for a long course

of centuries. On the contrary, in the mind of Christ the kingdom of heaven together with the end of the world was about to come immediately.

53. The organic constitution of the Church is not immutable. Like human society, Christian society is subject to a perpetual evolution.

54. Dogmas, Sacraments and hierarchy, both their notion and reality, are only interpretations and evolutions of the Christian intelligence which have increased and perfected by an external series of additions the little germ latent in the Gospel.

55. Simon Peter never even suspected that Christ entrusted the primacy in the Church to him.

56. The Roman Church became the head of all the churches, not through the ordinance of Divine Providence, but merely through political conditions.

57. The Church has shown that she is hostile to the progress of the natural and theological sciences.

58. Truth is no more immutable than man himself, since it evolved with him, in him, and through him.

59. Christ did not teach a determined body of doctrine applicable to all times and all men, but rather inaugurated

a religious movement adapted or to be adapted to different times and places.

60. Christian Doctrine was originally Judaic. Through successive evolutions it became first Pauline, then Joannine, finally Hellenic and universal.

61. It may be said without paradox that there is no chapter of Scripture, from the first of Genesis to the last of the Apocalypse, which contains a doctrine absolutely identical with that which the Church teaches on the same matter. For the same reason, therefore, no chapter of Scripture has the same sense for the critic and the theologian.

62. The chief articles of the Apostles' Creed did not have the same sense for the Christians of the first ages as they have for the Christians of our time.

63. The Church shows that she is incapable of effectively maintaining evangelical ethics since she obstinately clings to immutable doctrines which cannot be reconciled with modern progress.

64. Scientific progress demands that the concepts of Christian doctrine concerning God, creation, revelation, the Person of the Incarnate Word, and Redemption be re-adjusted.

65. Modern Catholicism can be reconciled with true science only if it is transformed into a non-dogmatic Christianity; that is to say, into a broad and liberal Protestantism.

The following Thursday, the fourth day of the same month and year, all these matters were accurately reported to our Most Holy Lord, Pope Pius X. His Holiness approved and confirmed the decree of the Most Eminent Fathers and ordered that each and every one of the above-listed propositions be held by all as condemned and proscribed.

PETER PALOMBELLI, Notary of the Holy Roman and Universal Inquisition

MIT BRENNENDER SORGE

POPE PIUS XI ON THE CHURCH AND THE GERMAN REICH—1937

✠ To the Venerable Brethren the Archbishops and Bishops of Germany and other Ordinaries in Peace and Communion with the Apostolic See.

Venerable Brethren, Greetings, and Apostolic Blessing.

It is with deep anxiety and growing surprise that We have long been following the painful trials of the Church and the increasing vexations which afflict those who have remained loyal in heart and action in the midst of a people that once received from St. Boniface the bright message and the Gospel of Christ and God's Kingdom.

2. And what the representatives of the venerable episcopate, who visited Us in Our sick room, had to tell Us, in truth and duty bound, has not modified Our feelings. To consoling and edifying information on the stand the Faithful are making for their Faith, they considered themselves bound, in spite of efforts to judge with moderation and in spite of their own patriotic love, to add reports of things hard and unpleasant. After hearing their account, We could, in grateful acknowledgment to God, exclaim with the Apostle of love: "I have no greater grace than this, to hear that my children walk in truth" (John iii. 4). But the frankness indifferent in Our Apostolic charge and the determination to place before the Christian world the truth in all its reality, prompt Us to add: "Our pastoral heart knows no deeper pain, no disappointment more bitter, than to learn that many are straying from the path of truth."

3. When, in 1933, We consented, Venerable Brethren, to open negotiations for a concordat, which the Reich Government proposed on the basis of a scheme of several years' standing; and when, to your unanimous satisfaction, We concluded the negotiations by a solemn treaty, We

were prompted by the desire, as it behooved Us, to secure for Germany the freedom of the Church's beneficent mission and the salvation of the souls in her care, as well as by the sincere wish to render the German people a service essential for its peaceful development and prosperity. Hence, despite many and grave misgivings, We then decided not to withhold Our consent for We wished to spare the Faithful of Germany, as far as it was humanly possible, the trials and difficulties they would have had to face, given the circumstances, had the negotiations fallen through. It was by acts that We wished to make it plain, Christ's interests being Our sole object, that the pacific and maternal hand of the Church would be extended to anyone who did not actually refuse it.

4. If, then, the tree of peace, which we planted on German soil with the purest intention, has not brought forth the fruit, which in the interest of your people, We had fondly hoped, no one in the world who has eyes to see and ears to hear will be able to lay the blame on the Church and on her Head. The experiences of these last years have fixed responsibilities and laid bare intrigues, which from the outset only aimed at a war of extermination. In the furrows, where We tried to sow the seed of a sincere peace, other men -- the "enemy" of Holy Scripture -- oversowed the cockle of distrust, unrest, hatred, defamation, of a determined hostility overt or veiled, fed from many sources and wielding many tools, against Christ and His Church. They, and they alone with their accomplices, silent or vociferous, are today responsible, should the storm of religious war, instead of the rainbow of peace, blacken the German skies.

5. We have never ceased, Venerable Brethren, to represent to the responsible rulers of your country's destiny, the consequences which would inevitably follow the protection and even the favor, extended to such a policy. We have done everything in Our power to defend the sacred pledge of the given word of honor against theories and practices, which it officially endorsed, would wreck every faith in treaties and make every signature worthless. Should the day ever come to place before the world the account of Our efforts, every honest mind will see on which side are to be found the promoters of peace, and on which side its disturbers. Whoever had left in his soul an atom of love for truth, and in his heart a shadow of a sense of justice, must admit that, in the course of these anxious and trying years following upon the conclusion of the concordat, every one of Our words, every one of Our acts, has been inspired by the binding law of treaties. At the same time, anyone must acknowledge, not without surprise and reprobation, how the other contracting party emasculated the terms of the treaty, distorted their meaning, and eventually considered its more or less official violation as a normal policy. The moderation We showed in spite of all this was not inspired by motives of worldly interest, still less by unwarranted weakness, but merely by Our anxiety not to draw out the wheat with the cockle; not to pronounce open judgment, before the public was ready to see its force; not to impeach other people's honesty, before the evidence of events should have torn the mask off the systematic hostility leveled at the Church. Even now that a campaign against the confessional schools, which are guaranteed by the concordat, and the destruction of free election, where Catholics have a right to their children's Catholic education, afford evidence, in a matter so essential to the life of the Church, of the extreme gravity of the situation and the anxiety of every Christian conscience; even now Our responsibility for Christian souls induces Us not to overlook the last possibilities, however slight, of a return to fidelity to treaties, and to any arrangement that may be acceptable to the episcopate. We shall continue without failing, to stand before the rulers of your people as the defender of violated rights, and in obedience to Our Conscience and Our pastoral mission, whether We be successful or not, to oppose the policy which seeks, by open or secret means, to strangle rights guaranteed by a treaty.

6. Different, however, Venerable Brethren, is the purpose of this letter. As you affectionately visited Us in Our illness, so also We turn to you, and through you, the German Catholics, who, like all suffering and afflicted

children, are nearer to their Father's heart. At a time when your faith, like gold, is being tested in the fire of tribulation and persecution, when your religious freedom is beset on all sides, when the lack of religious teaching and of normal defense is heavily weighing on you, you have every right to words of truth and spiritual comfort from him whose first predecessor heard these words from the Lord: "I have prayed for thee that thy faith fail not: and thou being once converted, confirm thy brethren" (Luke xxii. 32).

7. Take care, Venerable Brethren, that above all, faith in God, the first and irreplaceable foundation of all religion, be preserved in Germany pure and unstained. The believer in God is not he who utters the name in his speech, but he for whom this sacred word stands for a true and worthy concept of the Divinity. Whoever identifies, by pantheistic confusion, God and the universe, by either lowering God to the dimensions of the world, or raising the world to the dimensions of God, is not a believer in God. Whoever follows that so-called pre-Christian Germanic conception of substituting a dark and impersonal destiny for the personal God, denies thereby the Wisdom and Providence of God who "Reacheth from end to end mightily, and ordereth all things sweetly" (Wisdom viii. 1). Neither is he a believer in God.

8. Whoever exalts race, or the people, or the State, or a particular form of State, or the depositories of power, or any other fundamental value of the human community -- however necessary and honorable be their function in worldly things -- whoever raises these notions above their standard value and divinizes them to an idolatrous level, distorts and perverts an order of the world planned and created by God; he is far from the true faith in God and from the concept of life which that faith upholds.

9. Beware, Venerable Brethren, of that growing abuse, in speech as in writing, of the name of God as though it were a meaningless label, to be affixed to any creation, more or less arbitrary, of human speculation. Use your influence on the Faithful, that they refuse to yield to this aberration. Our God is the Personal God, supernatural, omnipotent, infinitely perfect, one in the Trinity of Persons, tri-personal in the unity of divine essence, the Creator of all existence. Lord, King and ultimate Consummator of the history of the world, who will not, and cannot, tolerate a rival God by His side.

10. This God, this Sovereign Master, has issued commandments whose value is independent of time and space, country and race. As God's sun shines on every human face so His law knows neither privilege nor exception. Rulers and subjects, crowned and uncrowned, rich and poor are equally subject to His word. From the fullness of the Creators' right there naturally arises the fullness of His right to be obeyed by individuals and communities, whoever they are. This obedience permeates all branches of activity in which moral values claim harmony with the law of God, and pervades all integration of the ever-changing laws of man into the immutable laws of God.

11. None but superficial minds could stumble into concepts of a national God, of a national religion; or attempt to lock within the frontiers of a single people, within the narrow limits of a single race, God, the Creator of the universe, King and Legislator of all nations before whose immensity they are "as a drop of a bucket" (Isaiah xl, 15).

12. The Bishops of the Church of Christ, "ordained in the things that appertain to God (Heb. v, 1) must watch that pernicious errors of this sort, and consequent practices more pernicious still, shall not gain a footing among their flock. It is part of their sacred obligations to do whatever is in their power to enforce respect for, and obedience to, the commandments of God, as these are the necessary foundation of all private life and public morality; to see that the rights of His Divine Majesty, His name and His word be not profaned; to put a stop to the blasphemies, which, in words and pictures, are multiplying like the sands of the desert; to encounter the obstinacy and provocations of those who deny, despise and hate God, by the never-failing reparatory prayers of the Faithful, hourly rising like incense to the All-Highest and staying His vengeance.

13. We thank you, Venerable Brethren, your priests and Faithful, who have persisted in their Christian duty and

in the defense of God's rights in the teeth of an aggressive paganism. Our gratitude, warmer still and admiring, goes out to those who, in fulfillment of their duty, have been deemed worthy of sacrifice and suffering for the love of God.

14. No faith in God can for long survive pure and unalloyed without the support of faith in Christ. "No one knoweth who the Son is, but the Father: and who the Father is, but the Son and to whom the Son will reveal Him" (Luke x. 22). "Now this is eternal life: That they may know thee, the only true God, and Jesus Christ whom thou has sent" (John xvii. 3). Nobody, therefore, can say: "I believe in God, and that is enough religion for me," for the Savior's words brook no evasion: "Whosoever denieth the Son, the same hath not the Father. He that confesseth the Son hath the Father also" (1 John ii. 23).

15. In Jesus Christ, Son of God made Man, there shone the plentitude of divine revelation. "God, who at sundry times and in divers manners, spoke in times past to the fathers by the prophets last of all, in these days hath spoken to us by His Son" (Heb. i. 1). The sacred books of the Old Testament are exclusively the word of God, and constitute a substantial part of his revelation; they are penetrated by a subdued light, harmonizing with the slow development of revelation, the dawn of the bright day of the redemption. As should be expected in historical and didactic books, they reflect in many particulars the imperfection, the weakness and sinfulness of man. But side by side with innumerable touches of greatness and nobleness, they also record the story of the chosen people, bearers of the Revelation and the Promise, repeatedly straying from God and turning to the world. Eyes not blinded by prejudice or passion will see in this prevarication, as reported by the Biblical history, the luminous splendor of the divine light revealing the saving plan which finally triumphs over every fault and sin. It is precisely in the twilight of this background that one perceives the striking perspective of the divine tutorship of salvation, as it warms, admonishes, strikes, raises and beautifies its elect. Nothing but ignorance and pride could blind one to the treasures hoarded in the Old Testament.

16. Whoever wishes to see banished from church and school the Biblical history and the wise doctrines of the Old Testament, blasphemes the name of God, blasphemes the Almighty's plan of salvation, and makes limited and narrow human thought the judge of God's designs over the history of the world: he denies his faith in the true Christ, such as He appeared in the flesh, the Christ who took His human nature from a people that was to crucify Him; and he understands nothing of that universal tragedy of the Son of God who to His torturer's sacrilege opposed the divine and priestly sacrifice of His redeeming death, and made the new alliance the goal of the old alliance, its realization and its crown.

17. The peak of the revelation as reached in the Gospel of Christ is final and permanent. It knows no retouches by human hand; it admits no substitutes or arbitrary alternatives such as certain leaders pretend to draw from the so-called myth of race and blood. Since Christ, the Lord's Anointed, finished the task of Redemption, and by breaking up the reign of sin deserved for us the grace of being the children God, since that day no other name under heaven has been given to men, whereby we must be saved (Acts iv. 12). No man, were every science, power and worldly strength incarnated in him, can lay any other foundation but that which is laid: which is Christ Jesus (1 Cor. iii 11). Should any man dare, in sacrilegious disregard of the essential differences between God and His creature, between the God-man and the children of man, to place a mortal, were he the greatest of all times, by the side of, or over, or against, Christ, he would deserve to be called prophet of nothingness, to whom the terrifying words of Scripture would be applicable: "He that dwelleth in heaven shall laugh at them" (Psalms ii. 3).

18. Faith in Christ cannot maintain itself pure and unalloyed without the support of faith in the Church, "the pillar and ground of the truth" (1 Tim. iii. 15); for Christ Himself, God eternally blessed, raised this pillar of the Faith. His command tO hear the Church (Matt. xviii. 15), to welcome in the words and commands of the Church His own words and His own commands (Luke x. 16), is addressed to all men, of all times and of all countries. The Church founded by

the Redeemer is one, the same for all races and all nations. Beneath her dome, as beneath the vault of heaven, there is but one country for all nations and tongues; there is room for the development of every quality, advantage, task and vocation which God the Creator and Savior has allotted to individuals as well as to ethnical communities. The Church's maternal heart is big enough to see in the God-appointed development of individual characteristics and gifts, more than a mere danger of divergency. She rejoices at the spiritual superiorities among individuals and nations. In their successes she sees with maternal joy and pride fruits of education and progress, which she can only bless and encourage, whenever she can conscientiously do so. But she also knows that tO this freedom limits have been set by the majesty of the divine command, which founded that Church one and indivisible. Whoever tampers with that unity and that indivisibility wrenches from the Spouse of Christ one of the diadems with which God Himself crowned her; he subjects a divine structure, which stands on eternal foundations, tO criticism and transformation by architects whom the Father of Heaven never authorized to interfere.

19. The Church, whose work lies among men and operates through men, may see her divine mission obscured by human, too human, combination, persistently growing and developing like the cockle among the wheat of the Kingdom of God. Those who know the Savior's words on scandal and the giver of scandals, know, too, the judgment which the Church and all her sons must pronounce on what was and what is sin. But if, besides these reprehensible discrepancies be between faith and life, acts and words, exterior conduct and interior feelings, however numerous they be, anyone overlooks the overwhelming sum of authentic virtues, of spirit of sacrifice, fraternal love, heroic efforts of sanctity, he gives evidence of deplorable blindness and injustice. If later he forgets to apply the standard of severity, by which he measures the Church he hates, to other organizations in which he happens to be interested, then his appeal to an offended sense of purity identifies him with those who, for seeing the mote in their brother's eye, according to the Savior's incisive words, cannot see the beam in their own. But however suspicious the intention of those who make it their task, nay their vile profession, to scrutinize what is human in the Church, and although the priestly powers conferred by God are independent of the priest's human value, it yet remains true that at no moment of history, no individual, in no organization can dispense himself from the duty of loyally examining his conscience, of mercilessly purifying himself, and energetically renewing himself in spirit and in action. In Our Encyclical on the priesthood We have urged attention to the sacred duty of all those who belong to the Church, chiefly the members of the priestly and religious profession and of the lay apostolate, to square their faith and their conduct with the claims of the law of God and of the Church. And today we again repeat with all the insistency We can command: it is not enough to be a member of the Church of Christ, one needs to be a living member, in spirit and in truth, i.e., living in the state of grace and in the presence of God, either in innocence or in sincere repentance. If the Apostle of the nations, the vase of election, chastised his body and brought it into subjection: lest perhaps, when he had preached to others, he himself should become a castaway (1 Cor. ix. 27), could anybody responsible for the extension of the Kingdom of God claim any other method but personal sanctification? Only thus can we show to the present generation, and to the critics of the Church that "the salt of the earth," the leaven of Christianity has not decayed, but is ready to give the men of today -- prisoners of doubt and error, victims of indifference, tired of their Faith and straying from God -- the spiritual renewal they so much need. A Christianity which keeps a grip on itself, refuses every compromise with the world, takes the commands of God and the Church seriously, preserves its love of God and of men in all its freshness, such a Christianity can be, and will be, a model and a guide to a world which is sick to death and clamors for directions, unless it be condemned to a catastrophe that would baffle the imagination.

20. Every true and lasting reform has ultimately sprung from the sanctity of men who were driven by the love of

God and of men. Generous, ready to stand to attention to any call from God, yet confident in themselves because confident in their vocation, they grew to the size of beacons and reformers. On the other hand, any reformatory zeal, which instead of springing from personal purity, flashes out of passion, has produced unrest instead of light, destruction instead of construction, and more than once set up evils worse than those it was out to remedy. No doubt "the Spirit breatheth where he will" (John iii. 8): "of stones He is able to raise men to prepare the way to his designs" (Matt. iii. 9). He chooses the instruments of His will according to His own plans, not those of men. But the Founder of the Church, who breathed her into existence at Pentecost, cannot disown the foundations as He laid them. Whoever is moved by the spirit of God, spontaneously adopts both outwardly and inwardly, the true attitude toward the Church, this sacred fruit from the tree of the cross, this gift from the Spirit of God, bestowed on Pentecost day to an erratic world.

21. In your country, Venerable Brethren, voices are swelling into a chorus urging people to leave the Church, and among the leaders there is more than one whose official position is intended to create the impression that this infidelity to Christ the King constitutes a signal and meritorious act of loyalty to the modern State. Secret and open measures of intimidation, the threat of economic and civic disabilities, bear on the loyalty of certain classes of Catholic functionaries, a pressure which violates every human right and dignity. Our wholehearted paternal sympathy goes out to those who must pay so dearly for their loyalty to Christ and the Church; but directly the highest interests are at stake, with the alternative of spiritual loss, there is but one alternative left, that of heroism. If the oppressor offers one the Judas bargain of apostasy he can only, at the cost of every worldly sacrifice, answer with Our Lord: "Begone, Satan! For it is written: The Lord thy God shalt thou adore, and Him only shalt thou serve" (Matt. iv. 10). And turning to the Church, he shall say: "Thou, my mother since my infancy, the solace of my life and advocate at my death, may my tongue cleave to my palate if, yielding to worldly promises or threats, I betray the vows of my baptism." As to those who imagine that they can reconcile exterior infidelity tO one and the same Church, let them hear Our Lord's warning: -- "He that shall deny me before men shall be denied before the angels of God" (Luke xii. 9).

22. Faith in the Church cannot stand pure and true without the support of faith in the primacy of the Bishop of Rome. The same moment when Peter, in the presence of all the Apostles and disciples, confesses his faith in Christ, Son of the Living God, the answer he received in reward for his faith and his confession was the word that built the Church, the only Church of Christ, on the rock of Peter (Matt. xvi. 18). Thus was sealed the connection between the faith in Christ, the Church and the Primacy. True and lawful authority is invariably a bond of unity, a source of strength, a guarantee against division and ruin, a pledge for the future: and this is verified in the deepest and sublimest sense, when that authority, as in the case of the Church, and the Church alone, is sealed by the promise and the guidance of the Holy Ghost and His irresistible support. Should men, who are not even united by faith in Christ, come and offer you the seduction of a national German Church, be convinced that it is nothing but a denial of the one Church of Christ and the evident betrayal of that universal evangelical mission, for which a world Church alone is qualified and competent. The live history of other national churches with their paralysis, their domestication and subjection to worldly powers, is sufficient evidence of the sterility to which is condemned every branch that is severed from the trunk of the living Church. Whoever counters these erroneous developments with an uncompromising No from the very outset, not only serves the purity of his faith in Christ, but also the welfare and the vitality of his own people.

23. You will need to watch carefully, Venerable Brethren, that religious fundamental concepts be not emptied of their content and distorted to profane use. "Revelation" in its Christian sense, means the word of God addressed to man. The use of this word for the "suggestions" of race

and blood, for the irradiations of a people's history, is mere equivocation. False coins of this sort do not deserve Christian currency. "Faith" consists in holding as true what God has revealed and proposes through His Church to man's acceptance. It is "the evidence of things that appear not" (Heb. ii. 1). The joyful and proud confidence in the future of one's people, instinct in every heart, is quite a different thing from faith in a religious sense. To substitute the one for the other, and demand on the strength of this, to be numbered among the faithful followers of Christ, is a senseless play on words, if it does not conceal a confusion of concepts, or worse.

24. "Immortality" in a Christian sense means the survival of man after his terrestrial death, for the purpose of eternal reward or punishment. Whoever only means by the term, the collective survival here on earth of his people for an indefinite length of time, distorts one of the fundamental notions of the Christian Faith and tampers with the very foundations of the religious concept of the universe, which requires a moral order.

25. "Original sin" is the hereditary but impersonal fault of Adam's descendants, who have sinned in him (Rom. v. 12). It is the loss of grace, and therefore of eternal life, together with a propensity to evil, which everybody must, with the assistance of grace, penance, resistance and moral effort, repress and conquer. The passion and death of the Son of God has redeemed the world from the hereditary curse of sin and death. Faith in these truths, which in your country are today the butt of the cheap derision of Christ's enemies, belongs to the inalienable treasury of Christian revelation.

26. The cross of Christ, though it has become to many a stumbling block and foolishness (1 Cor. i. 23) remains for the believer the holy sign of his redemption, the emblem of moral strength and greatness. We live in its shadow and die in its embrace. It will stand on our grave as a pledge of our faith and our hope in the eternal light.

27. Humility in the spirit of the Gospel and prayer for the assistance of grace are perfectly compatible with self-confidence and heroism. The Church of Christ, which throughout the ages and to the present day numbers more confessors and voluntary martyrs than any other moral collectivity, needs lessons from no one in heroism of feeling and action. The odious pride of reformers only covers itself with ridicule when it rails at Christian humility as though it were but a cowardly pose of self-degradation.

28. "Grace," in a wide sense, may stand for any of the Creator's gifts to His creature; but in its Christian designation, it means all the supernatural tokens of God's love; God's intervention which raises man to that intimate communion of life with Himself, called by the Gospel "adoption of the children of God." "Behold what manner of charity the Father hath bestowed on us, that we should be called and should be the sons of God" (1 John iii. 1). To discard this gratuitous and free elevation in the name of a so-called German type amounts to repudiating openly a fundamental truth of Christianity. It would be an abuse of our religious vocabulary to place on the same level supernatural grace and natural gifts. Pastors and guardians of the people of God will do well to resist this plunder of sacred things and this confusion of ideas.

29. It is on faith in God, preserved pure and stainless, that man's morality is based. All efforts to remove from under morality and the moral order the granite foundation of faith and to substitute for it the shifting sands of human regulations, sooner or later lead these individuals or societies to moral degradation. The fool who has said in his heart "there is no God" goes straight to moral corruption (Psalms xiii. 1), and the number of these fools who today are out to sever morality from religion, is legion. They either do not see or refuse to see that the banishment of confessional Christianity, i.e., the clear and precise notion of Christianity, from teaching and education, from the organization of social and political life, spells spiritual spoliation and degradation. No coercive power of the State, no purely human ideal, however noble and lofty it be, will ever be able to make shift of the supreme and decisive impulses generated by faith in God and Christ. If the man, who is called to the hard sacrifice of his own ego to the common good, loses the support of the eternal and the divine, that comforting and consoling faith in a

God who rewards all good and punishes all evil, then the result of the majority will be, not the acceptance, but the refusal of their duty. The conscientious observation of the ten commandments of God and the precepts of the Church (which are nothing but practical specifications of rules of the Gospels) is for every one an unrivaled school of personal discipline, moral education and formation of character, a school that is exacting, but not to excess. A merciful God, who as Legislator, says -- Thou must! -- also gives by His grace the power to will and to do. To let forces of moral formation of such efficacy lie fallow, or to exclude them positively from public education, would spell religious under-feeding of a nation. To hand over the moral law to man's subjective opinion, which changes with the times, instead of anchoring it in the holy will of the eternal God and His commandments, is to open wide every door to the forces of destruction. The resulting dereliction of the eternal principles of an objective morality, which educates conscience and ennobles every department and organization of life, is a sin against the destiny of a nation, a sin whose bitter fruit will poison future generations.

30. Such is the rush of present-day life that it severs from the divine foundation of Revelation, not only morality, but also the theoretical and practical rights. We are especially referring to what is called the natural law, written by the Creator's hand on the tablet of the heart (Rom. ii. 14) and which reason, not blinded by sin or passion, can easily read. It is in the light of the commands of this natural law, that all positive law, whoever be the lawgiver, can be gauged in its moral content, and hence, in the authority it wields over conscience. Human laws in flagrant contradiction with the natural law are vitiated with a taint which no force, no power can mend. In the light of this principle one must judge the axiom, that "right is common utility," a proposition which may be given a correct significance, it means that what is morally indefensible, can never contribute to the good of the people. But ancient paganism acknowledged that the axiom, to be entirely true, must be reversed and be made to say: "Nothing can be useful, if it is not at the same time morally good" (Cicero, De Off. ii. 30). Emancipated from this oral rule, the principle would in international law carry a perpetual state of war between nations; for it ignores in national life, by confusion of right and utility, the basic fact that man as a person possesses rights he holds from God, and which any collectivity must protect against denial, suppression or neglect. To overlook this truth is to forget that the real common good ultimately takes its measure from man's nature, which balances personal rights and social obligations, and from the purpose of society, established for the benefit of human nature. Society, was intended by the Creator for the full development of individual possibilities, and for the social benefits, which by a give and take process, every one can claim for his own sake and that of others. Higher and more general values, which collectivity alone can provide, also derive from the Creator for the good of man, and for the full development, natural and supernatural, and the realization of his perfection. To neglect this order is to shake the pillars on which society rests, and to compromise social tranquillity, security and existence.

31. The believer has an absolute right to profess his Faith and live according to its dictates. Laws which impede this profession and practice of Faith are against natural law. Parents who are earnest and conscious of their educative duties, have a primary right to the education of the children God has given them in the spirit of their Faith, and according to its prescriptions. Laws and measures which in school questions fail to respect this freedom of the parents go against natural law, and are immoral. The Church, whose mission it is to preserve and explain the natural law, as it is divine in its origin, cannot but declare that the recent enrollment into schools organized without a semblance of freedom, is the result of unjust pressure, and is a violation of every common right.

32. As the Vicar of Him who said to the young man of the Gospel: "If thou wilt enter into life, keep the commandments" (Matt. xix. 17), We address a few paternal words to the young.

33. Thousands of voices ring into your ears a Gospel

which has not been revealed by the Father of Heaven. Thousands of pens are wielded in the service of a Christianity, which is not of Christ. Press and wireless daily force on you productions hostile to the Faith and to the Church, impudently aggressive against whatever you should hold venerable and sacred. Many of you, clinging to your Faith and to your Church, as a result of your affiliation with religious associations guaranteed by the concordat, have often to face the tragic trial of seeing your loyalty to your country misunderstood, suspected, or even denied, and of being hurt in your professional and social life. We are well aware that there is many a humble soldier of Christ in your ranks, who with torn feelings, but a determined heart, accepts his fate, finding his one consolation in the thought of suffering insults for the name of Jesus (Acts v. 41). Today,

as We see you threatened with new dangers and new molestations, We say to you: If any one should preach to you a Gospel other than the one you received on the knees of a pious mother, from the lips of a believing father, or through teaching faithful to God and His Church, "let him be anathema" (Gal. i. 9). If the State organizes a national youth, and makes this organization obligatory to all, then, without prejudice to rights of religious associations, it is the absolute right of youths as well as of parents to see to it that this organization is purged of all manifestations hostile to the Church and Christianity. These manifestations are even today placing Christian parents in a painful alternative, as they cannot give to the State what they owe to God alone.

34. No one would think of preventing young Germans establishing a true ethnical community in a noble love of freedom and loyalty to their country. What We object to is the voluntary and systematic antagonism raised between national education and religious duty. That is why we tell the young: Sing your hymns to freedom, but do not forget the freedom of the children of God. Do not drag the nobility of that freedom in the mud of sin and sensuality. He who sings hymns of loyalty to this terrestrial country should not, for that reason, become unfaithful to God and His Church, or a deserter and traitor to His heavenly country. You are often told about heroic greatness, in lying opposition to evangelical humility and patience. Why conceal the fact that there are heroisms in moral life? That the preservation of baptismal innocence is an act of heroism which deserves credit? You are often told about the human deficiencies which mar the history of the Church: why ignore the exploits which fill her history, the saints she begot, the blessing that came upon Western civilization from the union between that Church and your people? You are told about sports. Indulged in with moderation and within limits, physical education is a boon for youth. But so much time is now devoted to sporting activities, that the harmonious development of body and mind is disregarded, that duties to one's family, and the observation of the Lord's Day are neglected. With an indifference bordering on contempt the day of the Lord is divested of its sacred character, against the best of German traditions. But We expect the Catholic youth, in the more favorable organizations of the State, to uphold its right tO a Christian sanctification of the Sunday, not tO exercise the body at the expense of the immortal soul, not to be overcome by evil, but to aim at the triumph of good over evil (Rom. xii. 21) as its highest achievement will be the gaining of the crown in the stadium of eternal life (1 Cor. ix. 24).

35. We address a special word of congratulation, encouragement and exhortation to the priests of Germany, who, in difficult times and delicate situations, have, under the direction of their Bishops, to guide the flocks of Christ along the straight road, by word and example, by their daily devotion and apostolic patience. Beloved sons, who participate with Us in the sacred mysteries, never tire of exercising, after the Sovereign and eternal Priest, Jesus Christ, the charity and solicitude of the Good Samaritan. Let your daily conduct remain stainless before God and the incessant pursuit of your perfection and sanctification, in merciful charity towards all those who are confided to your care, especially those who are more exposed, who are weak and stumbling. Be the guides of the faithful, the support of

those who fail, the doctors of the doubting, the consolers of the afflicted, the disinterested counselors and assistants of all. The trials and sufferings which your people have undergone in post-War days have not passed over its soul without leaving painful marks. They have left bitterness and anxiety which are slow to cure, except by charity. This charity is the apostle's indispensable weapon, in a world torn by hatred. It will make you forget, or at least forgive, many an undeserved insult now more frequent than ever.

36. This charity, intelligent and sympathetic towards those even who offend you, does by no means imply a renunciation of the right of proclaiming, vindicating and defending the truth and its implications. The priest's first loving gift to his neighbors is to serve truth and refute error in any of its forms. Failure on this score would be not only a betrayal of God and your vocation, but also an offense against the real welfare of your people and country. To all those who have kept their promised fidelity to their Bishops on the day of their ordination; to all those who in the exercise of their priestly function are called upon to suffer persecution; to all those imprisoned in jail and concentration camps, the Father of the Christian world sends his words of gratitude and commendation.

37. Our paternal gratitude also goes out to Religious and nuns, as well as Our sympathy for so many who, as a result of administrative measures hostile to Religious Orders, have been wrenched from the work of their vocation. If some have fallen and shown themselves unworthy of their vocation, their fault, which the Church punishes, in no way detracts from the merit of the immense majority, who, in voluntary abnegation and poverty, have tried to serve their God and their country. By their zeal, their fidelity, their virtue, their active charity, their devotion, the Orders devoted to the care of souls, the service of the sick and education, are greatly contributing to private and public welfare. No doubt better days will come to do them better justice than the present troublous times have done. We trust that the heads of religious communities will profit by their trials and difficulties tO renew their zeal, their spirit of prayer, the austerity of their lives and their perfect discipline, in order to draw down God's blessing upon their difficult work.

38. We visualize the immense multitudes of Our faithful children, Our sons and daughters, for whom the sufferings of the Church in Germany and their own have left intact their devotion to the cause of God, their tender love for the Father of Christendom, their obedience to their pastors, their joyous resolution to remain ever faithful, happen what may, to the sacred inheritance of their ancestors. To all of them We send Our paternal greetings. And first to the members of those religious associations which, bravely and at the cost of untold sacrifices, have remained faithful to Christ, and have stood by the rights which a solemn treaty had guaranteed to the Church and to themselves according to the rules of loyalty and good faith.

39. We address Our special greetings to the Catholic parents. Their rights and duties as educators, conferred on them by God, are at present the stake of a campaign pregnant with consequences. The Church cannot wait to deplore the devastation of its altars, the destruction of its temples, if an education, hostile to Christ, is to profane the temple of the child's soul consecrated by baptism, and extinguish the eternal light of the faith in Christ for the sake of counterfeit light alien to the Cross. Then the violation of temples is nigh, and it will be every one's duty to sever his responsibility from the opposite camp, and free his conscience from guilty cooperation with such corruption. The more the enemies attempt to disguise their designs, the more a distrustful vigilance will be needed, in the light of bitter experience. Religious lessons maintained for the sake of appearances, controlled by unauthorized men, within the frame of an educational system which systematically works against religion, do not justify a vote in favor of non-confessional schools. We know, dear Catholic parents, that your vote was not free, for a free and secret vote would have meant the triumph of the Catholic schools. Therefore, we shall never cease frankly to represent to the responsible authorities the iniquity of the pressure brought to bear on you and the duty of respecting the freedom of education. Yet do not forget this:

none can free you from the responsibility God has placed on you over your children. None of your oppressors, who pretend to relieve you of your duties can answer for you to the eternal Judge, when he will ask: "Where are those I confided to you?" May every one of you be able to answer: "Of them whom thou hast given me, I have not lost any one" (John xviii. 9).

40. Venerable Brethren, We are convinced that the words which in this solemn moment We address to you, and to the Catholics of the German Empire, will find in the hearts and in the acts of Our Faithful, the echo responding to the solicitude of the common Father. If there is one thing We implore the Lord to grant, it is this, that Our words may reach the ears and the hearts of those who have begun to yield to the threats and enticements of the enemies of Christ and His Church.

41. We have weighed every word of this letter in the balance of truth and love. We wished neither to be an accomplice to equivocation by an untimely silence, nor by excessive severity to harden the hearts of those who live under Our pastoral responsibility; for Our pastoral love pursues them none the less for all their infidelity. Should those who are trying to adapt their mentality to their new surroundings, have for the paternal home they have left and for the Father Himself, nothing but words of distrust, in gratitude or insult, should they even forget whatever they forsook, the day will come when their anguish will fall on the children they have lost, when nostalgia will bring them back to "God

who was the joy of their youth," to the Church whose paternal hand has directed them on the road that leads to the Father of Heaven.

42. Like other periods of the history of the Church, the present has ushered in a new ascension of interior purification, on the sole condition that the faithful show themselves proud enough in the confession of their faith in Christ, generous enough in suffering to face the oppressors of the Church with the strength of their faith and charity. May the holy time of Lent and Easter, which preaches interior renovation and penance, turn Christian eyes towards the Cross and the risen Christ; be for all of you the joyful occasion that will fill your souls with heroism, patience and victory. Then We are sure, the enemies of the Church, who think that their time has come, will see that their joy was premature, and that they may close the grave they had dug. The day will come when the Te Deum of liberation will succeed to the premature hymns of the enemies of Christ: Te Deum of triumph and joy and gratitude, as the German people return to religion, bend the knee before Christ, and arming themselves against the enemies of God, again resume the task God has laid upon them.

43. He who searches the hearts and reins (Psalm vii. 10) is Our witness that We have no greater desire than to see in Germany the restoration of a true peace between Church and State. But if, without any fault of Ours, this peace is not to come, then the Church of God will defend her rights and her freedom in the name of the Almighty whose arm has not shortened. Trusting in Him, "We cease not to pray and to beg" (Col. i. 9) for you, children of the Church, that the days of tribulation may end and that you may be found faithful in the day of judgment; for the persecutors and oppressors, that the Father of light and mercy may enlighten them as He enlightened Saul on the road of Damascus. With this prayer in Our heart and on Our lips We grant to you, as a pledge of Divine help, as a support in your difficult resolutions, as a comfort in the struggle, as a consolation in all trials, to You, Bishops and Pastors of the Faithful, priests, Religious, lay apostles of Catholic Action, to all your diocesans, and specially to the sick and the prisoners, in paternal love, Our Apostolic Benediction.

Given at the Vatican on Passion Sunday, March 14, 1937.

HUMANAE VITAE

POPE PAUL VI ON THE REGULATION OF BIRTH—1968

✠ To the Venerable Patriarchs, Archbishops, Bishops and other local Ordinaries in Peace and Communion with the Apostolic See, to Priests, the Faithful and all Men of Good Will.

VENERABLE BROTHERS *and Beloved Sons.*

✠ 1. The most serious duty of transmitting human life, for which married persons are the free and responsible collaborators of God the Creator, has always been a source of great joys to them, even if sometimes accompanied by not a few difficulties and by distress. At all times the fulfillment of this duty has posed grave problems to the conscience of married persons, but, with the recent evolution of society, changes have taken place that give rise to new questions which the Church could not ignore, having to do with a matter which so closely touches upon the life and happiness of men.

2. The changes which have taken place are in fact noteworthy and of varied kinds. In the first place, there is the rapid demographic development. Fear is shown by many that world population is growing more rapidly than the available resources, with growing distress to many families and developing countries, so that the temptation for authorities to counter this danger with radical measures is great. Moreover, working and lodging conditions, as well as increased exigencies both in the economic field and in that of education, often make the proper education of a larger number of children difficult today. A change is also seen both in the manner of considering the person of woman and her place in society, and in the value to be attributed to conjugal love in marriage, and also in the appreciation to be made of the meaning of conjugal acts in relation to that love.

Finally and above all, man has made stupendous progress in the domination and rational organization of the forces of nature, such that he tends to extend this domination to his own total being: to the body, to psychical life, to social life and even to the laws which regulate the transmission of life.

3. This new state of things gives rise to new questions. Granted the conditions of life today, and granted the meaning which conjugal relations have with respect to the harmony between husband and wife and to their mutual fidelity, would not a revision of the ethical norms, in force up to now, seem to be advisable, especially when it is considered that they cannot be observed without sacrifices, sometimes heroic sacrifices?

And again: by extending to this field the application of the so-called "principle of totality," could it not be admitted that the intention of a less abundant but more rationalized fecundity might transform a materially sterilizing intervention into a licit and wise control of birth? Could it not be admitted, that is, that the finality of procreation pertains to the ensemble of conjugal life, rather than to its single acts? It is also asked whether, in view of the increased sense of responsibility of modern man, the moment has not come for him to entrust to his reason and his will, rather than to the biological rhythms of his organism, the task of regulating birth.

4. Such questions required from the teaching authority of the Church a new and deeper reflection upon the principles of the moral teaching on marriage: a teaching founded on the natural law, illuminated and enriched by divine revelation.

No believer will wish to deny that the teaching authority of the Church is competent to interpret even the natural moral law. It is, in fact, indisputable, as our predecessors have many times declared,[1] that Jesus Christ, when communicating to Peter and to the Apostles His divine authority and sending them to teach all nations

His commandments,[2] constituted them as guardians and authentic interpreters of all the moral law, not only, that is, of the law of the Gospel, but also of the natural law, which is also an expression of the will of God, the faithful fulfillment of which is equally necessary for salvation.[3] Conformably to this mission of hers, the Church has always provided -- and even more amply in recent times -- a coherent teaching concerning both the nature of marriage and the correct use of conjugal rights and the duties of husband and wife.[4]

5. The consciousness of that same mission induced us to confirm and enlarge the study commission which our predecessor Pope John XXIII of happy memory had instituted in March, 1963. That commission which included, besides several experts in the various pertinent disciplines also married couples, had as its scope the gathering of opinions on the new questions regarding conjugal life, and in particular on the regulation of births, and of furnishing opportune elements of information so that the magisterium could give an adequate reply to the expectation not only of the faithful, but also of world opinion.[5]

The work of these experts, as well as the successive judgments and counsels spontaneously forwarded by or expressly requested from a good number of our brothers in the episcopate, have permitted us to measure more exactly all the aspects of this complex matter. Hence with all our heart we express to each of them our lively gratitude.

6. The conclusions at which the commission arrived could not, nevertheless, be considered by us as definitive, nor dispense us from a personal examination of this serious question; and this also because, within the commission itself, no full concordance of judgments concerning the moral norms to be proposed had been reached, and above all because certain criteria of solutions had emerged which departed from the moral teaching on marriage proposed with constant firmness by the teaching authority of the Church.

Therefore, having attentively sifted the documentation laid before us, after mature reflection and assiduous prayers, we now intend, by virtue of the mandate entrusted to us by Christ, to give our reply to these grave questions.

7. The problem of birth, like every other problem regarding human life, is to be considered, beyond partial perspectives -- whether of the biological or psychological, demographic or sociological orders -- in the light of an integral vision of man and of his vocation, not only his natural and earthly, but also his supernatural and eternal vocation. And since, in the attempt to justify artificial methods of birth control, many have appealed to the demands both of conjugal love and of "responsible parenthood," it is good to state very precisely the true concept of these two great realities of married life, referring principally to what was recently set forth in this regard, and in a highly authoritative form, by the Second Vatican Council in its pastoral constitution "Gaudium et Spes."

8. Conjugal love reveals its true nature and nobility when it is considered in its supreme origin, God, who is love,[6] "the Father, from whom every family in heaven and on earth is named."[7]

Marriage is not, then, the effect of chance or the product of evolution of unconscious natural forces; it is the wise institution of the Creator to realize in mankind His design of love. By means of the reciprocal personal gift of self, proper and exclusive to them, husband and wife tend towards the communion of their beings in view of mutual personal perfection, to collaborate with God in the generation and education of new lives.

For baptized persons, moreover, marriage invests the dignity of a sacramental sign of grace, inasmuch as it represents the union of Christ and of the Church.

9. Under this light, there clearly appear the characteristic marks and demands of conjugal love, and it is of supreme importance to have an exact idea of these.

This love is first of all fully human, that is to say, of the senses and of the spirit at the same time. It is not, then, a simple transport of instinct and sentiment, but also, and principally, an act of the free will, intended to endure and to grow by means of the joys and sorrows of daily life, in such a way that husband and wife become one only heart and one only soul, and together attain their human perfection.

Then, this love is total, that is to say, it is a very special form of personal friendship, in which husband and wife generously share everything, without undue reservations or selfish calculations. Whoever truly loves his marriage partner loves not only for what he receives, but for the partner's self, rejoicing that he can enrich his partner with the gift of himself.

Again, this love is faithful and exclusive until death. Thus in fact do bride and groom conceive it to be on the day when they freely and in full awareness assume the duty of the marriage bond. A fidelity, this, which can sometimes be difficult, but is always possible, always noble and meritorious, as no one can deny. The example of so many married persons down through the centuries shows, not only that fidelity is according to the nature of marriage, but also that it is a source of profound and lasting happiness.

And finally this love is fecund for it is not exhausted by the communion between husband and wife, but is destined to continue, raising up new lives. "Marriage and conjugal love are by their nature ordained toward the begetting and educating of children. Children are really the supreme gift of marriage and contribute very substantially to the welfare of their parents."[8]

10. Hence conjugal love requires in husband and wife an awareness of their mission of "responsible parenthood," which today is rightly much insisted upon, and which also must be exactly understood. Consequently it is to be considered under different aspects which are legitimate and connected with one another.

In relation to the biological processes, responsible parenthood means the knowledge and respect of their functions; human intellect discovers in the power of giving life biological laws which are part of the human person.[9]

In relation to the tendencies of instinct or passion, responsible parenthood means that necessary dominion which reason and will must exercise over them.

In relation to physical, economic, psychological and social conditions, responsible parenthood is exercised, either by the deliberate and generous decision to raise a numerous family, or by the decision, made for grave motives and with due respect for the moral law, to avoid for the time being, or even for an indeterminate period, a new birth.

Responsible parenthood also and above all implies a more profound relationship to the objective moral order established by God, of which a right conscience is the faithful interpreter. The responsible exercise of parenthood implies, therefore, that husband and wife recognize fully their own duties towards God, towards themselves, towards the family and towards society, in a correct hierarchy of values.

In the task of transmitting life, therefore, they are not free to proceed completely at will, as if they could determine in a wholly autonomous way the honest path to follow; but they must conform their activity to the creative intention of God, expressed in the very nature of marriage and of its acts, and manifested by the constant teaching of the Church.[10]

11. These acts, by which husband and wife are united in chaste intimacy, and by means of which human life is transmitted, are, as the Council recalled, "noble and worthy,"[11] and they do not cease to be lawful if, for causes independent of the will of husband and wife, they are foreseen to be infecund, since they always remain ordained towards expressing and consolidating their union. In fact, as experience bears witness, not every conjugal act is followed by a new life. God has wisely disposed natural laws and rhythms of fecundity which, of themselves, cause a separation in the succession of births. Nonetheless the Church, calling men back to the observance of the norms of the natural law, as interpreted by their constant doctrine, teaches that each and every marriage act (quilibet matrimonii usus) must remain open to the transmission of life.[12]

12. That teaching, often set forth by the magisterium, is founded upon the inseparable connection, willed by God and unable to be broken by man on his own initiative, between the two meanings of the conjugal act: the unitive meaning and the procreative meaning. Indeed, by its intimate structure, the conjugal act, while most closely uniting husband and wife, capacitates them for the generation of new lives, according to laws inscribed in the

very being of man and of woman. By safeguarding both these essential aspects, the unitive and the procreative, the conjugal act preserves in its fullness the sense of true mutual love and its ordination towards man's most high calling to parenthood. We believe that the men of our day are particularly capable of seeing the deeply reasonable and human character of this fundamental principle.

13. It is in fact justly observed that a conjugal act imposed upon one's partner without regard for his or her condition and lawful desires is not a true act of love, and therefore denies an exigency of right moral order in the relationships between husband and wife. Likewise, if they consider the matter, they must admit that an act of mutual love, which is detrimental to the faculty of propagating life, which God the Creator of all, has implanted in it according to special laws, is in contradiction to both the divine plan, according to whose norm matrimony has been instituted, and the will of the Author of human life. To use this divine gift destroying, even if only partially, its meaning and its purpose is to contradict the nature both of man and of woman and of their most intimate relationship, and therefore it is to contradict also the plan of God and His will. On the other hand, to make use of the gift of conjugal love while respecting the laws of the generative process means to acknowledge oneself not to be the arbiter of the sources of human life, but rather the minister of the design established by the Creator. In fact, just as man does not have unlimited dominion over his body in general, so also, with particular reason, he has no such dominion over his generative faculties as such, because of their intrinsic ordination towards raising up life, of which God is the principle. "Human life is sacred," Pope John XXIII recalled; "from its very inception it reveals the creating hand of God."13

14. In conformity with these landmarks in the human and Christian vision of marriage, we must once again declare that the direct interruption of the generative process already begun, and, above all, directly willed and procured abortion, even if for therapeutic reasons, are to be absolutely excluded as licit means of regulating birth.14 Equally to be excluded, as the teaching authority of the Church has frequently declared, is direct sterilization, whether perpetual or temporary, whether of the man or of the woman.15 Similarly excluded is every action which, either in anticipation of the conjugal act, or in its accomplishment, or in the development of its natural consequences, proposes, whether as an end or as a means, to render procreation impossible.16

To justify conjugal acts made intentionally infecund, one cannot invoke as valid reasons the lesser evil, or the fact that such acts would constitute a whole together with the fecund acts already performed or to follow later, and hence would share in one and the same moral goodness. In truth, if it is sometimes licit to tolerate a lesser evil in order to avoid a greater evil or to promote a greater good,17 it is not licit, even for the gravest reasons, to do evil so that good may follow therefrom;18 that is, to make into the object of a positive act of the will something which is intrinsically disorder, and hence unworthy of the human person, even when the intention is to safeguard or promote individual, family or social well-being. Consequently it is an error to think that a conjugal act which is deliberately made infecund and so is intrinsically dishonest could be made honest and right by the ensemble of a fecund conjugal life.

15. The Church, on the contrary, does not at all consider illicit the use of those therapeutic means truly necessary to cure diseases of the organism, even if an impediment to procreation, which may be foreseen, should result therefore, provided such impediment is not, for whatever motive, directly willed.19

16. To this teaching of the Church on conjugal morals, the objection is made today, as we observed earlier (no. 3), that it is the prerogative of the human intellect to dominate the energies offered by irrational nature and to orientate them towards an end conformable to the good of man. Now, some may ask: in the present case, is it not reasonable in many circumstances to have recourse to artificial birth control if, thereby, we secure the harmony and peace of the family, and better conditions for the education of the

children already born? To this question it is necessary to reply with clarity: the Church is the first to praise and recommend the intervention of intelligence in a function which so closely associates the rational creature with his Creator; but she affirms that this must be done with respect for the order established by God.

If, then, there are serious motives to space out births, which derive from the physical or psychological conditions of husband and wife, or from external conditions, the Church teaches that it is then licit to take into account the natural rhythms immanent in the generative functions, for the use of marriage in the infecund periods only, and in this way to regulate birth without offending the moral principles which have been recalled earlier.20

The Church is coherent with herself when she considers recourse to the infecund periods to be licit, while at the same time condemning, as being always illicit, the use of means directly contrary to fecundation, even if such use is inspired by reasons which may appear honest and serious. In reality, there are essential differences between the two cases; in the former, the married couple make legitimate use of a natural disposition; in the latter, they impede the development of natural processes. It is true that, in the one and the other case, the married couple are concordant in the positive will of avoiding children for plausible reasons, seeking the certainty that offspring will not arrive; but it is also true that only in the former case are they able to renounce the use of marriage in the fecund periods when, for just motives, procreation is not desirable, while making use of it during infecund periods to manifest their affection and to safeguard their mutual fidelity. By so doing, they give proof of a truly and integrally honest love.

17. Upright men can even better convince themselves of the solid grounds on which the teaching of the Church in this field is based, if they care to reflect upon the consequences of methods of artificial birth control. Let them consider, first of all, how wide and easy a road would thus be opened up towards conjugal infidelity and the general lowering of morality. Not much experience is needed in order to know human weakness, and to understand that men -- especially the young, who are so vulnerable on this point -- have need of encouragement to be faithful to the moral law, so that they must not be offered some easy means of eluding its observance. It is also to be feared that the man, growing used to the employment of anti-conceptive practices, may finally lose respect for the woman and, no longer caring for her physical and psychological equilibrium, may come to the point of considering her as a mere instrument of selfish enjoyment, and no longer as his respected and beloved companion.

Let it be considered also that a dangerous weapon would thus be placed in the hands of those public authorities who take no heed of moral exigencies. Who could blame a government for applying to the solution of the problems of the community those means acknowledged to be licit for married couples in the solution of a family problem? Who will stop rulers from favoring, from even imposing upon their peoples, if they were to consider it necessary, the method of contraception which they judge to be most efficacious? In such a way men, wishing to avoid individual, family, or social difficulties encountered in the observance of the divine law, would reach the point of placing at the mercy of the intervention of public authorities the most personal and most reserved sector of conjugal intimacy.

Consequently, if the mission of generating life is not to be exposed to the arbitrary will of men, one must necessarily recognize insurmountable limits to the possibility of man's domination over his own body and its functions; limits which no man, whether a private individual or one invested with authority, may licitly surpass. And such limits cannot be determined otherwise than by the respect due to the integrity of the human organism and its functions, according to the principles recalled earlier, and also according to the correct understanding of the "principle of totality" illustrated by our predecessor Pope Pius XII.21

18. It can be foreseen that this teaching will perhaps not be easily received by all: Too numerous are those voices -- amplified by the modern means of propaganda -- which are contrary to the voice of the Church. To tell the truth, the Church is not surprised to be made, like her divine

Founder, a "sign of contradiction",[22] yet she does not because of this cease to proclaim with humble firmness the entire moral law, both natural and evangelical. Of such laws the Church was not the author, nor consequently can she be their arbiter; she is only their depositary and their interpreter, without ever being able to declare to be licit that which is not so by reason of its intimate and unchangeable opposition to the true good of man.

In defending conjugal morals in their integral wholeness, the Church knows that she contributes towards the establishment of a truly human civilization; she engages man not to abdicate from his own responsibility in order to rely on technical means; by that very fact she defends the dignity of man and wife. Faithful to both the teaching and the example of the Savior, she shows herself to be the sincere and disinterested friend of men, whom she wishes to help, even during their earthly sojourn, "to share as sons in the life of the living God, the Father of all men."[23]

19. Our words would not be an adequate expression of the thought and solicitude of the Church, Mother and Teacher of all peoples, if, after having recalled men to the observance and respect of the divine law regarding matrimony, we did not strengthen them in the path of honest regulation of birth, even amid the difficult conditions which today afflict families and peoples.

The Church, in fact, cannot have a different conduct towards men than that of the Redeemer: She knows their weaknesses, has compassion on the crowd, receives sinners; but she cannot renounce the teaching of the law which is, in reality, that law proper to a human life restored to its original truth and conducted by the spirit of God.[24]

20. The teaching of the Church on the regulation of birth, which promulgates the divine law, will easily appear to many to be difficult or even impossible of actuation. And indeed, like all great beneficent realities, it demands serious engagement and much effort, individual, family and social effort. More than that, it would not be practicable without the help of God, who upholds and strengthens the good will of men. Yet, to anyone who reflects well, it cannot but be clear that such efforts ennoble man and are beneficial to the human community.

21. The honest practice of regulation of birth demands first of all that husband and wife acquire and possess solid convictions concerning the true values of life and of the family, and that they tend towards securing perfect self-mastery. To dominate instinct by means of one's reason and free will undoubtedly requires ascetical practices, so that the affective manifestations of conjugal life may observe the correct order, in particular with regard to the observance of periodic continence. Yet this discipline which is proper to the purity of married couples, far from harming conjugal love, rather confers on it a higher human value. It demands continual effort yet, thanks to its beneficent influence, husband and wife fully develop their personalities, being enriched with spiritual values. Such discipline bestows upon family life fruits of serenity and peace, and facilitates the solution of other problems; it favors attention for one's partner, helps both parties to drive out selfishness, the enemy of true love; and deepens their sense of responsibility. By its means, parents acquire the capacity of having a deeper and more efficacious influence in the education of their offspring; little children and youths grow up with a just appraisal of human values, and in the serene and harmonious development of their spiritual and sensitive faculties.

22. On this occasion, we wish to draw the attention of educators, and of all who perform duties of responsibility in regard to the common good of human society, to the need of creating an atmosphere favorable to education in chastity, that is, to the triumph of healthy liberty over license by means of respect for the moral order.

Everything in the modern media of social communications which leads to sense excitation and unbridled customs, as well as every form of pornography and licentious performances, must arouse the frank and unanimous reaction of all those who are solicitous for the progress of civilization and the defense of the common good of the human spirit. Vainly would one seek to justify such depravation with the pretext of artistic or scientific exigencies,[25] or to deduce an argument from the freedom allowed in this sector by the public authorities.

23. To Rulers, who are those principally responsible for the common good, and who can do so much to safeguard moral customs, we say: Do not allow the morality of your peoples to be degraded; do not permit that by legal means practices contrary to the natural and divine law be introduced into that fundamental cell, the family. Quite other is the way in which public authorities can and must contribute to the solution of the demographic problem: namely, the way of a provident policy for the family, of a wise education of peoples in respect of moral law and the liberty of citizens.

We are well aware of the serious difficulties experienced by public authorities in this regard, especially in the developing countries. To their legitimate preoccupations we devoted our encyclical letter Populorum Progressio. But with our predecessor Pope John XXIII, we repeat: no solution to these difficulties is acceptable "which does violence to man's essential dignity" and is based only on an utterly materialistic conception of man himself and of his life. The only possible solution to this question is one which envisages the social and economic progress both of individuals and of the whole of human society, and which respects and promotes true human values.26

Neither can one, without grave injustice, consider divine providence to be responsible for what depends, instead, on a lack of wisdom in government, on an insufficient sense of social justice, on selfish monopolization, or again on blameworthy indolence in confronting the efforts and the sacrifices necessary to ensure the raising of living standards of a people and of all its sons.27

May all responsible public authorities -- as some are already doing so laudably -- generously revive their efforts. And may mutual aid between all the members of the great human family never cease to grow: This is an almost limitless field which thus opens up to the activity of the great international organizations.

24. We wish now to express our encouragement to men of science, who "can considerably advance the welfare of marriage and the family, along with peace of conscience, if by pooling their efforts they labor to explain more thoroughly the various conditions favoring a proper regulation of births."28 It is particularly desirable that, according to the wish already expressed by Pope Pius XII, medical science succeed in providing a sufficiently secure basis for a regulation of birth, founded on the observance of natural rhythms.29 In this way, scientists and especially Catholic scientists will contribute to demonstrate in actual fact that, as the Church teaches, "a true contradiction cannot exist between the divine laws pertaining to the transmission of life and those pertaining to the fostering of authentic conjugal love."30

25. And now our words more directly address our own children, particularly those whom God calls to serve Him in marriage. The Church, while teaching imprescriptible demands of the divine law, announces the tidings of salvation, and by means of the sacraments opens up the paths of grace, which makes man a new creature, capable of corresponding with love and true freedom to the design of his Creator and Savior, and of finding the yoke of Christ to be sweet.31

Christian married couples, then, docile to her voice, must remember that their Christian vocation, which began at baptism, is further specified and reinforced by the sacrament of matrimony. By it husband and wife are strengthened and as it were consecrated for the faithful accomplishment of their proper duties, for the carrying out of their proper vocation even to perfection, and the Christian witness which is proper to them before the whole world.32 To them the Lord entrusts the task of making visible to men the holiness and sweetness of the law which unites the mutual love of husband and wife with their cooperation with the love of God the author of human life.

We do not at all intend to hide the sometimes serious difficulties inherent in the life of Christian married persons; for them as for everyone else, "the gate is narrow and the way is hard, that leads to life."33 But the hope of that life must illuminate their way, as with courage they strive to live with wisdom, justice and piety in this present time,[34] knowing that the figure of this world passes away.[35] Let married couples, then, face up to the efforts needed, supported by the faith and hope which "do not disappoint . . . because God's love has been poured into our hearts through the Holy Spirit, who has been given to Us"[36]; let them implore divine assistance by persevering prayer; above all, let them draw from the source of grace and charity in the Eucharist. And if sin should still keep its hold over them, let them not be discouraged, but rather have recourse with humble perseverance to the mercy of God, which is poured forth in the sacrament of Penance. In this way they will be enabled to achieve the fullness of conjugal life described by the Apostle: "husbands, love your wives, as Christ loved the Church . . . husbands should love their wives as their own bodies. He who loves his wife loves himself. For no man ever hates his own flesh, but nourishes and cherishes it, as Christ does the Church . . . this is a great mystery, and I mean in reference to Christ and the Church. However, let each one of you love his wife as himself, and let the wife see that she respects her husband."[37]

26. Among the fruits which ripen forth from a generous effort of fidelity to the divine law, one of the most precious is that married couples themselves not infrequently feel the desire to communicate their experience to others. Thus there comes to be included in the vast pattern of the vocation of the laity a new and most noteworthy form of the apostolate of like to like; it is married couples themselves who become apostles and guides to other married couples. This is assuredly, among so many forms of apostolate, one of those which seem most opportune today.[38]

27. We hold those physicians and medical personnel in the highest esteem who, in the exercise of their profession, value above every human interest the superior demands of their Christian vocation. Let them persevere, therefore, in promoting on every occasion the discovery of solutions inspired by faith and right reason, let them strive to arouse this conviction and this respect in their associates. Let them also consider as their proper professional duty the task of acquiring all the knowledge needed in this delicate sector, so as to be able to give to those married persons who consult them wise counsel and healthy direction, such as they have a right to expect.

28. Beloved priest sons, by vocation you are the counselors and spiritual guides of individual persons and of families. We now turn to you with confidence. Your first task -- especially in the case of those who teach moral theology -- is to expound the Church's teaching on marriage without ambiguity. Be the first to give, in the exercise of your ministry, the example of loyal internal and external obedience to the teaching authority of the Church. That obedience, as you know well, obliges not only because of the reasons adduced, but rather because of the light of the Holy Spirit, which is given in a particular way to the pastors of the Church in order that they may illustrate the truth.[39] You know, too, that it is of the utmost importance, for peace of consciences and for the unity of the Christian people, that in the field of morals as well as in that of dogma, all should attend to the magisterium of the Church, and all should speak the same language. Hence, with all our heart we renew to you the heartfelt plea of the great Apostle Paul: "I appeal to you, brethren, by the name of Our Lord Jesus Christ, that all of you agree and that there be no dissensions among you, but that you be united in the same mind and the same judgment."[40]

29. To diminish in no way the saving teaching of Christ constitutes an eminent form of charity for souls. But this must ever be accompanied by patience and goodness, such as the Lord himself gave example of in dealing with men. Having come not to condemn but to save,[41] he was indeed intransigent with evil, but merciful towards individuals. In their difficulties, may married couples always find, in the words and in the heart of a priest, the echo of the voice and the love of the Redeemer.

And then speak with confidence, beloved sons, fully convinced that the spirit of God, while He assists the magisterium in proposing doctrine, illumines internally the hearts of the faithful inviting them to give their assent. Teach married couples the indispensable way of prayer; prepare them to have recourse often and with faith to the sacraments of the Eucharist and of Penance, without ever allowing themselves to be discouraged by their own weakness.

30. Beloved and venerable brothers in the episcopate, with whom we most intimately share the solicitude of the spiritual good of the People of God, at the conclusion of this encyclical our reverent and affectionate thoughts turn to you. To all of you we extend an urgent invitation. At the head of the priests, your collaborators, and of your faithful, work ardently and incessantly for the safeguarding and the holiness of marriage, so that it may always be lived in its entire human and Christian fullness. Consider this mission as one of your most urgent responsibilities at the present time. As you know, it implies concerted pastoral action in all the fields of human activity, economic, cultural and social; for, in fact, only a simultaneous improvement in these various sectors will make it possible to render the life of parents and of children within their families not only tolerable, but easier and more joyous, to render the living together in human society more fraternal and peaceful, in faithfulness to God's design for the world.

31. Venerable brothers, most beloved sons, and all men of good will, great indeed is the work of education, of progress and of love to which we call you, upon the foundation of the Church's teaching, of which the successor of Peter is, together with his brothers in the episcopate, the depositary and interpreter. Truly a great work, as we are deeply convinced, both for the world and for the Church, since man cannot find true happiness -- towards which he aspires with all his being -- other than in respect of the laws written by God in his very nature, laws which he must observe with intelligence and love. Upon this work, and upon all of you, and especially upon married couples, we invoke the abundant graces of the God of holiness and mercy, and in pledge thereof we impart to you all our apostolic blessing.

Given at Rome, from St. Peter's, this 25th day of July, feast of St. James the Apostle, in the year 1968, the sixth of our pontificate.

PAULUS PP.VI.

Don de Mrs les membres de la Fabrique
Dequevauviller prt · Gossin · Malligand
Daviond · Grout · Odent · 1877
Delagroüe · Hermite · Quatremere

Vocation de St Pierre
Ravissement de St Paul

INDEX

ACKNOWLEDGMENTS

b: below, c: center, l: left, r: right, t: top

4br Mirek Hejnicki/shutterstock.com | 7bl Gunnar Bach Pedersen | 7br MattiaATH/Shutterstock.com | 9 Bojan Pavlukovic/Shutterstock.com | 10 grafalex/Shutterstock.com | 13 Tupungato/Shutterstock.com | 14 -15 mountainpix/shutterstock.com | 16l Hanay | 16b Vibrant Image Studio/shutterstock.com | 17 Pablo Debat/shutterstock.com | 18t Renata Sedmakova/shutterstock.com | 19t Musée des Beaux-Arts de Dijon/Rama | 20c Janericloebe | 21cl PennaPazza/shutterstock.com | 22bl DerHexer | 23br Ian McDonald/shutterstock.com | p25br Photo Chris Wimbush | 26t Torvindus | 26cl Nick Thompson | 26bl Stephen Chung/shutterstock.com | 26br Simone Ramella | 27b Heinz-Joachim Krenzer | 30b Musei Capitolini/Marie-Lan Nguyen | 31bl Grandpa Larry | 31br Heinz-Joachim Krenzer | 32tl Wmpearl | 32cl Fotowan/shutterstock.com | 32b Courtesy Wildwinds | 33bl KUCO/shutterstock.com | 36br Giovanni Dall'Orto | 37b Clemchambers | 38cl Mirek Hejnicki/shutterstock.com | 39b grafalex/shutterstock.com | 44 - 45 iofoto/shutterstock.com | 48r Museum für Indische Kunst, Berlin-Dahlem/Gryffindor | 50c Bocman1973/shutterstock.com | 50b Radosław Botev | 51cl Classical Numismatic Group, Inc. http://www.cngcoins.com | 51b piotrwzk/shutterstock.com | 53b Musee du Louvre, Paris/Marie-Lan Nguyen | 55cr Vassia Atanassova | 55cl Claudio Giovanni Colombo/shutterstock.com | 59b 663highland | 61bl Nevit Dilmen | 62cl Classical Numismatic Group, Inc. http://www.cngcoins.com | 63t Arpingstone | 63c Courtesy James Steakley | 65br Rob Wilson/shutterstock.com | 68b Wiggum | 69b Reiss & Sohn, Königstein im Taunus | 73b Anna Kucherova/shutterstock.com | 76bc jiawangkun/shutterstock.com | 76 br Courtesy Wildwinds | 77cl BasPhoto/Shutterstock.com | 78cl Classical Numismatic Group, Inc. http://www.cngcoins.com | 79br Vitvit | 80cl 12345678 | 81bl ever/shutterstock.com | 85tr Penn Libraries call number: Inc B-720, Penn Provenance Project | 87br Talk2winik | 88tr Antonio Abrignani/Shutterstock.com | 88cl Uwe Barghaan | 90c Awe Inspiring Images/Shutterstock.com | 90b gugganij | 91b Photo Pierre Kessler | 94b worldswildlifewonders/shutterstock.com | 95cl O.G.N., ogn-numismatique.com | 98bc JohnArmagh | 102-103 jorisvo/shutterstock.com | 109t Library of Congress, LC-USZ62-106736 | 109b ventdusud/shutterstock.com | 111br Anthony Ricci/shutterstock.com | 112cr Anilah/shutterstock.com | 113cl AndreasPraefcke | 113b Solodov Alexey/shutterstock.com | 114b ŁW | 116b Viacheslav Lopatin/shutterstock.com | 118br Bruce J Webber | 120c Nolege | 120b BMJ/Shutterstock.com | 121t Chris Bainbridge | 121b PHGCOM | 123bl © Andrew Dunn | 123br steve estvanik/shutterstock.com | 126b r.nagy/shutterstock.com | 127bl Yale Center for British Art, Paul Mellon Collection | 128tr Croberto68 | 129b Helge Høifødt | 130cl Aperitivi/Shutterstock.com | 131b Nanisimova/shutterstock.com | 132b Myrabella | 133t Hadrian/shutterstock.com | 133c Urban | 133b Narongsak Nagadhana/Shutterstock.com | 134cl Martin Geisler | 134b Classical Numismatic Group, Inc. http://www.cngcoins.com | 135c Cliff Lloyd/shutterstock.com | 134b Joe Dorward | 138b Claudio Divizia/shutterstock.com | 141 NicFer | 142b Professor John Palmer and George Slater, http://domesdaymap.co.uk | 143t cudak/shutterstock.com | 143b Urban | 144b G CHP | 145cl Mussklprozz | 145b Stan Shebs | 146cl Reinhardhauke | 147br Prinz Wilbert | 149b Patricia Drury | 152b Rob Bendall (Highfields) | 153b anshar/shutterstock.com | 154cr PurpleHz | 157b Luciano Mortula/shutterstock.com | 158cl Joshua Sherurcij | 159 Claudio Giovanni Colombo/shutterstock.com | 161br Mitya/shutterstock.com | 163t blackpixel/shutterstock.com | 163b Pawel Kowalczyk/shutterstock.com | 165t Luciano Mortula/shutterstock.com | 165b Kiril Stanchev/shutterstock.com | 170br Bertl123/shutterstock.com | 172tr Osado | 174br Alysta/shutterstock.com | 175br Berthold Werner | 176cl Gunnar Bach Pedersen | 177t PHGCOM | 177b Ray9 | 178t PHGCOM | 178r K.Weise | 178bl Japiot | 179c sailko | 180bl Neithan90 | 181bl PHGCOM | 182cl vector99/shutterstock.com | 184cl Frank Bach/shutterstock.com | 185tl PHGCOM | 185tr Claudio Giovanni Colombo/shutterstock.com | 185bl Shayno | 186tr Jastrow | 187cl Renata Sedmakova/shutterstock.com | 188tr claudio zaccherini/shutterstock.com | 188bl Jastrow | 190-191 wjarek/shutterstock.com | 193t ho visto nina volare | 193br Library of Congress, Southern Asian Collection, Asian Division | 194bl yvon52/shutterstock.com | 195b Acoma | 200tr claudio zaccherini/shutterstock.com | 201br Kenneth Dedeu/shutterstock.com | 203cr Claudio Giovanni Colombo/shutterstock.com | 203br Georgios Kollidas/shutterstock.com | 204b edella/shutterstock.com | 205t Fabio Bernardi/shutterstock.com | 210c Roberto Aquilano/shutterstock.com | 214cl LianeM/shutterstock.com | 215cr Radu Razvan/shutterstock.com | 216c Vlad G/shutterstock.com | 216br NCG/shutterstock.com | 219cl Daniela Pelazza/shutterstock.com | 222 Mi.Ti./shutterstock.com | 223b StevanZZ/shutterstock.com | 225t Danilo Ascione/shutterstock.com | 225b catwalker/shutterstock.com | 226tl & bl Georgios Kollidas/shutterstock.com | 227 byggarn.se/shutterstock.com | 228bl Gail Johnson/shutterstock.com | 230t Georgios Kollidas/shutterstock.com | 230b El Comandante | 235b JohnArmagh | 237b LianeM/shutterstock.com | 239t MM | 242b The lifted lorax | 246t Jastrow | 248 - 249 eZeePics Studio/istockphoto.com | 250b Samot/shutterstock.com | 252bl Jastrow | 254tl Jastrow | 255cr Stocksnapper/shutterstock.com | 255b 0399778584/shutterstock.com | 256cr John Copland/shutterstock.com | 257cl Georgios Kollidas/shutterstock.com | 257b Bocman1973/shutterstock.com | 261cl Pablo Alberto Salguero Quiles | 264r Claudio Giovanni Colombo/shutterstock.com | 264b Noelcr | 265b Antonio Abrignani/Shutterstock.com | 266cl Viacheslav Lopatin/shutterstock.com | 266b Georgios Kollidas/shutterstock.com | 267c Renata Sedmakova/shutterstock.com | 269tr Pavel K/shutterstock.com | 270b NARA/Still Picture Records Section, Special Media Archives Services Division (NWCS-S) | 271t Giovanni Rinaldi Photography | 272b NARA/Still Picture Records Section, Special Media Archives Services Division (NWCS-S) | 274cl Georgios Kollidas/shutterstock.com | 275t Neveshkin Nikolay/shutterstock.com | 275cl ultimathule | 276cl Georgios Kollidas/shutterstock.com | 277tr Roi Boshi | 278b Everett Collection/shutterstock.com | 279br Quintanilla/shutterstock.com | 280tl Library of Congress, LC-DIG-pga-01227 | 280bl Myrabella | 282tl Library of Congress, LC-USZC4-7498 | 283tr © Marie-Lan Nguyen/Wikimedia Commons/CC-BY 2.5 | 283cl Eve81/shutterstock.com | 283br Library of Congress, LC-USZ62-114673 | 284tl Library of Congress, LC-USZC4-8961 | 284cl Karol Kozlowski/shutterstock.com | 285cl Use the force | 285br Jane Rix/shutterstock.com | 286tl Library of Congress, LC-USZ62-55542 | 286br Jean-Pol Grandmont | 287cl Mrlopez2681 | 287br Library of Congress, LC-DIG-hec-31012 | 288b 4736202690/Shutterstock.com | 289c Library of Congress, LC-USW33-019081-C United States. Office of War Information Photograph Collection. | 289b Bundesarchiv, Bild 146-1972-026-11/Sennecke, Robert/CC-BY-SA | 291t Bernhardt Walter/Ernst Hofmann USHMM, courtesy of Yad Vashem | 291b NARA 208-N-43888 | 292b US Navy, KN 6935 | 293bl Bundesarchiv, Bild 183-B0628-0015-035/Junge, Peter Heinz/CC-BY-SA | 293br Darjac | 294br NASA | 295b US Army | 296cl Fotocamera | 296br NARA/Bill Fitz-Patrick | 297bl Vdp | 298bl NARA | 298br Julo | 298cr Gaj777 | 299t Thalion77 | 299b Neftali/shutterstock.com | 300tl ewg3D/istockphoto.com | 300b Northfoto/shutterstock.com | 301tl Agata Malchrowicz/istockphoto.com | 301c Giuseppe Fucile/shutterstock.com | 301b Dan Howell/shutterstock.com | 302tl Sergey Gabdurakhmanov | 302cl Alexander Z | 302b FEMA/Andrea Booher | 303tl West Midlands Police | 303cl manfredxy/shutterstock.com | 303br Dongliu/shutterstock.com | 304t EdStock/istockphoto.com | 304b J. Helgason/shutterstock.com | 305t EdStock/istockphoto.com | 305cr Lya_Cattel/istockphoto.com | 305br Migel/shuttestock.com | 306tl MattiaATH/shutterstock.com | 306c eZeePics Studio/shutterstock.com | 306bl dutourdumonde/shutterstock.com | 306br Jaber Al Nahian | 307tl Agência Brasil | 307c Zvonimir Atletic/shutterstock.com | 307b Sarin Kunthong/shutterstock.com | 386-387 Renata Sedmakova/shutterstock.com

The publisher wishes to thank all of the photographers (known and unknown) whose images appear in this book. We apologize in advance for any omissions, or neglect, and will be pleased to make any corrections in future editions.